EUROPEAN THOUGHT IN THE NINETEENTH CENTURY
CENTURY

Τοιοῦτος οὖν μοι ὁ συγγραφεὺς ἔστω, . . .
ξένος ἐν τοῖς βιβλίοις καὶ ἄπολις.
                                        —LUCIAN.

A HISTORY

OF

EUROPEAN THOUGHT

IN THE

NINETEENTH CENTURY

BY

JOHN THEODORE MERZ

VOL. III.

WILLIAM BLACKWOOD AND SONS
EDINBURGH AND LONDON
MCMXII

PREFACE.

I HAD originally intended to publish the two volumes which should form the second section of this work, dealing with the History of Philosophical Thought during the Nineteenth Century, together. With this intention I wrote the text of both volumes, with the exception of a closing chapter. When, however, after the lapse of many years I returned to the revision and the working up of the notes and references, I found that in the meantime the whole subject had in my own mind acquired a somewhat altered aspect, and that to give expression to this I had to introduce important changes and additions. As to carry these out much more time was required than I had expected, I have given way to the wish of some of my friends, as also to my own growing conviction, that it would be better to publish the third volume by itself and let the fourth follow as soon as possible. I cannot help feeling that this is somewhat unfair to my readers and critics, as the whole subject cannot so easily be divided into separate tolerably independent parts as seemed possible in the first section. I have, however, missed no

opportunity which offered to point incidentally to the
leading ideas which have guided me in this review of the
Philosophical Thought of the Century, and which should
come out more clearly and be brought to a final expression in a following volume. I have also, to facilitate
the study of the subject, added a preliminary index
which, when the fourth volume appears, will be cancelled
to make place for a more comprehensive index covering
both volumes.

As in the earlier volumes, I have again been assisted
by the advice and encouragement of many friends. To
the names given before I wish to add that of Prof.
W. R. Sorley of King's College, Cambridge, to whose
valuable suggestions I have, as will be seen, referred in
several instances. I must again express my deep sense
of obligation to Mr Thos. Whittaker, B.A., whose assistance has in this section exceeded in importance, if possible,
even that which he had so fully given me in the earlier
volumes.

The fourth volume will continue the plan described
in the Introduction to this volume by adding chapters,
Of the Beautiful, Of the Good, Of the Spirit, Of Society,
Of Systems of Philosophy, and will close with a summary
on the general outcome of Philosophical Thought during
the Nineteenth Century.

J. THEO. MERZ.

THE QUARRIES,
NEWCASTLE-UPON-TYNE, *November* 1912.

CONTENTS OF THE THIRD VOLUME.

CHAPTER I.

INTRODUCTORY.

Common-sense and speculation, 3 ; Language the instrument of common-sense, 3 ; New terms in philosophy, 4 ; Creative and critical eras, 6 ; Contrast between philosophical and scientific thought, 8 ; Seen especially in language, 10 ; The precept of science and that of philosophy, 12 ; External object common to all ; internal, peculiar to the observing subject, 13 ; Outer world in space ; inner world in time, 13 ; Distinction, however, not hard and fast, 15 ; Either language or bodily sensation can furnish a point of union, 15 ; Psycho-physical view of nature, 17 ; Kantian Idealism the antithesis to this, 18 ; Both methods overreach their limit, 19 ; Their permanent value, 19 ; Transition to the social point of view, 20 ; A characteristic tendency of recent thought, 21 ; Biology and the history of origins, 22 ; Reality added by thought to natural things, 24 ; Twofold aspect of the Real first recognised by Plato, 25 ; Mediæval philosophy and the modern break with it, 27 ; Community between Kant and Plato, 28 ; Evolution and the power of words, 30 ; The social point of view in history, 31 ; Application to the history of thought, 33 ; Differences as well as uniting ideas not to be neglected, 34 ; New point of view required, 34 ; Contrast to be dealt with, 34 ; Philosophical contrasted with scientific method, 35 ; Histories of philosophy, 37 ; Kuno Fischer, 39 ; National and international work in science and philosophy, 41 ; Auguste Comte, 43 ; English empiricism, 43 ; Social point of view in France and England, 43 ; Absence of the same in Germany, 44 ; Psychological, metaphysical, and positive interests, 45 ; A new character of philosophical thought in the century, 47 ; The term Criticism as used by Kant, 48 ; Criticism and history, 49 ; Growth and diffusion

of the critical spirit, 50 ; Hegel and Spencer, 51 ; Intermediate position
of philosophy between science and religion, 52 ; Monistic doctrines, 52 ;
Attempts at reconciliation of knowledge and belief, 54 ; Dualism in
philosophic systems, 55 ; Plan of this history, 56 ; Character and aims
of philosophical thought, 59 ; No consensus as to philosophical methods,
60 ; Philosophy is interested, science disinterested, 62 ; Philosophers as
educators and reformers, 64 ; Problems of science are many, problem of
philosophy is one, 65 ; Renunciation in recent philosophy, 66 ; Reversion
to common-sense, 68 ; "Scientific Philosophy," 69 ; Direction of Herbart
and Lotze, 71 ; E. Zeller, 71 ; Wilhelm Wundt, 72 ; Influence of Schopenhauer, 74 ; Materialism of the "Forties," 76 ; Schopenhauer's pessimism
an accident, 77 ; Realism of Nietzsche, 78 ; Comte's sociology, 80 ;
Temporary decline of philosophic interest, 81 ; Hints of its revival, 82 ;
"Voluntarism," 83 ; Relation of recent philosophy to religion, 87.

CHAPTER II.

ON THE GROWTH AND DIFFUSION OF THE CRITICAL SPIRIT.

Reversal of the position of science and philosophy, 91 ; Causes of the change,
93 ; Anarchy of recent philosophy, 93 ; Critical spirit, 95 ; Narrower
and wider sense of criticism, 96 ; Germany the home of criticism in the
wider sense, 98 ; Attempts to apply exact methods to philosophy, 100 ;
Reason of their failure, 101 ; Contrast between unities to which phenomena of nature and inner life are referred, 103 ; Loss of synoptic view
in recent philosophy, 104 ; Sapping effect of critical spirit, 105 ; How
has science escaped ? 106 ; The escape has not been complete, 106 ;
Reasons why science has not succumbed, 107 ; Peculiar strength in their
practical utility, 109 ; Besides, man cannot judge nature, 109 ; Criticism
a reflection of the mind on itself, 110 ; Three critical periods, 110 ; From
the last we have not yet emerged, 111 ; Its methodical character, 112 ;
Obstructions to it, 113 ; Winckelmann's reform of art by criticism, 114 ;
Ideal of humanity : its phases, 115 ; Lessing's revival of Spinoza, 118 ;
Kant and Spinoza the poles of German thought, 119 ; Spinoza and
German idealism, 121 ; Spinoza, Lessing, Kant, and the Higher Criticism, 123 ; Representative higher critics, 127 ; Göttingen and the critical
spirit, 127 ; Criticism an instrument of education, 130 ; Difference of
philosophical and historical criticism, 131 ; Two modes of treatment in
classical philology, 134 ; Criticism as practised by Hermann and Ritschl,
137 ; Encyclopædic aims of F. A. Wolf, 138 ; Sprach-philologen and
Sach-philologen, 139 ; Ritschl and Liebig compared, 145 ; Extension of
methods from classical to other branches of philology, 146 ; Bopp and

Grimm, 147 ; Extension to historical studies, 148 ; Broader view of history since Niebuhr, 150 ; Leopold von Ranke, 151 ; Ernst Curtius, 152 ; Theod. Mommsen, 156 ; Political temper in Mommsen, 158 ; Liberation of historical criticism from religious influence, 159 ; First application of criticism to religion by Fichte and Kant, 161 ; Schleiermacher's Religious Discourses, 162 ; Criticism of religious origins, 163 ; Eichhorn as successor of Astruc, 164 ; Influence of Hegel, 166 ; David F. Strauss, 166 ; F. C. Baur, 170 ; Philosophical criticism : Feuerbach, 174 ; Humanistic interpretation of Hegel, 174 ; Another interpretation, 174 ; Materialistic controversy, 176 ; Renunciation of premature solutions : Lotze, 178 ; Return from metaphysics to psychology : Herbart, 179 ; Fechner's psycho-physics, 179 ; Neo-Kantism : F. A. Lange, 179 ; Influence of Darwin and Riemann, 180 ; Unsettlement due to criticism, 182 ; Philosophical thought outside Germany, 183 ; French and English philosophy little known in Germany, 183 ; French and English philosophy uncritical in the German sense, 184 ; The philosophy of Renouvier, 185 ; Recent critical tendency in England, 186 ; Cousin's Eclecticism and philosophy of Common-sense, 186 ; Philosophy becoming international, 187 ; Criticism the common meeting-ground, 188.

CHAPTER III.

OF THE SOUL.

Philosophical and scientific thought again contrasted, 192 ; Aim at unification, 193 ; General conceptions ancient and modern, 194 ; Words marking leading philosophical problems, 195 ; The problem of the Soul or Psychology, 196 ; The 'Seelenfrage,' 197 ; Problems centering in this, 200 ; Empirical and rational psychology, 200 ; At the beginning of the century rational psychology mainly studied in Germany, 202 ; Empirical psychology chiefly British, 202 ; French physiological psychology, 203 ; Herbart, 204 ; Conceptions introduced by Herbart, 207 ; Exact method, 208 ; Beneke, 208 ; British introspective psychology, 209 ; Attempt to base psychology on elementary scientific principles, 211 ; Errors of this procedure, 212 ; Association psychology, 215 ; James Mill's mental chemistry, 218 ; Alex. Bain, 218 ; Want of system in British philosophy, 219 ; University teaching in Scotland, 221 ; Philosophy of common-sense, 224 ; British ideas carried over to France, 227 ; Reaction and development, 230 ; De Tracy and the idea of activity, 231 ; Maine de Biran, 232 ; Royer Collard and Cousin, 235 ; Influence of Kant and of German idealism, 236 ; Kant and psychology, 237 ; Epistemological development in Germany, 243 ; Kant's psychological programme, 248 ;

The way out of individualism, 248 ; General causes of this movement,
250 ; Disappearance of psychology in the older sense, 252 ; Individual
self merged into general self, 255 ; Creation of ideals, 256 ; The educational movement, 256 ; The political movement, 257 ; Return to empirical psychology, 258 ; J. F. Fries, 258 ; Influence of physiology, 259 ;
Feuerbach on Hegel, 260 ; Die Seelenfrage, 261 ; International contact,
262 ; Lotze, 264 ; Approaches philosophy from the side of medicine,
265 ; Connection with the classical period, 265 ; His psychology, 266 ;
His circumspection, 267 ; Various lines in recent psychology, 268 ;
Ribot, 269 ; Morbid psychology, 272 ; ' Mind ' and Croom Robertson,
275 ; James Ward, 277 ; Avenarius, 282 ; Hartmann, Spencer, and
Fouillée, 285 ; Spencer's evolutional psychology, 286 ; Idealistic antecedents of Hartmann and Fouillée, 286 ; The Unconscious in psychology,
287 ; Change in vocabulary, 289 ; Stress laid on activity and feeling,
290 ; Presentation-continuum, 291 ; Anthropology, 291 ; Discontinuity
—Renouvier, 291.

CHAPTER IV.

OF KNOWLEDGE.

Early appearance of the problem of knowledge, 294 ; Re-emergence characteristic of nineteenth century, 294 ; Fichte's *Wissenschaftslehre*, 295 ;
Erkenntnisstheorie, 296 ; Renouvier's Neocriticism, 296 ; Agnosticism
and Pragmatism, 297 ; Preparation in logic and psychology, 298 ; Influence of current literature and science, 299 ; Effect of the French
Revolution, 300 ; Later dominance of exact science, 300 ; J. S. Mill, 301 ;
Influence of social questions, 302 ; Influence of mathematics in France,
302 ; Reaction in British thought, 304 ; Dispersive character of earlier
British thought, 309 ; Its want of systematic unity, 311 ; Beginning of
search for a creed, 312 ; The first episode ends in Agnosticism, 315 ;
Continental efforts to transcend dualism, 316 ; Two lines of develop-
ment, 317 ; Union of these, 317 ; Continental thought began with
scepticism, 320 ; Descartes' constructive effort, 321 ; Mathematical
methods, 322 ; Spinoza and Leibniz, 324 ; Diverging directions after
Leibniz, 330 ; Aim at unity in Continental thought, 331 ; Spinoza and
Leibniz contrasted, 331 ; Leibniz and Bayle, 332 ; Systematisation of
Leibniz's ideas, 335 ; New way opened by Kant, 336 ; Relation to Locke,
Hume, and Leibniz, 339 ; Locke and Kant, 340 ; Kant's philosophy a
central point, 344 ; Relativity of Knowledge, 344 ; The sensible and the
intelligible, 345 ; The regulative ideas, 346 ; Acceptance of extant body of
scientific knowledge, 348 ; And of traditional psychology, 349 ; Apparent
want of unity, 349 ; Criticism predominant, 350 ; Reinhold, 351 ; Criti-

cism superseded by construction, 355 ; Fichte, 357 ; Fichte representative of a new generation, 363 ; Schelling, 366 ; Want of criticism and
exactness, 367 ; Hegel aims at supplying the want, 371 ; J. S. Mill's
Logic, 374 ; Ground common to Mill and Kant, 377 ; Sir W. Hamilton,
379 ; A. Comte, 381 ; Revival and deepening of the historical sciences,
386 ; Epistemology and exact sciences, 390 ; Greater precision, 391 ;
Conception of energy, 392 ; Darwin and development, 394 ; Cause and
effect defined, 397 ; Supersession of astronomical view, 400 ; Plenum
substituted, 400 ; Limitation of scientific knowledge, 403 ; Dualism in
the problem of knowledge, 406 ; Recognised by Lotze, 406 ; His doctrine
of Values, 408 ; Hegel's new conception of Logic, 410 ; Reaction against
this, 411 ; Lotze and English Hegelianism, 412 ; Bradley and Bosanquet,
414 ; Lotze and Spencer, 415 ; The 'Unknowable,' 416 ; Renouvier on
Discontinuity and Personality, 417 ; Schopenhauer's Voluntarism, 418 ;
Overthrow of extreme Intellectualism, 419.

CHAPTER V.

OF REALITY.

Epistemology and systems of philosophy, 421 ; Some systems start with
theories of Reality, 423 ; Interests of academic teaching and of practical
life, 424 ; Discredit of Metaphysics, 428 ; Revival of Metaphysics, 430 ;
Necessity of the word, 431 ; The problem of Reality, 432 ; Modern
problem of Reality centres in Kant, 435 ; The "Thing in itself," 437 ;
His objection to Idealism, 439 ; His "Categorical Imperative," 441 ;
Importance of his terminology, 441 ; Fichte on Kant's terms for Reality,
442 ; Fichte and Schelling, 445 ; "Intellectual Intuition," 445 ; Fichte's
practical aims, 447 ; "Self-realisation," 448 ; Fichte's Absolute is a
process, 450 ; Schelling, 453 ; His central position in German Idealism,
453 ; Practical and poetical interests, 456 ; Rehabilitation of Nature,
458 ; Formulæ of "polarity," 461 ; Hegel, 464 ; Philosophy of the
Absolute Spirit, 466 ; Logical process identified with world-process,
469 ; Reason of Hegel's success, 471 ; Compared with Bacon, 476 ;
Meaning of the identification of the Rational and the Real, 478 ;
Opposition to the monistic tendency, 479 ; Herbart, 481 ; Schopenhauer, 482 ; The term "positive," 487 ; Schelling's positive philosophy,
488 ; His religious turn, 489 ; New eclectic spirit, 491 ; Lotze, 491 ;
Defect in historical sense, 494 ; Doctrine of Values, 495 ; Ethics the
root of Metaphysics, 498 ; Detailed interest in phenomena, 501 ; At the
summit a religious conception, 503 ; Theory of knowledge and belief,
505 ; The problem of Reality since Lotze, 506 ; The idea of Personality,

507 ; The problem of Evil, 508 ; Ethical problems, 509 ; Ethical spirit
of British philosophy, 510 ; Return of British thinkers to Metaphysics,
510 ; Spencer's "Unknowable," 511 ; Wundt, 513 ; Lotze's, Spencer's,
and Wundt's phenomenalism contrasted, 516 ; Fechner and E. von
Hartmann, 518 ; Return to Ontology in England and France, 523 ; The
two movements of search in England : Realistic and Idealistic, 527 ;
Popular influences : the new monthly Reviews, 530 ; Caird, Wallace, and
Green, 532 ; Bradley's 'Appearance and Reality,' 533 ; Bradley and
Lotze, 534 ; Bradley's opposition to both atomistic and transcendental
view of Reality, 536 ; His Monism or Absolutism, 540 ; Phenomenalists
and Ontologists, 542.

CHAPTER VI.

OF NATURE.

Nature : a metaphysical problem, 544 ; Superseded by empirical studies, 545 ;
Changes in the thoughts of the age, 546 ; The exact study of Nature,
547 ; Naturalism of English poetry and art, 547 ; Philosophy of Nature,
547 ; Importance of this last, 549 ; Laplace, 550 ; Absence of organic and
subjective factors, 552 ; Biological appeal of Schelling, 553 ; An omitted
idea : Malthus, 554 ; Afterwards taken up by Darwin, 554 ; Statical
view of French science, 555 ; Insufficiency of this, 555 ; Vague ideas of
development kept back by mathematical spirit, 558 ; A premature
rationale in materialism, 560 ; Büchner, 561 ; Inadequacy, yet popularity, of "Matter" and "Force," 565 ; Inexactness of the popular term
Force, 566 ; Lotze's formula regarding mechanism, 570 ; Success and
failure of Materialism, 570 ; Change in scientific conceptions, 573 ; New
criticism of fundamental notions, 575 ; J. S. Mill, 575 ; Thomson and
Tait, Maxwell, 576 ; Kirchhoff, 578 ; Wundt and Mach, 578 ; Clifford
and K. Pearson, 579 ; Economy of Thought : Mach and Avenarius, 579 ;
Want of philosophical interest attaching to mechanical theories, 583 ;
Schopenhauer's philosophical view of Nature, 586 ; Opposed to Paulogism
and Mechanicism, 587 ; Schopenhauer an idealist and romantic, 589 ; As
also Von Hartmann, 590 ; The philosophy of the "Unconscious," 590 ;
The ideal view displaced by the naturalistic, 593 ; Wundt on Actuality,
595 ; Rise of the problem of Discontinuity, 597 ; Du Bois Reymond, 597 ;
Haeckel's Monism, 600 ; Loose use by naturalists of physical concepts,
603 ; Mach on the limitation of mechanical physics, 604 ; Effects of
modern analysis on view of nature as a whole, 606 ; Artistic view of
nature, 610 ; Goethe as representative of the synoptic view, 611 ; This

view indispensable in science also, 613 ; Double use of the word positive, 614 ; Fechner and Lotze, 615 ; Lotze's distinction between things, forms, and values, 615 ; New problems, 617 ; The problems of the Contingent and the Discontinuous outstanding, 619 ; Lachelier and Renouvier, 620 ; Transition to æsthetic and ethical aspects, 625.

A HISTORY OF EUROPEAN THOUGHT IN THE NINETEENTH CENTURY

PART II.

PHILOSOPHICAL THOUGHT

Ὁ μὲν γὰρ συνοπτικὸς διαλεκτικός, ὁ δὲ μὴ οὔ.

—Plato.

CHAPTER I.

INTRODUCTORY.

I.

COMMON-SENSE, in spite of the obloquy cast upon it in certain schools of philosophy, still asserts its position as the ultimate tribunal before which all speculation has to justify itself. It does so by certain distinctions which it makes and which every school of philosophy has been obliged to recognise: it may be by affirming or denying, but in any case by explaining them.

1. Common-sense and speculation.

These distinctions are crystallised and perpetuated in and by that great instrument of common-sense called language.[1] From the words and terms of language we

2. Language the instrument of common-sense.

---

[1] With this statement I revert to a position distinctly taken up in modern philosophy by Thos. Reid in the second half of the eighteenth century. This position is fully explained by Prof. Pringle - Pattison in his 'Balfour Lectures on Scottish Philosophy'—see especially 3rd ed., p. 122. "Reid's favourite appeal is to common - sense . . . 'the consent of ages and nations of the learned and unlearned.' . . . Reid, however, does not leave his authority so vague; he provides his scattered and inarticulate multi- tude with an accredited spokesman and interpreter; 'we shall frequently have occasion,' he says in the beginning of the Essays, 'to argue from the sense of mankind expressed in the structure of language.'" The common-sense philosophy of Reid has been unduly depreciated by German philosophers such as Kant and Hegel, partly owing to the fact that the German equivalents for "common-sense" are apt to lay stress upon the adjective "common" instead of the noun "sense"; mainly, however, because

have to start if we desire to make our thoughts accessible and intelligible to our fellowmen, and, although we can put these words and terms together in a more or less original manner, we have always to accommodate ourselves to the established usage, from which we can deviate only to a very small extent. In this way language exerts a control over the free movements of our thoughts and reflections which is not infrequently felt to be severe and irksome, and which is more than ever experienced in that great department of literature which is the embodiment of the philosophical thought of an age. More even than in science, we may say that in philosophy progress consists in finding an appropriate verbal expression, or, having found it, in conveying to our readers the clear definition of the meaning we desire to attach to it.

3.
New terms in philosophy.

Looking broadly at the philosophical literature of any period, we may divide its main representatives into two classes—viz., those who have introduced into the existing language new terms, the bearers of thoughts and ideas constituting a new message, and those others who, taking up these newly imported terms, have tried to define them more closely, to prescribe their exact usage,

neither of them—Kant even less than Hegel—seems to have had a sufficient acquaintance either with Reid's own writings or with the principal work of Hume which he criticised. This is fully brought out in Henry Sidgwick's Address on "The Philosophy of Common-sense" (1895), see 'Mind,' N.S., vol. iv. p. 145, &c. He there suggests that Kant was influenced by Priestley, who classes Reid along with Oswald and Beattie, writers of quite an inferior order of merit. When Hegel delivered his Lectures on 'The History of Philosophy' (1817-30), Reid's writings were principally known on the Continent through the influence they had acquired on French thinkers such as Royer Collard and Jouffroy, and are accordingly treated with more respect. With Hegel the contempt for British philosophy seems to have been directed mainly against English as distinguished from Scottish thinkers; see 'Werke,' vol. xv. p. 501 : "Of English philosophy there can no more be any mention."

and, by doing so, to bring home to the common understanding a sense of the deeper meaning or ideal content
which is embodied in them.

During the period which covers roughly ninety years,
from 1780 to 1870, the languages of the western
European nations have been enriched by a long list of
new terms.[1] Around these, separate philosophical schools
have grown up which have made them their watchwords.
These terms have not always been the outcome of abstract
philosophical reasoning; they have often been suggested
by practical demands or borne in the wake of political
and social movements. Thus the French Revolution in
its ˋshibboleths of liberty, equality, and fraternity has
furnished an inexhaustible material not only for political
agitation but also for philosophical speculation ever since.
In the more restricted province of philosophical literature
itself the names of Adam Smith, Bentham, and Mill in
this country, of Comte in France, of Kant and his successors in Germany, are connected with well-known words
and phrases, each of which has enriched common language
and made whole regions of thought accessible to the
general understanding which were unknown or unexplored before. "Free trade" and the "wealth of nations,"
the "greatest happiness of the greatest number," the
"categorical imperative," "intellectual intuition," "positivism," the "world as will and intellect," the "ob-

[1] The 'Critique of Pure Reason'
appeared in 1781 and gave to the
world the larger portion of the
vocabulary of the Kantian system,
which has played such a great part
in subsequent German, English,
and French philosophy. About the
year 1870 I believe the larger part
of the vocabulary of evolution had
been formulated. Probably no
philosophical treatise of any importance could now be written
without making free use of these
two vocabularies.

jective mind," and the "absolute" are only a few
examples of the many now familiar words which have
been introduced by philosophical thinkers into our everyday speech. Among the latest creations of the philosophical genius we may count the terms "unconscious"
and "unknowable," and more than all "natural selection,"
the "survival of the fittest," and many other terms
which are peculiar to the doctrine of "Evolution."

4.
Creative
and critical
eras.

The representatives of the creative era of philosophical
thought which terminated with the second third of the
nineteenth century have been succeeded by a large class
of thinkers whose principal task seems to be not so
much to put forward new ideas and brilliant generalisations as to survey critically and impartially the inheritance of the past, to put into order the abundant supply
of new words and terms which it contains, to reduce
each to its legitimate meaning, defining the limits of its
usage, and by so doing to promote that unity of thought
and harmony of expression of which the loss was frequently threatened by the extreme emphasis, not to say
the vehemence, with which many of those new ideas were
put forth at the moments of their birth. A foremost
representative of this later form of philosophical thought
is Hermann Lotze,[1] who, in a manner following Herbart

[1] As I shall, for various reasons
which will become evident in the
sequel, refer to Lotze's philosophy
as a kind of central point of reference for the movement of philosophical thought during the century, I
give here a list of his more important works. Lotze was born in
1817 and died in 1881. His
activity as a teacher is connected
with the University of Göttingen,
and his name will always be
associated with some of the
most illustrious professors at that
University. See, inter alia, Mr
Haldane's Address, "Universities
and National Life" (1910), p. 24,
&c.
'Metaphysik' (1841).
'Allgemeine   Pathologie   und

and inspired by Leibniz, seems to me to have impressed upon many of the prominent thinkers in Germany, England, and France of to-day the tone of their thought, and suggested the attitude they have taken up to the great philosophical problems.

From the foregoing it might appear as if the process of philosophical thought were similar to that which I have had occasion to point to in many passages in the earlier volumes of this work. I there showed how various terms handed down from earlier ages with a vague and undefined meaning have been raised to the rank of leading ideas by the scientific thought of recent times. Such terms were, *e.g.*, "attraction," "repulsion," " atom," "mass " and " motion," " energy," " form," " development," &c. By being clearly defined—*i.e.*, by having a fixed meaning attached to them—they have become centres around which the scientific thought of the century has gathered, and which have guided us in that survey which this History has undertaken.

It would appear as if an analogous process might guide us in our survey of the philosophical thought of the

Therapie als mechanische Naturwissenschaften ' (1842).
' Logik ' (1843).
Articles — " Leben," " Lebens-straft," " Instinkt," " Seele und Seelenleben," in Wagner's ' Handwörterbuch der Physiologie ' (1843-46).
' Ueber den Begriff der Schönheit ' (1845), and ' Ueber Bedingungen der Kunstschönheit ' (1847).
' Allgemeine Physiologie des Körperlichen Lebens ' (1851).
' Medicinische Psychologie oder Physiologie der Seele ' (1852).

' Microcosmus,' 3 vols. (1856-64).
' Streitschriften ' (1857).
' Geschichte der Aesthetik in Deutschland ' (1868).
' System der Philosophie ' (2 vols. ' Logik,' ' Metaphysik,' 1874-79).
The dictated Notes of his Lectures were published after his death in eight parts, and his ' Kleinere Schriften ' have been collected in four volumes and edited by Peipers (1885 - 91). English translations have appeared of the ' Microcosmus,' the ' System,' and the ' Dictate.'

century,[1] enabling us to bring some order into the tangled maze of speculative writing and to construct a road through the labyrinth of philosophical opinions. The sequel will show that, to a large extent, I shall avail myself of this method. For the moment I wish to dwell on this point with the object of giving to my readers a preliminary idea of the difference between philosophical and scientific thought. The full appreciation of this difference can, of course, only be reached during the course of the second portion of this History itself.

5.
Contrast
between
philosophi-
cal and
scientific
thought.

Science for long ages has lived, as much as philosophy still lives, under the control, not to say the tyranny, of language and of words.[2] It is well known that science for a long time formed merely a branch of philosophy,

[1] In fact, such a process has been suggested by a well-known authority : "a history of the language . . . in which the introduction of every new word should be noted . . . in which such words as have become obsolete should be followed down to their final extinction, in which all the most remarkable words should be traced through their successive phases of meaning, and in which, moreover, the causes and occasions of these changes should be explained,—such a work would not only abound in entertainment, but would throw more light on the development of the human mind than all the brain-spun systems of metaphysics that ever were written" (Archdeacon Hare, quoted by Trench, 'English Past and Present,' p. 2). "When the function of language in producing and maintaining community of knowledge among men is once considered, its philosophical import is seen to be of the most profound and far-reaching character ; and Reid with his 'common-sense' is to be blamed only for allowing the more important use of the word 'common' to be overshadowed by its other implication of 'ordinary' (as having relation to everyday experience and practice). In making what reference he did to language, he shadowed forth a surer method of philosophical analysis than Kant, with all his more laboured art, was able to devise." See G. Croom Robertson, in 'Mind,' O.S., vol. xi. p. 270 ; also 'Philosophical Remains,' p. 421.

[2] It was one of the idols which Bacon desired to destroy under the title of "Idols of the Market-place" : "For it is by discourse that men associate ; and words are imposed according to the apprehension of the vulgar. And therefore the ill and unfit choice of words wonderfully obstructs the understanding. . . . Words plainly force and over-rule the understanding and throw all into confusion, and lead men away into numberless empty controversies and idle fancies" ('Novum Organum,' book i., Aphorism xliii.)

and that only latterly has it established its independent position under the terms "Natural Philosophy" and "Natural Science." This process of emancipation has been carried out mainly through those clear and concise definitions referred to above. They have enabled it to abandon purely verbal discussions for actual description of facts. Now it will be interesting to note that the manner in which these definitions have been gained, the method of this clearing up, are not in general or to a large extent available in that domain of thought which still retains the name of philosophy proper. In order to rise, as science has effectually done, from merely verbal discussions to the consideration of realities—*i.e.*, to emancipate itself from the tyranny of words—philosophy proper will have to look out for a different method from that which is peculiar to science. Whenever the latter method is applicable we may say that science has established itself, and wrenched a new province from the common parent-land of philosophy.

Moreover, the method by which the different sciences have succeeded in defining the ideas with which they deal must have become abundantly clear in the course of our historical exposition. Scientific thought has always progressed by looking outside for definite things or processes in and through which the abstract terms it makes use of are exemplified in the external world—*i.e.*, in Nature. Wherever any doubt, vagueness, or ambiguity has shown itself, it has been dispelled by resorting to observations of special instances, by multiplying these, and thus attaining to generality, by experiments through which complicated cases have been analysed

into simpler elemental processes, by dealing with samples
or examples where the existing material was huge and
overwhelming, and by many similar devices. The
student of science has, in the course of the last hundred
years, learnt to apply these devices in numberless ways,
and to combine them with an astounding and ever-growing
ingenuity and resourcefulness which is the wonder of the
age. The scientific student has learnt to go from words
to things, from books to nature, and nature herself has
revealed to him her phenomena in ever-increasing wealth
and abundance. If nowadays any of the many problems of science have to be attacked, the foremost precept
will be: *circumspice*, look around you. The road of scientific inquiry is the way that leads outside.

6.
Seen es-
pecially in
language.

But starting, as we did, with language—*i.e.*, with
words and terms—we very soon find that language contains a vast number of expressions for which no outer
image can be readily found. Such words refer to what
are generally called abstract ideas or ideas *par excellence*.
If we try to define them—*i.e.*, to assign to them a definite meaning—we have, in many cases, not to look outside but to resort to contemplation, to retire into the
solitude of thought, to shut out as much as possible the
disturbing influence of things around us, and to concentrate our attention as much as ever we can upon the
images which arise within us. We have to look within,
not outside, if we wish to find and fix the exact meaning of the words we employ.

This difference which exists between the words in our
common speech has been noted by all philosophical
writers and urged with more or less clearness. To

mention only one or two instances, I refer first to the treatment of the subject in the writings of Locke, with whom one of the principal lines of modern philosophical thought originated.

But I prefer, for the sake of general interest, to quote what Edmund Burke says at the close of his ' Enquiry into the Origin of our Ideas of the Sublime and Beautiful,' which was published in the middle of the eighteenth century. The fifth part of this treatise deals with Words, and in the fourth section, " On the Effect of Words," he says: " If words have all their possible extent of power, three effects arise in the mind of the hearer. The first is, the sound; the second, the picture, or representation of the thing signified by the sound; the third is, the affection of the soul produced by one or by both of the foregoing. Compounded abstract words of which we have been speaking (honour, justice, liberty, and the like) produce the first and the last of these effects, but not the second. Simple abstracts are useful to signify some one simple idea without much adverting to others which may chance to attend it, as blue, green, hot, cold, and the like; these are capable of affecting all three of the purposes of words; as the aggregate words, man, castle, horse, &c., are in a yet higher degree."

In recent years, when the study of philosophy has again brought into the foreground the problem of language, Prof. Stout has fully discussed this passage of Burke, and in connection with it reviewed the opinions of other eminent thinkers.[1]

[1] G. F. Stout, 'Analytic Psychology,' 1902, vol. i. p. 80.

For my present purpose it is sufficient to say that, starting with language and words, two roads are open for our reflection—*i.e.,* for finding their underlying meaning : the one leads outside, the other inside; the precept of the first was, as we have seen, *circumspice,* look around you; the precept of the other is *introspice,* look inside you. Broadly speaking, the former is the precept of science, the principle of scientific thought and progress; the latter is the precept of philosophy, the principle of philosophical thought and insight.

7.
The precept
of science
and that of
philosophy.

This distinction between the two ways, which are those of scientific thought on the one side and of philosophical thought on the other, also helps us to realise the great difficulty which besets all philosophical reasoning. The way outside leads us into the world of the many things that exist not only for ourselves but also for our fellow-men whom we address. The scientific thinker, in appealing to the things and phenomena of nature, can invite the student or the reader to follow him into the observatory, the laboratory, the museum, the dissecting-room, or the world of nature herself, there to seek and find the same things as he describes, to repeat the observations which he has made, or to go through the experiments which he has instituted. Even the mathematical formula furnishes the same starting-point for him who first wrote it down as for him who follows. Thus the scientific thinker appeals to something that under certain conditions is accessible to others, being the common object of thought and investigation.

8.
External
object com-

It will at once be seen that this is not the case if we turn our thoughts inside, if we have to look for the meaning of words and phrases not outside but within our own minds. To each of us his own mind is only accessible to himself. For every one the object of internal reflection and observation is different. If the philosophical thinker addresses his hearers or his readers in terms of language, he invites them to do what he has done—*i.e.*, he desires that each of them, for himself alone, should retire into the depths of his own consciousness, into his own inner world. He expects that they will there find something analogous to that which he has seen and found within himself. But the objects are not identical, and that they are, in a greater or smaller degree, similar, rests upon an assumption which practice has taught us to make and which experience has shown to be justified and useful. Nevertheless the many misunderstandings, the endless controversies, the wearisome discussions which fill philosophical books, show sufficiently that this assumption is only very partially correct.

If the fact that the object of philosophical inquiry, viz., the inner world, is not the same for all of us, explains one of the great difficulties of philosophical thought, another feature which establishes an important difference between scientific and philosophical reasoning will at once be seen to give to the former an enormous advantage over the latter. This difference can be defined by saying that the outer world exists in space, whereas the inner world presents only succession in time. We have learnt to apply to things in space the methods of measurement, of exact definition, and of subsequent calculation. The history of scientific thought has shown that science has progressed in the same degree as the

[margin notes:] mon to all; internal, peculiar to the observing subject.

9. Outer world in space; inner world in time.

observation of things has taken the place of discussion of words, and further, as these things have been located in space, geometrically defined and subjected to mathematical calculation. As the conceptions of space, of location, and of definition in space are at the bottom of all processes of measurement, it is at once clear that philosophical thought is deprived of the benefit of that great instrument by which scientific thought has progressed.

But, though it can in general be admitted that the difference between the outer world and the inner, as well as the arrangement in space of the former, points to the radical difference which must exist between the study of nature and the study of mind, and that the former is placed in a much more advantageous position than the latter,—it would be a mistake to rest satisfied with this distinction, or to attach to it more importance than belongs to a merely preliminary statement or a first approximation. The outer and the inner worlds are not separated by a rigid line of demarcation; the one flows into the other, and there exists a large borderland which belongs to both in common and neither to the one nor the other exclusively. This is evident from the nature and structure of language itself; for this not only employs in close conjunction words the meaning of which is to be found in opposite directions, but also contains a great number of terms of which it would be difficult to say to which of the two great realms they apply, or that have a double meaning, being promiscuously and alternately used to denote the one or the other. This was already expressed in the above-quoted passage of Burke, who divided words not into two but into three classes. Language thus forms a common ground where our images or conceptions of the outer and the inner meet and have mutually to be accommodated to each other. There is another common meeting-ground between the outer and the inner worlds, and that is to be found in our bodily sensations. Many of these, though by no means all, have as it were two sides, and can be referred to either as things outside of us or as perceptions of ourselves. Such is notably the case with the sensations of colour or other visual and tactile sensations. Our bodies are for each of us just as much the meeting-ground of the outer and the inner world as are the language and the words we make use of.

10. Distinction, however, not hard and fast.

I might in fact have introduced my readers to the great difference which exists between the outer and the inner worlds of thought just as easily by starting with a psychological analysis of our bodily sensations, of that physical envelope which encloses the inner and shuts out the outer world. This is usually done in treatises on psychology. The reason why I have preferred to start with language is mainly this, that I am writing a history of thought, and that the great body of human thought is to be found in the written literatures of the different nations. The other means which we possess for expressing our thoughts, such as the various processes employed in the fine arts or in music, can, as we may have occasion to see later on, only be introduced into a history of thought to the extent that we are able to find an

11. Either language or bodily sensation can furnish a point of union.

analogue in words for that which they attempt to express
by other signs or symbols.[1]

But, whether we start with language or with our
bodily sensations—which according to a now generally
accepted view furnish all the material of our thoughts,—
it is clear that two roads present themselves, by following which we may hope to bring some order into our
discussions : these are the way outside into what we call
nature in the largest sense of the word, and the way
inside into what common language calls the mind. And
accordingly we can distinguish two great currents of
thought which govern all modern science and philosophy :
the course of scientific thought with which we have
become acquainted in the first part of this history, and
the way of philosophical thought which will form the
subject of the second part. The fact, however, that
neither an analysis of our sensations nor language itself
is able to draw a definite line of demarcation has given
rise to hopes on both sides that, starting on either
course, both regions, the outer and the inner, can be
ultimately reached and understood. We have seen,
notably in the eleventh chapter of the first part of this
work, how scientific thought has, within the last fifty
years, made great advances into the region of the inner,
mental, phenomena; how special devices have been introduced by which these phenomena can be subjected to
the same exact scrutiny which has proved so successful

[1] A recent Italian philosopher,
Signor Benedetto Croce, has made
this view the foundation of his
treatise on 'Æsthetics,' which he
considers to be "Science of Expression and General Linguistic."
According to this view language is
an art, and the arts are special
forms of general language. See
B. Croce, 'Esthétique.' French
translation by H. Bigot (1904).

in the abstract and the applied sciences of nature, and which even make it possible to employ those methods of measurement and calculation by which not only have natural phenomena and processes been more clearly described, but many have been discovered which otherwise would have remained for ever unknown. We there saw how these attempts, which I comprised under the title of the "psycho-physical view of nature," have caused the elaboration of two theories which, like all fruitful theories, have been domiciled in scientific literature by novel terms that have become widely current, and are being largely used with a more or less clear understanding of their meaning. The first of these is the theory of "psycho-physical parallelism," which—to put it briefly—maintains that every inner, psychical, phenomenon or process is accompanied by some outer physical phenomenon or process in the human body, and that the former can, to a great extent, be studied and understood through the latter, which is its counterpart; and this by the same methods as those by which other physical phenomena have been attacked. It is admitted that these phenomena are extremely intricate, not to say puzzling and mysterious; but, it is said, not more so than those exhibited in every other region of nature. A second term which characterises and popularises this view is the term "epi-phenomenon."[1] It has been introduced to give expression to the conception that there really exist only physical or bodily phenomena and processes, that what we call the inner states only intermittently and transiently accompany the physical processes which

12.
Psycho-
physical
view of
nature.

---

[1] In German, Begleiterscheinung,—a less illogical term.

18 PHILOSOPHICAL THOUGHT.

correspond to them, and which form the only real basis by which definite location in time and space and continuity of existence are secured.

In the sequel we shall see that about sixty years before the psycho-physical methods were invented an opposite view had been introduced into German philosophy mainly through the influence of Kant. Admitting the correctness of the position taken up by Locke and his followers, viz., that all the material for our thinking is furnished by the senses, he nevertheless pointed out, following a suggestion forcibly put by Leibniz, that in addition to the material supplied by the senses there must be the mind or intellect itself, which forms the centre and point of reference and effects the synthesis of all this material. The emphasis with which he urged this latter point suggested to his followers the possibility that it might be quite as legitimate and perhaps more promising to start from the centre than it would be to study and analyse the peripheral world of sensations themselves. The latter had been undertaken with considerable success by the contemporary school of philosophers in this country. To place oneself at once at the centre and point of reference of all our thinking, and to work from this outward, seemed a promising and novel way of proceeding. It was supported and greatly favoured by the circumstance that, about the same time, German literature, poetry, and art had taken an unexpected and unexampled development through which an ideal force was launched into the world which had the greatest practical influence not only in literature but also in education, legislation, and the political life of the

13.
Kantian
Idealism the
antithesis
to this.

nation. It does not seem unnatural that a movement so sudden and rapid, which resulted in such momentous changes and even formed an important factor in the great anti-Napoleonic revolution of Europe,[1] should find its counterpart in an idealistic school of philosophy which started in a lordly manner from the inner world of thought and the supposed data of consciousness, and looked down with a certain amount of contempt upon the opposite school of philosophy which dealt more exclusively with the problems of wealth, industry, and the interests of the masses.

The history of this movement, which may be called the idealistic movement of thought, and which will occupy us more in detail in the course of this work, has shown, quite as much as the history of the later or psycho-physical movement, that any exclusive method soon exhausts its resources. In trying to find the way outside into nature and life it very soon arrived at an impassable limit, just as I have had occasion to show that the psycho-physical methods by themselves lead to an impassable limit beyond which lies the inner experience or introspective view which alone reveals to us the specific nature of our mind.

14. Both methods overreach their limit.

Both methods, the one that works from inside out and the other that works from outside in, have been of great value. Perhaps one of the most important gains has been the conviction to which both lines of reasoning have led, that beyond the region from which each started separ-

15. Their permanent value.

---

[1] The history of this movement has been written in a masterly manner by the late Sir J. R. Seeley in his 'Life and Times of Stein,' a work which largely, as it seems to me, in consequence of its title, has not gained that popularity in this country which it richly deserves.

ately, there lies another region equally important though
not equally accessible by one and the same approach. It is
also interesting to see that both roads have met in that
common region to which I referred above, and in which
language forms the central and dominating feature. The
same spirit which lives in the philosophical systems of
the great idealistic movement in Germany, and which
went hand in hand with the revival of German literature,
lived also in the minds of the founders of that great
movement to which we owe the sciences of philology,
comparative and classical, of jurisprudence, of biblical
theology, of history in its many branches. Many of
these were indeed pupils of Kant or his successors,
and notably the last and greatest exponent of this line
of thought, Hegel, can count among his followers a
great array of names of the leaders in the various
branches of historical research. On the other side, the
school which calls itself pre - eminently scientific, and
which is represented in Germany and France by the
psycho-physical, in England by the evolutionist schools
of thought, has found it not only necessary to study
the phenomena of mind in their physical and physiological foundations, but also to attack and explore that
region in which the human mind has become, as it were,
an external and tangible thing, viz., human society
with its primitive or more advanced institutions. It is
needless to say that here again language presents itself
as the central creation. In and through it—in the
spoken and still more in the written word,—as also
through the creations of the fine and useful arts and of
music, external material and lifeless things have become

16.
Transition
to the social
point of
view.

the bearers of ideas ; while, on the other side, ideas, the work of the mind, have become, as it were, externalised and deposited for all time in tangible objects. What was once the creation and the hidden property of only one or of the few has, through this process of external- isation, become the common possession of the many, in whom, through it, a new life has been awakened which does not end within the narrow limits of our corporeal existence, but is itself capable of continuous growth and development.

Considering, then, the extreme difficulty which exists if we try, by the methods of introspection, to get hold of our inner life, it is no wonder that the study of mental phenomena should more and more take the direction of a study of their external manifestation in the institutions of society in its primitive and more advanced forms, of languages living and dead, of art, religion, science, and industry ; further, that this study, after having for a long time lingered over the more developed forms, should latterly have been directed more especially to the origins, the supposed primitive or elemental forms out of which the more advanced institu- tions and more finished productions have historically developed. This characteristic tendency of nineteenth century thought was not only favoured by the extreme difficulty of all purely introspective or subjective attempts, but quite as much by a kind of reaction against the sceptical attitude which found an extreme expression in the writings of David Hume. He had himself pointed out the path, when, after arriving at a deadlock in his purely logical and psychological writings, he gradually

17
A character- istic ten- dency of recent thought.

led the way, through his ethical and political essays, to the study of history.[1]

18.
Biology and the history of origins.

We have met with a similar tendency towards historical treatment and the study of origins in that great region of scientific thought comprised under the term Biology : the science of life. After the futility of all attempts to grasp the essence of life itself by a direct analysis had become apparent, the more extensive description and observation of living things themselves, of their forms, their habits, and their environment, infused new hope into the sciences of nature ; and, latterly, all these studies have converged in the direction of the study of origins,[2] whether these be found in the embryological beginnings of individual life (ontogenesis), or in the historical beginnings of genera and species (phylogenesis). Instead of trying to grasp the meaning of life through philosophical definitions, natural science has taken the more promising course of studying life in the great world of living things and their properties. Similarly the study of mind, after having met with much discouragement from the side of philosophical sceptics, as well as through the endless controversies peculiar to the introspective schools, has latterly gained new hope by turning to the external manifestations of mental life in the phenomena of society, religion, language, &c. The reality of mental life, which had gradually evaporated under the hands of

[1] See *supra*, vol. i. p. 47, and the passages there quoted from Leslie Stephen's ' English Thought in the Eighteenth Century.'
[2] I am indebted to Prof. J. Arthur Thomson, in his Review of the first part of this History (see ' Hibbert Journal,' vol. iii. p. 395), for the remark that it is not so much a study of genesis and origins as of genealogies and descent that the Darwinian view has introduced into biology.

the psycho-physicist or been reduced to a mere semblance, to a discontinuous epi-phenomenon, asserted itself in full force when philosophers looked around at the great structures of human history and civilisation, at the fabric of language, the institutions of society, the monuments of literature, art, and industry. Compared with the amount of external matter and energy which Nature even only on this small globe of ours works with, the actual material and energy, the substances employed, in all the literatures, the monuments of art, the compositions of music, or even the products of industry, are infinitesimal, a vanishing quantity; yet they are the greatest reality that surrounds us, being of more importance to us than all the rest of the world put together. How has this small assemblage of matter and energy, which is the bearer and preserver, the repository of all mental life and interest, acquired that additional reality? This is the philosophical question which a study of history forces upon us.

> "Oh, the little more, and how much it is,
> And the little less, and what worlds away!"

It is this little more or less that makes all the difference. It gives to the small piece of canvas the increasing value which all the bales of canvas in the world do not equal; it gives to the small block of marble, hewn out of the quarries of Pentelicon or Carrara, an importance as a unique object of art; it gives to the slab of stone, or the sheet of paper, valueless in themselves, the position of priceless monuments, to the score of music a meaning which could not otherwise be expressed; it distinguishes between the pile of bricks and mortar and the heap of rubbish into which any earthquake might convert it, and which would not be worth removing were it not for the fragments of the destroyed edifice which it contains. What was it that converted the Rosetta Stone, through the discovery of Thomas Young, from a simple piece of building material into the corner-stone of the great edifice of the science of Hieroglyphics? Surely something has been added to all these small and insignificant objects to raise them to the position of interest, not to say veneration, which they occupy in our estimate.

19.
Reality
added by
thought
to natural
things.

We feel that they have got a reality which they did not possess in themselves; they have, in some mysterious manner, become the repository of human thought, of the very essence of the human mind! Is it not important to ask the question: Whence came this added reality and what is its nature?

We come thus upon another definition of the object and aim of philosophy as distinguished from science. This definition is suggested by the twofold meaning of the words "real" and "reality." It furnishes one, and perhaps the most remarkable, instance of the twofold aspect which many words of language present to us. It is evident that, to find the meaning of the word "real," we have to look not only outside but likewise inside our own selves. No external examination, by all the methods of science, would reveal to us anything but the most unimportant side or portion of the reality which belongs to any of the objects just referred to. In order to get hold of the much more important side of this reality, we have to resort to a variety of mental processes, of inner contemplation, for which science gives us little or no help. To define and demonstrate, so as to produce general conviction, is to a large extent quite impossible. To gain understanding here is a task which each thinking and contemplating mind is bound to perform for itself alone.

An awakening to the consciousness that there are two realities in and around us which language and common-sense unconsciously recognise, but continually intermingle, marks probably the first important stage in the history of philosophy, and accordingly we find already with the great philosophers of Greece, notably with Plato, due recognition of this twofold aspect of the real, and a continued striving to find an appropriate expression for it.

20.
Twofold aspect of the Real first recognised by Plato.

We owe to Plato the greater part of the terms by which this central problem of philosophy is put before us in the writings of ancient and modern thinkers. He created at least one half of the vocabulary of mental philosophy; he first put prominently forward and expressed in words the conception that there is a world of ideas which has a definite existence not only in but above and outside of the world of material things. In speaking of that which is real or exists (τὸ ὄν) he puts forward the notion of that which is really (not only apparently) real (τὸ ὄντως ὄν), and likewise the complementary notion that, besides the real, there exists something which is not real (τὸ μὴ ὄν), and which, by its admixture with the truly real, deprives the latter of a portion of its true or pure reality, reducing it to an appearance or semblance. He also tries to answer the question: What is the nature or essence of the truly real? All these reflections, put forward in the Platonic dialogues in endless variety and illustrated from many sides, embodying many ideas contained in the writings of his predecessors or suggested by the conversations of Socrates, have formed the text for the discussions of more than one half of the great thinkers of ancient and modern times. Attempts have indeed been made, ever since the time of Descartes and Bacon, to escape from the influence of Plato's idealism; the fact, however, that hardly any philosopher who has attacked the highest problems of philosophy has succeeded in liberating himself from the use of Plato's terminology, or consequently from the influence of his ideas, proves to us how important a part the great problem of the twofold aspect of reality plays in all our most serious reflections. Of modern languages the German has certainly assimilated more than any other the wealth of expressions which Greek philosophers, notably Plato and Aristotle, have bequeathed to posterity. Other languages, especially the English, have only tardily followed; but during the latter part of the nineteenth century, when the British mind turned again to those deeper problems which, after the original and isolated treatment contained in the writings of Bishop Berkeley, had been pushed aside and neglected, the necessity was felt to enrich the English language by a variety of terms, most of which are directly or indirectly imported from ancient philosophy, or at least, through their German equivalents, suggested by it.[1] It is especi-

[1] The translation of Plato's 'Dialogues' by some of the foremost thinkers in the three countries during the nineteenth century has done much to promote idealism. Thus we have in Germany Schleier- macher's Translations (1804-28), in France Victor Cousin's Translations (1822-40), and in England Jowett's Translations (1871, &c.) Nor is it unimportant to note that one prominent representative of

ally interesting to see how in the writings of one of the latest representatives of the ideal school of philosophy in this country, and one who has had a very marked influence, we find a continual striving to find an expression for the twofold aspect of reality and for the essence of the truly real, similar to that which we meet with in the writings of Plato.[1]

The patristic and scholastic philosophies are full of a recognition of the twofold aspect of reality; but they find a solution of the question as to the truly real in the Christian doctrine of a higher life. Modern philosophy started in England in the teaching of Bacon, and on the Continent in that of Descartes, with a reaction against the neglect with which mediæval philosophy had treated the problems of this world. It led, though in very different ways, to the culture of those branches of knowledge which have to do with the outer world—*i.e.*, with Nature in the largest sense of the term. This interest, as well as the fact that Plato's writings are wanting in due appreciation of the importance of the exact and natural sciences,—with the sole exception of mathematics,—was probably the reason why, for a long time, Plato's works remained little known to philosophical students. With a deeper recognition, however, that the question as to the truly real was not only of re-

21.
Mediæval
philosophy
and the
modern
break
with it.

modern, positive and evolutionary, thought, M. Fouillée in France, started on his philosophic career with a study of Plato. In each of the three countries the prominence given to Platonic studies through these translations was followed by a reaction more or less associated with the study of Aristotle, in Germany by Trendelenburg ('Elementa Logices Aristot.,' 1836, 'Logische Untersuchungen,' 1840), in France by Barthélemy-Saint Hilaire (1844, &c.), in England by the recent Aristotelian studies at the University of Oxford.

[1] See Mr F. H. Bradley's 'Appearance and Reality,' 1st ed., 1893.

ligious but likewise of supreme philosophical interest, a revival of the study of Plato went hand in hand; Leibniz being probably one of the first of the great philosophers of modern times to appreciate the Platonic idealism. Towards the end of the eighteenth century the old problem which was before the mind of Plato received a new expression in the philosophy of Kant, and this expression has dominated most of the great systems of nineteenth century philosophy. Even the positive philosophy in France and the philosophy of Evolution in England which, in their great representatives, professed to break with the historical traditions of philosophy, as Descartes and Bacon had done before them, have led, through the reaction which they provoked, to a profound appreciation of the form in which this central problem of philosophy presented itself to Plato and Kant.[1] Philosophical thought in the nineteenth century indeed not only started from, but, as we shall see, continually reverts to, Kant's statement of the great problem.

22.
Community
between
Kant and
Plato.

[1] This view of Kant's philosophy as belonging to the Platonic tradition is strongly brought out by Fr. Paulsen. "Kant's metaphysical conceptions through all their changes remained essentially the same : they consist of an idealism under the directing influence of Leibniz (and Plato)." Paulsen, 'Immanuel Kant,' 4th ed., p. 83 ; cf. also pp. xi, 97. This view has been attacked by some of Paulsen's critics.

One of the leaders of what is termed in Germany Neokantianism, a revival of the study of Kant's Works, following upon the publication of Kuno Fischer's 'Exposition of Kant's System,' in the 3rd and 4th volumes of his 'History of Modern Philosophy' (1860), F. A. Lange, has fully entered upon the influence of Platonism upon subsequent ancient and modern philosophy, and has in his 'History of Materialism' (Engl. transl. by E. C. Thomas, in 3 vols., 1877, 1880, 1881) denounced it as one of the great errors in philosophic thought. At the same time he recognises its great historical importance and its abiding value from a different point of view, which he places in opposition to the methodical treatment that belongs to science and philosophy. Of this important distinction, which is independently upheld by other thinkers besides Lange, I shall treat in a later chapter.

It is influenced throughout by the conviction that finds its most eloquent expression in the words which Kant placed at the end of his work on Ethics: "Two things fill my mind with ever new and ever growing wonder and reverence, the more often and continuously my thoughts are occupied with them: the starry heavens above me, and the moral law within me. Neither of these ought I to seek for or merely to assume, as if they lay outside my horizon, clothed in darkness and the unreachable. I see them both before me and connect them directly with the consciousness of my existence. The first begins with the place which I occupy in the outer world of the senses and expands the connections in which I stand into the invisibly great, with worlds upon worlds and systems upon systems, moreover, into limitless ages of their periodic motion, its origin and duration. The second begins with my invisible Self, my personality, and represents me as standing in a world which has true Infinity, but is accessible only to Reason, and with which I stand not only—as is the case with the outer world—in accidental, but in a general and necessary relation." [1]

We shall see in the sequel how the ideas contained or suggested in this remarkable passage, in which Kant sums up the final result of his teaching, have governed consciously or unconsciously the various directions which philosophical thought has taken during the nineteenth century. We shall also see how Kant replied, in no uncertain manner, to the question which of the two worlds is the truly real one.

[1] See Kant, 'Kritik der praktischen Vernunft,' 1st ed., 1788, conclusion.

II.

23.
Evolution
and the
power of
words.

No better instance of the control—not to say the tyranny—which language exerts over our thoughts can be found than the modern use of the word Evolution. In every department of literature, scientific, philosophical, or general, systematic or unsystematic, the word occurs again and again; it seems to satisfy authors as well as their readers. By it they seem to have found the right position from which to treat or comprehend almost any subject, to have gained the right attitude of contemplation.[1] In most cases, when the word is used on the title-pages of books, in introductions, reviews, or leading articles in the daily papers, it would be needless to ask the question what is really meant by the term; every-

[1] This refers mainly to English literature, where the term has been appropriated by Herbert Spencer to characterise his synthetic philosophy, and has since been generally used to signify development, physical or mental, much on the lines indicated by Schelling and Hegel in Germany at an earlier period. Latterly the term has also been largely used in French literature in a similar sense, though it had been current there already in the eighteenth century. In Germany the word has never become current in philosophical literature, and remains identified with the philosophy of Spencer, although isolated instances of its use are already to be found in the writings of Herder. On the history and the older meaning of the word, see Huxley's 'Science and Culture' (1888). "In the former half of the eighteenth century the term 'Evolution' was introduced into biological writings in order to denote the mode in which some of the most eminent physiologists of that time conceived that the generation of living things took place, in opposition to the hypothesis advocated in the preceding century by Harvey, &c." (p. 274).

"Evolution, or development, is at present employed in biology as a general name for the history of the steps by which any living being has acquired the morphological and the physiological characters which distinguish it" (p. 282).

"The terms 'Development,' 'Entwickelung,' and 'Evolutio,' are now indiscriminately used . . . by writers who would emphatically deny . . . the sense in which these words were usually employed by Bonnet or by Haller" (Ibid.)

body is supposed to understand it; to every one it seems to suggest a useful meaning.

In the scientific portion of this history we have seen how the word has been introduced, notably through cosmology and geology, to denote gradual succession of slow developments and changes; how it was then taken up by biology, and how, in these three fields of research, it marks a contrast to two other views, the uniformitarian and catastrophic views, of which the former emphasised the fixity, the latter, the suddenness of change in natural things and processes. From this more restricted and well-defined use the word has been introduced into other regions of science, history, and thought with less well-defined meanings.

To historians and philosophers the word recommends itself for yet other reasons, which seem to stand in no immediate connection with the movements of scientific thought to which I just referred.

A great change has come over the writing of history in the course of the nineteenth century. History, even if it be only political history, no longer consists solely of a record of wars, battles, invasions, and revolutions, nor in the biography of kings, rulers, warriors, and statesmen. An account of the manners and customs of different peoples in different ages is not relegated to isolated chapters, or to the meagre appendix of a political history.[1] The idea, which was already expressed by

24.
The social point of view in history.

---

[1] As it was by David Hume, who nevertheless emphasises the importance of these subjects. "Where a just notion is not formed of these particulars (viz., government, manners, finances, arms, trade, learning), history can be little instructive and often will not be intelligible" ('History of England,' Appendix to chap. xlix.)

older historians, that the progress of culture and civilisation, that laws, art, science, and industry and the life of
the people form by far the most interesting side of
history, has been realised in some of the later historical
works which the nineteenth century has produced. We
have now, at least, the beginnings of a history of the
popular masses,[1] of their occupations, habits, and interests. The result of this has been that historians
now deal more with the continuous, not so much with
the discontinuous, forces of historical life; with the properties of the masses, rather than with the characters of
individuals. One of the principal properties of masses
is this, that they possess inertia and move slowly. Like
the changes in Nature, their changes are gradual and
imperceptible, not sudden and catastrophic. Accordingly
historians deal now more with those phenomena which
are analogous to the slow-moving processes of Nature,
and the term Evolution has come in appropriately to
define the nature of the things and changes which they

[1] It is needless to refer English
readers to the constitutional histories of Hallam, Stubbs, and others,
or to J. R. Green's 'History of the
English People.' In countries like
France and Germany, where, within
recent times, constitutional history
hardly existed before the French
Revolution, the transition from political history to the social history
of the people did not take place
through the writing of constitutional
histories; but in the course of
the nineteenth century important
works, dealing with popular interests, have appeared, such as H.
Taine's 'Origines de la France
Contemporaine.' In Germany Gustav Freitag in his 'Bilder aus der
Deutschen Vergangenheit' (1859-
62), and notably W. H. Riehl,
'Naturgeschichte des Volkes'
(1853-69), 'Die Deutsche Arbeit'
(1861), 'Land und Leute,' and
many other books, made a beginning
of a history of the German people,
and at the end of the century we
have Karl Lamprecht's 'Deutsche
Geschichte,' in twelve volumes
(1891, &c.), written mainly from
an economic point of view. The
real historians of the people are,
however, the great novelists, and
it is interesting to note that the
modern social and historical novel
made its first appearance simultaneously with the rise of modern
historiography, and this in all the
three countries alike.

are attempting to record.   They deal, not so much with persons and events, as with the gradual development of constitutions, the growth of nationalities and societies,— in fact, with the life and interests of the masses.

The history of thought seems similarly to lend itself very readily to such treatment.   It is easy to fix upon one or several leading ideas or movements of thought, and to trace their slow growth and gradual diffusion and influence.   Important historical works, comprising sometimes many volumes, have been written or planned from this point of view.   It is seldom, however, that we do not rise from the perusal of such works with the feeling that they have only taken notice of one side, and that there are other sides which must also be taken into account if we wish to arrive at a fair judgment or a comprehensive view.[1]

Thus, although it is the object of this history to dwell

25.
Application
to the
history of
thought.

[1] The prominent examples of this manner of treating the History of Thought are Comte's 'Philosophie Positive,' Thos. Buckle's 'History of Civilisation,' and Hegel's 'Philosophy of History.' With these I shall be largely occupied in future chapters.   Of smaller Works we have Guizot's Lectures on 'History of Civilisation in Europe' and 'History of Civilisation in France' (1828); Lecky's 'History of the Rise and Influence of Rationalism in Europe' (1865), 2 vols.   German literature is particularly rich in monographs on special ideas or movements of thought, such as Lange's 'History of Materialism,' already quoted, Lasswitz' 'Geschichte der Atomistik,' 2 vols. (1890); Tholuck's 'Vorgeschichte des Rationalismus' (1853-62); 'Geschichte des Rationalismus' (1865); A. Ritschl's 'Geschichte des Pietismus' (1880-86); A. Drews' 'History of German Speculation since Kant,' containing mainly a history of the idea of Personality. Of course, by far the most important idea or cluster of ideas in modern times has its special development and history in the vast theological literature dealing with Christianity in its two great manifestations, 'Christian Church' and 'Christian Doctrine.' As this rests on a unique historical foundation, it will not be specially dealt with in the present section of this history.   It belongs to the religious thought of the century. Only where it comes into immediate contact with philosophical doctrines, as it certainly has done very frequently, shall I have occasion to refer to it.

by preference on the uniting ideas which underlie the Thought of the nineteenth century, I feel that it would

26.
Differences as well as uniting ideas not to be neglected.

be a mistake were I to undervalue the many differences and contrasts which have existed within the great realm of thought during that whole period.

I think it will be more helpful to my readers if, when entering on a new portion of my subject, I impress upon them the necessity of adopting an entirely different point of view from that to which they may have become accustomed by the perusal of the former

27.
New point of view required.

volumes. So strongly do I feel the necessity of this, that I am inclined to say, that except they are prepared to familiarise themselves with an entirely altered set of interests, problems, and methods, I shall fail to gain, or to retain, their attention in that which follows.

Unity or harmony of thought may be the desired end, it may even be a growing tendency which has become more and more evident; it certainly has not been the prominent external feature of nineteenth cen-

28.
Contrast to be dealt with.

tury Thought. The historian must first take note of the differences, the contrasts, and controversies before he can hope to trace the secret and underlying agreement. The former present themselves wherever we look, the latter is hidden—a subject rather of speculation and conjecture.

Similarly in the line of political history, of biography, of the histories of literature, or of practical life, a fuller and correcter insight is frequently gained by emphasising differences, be they national, personal, or local, than by dwelling on those features which belong to all forms of human life and progress alike. I desire, then, first of all, to impress on my readers the great difference, and indeed the contrast, which has existed all through the century, between that great domain of Thought of which I treated in the former volumes, under the name of Scientific Thought, and that equally important, though perhaps not equally coherent, region which we now approach, and which I comprise under the name of " Philosophical Thought."

Earlier philosophical systems of the century aimed at comprising under the term philosophy a well-arranged system of all knowledge : modern science inclines in the opposite direction of reducing philosophy to the position of being merely a formal introduction to science —or the most abstract outcome of scientific reasoning. Nevertheless, a glance at the scientific and philosophical literatures of Germany, France, and England forces upon us a strong conviction of the essential difference, of the contrast and antagonism in the aims and interests, in the style and the methods which are peculiar to science on the one side and to philosophy on the other. It was once as difficult to find a way from the abstractions of the great idealistic systems into the broad expanse of natural science, as it is now to ascend from this to the leading conceptions which form the basis of our moral and social life, the ideals of art and the truths of religion. The consequence has been that, a century ago, natural science took its own course, untrammelled by the theories of philosophers, and that we find in our days little inclination on the part of practical legislators, of statesmen, and of politicians, still less of artists and religious teachers, to refer for help

29.
Philosophical contrasted with scientific method.

to the doctrines of pure science. The ethics and religion of science which the latter half of the century
has variously elaborated meet with even less recognition by practical teachers than did the "philosophy
of Nature" of Schelling and of Oken a hundred years
ago on the part of the leaders of Science. Science and
the philosophy of Life, knowledge and wisdom, still
live mostly far apart, or are found united only in rare
and isolated instances. Looking, then, from a broad and
general point of view at the two great branches of
methodical thought of the past century, we may say
that there existed two main problems. For the philosopher who started with the highest interests before
his mind, the question arose, how was he to find a way
into the broad expanse of natural phenomena? What
was the principle by which these phenomena could be
grasped and studied? And for the student of Nature,
who started from the observation of nature herself in
her endless variety, the question presented itself: how
could he ascend to a conception and understanding of
the highest principles which govern and regulate the
mental life of man and mankind? The first of these
two problems has in a measure been solved by the
methods and principles of exact science, as I have
explained them in the former volumes; they are the
scientific, exact, or mathematical methods. The second
has occupied the greatest thinkers in the course of the
century, but a generally accepted answer has not been
arrived at.

We have seen that the methods of the exact sciences
by which the exploration of nature in the largest sense

of the word has been carried out have, in many instances, led to problems for which the exact or mathematical methods do not suffice. The question still awaits a universally approved answer: " Where and how can the thinking mind grasp the whole of that region which we broadly define as the life of the mind ? " Many ways and many answers have suggested themselves. The history of Philosophical Thought is mainly concerned with tracing and explaining them.

Having thus arrived at a crude definition of the task which the history of philosophical Thought has to fulfil, the question arises how the whole subject can be conveniently grouped and divided. The courses of philosophical Thought have been so numerous and intricate, crossing and recrossing each other so frequently, that the historian has no little difficulty in choosing a starting-point. Histories of philosophy have indeed been written in great number.[1] They have generally taken up the

30.
Histories of philosophy.

---

[1] By far the greater part of the work has been done by German historians, among whom during the nineteenth century the most prominent are—H. Ritter ('Geschichte der Philosophie,' 12 vols., 1836-53, of which several parts have been republished), Chr. Aug. Brandis ('Handbuch der Geschichte der Griechisch-Römischen Philosophie,' 1835-60, and a smaller work in 2 vols., 1862-64), J. E. Erdmann ('Versuch einer Wissenschaftl. Darstellung der neuer. Philos.,' 1834-53). After these pioneer works, written under the influence of Schleiermacher and Hegel, had to some extent cleared the ground, laid bare the sources and amassed an enormous amount of material, we come upon a second period of philosophical historiography in the more comprehensive and finished works of E. Zeller ('Die Philosophie der Griechen,' 3 vols., 1844-52, and subsequent editions much enlarged), Kuno Fischer ('Geschichte der neuern Philosophie,' 8 vols., 1854-99), and a new work by Erdmann (2 vols., 1865, and subsequent editions) embracing the whole history of Philosophy. The three last-mentioned works are all inspired by the Hegelian philosophy, from the stricter formulæ of which the authors have gradually emancipated themselves, most of all Zeller, who was much influenced by Strauss and, together with him, by modern scientific notions. After these

chronological point of view—dealing with the different
systems as they have rapidly followed each other,
especially on the Continent, casting side glances at the
smaller developments which have issued from them.
The classical model in this line is the 'History of
Modern Philosophy,' by Kuno Fischer. In spite of
much that may be said against the plan and method
adopted in this work, it remains the greatest performance which the last fifty years have witnessed in the
history of recent speculation, a worthy counterpart to
Edward Zeller's equally monumental 'History of Greek
Philosophy.'

works, which still form fundamental treatises, we come to a
third period of philosophical historiography in Germany which is
characterised by a freer treatment
of the subject, inclining more in
the direction which this history is
following — i.e., towards a history
of philosophic thought rather than
of philosophic systems or individual
thinkers. Prominent among these,
so far as recent philosophy is concerned, are Falckenberg ('Geschichte der neuern Philosophie,' 1886,
and many subsequent editions) and
W. Windelband ('Geschichte der
Philosophie,' 1893, 'Geschichte der
neuern Philosophie,' 2 vols., 1878-
80, both in several editions). For
purposes of reference Ueberweg's
'Grundriss' (re-edited by Heinze,
Part iv., 10th ed., 1906) is invalu-
able. In addition to these standard
works there exist an enormous
number of historical treatises on
special subjects, or written from
special points of view; among these
the historical works of E. von Hartmann are conspicuous. To such
works I shall refer in the course of
this History, but I am by no means
acquainted with all of them. Most
of the larger works which I mention confine themselves, so far as

the nineteenth century is concerned,
mainly to German philosophy, and
only the very latest have begun
to take notice also of philosophy
in France, England, and other
countries. Ueberweg's 'Grundriss'
has indeed elaborate additional sections on modern philosophy in
other than German countries. As
they are, however, written by separate authors belonging to the
respective countries, the whole
work does not afford a survey
from an international point of view.
The only comprehensive work written in this spirit is the 'History
of Modern Philosophy,' by Prof.
Harald Höffding (Engl. transl., 2
vols., 1900). Like his countryman G. Brandes, not being identified with any of the principal
movements of modern literature
or thought, he has been able, more
than other writers, to do justice
to the separate work of different
nationalities, taking up an impartial
cosmopolitan attitude; though Höffding admits that even in his later
supplementary historical works on
"modern problems of philosophy"
and "modern thinkers" his exposition is still defective, especially
for French philosophy.

Of the eight volumes of Kuno Fischer's work, six treat of the philosophy of Kant and his successors. There is no doubt that many students of philosophy owe their first introduction to this difficult subject to the luminous pages of this foremost historian of modern philosophy. The appearance of each of the successive parts has marked a revival in the interest which has been taken, not only abroad but also in this country, in philosophy generally, and in the special systems which it dealt with in particular. If I do not take this work as a guide through the labyrinth of philosophical theories, it is not for want of appreciation of its unique contribution to the philosophical literature of the second half of the nineteenth century, nor of gratitude for the insight I myself have gained through it, but because I am not primarily interested in expounding the different philosophical systems, but rather in tracing the leading ideas which have survived these systems themselves and become the common property of the philosophical mind at the present day.[1]

[1] Kuno Fischer's History (latest ed. in 9 vols.) may appropriately be termed a history of modern Idealism; which starts with Descartes and develops through Spinoza, Leibniz, Kant, Fichte, and Schelling to its consummation in Hegel. Other important movements in philosophy, both German and foreign, are treated as side issues or antitheses to the idealistic movement. Of other writers full attention is given only to Schopenhauer. Hegel's philosophy is looked upon as the dominating philosophy of the century, as its underlying Thought; its main characteristics being that it is speculative and not positive (Comte); that it is metaphysical and not psychological (Beneke); that it is monistic and not dualistic (Günther and Hermes); that it identifies Thought and Being in contrast to their essential difference (Herbart); that it finds the truly Real in logical thought or reason, not in the unreasoning Will (Schopenhauer) or the "Unconscious" (v. Hartmann) (see vol. viii., pt. 2, p. 1176 *sqq.*) The only promising further development of the Hegelian scheme is seen by Fischer in the philosophy of Lotze, who, as I shall have occasion to explain in the sequel, is historically connected with Hegel through his master, Ch. H. Weisse, and to whom belongs, according to Fischer, a position of unusual importance among German philosophers; his

In the earlier volumes of this history it was, of course, not my intention to give anything like an exhaustive record of scientific discoveries : I referred to these only in the way of illustration, or to the extent that they reacted upon Scientific Thought. So also in the present case, I shall only refer to special philosophical theories or systematic attempts as instances in and by which these permanent ideas have found expression which has survived writers and systems of philosophy alike. As we saw that the scientific activity of the century resulted in the firm establishment of a small number of leading conceptions, so I shall now endeavour to show how the huge and frequently conflicting philosophical literature has left behind it a small

main thesis being defined as the conviction that the world is not only a fact, but has also a meaning. Without this latter addition philosophy remains unphilosophical, "standing in the midst of the darkness and thicket of facts, what Bacon termed the *silva silvarum*, the forest of forests." See vol. viii. p. 1176, &c. Prominent in Kuno Fischer's History are the intimate relations which he establishes between philosophical idealism and the classical and romantic literature of Germany, of which he has a thorough knowledge and a unique conception, being popularly quite as well known through his writings in literary criticism as through his 'History of Philosophy.' Among his followers and pupils a recognition of this intimate connection of thought with literature and life is still more conspicuous. More than any other German historian has Fischer refused to recognise that other modern countries have elaborated philosophies of their own. In fact,

whenever important foreign names are mentioned it is only in contrast to the dominating current of Hegelian thought, or, as for instance with Darwin, as special examples of the Hegelian idea of development ; besides, important movements, even in German philosophy, are almost entirely omitted, as notably the great movement in religious philosophy which has its origin in Schleiermacher. In consequence of these omissions Kuno Fischer's History, though an inspiring work, is hardly a safe guide through the labyrinth of philosophical thought in Western Europe during the nineteenth century. It is interesting to note that Erdmann likewise closes his 'History of Modern Philosophy' with an even more elaborate appreciation of Lotze's views. In this respect both Fischer and Erdmann form a contrast to Zeller, who in his 'History of German Philosophy' (Munich, 1873) has only a slight and quite inadequate reference to Lotze.

body of guiding ideas which form the enduring bequest of nineteenth century speculation.

In dealing with scientific Thought I had frequent opportunity of pointing out how, in the course of the century, science has become more and more international, whereas in the beginning of the century the three principal nations with which we are dealing took up different and independent positions in their scientific work. A similar observation applies to philosophical Thought, although in this case the change from national to international work and co-operation has come much later and is less pronounced.

32.
National
and inter-
national
work in
science and
philosophy.

At the end of the century the philosophy of the three countries preserves more of the specific national characteristics than does their science, and whilst in the beginning of our period we meet with a lively though somewhat casual scientific intercourse and exchange, the philosophy of the Continent, notably of Germany, sprang up and developed without producing for a long time any important influence on France and England. In fact, we may say that the powerful mutual influence of French, English, and German philosophy produced in former centuries by the teaching of Descartes, Locke, Leibniz, and Hume, had given way to specific developments, chiefly in the Scottish and the German schools. If we wish to characterise broadly and without going into minute details these two opposite developments which sprang out of the common root of David Hume's scepticism, we may say that Scottish philosophy cultivated the field of psychological research, whereas German philosophy centred in metaphysics : the consequence being that we owe to the

former almost exclusively the development which psychology underwent during the first half of the century;
to the latter almost all the important constructive
efforts in modern philosophy.   These two quite independent movements met on common ground when
they approached, from different sides, the theories
of logic and philosophical method.   To this common
task British psychologists were led, mainly under the
guidance of John Stuart Mill, when they desired to
extend their methods and theories so as to deal with
economic and social phenomena : German metaphysicians
were led to similar investigations through a criticism of
the dialectic (or metaphysical logic) of Hegel, the leader
in this movement being the Aristotelian scholar, Adolf
Trendelenburg.   From these two independent modes of
approach, which met over a discussion of Hume's and
Kant's criticisms, the modern theory of Knowledge
(Erkentniss-theorie) arose.   On this ground British and
German philosophy met again after a separation of more
than half a century.

One would have thought that the great achievements
of the exact methods in France at the end of the
eighteenth century, resulting as we saw in many instances in a creation of new sciences or a complete
remodelling of older ones, would have led on to a similar
revolution in mental and moral science.   Such a process
indeed seemed to make a beginning in the school of
De Tracy and the ' Idéologues '; but for reasons which
have been explained in an earlier section of this work,
this development was stifled in its inception.[1]

[1] See this History, vol. i. p. 149.

French philosophical Thought, for a considerable period, preserved a purely eclectic character, and did so even long after an independent and novel system of philosophy had been elaborated in its midst, which was destined to exert a very powerful influence, first in England and later in France itself. This system, the philosophy of Auguste Comte, did not seek an extension of scientific research in the direction of psychology, which indeed it discouraged in a very peremptory fashion; it attached itself to that line of Thought which has always marked the strongest side of French genius; the mathematical rather than the essentially empirical development of knowledge. Those three great characteristics of German, English, and French philosophy during the first half of the century, the metaphysical, the psychological, and the mathematical, are intimately connected with the state of higher culture in these three countries during that period.

33. Auguste Comte.

England had developed, ever since the time of Bacon, the experimental or empirical philosophy of nature: it was only natural that a similar empirical treatment of mental life should suggest itself as the necessary complement of that philosophy. The brilliant achievements of French Science, building upon the mathematical foundations laid by Newton and Lagrange, suggested in the mind of Auguste Comte the idea of a positive or exact philosophy.

34. English empiricism.

But in one point the British and the French mind were in harmony, and this accounts for the interest which England took in Comte's philosophy in the middle of the century. Both countries had witnessed in the

35. Social point of view in France and England.

course of the seventeenth and eighteenth centuries large national developments, with this difference: that in England, the national development brought with it preeminently the industrial and economic problems, which only come to the fore when a more or less settled state of society has been reached; whereas the national development of France resulted in the great cataclysm of the Revolution, bringing with it the many doubts, theories, and constructive attempts which surround the question of the groundwork of state and society. Comte was the first to proclaim Sociology as the science of the nineteenth century—*i.e.*, the problems connected with the life of man, not as an individual but as a member of a social organisation.

This view appealed strongly to John Stuart Mill, in whose mind the sociological problem, which in his forerunners had been limited more or less to industrial, economic, and legal questions, began to acquire that larger meaning and greater importance which it has finally attained in the writings of Herbert Spencer.

36.
Absence of
the same in
Germany.

No such inducement to attempt the solution of practical questions referring to State and Society existed in Germany at the end of the eighteenth century. There existed there no great industrial developments and no great national expansion as in England, nor did the Revolution offer to German thinkers much more than a subject for theoretical contemplation. But, as I have had occasion to point out before, the dispersive nature of Germany's political life and the absence of national unity had resulted in a greater diffusion of culture and in the development of the great educational systems,

notably in the establishment of the German university
system which trained teachers and servants of the State,
and which in the philosophical faculty had organised a
comprehensive theoretical treatment of all problems of
mind, life, and nature alike.   It was natural that the
problem of knowledge as such should be taken up in a
novel and quite general manner and with direct recognition of the results of ancient and modern philosophy.
This explains the interest and appreciation with which
so abstract a work as Kant's philosophy was received.
It was purely logical, or rather metaphysical, and it
stood in immediate connection with Aristotle, Leibniz,
and Hume.   The sociological problem was taken up in
Germany at a much later period; but we must not
forget that meanwhile an important step in the practical
advancement of it had been made in the development of
the system of popular as distinguished from learned
education : a contribution to the solution of that problem
of the nineteenth century which for a long time was
wanting both in England and in France, and the far-
reaching consequences of which are only now beginning
to be realised.   This movement was greatly influenced
by the leaders of philosophical thought themselves, by
Lessing, Herder, Kant, Schiller, Fichte, Schleiermacher,
and Herbart, who inspired the leaders of education and
the founders of the many seminaries or training schools
for teachers in the elementary schools.

Looking, then, at the different national interests which
promoted philosophical Thought in the three countries,
we are led to a first division of this great subject which
is given by the terms, psychological, metaphysical, and

37.
Psychologi-
cal, meta-
physical,
and positive
interests.

positive. We can speak of a psychological, a metaphysical, and a positive movement in philosophical
Thought—that is, we can distinguish between a pre-
eminently psychological, a metaphysical, and a positive
or exact treatment of philosophical problems. To this we
may add, as equally important aspects, the logical and
the sociological; but we must note that the three former
terms refer to the subjects, the two latter to the method
and purpose, of philosophical reasoning. Accordingly,
I shall in the sequel treat separately of the development
of psychology, of metaphysics, of scientific method, and
the theory of knowledge. A later portion of this section
will have to deal with the question, to what extent the
social problem, which in the meantime has more and
more forced itself upon the attention of thinkers of every
school, has been defined and brought nearer to a solution.
The social problem is in time one of the latest, as it is
in subject one of the most complex, problems which the
nineteenth century has taken up. In the beginning of
the century it was still largely in the hands of enthusiasts
and visionaries, to whom, it may be noted in passing, we
owe almost all the great ideals in our higher life, and
from whom they pass into the hands of the thinker and
the philosopher, by whom they are in turn handed over
to the practical man, to the legislator, the statesman,
the leader of society, industry, or labour.

Confining ourselves, then, in the beginning, to the three
earlier philosophical developments — the metaphysical,
the psychological, and the positive—it is next important
to observe that in due course they underwent certain
changes. These changes are common to them all alike,

as they are indeed characteristic of all recent Thought
which is not purely scientific or mathematical. As this
points to a general feature of nineteenth century philosophy, and has led to special doctrines of great importance and widespread influence, it will be helpful to take
note of it in advance.

38.
A new char-
acter of
philosophi-
cal thought
in the
century.

Philosophical thought has acquired the general character I refer to, mainly under the influence of the
German mind. We owe it to that organisation for
abstract research which we find typified in the philosophical faculty at the German universities. This is the
home and nursery of pure science in the broader sense of
the word, denoted by the term " Wissenschaft "—*i.e.*,
science and erudition combined.

When the leaders and founders of the German
university system, at the end of the eighteenth century,
undertook to start afresh higher instruction in all
branches of knowledge, they found themselves face to
face with an enormous accumulation of erudition and of
philosophical doctrine. This had been brought together
by ancient and modern thinkers, by scattered research,
by no generally recognised method, and with no common
aim and purpose. It was the tradition, and constituted
the inheritance from former ages. More and more it
became evident that this great accumulation of knowledge, of learning, and of doctrine required to be put in
order and to be sifted, so that truth could emerge and
falsehood be discarded. Historical records had to be
traced to their sources, theories had to be followed up to
their origin or shown to be valid and consistent; dogmas
had to show the authority upon which they rested; in

fact, the whole edifice of knowledge, learning, and doctrine, as handed down from former generations, had to be put in order and newly arranged.

The precept of Leibniz had to be carried out in its integrity, "Didici in mathematicis ingenio, in physicis experimentis, in legibus divinis humanisque auctoritate, in historicis testimoniis nitendum esse." [1]

Such process of sifting or arranging, of confirming or discarding, existing opinions, and generally of establishing the true canons of research in dealing with historically accumulated material, had already been sporadically set agoing in various branches, but notably in the domain of classical learning, about the time when the natural and exact sciences had been put upon an independent and secure foundation by the great natural philosophers of the sixteenth and seventeenth centuries. We have to go back to the names of Erasmus, of Scaliger, of Casaubon, and of Bentley if we wish to trace the beginnings of that great volume of learning and research which has gradually acquired the generic name of Philological Criticism.

Towards the end of the eighteenth century the term criticism had been introduced in this country to denote discussions relating to subjects of fine art and literature.[2]

39.
The term
Criticism
as used by
Kant.

We find Kant in Germany introducing the term to denote preparatory investigations which he deemed necessary in order to place philosophy upon a secure foundation, and to refute the scepticism of Hume and the

---

[1] "I have learnt that in mathematics we have to rely on genius, in physics on experiment, in law, human and Divine, on authority, in history on testimony."

[2] See especially Henry Home, Lord Kames' 'Elements of Criticism' (1761).

metaphysics of Leibniz. In the first half of the nineteenth century a similar process of sifting and analysing was infused into scientific theology in Germany, whilst critical philology under the hands of F. A. Wolf and his successors attained, during the second third of the century, that rigid, methodical development which for a long time gave it the leading influence in the higher secondary and learned schools of Germany.

All these resultants of the desire to sift, to arrange, and to judge historically transmitted material, be it facts, records, or theories, testify to the working of the critical spirit. This latter, together with the purely scientific or exact spirit, marks probably the most important characteristic of nineteenth century Thought. It is accompanied by its necessary and inevitable ally—historical research and learning.

All methodical thought which cannot adopt, or is not yet ready to adopt, the canons of exact or scientific thought, such as have been set out in the earlier portion of this work, has been all through the nineteenth century, and is still, under the undisputed sway of the historical and critical spirit; all philosophical theories, be they logical, psychological, or purely scientific and enunciated for whatsoever end or purpose, are dominated by criticism and history. So much is this the case that in many instances research has almost lost itself in history and criticism, to the damage of the positive interests which originally prompted it. We notice this, for instance, in the work of many distinguished representatives of critical theology abroad : the religious interest has not infrequently given way to a purely literary or learned interest.

40.
Criticism
and history.

Before entering upon a more detailed account of psychological, logical, and positive lines of reasoning, and before dealing with the Sociological Thought of the century, I therefore propose to pass under review the growth and diffusion of the critical and historical spirit in the three countries, in a manner similar to that which I adopted when dealing with the growth and diffusion of the scientific spirit in the earlier part of this history.

41.
Growth and
diffusion of
the critical
spirit.

In the present case, as Germany is the centre of the critical phase of Thought, and has carried criticism into every branch of learning, literature, and art in the most complete manner, I shall begin with the critical spirit in Germany, after which I shall treat of the diffusion of criticism in England and France. After this I propose to take up in the four following chapters the psychological, the logical, the metaphysical, and the positivist movements of Thought, up to the point at which they came under the decided influence of the critical and historical spirit. It will then be shown that this resulted in the creation of two distinct lines of speculation, the first of which started from the foundation of the logical and metaphysical systems of the Continent, the other from the psychological and positivist doctrines of France and England. Both of them are historical, and have in the detail of their research had to resort to special critical methods : we may comprise them under the general term of theories of development. Continental Thought, under the influence of the Hegelian system and the great historical studies which were there prevalent, adopted the name of history of culture or civilisation in a more general sense ; whereas, under the combined influence of natural science and the positivist philosophy, the word Evolution has been introduced by Herbert Spencer to denote that form of development which is based upon mechanical or physical principles.

All through the present section of this History the idea of development in these two distinct forms will be shown to have influenced philosophical thought and given to philosophical problems an entirely altered complexion. It has, moreover, tended latterly to bring together scientific and philosophical thought, rendering, as it appears, the former more philosophical and the latter more scientific. The two aspects which the idea of development has assumed centre respectively in the philosophies of Hegel and of Herbert Spencer.

42.
Hegel and Spencer.

There exist for our human mind only two intelligible forms of spontaneous, that is, inevitable and never-ceasing, change—namely, physical motion on the one side and the movement of thought on the other. Neither can be arrested or annihilated : they form the simplest examples, which cannot be further analysed, of the process of development, and they underlie respectively the systems of Herbert Spencer and of Hegel.[1]

[1] Before the modern conceptions of Evolution were distinctly formulated, this view was prominently brought forward in a criticism of Hegel's as well as of Herbart's system, by Adolf Trendelenburg in his 'Logische Untersuchungen,' of which the first edition appeared in 1840. It marks at the same time a reversion to Platonic and Aristotelian ideas, to that era of Thought when science and philosophy were not yet divided. In the Preface to the second edition (1862) we find the following remarkable passage :— "The prejudice of the Germans must be abandoned that for the philosophy of the future a new principle had to be discovered. The principle has been found ; it lies in that organic conception of the Universe which has its foundation in Plato and Aristotle, and which, continuing from them, will have to complete itself in a profounder examination of fundamental ideas and through an interchange with the

But there still remains a large and important section of the philosophical literature of the century in all the three countries which is not covered by the foregoing developments, but into which they all enter. This arises out of the peculiarity of philosophical thought to which I referred in the third part of the general introduction to this history.

**43.
Intermediate position of philosophy between science and religion.**

I there tried to show how philosophy occupies an intermediate position between scientific thought which is capable of clear definition and enunciation and that other and opposite region of thought which I have variously termed Individual, Subjective, or Religious Thought. In fact, we may say that one of the objects of philosophy has always been to effect a reconciliation between science and religion, or, expressed in different words, to show the relations between definite and detailed knowledge on the one side and our beliefs and convictions on the other. The philosopher is bound to have an eye as much for the latter as for the former.

**44.
Monistic doctrines.**

There have indeed existed many philosophical attempts to establish what is usually termed the monistic view by starting from one undisputed principle, or from one coherent and self-consistent body of facts, and to discountenance any compromise between apparently contradictory regions of thought. Especially in the course of the nineteenth century various efforts were made to

science of reality." Trendelenburg's criticisms, though they influenced several prominent living thinkers, have generally been too little appreciated, especially out of Germany. When he wrote, the philosophical mind still hoped for a new constructive effort, and was more easily satisfied by the brilliant constructions of Schopenhauer and v. Hartmann than by the historicism and eclecticism of Trendelenburg or the cautious and circumspect analysis of Lotze.

base all philosophy upon a purely Scientific foundation. It is not necessary, at present, to examine what has been the nature and the result of these efforts. We shall come across them in the sequel when dealing with special philosophical problems. At present it is sufficient to note that these attempts have not been found generally acceptable, and have had little practical influence. It must be admitted that individual beliefs and convictions still play a very large part in the region of thought; that they have quite as much the right to be regarded as facts as any more definite, scientific, or historical knowledge. For although it is true that it will rarely be possible for two persons to agree exactly where beliefs and convictions are in question, it is just as true on the other side that these beliefs and convictions, in their collective aggregate, exert upon our practical life an even greater influence than exact knowledge and science itself.

Most persons are unable or unwilling to take a correct inventory of their beliefs and convictions; they nevertheless, willingly or unwillingly, submit more or less to the existing laws of the society in which they live, and to manifold restrictions and ordinances of a legal, moral, and religious nature.

They do so consciously or unconsciously, admitting in this manner that the convictions and beliefs of which these laws and ordinances are the outcome have a marked reality and are of paramount importance. And if we consider all the more important steps which we take, either in our individual or in our social and political life, and try to analyse the motives

which have led to them and to gauge the amount
of actual and undisputed knowledge by which we are
guided, it will probably be found that the latter plays
only a very small part, and that beliefs and convictions
constitute the much larger portion of the considerations
which have led up to them. The task not only of
placing these convictions and beliefs in a clearer light,
but also of bringing them into some definite and intelligible relation with the results of scientific thought, will
therefore always present itself; and to many thinking
minds it will be the most important function of philosophical speculation.

45.
Attempts at
reconcilia-
tion of
knowledge
and belief.

The endeavours to fulfil this task, to reconcile Knowledge and Belief, constitute a large department of the
philosophical thought of the century. They will claim
our attention in the later chapters of this section, which
will respectively deal with the time-honoured problems
of the Beautiful (Æsthetics), the Good (Ethics), and the
Spirit (Philosophy of Religion), further with the more
recent problem of Society. A last chapter will deal
exclusively with the several attempts towards a unification and systematisation of thought in which the
nineteenth century has been particularly rich.

Perhaps we shall have to state that those endeavours
towards a reconciliation of the scientific and religious
aspects have not been very successful, and shall thus
have to confirm a widespread opinion which looks upon
such attempts with disfavour. But even if this should
be the case, we shall be much impressed with the discovery that all through the century, and from apparently
divergent points of view, the fact has been recognised

that all human thought as well as all mental and natural development reveal the existence of two factors,—that there exist, as it were, two poles which form independent centres of life and development.

In the same degree as the desire has become more pronounced to unify Thought and Knowledge, the apparent dualism, so evident to common-sense, has become more and more accentuated. In fact, as I stated in the beginning of this Introduction, the desire to discover the underlying unity has primarily revealed the existing contrast and the necessity of first clearly defining and understanding it.

Accordingly we find running through nearly all the philosophical theories and speculations of the different schools, the attempt to grasp more completely and define more clearly that inherent dualism, frequently, indeed, with the tacit or pronounced intention of dissolving it in some unifying conception. Nearly every phase of philosophical thought has thus coined its special terms wherewith to define this two-sidedness or polarity which exists everywhere in and around us. Kant spoke of " phenomena " and " noumena," of " pure theoretical " and " pure practical reason "; Schopenhauer writes of " the world as Will and Intelligence "; Schelling strove all through the many phases of his philosophical career to complete the " negative " by a " positive " philosophy; Herbert Spencer places " the Unknowable " in opposition to " the Knowable," and even Comte's philosophy finds room for " the Incognoscible."

46.
Dualism in philosophic systems.

Of all these different terms in which the same idea finds various expression, that which gives to the active principle in human nature, to the Will, an important, not to say the most prominent, position, has probably succeeded more than any other in impressing the philosophical consciousness of the present age. This explains why the philosophy of Schopenhauer, neglected for a long time, and repellent in many of its features, has nevertheless latterly attracted and held the attention of thinkers of very different schools, and has led to so many minor developments.

The dualism which pervades all modern thought will occupy us quite as much as the attempts towards unification. At the same time, the study of the various attempts to give expression to the idea that in the life of the mind, be it in the individual, society, or history, the active principle occupies the primary position, will lead us naturally on to the social question which, as I said, will form the subject of one of the last chapters of this section. In many ways we shall find that all other developments more or less converge upon it.

47.
Plan of this history.

It will be seen from this rough sketch of the manner in which I propose to subdivide the wide region of philosophical thought, that I do not intend to follow in any strictness either a biographical, or a systematic, or a chronological arrangement.[1]   In fact, I intend as little

---

[1] The plan I have adopted may best be understood by saying that the History of Philosophical Thought is considered to be identical with a History of Philosophical Problems. Most of these problems are as old as philosophy itself, and go back into antiquity, although some of them, such as the problem of Knowledge, the problem of the Beautiful, the problem of Religion, and the problem of Society, have only in recent times been independently treated and received special names. The attempt to deal with History of Philosophy according to this plan is not new, but has been more or less definitely adopted by various prominent thinkers of this age. I have only become more intimately

to write a history of philosophy, or the philosophers of the century, as in the earlier part of the work I proposed to write a history of science. Histories of philosophy, as a whole, or of the various schools of philosophy, have been written in great number; in the right place I shall fully refer to them. It will then become abundantly evident how little my own work could have been written without the assistance which at every step I have received from them. But though it may appear as if the proposed manner of dealing with the subject could hardly afford that systematic completeness which a more chronological method might secure, it will in the sequel

acquainted with their writings after having sketched out for myself the plan of this section ; but I gratefully acknowledge the assistance I have received from them in working out the scheme. Foremost among them are : Prof. Windelband's brilliant ' History of Philosophy,' of which I have before me the 4th German edition (1907); an English translation by J. F. Tufts appeared in 1893. In a prospectus to the 1st edition (1889) Prof. Windelband defines his subject to be " a history of the problems and of the notions which have been formed for their solution." In referring to the 6th and 7th sections of his History my readers will be able to see how his arrangement and definition of the problems differs from those I have adopted. More distinctly and concisely, the ' History of Philosophy ' as a History of Problems has been written by Harald Höffding (1st ed. 1894, Engl. transl. 1900). In the Introduction he says : "The investigation of the History of Modern Philosophy which I have here undertaken has confirmed me personally in the view . . . that philosophical investiga-

tion centres in four main problems." He then characterises these problems as—
1. " The Problem of Knowledge (the logical problem)."
2. " The Problem of Existence (the cosmological problem)."
3. " The Problem of the Estimation of Worth (the ethico-religious question)."
4. " The Problem of Consciousness (the psychological problem)."
We have further from the same eminent author, with a slightly different arrangement of the four problems, a series of Lectures delivered in the University of Upsala (1902) and published under the title ' Philosophische Probleme ' (1903), and a Review of recent thinkers in a series of Lectures delivered in the same year in Copenhagen and published under the title ' Moderne Philosophen ' (1905) ; a French work on somewhat related lines with the title ' A History of the Problems of Philosophy ' has been written by Paul Janet and Gabriel Séailles and translated by Ada Monahan (Macmillan, 1902).

become evident that in relation to those several distinct aspects which I have defined, all the important doctrines of philosophy and many underlying and hidden currents of thought will come under review. Frequently, also, lines of reasoning otherwise far apart and apparently diverg- ent will be shown to reveal the same or similar ten- dencies. Thus the logical and metaphysical development of thought will not only deal with the philosophies of Kant and his immediate successors, but also with that independent development which centres in John Stuart Mill. Psychology will not only embrace the Scottish school of philosophy, but also that of Herbart, Fechner, and Wundt in Germany, as well as the more recent contributions of the French school; positivism will for us mean not only the philosophy of Comte, but also many cognate developments in England, though they refuse allegiance to Comte, as also the latest theory of scientific knowledge which we connect with the name of Professor Ernst Mach. The great idea of develop- ment will, as has been stated above, have two sides, of which, far distant as they otherwise appear, Hegel and Herbert Spencer are nevertheless together the main representatives. Almost all the leading thinkers of this century have, to a greater or less extent, attacked the problem of monism or dualism, which historically can be traced back to Leibniz, whose ideas in one form or another meet us again in the speculations of very oppo- site schools of recent philosophy. We cannot understand the position which philosophy has taken up towards the religious question without recalling the influence of Jacobi and Schleiermacher abroad, or of Hamilton and

Mansel in this country. All the different lines of philosophical thought converge, however, as I have already
said, towards the practical or social question which has
increasingly asserted itself in many forms as the great
philosophical problem of the age.

This treatment will at the same time force upon us a
recognition how little has yet been done by scientific or
philosophical thinkers towards the solution of the many
burning questions which it involves, and how much, on
the other hand, we are still beholden to that vast army
of writers, thinkers, and practical workers who are
inspired by convictions and beliefs which have not yet
found any full and adequate scientific or philosophical
recognition.

In this way the study of philosophical Thought will
lead us on to that large volume of unsystematic and
unmethodical Thought which I have variously defined
as subjective, individual, or religious, and which should
form the subject of the third and concluding section of
this History.

III.

Before entering upon a detailed account of the development of the different philosophical ideas in the course of
the nineteenth century, it may be useful to my readers
if I try to give a general and comprehensive view of the
character and aims of philosophical Thought during that
period. In attempting this I do not find myself so
favourably situated as when I started on our survey

48.
Character
and aims
of philo-
sophical
thought.

of Scientific Thought. There we were from the beginning able to give a simple and intelligible account of the aim and purpose of all scientific reasoning ; this consisted in the application of one and the same method to all objects and events of Nature as they exist or have existed in the past. This method was the simple method which begins with observation and proceeds through description and clear definition, to measurements, and ultimately to calculation : only to the extent that the latter and highest process—viz., that of calculation—has become applicable, has it been found possible to deal not only with present and past phenomena and occurrences, but also to some extent to foretell the future, or to penetrate with our knowledge into those recesses of nature which are, through distance in time and space, through magnitude or minuteness, unreachable by actual observation.

49.
No consensus as to philosophical methods.

It is not possible to comprise all successful philosophical thought within an equally simple formula. This defect may be traced to two definite causes. The first of these is the fact that no general consensus exists regarding the method of philosophy, such as exists with regard to the methods of science. The methods of the latter, though their logical nature has been variously defined, are nevertheless so simple in their application that little time need be spent by the student of science in learning them. The best way of acquiring a knowledge of them is practice itself. This gives such proficiency that even the greatest minds that have applied these methods with unfailing success have not generally spent much time in giving an account of the processes of thought which they have used. If they have done so it has usually been after they had successfully used them, and then even their account has not always been marked either by particular clearness or consistency. In fact, the practice of the scientific method, now universally admitted, resembles very much the use of language which is not primarily acquired by the study of grammar and syntax, but by the practice of speaking and reading. Some of the greatest writers, especially in this country, would probably be quite unable to give an account of the correctness and beauty of their style, which is rather an unconscious expression of their individuality.

In the case of philosophy, we seem still to be in the position of the learners of a foreign tongue ; we have to go through all the intricate rules of etymology and syntax. The stylistic handling of these subjects has not become a second nature to us like the use of a language in which we have got beyond the tuitional stage. Accordingly we find all through the century an endless discussion and ever-repeated attempts referring to the fixing of the right method and procedure ; some maintaining that the method of philosophy is purely logical or metaphysical with as much emphasis as others denounce the logical method as empty, ridicule metaphysics as pernicious, and preach the pure application of scientific methods as the only promising and fruitful way. By doing so, we may point out, they again expose themselves to the just retort of their opponents, that their chosen method is only applicable to a very small number of philosophical questions, and these the least important and interesting.

But this uncertainty as to the method is probably not

the most important feature which divides philosophical from scientific thought. There exists a much more radical difference, and one which affords a deeper insight into the real nature and aim of philosophy. Probably the simplest way of letting my readers realise this great difference is by saying that philosophy is interested, science is disinterested.

The ideal man of science should care only for the correctness of his observations, the consistency of his inferences, and the formal truthfulness of his calculations and deductions. No higher interest in maintaining a preconceived notion, in serving a practical end, or in supporting a pet theory, should be allowed to interfere with the even and passionless tenor of the scientific judgment. That this does not exist to perfection is the consequence, not of the faulty method of science, but of the frailty of all human nature. The scientific mind should acquire, or try to acquire, an attitude as dispassionate and as evenly balanced as that of a judge to whose care the most momentous issues concerning life, happiness, or misery are intrusted. We know from history how many centuries elapsed before the purity of scientific method was not only preached and accepted, but also manifested through practice. We have heard much of the baneful effect of the influence of theological dogmas and metaphysical theories.

The nineteenth century is justly proud of having finally established and successfully practised the pure scientific method. The greatest representatives of science in all the three countries we are specially interested in have bequeathed to us models of research, conducted without fear or favour, with the sole object of arriving at that natural knowledge which was proclaimed by Francis Bacon, for which the great Societies and Academies of Europe were founded, and which probably attained its most brilliant expression in the work of the German Universities during the first two-thirds of the century. It cannot, however, be held that this serene temper of the scientific mind has been left undisturbed within the last forty years. Hardly escaped from the trammels of theology or the control of metaphysics, a new danger seems to threaten pure science. This danger comes from the side of the practical usefulness of scientific discoveries, and from the many problems which the Arts and Industries place before the scientific mind in an ever-increasing degree. There seems to be as much danger nowadays of science becoming the prey of commercial, industrial, and financial interests, as there was formerly that it should lack independence through being regulated by theology and metaphysics.

Philosophy, as distinguished from Science, does not profess to start on its career without a distinct interest in the results which it will attain to. The ultimate answers to the highest questions of life and society, of duty and happiness, are not indifferent to the philosophical thinker, and if we occasionally meet with some secluded sage who professes to have attained to that unbiassed attitude which characterises pure thought, we shall have to admit that his speculation suffered from the want of contact with things real ; nor is it an infrequent occurrence to find that his followers have speedily undertaken to show the practical bearing of his refined and abstract theories. It seems as if even the most abstract and serene thought could not live long without coming into contact — for mutual good or evil — with the affairs of practical life.

These affairs and interests of practical life form the highest subject of philosophical thought; with their furtherance, be it to strengthen, to reform, or to develop them, philosophical thought is mainly occupied. The whole fabric of Society, all the work of Culture, all the achievements of civilisation, are bound up with certain existing fundamental convictions which cannot be attacked or lost without the most serious consequences. In the face of this circumstance it would be futile to maintain that any earnest thinker could approach these momentous problems without a feeling of the great responsibility which must attach to his utterances. It is not too much to say that the whole weight of the moral world presses upon the minds of those who deal with these fundamental problems.

51.
Philo-
sophers as
educators
and re-
formers.
The great philosophers of the past century have shared this feeling of heavy responsibility with the great thinkers of former ages, and the fact that that century has probably produced a greater number of leading thinkers fully conscious of the educational and reforming task which lay before them, is a sign that more has been expected in these recent times from philosophical speculation than in any former age during the whole course of civilised history. The only age which could be compared with the nineteenth century was that which during the fourth and third centuries B.C. witnessed the disintegration of the ideals of Grecian

Culture. Considering these enormous responsibilities, these momentous issues which have lain heavily on the philosophic mind in recent times, it is not surprising to find that many philosophic thinkers have taken refuge in studies which are subsidiary or purely preliminary. Frightened, as it were, by the overwhelming importance of the final problems, they have contented themselves with taking up a position similar to that which is habitual and customary among men of pure science.

There it has long been recognised that progress can only be attained by specialisation. The scientific problem, as a whole, does not exist. It can only be solved in parts. The science of any age consists in the summation of numberless contributions. But the problem of philosophy, which is the problem of Life, is *one* and undivided. Those who only take up special aspects must do so with the conviction that their work is incomplete, not only in the sense that all human work is incomplete, but in that sense which is the only important one from a philosophical point of view, viz., in its bearing upon the whole and undivided issue. The only escape from that depressing conviction of inadequacy which the resignation of the philosophical specialist necessarily produces, lies in the belief that the solution of the problem of Life is worked out by different means, and in a different sphere, from those peculiar to philosophical thought. I shall point out in the sequel how certain scientific and philosophical notions which have become current in the latter half of the nineteenth century — notably the theories of Evolution and the tendency to consider everything

52.
Problems of science are many, problem of philosophy is one.

from the historical point of view — have the effect of
seemingly exonerating the thinking mind of the individual or of the age from that heavy responsibility
which the leading thinkers of former times felt to rest
on their shoulders.

Thus it has come about that the greater part of the
philosophical writings of the last quarter of the century
exhibit an entirely different character from those belonging to the earlier part of our period.[1] In the
earlier period we meet with a great array of comprehensive philosophical systems which approach con-
fidently and hopefully the great world-problem ; and
although these systems belong mostly to Germany, we
find, somewhat later, France and England taking prominent part in the attempt to unite all knowledge into
all-embracing systems—the systems of Positivism and
Evolution—and to arrive at formulæ which should, as
it were, lead to a solution of all the great practical
problems of life and society. It is perhaps safe to say
that all these systems have had their day, that the

[1] When in 1876 the late Prof.
Croom Robertson, with the generous support of A. Bain, started
the quarterly review 'Mind,' he
induced prominent thinkers of the
different countries to write summary accounts of the state of philosophy with them. These are to
be found in the two first volumes,
and are still well worth reading,
notably those by Mark Pattison
(Oxford), H. Sidgwick (Cambridge),
Veitch (Scotland), G. C. Robertson
(London), Th. Ribot (France), and
W. Wundt (Germany). Before
that time Ravaisson had written
a highly interesting report on
French philosophy (1867), and M.
Boutroux has taken up the subject
for the last third of the century in
the 'Revue de Métaphysique et de
Morale' (1908). In the same
volume will be found articles on
the philosophical movement in
other countries. For German contemporary thought the publication
of a memorial to Kuno Fischer,
entitled ' Die Philosophie im
Beginn des 20ten Jahrhunderts '
(1904), is to be recommended, also
the earlier publication of Lexis,
' Die deutschen Universitäten '
(vol. i., Article by J. Baumann,
p. 427, 1893).

formulæ of Comte and Spencer, no less than those of Schelling, Hegel, and Schopenhauer, have been tried and found wanting. Not indeed without leaving lasting marks of their originality and power in special directions, affording many fresh glimpses which had escaped the glance of earlier thinkers. To show to what extent they have done this will form the main task of the following pages. During the last quarter of the century, systems of philosophy have been rare, if one can say that they have been produced at all. The largely increased number of students and writers on philosophy are content to devote themselves to the examination of special questions, to write preliminary and preparatory treatises,[1] to content themselves at best with a kind of eclecticism, following the course begun by Victor Cousin in France, and adopting the maxim of Lotze, " that after such a lengthy development of philosophy, during which every point of view has been set up, abandoned, and tried again, there no longer exists any merit in originality but only in accuracy." [2] Others have put forward their attempts towards a Unification of Knowledge as subjective endeavours, in the same way as

[1] The first among the leading philosophers of the earlier part of the century who adopted this position was Herbart, whose 'Lehrbuch zur Einleitung in die Philosophie' was published in 1813, and went through several editions. It is also characteristic of Herbart that he never attempted a systematic exposition of his philosophical ideas, and left some of the highest problems, notably that of Religion, undiscussed. Since his time the writing of Introductions to Philosophy has been, in Germany, quite the order of the day. Among these, those of Wundt, Paulsen, and Külpe, have a large circulation. Prof. Wundt has crowned the large array of his separate philosophical Treatises by publishing in 1889 his 'System of Philosophy.' He is almost the only thinker of the last generation with whom we shall have to deal at length in the last chapter of this section, which will bear the title " Of Systems of Philosophy."

[2] See Lotze, ' Streitschriften ' (1857), p. 5.

Lotze himself had done, or as fanciful and half poetic creations. Here Fechner is the most original example. The lack of originality, combined with an increased accuracy, shows itself in the great predilection for historical studies, in the revival of older theories and systems, in the love of the past. In a similar manner this retrospective interest has shown itself wherever Art and Literature have left behind them an age of original production and the sources of inspiration seem for the time exhausted. Such phases in the history of thought or of artistic creation are characterised by minuteness of research, by formal excellence, by critical acumen, by elaboration of detail. They mark the twilight of the waning day which again, after the longer or shorter absence of the full light, may lead to the dawn of a new day. It is not the object of the historian to indulge in prophecies or fanciful anticipations; yet it is his duty to note whether his age shows any sign of revival and of the return of the creative faculty.

To this latter question I shall revert later on; in the meantime it is useful to note that the last generation, devoid as it has been of any distinct creative effort in philosophical thought, has been characterised by two generalised movements of thought, and this in all the three countries alike. The first of these tendencies has already been noted at the beginning of this Introduction; we may call it the reversion to common-sense. On this I need not at present dwell at any greater length, as the special forms which this general tendency has assumed in the different literatures and schools will

54.
Reversion
to common-
sense.

occupy us in the sequel. The second tendency is perhaps more prominent, and in the eyes of many thinking persons more promising. Allured by the enormous progress and the stupendous triumphs of the Natural Sciences, thinkers of the last generation have attempted to remodel the whole of philosophy according to the methods of science. The word science in France and England has acquired a larger meaning than it used to have in the earlier part of the century. We now hear much of the scientific treatment of philosophical problems. Definite well marked-off provinces have been separated from the whole realm of philosophy and placed, as it were, under special management; thus in psychology, logic, and ethics, more or less successful attempts have been made to establish independent and self-consistent doctrines upon the basis of a small number of self-evident principles which, just as in the various Natural Sciences, enable a large amount of empirical material to be described, arranged, and methodically expounded. Even in Germany, where philosophy has always ranked as a Science in that larger sense of methodical Thought which is conveyed by the term "Wissenschaft," the last twenty-five years have witnessed the growth of an "exact" or "scientific" philosophy,[1] an attempt, the

55.
"Scientific Philosophy."

---

[1] In 1861 the first number of the 'Zeitschrift für exacte Philosophie' (edited by Allihn, Ziller, and Flügel, pupils of Herbart) appeared, and was continued till 1875, and with certain changes up to 1896. Its programme was to explain clearly the proper tasks of philosophy and of the separate philosophical sciences, &c. Latterly the memory of Herbart has been mainly preserved, through his influence in the sphere of education, in the 'Zeitschrift für Philosophie und Pädagogik' (since 1894). In 1877 Avenarius started the 'Vierteljahrsschrift für Wissenschaftliche Philosophie' with the professed object of founding Philosophy as a science upon experience alone without specifically or narrowly defining this term.

significance of which did not remain unnoticed by the representatives of the older schools of philosophical thought. This so-called scientific philosophy does not necessarily exclude a regard for the highest questions of systematic philosophy, an interest in the great realities, the quest for which has always been the principal prerogative of philosophy; but this interest is being kept in suspense as premature, forming frequently the inevitable background and sustaining impulse, but not the object of philosophic thought in our day. On the other hand, some representatives of this scientific philosophy have openly disavowed all intention of dealing with the great World-and-Life problem; separate schools have reproached each other with a taint of metaphysics, maintaining that such a study does not legitimately exist at all, being merely a waste and corruption of useful thought. Modern language, notably in France and England, has coined such terms as " the Unknowable," " the Incognoscible," and " Agnosticism," in order to give expression to this extreme view. Others have been more cautious, taking refuge in some current phrases such as " the Unconscious," " the Subconscious," or " the Subliminal self." To all these thinkers, whether they belong to the bolder or to the more cautious school, general philosophy, apart from the several philosophical sciences, still has a special and well - defined meaning. They recognise that you must step outside of the separate sciences and assume a more general position if you wish to satisfy the intellectual craving of the human mind. They demand an analysis and a critical estimate of the ultimate principles and fundamental notions which the separate natural and philosophical sciences take for granted. With this we find frequently connected the desire to unite these different and detached principles into a consistent and united scheme. As this can only be done by a process of reconstruction, by remodelling those principles as they primarily present themselves, these thinkers follow to some extent in the footsteps of Herbart and of Lotze. By such a process of reconstruction they may then arrive at some kind of system, which will nevertheless differ very materially from those earlier systems which have for centuries led human thought. These mostly sprang from a deep-seated conviction that some one Supreme Idea had been found, which afforded, as it were, an insight into the very essence and nature of things, a glimpse of the underlying reality of the All. The most noteworthy example of that other and more modest form of philosophy is probably to be found in Professor Wundt's ' System of Philosophy ' and in the elaborate expositions contained in his other philosophical works. Other recent thinkers have altogether abstained from systematic ventures, contenting themselves with a general theory of knowledge. In their endeavours they have been mostly influenced by Kant, who, as many declare, abstained for himself from metaphysics. In fact, they try to do better and more thoroughly what Kant had attempted to do in his celebrated three " Critiques."

56.
Direction
of Herbart
and Lotze.

Eduard Zeller, the renowned historian of Greek philosophy, gave expression to this attitude of thought in

57.
E. Zeller.

his Heidelberg Address of the year 1862, " On the meaning and importance of *Erkenntniss-Theorie*." [1] The introduction of this term forms a kind of landmark in the history of German philosophy, which has since largely moved in the indicated direction. The term has been translated into English by the word " Epistemology "; a general theory of knowledge, of its principles and limits. John Stuart Mill had worked in a similar direction long before the modern term had been introduced.

Neither the conception of such a science, nor an adequate designation of it, has ever found much favour among French philosophers.[2]

About the same time that this more modest programme of philosophical inquiry was placed before the thinking public by Zeller, another public address delivered in the same place by Prof. Wundt announced to the world in more confident tones the advent of a new philosophy. It meant the development of that line of thought and research of which, only two years before, Fechner had given a brilliant example in his ' Elements of Psycho-physics.' Of this I treated in the

58.
Wilhelm
Wundt.

---

[1] This Address is reprinted in the 1st vol. of Zeller's ' Gesammelte Abhandlungen.'

[2] The only French thinker who has persistently laboured in a similar direction is Charles Renouvier (1818-1903). His critical writings, notably his ' Essais de Critique Générale' in four parts (1854-64, second enlarged edition 1875-96), have had a wide influence on French thought. He can, however, though starting from Kant, hardly be called a Kantian, as he opposes most of the original conceptions through which Kant created a revolution in philosophical thought. He repudiates the "Thing-in-itself," the "noumenon," and the "transcendental" nature of human freedom. Though an empiricist his philosophical tendency is idealistic. In his later writings he inclines in the direction of Leibniz. He has introduced the word "Criticisme" into the French language and terms his philosophy "Néocriticisme," to distinguish it from Kant's. If we define Kant's philosophy as "Noumenalism" or "Transcendentalism" we may define Renouvier's as "Phenomenalism."

eleventh chapter of the first section of this work.   Investigations similar to those carried out or suggested by Fechner and Wundt were stimulated by the appearance of Helmholtz's two celebrated treatises on ' Physiological Acoustics' and ' Physiological Optics,' and by the original philosophical interest associated with them in the mind of their author, leading him to a serious study of Kant's works.   However different the programme of Zeller might at the time have appeared to be from that of Wundt, both had this in common, that they practically abandoned the speculative line of thought which in Germany had reigned supreme during the first half of the century.   Zeller himself was brought up in the Hegelian School; Wundt, on the other side, connected for some time with Helmholtz in his academic teaching, had been brought up in the school of Exact Science.   The hopelessness of the later developments of the Hegelian School, which had split into two exactly opposite factions, seemed to produce, on one point, the same results in the mind of Zeller as did in the mind of Wundt the hopefulness with which, in the School of Johannes Müller, Helmholtz and others approached the borderland of physical and mental phenomena.   The common conviction arose that speculative philosophy, the orthodox form of metaphysics, was played out.   Both Zeller, who was a leader in historical and critical studies, and Wundt, who was equally so in physiological work, emphasised those lines of study in which each of them had attained his early successes,—the one pointing to criticism and history, the other to the exact methods of research.   The historical spirit in Hegel's school pre-

vented Zeller from becoming too exclusively logical and
critical, whilst, no doubt, the ideal side of Fechner's
philosophy, which exerted an increasing influence upon
Wundt, helped him to recognise that exact methods alone
would lead only to one - sided results, that philosophy
meant a Unification of thought; it resulted in his increasingly pronounced endeavour to find a formula in
which the spiritual side of things should be adequately
expressed.

59.
Influence of
Schopen-
hauer.

About the same time a third influence began to make
itself felt in philosophical circles in Germany. This was
the belated influence of the philosophy of Schopenhauer,
whose principal work had been more than forty years
before the world.[1] It had remained unappreciated, and

[1] Of all the leading philosophers
of Germany the personality of
Schopenhauer has created the
greatest interest. His philosophy
was so much an outcome of his subjective character and experience,
and so little influenced by the
necessities and considerations of
academic teaching, that he resembles rather independent thinkers
like Descartes, Spinoza, and
Leibniz, than the leaders of the
philosophy taught at the German
universities from Wolff down to
Hegel and Herbart. Among these
he only recognised Kant as his
immediate predecessor, and carried
on a lifelong protest against the
official philosophy at the universities. The unique and solitary life
which he led, away from intercourse
with any of the leading thinkers or
scholars of his age, gave him the
reputation of a philosophical curiosity, and added much to the
popular interest which surrounded his eccentric teaching. After
the publication of a volume of
Essays in 1851 with the title of

'Parerga and Paralipomena,'
and of the 'Letters on Schopenhauer's Philosophy' by Julius
Frauenstädt (1854), Schopenhauer
began to be known to a wider
circle of philosophically interested
readers. Three important earlier
notices of Schopenhauer's system
by Herbart (1820, 'Works,' vol.
xii. pp. 369-91), Rosenkranz in his
'History of the Kantian Philosophy'
(1840), 'Kant's Works' (vol. xii.),
and Erdmann 'Geschichte der
Neueren Philos. (vol. iii., part 2),
as well as some notices by less
well-known authors, failed to attract due attention. When the
writer of this History came to
Göttingen in 1860 Schopenhauer's
name was hardly known even
amongst students of philosophy,
no reference being made to him in
philosophical lectures ; and it was
only after his death, in September
of that year, that through various
obituary notices and through a biography by his personal friend, W.
Gwinner (1862), Schopenhauer became for a time the most interesting

little known, till the death of the philosopher in 1860 drew the attention of wider circles to the originality of his writings. Within a few years Schopenhauer became the most popular philosopher in Germany. The reasons for this are not difficult to understand. After Kant had passed away, the more ambitious of his followers had proclaimed in various promising announcements the advent of a new era of thought which should do justice to the high aspirations of the nation. These had found expression in a literature which has since become classical, in a revival of art and in all the ideals which produced and accompanied the battle for freedom and the Anti-Napoleonic Revolution in Europe. Philosophy was to do justice to the logical emancipation of the older Rationalism and the newer Criticism, as much as to the inwardness of the older Mysticism and the more recent spiritualism of the Romantic School. It was to unite Science, Art, and Religion, the intellectual and spiritual interests, into one comprehensive view. The age was one of hopefulness and expectancy, of a high optimism, of ideals and strivings. The youth of Germany and the thoughtful public listened with enthusiasm and confidence to dozens of academic lecturers. It was the same age which witnessed, besides the political liberation of Germany, one other

philosophical phenomenon of the day, being discussed in Reviews and pamphlets both in Germany and abroad. Since that time, and still more after the appearance of v. Hartmann's 'Philosophy of the Unconscious' (1st ed. 1869), the literature on Schopenhauer has grown to enormous dimensions, as can be seen from Ueberweg's Handbook (vol. iv.), where also his influence in other countries is referred to. In England translations have appeared of his principal work by Haldane and Kemp (3 vols. 1883-86), and of his Essays by T. B. Saunders (1891). Prof. Sully treats of him at length in his 'History of Pessimism' (1877), and Mr Thos. Whittaker has recently published a concise and spirited sketch of his Philosophy (1909).

great practical achievement—the foundation of that great
scheme of higher and popular education which other
nations have found it impossible to imitate. When,
however, after a considerable lapse of time, the outcome
of the new philosophy proved to be delusive, when it
failed to appreciate the growing importance of the
Natural Sciences, when it entered into an alliance with
the reactionary movement in politics and the intolerance
of ecclesiastics, when finally it appeared that the canons
of the Hegelian philosophy were used alike by the
orthodox and by unbelievers, the popular interest and
belief in this philosophy began to wane. For a moment
it appeared as if the belief in Idealism might be replaced
by that in Materialism : there is no doubt that a certain
section of the intelligent public in Germany was, and still
is, strongly imbued with and influenced by the teachings
of the materialistic writers of the Forties. For the more
thinking section these crude doctrines could, however,
have no lasting attraction. At that moment there
existed in Germany only two thinkers who might have
met the much felt need of a new doctrine, namely,
Lotze and Fechner. The causes which prevented either
of them forming a school of followers will have our
attention in the sequel of this History ; perhaps it is
sufficient to say here that neither of them, for different
reasons, took up a clearly defined position, or summed
up his teachings in an easily intelligible formula,[1] such
as the speculative mind had been accustomed to find in

60.
Materialism
of the
" Forties."

[1] Lotze was, in the beginning, quite misunderstood. His real position came out clearly only in his later writings ; and as regards Fechner, he was known at that time as a scientific writer and as a humourist under the pseudonym of Dr Mises.

the earlier systems. A general scepticism settled upon men's minds, a deep-seated doubt as to the capacity of the human intellect to solve its highest problems. At the same time the failure of the theoretical politicians, which the events of the year 1848 had made only too evident, assisted in producing a general discouragement, so far as the highest practical, as well as intellectual, interests were concerned.

Under these circumstances the philosophy of Schopen-hauer came to many younger minds as a kind of revela-tion. It was sufficiently speculative to satisfy the idealistic craving; it summed up its teaching in an intelligible formula; it supported its doctrines by a great wealth of artistic insight; and it contrasted favour-ably with the writings of Hegel by the elegance and lucidity of its literary style. Add to this, that it was highly spiced by brilliant and unsparing invective against the philosophers who had so long, by unfulfilled promises, led the nation astray; it was also the first attempt in Germany to drop, in the discussion of the highest problems, the professorial and academic tone, which to many practically minded people had assumed too much of self - assurance and the pride of infallibility. Un-fortunately the theoretical principles of Schopenhauer's philosophy were, in their practical application to ethical problems, joined to a pessimistic view of the world and life. This had its origin in personal traits of character, and was fostered through the study of the philosophy of the East, then newly introduced into Europe. It was opposed to the spirit of Plato, which likewise influenced Schopenhauer, and it stands in no logical connection with

61.
Schopen-
hauer's
pessimism
an accident.

his abstract principles. Allied as it was to that sensation of world-sickness which ran through a large portion of Continental literature, it appealed to many youthful and ardent spirits who found the ideals of a former generation destroyed and its hopes abandoned.

It gave, as it were, a philosophical explanation of the general and growing feeling of disappointment. Similar causes may have worked to secure the phenomenal popularity of Eduard von Hartmann's [1] 'Philosophy of the Unconscious.' Further developments of this line of sentiment rather than of thought, in which the highest virtues were considered to be those of resignation, of fortitude in suffering, and of sympathetic compassion with existing evils, have led many minds to a philosophy of despair. It took a singular turn in the writings of Friedrich Nietzsche, where it produced a reaction in the direction of an extreme individualism, which preached the necessity of a superhuman effort through which to overcome the indifferentism of the age, and lead it to a renewed grasp of the great Realities.

62.
Realism of
Nietzsche.

In the foregoing rapid sketch I have confined myself almost exclusively to German philosophy. For a long time indeed, German philosophy was the philosophy *par excellence*. In Germany itself, where many histories of

[1] Prof. Sully in his interesting volume on ' Pessimism ' mentions in the Preface to the 2nd edition several other pessimistic writers whose works have had considerable popular influence in Germany. Among these the most extreme is probably Philipp Mainländer (pseudonym for Philipp Batz), who wrote a ' Philosophy of Redemption ' (1876), which ran through several editions.

It is, however, well to note that, though not so conspicuously as in the case of Hegel, the philosophy of Schopenhauer lends itself to a twofold development. Not only have we the reaction in Nietzsche, mentioned in the text, but we have also the remarkable writings of Paul Deussen, of whom more in the sequel.

modern philosophy have been written, scarcely any notice was taken during the first two-thirds of the century of philosophy outside of Germany; in fact, such did not exist, according to the opinion of many eminent German thinkers. The contempt with which the Scottish philosophy of Common-sense and the French Eclecticism of Victor Cousin were regarded, prevented for a long time a due appreciation of many valuable new ideas, which with less ostentation, nevertheless, made their way in neighbouring countries. The enormous bulk of work which issued annually from the German Universities, in almost every field of knowledge, absorbed the attention to such an extent that no space or time was left for the recognition of what was done outside of academic circles or in other countries. As I mentioned before, the writings of Schopenhauer did a great deal to break down the supposed privilege of a professorial class to settle the highest and most important questions. About the same time two eminent foreigners began to attract the attention of German students as well as of the non-academic public. These were Ernest Renan in France and Charles Darwin in England. A knowledge of Auguste Comte, though so much before Renan, and still more, an appreciation of the earlier English psychology of Mill, Bain, and Spencer, belongs to even a later period of German philosophy. Nevertheless, these less ostentatious beginnings of the new thought in England and in France have probably done more than the voluminous writings of German philosophers to place philosophical thought in an entirely altered position during the last quarter of the century.

I have already referred to the fact that, whereas philosophical thought in the beginning of the century moved mainly in the realm of logic, metaphysics, and psychology, at the end of the century the study which seems to be gradually superseding all others is the study of Sociology, a term which was introduced by Auguste Comte, and has latterly become a watchword in the literature of the whole of Western Europe— latest in Germany. This phenomenon has various and very deep-seated causes, which have shown themselves in all the three countries, but in different forms. They showed themselves first of all, and most drastically, in France, where the Revolution had made a clean sweep of many of the older foundations of society, and where men of the highest order and in almost every depart- ment of science and literature had speculated or prac- tically worked in the direction of a reconstruction of society. A temporary check was indeed put upon these endeavours by the reactionary movement during the Restoration. Nevertheless, all through the cen- tury, French literature has systematically, or in more general ways, worked at the great social problems. In England, though the movements were less convulsive, the interests of the Masses, as opposed to those of the Classes, have increasingly occupied the attention of both statesmen and thinkers, the reform movement having been the leading feature of internal politics during the greater part of the century. It was in England that the problem of population and the evils of overcrowding were first openly discussed, and it is not too much to say that the misery of the residuum which the con-

63.
Comte's
sociology.

centration in large cities has brought about has gradually become in general literature, as well as in philosophical, ethical, and religious writings, the great topic of the day.

The impossibility which not only philosophical theorists, but also religious workers, have experienced in dealing with this great problem, which we may, for the moment, call the salvation of society, has in this country brought about a widespread feeling of dismay, and deprived not only philosophical doctrines of their interest, but also religious beliefs of that hold which they once had on the minds of men.   In Germany the older forms of religious belief had in the eighteenth century been largely superseded by rationalism; this again for a time looked as if it would yield to the deepening and spiritualising influence of the idealistic philosophy. But when the latter appeared to many to be uncertain in its results and delusive in its promises, a reaction set in which produced for a long time an indifferentism, not only towards religious, but also towards philosophical teaching.   Add to this that the growing industrialism of the age, the commercial spirit, and the increasing wealth of the upper and middle classes, had found a convenient and comfortable popular philosophy in the shallow tenets of materialism.   Thus we can say that philosophical thought of the highest order — i.e., the intellectual search for the great Realities which underlie and sustain everything, the quest for the truly Real—has suffered bankruptcy, in Germany mostly through theoretical, in England through practical, causes.   Nevertheless, it must be added that the very recognition of all these

64.
Temporary decline of philosophic interest.

destructive agencies, both in the realms of theory and practice, of science, literature, and life, has in many minds already produced a revulsion of feeling. A desire is everywhere manifested once more to probe to the bottom the various agencies, intellectual, moral, and material, which have led to this apparent collapse. Somehow or other the conviction seems to be gaining ground that the great Realities, which in former times religious faith and philosophical reasoning had combined to bring home to the human soul, have not disappeared, but have only been removed to a greater distance in time and space, as well as in the region of thought. All the various formulæ which modern philosophy has introduced in this country and abroad, such as " the unknowable," " the unconscious," " the incognoscible," do not signify a straightforward denial of the spiritual essence of everything, but indicate merely that the same is far removed from the reaches of the human intellect. For all that the agnostic can say, the Spiritual Reality may still be there, though it seems to him inaccessible to the purely intellectual grasp. The human mind can never remain, for any length of time, in a state of suspense, of doubt, and uncertainty. Individual thinkers and specialists, living in a community which is built up upon the foundation of certain time-honoured beliefs, may indulge in the luxury of withdrawing from the actual quest after the Real, leaving the same to others who are not troubled by their scruples; the agnostic may proclaim ever so loudly the impossibility of knowledge regarding the fundamental questions; the critical philosopher may define ever so clearly the limits of

65.
Hints of
its revival.

human reason; the more confident these self-denying assertions, the sooner will a reaction set in. The question then for us is this: Has philosophical thought merely exhausted its powers, or has it, at the very moment when materialism, naturalism, and agnosticism appear to rule supreme, still discovered some untried path and some unrecognised resources? Has the ruling pessimism and indifferentism of the age given way at all to any signs of hope that the veil will once more be lifted and confidence restored? Whoever has read attentively the philosophy of the last ten years in all the three countries cannot, I think, have failed to discover signs of the recurrence of a more hopeful line of thought. I shall have many opportunities of pointing to this in greater detail and with more definiteness in the later chapters of the present section of this History.

For the moment it may be of interest to refer, as I have done so often before, to the changes which the philosophical vocabulary of the three countries is undergoing, to the increasing array of new terms with which philosophical thought is being enriched, all pointing to the advent of some new era of thought. Without defining at present what is frequently only dimly foreshadowed in this new vocabulary, I will refer only to the term "Voluntarism" which Paulsen has coined and Professor Wundt has adopted to describe his ultimate philosophical position, to the philosophy of the "Idées-forces" of M. Alfred Fouillée, and the "Philosophie de l'Effort" in France, to the "Pragmatism" of the recent Oxford school of Thought, and to William James's "Will to

66
"Voluntarism."

believe." Many of these writers have been influenced, consciously or unconsciously, by the great truth, amounting almost to a discovery, contained in the philosophy of Schopenhauer, which emphasised the independence of the Will in its relation to the Intellect, and found the very essence of Reality, the truly Real, in a principle of Action. As I remarked above, it was unfortunate for the reputation of Schopenhauer, as well as for the development of German philosophy, that Schopenhauer saw in the Will, in the active principle, not a source of good, but of evil, and that in consequence his writings, which otherwise might have had an inspiring and reassuring influence, became on the contrary the gospel of pessimism which has blighted so many hopes and deadened so many aspirations.

It is interesting to note that the necessity of a development such as is aimed at in many modern schools of philosophic thought was not unexpected by earlier thinkers during the century; that Lotze, after reviewing all the doubts and difficulties which beset the acceptance of the belief in a spiritual and personal Creator and Ruler, declared that belief was "a resolution of the character" and not of the intellect.

It cannot be said that the tendency to which I refer, and which permeates much of recent philosophical literature, has yet attained that clearness which belongs to some earlier speculations. Perhaps the very nature of it will prevent it from ever submitting to the ordinary categories of logic, though the very fact is significant that logic itself, which for a long time was supposed to be permanently crystallised in Aristotelian formulæ, has during the last twenty-five years become again more fluent, more accommodating to the needs of modern thought. At the moment it looks more likely that philosophy has handed over the next great advance in human thought to the practical worker, and that the purely intellectual grasp of the new truths will have to await their actual realisation; that they will have to become efficient forces in the life of society at large before some individual genius will find the logic and metaphysics of their essence, the intelligible rationale of their activity.

There is no mistaking the signs of the times; the tide is running away from abstract dogmas and metaphysical speculation. Both these have been tried and found wanting, so far as the great practical problems are concerned. Theology has failed to evangelise the masses, and philosophy to enlighten them. For a time all hopes were concentrated upon exact science, but this also has shown itself powerless to deal with fundamental questions, or to approach the ground and origin of things. Truth, in the higher sense of the word, as an expression of the truly Real, is no longer an object of scientific research. Exact science does not profess to deal with essences and existences, but only with what is apparent. This it is content to describe and interpret in the most consistent, the simplest, and the most useful manner. The value of science lies in its applicability to problems of industry, commerce, the useful arts, and, in a limited sense, the problems of administration. The latest leading ideas which have been introduced into Scientific Thought have done much to remove still further out of our reach the

elements in space and the origin in time of the existences which are in and around us.   The hopefulness
which characterised philosophy in Germany and science in
France in the beginning of the nineteenth century, and
which, so far as the latter is concerned, found an expression in the teaching of Comte, has not been realised in
the course of the last half of the century.   A large portion of the population of the most cultured nations, in
spite of educational efforts, still partakes to a very
small extent of the intellectual advancement which
philosophy and science afford to a select few, not to
mention the utter hopelessness in which large numbers
of the population, in the great centres of so - called
culture, have to pass their lives.   Is it then to be
wondered at that a distrust, not to say contempt for
philosophical speculation, has taken hold of the public
mind ? and that the belief in pure science is not based,
as it used to be, on the love of truth, but that it has
increasingly what Bolingbroke used to call "a metallic
flavour" ?   Nevertheless, as I stated above, the search
for the truly Real is not abandoned, but looks for the
effort of the practical worker.   If the realisation of the
great ideals which Christianity has set before us, and
philosophy has endeavoured, perhaps not altogether successfully, to support, is the sole and only object of all
practical Religion, then we may say with some confidence
that an increasing number of the thinkers of our age
expect the next step in the solution of the great problems of life to be taken by practical Religion.   Assuming they are not mistaken in this, as I firmly believe
they are not, the first signs that this advance has to

some extent succeeded will react again upon the purely intellectual courses of thought and imbue them with fresh vigour and hopefulness. Should we, however, be mistaken in this expectation, we can say this with certainty, that neither the most refined theories of science, nor the speculations of philosophy, nor the dogmas of theology will prevent the utter loss of our ideals, the ruin of the higher life of mankind.

It has been frequently asserted that the philosophy of the day is irreligious. This is only partially correct. Many earnest thinkers in England and abroad are intently occupied with trying to understand the psychological foundation and the historical growth of religion, which they look upon as a great Reality, having an independent existence outside science and philosophy. If, at the same time, they refuse to draw into philosophical discussion those great Divine and human Truths, such as the nature of God and the scheme of redemption, which philosophical writers of the preceding age frequently dealt with in a prolific manner, we may look upon this as a sign of increasing reverence, and as an acknowledgment of the existence of other powers in the human soul than those of merely external sensation and logical inference. These thinkers are, in their writings, merely preparing the way for the new light.

In the general Introduction I pointed out that I propose in this History to look upon philosophical thought as occupying an intermediate position between scientific and religious thought. What has been said in the last few pages confirms this view, by pointing

67.
Relation of recent philosophy to religion.

to the position which philosophical thought seems to occupy in our day. It would appear as if, at the end of the nineteenth century, philosophy was paving the way for a fuller and more original display of the creative forces of the human soul, such as manifest themselves in poetry, art, and religion; for it is a fact, that for the moment these creative powers appear to have receded somewhat into the background, whilst, at the same time, much is expected from them. Wherever the vital forces in a society, or in an age, have not been absolutely exhausted—and I can find no sign of this in the present civilisations of Western Europe—such periods, where the higher creative and spiritual powers seem to be temporarily in abeyance, have always, sooner or later, been followed by periods of greater vigour and productiveness. Auguste Comte, in studying the historical developments of human thought, felt himself justified in laying down his well-known law of the three states, —the theological, the metaphysical, and the positive,— as the rationale of the development of the human mind in its intellectual progress. Formulæ such as that of Comte, or those contained in the doctrines of Hegel or Spencer, all suffer from the defect that they give no intelligible answer to the question, "What is going to happen when the final stage is arrived at?" All historical evidence goes to show that no agency of progress has ever continued to work unchallenged and uninterrupted. All processes in nature and society seem, in course of time, to exhaust themselves and call forth counter-movements which gain force, as it were, through reaction and contrast. This has, in modern times, been abundantly evident in the rapidly succeeding phases of modern history. It has also been recognised by philosophical writers. Let us then try to correct the formula of Comte so as to bring it into harmony with the larger experience of the day. We might feel disposed to say that Comte was right in assigning to philosophical thought an intermediate or transitional position, preferring, on our part, to speak of philosophy rather than of metaphysics—as the latter term, though perfectly legitimate and useful, has acquired in the eyes of many persons a doubtful meaning. We might then go on to say that the stage of positive or exact thought having been reached in the course of the nineteenth century, this itself is producing the desire for a new departure, a counter-movement which will call forth and urge the active rather than the purely intellectual powers of the human soul. Philosophy thus occupies still the intermediate or transitional stage assigned to it by Comte; only that we now find ourselves, as it were, reversing the Comtian process of development, passing from the one-sided sway of exact or positive thought through philosophy to a renewed life, not of dogmatic Theology, but of practical Religion, bringing with it a fresh display of the creative powers of the human mind.

In offering this concluding formula, I do not desire to attach much importance to any scheme which unduly abbreviates my task of exhibiting the mental forces of our century in the fulness of their life and their many-sided significance; but conducting my readers, as I am proposing to do, through the labyrinthine mazes of philosophical thought, I believe they may be thankful for some guiding idea, though this at best is only tentative. The sequel will give them ample material and opportunity to confirm or to contest this preliminary generalisation.

CHAPTER II.

ON THE GROWTH AND DIFFUSION OF THE CRITICAL SPIRIT.

I.

NOTHING probably strikes the impartial student of the progress of scientific and of philosophical thought more than the changing and opposite attitudes which the exponents of these two forms of thought have assumed in the course of the nineteenth century. This change has been more and more evident as the century has progressed. To a great extent we may even say that the attitudes have been reversed. The difference I refer to may be expressed concisely by saying : Science has more and more acquired the character of definiteness and the attitude of assurance ; Philosophy, on the other hand, has become more and more uncertain and timid.

In the beginning of the century, both in Germany and England, science and scientific thought played only a secondary part in literature and teaching. France was the only country in which it had early acquired that position and commanded that esteem which it now enjoys everywhere.[1] In Germany philosophy led the way, and even in this country, where it could not boast

1.
Reversal of the position of science and philosophy.

---

[1] See vol. i. p. 105 *sqq.* of this History.

of the same systematic treatment, philosophical subjects
such as Economics, Politics, and questions of taste and
literary criticism filled the pages of those numerous
and popular reviews which form such an important
department of nineteenth century literature.[1]

[1] In this country before the beginning of the nineteenth century
there existed no important periodical literature which appealed to a
larger circle of cultivated readers.
The British Essayists, headed by
Steele and Addison, possessed their
peculiar interest and have acquired
the standing of classics. Some of
them had European reputation and
much influence, notably on German literature. The 'Gentleman's
Magazine,' founded in 1731, had a
wide circulation, and imparted a
large amount of varied and desultory
information. The 'Monthly Review' (1749) and the 'Critical Review' (1756) had no commanding
influence. The Reviews existing
in the beginning of the nineteenth
century were said to be in their
dotage. At this time new life was
infused into periodical literature
from a quite unexpected quarter.
The 'Edinburgh Review,' edited
during twenty - seven years by
Jeffrey, began its brilliant career
with quite unforeseen success in the
year 1802, and very soon became
the organ of a distinct political
party with a definite programme of
reform in things political, social,
and literary. It provoked in the year
1809 the foundation of a literary
organ for the opposite party, in
defence—as was said—of Church,
Tory, and War Principles. "The
defence was a consequence of the
attack. And it is fortunate that it
was so. For besides getting these
opinions fairly discussed, the party
excesses natural to any unchecked
publication were diminished ; and
a work arose which, in many respects, is an honour to British

literature, and has called out, and
indirectly reared, a great variety of
the highest order of talent " (Cock-
burn's 'Life of Lord Jeffrey,' vol. i.
p. 192). But this critical attitude,
this spirit of "accuse and defence,"
peculiar to leaders in the legal profession who launched this whole
enterprise into existence, was not
favourable to a just appreciation of
the scientific spirit, and both the
'Edinburgh,' as in the case of
Thomas Young, and the 'Quarterly,'
as in the case of Charles Darwin,
have shown themselves singularly
incompetent in the discussion of
novel and leading scientific ideas.
The scientific interest was not introduced into general literature
either in Germany or in this country before the fourth decade of
the century. In England it was
characteristically introduced in connection with Economic questions.
In Germany its introduction was
partly through French models
which had a great influence upon
men like Humboldt and Liebig ; and secondly, also through
some of the representatives of the
philosophy of nature such as Oken,
Schubert, Steffens, and Oerstedt.
Under the influence of these very
different interests, review literature
in Germany and in England has in
the course of the century become
more and more expository and
representative rather than critical
—its object being to spread knowledge and information and to abstain
from premature criticism. All this
is due to the increasing prevalence
of the scientific as against that of
the critical spirit.

I propose now to inquire into the causes which have brought about this change which, as I said, amounts in many cases to a complete reversal of the estimation in which the mathematical and natural sciences on the one hand, the historical and philosophical on the other, are held. The earlier part of this History has furnished the answer to the first half of the problem: I there endeavoured to show that the success and assurance of scientific thought has grown with the growth and diffusion of the scientific spirit, which has been more clearly defined as the exact or mathematical spirit. It is however very likely, nay, almost certain, that the employment of these methods alone would not have secured for science that triumphant, not to say that boastful, position to which it has universally attained. This is greatly owing to the practical applications to commerce and industry which have followed the discoveries of that long line of intellects of a high order to whom the recent progress of science is due. It must in justice be added that it is not in their own writings and deliverances that we, as a rule, meet with that tone of assurance. This is more frequent among those who are occupied with the popularisation and diffusion rather than with the extension of scientific knowledge.

The second part of this History will have to answer the other half of the above question, namely, what are the causes that have brought about that great change in the general and popular appreciation of philosophical discussions? How is it that instead of one or two dominant systems of thought we have now what may

2. Causes of the change.

3. Anarchy of recent philosoph

be called a complete anarchy, or, at best, a bewildering eclecticism ? How is it that instead of stepping boldly forward with finished and assertive systems as did Fichte, Hegel, and Schopenhauer in Germany, Auguste Comte in France, and Herbert Spencer in England, the thinkers of the day require us to be content with introductions to philosophy, with preliminary discourses, or with dissertations of an historical character which not infrequently do little more than hint with reserve and qualification at a possible solution which is promised but not given ? [1]

---

[1] That anarchy and inconclusiveness are characteristic of the philosophic thought of the day has been very generally expressed from very different quarters, and is shown in many important publications. Among these I only mention a few. Prof. Ludwig Stein, the learned editor of the ' Archiv für Philosophie ' (appearing in two series, historical and systematic), has given full expression to the state of unrest, not to say bewilderment, in contemporary philosophical literature in his recent publication, ' Philosophische Strömungen der Gegenwart ' (1908), notably in the first chapter, which treats of the Neo-idealistic movement of thought. Another not less significant indication is to be found in one of the volumes of a compendious German publication, ' Die Kultur der Gegenwart ' (ed. Paul Hinneberg). The volume in question bears the title of ' Systematic Philosophy,' but is in reality what must appear to many a very unsystematic exposition of recent speculation, inasmuch as it is a collection of mostly brilliant essays on various philosophical problems from very different and frequently opposing points of view, without an attempt towards reconciliation or completeness. If we turn to French philosophy, neither the earlier ' Rapport ' by Ravaisson (1867) nor the shorter Review by Ribot (' Mind,' 1877, p. 366), nor the quite recent sympathetic Review by Boutroux (' Revue de Métaphysique et de Morale,' vol. 16, 1908), can fail to produce upon the reader a sense of bewilderment, of the total absence of dominant ideas in the voluminous and interesting philosophical literature of the country. In this country, where systematic philosophy has only one prominent representative, viz., Herbert Spencer, the diversity of philosophic opinion is not felt so keenly as in France and Germany, where elaborate systems have in succession directed philosophic thought. Nevertheless we meet here also with the complaint of inconclusiveness. In the Introduction to a recent publication with the title ' Idola Theatri,' which purports to be a " criticism of Oxford Thought " (1906), Mr Henry Sturt gives us the final impression which the teaching of T. H. Green and his followers left on young minds : " I came to feel, in common, I believe, with not a few of my contemporaries, that the teaching we got was hardly strong enough in the explanation of definite problems. Some such

I will at once answer this question. The great change referred to is owing to the growth and diffusion of the Critical Spirit, taking this term, as I shall immediately proceed to show, in its widest sense. In order that my readers may have before them as clear an idea as possible of the main drift of the second part of this History, I may say that its principal object will be to exhibit the workings of the critical spirit and the critical methods, just as the main object of the first part was to exhibit the workings of the scientific or exact spirit and methods. In doing so I shall follow a similar plan to that adopted in the first part : trying first to trace the growth and diffusion of the critical spirit in general, leaving it to separate chapters to deal with the separate results which the application of the critical methods has brought about in the various courses in which philosophical thought has habitually moved.

thought, I remember, haunted me on hearing, for example, the logic lectures of the late Lewis Nettleship. He told us elaborately and often what knowledge was *not*, but having thus awakened expectation, he did little to satisfy it : we seemed to be always on the verge of a great secret which our teacher would never disclose. T. H. Green, whose 'Prolegomena to Ethics' I read somewhat later, was much more definite than Nettleship : but even his great doctrine of the Spiritual Principle, though it gratified religious aspiration, did not seem to be clearly reasoned out ; nor could any one be sure how far it would go in explaining the religious consciousness. Meanwhile, no open-minded student, I am certain, was quite at ease about the attitude of the Oxford Idealists to modern science. . . . The want of receptivity, together with its own limited explanatory power, cast upon the Oxford philosophy of 1885 a suspicion of reactionism and unreality which even an eager disciple could scarcely ignore" (pp. 1, 2). "The net result for Oxford of this remarkable literature, which together with much exegetical work of a similar tendency shows the highest speculative quality, was that philosophy went down seriously in academic consideration from the position which it held at Green's death. The man of average calibre took more and more to commentating : and an Alexandrian period threatened to set in," &c., &c. (p. 3). This is almost identical with Prof. Wundt's well-known dictum, "Wir sind Alle Epigonen."

The word Criticism has been used in a narrower and in a wider sense. In English literature it acquired a definite meaning through Pope's "Essay on Criticism." This essay is written very much in the spirit of the French writers of the seventeenth century, notably of Boileau, who, on his part, followed in the steps of Horace and the ancients. In fact, criticism in this narrower sense is in modern literature a creation of the French mind; it means a kind of philosophy of taste, and is an expression of the literary, artistic, or æsthetical conscience of the age. In this sense it was used by Henry Home, Lord Kames, whose 'Elements of Criticism' appeared in 1761, and quite recently Professor Saintsbury has thus used the word in his valuable ' History of Criticism and Literary Taste in Europe.'[1] But the country which has not only produced separate and isolated works on criticism in this narrower sense, but has consecutively produced a literature of criticism, is France. M. Brunetière says in this regard: " Even if the Italian and English critics are not isolated in the history of their literatures, one may say that they form a kind of exception, and that nowhere else than in France has criticism had for the last three centuries what we call a consecutive history. Must I add that it has been truly the soul of French literature? I, at least, see from Ronsard to Victor Hugo a revolution of taste and of literature which, with us, has had for its origin and

---

[1] 3 vols., Edinburgh, Blackwood, 1900-1904 : Prof. Saintsbury defines the "criticism" with which he deals as "that function of the judgment which busies itself with the goodness or badness, the success or ill-success, of literature, from the purely literary point of view" (vol. i. p. 3).

guide a development of criticism." No other nation possessed an institution like the Académie Française, which, as the same author says, had according to the intention of its founder the special mission of establishing "a system of absolute confidence in the power of definite rules and of watching over their observation."[1] It may be of further interest to note that the English term "criticism" is synonymous with the French word "critique," and that the French word "criticisme" has been reserved to denote the philosophy of Kant and its developments.[2]

In Germany the word "Kritik" has never been confined to that narrower meaning which is still largely current in this country :[3] it has always been employed

---

[1] M. Brunetière defines the object of criticism as follows : "l'objet de la critique est de juger de classer d'expliquer les œuvres de la littérature et de l'art" (Art. "Critique," 'Grande Encyclopédie,' vol. xiii. p. 447—*loc. cit.*, p. 414, p. 6).

[2] This special meaning was introduced by one of the two original thinkers who have swayed philosophic thought in France since the time of Cousin, and outside of the Thomistic movement within the pale of the Roman Catholic Church. These two thinkers are Auguste Comte and Charles Renouvier (1818-1903, 'Essais de Critique Générale,' 1st ed., 1854). Comte coined the term Positivism, Renouvier, the term Néo-criticisme, to characterise their respective philosophical points of view. In this respect the latter occupies an important place in the diffusion of the critical spirit in the wider sense of the word. It is "Criticisme" in the Kantian sense, as distinguished from that philological learning and criticism which was succesfully practised by some eminent members of the eclectic school of Victor Cousin.

[3] Carlyle had already pointed to the use of the term in a larger sense than that prevalent in England. In his Essay on the "State of German Literature" (1827, 'Collected Works,' vol. vi. p. 60) he wrote : "Far from being behind other nations in the practice or science of Criticism, it is a fact, for which we fearlessly refer to all competent judges, that they [the Germans] are distinctly and even considerably in advance. We state what is already known to a great part of Europe to be true. Criticism has assumed a new form in Germany ; it proceeds on other principles, and proposes to itself a higher aim. The grand question is not now a question concerning the qualities of diction, the coherence of metaphors, the fitness of sentiments, the general logical truth in a work of art, as it was some half-

in the larger sense to denote a definite attitude of the inquiring mind towards any subject which is accessible to a critical treatment. Accordingly we may look upon Germany as the real home of the critical spirit and the critical methods in their widest sense and in their most unfettered development, as we may look upon France as the birthplace of modern philological and literary criticism. In the former country a philosophy sprang up at the end of the eighteenth century which called itself critical *"par excellence,"* and which, in spite of many brilliant attempts to supersede or dislodge it, still constitutes the rallying-point for most of the systematic thought which has not come under the influence of the scientific or exact methods. Although, therefore, we

6. Germany the home of criticism in the wider sense.

century ago among most critics ; neither is it a question mainly of a psychological sort, to be answered by discovering and delineating the peculiar nature of the poet from his poetry, as is usual with the best of our own critics at present ; but it is, not indeed exclusively, but inclusively of those two other questions, properly and ultimately a question on the essence and peculiar life of the poetry itself." Carlyle also pointed out that Herder, Schiller, Goethe "are men of another stature of form and movement whom Bossu's scale and compasses could not measure without difficulty, or rather, not at all." And yet Carlyle does not use criticism in the wider sense in which I am now using it. The representative of the latter usage in this country is Matthew Arnold, who, in various writings, but notably in his ' Essays in Criticism' (1865), took the wider view opened out to him as much by the earlier and the more recent French critics as by Goethe and by the constructive criticism of Nie-

buhr, introduced into this country by his father, Thomas Arnold, of Rugby. In the first of the Essays, "On the Function of Criticism at the present Time," he defines as "the business of the critical power, in all branches of knowledge, theology, philosophy, history, art, science, to see the object as in itself it really is. Thus it tends, at last, to make an intellectual situation of which the creative power can profitably avail itself. It tends to establish an order of ideas, if not absolutely true, yet true by comparison with that which it displaces ; to make the best ideas prevail. Presently these new ideas reach society, the touch of truth is the touch of life, and there is a stir and growth everywhere ; out of this stir and growth come the creative epochs of literature" (p. 6). Matthew Arnold also points out how the political and party interest so prevalent in England is detrimental to this higher form of criticism, "the rule of which should be disinterestedness" (p. 18).

cannot find in modern German literature the source or origin of any definite branch of criticism, we nevertheless are justified in selecting the modern literature of Germany as exhibiting more than that of any other country the working in a comprehensive style of the critical methods, the triumphs as well as the ravages of the critical spirit.[1]

[1] To those who have been brought up in the centre of the thought and learning of Germany during the nineteenth century it may appear as if criticism exhibits there two very different aspects, being, on the one side, eminently sympathetic and constructive (as manifested in the great edifice of classical philology), and, on the other side, unsympathetic and destructive (as shown by much of biblical criticism since the time of Strauss and the Tübingen school) : accordingly, they might object that two such opposite tendencies cannot be brought together as manifestations of the same, the critical spirit. In defence of the position I have taken up, and after fully considering the pertinence of this remark, I have to urge that I regard the whole of German thought from an extraneous or international point of view. Now, not only do foremost representatives of German criticism in all its different branches use the term " Kritik," without any special definition, as quite intelligible to their readers, but there are also notable instances in which destruction and construction are taken for granted as being two essential sides of the same critical process. As an example, I refer to the writings of Eduard Zeller, one of the few who displayed his great critical ability as much in his theological as in his philological writings. Notably in his collected Essays, where he discusses at great length the critical writings of Strauss, Baur, and the Tübingen school (see ' Vorträge und Abhandlungen,' vol. i.), there is no indication that there is any difference between the criticism employed by them in biblical matters and that employed by himself in his ' Philosophy of the Greeks.' Mr Whittaker also remarks that with philological criticism, when dealing with literary creations, the origins of which, like those of the biblical records, have to be traced, not in the full daylight, but in the twilight of history—such as the poems of Homer, Hesiod, Theognis, and the beginnings of Greek and Roman history—similar disintegration and unsettlement of opinion has resulted. The fact that, in reviewing the labours of English and French scholars and historians, German authorities have so frequently stigmatised them as unscientific and uncritical, has done more than anything else to identify, in the English mind, the historical and philosophical literature of Germany with a critical tendency which sometimes—as, e.g., when dealing with the Scriptures or with the creations of polite literature and art—has missed the essence of its subject and become unsympathetic through excessive minuteness or preconceived ideas. Evidence of this opinion among English writers may be found, e.g., in many passages of Prof. Saintsbury's ' History of Criticism and Literary Taste.'

7.
Attempts to
apply exact
methods to
philosophy.   It may already have occurred to some of my readers
to ask the question : If it is true that the critical spirit
has done so much to unsettle the philosophical mind as
is the case according to the view I have taken above,
and if, on the other side, the scientific or exact methods
have been so successful in producing definiteness and
assurance, how is it that the latter methods have not
been applied to philosophical subjects in the same way
as they have been applied to the exploration of nature ?
With this question we strike upon one of the cardinal
points which have been brought out in the course of the
nineteenth century.   For only towards the end of that
period has the thinking mind awakened to a consciousness of the weakness and limitations of the scientific
methods,—points which have not even partially been
settled without much controversy and many abortive
trials.   Ever since the exact methods of research have
been fully recognised in their power and fruitfulness, a
tendency has set in to apply them, not only to scientific
but to every kind of knowledge.   This tendency is
already clearly expressed in some of the writings of the
great French mathematicians at the end of the eighteenth
century ; [1] it became very marked in the middle of the
nineteenth century in Germany,[2] where periodicals were

---

[1] It was notably through Con-
dorcet and Laplace that an exaggerated opinion as to the value
and fruitfulness of the theory of
probabilities in the realm of moral
and social questions was spread.
This was noted by John Stuart
Mill, who, on his part, aimed
at introducing into Economics
that spirit of precision which
belonged to what has been termed

in this country natural knowledge.
[2] I do not here refer to the
illegitimate use, in quasi - philosophical writings, some of which
have attained to great popularity,
of such scientific terms as Matter,
Force, Energy, Substance, &c.,
even if used by scientific authorities
like Carl Vogt, Ernst Haeckel, or
Wilhelm Ostwald.

started for exact philosophy, and where the new school of psychology, heralded by Fechner, and brilliantly represented by Wundt and his pupils, was put forward as a kind of opposition to the older metaphysical methods which were considered obsolete and misleading. I have had occasion to refer to this school of thought in the eleventh chapter of the first section, where I treated of the psychophysical view of nature. I have there also referred to the restricted area within which the new methods have been successfully applied. Nor is it difficult to find the reason why these attempts, which were frequently put forward with so much self-assurance, have on the whole failed. What I have said in the introduction to the second part of this History about the difference between philosophy and science, between mind and nature, contains an explanation of the point in question. The exact methods of science, whether they consist in observation, measurement, or calculation, or in the combination of all three processes, can only be successfully applied to things or phenomena which have a definite location in space or in space and time. Definition in this sense is the first condition of the scientific process; nor would the scientific worker be satisfied if this fixing of his object in time and space were merely the result of one or a few observations and their record. The scientific mind is nowadays so fully aware of the numberless subjective and casual influences which tend to vitiate or make uncertain every single observation,[1] that one of the first requisites is to

8.
Reason of their failure.

___

[1] Not only is the subjective character of single observations fully recognised and corrections everywhere introduced, but even processes of logical deduction in some of the purely mathematical sciences

eliminate, by numerous repetitions and many co-operators, the subjective errors, the "personal equation" which attaches to every single observation and record.

Now it will be seen at once that, as all the incidents of mental life are accessible only to one observer, and never repeat themselves even to him, this method of repetition and co-operation, so essential and indispensable in all scientific work, is inapplicable where we have to do with purely introspective or mental phenomena. In fact, the material cannot be prepared and got ready to be handled with the instruments of science in the same way as the material of the scientific worker. In a great many cases also it is only by the fugitive and changing meaning of words that we can transiently fix, to a small extent, the object with which we are dealing. If we try to rid it, as the scientific worker does, of its subjective colouring or its personal equation, nothing remains; whilst attempting to remove the shell we find that we have lost the kernel.

There is a further point which is almost equally important in dealing with philosophical subjects, and this is that we involuntarily refer every mental, psychical, or introspective phenomenon to a personal unity or whole which we denote by the word mind, soul, consciousness, spirit, or some other similar term, and that we can only

are recognised to be not infrequently fallacious. Nowhere is this more the case than in the calculus of probabilities and its applications, as, for instance, in the kinetic theory of gases (see, e.g., O. E. Meyer, 'Die Kinetische Theorie der Gase,' passim). At one time it was thought that there existed only one type of a fluid ellipsoid in motion, till Jacobi discovered another. Also the motion of bodies under the Newtonian law of attraction seemed for a long time confined to conic sections, till G. W. Hill showed the usefulness of dealing with other forms of periodic orbits in the planetary and lunar theories (see H. H. Turner, 'Modern Astronomy,' 1901, p. 257 sqq.)

with difficulty divest ourselves of the notion that the single phenomenon with which we are dealing is the transient appearance or experience of some underlying reality, subject, or person.   Now it is quite true that, when dealing with external or natural phenomena, we are equally in the habit of introducing a fictitious unity or whole which we call nature, the outer world, or the universe.   This reference, however, to nature as a whole or a unity has little or no meaning for by far the greater part of all scientific work.   In fact, the progress of science and of its applications is marked by an increasing tendency to restrict the field of observation and research, and leave out of sight the position which the special subject under review has to the whole.   Indeed, we can say that the whole or totality is for the scientific worker simply the sum of its parts, and that, as the number of these parts is continually and rapidly increasing, the whole or comprehensive unity is more and more receding into the background and into a shadowy distance.   But the unity or whole of mental phenomena which we term our mind, soul, or consciousness is always before us, accompanies all our reflections, and cannot be got rid of. The process of isolation and abstraction so fruitful in scientific research and in the acquisition of natural knowledge is inapplicable to the phenomena of inner life.

9. Contrast between unities to which phenomena of nature and inner life are referred.

Thus, though the attempt has frequently been made in modern times to deal after the manner of exact science with the phenomena of the inner or mental world, this attempt has succeeded only to a very small extent; we may, moreover, truly say that wherever it

has succeeded, in ever so small a degree, it has destroyed
that truly philosophical interest which originally attaches
to all phenomena of the inner world.   While science has
gained by the methods of abstraction and isolation, which
we may term the analytical methods, philosophy has lost.

10.
Loss of
synoptic
view in
recent
philosophy.

It is important to bear this in mind whenever we
desire to form an opinion of the value of by far the larger
portion of recent philosophical writings.   That they are so
frequently deficient in depth, interest, and suggestive-
ness, if we compare them with the writings of the
great philosophers of ancient and modern times down
to the middle of the nineteenth century, is just owing
to this, that they intentionally confine themselves to
detailed discussions and special analyses, purposely
abstaining from a reference to the great central problems which alone give to philosophy its real interest
and importance.   Concentrating themselves on analysis,
they rarely venture upon the opposite process of synopsis
and synthesis.   Just as we have excellent treatises
on biology which contain no definition of life, so it
is supposed that we might have psychology without
a soul, ethics without obligation or sanction, religion
without a Deity and an object of reverence.   The great
thinkers of ancient and modern times, from Plato and
Aristotle down to Schopenhauer, Comte, and Herbert
Spencer, did not write on philosophical subjects before
they had gained a firm foothold, a central and governing
idea, a synopsis of their whole subject which threw light
on the whole of their detailed and special discussions.[1]

[1] Herbert Spencer, giving expression to this idea, terms his philosophy "Synthetic philosophy," and

Comte, on his part, though originally a mathematician and analyst,
had a very clear conception of the

This attitude has almost disappeared in the philosophical literature of our day; most philosophical writers have lost the "magnet of their course"; hence the anarchy of opinions and the labyrinthine meanderings of modern philosophical thought to which I referred above.   They do not write philosophy; they write about philosophy or philosophical subjects.[1]

This state of things has been brought about by the workings of the critical spirit.   It will be one of the main objects of the following pages to show how criticism has undermined one after the other of the foundations upon which former systems have built, how it has destroyed the central ideas from which emanated the light that illuminated the speculations of former ages.

11. Sapping effect of critical spirit.

"For who, without some far-off light, his own soul ponders o'er,
  Is like the bark that compassless would reach a distant shore."

Just as the question presented itself above: Why has philosophical thought not availed itself of the methods of science which have given so much definiteness and assurance? we may now put the reverse question: Why has the critical spirit, which has had such free access to every department of knowledge and thought, not wrought similar havoc in the regions of

necessity of complementing the analytical process, the "esprit d'analyse," by a synoptical process, the "esprit d'ensemble."   To this I have drawn attention in a paper published in the 'Proceedings of the Philosophical Society of the University of Durham,' vol. iii., entitled "On a General Tendency of Thought in the Second Half of the Nineteenth Century"; see also

'Edinburgh Review,' April 1911. I shall revert to this subject at the close of the present section.
[1] I have adopted this distinction from a remark made by the late Professor Sylvester regarding the mathematical writings of Augustus de Morgan.   He said — whether justly or unjustly—that De Morgan did not write mathematics, but about mathematics.

science, how is it that science has escaped the ravages of the critical spirit ?   The answer to this question will introduce us to another large department of the philosophical thought of the nineteenth century—that which deals with the foundations, the validity, and the value of scientific thought and knowledge.   Ever since Kant wrote his 'Critique of Pure Reason' the questions regarding the principles of science and the nature of mathematical reasoning have formed a very important chapter of philosophy.   The subject has been approached from the side of logic, psychology, metaphysics, and science itself; both philosophical and scientific authorities have contributed towards the solution of the problem; perhaps it may be said that it marks one of the few provinces of philosophical thought in which we seem to be approaching a consensus of opinion, to be attaining to a tolerable agreement between philosophical and scientific thinkers.   There are few other instances in the large region of philosophical thought where as much as this could be said.   These questions centre in the changed view which we take of nature and natural knowledge, the altered meanings which we attach to these words.   In the sequel I shall devote a special chapter to this subject.

In the meantime it is sufficient to say that science, scientific knowledge, and scientific theories have not escaped the attacks of the critical spirit.[1]   The main

---

[1] I do not here refer to the never-ending cavillings, on the part of theologians, against the results and teachings of scientific thinkers. I refer to investigations into the principles of scientific reasoning and the nature of scientific evidence, be it that of the senses or of the logical processes. In modern times these investigations start with Locke, and were continued in his spirit by Mill; more

reason why they have not succumbed, sharing the same
fate as the purely philosophical theories of earlier times,
can be traced to the following causes.   The first consists
in this, that science has a definite object to deal with—
namely, the phenomena of nature, which present at least
as much uniformity and regularity as is necessary to
afford a firm and unaltering foundation for human thought,
a strong foothold for the searcher and explorer.   Of
this *sine qua non* scientific workers have continually
availed themselves wherever their results have been
attacked; they have always retired into the stronghold
of a small number of undisputed facts based upon
observation and verifiable by every beginner or any
critic who is qualified or willing to take the trouble.
The philosophical or introspective thinker cannot do the
same, and this is owing partly to the subjective nature
of the object of his research, but equally perhaps to the
fact that he is not so far removed from his object as is

14.
Reasons
why science
has not
succumbed.

---

recently by Stanley Jevons and
Karl Pearson.   In Germany they
have two quite independent beginnings, the first in the 'Critique'
of Kant, who looked upon mathematics and natural philosophy as
proving by their existence and their
results the possibility of scientific
knowledge.   Somewhat later, and
for a long time unknown to the
scientific world, the great mathematician Gauss began to question for
himself, and in correspondence with
some friends, the fundamental
axioms of geometry.   In the sequel
there arose out of these speculations
the non - Euclidean geometry of
Vasiliev Lobatchevsky and others.
As this seeming paradox led to an
extension of geometrical ideas, so
in arithmetic the so-called imaginary quantities led Gauss in Germany, De Morgan and Hamilton in
England, to an extension of our
algebraical and arithmetical conceptions.   Kirchhoff, and following
him Mach, in Germany, and, as it
appears, independently, Karl Pearson in England, defined more clearly the real processes of dynamical reasoning and the fundamental
notions of mathematical physics.
Of this subject, which belongs as
much to science as to philosophy,
I have treated in the last chapter
of the first section of this History.
In so far as it affects philosophical
thought, I shall deal with it in a
later chapter of the present section,
which will be occupied with the
problem of Nature as a whole.

the scientific worker; that he lives in much greater intimacy with it, and that, above the endless changes and the bewildering detail, he finds it difficult or impossible to rise to a conception of that regularity, uniformity, and continuity which seem to be the first conditions of all human certainty.

It may here be mentioned that in the course of that searching investigation, that scrutiny to which scientific thought has been subjected during the nineteenth century, we have come to see that those three requisites of scientific certainty, those foundations of natural knowledge—regularity, uniformity, and continuity,—may after all be to a large extent fictitious, having their origin not so much in nature itself as in the powers and limitations of the human mind. I have had occasion to point to this in the earlier part of this History, and to point out how the degree of certainty in the various sciences depends almost entirely upon the amount of abstraction to which they have attained, that the closer we approach the single facts, things and phenomena of nature as they present themselves in the actual world itself and not in the artificial world—such as the laboratory, the museum, or the dissecting-room,—the more we come, so to speak, to close quarters with nature itself, the more uncertain and imperfect becomes our knowledge. Such is notably the case with the phenomena of Life, be it in the Individual or in Society.

But there is another equally important feature peculiar to scientific knowledge, which has become more and more prominent during the nineteenth century, and with which the scientific student will always defy

the critical scholar.   He can increasingly maintain that
his theories, be they philosophically valid or not, are
practically useful, that they *work*, that his methods are
at least clear and definite, his path distinctly marked
out, his conclusions logically consistent, that his knowledge is daily increasing, and that, above all, he can
foretell in many cases what will happen, discover that
which has been hidden, and that the practical applications and triumphs of technical science are the most
eloquent testimony to the value of his pursuits, suffic-
ing to dispel all critical doubts in the mind of any
reasonable person.

15.
Peculiar
strength in
their prac-
tical utility.

Moreover, it should not be forgotten that the object
of scientific research, the facts and processes of nature,
are not really accessible to human criticism.   Criticism
implies a standard from which we can judge the object
of our reflection.   It further implies that what we
criticise might have been different.   Now we have
no standard from which we can judge Nature herself,
and we have no justification for the assumption that
facts and events in the natural world might have been
different from what they are.   Nature is simply what
she is, and if we attempt to pass judgment upon her
phenomena we transcend the limits of natural knowledge, we import considerations which are foreign to
science.   Nature may be an object of curiosity, of
admiration, wonder, or awe ; she is not an object of
criticism.   Criticism is only possible where we can
apply such categories as true or untrue, good or bad,
beautiful or ugly, useful or useless.   These categories,
however, contain a reference to the human mind.   Nature

16.
Besides,
man cannot
judge
nature.

by herself is neither true nor untrue, neither good nor bad, neither beautiful nor the reverse, neither useful nor useless.

Our statements and observations of nature may be true or false, the things of nature may be beautiful to us, the beholders, natural things and events may be good and useful for our purposes or the reverse; but all such considerations import into our reflections a foreign, subjective, or personal element which the purely scientific view must get rid of.   Although therefore the writings of scientific authorities have been subjected to severe criticism, this criticism does not affect nature herself—that is, the object with which science has to do—but only the methods of the human mind, which subjects nature and natural things to the mental processes of observation, registration, measurement, and calculation. These processes can be conducted correctly or incorrectly, elegantly or inelegantly, usefully or uselessly, and are therefore subject to criticism.   In fact, criticism means a reflection of the human mind upon itself.   It is an introspective process.   In the course of history the stage of criticism has only been reached when and where a large amount of mental work, of thought in the widest sense, has accumulated.   Wherever this accumulated mental work, this body of thought, has itself become an object of contemplation, criticism has set in.   In the course of the history of thought we have three great critical periods, which coincide with the age of Socrates in antiquity, the age of Descartes in the seventeenth century, and the great critical movement of the nineteenth century.

17.
Criticism a reflection of the mind on itself.

18.
Three critical periods.

Of these three periods the last interests us at this moment.   As mentioned above, its representatives took the word "criticism" in the widest sense, and it may be said that in length of duration it has far exceeded any earlier critical period.   It has now lasted more than a century, and we cannot say that we have yet emerged from it.   The critical movements of former times were quickly followed by renewed creative activity, by novel constructive efforts, by the dogmatism of new systems and schools of thought.[1]   It is true that the critical movement so splendidly represented in Germany by Lessing (1729-81) and Kant (1724-1804) was followed by the great productive era of classical literature and a brilliant succession of speculative systems of philosophy which for the greater part of half a century forced into the background the workings of the critical spirit.   These workings, nevertheless, proceeded without interruption, and became so much the more evident and effective when the productive powers of German poetry, literature, and philosophy had exhausted themselves.   Although therefore the beginning of the great critical movement in Germany may be placed in the middle of the eighteenth century, its full effect upon the whole of German thought and culture did not become evident before the middle of the nineteenth century.   Since then it has reigned supreme, leaving almost the whole of the constructive work of thought to the workers in the fields of

19.
From the
last we have
not yet
emerged.

[1] Matthew Arnold, in the Essay quoted above (p. 97 note 3), looked in this manner upon the critical spirit as paving the way for the creative spirit.   This statement is borne out by the experience of former periods of criticism, but, as I mentioned in the text, the critical movement which still prevails has not as yet shown any signs of making room for a creative era of thought.

exact science.   We may ask the question : What is the reason that, in former instances, the critical movement was so soon superseded by constructive efforts, whereas modern criticism, notably in Germany, has become a growing, all-destructive, and dominant current ?   The answer to the question is this : Criticism in former times was not really methodical ; it was casual, in many cases brilliant, but it was not conducted on any fixed principles, and was therefore easily overpowered by novel and daring speculations and by that enthusiasm of creative effort which is always absent in purely negative movements.

20.
Its method-
ical char-
acter.

The critical movement both in the age of Socrates and in the age of Descartes developed very rapidly into scepticism, which, as it marks the last stage of the destructive movement of thought, has not in itself the germs of any further development, and is usually followed by a complete reaction in favour of an un-critical acceptance of some dogmatic position.   Kant was the first great thinker who desired to interpose between the sceptical stage—which had been reached in England and France through the influence of Locke and Hume, of Bayle and Voltaire—and a new posi-tive philosophy, which he had in view, a methodical examination of the ways and means by which the human mind could arrive at certainty and knowledge. He laid the foundation of a special philosophical dis-cipline which has latterly received the name of " Erkenntnisstheorie " (theory of knowledge) in Germany, and which has become domiciled in England under the name " Epistemology."   But neither Kant, in the purely philosophical, nor Lessing, in the wider field of criticism, was really radical enough. In their critical attempts they did not go to the root of the matter. Their successors have tried to improve upon them and to penetrate deeper into the recesses of all mental life and activity. With what results we shall see in the sequel. The reasons why both Lessing and Kant halted, as it were, half-way in their critical discussions were probably twofold. To begin with, they had an overwhelming material to deal with, all the inherited systems of ancient and modern philosophy and all the products of ancient and modern literature and learning, all the creations of ancient and modern art and poetry. In the middle of the eighteenth century, when Lessing and Kant started on their literary enterprises, the means of acquiring a tolerably comprehensive view of the great field of the mental labours of the past were exceedingly meagre. It was the time when the French Encyclopædists started the first attempt to arrange methodically the whole body of accumulated knowledge and learning ; in fact, it was the beginning of what I have termed before the age of the encyclopædic treatment of knowledge and learning which lasted for a century.[1] This attempt to arrange methodically and to make inventory of knowledge went parallel with the critical movement. During that period we find continually that the greatest critics had to interrupt their critical work in order to gather the necessary information without which criticism was impossible or premature. We find this notably in the work of Lessing. And

21. Obstructions to it.

[1] See vol. i. p. 34.

still more is it the case with his great younger contemporary and follower Herder (1744-1803), who,
starting with so-called critical dissertations in the manner
of Lessing, was very soon drawn away into new and
unexplored regions which it was more interesting, useful, and congenial to his mind to explore than to
criticise.

The second fact which interfered with a thorough-
going criticism and impeded the free development of the
critical spirit was this, that German literature and
thought had for some time past been moving in a
restricted area, had been under the dominating influence
of special schools of taste and thought.   Out of these
limited regions, prescribed in literature by the canons
of French taste and in philosophy by a mutilated version
of Leibniz's ideas, the German mind broke loose under
the influence of English literature and philosophy.

22.
Winckel-
mann's
reform of
art by
criticism.
At the same time Winckelmann (1717-1768) initiated
in Germany quite a new era of artistic reform through
his anonymously published ' Reflections on the Imitation of the Grecian Works in Painting and Sculpture '
(1755).   Through the discovery in Germany of those
great artistic creations, which had been previously disregarded, of the glories of Grecian sculpture by
Winckelmann on the one side and of the titanic and
elemental greatness of Shakespeare by Lessing on the
other, the purely critical attitude was changed into that
of a comparison of the modern French creations with
those of ancient Greece and of the Elizabethan period
of English literature.   As so frequently afterwards, the
purely critical were changed into comparative studies,

the historical took the place of the analytical treatment.
In the desire for something freer, better, and greater,
it was more natural to turn to the long neglected but
recently discovered models of ancient and modern times
than to develop something entirely original and novel.
For it must not be forgotten that, whilst Lessing and
Kant were the two great representatives of the critical
spirit in the wider sense of the word, they were not
essentially negative minds, and that they opposed the
purely sceptical and destructive movement of which
Voltaire in France was the most brilliant and popular
exponent. Their object was not to destroy but to build
up, to lead taste into new channels and to establish
philosophy upon a firmer foundation; thus they were
more attracted by Rousseau, his gospel of nature and
his educational ideals, than by Voltaire, whose flippancy
and artificiality were opposed to their innermost convictions. In fact, they had definite ideals. They
initiated what we may call the age of ideals, which
governed the German mind for the greater part of a
century. It may have been difficult at that time to
express in words what these ideals really consisted in,
and more easy for their upholders to say what they
were not, what they opposed and disapproved of. But
Lessing and Kant had a strong faith in the existence
of eternal standards of the true, the beautiful, and the
good, and they strove for a general recognition and
appreciation of them.

If, in the light of history and subsequent events, we
ask ourselves the question what this ideal which they
were striving after consisted in, we meet with an

23.
Ideal of
humanity:
its phases.

expression which, ever since the times of the Renaissance and the Reformation, has been adopted by very different schools of taste and thought. It is the term Humanity. This term used to characterise a movement during the sixteenth century of which Erasmus and Melanchthon were the great representatives on the Continent. It was used to define the liberal studies of the Protestant Universities in this country and abroad. Still later the ideal of humanity was the term introduced to characterise the classical works of German literature in their contrast to the productions of the age of enlightenment (Aufklärung).[1] A century after we come again across

[1] The history of these two movements of what is termed in Germany "Humanismus" or "das Ideal der Humanität" has been written in recent times by Fr. Paulsen in his important 'Geschichte des gelehrten Unterrichts auf den Deutschen Schulen und Universitäten vom Ausgang des Mittelalters bis zur Gegenwart' (2 vols., 2nd ed., 1896, 1897). He there distinguishes two periods in this movement of thought in modern history. He deals both with the older form of "Humanismus" in the second half of the fifteenth century, which came to an end at the beginning of the eighteenth century, and with the second or more recent form which started in the middle of the eighteenth, and as he maintains is coming to an end at the present time. Regarding the ideal of culture developed in the former period he gives the following definitions: "The aim of education as it was developed under the influence of 'Humanismus' and the Reformation during the sixteenth century consists in : literary culture and confessional orthodoxy or, to use the formula of Jos. Sturm, 'litterata pietas.' Literary culture is manifested in 'eloquence,' that is, in the ability to write classical Latin in prose and verse. To this the older humanistic teaching is directed ; imitation of the ancient orators and poets is the road to eloquence. The second epoch, the epoch of 'Neuhumanismus,' is primarily characterised by giving up this aim. The Latin imitation-eloquence and imitation-poetry had, in the course of the seventeenth century, become obsolete ; into their place there now stepped first of all the French and alongside of it the German poetry and eloquence, themselves an imitation of Roman literature. From the days of Klopstock, Lessing, Herder, Goethe, there arose an independent German literature, the poetry of original genius. This was enthusiastic for Greek literature as the more original literature compared with the Roman. It heralded the Græco-German 'Humanismus.' Under its influence a study of Greek language and literature becomes the main object and professedly the main subject of instruction in the German Higher Schools. Through it the object of

the term in the later writings of Auguste Comte, and in our days the word is being used by a young school of thinkers in Oxford who have come under the influence of the original writings of the late Prof. Wm. James.

The fact that the critical labours of Lessing found a first resting-place in an admiration of the Greeks, notably Sophocles, and of Shakespeare,—an admiration which was transmitted, deepened and widened, by Goethe and the Romantic school,—has exposed the whole of German literature to the remark that it was largely an imitation of the ancient classics on the one side, and of Shakespeare and the English on the other. As a matter of fact, it was only through the personality and originality of the small number of its greatest representatives that the German mind, after going through the school of the ancients and of Shakespeare, emancipated itself and rose to the production of a few works of the highest order, equalling, though not excelling, the great models which were its masters. To follow up this development would, however, lead us far away from the history of the critical movement, and belongs really not

---

classical studies is changed; the aim of the Neo-humanistic school work is not imitation, either in the Greek or in the German language, but the culture of mind and taste through intercourse with the ancient authors in every branch of literature" (vol. i. p. 3).

The ideal of humanity in the classical literature of Germany is also brilliantly dealt with by Hettner in his 'Literatur-Geschichte' (quoted vol. i. p. 50), and by Carl Schmidt in his 'Geschichte der Pädagogik' (ed. W. Lange, vol. iv., 1876). It will be seen from this extract from Paulsen that German "Humanismus," neither in its earlier nor in its later form, had any sympathy with the contrast emphasised in Auguste Comte's 'Religion of Humanity,' namely, the opposition to religion with a personal Deity. It is also quite different from what has been termed "Humanism" in the new Oxford School, which would more appropriately be termed "Personalism" if this word had not already been appropriated by Renouvier for the religion of his Neo-criticism.

to the philosophical portion of this History but to that
which will deal with individual and poetical thought.
It may here suffice to say that this deeper movement
consisted in a still greater widening of the meaning of
Criticism : it meant not only literary, philosophical,
theological, and æsthetic criticism,—it meant Criticism
of Religion, Morality, and Life. It is represented in
England by Coleridge, Carlyle, and Matthew Arnold, in
France by Renouvier.

The influence of Lessing and that of Kant did not
run in the same channels. That of the former was
most marked in the domain of general literature and
of historical studies. In these two directions the
influence of Kant was scarcely felt, or only indirectly
asserted itself. But in the dominion of philosophy
and theology the influence of both thinkers was
combined, although their direction was by no means
identical. So far as philosophy is concerned, the
purely critical movement which emanated from Kant,
and which down to recent times has prevented the due
appreciation of the positive side of his philosophy, was
to a great extent opposed by the peculiar turn which
philosophical thought took largely under the influence of
Lessing. For it was one of Lessing's great merits that
he drew attention to the forgotten and neglected works
of Spinoza. In fact, it has been maintained by F. H.
Jacobi and by several of Lessing's biographers that
Lessing was a Spinozist. At any rate, whether this was
so or not, the discussion over the point which sprang
up through Jacobi's publication of a conversation
which he had with Lessing shortly before the death of

24.
Lessing's
revival of
Spinoza.

the latter on the subject of Spinoza, drew attention to the works of that remarkable man, and introduced him to the notice of such original minds as Herder, Goethe, Fichte, and Schelling. In fact, it may be said that Spinoza was to the poetical mind of the great German classics a much more congenial thinker than Kant. The philosophy of Spinoza from that moment became and has remained one of the great agencies, not to say sources, of inspiration in the development of the idealistic systems which for fully thirty years pushed the critical philosophy of Kant into the background.

It has been truly said that Kant and Spinoza form the two poles around which the deeper thought of Germany at that time revolved.[1] This twofold attraction started about the same time, for Kant's ' First Critique ' appeared in the year 1781 and Jacobi's ' Letters on the Doctrine of Spinoza ' appeared four years after, in 1785. But the very different ways in which Kantism and Spinozism made their appearance — the former in a strictly philosophical treatise, the latter in a literary discussion [2]—correspond to the abstract logical character

25.
Kant and Spinoza the poles of German thought.

[1] " A momentous coincidence willed it that just at the time when the ' Critique ' of the all-destroying man of Königsberg began to make headway, the most firmly jointed and effective of all metaphysical systems, the type itself of dogmatism, became known in Germany : namely, Spinozism. Through the controversy between Jacobi and Mendelssohn, which referred to Lessing's position with regard to Spinoza, the doctrine of the latter had become the subject of the most lively interest, and this through the deep contrast that exists between them. Kant and Spinoza became the two poles around which the thought of the following generation revolved " (Windelband, ' Geschichte der Philosophie,' 4th ed., p. 475).

[2] It appears that Goethe during his Strassburg period became acquainted through Hamann and Herder first with the writings of Giordano Bruno, and was led from them to occupy himself with Spinoza, one side of whose doctrine, the mystical and pantheistic, attracted him. He could not agree with Bayle, who speaks of the

of the former as compared with the vague, even mystical, meaning of the latter. That Kantism was not as abstract a doctrine as it *prima facie* appeared to be was made abundantly clear by the publication of Kant's later writings, which attracted not only philosophers by profession but also poetical minds like Schiller and even Goethe. On the other side, the strictly logical, not to say mathematical, formalism of Spinoza repelled his earlier admirers, such as Lessing, Goethe, and Herder. It was clearly brought out and appreciated in its consistency and in its ultimate conclusions at a much later

impiety and absurdity of Bruno, and treats Spinoza not less unfairly. In the year 1773 Goethe wrote the Fragment entitled 'Prometheus,' in which some passages are quite in the spirit of Spinoza, and he tells us in his 'Autobiography' ('Dichtung und Wahrheit,' bk. 14 and 16) how Spinoza became a common and uniting subject of interest when, in the year 1774, he met F. H. Jacobi. Having only cursorily dipped into Spinoza himself, Goethe tells us that, whilst repelled by Lavater's orthodoxy and Basedow's didactics, he experienced an inner harmony with Jacobi's manner of approaching the Inscrutable for which to some extent he had been prepared by "assimilating the attitude of thought of an extraordinary man." "This man who impressed me so decidedly, and who was to have such an important influence on my whole way of thinking, was Spinoza. For, having everywhere searched in vain for a means of culture for my own perplexing self, I at last came into contact with 'The Ethics' of this thinker. . . . A large and liberal view into the sensuous and moral world seemed to be opened out to me. But what attracted me most in him was the boundless unselfishness which appeared in every one of his sentences." Goethe also refers to the totally inadequate article on Spinoza in Bayle's celebrated Dictionary,—"a book which through erudition and acuteness was quite as estimable and useful as it was, through gossip and sermonising, ludicrous and harmful." In the year 1780, not long after the meeting of Jacobi and Goethe, the former paid a visit to Lessing, and being desirous to learn more about Lessing's opinion regarding Spinoza, entered into a conversation with him which he introduced by showing Lessing a copy of Goethe's 'Prometheus.' The purport of this conversation Jacobi, after the death of Lessing, published in his 'Letters on the Doctrine of Spinoza' (1785). This created an enormous sensation, and no doubt promoted very much the study of Spinoza, who had, in a one-sided manner, been considered by the popular philosophy of the day as an atheistic writer. This feeling was entirely reversed by the leaders of the New Thought.

date. A great authority on Spinoza, who, for the first time, put before the English public an exhaustive study of his personality and teachings, sums up his appreciation of this remarkable thinker in the words: "Spinozism, as a living and constructive force, is not a system but a habit of mind, and as science makes it plainer every day that there is no such thing as a fixed equilibrium either in the world without or in the mind within, so it becomes plain that the genuine and durable triumphs of philosophy are not in systems but in ideas. Wealth in vital ideas is the real test of a philosopher's greatness, and by this test the name of Spinoza stands assured of its rank among the greatest." [1]

As these words express most clearly likewise the position which in this History I am taking up, not only to philosophical but also to scientific thought, it may be well to note here that the breaking up of the strict logical formalism introduced into German philosophy by Wolff, and continued by Kant, through the Spinozistic thought of viewing everything *sub specie œternitatis*, marks one of the great characteristics not only of German Idealism but indeed of the whole of the classical and romantic literature in that country from 1780 up to 1840,—a characteristic which is totally absent in contemporary philosophical literature in France as well as in this country. English philosophers about the year 1860 began to make a serious study of modern German Idealism, starting with Hegel and going back to Kant as its origin. Twenty years later they recognised that

26.
Spinoza and German idealism.

[1] Sir Frederick Pollock, 'Spinoza: His Life and Philosophy,' 1st ed., p. 408.

it is quite as necessary, for the understanding of this remarkable movement, to go back to Spinoza,[1] who, if not forgotten, was certainly neglected and egregiously, not to say shamefully, misrepresented[2] by eminent writers in both countries. And, anticipating, we may go a step further in mapping out philosophical currents on the Continent, notably in Germany, by remarking that the current of philosophic thought which set in, in the middle of the nineteenth century, in opposition to the Hegelian attitude, may not

[1] This interest in Spinoza produced four important publications. Leaving out what was done by G. H. Lewes, who was probably led to Spinoza when writing his 'Life of Goethe,' and by F. D. Maurice, who inherited Coleridge's interest in him, also Matthew Arnold's brilliant Essay (1865), we meet with the first fairly impartial and lucid exposition of Spinoza's teaching in J. A. Froude's article in the 'Westminster Review,' 1854. But foremost among all stands the work of Sir Frederick Pollock, from which I have just quoted. It appeared in the year 1880, and gives in addition to an account of his life and philosophy a complete bibliography of English and foreign books on Spinoza in the Introduction, and a history of Spinozism in the twelfth chapter, "Spinoza and Modern Thought." Almost simultaneously James Martineau had occupied himself with Spinoza, and brought out in 1882 'A Study of Spinoza.' In the last chapter of this treatise special attention is drawn to his work as a critic approaching the biblical records from an historical as well as a philosophical point of view. A few years later, 1888, there appeared in Blackwood's Philosophical Class-ics a volume on Spinoza by John Caird. This treatise, which deals with the "apparent inconsistencies" and "underlying unity" of his system, is written from a point of view influenced by Hegelian thought, which at that time was prominently represented in this country by the author and his brother, Edward Caird. These four works in the English language may be said to have corrected the many misrepresentations and misunderstandings regarding Spinoza's person and teaching which abounded in the earlier literature of this country.

[2] There seems no doubt that Malebranche and Bayle between them must be blamed for having, through their superficial treatment of Spinoza, prevented for a long time an adequate estimation of the importance of his doctrine, not only among their countrymen—such as Voltaire, Montesquieu, and the Encyclopædists—but also in this country, where, for instance, even so temperate a thinker as David Hume betrays a lamentable ignorance of the subject, calling Spinoza a "famous atheist" and his fundamental principle a "hideous hypothesis" ('Treatise of Human Nature,' part 4, sec. 5).

incorrectly be described as an importation into the
critical atmosphere then everywhere prevailing of the
spirit of Leibniz.   The foremost representative of this
widely different "habit of thought" is Hermann Lotze.
On the other side, the strictly logical monism of Spinoza,
as detached from his mystical pantheism, has latterly
found favour among prominent representatives of
Naturalism, or even Materialism.   Be this as it may,
Lessing and many of his followers certainly found in
the philosophy of Spinoza a resting-place and refuge
from the prosaic moralising and shallow rationalism of
the Deists in England and the Encyclopædists in France.
Compared with these Spinoza rose before them as an
inspired writer, as one who looked at the great life problems not from a utilitarian and narrowly moralising
point of view but *sub specie æternitatis*.

Now though Spinoza is commonly instanced as a
decided dogmatist in opposition to Kant's criticism, and
though Kant himself knew little of Spinoza and never
mentions Lessing, these three thinkers nevertheless
contributed, each in his way, to cultivate an important
field of modern research which, perhaps more than any
other, exhibits the workings of the modern critical
spirit.   Each in his way helped to establish what has
been termed the Higher Criticism in Theology.   The
two great critical movements in modern German Theology,
Higher Criticism as applied to the biblical records on
the one side, and the philosophical interpretation of
religious beliefs on the other, can both, to a large extent,
point to Spinoza, Lessing, and Kant as their earliest
representatives.

27.
Spinoza,
Lessing,
Kant, and
the Higher
Criticism.

Lessing was not a university professor; he moved in wider literary and artistic circles at Berlin and Hamburg, and at last became librarian at Wolfenbüttel. His influence was not that of an academic teacher; like Leibniz before him, he did not gather around him a circle of pupils. Accordingly criticism with him was not reduced to a teachable method, but remained an original and personal feature of his literary genius. It was especially in his style that he marked an era in German literature.[1] In this respect he resembled Diderot in France, for whom he had the greatest admiration. As for Kant, his academic activity moved in the traditional courses of philosophical teaching, and his peculiar method was made known to the world mainly through his writings. His pupils

[1] Carlyle in his Essay ('Edinburgh Review,' 1827) on the "State of German Literature," being a review of two books on German literature by Franz Horn, says of Lessing: "It is to Lessing that an Englishman would turn with readiest affection. . . . Among all the writers of the eighteenth century, we will not except even Diderot and David Hume, there is not one of a more compact and rigid intellectual structure who more distinctly knows what he is aiming at, or with more gracefulness, vigour, and precision sets it forth to his readers. He thinks with the clearness and piercing sharpness of the most expert logician; but a genial fire pervades him, a wit, a heartiness, a general richness and fineness of nature, to which most logicians are strangers. He is a sceptic in many things, but the noblest of sceptics; a mild, manly, half-careless enthusiasm struggles through his indignant unbelief; he stands before us like a toilworn but unwearied and heroic champion, earning not the conquest but the battle; as indeed himself admits to us, that 'it is not the finding of truth, but the honest search for it, that profits.'"

In spite of this appreciation of Lessing and of his style, which "will be found precisely such as we of England are accustomed to admire most," Lessing is probably, of all the German Classics, the one who is least known, read, or written about, either in France or England. This is partly owing to the fact that he is characteristically German, having, next to Luther, done more than any other writer to create modern German style, of which he is one of the very few really great representatives, but still more owing to the fact that in all his critical writings he was a pioneer, and that, as such, his views have been either largely developed or superseded by those who followed him.

and followers, who soon filled to a large extent the philosophical chairs at the German Universities, were less interested in studying and promulgating his peculiar method than in expounding a few characteristic points or doctrines which for a long time became the watch-words of the Kantian School in a very uncritical fashion. Such were, *e.g.*, the doctrine of the Ideality of Time and Space, of the Noumena (or things in themselves) as opposed to Phenomena, of the difference of the theoretical and the practical Reason, of the supremacy of the latter, and of the Categorical Imperative as the fundamental principle of Ethics.   The really critical work which Kant began, and which he only carried out to a very limited extent, was followed up by such men as Reinhold and Fries, and later by Herbart; to some extent also by Schopenhauer, but in the case of the latter, as well as of Herbart, from original and independent points of view which they had gained.   The exclusively critical task of deciding as to the powers and limits of the human intellect and the nature of scientific knowledge was taken up as a definite problem much later on, partly as a continuation and confirmation of Kant's views, partly also in opposition to them.   The solution of this problem was very much assisted and influenced by two independent lines of research.   The first of these was the analysis of the methods of science, of which John Stuart Mill was the great representative; the second was the revival of Aristotelian studies, in which Trendelenburg of Berlin was the principal leader.   It was only after these different lines of research had been pursued for some time that the new critical discipline of Epistemology

(*Erkenntnisstheorie*) was established and named by
Eduard Zeller (1862). Since that time it has become
and remained a favourite subject for lectures at the
German Universities.[1]

II.

The great influence of the critical spirit in Germany,
of which we have considered Lessing to be the first and
most liberal representative, did not emanate either from
him or from the great heroes of the classical period in
German literature, but made itself felt only when it
became introduced into academic teaching as a definite
method, when it became domiciled at the German
Universities. This took place, about the time when
Lessing published his first critical writings, at the
University of Göttingen. It there met another important tradition, which assisted, and in many ways
strengthened it : the connection with English literature
and learning. Many academic teachers contributed
there to introduce and establish what may still be con-

---

[1] It may here be mentioned that
Lotze forms in this respect an
exception among modern German
philosophers. In many passages of
his writings he has denounced
what, he maintains, has been falsely
considered to be Kant's real object,
by "drawing attention to the inevitable circle in which a theory of
knowledge must move." Most
clearly has he put this in one of
his last deliverances ("Philosophy
in the Last Forty Years," 1880,
'Contemporary Review'): "It is no
matter whence our ideas come, and
how they form themselves within
us psychologically, but what is of
consequence is to know whether,
when we have them, we may halt
with them, or must go farther and
necessarily make judgment upon
them, in order to secure the complete harmony of our reason with
itself and with the given facts, the
only goal which is at all attainable by us" (reprinted in 'Kleine
Schriften,' ed. Peipers, vol. iii.)

sidered the highest standards of academic teaching and method. For our purposes it will be sufficient to single out a few names as leaders and representatives of the critical method which then already received the name of the "Higher Criticism." [1] These names were J. M. Gesner (1691-1761), C. G. Heyne (1729-1812), and J. G. Eichhorn (1752-1827). I select these three names, as from them emanated two prominent streams into which the critical spirit poured its refreshing as well as its devastating waters, namely, classical criticism (philology) on the one side, and biblical criticism (exegesis) on the other.

28.
Representative higher critics.

I have already on a former occasion (vol. i. p. 164) mentioned how the foundation of the University of Göttingen marked an era in the history of German thought. It not only initiated the modern conception of liberal studies in Germany, it also gathered into a focus intellectual developments which had before been

29.
Göttingen and the critical spirit.

[1] Higher Criticism is frequently distinguished from Lower Criticism. The latter is occupied mainly with the text of writers, its emendation, purification, and restitution : Higher Criticism introduces the historical and philosophical aspects. It studies the genesis, historical surroundings, and antecedents of its subject, and advances to an interpretation of the meaning of prominent writers, notably the ancient Classics and the Holy Scriptures, aiming, in the last instance, at a reconstruction of the thought and culture of important periods of history. This Lower and Higher Criticism is, as I have already remarked, quite different from that criticism which is allied to rhetoric on the one side and to the history of literary taste on the other—two distinct studies which have in modern literature been carried on consistently and continuously only in France. Prof. Saintsbury in the work already referred to (*supra*, p. 96) separates this criticism from that kind of criticism I am now dealing with, which is, in its development, though not in its origins, a characteristic creation of the modern German mind. For this criticism, with its philological, philosophical, and theological branches, Prof. Saintsbury has evidently only scant appreciation (see *loc. cit.*, vol. i. p. 4). On the term Higher Criticism, as connected with Bible studies, see H. S. Nash, 'The History of the Criticism of the New Testament' (1900), especially p. 12, &c.

geographically separated.   It inherited the taste for
classical studies, of which Thuringia and Saxony had
been the traditional homes.[1]   With this it now united
the study of English literature and learning.[2]   It also
stood in intimate connection with the polite literature of
Germany,[3] one of the earliest organisations of the new

[1] A beginning had been made in
this direction already by the foundation of the University of Halle
(1693). But "free inquiry" was
there still hampered by Wolff's
Rationalism on the one side and
Francke's Evangelicalism on the
other. Speaking mainly of philological studies, Professor Ulrich
von Wilamowitz-Moellendorff says
(Lexis, 'Die Deutschen Universitäten,' vol. i. p. 458): "It was
first of all the foundation of the
University of Göttingen (1737) by
the electoral House of Hanover,
which was at the same time the
reigning House of Great Britain,
that created an epoch in the history
of philology."

[2] This influence was prominently
represented at Göttingen by a remarkable man, who forms a unique
figure in German literature. This
was G. Chr. Lichtenberg (1742-
1799). He was Professor of Natural
Philosophy, and his name is preserved in the History of Science
through the Lichtenberg figures of
Electric Discharge, the memory of
which has been revived in recent
times through Lord Armstrong's
work on 'Electrical Discharge in
Air and Water' (1899). But
though a much valued scientific
teacher, his importance lies in this,
that he is one of the few great
humourists in German literature,
forming a link between the British
humourists—Swift, Sterne, Defoe,
and others—on the one side, and
Jean Paul on the other. The
union of scientific studies with
polite literature is rare, especially

in Germany. But that country
possesses another prominent example in more recent times, in
G. T. Fechner — a thinker little
known in this country except as
the founder of psycho - physics.
Lichtenberg was a very popular
writer, and many of his witticisms
have survived in popular literature.
Cast into the shade through the
creations of the classical literature
of Germany, and more or less forgotten about the middle of the
nineteenth century, his memory has
been revived again by the republication of his Collected Works,
and notably by a collection
of extracts from them by Ed.
Grisebach (1871), the well - known
editor of Schopenhauer, and himself
a humouristic writer of merit. It
was especially the great actor Gar-
rick and the painter Hogarth who
became known to Germany through
Lichtenberg's 'Letters' and 'Explanations.' It is interesting to see
how ideas on the relation of philosophy, science, and religion now
current, flitted prematurely through
the mind of Lichtenberg more than
a century ago.

[3] The importance of Göttingen
as a centre of literature, as well as
of science, is little appreciated,
especially in foreign works dealing
with German thought and literature. Nevertheless, what is termed
the Göttingen school marks an important development in the polite
literature of the country, from
which emanated much that has
been of great value. Histories of
German literature, like those of

literary spirit, the "Hainbund," [1] having been founded in its midst. During the last third of the eighteenth century the University of Göttingen launched into existence the methodical treatment of classical, historical, theological, legal, and economic studies in such a way that in all these five branches the great teachers of Göttingen became the founders of definite schools which gradually spread over the whole of Germany and of the German - speaking countries. Criticism which before that, and in other countries, had frequently degenerated into scepticism or wasted itself in polemics, lowering itself not infrequently to personal invective, became in the hands of the great Göttingen professors and their pupils an academic method and an instrument of

Gervinus and Hettner, give full information on this subject. The migration of the centre of German literature, as distinguished from science and learning, from Göttingen to Weimar, was followed by independent growth on both sides. The literary and poetical genius of the nation liberated itself from the oppressive influence which academic learning or scientific ideas have frequently exerted in other literatures. On the other side, science and criticism were for a considerable period thrown upon their own resources, which led to much original work of the highest order, but also to a deterioration of style and a greater estrangement from polite literature than has been the case either in this country or in France. To mention, however, one instance in which the Göttingen school made a lasting impression on German literature, we need only refer to J. H. Voss, who, much influenced by Heyne's teaching, betook himself to the translation of Homer. His work

has become a classic, much more than translations in any other country, and has domiciled the hexameter as a form of poetic diction in Germany. Voss's 'Luise' and Goethe's 'Hermann and Dorothea' are other examples.

[1] Founded 1777 by Boie. The term "Hain"—the forest, copse, or grove—plays a great part in German mythology, and in the Germanising school, of which Klopstock in the later part of his life became a centre. This term, as expressive of the religious and poetical cult of the Ancient Teutons, was opposed to Parnassus as the home of the Greek Muses, and was chosen as the name of the school of German poetry which originally exalted Klopstock and opposed the Franco-classical style represented by Wieland. On the occasion of their early gatherings they decorated Klopstock's portrait and works with laurels, while they burnt and otherwise defaced the writings of Wieland.

education. For it was mainly under influences coming from Göttingen that a change in the higher education of Germany took place. This consisted in taking the leadership in the learned schools out of the hands of theological and placing it in the hands of classical teachers. Under the enlightened guidance of these the German gymnasium attained its great influence, which has lasted for nearly a century. The mental discipline and intellectual atmosphere at these schools during that period was really owing to the workings of the critical spirit in the wider sense of the word; of free inquiry, based upon methodical study: it took the place of the theological spirit, which had ruled before but has had in the end largely to give way to the ruling of the scientific spirit in the narrower sense of the word that is synonymous with the term exact or mathematical.[1]

[1] All this is brought out very clearly in Paulsen's work mentioned above (p. 116 note). As it deals mainly with the teaching in the learned schools, it casts only side glances at literary criticism on the one side and theological on the other. Those who wish to convince themselves at first hand of the part that criticism has played in German thought and literature, and how, for the greater part of the century, it ruled supreme at the German Universities, need only refer to the histories of the different sciences published by the Munich Academy (1864, onward). Note especially the volumes by Dorner, Protestant Theology; Bursian, Classical Philology; Benfey, Comparative Philology; Wegele, Historiography; Roscher, Economics; Bluntschli, Staatswissenschaft; Zeller, Philosophy. Lotze's volume on the 'History of Aesthetics in Germany' is a unique example in the whole series of a different treatment of an important subject, inasmuch as little attention is given to the influence of criticism, and much more to the constructive ideas which made themselves felt in that field of inquiry.

Another publication to which I am much indebted, and which, though not professedly a history of the critical movement of thought, yet leaves the impression of its supremacy on the mind of the reader, is the history of the German Universities written for the Exhibition at Chicago ('Die Deutschen Universitäten,' 2 vols., 1893), and edited by Prof. W. Lexis. It contains a valuable general Introduction by Paulsen. The different subjects are treated in the order of the different Faculties of the German Universities, under a large number of headings, by leading representatives in each department.

The necessity of becoming an educational instrument had a twofold influence upon the development of criticism in the wider sense of the word.   Criticism had to afford a mental discipline to the learner, and it had to become communicable and teachable.   With these objects in view, it became specialised and more or less reduced to forms and methods.   In the course of time it also became more and more evident that criticism could be carried on from two entirely different points of view.   These were not clearly separated by the earlier representatives of the Higher Criticism.   In dealing with mental phenomena, such as the literatures and culture of the past, and with opinions and bodies of doctrine which have been handed down, we can pass judgment upon them either from the purely philosophical or from the historical point of view.   The first point of view implies the existence of definite standards and clear principles; the latter leads us to the great problem of historical genesis.   In the first instance we refer the subject we are interested in to standards and principles which we must either assume or demonstrate; in the latter case we connect the object of our study historically with its antecedents and surroundings in time and place.   Considerations of both kinds were before the minds of all the great critics in ancient and modern times; but they were not clearly separated, they were introduced promiscuously.   It is one of the most marked characteristics of the learned literature of the nineteenth century, especially in Germany, that in the course of its development the fundamental difference of historical and philosophical criticism has been brought

31.
Difference of philosophical and historical criticism.

out.   Accordingly, we find in all the different fields into which the stimulating, and frequently destructive, waters of criticism have flowed, a growing differentiation of the historical and the philosophical points of view.   In theology, and what has more recently been called the science of religion, we have the historical school and the philosophical school.   The first tries to find its sanction, the justification of its doctrines, in their historical origins ; the latter looks for their philosophical meaning and value.   In the study of law, termed in Germany juris-prudence, we have early in the century the opposition of the historical school founded by Savigny to the older philosophical school represented by Thibaut.[1]

[1] Nowhere has the critical spirit in its quest for leading principles of research or for the origin and genesis of existing doctrines been more evident in Germany than in the older science of jurisprudence and the more modern science of sociology. To the latter, as a crea-tion of European thought during the nineteenth century, I shall have special opportunity to refer in a subsequent chapter ; the former may be mentioned here as a strik-ing example of the working of the critical spirit, exhibiting an enor-mous amount of learning little known in this country, though not wanting in dramatic incidents. Among the latter I may mention a controversy which began in the early years, and reached something like a conclusion at the end of the cen-tury.   The beginning is connected with the celebrated names of Thibaut (1772-1840) and Savigny (1779-1861) ; the end with the completion and introduction of the German Civil Code (1888). Thibaut belonged, as one of the latest representatives, to the school of legal studies of which Samuel Puffendorf, of European renown, is considered the founder.   It aimed at establishing the so-called "Na-turrecht" or Natural Law, "the principles of which were taken to be a measure for the value of the existing Roman Law" (E. Eck, in Lexis, loc. cit., p. 301).   "When, after the conclusion of the War of Liberation and of the French supremacy, a feeling of German unity was kindled, many, and among them not the least patriotic, saw in the establishment of a German national code of law a desirable object, and one which was at the time also attainable.   This move-ment found its most prominent spokesman in the Heidelberg pro-fessor of Roman Law, Thibaut, who gave it emphatic and eloquent ex-pression in his pamphlet on 'The Necessity of a General Civil Code for Germany' (1814).   He was op-posed by no less an authority than F. C. von Savigny, who in his treatise 'On the Task of our Age for Legislation and Jurisprudence' furnished the programme of the

In economics, we have the great historical school, of which Roscher may be considered the foremost representative, and the earlier dogmatic school, which dates back to the great influence of Adam Smith. In the many and far-reaching studies which deal with public or private ethics or the problems of the state and government,[1] we have the two opposite tendencies, seeking for

historical school" (E. Strohal, in Lexis, *loc. cit.*, p. 327). In it he successfully opposed the idea of such a codification, and maintained that the most "pressing task consisted rather in the historical understanding of the ruling jurisdiction." His position has been criticised as too supremely academic and unsympathetic towards the practical demands of the age. Nevertheless it remained victorious for a long time in scientific circles, though practically of little effect, seeing that even the "Code Civil," which Napoleon had forcibly thrust upon a large district in Western Germany, remained in popular force and favour. On the other side, the programme of Thibaut was revived when, on the 22nd June 1874, the German Imperial Diet charged a commission of eminent jurists with the drafting of a civil code. The first outcome of this was submitted to the public in the year 1888, and has since, after being subjected to elaborate criticism and emendation, passed into law.

[1] I wish to remind my readers that I am dealing with the diffusion of the critical spirit, and am not attempting even a mere sketch of the history of Higher Criticism in Germany. Such would have to take special note of a large cluster of studies peculiar to the German universities, but which are only very incompletely, if at all, cultivated in the learned schools of

France and England. It is not only that all German universities contain a legal faculty ; such existed in early times already in the French university system of the Middle Ages, and has from this likewise been transferred to the Scottish universities. The German universities contain, in addition, special faculties and curricula for the study of what are termed "Cameralia," the word camera, or chamber, being used in the sense in which it has survived in such terms as "Chamber of Deputies," "Chamber of Parliament," "Chamber of Commerce," &c. Students of Cameralia are such as prepare specially for the lower and higher positions in the administration. They are incorporated in the ever-widening circumference of the philosophical faculty, or they constitute, as at Strassburg, Würzburg, Munich, and Tübingen, separate faculties, which have incorporated in various ways such of the legal branches as are of special importance for administrative purposes (see Lexis, *loc. cit.*, vol. i. p. 279, &c.) Their studies, termed in German "Staatswissenschaften," approach on the one side branches of legal study such as "Staatsrecht," and on the other side the statistical sciences, which in the course of the nineteenth century have become more and more mathematical. With such a very definite conception of the training which the lower and higher officers and servants of the State require, it is interesting

historical or psychological origins and sources on the one side, for philosophical or actual justification on the other. In general it may be said that the interest has gradually moved away from the philosophical or purely theoretical to the historical treatment in all these and many other departments. This tendency has been very much strengthened, not only from outside by the view which has been independently established in the natural sciences under the influence of Darwin, but also from inside, *i.e.*, in the very heart of the learned schools themselves, upon which the spirit of the Hegelian philosophy, with its motto " that everything real is reasonable," has consciously or unconsciously exerted an enormous influence. This contrast between what we may call the historical and the philosophical treatment has also existed in that great cluster of studies, in that stupendous edifice of learning which the genius of the German nation has erected in the course of the nineteenth century—classical philology. Only here the opposition to the broad historical treatment of classical studies which emanated from Göttingen has not been what we can term philosophical, but chose rather for its foundation the systematic and methodical study of the two classical languages. It is, however, interesting to note that the greatest exponent of this the most influential of classical schools abroad, Gottfried Hermann of

32.
Two modes
of treatment
in classical
philology.

to note that a profession which deals practically with such matters has not received as yet any independent recognition or standing in Germany. I refer to what the more practical tendencies of this country have created as the special profession of accountants and auditors. The duties and qualifications of this specifically British body of professional men are still difficult to explain to foreigners. I believe that in most cases the duties of the auditor are performed in Germany by members of the legal profession, who have all a university training.

Leipzig (1772-1848), got his philosophical training in the school of Kant.

From what was said in the introduction to this portion of the history of thought, on the importance of language in the study of philosophical problems, it will be seen that the position taken up by the great representatives of what has been called "Sprachphilologie" was quite natural and consistent. Language itself, notably the highly developed languages of classical antiquity, forms a firm basis from which we can penetrate into the meaning and ideas of ancient civilisation in its most perfect examples. In the two classical languages, the mental achievements of two great ages, upon which all modern civilisation is grafted, have found a definite expression. The study of these languages, of the literatures of Greece and Rome, of the words, flexions, syntax, and metrical forms which they contain and exhibit, thus affords the best introduction to the study of antiquity. The emendation of corrupt texts, conjectures as to doubtful readings, rehabilitation of missing passages, all that is usually comprised in the term text-criticism, furnishes an enormous field for research, and gives ample opportunity for the exercise of ingenuity and the application of learning. It marks a well-defined object, upon which both master and pupil can direct their attention, and, under favourable circumstances, assist each other. No subject can form a better opportunity for the work of education and training in the higher sense of the word. The exercises are concentrated upon an object which is sufficiently defined and compact to counteract vagueness, and yet sufficiently

flexible to lead to a variety of emendations and interpretations, forming a very suitable opportunity for
oral discussion and combined work.[1] This was recog-

[1] "On a philosophical foundation Hermann appears to us as
the φιλόλογος κατ᾽ ἐξοχήν, as a
philologist in the real sense of the
word, i.e., as the propounder of the
λόγος in its twofold and inseparable
nature, ratio and oratio, thought
and word in one ; the former representing the inner, the latter
the outer side of the activity
which constitutes the essence of
Mind. A thought becomes fully
apparent only when it is spoken ;
the word without the full content
of the thought is an empty sound.
From this peculiarity of Hermann's
nature, combined with his absolute
truthfulness, there follows with
psychological necessity his indifference towards everything that cannot be clearly thought and spoken,
. . . and even out of this peculiarity
there sprang with the same necessity the comprehensive conception
which Hermann had of his science,
and which he followed throughout.
Language is to him the highest
artistic production of the human
mind ; hence it appears, in spite
of its natural origin, frequently
as the result of conscious incisive
thought. Thus voice and language
are the picture of mind and
life. Language exists, therefore,
not only to be empirically used, but
also to be rationally understood ; it
has its definite laws, which it is
the object of science to discover in
general and in detail. In this way
Hermann conceived of language at
a time when there could yet be no
mention of a general science of
language. The languages of the
two civilised peoples of antiquity
—foremost the language of the
Greeks—are as such alone worthy
of study, but still more so as the
means of giving us an understanding of the greatest masters
who have ever lived, for their
written monuments are the greatest
works of art which we possess ; and
they are, further, likewise the best
—indeed, the only means by which
we can understand also the other
monuments ; they alone speak to us ;
other monuments without them remain to us dumb. Thus the correct
understanding and the thorough-
going interpretation of the ancient
authors is the main task of philology ; criticism and exegesis are
indissolubly united. . . . In this
sense also Hermann is the model of
the genuine philologist."—('Gottfried Hermann,' by H. Koechly
(1874), p. 13, &c.) In the same
sense a much later writer says :
"There still remains what the
nineteenth century, especially also
in Germany, has considered to be
the very kernel of philology—criticism and interpretation of authors.
To this also has reference the
much-lauded philological method,
which came to be appraised as
being the best preparation for
all the mental sciences, just as
formerly Latin used to be considered in the schools. . . . The
belief in the possession of a method
as an ever-ready sorcerer's wand
was the most precious gift that
the numerous pupils of Ritschl received from this teacher, whose fascinating personal activity can only
be compared with that of Hermann. He who reads, e.g., Ritschl's
'Parerga' and Haupt's earliest
'Berlin Programmes' has indeed
the sense of a quite peculiar confidence through a dialectic which
certainly produces at times quite
insignificant results ; at times also
such as have since been found to be
erroneous. These writings will as

nised by the great teachers of text-criticism in Germany, who, following the example of Richard Bentley, introduced his methods into their philological seminaries or training schools. These reached their highest development and most perfect organisation first under Hermann, and then under the greatest among his independent followers, Friedrich Ritschl (1806-1877). The philological seminary of the latter has become a model for the highest form of university instruction.

33.
Criticism as practised by Hermann and Ritschl.

And yet it cannot be denied that in the larger movement of thought this criticism of texts, with all its elaborate and ingenious machinery, forms only a temporary resting-place. In this respect we can compare it to the temporary stages which in scientific thought have furnished firm foundations for great scientific developments. As such we had to regard, for instance, the atomic theory, the older undulatory theory of light, or the dynamical theory of gases. None of these theories, any more than the theory of gravitation, can be regarded as ultimate foundations, though they for a long time furnished convenient, well-defined, and practically useful standing-ground for research, and will continue to do so for teaching purposes, even after their merely preliminary character has become scientifically recognised.

In opposition to the grammatical and textual studies which formed the main part of Gottfried Hermann's labours, we have in Göttingen the development of Gessner's and Heyne's seminary under the influence of

little become antiquated as Bentley's dissertation on the 'Letters of Phalaris' or Lessing's 'Antiquarian Letters,' and will continue to be the student's introduction to method" (see Wilamowitz - Moellendorff, in Lexis, *loc. cit.*, vol. i. p. 471).

F. A. Wolf (1759-1824), who was the first to inscribe
himself as a student of philology, and who was also the
first to define philology as the Science of Antiquity.
Through him classical and archæological studies were
transported from the University of Göttingen into the
Prussian state. Wolf's greatest activity, through which
he created an era in the historical and classical studies
of Germany, belonged to the years 1783-1806, at the
University of Halle. He explained his ideas on the
encyclopædic treatment of the studies of antiquity in
an essay (1807) which was dedicated to Goethe. He
saw in the art and culture of the two classical
nations the grasp and firm hold which they had
attained of the highest aims of humanity, and in the
communication of this conception to the younger generation the means of elevating them above the narrow
arena of ordinary life and petty circumstance. Wolf
lived in intimate friendship with Goethe and Schiller
and inspired Wilhelm von Humboldt, through and in
whom the study of language and literature was brought
into immediate contact with the objects of government,
administration, and higher education. It was largely
through Wolf's influence that the idea of founding the
University of Berlin matured in the mind of his great
friend. When in the year 1806 the University of Halle
was closed owing to the Napoleonic occupation, the
plan of a University in Berlin was formed; it offered
to Wolf as well as to many others among the greatest
teachers of Germany a new sphere of activity. As
Ritschl represents the highest development of that line
of activity and classical learning which was initiated

34.
Encyclo-
pædic aims
of F. A.
Wolf.

by G. Hermann, so the programme sketched by Wolf was elaborated by his pupils and followers ; but it is significant that, whereas the former school, which was characterised by concentration and logical acumen, found a centre and its classical expression in the one person of Friedrich Ritschl, the school of Wolf, which was char-acterised rather by breadth than exactitude of view, spread out into a number of branches represented by men of very varying ability and interests, among whom in the first generation may be mentioned Niebuhr, Böckh, Welcker, Otfried Müller. The two schools represented by Hermann in Leipzig on one side, by Wolf and Böckh in Berlin on the other, carried on for some time the celebrated feud of the "Sprach-philologen" v. the "Sachphilologen," but it is gratifying to know that the two great masters themselves, Hermann and Böckh, who, according to the statement of the latter, stood in the remarkable relation "of a friendship maintained by mutual recriminations," ended their lives with the expression of mutual appreciation and personal esteem.

35.
Sprach-
philologen
and Sach-
philologen.

The critical spirit reached its highest development in the hands of representatives who, like Hermann and Ritschl, knew how to circumscribe the field of their research, how to define their object, and how to concentrate their attention and ingenuity. Most of the texts of the classical authors were at that time in a state of great corruption and mutilation. The work of editing and restoring these neglected relics, the study of the remains of antique life, the work of extricating and reviving, the collation of manuscripts, the deciphering of inscriptions, formed a large and fairly well-defined task which occupied the many pupils of Hermann and Ritschl for the greater part of the century.[1] A large portion of this work could be carried on by those whose main duty was to devote themselves to higher instruction at schools and universities. As such it had a great and elevating influence upon the teaching profession, which no one knew better how to exert, recommend, and

[1] Many striking incidents might be quoted ; one will suffice to show the zeal with which these studies were carried on and the dramatic interest which attached to purely philological work such as the restoration of ancient texts. Hermann had, in an open letter addressed to Ritschl in 1837, expressed his doubts as to the principles, differing from those of Bentley, which had been employed in an edition of one of the Plays of Plautus. Ritschl had in the meantime undertaken the examination and collation of the Plautine palimpsest which had been recently discovered by Cardinal Mai in the Ambrosian Library of Milan. These labours had convinced Ritschl of the correctness of Hermann's views, which amounted almost to a divination. " I still remember," says Koechly (loc. cit., p. 46), "the immense impression which Ritschl's celebrated letter to Hermann on the Ambrosian codex produced upon us students. Written in 1837 in Milan, the letter appeared in August in the same periodical ('Zeitschrift für Alterthumswissenschaft'). A few months before this the Professor-elect of Archæology, Adolf Becker, had started his course in the customary manner with a public disputation ; . . . the dissertation which he defended . . . was mainly intended to uphold the traditional Plautine text against the ingenious audacity of Hermann's metrics and its consequences. It was natural that the old teacher—his official opponent—and the new professor should hit each other pretty hard ; whereby the contest ultimately resulted in the establishment of a difference in principles. . . . Hermann adhered to the principles and conclusions of his metrical doctrine, Becker appealed to the traditional text of Plautus in the Palatine manuscripts which, on the whole, appeared to him to be correct. We had followed the contest with the greatest attention, with eagerness we expected the decision of Ritschl, who at that moment was occupied in Milan with the thorough deciphering of the Ambrosian text. And the decision arrived ; it was that letter which did honour as much to the writer as to the receiver, that letter in which Ritschl, from the correcter tradition of the Ambrosian text, proved that Hermann's ingenious divination, in spite of apparent arbitrariness and audacity, had nevertheless hit upon the right thing,—that it had, in short, in spite of all rational and methodical calculation, celebrated a splendid triumph. What joy on our side, what embarrassed silence on the other ! "

organise than Friedrich Ritschl himself. Under this influence not only did the few remaining classical schools in Thuringia and Saxony become the models upon which secondary education in the middle and south of Germany was reformed, but the exclusive character of these older schools was removed [1] and a universal system of educa-

[1] Among these the three most celebrated and influential were Pforta, Meissen, and Grimma. Many of the leaders of the sciences of antiquity and history had been themselves alumni of these celebrated high schools, among them notably Hermann himself and his pupil Fr. Thiersch. The latter undertook the reform of the high school system in Bavaria, and published interesting polemical records on this important side of his own activity. In these he came into conflict with the less exclusively classical system which was being introduced from Berlin in the high schools of Prussia and North Germany. The leader of this movement, himself in later years largely dependent upon Ritschl's advice, was Johannes Schulze (1786-1869), who in 1818 undertook the leadership of higher instruction in the Prussian Ministry under Altenstein, whose right hand in educational matters he remained up to the year 1840. He had himself studied both theology and philology, had been at Halle a member of F. A. Wolf's seminary, and an enthusiastic hearer of Schleiermacher's lectures. His experience was very wide and varied. For some time a teacher himself, as well as a preacher, he possessed to the end of his days an almost "convulsive liveliness" and the capacity of enthusiasm for things and persons. After living in the literary circles at Weimar he came, when called to

Berlin, under the influence of Hegel, whose lectures he attended together with other privy councillors, considering that for educational purposes a comprehensive study of philosophy in its latest system was most suitable. "To this end," he says, "I attended, from 1819 to 1821, during two evening hours daily, all Hegel's lectures on Encyclopædia, Logic, Psychology, Philosophy of Law, History of Philosophy, Philosophy of Nature, Philosophy of Art, History, and Religion, and did not shirk the trouble to impress upon myself the contents of all these lectures in carefully elaborated lecture notes. Hegel used to visit me after he lectured, and then, or in the course of a ramble, to enter into my questions." And Schulze specially remarks that Hegel was to him at all times a faithful, wise, and unselfish counsellor in matters of higher instruction. See for further detail and quotations from an enormous literature dealing with the reform of the high schools in Germany, Paulsen's 'History' (ante, p. 116 note), 2nd ed., Book 5. According to Paulsen, the Prussian system under Schulze was more liberal in facilitating the entrance into the curricula of the high schools of other than purely classical studies such as Modern Languages, Mathematics, and Natural Sciences. These schools thus formed a transition to the more modern type.

tion introduced for all those whose schooling extended beyond their thirteenth or fourteenth year. One of its most important results is to be found in the complete destruction of that difference of class which clung to the few older and celebrated classical schools. These resembled in some ways the public schools of England, through which class distinctions are still intentionally or unintentionally upheld.[1]

For the moment this subject is for us only of collateral importance, our present object being to follow the critical spirit in its various developments. That, applied to the study of the classical authors, it led to the establishment of a rigid method and a strict discipline was one of its chief recommendations in the eyes of educationalists. This brought about its wide-spread introduction in the learned schools. In the year 1872, thirty - eight headmasters and thirty - six professors were counted as belonging to the school of Ritschl.[2] But at that time the critical spirit

[1] The difference of class which in England is expressed by the term higher and middle class was, through the teaching at the older Fürstenschulen of Saxony, exhibited rather in the distinction between classical and non-classical education ; the absence of a thorough knowledge of Latin in reading, writing, and poetical composition being considered by many as equivalent to an absence of real culture. This standard shut out not only the uneducated, the industrial, and the tradesman, but also those who possessed merely literary attainments such as polite learning and proficiency in modern languages.

[2] Of Ritschl's enormous activity and extraordinary personal influence both at Bonn and later in Leipzig, a full account is given in Otto Ribbeck's 'Life of Ritschl' (2 vols., 1879-1881; see especially vol. ii. pp. 42, 299, 408, &c., also the long list of eminent classical scholars who were trained in Ritschl's seminary, p. 560, &c.) A very interesting and spirited picture of Ritschl's personality and influence during the heyday of his career is to be found in the Biography of Fr. Nietzsche by his sister E. Förster-Nietzsche (3 vols., 1895-1904). It is, however, interesting to note that Nietzsche, in spite of his admiration for Ritschl, had some misgivings that the value of the method might

did not rule supreme; by its greatest representatives, and even by those who took the extreme view and opposed the more liberal and vaguer conceptions which grew up in the school of Wolf, criticism was regarded as a means to an end, namely, the reconstruction of the culture of classical antiquity or, in more modest phrase, of the texts and works of the classical authors. Something positive was to be done, something definite was to be attained. The result was that critical labours were very frequently cut short and reconstructions attempted long before the necessary material had been collected or the sifting process carried far enough. The preliminary nature of their constructions was probably not always clear to the minds even of such men as Bentley when he wrote his letters on Phalaris, of Niebuhr in his fanciful reconstruction of early Roman history, or of Ritschl in his rehabilitation of archaic Latin and the text of Plautus. What are now looked upon as merely brilliant examples of method, were to their authors the very aim and object of their studies, and not merely tentative results of subjective criticism and ingenuity.[1] At a much later date, when the histori-

be overestimated, and the drift given through it to philology one-sided (see vol. i. p. 282, &c.) His manuscript notes of the year 1868, there quoted, close with the following sentence : "Where may the fructifying power of philology lie so that we may become somewhat reconciled with her and admit that out of all this immense exertion some germs have sprung up? Wherever these studies touch upon something of general human interest. Thus her fairest triumph is comparative linguistic with its

philosophical perspective." This is hardly spoken in the spirit of Ritschl himself.

[1] See specially on this point what Wilamowitz says in Lexis, *loc. cit.*, vol. ii. p. 472, &c.

The great Niebuhr himself, whose celebrated reconstruction of earlier Roman History made, especially in this country, so great a sensation, but has hardly stood the test of subsequent research (see Wilamowitz, *loc. cit.*, p. 464, also Wachsmuth, 'Einleitung in das Studium der

cal spirit had spread over other fields of research, we
find a similar stimulating audacity in the direction of
premature and problematical constructions.   A notable
example is furnished soon after the Darwinian points of
view had gained favour, in such works, *e.g.*, as Haeckel's
' Generelle Morphologie ' (see *supra*, vol. ii. p. 347, s. 99).
If we now ask the question : What was it that stood in
the way of the unimpeded march of the critical spirit,
what was it that checked and tempered it in its greatest
exponents, we may say that it was the influence of those
high ideals which lived in the minds of the great heroes
of the classical literature of Germany and which, through
their original creations, influenced even those more
methodical searchers and thinkers who were most
inclined to draw a sharp distinction between the highest
fruits of academic method and erudition on the one
side and the dilettante creations of the purely literary
genius on the other.[1]

Alten Geschichte,' 1895, p. 29),
had stated already, in the preface
to the first edition of his Roman
History (1811), that criticism
alone was not sufficient.   "We
must try to separate fiction from
falsification, and strain our gaze
so as to recognise the lineaments of
truth liberated from those retouch-
ings.   The removal of the fabul-
ous, the destruction of what is de-
ceiving, may satisfy the critic ; he
only desires to expose a deceptive
story. . . . The historian, however, requires something positive ;
he must discover at least some
probable connection and put a
more plausible narrative in the
place of that which he has had to
sacrifice to his conviction " (quoted
by Wachsmuth, *loc. cit.*, p. 28).
  [1] See for instance what Niebuhr

himself says, in the year 1826,
reviewing his early labours after
fifteen years (Pref., p. ix) :—
  " Towards the beginning of the
present century a new epoch dawned
for our nation.   Superficiality nowhere gave satisfaction : empty
words, half understood, had no
longer any currency : but neither
did mere destruction, in which the
past age had indulged, satisfy any
longer : we strove for definiteness
and positive insight, as our
ancestors did ; but the latter had
to be true instead of illusory, like
that which had been destroyed.
We now possessed a literature
worthy of our nation and language ;
we had Lessing and Goethe ; and
this literature comprised, what no
other literature had done, a large
portion of that of the Greeks and

We may compare the philological seminary of Heyne and Wolf, of Hermann and Ritschl, in the great influence which it had upon all humanistic studies, with the corresponding influence which the chemical laboratory of Liebig at Giessen had upon scientific research.   In many ways also the personal influence and activity of Ritschl resembled that of Liebig ; both were masterful personalities ; sovereign minds, capable and desirous of exerting a commanding influence ; both were masters of method, which they perfected if they did not create it ; both were led by ideal aims and opened out large fields of research, which required the co - operation of many talented pupils whom they inspired ; both had also an eye for the practical application of their theoretical ideas : Liebig showed this through the emphasis he laid upon the economic value of the researches which he led, Ritschl in the reform which the instruction at the universities underwent through the labours of his pupils and through his talent of organisation which he also manifested in various other directions ; both also showed unmistakably an intolerance of mediocre work, an impatience with mercenary labours and the βαναυσία of the scientific or literary tradesman. Their influence upon the highest university training in Germany cannot be overestimated, but it was also unique and cannot be

36.
Ritschl and Liebig compared.

Romans, not in the way of imitation but as a second creation. For this Germany is indebted to Voss, whom 'the grandson's child and grandchild' must praise as a benefactor : from whom starts a new era for the understanding of antiquity ; for he knew how to discover in the classical authors themselves what they took for granted, such as their notions of their gods and the earth, their life and household ; he understood and interpreted Homer and Virgil as if they were distant contemporaries separated from us only in space. His example acted on many, on me from early childhood, as indeed did also the personal encouragement of this paternal guest."

repeated. It was a product of the idealism of the age, and it led itself to developments which superseded it. The educational work commenced by Liebig has been used more and more for commercial and industrial purposes. We shall now see what was the fate of the critical methods perfected and used with signal success by Ritschl. It has been truly said that the refined dialectic which is to be found, *inter alia*, in Ritschl's Parerga, is not a monopoly of classical philology; Lachmann, *e.g.*, who handled this art in a masterly manner, edited not only the works of Lucretius but also old German manuscripts, as well as the works of Lessing; in fact, " every editor must handle this method whatever be the language of his text. Although therefore the ancient texts make peculiarly complicated demands upon the editor, philology, if confined to criticism of texts, ceases to be necessarily tied to classical antiquity. The view that it should be so is untenable though historically intelligible." [1] Accordingly the methods of Hermann and Ritschl, which were matured whilst dealing with classical texts, have been introduced into all the modern branches of philology, notably at the German universities. We have there Germanic, English, Romance, Oriental, Indian, and other philologies. [2] The rapid widening of

37.
Extension
of methods
from classi-
cal to other
branches of
philology.

[1] Wilamowitz, *loc. cit.*, p. 472.
[2] A very interesting and comprehensive account of the gradual growth of these other philologies, of the diffusion of criticism over the whole study of languages, literature, and antiquities all over the globe, will be found in the second volume of Lexis, pp. 475-549. There the reader will also find what an important part the University of Göttingen played in these studies, which belong almost exclusively to the nineteenth century : also the connection through Göttingen teachers, notably through Heyne, with English literature is well brought out. See especially Professor Brandl's report on " English Philology at the German Universities."

the circle of studies—which Ritschl and others viewed
not without apprehension that the method might suffer
—was assisted by the much larger circle of interests
which from the beginning characterised the programme
of F. A. Wolf. The multitude of problems involved
in the vast study of antiquity, which embraced archæology, history of ancient art, palæography, the study
of ancient commerce, industry, and administration, &c.,
counteracted in many instances that concentration of
talent and ingenuity upon which the older criticism
of texts prided itself so much. The enormous material
had a tendency to lead to that kind of erudition which
was represented in earlier ages by the great French
school of philologists of which Joseph Justus Scaliger
(1540 - 1609) was considered the most prominent
representative, but it also encouraged premature
generalisations with the legitimate desire to grasp the
vast material and to bring some kind of unity into
studies which would otherwise have fallen asunder. A
similar influence came from an entirely different quarter,
mainly through the growth of comparative philology.
This can be said to take its beginning with the introduction of the study of Sanscrit. It is marked by the
appearance, in the year 1816, of F. Bopp's work, 'On
the System of Conjugation of Sanscrit compared with
that of the Greek, Latin, Persian, and Germanic
Languages.' In the year 1819 Jacob Grimm published
at Göttingen the first part of his German Grammar.
A. F. Pott's etymological researches followed in 1833,
Benfey's Grecian Root-lexicon in 1839. But the first
to utilise these researches for the purposes of class-

38.
Bopp and
Grimm.

ical philology and to establish a connection between the latter and comparative philology was Georg Curtius (1820-85), whose influence as teacher equalled that of the great classical masters, and whose Greek Grammar has become a standard educational work in this country as well as abroad.

39.
Extension to historical studies.
The philological seminary with its characteristic feature of textual and higher criticism was in the course of the century imitated by similar institutions in other departments of learning. Such were the historical studies, in the narrower sense of the word, within which the academic influence, but also the exclusiveness, of Georg Waitz is prominent. In jurisprudence, *i.e.*, in the law faculty, these seminaries with their exegetical exercises were introduced in the middle of the century, first at Halle; they exist now at nearly all the German universities. In the departments which deal with economics, statistics, and administration, the first seminary was started at the University of Jena in 1849. Since that time they have become very general. There are also archæological, philosophical, and even art seminaries. The work in these institutions or training schools is more defined and severe in proportion as the subjects they deal with are themselves circumscribed, or as a definite, practical end and aim exists for which the pupil is to be trained. Such is the case in the study of law, and in some branches of those sciences which in Germany are comprised under the name of "Staatswissenschaften." In other departments, such notably as history and philosophy, where neither of these two features is well-

marked, the introduction of a strict system is more difficult. Criticism with its defined methods is there limited almost entirely to the study and emendation of manuscripts and texts and to interpretation of authors and documents, *i.e.*, to an introduction of those exercises which form the groundwork in the older philological seminaries. In the same degree as it has been found necessary to extend the field of research beyond the precincts of the universities, the rigid application of critical methods has relaxed. In many instances the work of specialists and practical experts, of explorers and travellers, of untrained amateurs with the assistance of large capital, has accumulated, at random, such an enormous amount of new material, usually out of the reach of the academic teacher, that the process, as it were, of digestion, of critical arrangement and sifting, has hardly begun. In the light of these vast and overwhelming discoveries, the results of earlier scholars and students who worked in a restricted area with small means and scanty material appear naturally insignificant and immature. Conclusions which they drew with much confidence from narrow premises and insufficient data have been disproved; whilst conjectures which at one time appeared fantastic and were ridiculed by men of the school have unexpectedly turned out to be true. All this has tended to bring the critical methods, or what is now called higher criticism, into some discredit, as a line of research which has no finality, and succeeds only in matters of detail; or, where larger problems are at stake, only by the aid of leading ideas and commanding points

of view which have themselves outrun criticism, being
the spontaneous outcome of the inspired and divining
genius.

This has notably been the case in the treatment of
larger historical subjects, and is probably the reason
why the historical literature of Germany till within
recent times cannot be compared with that of France
and of Great Britain.   It is only since the time of
Niebuhr, who was followed by Ranke and his school,
that Germany has produced historians who have had
great influence outside of Germany : this reputation
rests not so much and perhaps not mainly upon the
critical preparation of the material with which they
dealt, as upon the general aspects from which their
histories were written.   These were not gained exclusively through critical studies, but were imported,
as it were, from outside and combined with vast
erudition, which itself was acquired through academic
training.   To mention only a few examples : Fr. Chr.
Schlosser (1776-1861) wrote the history of a period,
the eighteenth century, from a philosophical point of
view.   He was one of the first who, on a large scale,
showed the connection and mutual influence of politics
and literature as it characterises the period of enlightenment, the philosophical century.   Schlosser's point of
view was adopted and enlarged by his disciple G. G.
Gervinus, who was the first to conceive the idea of
writing the history of the poetical genius of a nation,
treating of the same in its spontaneous development and
its dependence upon external conditions : a conception
which could only have grown up under the inspiration

40.
Broader
view of his-
tory since
Niebuhr.

of Lessing, Herder, and the classical literature of the beginning of the nineteenth century. The greatest example of the fruit of German erudition and philological criticism in union with the large philosophical aspects which the first third of the century produced were the historical works of Leopold von Ranke, beginning with his 'History of the Popes' and continued through his 'German History at the Time of the Reformation' and his 'French and English Histories' of the sixteenth and seventeenth centuries. In these works Ranke dealt, from a universal point of view, with the great political, literary, and religious agencies which were at work in the formation of modern Europe. No other historian of modern times had shown so much combined erudition and critical acumen in handling the enormous volume of documentary evidence which became accessible when the archives of Europe were for the first time opened. But this alone would not — as Ranke himself admitted— have sufficed to found and secure his reputation, had it not been for the art of historiography which he possessed. The artistic side did not suffer, as it did in many other German historians, by the weight of material on the one side or by abstract philosophical reflections on the other.[1]

41.
Leopold von Ranke.

[1] A great deal has been written not only in Germany but also in other countries concerning the real methods of Niebuhr as well as quite recently on the "Ideas" of Ranke. What was in both a result of artistic genius and insight has now to be dissected and analysed as biologists have endeavoured to find out and define the principle of life by dissecting and analysing living organisms. In both cases the living principle disappears under the hands of the critic, as, indeed, it was not produced by synthesis. So far as Niebuhr is concerned, his views regarding early Roman history have been criticised and discussed in this country—where he produced quite as great an impression as in Germany —notably by Sir George Cornewall Lewis in his 'Enquiry into the Credibility of Early Roman History.' Among recent German writers we find, e.g., the statement that the

How little the standpoint and the methods of pure
criticism are able to deal with larger historical subjects
is nowhere more visible than if we consider two historical works which have had a considerable influence
and reputation outside of Germany; they themselves
differ from each other greatly in their general character
and in the historical conception of their authors. These
two works are Theodor Mommsen's 'Roman History'
and Ernst Curtius' 'Greek History.' I will deal first

42.
Ernst
Curtius.

with the latter. Ernst Curtius (1814-96) was brought
up under the influence of that conception of the task of
philology which had been elaborated in the school of
F. A. Wolf mainly by Böckh (1785-1867), Welcker
(1784-1868), and Otfried Müller (1797-1840). The
life-plan of the latter, to write a comprehensive history

whole of Niebuhr's conception
regarding the sources of the Republican History of Rome "can,
of course, not really be proved, but
that it is supported by the analogy
of German and Italian Chronicles,
the development of the Florentine
Chronicles especially serving as an
example" (Wachsmuth, *loc. cit.*, p.
30). And Wilamowitz (in Lexis,
loc. cit., vol. ii. p. 464) says :
"Niebuhr's greatness lay, certainly
not in his Roman History, which
he did not continue beyond the age
about which no real history can be
written ; it lay rather in this that
he, for the first time, carried in his
mind a comprehensive picture of
the history of the old world, which,
in spite of all the casualty of reports preserved or lost, he formed
for himself out of the large connections of events and political
forces." The same writer refers
also to the overwhelming impression
which must have been produced by

his Lectures on Ancient History at
Bonn, where he exchanged the
activity of statesmanship and diplo-
macy for that of a professorial chair.
But Richard Garnett tells us ('Encyclopædia Britannica,' 9th ed., p.
493) that the notes of Niebuhr's
Lectures on Ancient History and
Geography "disappointed expectation," and "would not of themselves have made a great reputation." As to Ranke, I shall, in a
later chapter, have an opportunity of
dealing with the school of historiography which has arisen in Germany
in opposition to what is termed
the school of Ranke ; here it may
suffice to refer the reader to the
careful analysis of Ranke's method
in O. Lorenz's 'Die Geschichtswissenschaft,' vol. ii., 1891 ; also
the Articles by W. Freytag on
Ranke's 'Conception of History'
in the 'Archiv für Systematische
Philosophie,' vol. vi. p. 129, &c. ;
p. 311, &c.

of Greece, was, owing to his premature death whilst on a visit to that country itself, frustrated, only preliminary studies on the 'History of Hellenic Tribes and Places' having been published.[1] But this plan was to some extent carried out in later years by his friend and pupil Curtius, who was the first German historian after Niebuhr to qualify himself for his task by spending a considerable time away from the books and lecture-room of the professor, on the very scenes where the great events which he was narrating had taken place. In this respect he may be compared with A. von Humboldt (1769-1859) and Carl Ritter (1779-1859), who both in a peculiar and original manner did more than any other of their contemporaries to widen the horizon of the man of science as well as that of the historian.[2] During his

[1] Vol. i., 'Orchomenos' (1820), vol. ii., 'The Dorians' (1824)—Eng. trans.

[2] Ernst Curtius occupies a unique position, as he was not only a historian and an archæologist, but belonged to that small number of scholars who combine with their scholarship a poetical and artistic comprehension of the totality of the subject they treat. It is remarkable that his important description of the Morea ('Peloponnesus,' a historico-geographical description of the Peninsula, 2 vols., 1851-52), which is considered to be his greatest work, is little known, having been out of print for many years. In it he connects himself with writers of an entirely different order, such as Georg Forster, A. von Humboldt, and Carl Ritter in Germany, in whom the descriptive view and the artistic conception of nature and landscape is much more developed than the critical. Through this rare mental gift he stands in close relationship to many British travellers, notably to William Martin Leake (1777-1860), who on his military and diplomatic visits to Turkey, Greece, and Egypt during the early part of the century had gathered a large amount of topographical and antiquarian knowledge which he published in a series of Works on Athens (1821), Asia Minor (1824), the Morea (1830), and Northern Greece (1835). Of him Curtius himself says ('Alterthum und Gegenwart,' vol. ii. p. 319) : "William Leake occupies in the history of science, indeed we may say of modern civilisation, an important position, which deserves so much more acknowledgment as the man himself was so modest and unassuming in his work. But we dwell with peculiar interest on such scholarly endeavours as stand apparently in no connection with the labours of others ; which originated through accidental circum-

lengthened residence in Athens and his travels all over
Greece and the Grecian Archipelago, as also through his
subsequent repeated visits to these countries, Curtius
formed for himself a vivid picture of the topographical,
geographical, and ethnographical characteristics of the
Grecian landscape, of the soil, the climate, and the locali-
ties that produced the different Grecian races which together formed Ancient Greece with its different centres
of civilisation, in Sparta, Asia Minor, and Athens, in
Olympia and Delphi. From this comprehensive point
of view which had been prepared by some of the English
historians and travellers, and which was entirely in the
spirit of his teacher, Otfried Müller,[1] Curtius undertook

stances, but stand, nevertheless, in
a large historical connection, and
arose, as it were, with a certain necessity. . . . He devoted his life to
the rediscovery of the Old World,
which has its history quite as much
as the discovery of the New World,
and for which Leake was the true
Columbus. . . . He is an intellectual relative of Rawlinson,
Layard, Sir Charles Fellowes, who
have rediscovered whole worlds of
ancient culture, and if England
may be proud of anything, it is of
the fact that whilst on the Continent the devastating spirit of the
Revolution was still dominant, there
a high-minded and enlightened
enthusiasm for Grecian art had
captured the first intellects of the
nation."

[1] As also of Carl Ritter, who,
together with his more celebrated
contemporary, A. von Humboldt,
established what I have termed
the panoramic view of nature. He
is considered to be the greatest
geographer the nineteenth century
has produced. If Humboldt's view
of nature was essentially cosmical, Ritter's was more strictly

confined to the terrestrial aspect.
" The last and highest truths of
the geographical sciences find expression in the recognition that the
formation of the surface of the
earth and the difference of climate
depending thereon have governed
the development of our species
and defined the changing homes of
human culture in such a way that
a glance at the terrestrial landscape
leads us to see in the distribution
of land and water, of plains and
heights, a definite—we might say an
intentionally prescribed—course of
human affairs. Since Strabo, down
to our century, nobody approached
these deep secrets. Besides the
many thoughtful ideas which A.
von Humboldt expressed or suggested, the greatest revelations
have come from the mouth of Carl
Ritter, of whom we may well say
that he has put a soul into our
natural knowledge of the earth,
that he, for the first time, suspected
in the aspect of the different con-
tinents, which he termed the great
individuals of the earth, secretly
active personalities, or that he at
least traced their activities in the

to write the history of Greece down to the end of the classical period. It is an artistic conception, born in the mind of a poetical nature, and it is embodied in language the beauty of which has few rivals in modern German prose literature. Details of this poetical conception, which may be compared with that of a great landscape painter, had been given to the world in Curtius' earliest work on the Peloponnesus, and were subsequently further elaborated in a series of addresses which he, as "professor eloquentiæ," delivered at Göttingen and Berlin. There, with the touch of an artist, he showed the finer mouldings of the Grecian mind as it appeared to a loving and enthusiastic admirer of the noble side of Grecian culture. That such a work as

history of the human race" (O. Peschel, 'Geschichte der Erdkunde,' 2nd ed., Munich, 1877, p. 16, &c.) "He revealed to us that the ancient world, in which all continental phenomena appear sharpened, exhibits more powerful outlines than the New World, which is poor in contrast, like all creatures of the ocean, for water, he remarks, removes individuality. Europe, on the other side, slim and delicately formed, with stretching out members and deep penetrating water-courses, appears as a continent with higher organisation, as a thoughtfully planned nursery of human society" (Ibid., p. 812). Ideas similar to these lived in the mind of Ernst Curtius. With Ritter he had also in common the religious point of view; for the method of the latter "did not lie," as he himself says, "in the truth of a logical notion but in the totality of all truths, i.e., in the domain of faith. It rests on an inner intuition which is formed during his life in nature and the human

world" (Bögekamp, 'Karl Ritter,' 1860, p. 8). If Curtius, on the one side, assimilates much of Ritter's conception, on the other side he had also a full appreciation of that artistic and poetical view which the study of the ancient world of Greece had produced in many of the leading thinkers of the classical period, and which found expression in a transient phase of Schelling's philosophy. Though Curtius had as little sympathy with the logical systems of contemporary speculation on the one hand as he had with extreme criticism on the other, he nevertheless admired Schelling's view as laid down, e.g., in his celebrated Discourse (1807) " On the Relation of the Plastic Arts to Nature." We may also trace an intellectual kinship between Curtius and a thinker of a very different order, the eminent naturalist, Karl Ernst von Baer, for some of whose writings Curtius expressed much appreciation.

that of Curtius could not have come out of the school
of Hermann or Ritschl is evident. Those who represented the ideals of that school had ample occasion to
find fault with the want of erudition and critical acumen,
which—it goes without saying—can never be great
and deep enough in any historian. Some of Curtius'
favourite theories, notably those referring to prehistoric
times, were put down as fanciful and premature, but we
may now ask, were the constructions of David Strauss
in his ' Life of Jesus,' nay, even the views of Niebuhr,
less so ? Subsequent scholars have disposed of the constructions of the two last-named authors, whilst many
of the ideas of Curtius may still await the final verdict
of the archæologist.

The historical labours of Curtius must convince us
how little the purely critical process could have produced
such work. For an explanation of Curtius' literary
genius we have to look to the traditions and inspirations
of the classical age of German literature. The work of
Mommsen introduces us to entirely different courses
of thought, which crossed and intermingled with the
methods of the criticism of texts and documents. In
order to bring unity into his view of Roman history,
Mommsen started from that bequest of Roman civilisation which has, especially in Germany, exerted the
greatest influence on modern life and society : the great
edifice of Roman law. This had been a favourite study
at the German universities, where it formed, alongside of
purely philological, and later on of mathematical studies,
one of the principal subjects of mental discipline.

The foundation of Mommsen's Roman History was

43.
Theod.
Mommsen.

prepared by him in two great undertakings which occupied him during the larger part of his life, and which, from a learned point of view, will probably entitle him to greater and more lasting renown than the history, which he wrote at the request of a prominent Berlin publisher. This formed, together with Curtius' 'History of Greece' and some other text-books and editions of classical authors, the first attempt to put before the educated public the results of learned labours in a popular and attractive form. The two lines of study referred to resulted in the publication of his work on 'Roman Constitutional Law,' and in his edition of the 'Latin Inscriptions.' As stated above, Roman law, as the foundation of the Roman State, formed for Mommsen the key to Roman history. But there was another influence which formed the background of his historical conceptions. This was the peculiar position which he took up with regard to the political events of his time. Political views had already, before his time, played a great part in German historiography. In most cases, however, a strong political bias, exhibited in favour of or against the existing *régime* and generated under the influence of the startling events which followed the great French Revolution all through the nineteenth century, sufficed to place their authors outside of the pale of genuine scholarship, which should be founded on the unbiassed results of historical criticism. Ranke had kept singularly aloof from the politics of the day; his works really grew up on the older foundation of the idealism of the first third of the nineteenth century to which I have so often referred. Mommsen was probably

44.
Political
temper in
Mommsen.
the first great German historian in whom an unrivalled
mastership in the critical methods and an unparalleled
erudition was mingled with the modern political temper.[1]
He had lived through the great political crisis of the
middle of the century which had swept away all the
older landmarks, many of the great aspirations of the
earlier period, and also that religious spirit which—in an
unconfessional and unorthodox form—lived in the great
heroes of the classical epoch and in those who were
inspired by them.

In the General Introduction to this work I have
used the word Religion as denoting what is to us of
the deepest personal concern, our innermost faith and
convictions, finding expression in individual subjective
thought; not infrequently also in poetic or artistic
creation.   In this sense I may now refer to that

---

[1] "In Mommsen's Work the
whole receives a peculiarly vivid
colouring which evidently stands
in connection with the political
mood which recent experiences had
produced in many patriotic minds.
The 'Ideologues' are ridiculed
with caustic bitterness, and again
and again we are told with an
impetuous accent that only those
can count on a statesmanlike influence who understand how to
calculate calmly and to utilise
existing political forces.   Conspicuous is the contrast with the
solemn gravity and the old - fash-
ioned stiffness of what has been
called 'dignity of historic style'
. . . : men and things are conceived
with   fresh   immediateness   and
brought out with drastic vivacity.
In particular the active persons are
not mere shadows, but are full of
pulsating freshness of life. . . .

In all this the polemical tendency
which pervades the whole work
makes itself felt with an energy
characteristic of an opposition based
upon fundamental principles. . . .
The political estimate of the whole
development of the Roman Republic
in its different phases produces
everywhere original and suggestive
points of view ; . . . the defects
of the republican constitution are
pointed out ; the events of the last
century are placed in quite a new
light as preparatory to the military
monarchism of Cæsar ; the importance of which is pictured with
evident preference. . . . The educated public in Germany which had
lost nearly all interest in home
labours referring to the ancient
world was won with one stroke
for Roman history " (Wachsmuth,
'Einleitung,' &c., p. 48 *sqq.*)

influence which tempered criticism in all its greater exponents during the first half of the century in Germany as the religious or spiritual influence of German idealism. I emphasise again that I do not limit the term "religion" by any strict dogmatic or confessional, by any orthodox or rationalistic definition. From this background of a religious conviction which found its expression sometimes in traditional forms, more frequently in poetical or philosophical rendering, historical criticism in Germany liberated itself more and more through and after the revolutionary crisis of the middle of the century. From that time the religious influence loses its tempering and controlling effect. Inasmuch, however, as criticism alone is not sufficient to lead to any definite results or any positive view in any extensive department of learning, other influences had gained ground, of which the political, the naturalistic, and the industrial are the most prominent. In no department of knowledge which, through the great battle of free inquiry with tradition, was rescued during the first half of the century from the control of inherited views, have these modern influences shown themselves more prominently than among recent German historians. To follow this up is not my present task ; for it would be necessary to enter in greater completeness and detail into the development of German historiography,[1] which, as has been said, begins to be of

45.
Liberation of historical criticism from religious influence.

[1] Readers who are interested in this will find full information in F. X. von Wegele, 'Geschichte der Deutschen Historiographie' (1885, p. 975 to end) ; in O. Lorenz, 'Die Geschichtswissenschaft' (2 vols., 1886-91) ; in the chapter on "Mediæval and Modern Historiography at the German Universities," by Theodor Lindner (Lexis, *loc. cit.*, vol. ii. p. 549 *sqq.*) ; and lastly, in Ernst Bernheim, 'Lehrbuch der Historischen Methode' (1st ed., 1889 ; 6th ed., 1908).

general European interest only in the third decade of
the century.[1] For the History of European Thought it
is important, but also sufficient, to show how the critical
spirit entered more and more into regions of research
and learning which, before that time, were cultivated
without the conscious application of any definite method.
To do this I have, as it were, merely sampled an
enormous material, having dealt with a few prominent
representatives—such as Niebuhr and Ranke, Ritschl
and Mommsen—who are now recognised by authorities
all over Western Europe, or with others—such as Carl
Ritter and Ernst Curtius—who exhibit what is peculiarly
characteristic and unique among the contributions of the
German mind to this department of European thought.

In one of the later chapters of this section I shall
have an opportunity of showing how philosophical
criticism has latterly approached, among other subjects,
the historical problem also from a different side, having
been led to deal with it as one of the principal aspects
of a much larger question, of what I have termed "the
problem of society."

III.

As stated above, we may trace back philosophical
criticism, or criticism par excellence, to the writings of
Kant. They appeared somewhat later than those of
Lessing, whom we have regarded as the first representative in Germany of that critical movement which,

---

[1] By Lord Acton, in the 'English Historical Review,' vol. i. p. 7.

in the form of literary, philological, and historical criticism, permeated, and ultimately dominated, the scholarly literature of that country.   One of the first fruits of that other and independent line of thought which we trace back to Kant was the appearance in the year 1791 of Fichte's anonymously published 'Criticism of Revelation.'   It created such a stir that it was in the beginning taken for a work of Kant himself.   It was followed, in the year 1793, by Kant's work, entitled 'Religion within the Limits of Pure Reason.'   In these writings, as also in those of many other followers of Kant and Fichte, an idea was more systematically worked out, which we find already in Lessing, and in a vaguer form in Herder : the idea of regarding religion in its historical development, and especially revealed religion, as an educational process, which, under Divine guidance, has led mankind on to a purer morality and a more spiritual life.   This idea was worked out from various points of view, more or less poetically, intellectually, ethically, or spiritually, according to the personal bias and tastes of different writers.   From the position taken up in this respect by Lessing, Herder, Kant, and Fichte, the way could easily be found into all shades of orthodoxy or rationalism, of deism or supernaturalism, of theism or pantheism, of a prosaic moralising or a poetical idealisation.

As history has shown, none of these ways remained untrodden,[1] so great was the perplexity in which thinkers found themselves involved, so great the desire

46.
First application of criticism to religion by Fichte and Kant.

[1] This is fully brought out in the 'History of Protestant Theology in Germany' by J. A. Dorner (Eng. trans. by Robson and Taylor, 1871), see vol. ii. pp. 293-344, and especially the retrospect, pp. 345-47.

to find a way out of it.[1] It is therefore not surprising
to see how other courses of thought which bore on
the same subject were hailed with interest or with
enthusiasm as they presented themselves about the same
time, *i.e.*, at the end of the eighteenth century. Among
these must be mentioned, as perhaps the most important
and fruitful, the appearance of Schleiermacher's 'Religious
Discourses' (1799). These discourses were published
with a significant sub-title, as addressed to the "educated among the despisers" of religion. It is not my
intention to enter now into an adequate consideration
of Schleiermacher's views, which will occupy us fully on
a future occasion, as they mark probably the most
important attempt during a long period to get out of

47.
Schleier-
macher's
Religious
Discourses.

[1] This perplexity is well brought
out by Reinhold in his 'Letters on
the Kantian Philosophy,' which
appeared in two volumes in 1790
and 1792. They are admirably
analysed in Kuno Fischer's work
on 'Fichte and his Predecessors,'
which forms the fifth volume of
his 'History of Modern Philosophy'
(see especially p. 54, &c.) Kant
started in his first 'Critique' with
a purely logical problem which he
expressed in the abstract question :
How are synthetical judgments *a
priori* possible? His answer to
this question was partly logical,
partly psychological. A strictly
scientific examination of the solution he gave belongs, as I stated
above (p. 125), to a much later
period, when both logic and psychology had been much further
developed. Kant's age was hardly
prepared to give an exhaustive and
satisfactory reply ; but the abstract
question presented itself to that
age in various concrete forms which
were intelligible to the reasoning of

a much larger circle of educated
persons. Among these, three problems stand out most prominently :
1. How is scientific knowledge possible? 2. How is morality or moral
obligation possible? 3. How is religion possible? That scientific knowledge did exist — notably mathematics and natural philosophy—
there was no doubt ; that a moral
code must exist, and that this is
closely connected with a higher or
spiritual view of things, was not denied,—neither by such destructive
sceptics as Voltaire in France, nor
hardly even by such radical thinkers as David Hume in England.
The more practical forms in which
the abstract question of Kant
presented itself, the desire to have
a philosophy which made it intelligible how science (presupposing a
natural order), a supreme law of
conduct (presupposing a moral
order), and religious belief could
exist together and in harmony,
appealed at once to the age in
which Kant lived.

the purely critical position. In this connection, where I am occupied in following the movements of the critical spirit, it is important to note that these addresses put into the foreground a new problem which lent itself as much to philosophical as to historical treatment. It is characterised by the endeavour, already latent in F. H. Jacobi's writings, to look upon religion from a psychological point of view. All the many attempts to investigate and define the place which belongs to religion in the life of the human soul, individually or socially, down to such recent writings as those of F. B. Jevons, William James, and Wilhelm Wundt, can be traced to their beginnings in the work of Schleiermacher.[1] Religion was there looked upon as a psychological phenomenon, and it is only in proportion to the culture of psychological studies themselves—which constitute a principal feature of nineteenth century thought—that the problem of Schleiermacher has been seriously attacked.

But there is another movement of thought which had grown ever since the middle of the eighteenth century, and which was represented at the University of Göt-

48.
Criticism
of religious
origins.

---

[1] The books written in Germany with titles such as ' Das Wesen der Religion,' or ' Das Wesen des Christenthums,' have been legion. They are much rarer in the French and English languages. In the latter Dr F. B. Jevons' ' Introduction to the History of Religion ' (1896) deserves special notice, as does also the late Prof. Wm. James' ' Varieties of Religious Experience' (Gifford Lectures, Edinburgh, 1901-2). Both these books have received much attention also in German literature. The latter work is purely psychological, with a strong leaning towards modern physiological psychology. Unfortunately " a later work " which was promised, and which would have dealt more exhaustively with the author's own views, has not been published. On the other side Dr Jevons' book deals more with that side of religion upon which anthropological psychology has thrown some light. Prof. Wundt's large work on 'Anthropology' (' Völcker-psychologie,'vol. i. 1900, further vols. 1905 and 1909) is still incomplete.

tingen by the writings of the Orientalist J. D. Michaelis (1717-91), and more prominently by Eichhorn, whom I mentioned above, as being, alongside of Heyne and Wolf, one of the principal leaders in historical criticism. The vaguer attacks which had been made all through the eighteenth century, both in England and notably by Voltaire in France, upon the historical books of the Old Testament and the truthfulness of the Mosaic records, received a more tangible form and a definite starting-point through the anonymous publication in 1753 of a work entitled 'Conjectures sur les mémoires originaux dont il parait que Moyse s'est servi pour composer la Genèse.' The book was written by a French physician, Jean Astruc (1684 - 1766), otherwise well known through a variety of medical works. Eichhorn at Göttingen was the first to draw attention to Astruc's important discovery of the twofold name under which the Divine Being is introduced into the Mosaic records— viz., alternately as Jehovah and Elohim. This discovery the author had made use of to demonstrate the twofold origin of the sacred histories, and to separate them into two records, which partly agreed and partly differed from each other. The most important work in which Eichhorn made the beginning of what is now called Old Testament exegesis was his 'Introduction to the Old Testament,' which appeared from 1780 up to 1824 in four editions, latterly in five volumes.[1] In this

49.
Eichhorn as
successor
of Astruc.

[1] With Eichhorn "the interest in these (Old Testament) studies is only to a small extent theological, nay, hardly even religious, but almost exclusively archæological, literary, and critical. The contribu- tions towards a comprehension of the antiquities of the Bible as they could be gathered from the manners and customs of the present Orient appear here as the principal thing." Also in the study of the Mosaic

work, which exerted a great influence all through the
century on biblical studies abroad, he is considered as
having, for the first time, assumed the truly scientific
position in the larger sense of the word, having applied
"the principles of philological and historical criticism,
the use of which he had learnt under Heyne in the
domain of archæology, to the study of the Old Testament." [1]   This beginning of biblical criticism, which was
not applied methodically to the books of the New Testament till much later, had for a considerable time but
little influence upon religious, theological, or even philosophical thought, which was rather under the influence
of the purely philosophical writings mentioned above or
of the poetical views elaborated by Herder.[2]   Appar-

records following Astruc, criticism
"has so little notion of the prevailing spirit which is to be found
also in apparently heterogeneous
portions that it sees the solution of
the problem in accepting a number
of unconnected and irreconcilable
fragments" (E. Krautsch in Lexis,
loc. cit., vol. ii. p. 181).   It is interesting to note that from the
Göttingen school, and especially
from Michaelis, emanated the plan
of exploring the countries of the
East in the interest of theological
science.   This led to such travels
as those of the elder Niebuhr and
others which were supported by
the Danish Government.
[1] Siegfried in 'Deutsche Biographie.'
[2] In this connection it is important to draw attention to
Herder's relations to Göttingen,
especially to Eichhorn, and how he
and the latter represent two sides
of biblical study, the poetical and
literary on the one side, the critical
and archæological on the other.
That Herder himself recognised

the difference is evident from his
correspondence with Eichhorn, and
is fully dealt with in R. Haym,
'Herder,' 2 vols., 1880 - 85   (see
vol. ii. p. 166 sqq.)   Herder's most
important work in this direction
was that on the 'Spirit of Hebrew
Poetry' (1782).   Although, as is
stated in the Preface, the position taken up is original, it
was no doubt to a considerable
extent suggested by an English
writer whom Michaelis in Göttingen had brought prominently
before the German literary world,
namely,   Robert   Lowth   (1710-
87),   Bishop of London, who, as
Professor of Poetry at Oxford
(1741),   delivered   'Prælectiones
Academicæ de Sacra Poesi He-
bræorum.'   These were published
in Latin in 1753.   A second edition appeared in 1763, and was
republished   at   Göttingen,   with
Notes by Michaelis in 1770, and
translated, with the Notes, into
English by G. Gregory (1787).
Though Lowth is now recognised
as one of the pioneers in the

ently Schleiermacher was the first to come under the influence of both movements and to give to them a new and original expression.

Through the doubts which he threw out regarding the authenticity of the First Epistle to Timothy (1807), he has been considered to have inaugurated a new line of criticism——viz., the literary criticism of the books of the New Testament. It is not unlikely that he would have occupied in critical theology the position which he himself aimed at, doing for theology what Kant had done for philosophy, had it not been that the interest of religious thinkers was attracted in a different direction.

50.
Influence
of Hegel.

This came from the side of the Hegelian philosophy,[1] which for a time kept theological speculation spellbound. It was only after the fascination which Hegel exercised on many minds was removed, and many expectations had been disappointed, that the influence of Schleiermacher made itself felt in wider circles. The change, which amounted almost to a crisis, in German theology, was brought about in the year 1835 by the

51.
David F.
Strauss.

publication of D. Fr. Strauss's (1808-74) 'Life of Jesus.' This work furnishes another proof of the correctness of a remark I have had frequent occasion to make, how little the higher criticism alone is capable of dealing in a comprehensive manner with any large subject or any great problem; how necessary it is to import the

literary and critical study of the Old Testament, the impression he made abroad was much greater than in England. Together with Macpherson's 'Ossian' and the 'Percy Ballads,' he had a very important influence upon German literature.

[1] It is interesting to note that the year in which Schleiermacher published the critical investigation mentioned in the text was also the year which brought forth Hegel's first great work, the 'Phenomenology of Mind.'

unifying principle from some other region of thought. In the case of Strauss's work, the larger aspect was gained under the influence of the philosophy of Hegel, which has had such a dominant influence, consciously or unconsciously, and for good or for evil, upon so many other prominent students of history. Strauss, who was brought up in the narrow surroundings and contracted views of the Tübingen theological training-school, went for the completion of his studies to Berlin, where he came under the influence of both Hegel and Schleiermacher, two luminaries of the first magnitude, who moved in separate orbits.[1] Thus it came about that the

[1] A great deal has been written upon the distinct and very different positions which were prepared and represented respectively by Hegel and Schleiermacher in German thought, and especially in German theology. For a long time the importance of Schleiermacher as a philosopher was neglected in favour of his theological influence. This was owing, to a large extent, to the fact that he published no works on pure philosophy, and that his position, so far as the latter is concerned, was known only through his oral teaching and to a small number of philosophers, among whom Brandis and Ritter are conspicuous, and spread into wider circles only through the posthumous publication of his Lectures. The principal reason, however, must be found in this, that Hegel absorbed all philosophical interest, and that even after this interest had gradually almost disappeared, nevertheless nearly all historians of modern philosophy belonged to the school of Hegel and were inspired by him; the historical labours in Schleiermacher's school being mostly directed to ancient and mediæval speculation. "Schleiermacher was infinitely different from Hegel in his personality as well as in his teaching. The two never stood in close connection though they were placed so near to each other in their common activity at the newly founded University of Berlin, the centre of German scholarship, from which at that time an unparalleled fructifying power spread over the whole of recently liberated Germany. Among the first minds of the nation, which were here assembled, these two men stood in the first rank. But they came in contact only to repel each other; a deep-seated antipathy filled them to the last. Strauss somewhere compared two theologians, Daub and Schleiermacher, in the radical difference of their character, with Homer's heroes, Ajax and Ulysses. Perhaps this comparison might with the same right be applied to Hegel and Schleiermacher. For as Hegel's peculiarity was substantial thoroughness, which penetrated into the last ground of things, into the unexplored depths of the Universe; so, on the other side,

categories of Hegel's metaphysics were applied in the
mind of Strauss to the theological subjects which were
dealt with in Schleiermacher's lectures.[1]   From Hegel
Strauss adopted the speculative principle of his work.
This may be variously expressed.   For Strauss it took
the form of the immanence of the Divine Spirit in the
world.   This signifies that the Divine Spirit works in
the world from inside, not from outside, that its activity
is orderly, continuous, and connected, excluding everything that is miraculous as an external influence, as
a casual interference or interruption.   How this idea
was worked out by the interpretation of the gospel
records as mythical creations, and how the whole conception was upheld by a formidable array of critical and
exegetical erudition, need not occupy us at the moment.
It is sufficient to emphasise the fact that it was by no
means a sober, critical investigation, but rather a speculative construction, under the sanction of the canons of
Hegel's philosophy, which made Strauss celebrated;
perhaps also not less the fact that what appeared
abstruse and unintelligible in Hegel was set out and

Schleiermacher was in life and
learning the representative of subjectivity, the man of the most
restless mobility, of biting wit, as
well as easily stirred feeling. There
was in him a wonderful elasticity
and agility of mind. . . . To state
it concisely, there was in him a
rare combination of deep and sublime religious feeling, of mysticism,
in the best sense of the word, and
of an intensely mobile logical
intellect " (see Carl Schwarz,
'Zur Geschichte der Neuesten

Theologie,' 3rd ed., 1864, p. 29,
&c.)
    [1] Notably to the 'Life of Jesus,'
on which subject "Schleiermacher
was the first to deliver lectures full
of dissolvent scepticism and with
great power of combination. Principally in order to hear them David
Strauss—then a lecturer on theology—went in 1831 from Tübingen
to Berlin. They gave him the
strongest impulse to his later destructive work " (Ibid., p. 28).

applied in a lucid form and in elegant language by his pupil.[1]

The effect of Strauss's work was enormous, and not less so because the conclusions he came to were premature. To the more sober - minded, who were aware how in many instances Strauss had forestalled

---

[1] Allowing that the greater part of Strauss's work has become obsolete through subsequent criticism, the Introduction to the first volume and the Conclusion to the second are still well worth reading by those who desire to receive information on two points. First of all, we get in the Introduction a vivid picture of the perplexity and unsettlement which had penetrated into theological circles through the influence of English deism, German rationalism, lifeless traditional orthodoxy, and the Kantian philosophy. We also learn how the idea, which Strauss professes to have worked out in its completeness, the mythical or legendary character of the biblical records, had been prepared, but only partially applied, by previous religious and philosophical thinkers. What he means by the mythical point of view he defines himself. (1st ed., Introduction, p. 75.) "Putting everything together, little stands in the way of finding the mythical in all parts of the Gospel Story. The word 'myth' will, however, give as little umbrage to sensible persons as any mere word should ever do; for all the ambiguity which, through the suggestion of heathen mythology, clings to that word, should disappear through the explanation, according to which the myths of the New Testament are nothing else but quasi-historical representations of genuine Christian ideas grown through unintentional poetical legends." Further, in the Conclusion to the second volume (p. 729), Strauss refers to Schelling and Hegel as the leaders of that recent philosophy through which the narrow conception of the relation of the Deity to the world, as also the purely moralising theory of Kant, had been overcome. "If God is conceived as Spirit, there is contained in this statement, as man also is spirit, that both are not essentially different. . . . God is not conceived as the rigid Infinite over and outside of the Finite, but as entering into the latter; the Finite nature and mind being His external appearance out of which He ever returns again into unity with Himself. As little as the human exists truly only in its finitude; as little has God reality only in His self-contained Infinitude. But the Infinite is only truly Spirit when He unfolds Himself in finite spirits; as the Finite Spirit is likewise only real if He dives into the Infinite. The real and true existence of the Spirit is therefore neither God alone nor man alone, but the God - man." With these two presuppositions—the legendary envelope which surrounds the biblical records and the Hegelian conception of the idea which he himself compares with Plato's Ideology — Strauss with much erudition expounds and explains all the main incidents of the Life of Jesus.

results to support or refute which would take a long period of research and much sifting of material which had hardly yet been brought together, the correct thing seemed to be to postpone the verdict on the many cardinal questions which he had raised and to pursue patiently the work of historical criticism ; subjecting the books of the New Testament to the same methodical examination as had been practised for some time already with reference to the books of the Old Testament, and still more in the philological treatment of the profane classics.   For a considerable time this work was carried on in the " Tübingen School," at the head of which stood Ferdinand Christian Baur (1792-1860), who, after the death of Schleiermacher in 1834, may be regarded as the most prominent leader in German theological science.   His publications had already begun ten years before Strauss's work appeared.   In the same year with the latter, Baur published a work on Christian Philosophy of Religion.[1]   This work may be considered, as much as that of Strauss, to be an outcome of Hegel and Schleiermacher's combined speculations.   Like Strauss in his 'Life of Jesus,' Baur, in this work, professes to continue and to carry out, more consistently, views which had been prepared by his predecessors,[2]

52.
F. C. Baur.

[1] 'Die Christliche Gnosis oder die Christliche Religions - Philosophie in ihrer Geschichtlichen Entwickelung,' Tübingen, 1835.

[2] Among these he mentions three: René Massuet, a Benedictine Monk (1666-1716), the editor of the Works of St Irenæus and St Bernard ; J. L. von Mosheim (1694-1755), one of the celebrated early professors of the University of Göttingen, author,

among other writings, of a 'History of Heresy' (2 vols., 1746-48), and J. A. W. Neander (1789-1850), the well-known historian of the Christian Religion and Church.   It is especially in connection with the early sects of the Gnostics and their position to the orthodox doctrine of the Church, that Baur develops his wider conception, that a comprehension of the Gnostic view can

and to trace the endeavour to fathom philosophically
and systematise the Christian doctrine, from the
beginning which was made by the Gnostics, through the
patristic and scholastic philosophies of the middle ages
down to the theosophy of Jacob Böhme, and from him
to Schelling, Schleiermacher, and Hegel. It was one of
the first and most important elaborations of Hegel's
grand conception of historical development. The same
idea was followed out in a series of works—down to the
year 1860—on the historical development of separate
Christian dogmas and ultimately of the Christian Church
itself. "The characteristic feature in these works is
that the history of ecclesiastical and especially dogmatic
development is considered as a necessary mental process
which is dialectically carried on ; that, however rich the
details may be, no single feature has as such any value,
but only if it is placed in the whole and considered as
a moment in the process of the general idea which
governs everything. Thus the philosophical treatment
of history is here taken seriously and based on the
foundation of so much learned research and acute combination that the ordinary reproach of abstract constructions which is rightly advanced against so many of
Hegel's disciples is silenced in the presence of such an
author and such labours. Nevertheless, though Baur
is favourably distinguished among other members of
Hegel's school by his genuine erudition, it cannot

only be found "in the idea of philosophy of religion itself, as it belongs
to the essence of such philosophy
again and again to enter upon the
same path which had been trodden
by the ancient Gnostics " (loc. cit.,
p. 9), a view which Baur had already
explained in his inaugural dissertation of the year 1827.

be denied that in his case also a certain dualism becomes evident, a general aspect being frequently only a ready-made logical category, in which the single facts are caught as in a loop, being like a label externally attached to them." [1]

Strauss was well aware that historical criticism forms only one side of the critical process, that it must be supplemented by philosophical criticism. Ever since Jacobi and Schleiermacher raised the question as to the psychological origin and essence of faith and religion, it has become indispensable for every philosopher to answer the question regarding the nature of religion and its relation to other mental processes. The conception which Schleiermacher insisted on, that faith has an independent origin in the human soul alongside of the intellectual and active powers, that, in consequence, religion occupies a region for itself among human interests, was for a long time lost sight of, owing to the absence of a truer and fuller psychology. Notably in the philosophy of Hegel, religion was looked upon as a purely intellectual process, which process found its consummation in philosophy. Belief was an inferior stage in the development of thought, which must be superseded by knowledge. This process of the self-destruction of faith in its progress towards knowledge was worked out by Strauss in detail in his second great work, on 'Christian Dogmatics in their Historical Development and in their Battle with Modern Science.' In this work he tries to show how the general process

[1] Carl Schwarz, 'Zur Geschichte der Neuesten Theologie' (3rd ed., p. 149, &c.)

of dissolution of faith through thought, of religion through philosophy, is manifested historically in the dissolution of the various dogmas. " The real critique of the dogma is its history.   It is first of all to be found in a naïve and indefinite form in the Scriptures ; in the analysis and closer definition of it the Church splits into factions, which may develop into heretical extremes ; then comes the fixing of it in the symbols, and these are elaborated into theological dogmas ; but gradually criticism awakens, the mind distinguishes itself from the reality which it has assumed in the doctrine of the Church.   The subject retires from the substance of its beliefs and negatives them as truth.   This is only done because the mind has discovered another truth, though in an undeveloped form ; and all now depends on this, whether this new speculative truth is the same as the old dogmatic truth, or whether it is foreign and opposed to it, or lastly, whether a middle way can be found." [1] A large section of German theologians were for a long time occupied in looking for this middle way.   Strauss himself indicated a solution by adopting the Hegelian formula, according to which " the Divine Being is not a personality, but becomes personal through an infinite process of personification."

With Baur, as well as with Strauss in his earlier writings, criticism was limited to exegetical work on the one side and to the interpretation of existing texts and historical records in the light of some philosophical idea or of some unproved but plausible generalisation on the other.   With them criticism had not penetrated to

[1] 2 vols., 1840-41.   The quotation in the text is to be found vol. i. p. 71.

the philosophical foundations upon which they built
their constructive attempts. They lived, like so many
other of their contemporaries, under the spell of Hegelian
speculation; but this spell was to be broken, the very
foundations themselves, on which they built, were to
become the subject of a not less unsparing logical or
philosophical criticism. This process of philosophical
criticism culminated in the work of another disciple of
Hegel's: that of Ludwig Feuerbach (1804-72), whose
'Essence of Christianity' (1841), followed (in 1845) by
his 'Essence of Religion,' produced in this line of criticism
a crisis similar to that produced by Strauss some years
earlier in historical criticism. If the Divine Being,
according to Hegel and Strauss, is not a person, but an
infinite process of personification, this means that the
Divine becomes identical with the Human, because in
human history alone do we meet with this process of
development. We are thus obliged to identify Divinity
with Humanity: we are led to the religion of Humanity
and to Feuerbach's definition of religion "as the relation
of Man to himself, i.e., to his own Being, but as if it
were another Being."

It is needless to remark that the Hegelian view was
capable of another and quite different interpretation.
The process of personification of the immanent spirit can
also be looked upon as the gradual manifestation in time
and history of the Divine Mind, which was there from
the beginning and only hidden to the human observer.
From this point of view the highest form of human life
and thought is not an analogue of the flower in which
the life of a plant is consummated and eventually

Marginal notes: 53. Philosophical criticism: Feuerbach. 54. Humanistic interpretation of Hegel. 55. Another interpretation.

consumed; it is more like the mind of a poet or an artist which manifests itself to the world in its creations, but does not exhaust itself in them. The latter, as the more likely view, was adopted by those who considered themselves the true disciples and followers of Hegel, and it was also the formula which proved to be so fruitful and inspiring in the hands of many of the greatest representatives of historical research. This view has been elaborated in many forms in German philosophical and theological literature up to the present day, though, it must be admitted, with decreasing vitality.[1] At the

[1] The literature of this school of thought is very large, but not having apparently exercised any influence outside of Germany it does not really belong to a History of European Thought. Several works have been written in which these speculations are fully discussed. To them I must refer readers who are desirous of learning more about the now almost forgotten school of "speculative theology." Foremost stands the very spirited book of Carl Schwarz already referred to. It is extremely well written, but it comes from a period when the real, though small, value of speculative theology was not quite clearly recognised. The author still stands with one foot in speculative philosophy and expects from it a regeneration of theological science : see notably his account of the philosophies of the younger Fichte and of Weisse, who are about the only contemporary religious philosophers who escape his trenchant and well-directed criticisms. Still more immersed in the speculative aspect is J. A. Dorner in his ' History of Protestant Theology,' the only book, I believe, belonging to this class which has been translated into English. For an English reader it will probably suffice to read such passages as that introductory to the chapter on Schelling, Hegel, and Schleiermacher (vol. ii. p. 357 *sqq.*), to feel convinced how little religious interest, in any other than the German mind, could feel itself attracted by such a line of thought. Dorner is himself likewise still immersed in speculative theology. From quite a different point of view is written the posthumous publication by H. R. von Frank ('Geschichte und Kritik der Neueren Theologie,' 1st ed. by Schaarschmidt, 1894, 4th ed. revised and continued by Grützmacher, 1908). The author belongs to the positive or orthodox school of theology, and has accordingly less sympathy with the avowed, or implied, tendency of the opposite school to base theology on — or support it by — philosophy. His criticisms are, however, in general much more cautious than those of Schwarz. The book has the further advantage of being written at a time when the belief in constructive systems of philosophy had almost entirely disappeared, and when the opposite school, under the influence of A. Ritschl, had likewise broken away from philosophical traditions.

time when Feuerbach published his celebrated treatise, the view he took had much to recommend it in the eyes of many intelligent persons, and it must be admitted that it has gained much support from that other great movement of nineteenth century thought, which has alone resisted the disintegrating action of the critical spirit: the astounding progress of natural philosophy under the influence of the exact or mathematical methods. The latter had, at the time when Strauss's and Feuerbach's writings appeared, at last attained to a firm position in German thought and become domiciled at the German universities. Moreover, it had done so with a silent disregard of—or in ostentatious opposition to—that current of thought which, through the systems of Schelling and Hegel, had for a long time the upper hand in the German mind. There now resulted from all this an open conflict, which is usually termed the materialistic controversy. It broke out about the time when a general wave of radicalism swept over Continental Europe, — an open revolt, without any very definite programme, against the spirit of reaction which had gradually supervened in all the larger and smaller German States, and which had allied itself in single instances with Hegelian philosophy and ecclesiastical orthodoxy. The result

56.
Materialistic controversy.

From a purely philosophical point of view we have the elaborate work of Arthur Drews ('Die Deutsche Spekulation seit Kant,' 2nd ed., 2 vols., 1895), which deals specially with the central problems of the Absolute and of Divine Personality, and treats of theological as well as of purely philosophical writers. Although the author leads up to the idea of the "Unconscious," which he traces like a red line through all previous speculation down to its clear enunciation by E. von Hartmann, his historical analysis, like that contained in Hartmann's own critical and historical works, is extremely minute and instructive.

was a general unsettlement of religious and political beliefs, which was followed by two distinct tendencies in German thought. The first and more popular tendency manifested itself among those who felt the need of some practical philosophy which should take the place of those doctrines that had, through the conflict within the schools themselves or through the attacks of criticism, lost their stability and the hold which they once possessed over the thinking mind. It showed itself in the readiness with which they threw themselves into new systems, in the hope that these would afford some relief in the general perplexities with which they were surrounded. Of the various new philosophies put forth, two stand out as having apparently captured and retained the attention of large classes of thinking persons. Neither of them grew up within academic circles, in which they have never found a real home. They are : the materialistic philosophy, the gospel of which is Ludwig Büchner's 'Kraft und Stoff' (1855), and the philosophy of Arthur Schopenhauer, which, though of much earlier date, did not become generally appreciated till after the death of its author in 1860.

From this, the effect upon the more serious thinkers, who in the German universities presided over and led the higher education of the nation, differed widely. To them it seemed necessary to discard as premature all attempts to solve by an omnipotent formula, after the manner of Hegel, the great fundamental problems which presented themselves. They therefore discarded all hurried generalisations and advocated a sober examination and survey of the large field of new knowledge and research which had been opened out from many sides during the first half of the century. This survey had to be undertaken with a pronounced regard for those higher ethical and religious interests which were in jeopardy through the scientific, philosophical, social, and political convulsions of the middle of the century. By far the most important representative of this attitude, which, moreover, was very widespread, was Hermann Lotze (1817-81), who was better qualified than any other thinker of that time to do justice to the many potent influences and constructive ideas which had sprung up in such abundance between the years 1780 and 1850. To find the rationale of all this accumulated thought was indeed a task to which few were equal. Most of those who in essentials probably agreed with Lotze's great aim, betook themselves to the cultivation of more restricted regions. They succeeded in establishing, in the widest sense of the word, the spirit of free inquiry or of historical and philosophical criticism which had, up to that date, been loudly proclaimed, but had usually been hampered in its full and free development by the overpowering influence of certain dominant ideas which, mainly through the literature of the great classical period, swayed the German intellect.

57.
Renuncia-
tion of
premature
solutions:
Lotze.

Also the several systems of philosophy which the classical period of German literature had produced or suggested furnished new material for the critical process, both from an historical and from a logical point of view. Their principles had to be justified or refuted, their historical antecedents and logical foundations had to be examined and laid bare. In fact, what Kant had attempted to do, but only imperfectly performed, had to be done on a larger scale and with more abundant material. In addition to this, that province of philosophy which had been neglected in favour of metaphysical constructions, the analysis of the human mind, had been cultivated afresh by Herbart and Beneke. Almost simultaneously, but independently, the modern science of empirical psychology took a fresh start in this country as well as in Germany. Shortly after this revival had taken place through Herbart in Germany, through Mill and Bain in England, a new impetus was given to these studies by the appearance, in 1860, of Fechner's " Psycho-physics," which seemed to hold out the prospect of introducing into philosophical discussions that definiteness and methodical treatment which had done so much for the natural sciences. It is therefore not to be wondered at that about that time the general cry arose for a " return to Kant." The leader of this so-called Neo-Kantianism which, however, differed as much from Schelling and Hegel as it did from Plato and Spinoza among earlier, and from Lotze among modern thinkers, may be considered to be Friedrich Albert Lange, whose ' History of Materialism ' appeared in many editions and was translated into several languages. The tendencies of this line of thought were strengthened by a general movement which had its origin equally in historical, logical, and psychological studies ; it was prepared independently in England and in Germany, it resulted in the definition of a new and independent philosophical discipline, termed

58.
Return from metaphysics to psychology : Herbart.

59.
Fechner's psycho-physics.

60.
Neo-Kantianism : F. A. Lange.

Erkenntnisstheorie, the theory of knowing, or Epistemology. All these recent developments, however much they may differ amongst each other, have this in common, that they are an outcome of the modern critical spirit, of that professedly free and unprejudiced inquiry into the historical, logical, and psychological foundations of the whole structure of knowledge and belief as it has grown up in history or as it presents itself to individual minds. Criticism, in fact, had at this stage arrived at the study of fundamentals and origins. With these it is still everywhere occupied, without any immediate prospect of arriving at such tolerable unanimity as would secure the foundation for any generally acceptable system of philosophy.

The study of origins and fundamentals at which the process of critical examination had thus arrived about the year 1860 met with great encouragement and support from two independent lines of research which had their beginning within the region of the exact and natural sciences. These were started by the appearance, in 1859, of Darwin's ' Origin of Species,' and by the posthumous publication, in 1868, of Riemann's dissertation (written already in 1854) on the ' Hypotheses of Geometry.' The latter was immediately followed by Helmholtz's equally important paper on the " Data which lie at the Foundation of Geometry." In fact, the study of origins and fundamentals had been taken up by men of science independently of the critical movement in philosophical and historical thought, and contributed very largely to the strengthening of the critical movement. For a moment the hope existed that here at

61.
Influence of
Darwin and
Riemann.

last, in these two very different regions, a firm foundation and universal principles had been discovered which would work in with the general tendency of philosophical thought as it was announced in the critical works of Kant, temporarily pushed aside by the idealistic movement and recently revived by the proclamation of the necessity of a return to Kant. It was then remembered that Kant himself had made the existence of geometrical and dynamical knowledge a starting-point in his critical attempt to refute the scepticism of Hume, and it was only natural that this appeal to the certainty of mathematical knowledge should be repeated and urged afresh in the light of the mathematical investigations which led Riemann, and the physiological which led Helmholtz, to the critical study of our space-conceptions. On the other side, it was also remembered how Kant was one of the first to study the mechanism of the universe from a genetic point of view, and that in one of his three ' Critiques ' he put into the foreground the study of teleology — *i.e.*, of final causes and of purpose in the living creation, a feature the mechanical explanation of which was suggested in the ' Origin of Species.'

It is not necessary at present to do more than merely refer to the enormous literature and the endless discussions which during the last third of the century circle round the problem of the foundations of mathematical knowledge on the one side and of the principle of organic evolution on the other. It is sufficient at present to note how criticism in all its branches has been influenced by one or the other of these lines of research, or by both combined, as we shall have abundant opportunity of showing in detail in the following chapters.

It is of greater importance for my present purpose to bring under the preliminary notice of my readers the fact that in the course of the last forty years the attitude of the critical mind towards this problem of fundamentals and origins, of the foundations in thought and the beginnings in time, has gradually and radically changed. The confidence with which, from many sides, the ideas of Darwin and Helmholtz were received, has gradually vanished, so far at least as the hope is concerned that on those lines of research any finality may be attainable. The study of origins appears to us now to mean, not the study of the beginnings, but only that of an endless process without beginning or end; the genetic process has reduced itself to a genealogical record.[1] Nor has the study of foundations and fundamentals revealed to us any secure basis of thought; it has rather indicated that even the seemingly most certain of sciences, geometry and dynamics, rest upon conventional assumptions, as indeed David Hume had already foreshadowed. At the end of the century, the critical process has thus not realised the expectations with which both in theoretical and practical questions it was methodically started a hundred and twenty years ago. Rather it has resulted in a general unsettlement favourable both to scepticism and pessimism, and to a

62.
Unsettlement due to criticism.

[1] From this point of view the title of Darwin's work is really misleading, as it deals with the problems of transformation and descent rather than with that of origin—a problem which, as Darwin himself admitted in later years, was really insoluble.

general distrust and agnosticism with regard to the powers of the human mind, by any form of methodical thought, be it scientific or philosophical, to arrive at that certainty which, if not theoretically necessary, is at least practically indispensable in order to secure definite aims and steadfastness of purpose in practical life.

In dealing with the subject of this chapter,—the growth and diffusion of the critical spirit or of the spirit of free inquiry,—my readers will have noticed that only little reference has been made to the course which philosophical thought has taken outside of Germany. It is only through a few great names belonging to France and Great Britain, that in the course of the nineteenth century German thought has been influenced at all. This explains why the histories of modern philosophy which have appeared in Germany have up to quite recent times taken little notice of the contributions of French and English thinkers during the last hundred years. It is only since Auguste Comte's and Herbert Spencer's systems have become known in Germany that German students of philosophy have realised the fact that both England and France had developed systems of their own, which had but little, if any, contact with German thought. This is notably the case as regards the philosophy of Herbert Spencer, who professedly did not study the system of any other contemporaneous thinker, and, in fact, declared that he refrained from reading any philosophical work from which he found that he differed on perusal of the first pages. Nothing is more striking than that the author

63.
Philosophical thought outside Germany.

64.
French and English philosophy little known in Germany.

of a system of philosophy which emphasises progress and evolution, should concern himself so little about other earlier or later lines of thought; in one word, that he should show so little genuine historical interest or critical spirit. The followers of Herbert Spencer might retort that, if their master was deficient in the spirit of historical criticism, contemporary German philosophy on the other side was suffocated by it, and that the only original thinker in Germany after the middle of the century, Hermann Lotze, was likewise averse to the historical method and treated the history of philosophy in a purely subjective manner.

65.
French and
English
philosophy
uncritical in
the German
sense.

From the German point of view, the contemporary philosophies of France and England are mostly unscientific in the larger sense of the word, which is identical with saying that they have till quite recently been uncritical. This does not imply that they have not occasionally produced brilliant ideas, or that they have not succeeded every now and then in coining philosophical terms which have become the shibboleths of great schools of thought and instruments for the handling of large and original conceptions. The reasons why French and English thought has been deficient in that methodical, continuous, and exhaustive treatment which characterises German philosophical and historical learning during the nineteenth century are manifold. For a long time after David Hume had discouraged metaphysics, the philosophical interest in England centred in definite problems, mostly suggested by the social and industrial condition of the nation, or reverted to an analysis of the data of common-sense, preparing the way and gathering large materials for the modern science of psychology. Through the first-named tendency it came into intimate relations with French philosophy, from which it had, indeed, already during the eighteenth century learnt much in economic science. In France the rupture with all the traditions of the past which was produced by the Revolution urged the necessity of reconstructive work in two distinct and opposite directions, of which the one relied upon the rehabilitation of older authorities, whilst the other trusted to empiricism.

Nevertheless, it may be said that the critical spirit has entered fully into the philosophical literatures of France and England during the last quarter of the century. In France the philosophy of M. Renouvier has adopted the name of Neo-Criticism. It emanated from Kant's ' Critique,' which it remodels in important points.[1] Before Renouvier, critical and historical studies in philosophy had been largely cultivated in the school and by the pupils of Victor Cousin.[2] In England by far the most important philosophical works, outside of the writings

66.
The philo-
sophy of
Renouvier.

[1] I am inclined to think that no recent philosopher has grasped the meaning of Criticism in a larger sense than Renouvier. It is also significant that of the several larger encyclopædic works published in the three countries the ' Grande Encyclopédie' alone has an article on " Criticism," in which all the different sides of its function, as I have endeavoured to sketch them in this chapter, are referred to.

[2] Quite recently what may be called a new school of criticism has come to the fore mainly through the work of Dutch and French critics, beginning with Maspero and continued through the labours of Salomon Reinach, Ed. Dujardin, Maurice Vernes, Ernest Havet, and others. Mr Whittaker, in a recent work ('Priests, Philosophers, and Prophets,' A. & C. Black, 1911), has made an attempt to give a synoptic, as distinguished from a specialist view, of the results of the anthropological school of inquiry of religious criticism. He terms the latter the "new criticism" as distinguished from the "higher criticism," which is mainly the work of German and Dutch theologians, and has largely influenced theology in this country.

of Herbert Spencer, are either critical, such as Henry Sidgwick's 'Methods of Ethics' (1875), "Criticism of the Critical Philosophy" (in 'Mind,' 1883), F. H. Bradley's 'Ethical Studies' (1876), 'Principles of Logic' (1883), and 'Appearance and Reality' (1893), and James Ward's 'Naturalism and Agnosticism' (1899); or they are occupied with an analysis of the principles of the critical and allied philosophies. Among the latter I may mention two works which mark epochs in English thought: J. S. Mill's 'Examination of Sir William Hamilton's Philosophy' (1865), and Edward Caird's two critical works on the 'Philosophy of Kant' (1877), and a larger work in two volumes (1889).

What prevented the critical and historical spirit taking more complete possession of the philosophical mind in France and England at an earlier date were two distinct forms or phases of thought which for a long time ruled in their respective countries, and which, in one form or the other, have come to be characteristic features of the philosophic thought of to-day in all the three countries. I am referring to the Eclecticism of Victor Cousin in France and the philosophy of Common-Sense in Britain. The philosophical positions which may be characterised by the terms "eclecticism" and "common-sense" originated in the desire to counteract the sceptical tendencies of Hume's philosophy in England and the extreme form of the sensational philosophy developed by Condillac and his followers in France. German philosophers for a long time regarded both the eclectic and the common-sense philosophies as dilettante. In looking back, however, over the development of

67.
Recent critical tendency in England.

68.
Cousin's Eclecticism and philosophy of Common-sense.

philosophical thought during the nineteenth century, it
cannot be denied that the free development of the critical
process has not only been actually delayed or interrupted
by the philosophy of common - sense in Britain, the
eclectic school in France, and the idealistic school in
Germany, but that even at the present day we have to
resort to one or the other of the expedients offered respectively by idealism, eclecticism, or common-sense if we
desire to relieve the purely expectant attitude which the
critical method forces upon us; in other words, if we
desire to arrive at some positive answer to the great
philosophical problems.   The renewed interest which has
of late been taken in the systems of Hegel and of Leibniz
and in the philosophy of the Scottish school proves the
correctness of this observation.   It has been truly said
that at the end of the nineteenth century Philosophy has
become international; we had occasion to make a similar
remark with regard to Science.   This stage of what we
might call Co-operation in the higher regions of Thought
was reached earlier by Science than by Philosophy.   The
first great scientific idea to be worked out by the aid of
thinkers of all the civilised nations combined was that
of which we treated in the earlier part of this history
under the title of "The Physical View of Nature": the
conception of energy.   Somewhat later the working out
of the Darwinian programme, the theory of descent, has
still more closely united the thinkers in many countries.
Co-operation in philosophical labours was established
still later, and not till England had become thoroughly
acquainted with Continental philosophy by studying, in a critical spirit, consecutively the philosophies

69.
Philosophy
becoming
inter-
national.

of Comte, Kant, Spinoza and Hegel; not till Germany
on her part had recognised the originality of Comte and
Spencer, and France had by renewed study of Kant
assimilated in an independent manner the principles of
the critical philosophy. It is thus that we find philosophical criticism to have become at the end of the
century a common meeting-ground for the philosophical
thought in all the three nations. It is the spirit of the
Kantian philosophy, only that critical inquiry at the end
of the nineteenth century starts from beyond the premises
which seemed to afford a firm foundation and starting-
point to Kant himself. The new science of Psychology,
towards which England was the largest contributor, is
now cultivated by international co-operation; as likewise the critical examination of the fundamental conceptions and axioms in the exact sciences is prosecuted
with equal interest and success in Germany, France, and
England. In these two original branches of modern
criticism we see how a deeper level is being reached
from which to start afresh on the solution of the critical
problem formulated by Kant.

Compared with this international work of critical exploration, the constructive efforts in all three countries,
though numerous, are nevertheless insignificant. If in the
writings of the most eminent thinkers of to-day we were to
strike out all that is purely historical, polemical, and critical, how little would remain! And yet in this small total
of constructive effort we can distinguish in the contributions of the three nations that traditional bias which
has in the past been characteristic of their philosophical attitudes. The English mind, whenever hopelessly

70.
Criticism
the common
meeting-
ground.

baffled and perplexed to find a way out of the labyrinth of criticism, still resorts to the remedy which Hume so graphically describes in the closing pages of the first book of his ' Treatise of Human Nature.'

" Where am I, or what ?   From what causes do I derive my existence, and to what condition shall I return ?   Whose favour shall I court, and whose anger must I dread ?   What beings surround me ? and on whom have I any influence, or who have any influence on me ?   I am confounded with all these questions, and begin to fancy myself in the most deplorable condition imaginable, environed with the deepest darkness, and utterly deprived of the use of every member and faculty. Most fortunately it happens that, since reason is incapable of dispelling these clouds, nature herself suffices to that purpose, and cures me of this philosophical melancholy and delirium, either by relaxing this bent of mind or by some avocation and lively impression of my senses which obliterate all these chimeras.   I dine, I play a game of backgammon, I converse and am merry with my friends ; and when, after three or four hours' amusement, I would return to these speculations, they appear so cold and strained and ridiculous that I cannot find in my heart to enter into them any farther."

To the Englishman the way out of metaphysics is still common-sense, the overwhelming evidence of the things around us.   One of the latest and greatest of English thinkers, Henry Sidgwick, has given expression to this feature of the English mind in his recurrence to the philosophy of Thomas Reid.   If we turn to France we find a preponderant inclination to revert to those philosophies which are allied to or based upon exact, that is, mathematical thought: the philosophies of Descartes and Leibniz. Even leaving out the professedly positive philosophy of Comte, the French mind, in which, as we have seen, the scientific spirit is represented in its purest form, is involuntarily drawn to that attitude which is characteristic of the exact and natural sciences. Now we have seen in the earlier volumes of this History how in the course of the nineteenth century the method in the sciences has more and more tended to become one and the same, whilst the objects and fields of scientific research have become more and more diverse and widely separated, depending upon an increasing division of labour. The process of unification is going on from various well-defined centres, with little more than a far-off hope of ultimate and complete unification. This, however, if viewed philosophically, is the Eclectic state of mind in its highest form, which is not that with which the celebrated Eclecticism of Victor Cousin was so often and perhaps unduly reproved, an uncritical and un-methodical assemblage of unreconciled truths; but rather an orderly co-ordination of definite scientific aspects which, though preliminary, do not in their preliminary character militate against a closer approximation and an ultimate harmony. If we now, lastly, turn to German Thought, there is no doubt that, while standing on the common critical foundation everywhere recognised, it preserves, though to a diminishing extent, its traditional idealistic bias. The idealistic temper, though more and more overruled at the present time by industrialism and imperialism, still forms the ground-note. The ideals incorporated in classical literature and the great philosophical systems of the first half of the century form still for the German thinker the place of refuge where he can find shelter and refreshment when he is fatigued by too much criticism and disheartened by materialism and pessimism. These ideals are still to him a real world which, as with Plato in ancient times, is spread above the world of common-sense. If we join this peculiarity of the German mind to a critical and eclectic survey of the facts of nature and history, we arrive at that kind of philosophy of which the system of Lotze may be considered to be the latest and greatest example.

CHAPTER III.

OF THE SOUL.

I.

1.
Philo-
sophical
and scien-
tific thought
again con-
trasted.

I HAVE had in the past many occasions to refer to
the difference of scientific and philosophical thought.
Entering now on a more detailed review of the progress
of philosophical thought during the nineteenth century,
it will be of use to emphasise again this difference.
Philosophical thought proceeds invariably with the
object of arriving at a comprehensive view of the subject it deals with and ultimately of the totality or
connection of things.[1] Although therefore philosophical

---

[1] As I shall have repeated occasion to urge this distinction, which
has become better defined in the
course of the century, it may be of
interest to note how two leading
thinkers in the beginning of our
period gave expression to this
idea. Foremost stands Goethe, who
with remarkable insight unconsciously anticipated many of the
leading thoughts of the century
which followed him. In that well-
known tract, first published in the
year 1790, on the ' Metamorphosis
of Plants' ('Versuch die Metamorphose der Pflanzen zu erklären,'
Gotha, 1790), he became a pioneer
in a line of thought which at that
time was rare, and which was fully
recognised only when the phenomena of descent and environment,
i.e., of the contiguity in time and
space or of the "Together" of
things natural, had been brought
into view, mainly through Darwin,
in natural science. In subsequent
writings, notably in the revision and
republication of this tract in later
years, we find a clear expression of
the two aspects which nature presents to the contemplating mind,
the purely scientific on the one side,

discussions may lead to matters of detail and confine themselves frequently to restricted problems, they would cease to be philosophical in the true sense of the word if they should rest content with such restricted and detailed discussions and not take note of their bearing on the great task of the unification of knowledge and thought.

2.
Aim at
unification.

In that portion of this history which traced the

the philosophical on the other. "If we regard objects of nature, but especially those which are living, with the intention of gaining an insight into the connection of their being and acting, we believe that the best way to arrive at this is through separation of their parts; as indeed this way really leads us a good space onward. We need only recall to the memory of all friends of knowledge what chemistry and anatomy have contributed to an insight and comprehension of nature. But these dividing operations, ever and ever continued, produce likewise many a disadvantage; the living is indeed analysed into elements, but it cannot possibly be brought together again out of them and animated. This is even true of many inorganic and not only of organic bodies. Accordingly we find among scientific persons at all times the desire manifesting itself, to recognise living things as such, to regard their external, visible, and tangible parts in their connection, to view them as indications of the internal, and thus to command, as it were, a view of the whole. How intimately this desire is connected with the artistic and imitative tendency need not be elaborately pointed out" ('Zur Morphologie,' Jena, 1807, Werke, Weimar edition. II. Abth., vol. vi. p. 8). In the latter sense Goethe has referred to the same idea in many passages of

his morphological writings. The second prominent thinker who seems to have been impressed with this view is Auguste Comte, who had moreover the merit of coining a term which denotes the difference of the two aspects. Already in an early tract of the year 1825 ('Considérations sur les Sciences et les Savants'), he employs the term *esprit d'ensemble*, which he considers has been lost and can only be restored again by the positive philosophy. It is true that in his first great work he urges this aspect mainly when discussing the method of the biological sciences as compared with those sciences which deal with inorganic nature or with abstract mechanics. The translators of Comte's tract, which was reprinted by him at the end of the 4th volume of his second large work, in the year 1854, do not seem to have been able to find an English equivalent for this term. The best rendering of it seems to be that proposed by my friend, Prof. W. R. Sorley, viz., the synoptical view. The *ensemble* of things denotes their actual "Together" in nature, and is very different from that unification aimed at by Herbert Spencer and successfully carried out in what we may, in a restricted sense, call the scientific study of nature (see Eng. trans. of the 'System of Positive Polity, Paris, 1854,' vol. iv. p. 607).

VOL. III.

N

development of scientific thought during the century,
I followed an idea most clearly expressed by Herbert
Spencer, according to which science is partially unified
thought. There I took up those ideas and aspects
under the guidance of which a partial unification of
our knowledge of natural things has become possible.
Now—in treating of the development of philosophical
thought—I select those further conceptions which have
been used to arrive at a more complete if not an
ultimate unification of thought. As has already been
stated in the introductory chapter to this section, these
further conceptions are not to be found by looking
around us and outside, but rather by looking inside, by
introspection. They have become crystallised in certain
terms or words familiar in all the languages of the
civilised world.

3.
General
conceptions
ancient and
modern.

The conceptions under which we found it convenient
to arrange the historical development of scientific thought
were mostly known already to the ancients. Modern
times, notably the nineteenth century, have more clearly
defined them, increasing them indeed by one or two
additional ideas—such as energy and the doctrine of
averages. If we now look at the general conceptions,
expressed in definite words, which have governed modern
philosophical thought, we are still more struck by the
fact that they are not of modern origin. Although the
philosophical vocabulary has in the course of the nineteenth century enormously increased, it cannot be said that
any novel central idea is to be met with. All that has
been done by the enrichment of philosophical language
has been to attain to a clearer definition and under-

standing of the hidden meaning which underlies those
time-honoured terms, those traditional expressions which,
almost from the dawn of thought, have not only governed
philosophical reasoning but also embody all that is
most valuable in poetry and literature. These time-
honoured words describe in fact and tend to fix the
eternal problems which force themselves upon the human
mind, denoting its highest interests and aspirations. The
problems of science may and will change with the progress of knowledge, with altered attitudes of thought, and
with novel practical demands: the great problems of
philosophy remain always the same. With the intention
of emphasising this, as also with the desire to accommodate myself to the usage of language and common-
sense and the interests of all intelligent readers, I
propose to arrange my narrative of the courses and
development of philosophical thought under well-known
words or terms which will, without special definition,
introduce us into discussions which have always been,
and still are, of foremost importance. Such words, 4.
e.g., as the Soul, Truth or Knowledge, Reality, Nature, Words marking
Duty, Beauty, the Spirit, Society, &c., convey to the philosophical
mind of every thinking person, without any laboured problems.
definition, an idea of some momentous subject immediately connected with our deepest interests and practical endeavours. The whole of philosophical thought
can thus be arranged as the attempt to answer such
questions as, What is the Soul? What is meant by
truth, duty, reality, &c.? The adoption of such familiar
words will serve a double purpose. It will connect
philosophical thought with general literature and lan-

guage, neither of which can dispense with them; and it will also, to many minds, suggest a second very obvious reflection: a moment's thought will convince us that it is almost impossible to discuss separately any of the great problems indicated by those words; that the discussion of each leads involuntarily to that of the others, driving us onward to the conception of the Whole, the All, *i.e.*, to the discussion of the world-problem, the connection or actual "Together" of things. This is the highest, the central philosophical problem, the attempted solutions of which in the course of the nineteenth century I shall deal with in one of the last chapters of the present portion of this History. It will appropriately bear the title: "Of Systems of Philosophy."

5.
The problem
of the
Soul or
Psychology.
I have headed this first chapter which deals with a definite philosophical problem: "Of the Soul." I might have chosen several other words which would have equally introduced us into that portion of philosophical literature with which I am now concerned. Such terms would be, *e.g.*, the mind, consciousness, the inner world, &c. The province of philosophy with which I am dealing is usually in recent literature called Psychology. The oldest treatise on the subject is that of Aristotle, which bears the title περὶ ψυχῆς, De Anima. I have preferred to introduce the subject of this chapter by using the original term, which at once suggests problems, such as the nature of the soul, the fate of the soul, the whereabouts of the soul, and many others which command a continued interest, denoting some of the deepest questions which inquiring and thinking

persons may put to the philosopher. In the beginning of the century, both the word soul and the term Psychology were more frequent in the philosophical literature of Germany than they were in that of France or England. In the two latter countries, treatises on similar subjects were more commonly put forth under such titles as: On man, On the human mind, &c.; the word soul being more generally reserved for discussions referring to what we may term the emotional and spiritual side of human nature. That I nevertheless prefer to speak of the soul and not of the human mind or human nature, may be justified by the fact that the word soul introduces us at once into an historical discussion, which took place in the middle of the century in Germany, and which may be considered to mark one of the great changes that have come over our way of regarding all questions connected with the mental life.[1] What

6.
The 'Seelen-frage.'

[1] A good account of this controversy is given by F. A. Lange in his celebrated 'History of Materialism' already referred to. This history traces the materialistic hypothesis from its beginnings in ancient philosophy, where it found a brilliant exposition in Lucretius' celebrated poem on the 'Nature of Things.' Lange then sets out the revival of materialism as it accompanied the rise of the modern scientific spirit, following it through the writings of Gassendi on the Continent and Hobbes in England, the peculiar combination of scientific materialism with religious belief in Boyle and Newton, in Hartley and Priestley, and its dying out in the writings of Toland in the course of the eighteenth century. From England the materialistic movement of thought spread into France, where it received a classical expression in the works of La Mettrie and Holbach. In Germany the great influence of Leibniz counteracted for a long time the materialistic in favour of a spiritualistic view; materialism, however, gained a permanent foothold in German thought in the middle of the nineteenth century, and this, under the influence of two distinct lines of thought. The first was that of French medical science, dating back to the writings of Cabanis and Broussais, and continued through Flourens, Magendie, Longet, and others. The second came quite independently through the reaction against the idealistic systems of Schelling and Hegel as well as through the development of certain elements in these. The philosopher who brought these in-

was called at the time "Die Seelenfrage" occupied the foremost place in philosophical discussions carried on both by philosophers and by naturalists. Psychology (in German "Seelenlehre") formed a kind of reaction in the writings of Herbart and Beneke against the then ruling philosophy of the mind, and, on the other side, it embodied, as notably in the writings of Lotze, the matured discussion of the materialistic hypothesis advanced by Vogt, Moleschott, and Büchner. As the stormy discussions which were then carried on in

fluences together was Lotze, who early recognised quite as much the necessity of purifying the principles of the biological and medical sciences as of gaining an independent foundation for an idealistic or spiritual view of things. In the former endeavour he went further than contemporary French thinkers by combating the conception of vital forces current among them. His connection with Rudolph Wagner as a contributor to the physiological dictionary edited by the latter, and as his colleague at the University of Göttingen, made this side of his writings accessible to medical students, whereas his simultaneous metaphysical and logical treatises (see p. 6 note, *supra*) remained unknown. The result has been that Lotze may be considered as having, in a way, both suggested and combated the extreme materialistic conception, being, later on, its most competent and thorough-going critic and opponent. The principal writings in which German materialism found expression are Moleschott (1822-93), 'Der Kreislauf des Lebens' (1852, frequently re-edited and enlarged); Karl Vogt (1817-95), 'Physiologische Briefe' (1845-47), 'Bilder aus dem Thierleben' (1852), and

'Köhlerglaube und Wissenschaft' 1854). The former was provoked by and opposed certain passages in Liebig's 'Chemical Letters,' the latter bore a similar relation to Wagner's 'Physiologische Briefe' (1852). The whole question led to a celebrated discussion at the German Naturforscher-Versammlung at Göttingen in 1854, where Wagner expressed himself in favour of a dualistic conception of nature, allowing both for mechanism and spiritualism—a view ridiculed by Vogt as a kind of philosophical "book-keeping by double entry." It created a flood of literature on both sides. Ludwig Büchner (1824-99) followed in 1855 with his well-known, frequently republished and translated treatise, 'Kraft und Stoff,' which held its own in Germany as the gospel of materialism till it was followed, and to some extent superseded, by Ernst Häckel's 'Welträthsel' (1899, and many following editions). There is no doubt that these two books have successfully originated and perpetuated among the middle class intellect of Germany not only philosophical materialism, but also a material as opposed to an ideal and spiritual view of the world and life.

Germany, and which were echoed in a more sober manner in French and English literature, mark probably one of the most important changes that have come over philosophical thought in the course of the century, it seems appropriate to start the history of philosophical thought with an account of the problems which centre in the word soul.[1]

[1] In order to assist my readers, I anticipate what will be more fully explained in this and following chapters, by defining the great change which I refer to in the text, in a telling phrase invented by Lange. He speaks of a "psychology without a soul." This truly indicates the position which most English psychologists before the middle of the century had already —though unconsciously and generally without denying the existence of the soul—adopted, and which has become almost universal among psychologists since that time. It corresponds to similar positions taken up in physics and biology since they have submitted to rigorous scientific treatment. The former does not now concern itself with a definition of matter nor the latter with a definition of life ; see, e.g., the Appendix to P. G. Tait's 'Properties of Matter,' quoted in an earlier volume of this History (vol. ii. pp. 388-425), and Huxley's article on "Biology" in the 9th ed. of the 'Ency. Brit.' Earlier biologists, such as Cuvier, attempted to give a definition of life. This task, as also the definition of matter, is now admitted to be not a scientific but a philosophical problem. In the same way, since psychologists have very generally put aside the question as to the essence of the soul, confining themselves to the description of psychical processes and phenomena, psychology has become an independent science, and is, as such, an introduction to, but hardly a branch of, philosophy. It is, however, well to remark, that we have in Germany a prominent exponent of the older position in Prof. J. Rehmke ; see notably his small treatise, 'Die Seele des Menschen' (3rd ed. 1909), which is divided into two sections on the "Essence" and on the "Life of the Soul." Whilst revising the text of this chapter, which was written six years ago, I came across Prof. Henri Bergson's "Huxley Lecture" (delivered in Birmingham, 29th May 1911), and also the Report of his four Lectures "On the Soul," delivered October 1911 at University College, London. In the first-named lecture he complains that philosophers have gone away from vital questions such as : "What are we ?" "What are we doing here ?" "Whence do we come and whither do we go ?" (see 'Hibbert Journal,' October 1911, p. 24). Accordingly, M. Bergson, ever since the appearance of his two earlier works ('Les Données Immédiates de la Conscience,' 1889, and 'Matière et Mémoire,' 1896), has been considered to represent a new school of psychology ; see, e.g., M. Boirac in the 'Grande Encyclopédie,' article "Psychologie" : "Bergson et toute la jeune école qui le suit, maintiennent énergiquement l'indépendance et l'originalité de la psychologie en face des sciences proprement dites auxquelles on ne peut, selon eux, l'assimiler sans la défigurer ou plutôt sans la détruire."

7.
Problems
centering
in this.

The discussions which centred in the materialistic controversy referred really to three separate problems which at the time were not kept sufficiently distinct. These problems were familiar to philosophical writers in all the three countries before the middle of the century, but it is useful to note that each of the philosophical literatures had been occupied up to the middle of the century pre-eminently with one out of the three problems. After the middle of the century, and no doubt to a large extent owing to the vehemence with which the controversy had been carried on in Germany, thinkers in each of the three countries found it necessary to take up a definite position with regard to all the three questions involved. In stating separately these questions as they have been more clearly defined in the course of the last fifty years, we shall at the same time acquire some insight into the separate character of French, German, and English thought during the first half of the century.

8.
Empirical
and rational
psychology.

To begin with, the older German philosophy of the eighteenth century had already distinguished two kinds of Psychology, i.e., two ways of acquiring knowledge on matters connected with the Soul or the inner life. Calling the doctrine which embraced these subjects " Psychology," [1] it distinguished between Empirical and

[1] The term seems to occur for the first time in Germany, where Rudolph Göckel, or Goclenius (1547-1628), Professor at Marburg, published towards the end of the sixteenth century a work with the title ΨΥΧΟΛΟΓΙΑ. On this Mr Whittaker remarks : " I have met with the information that ψυχολογία first occurs in a false reading in Proclus. The true reading, if I remember rightly, is ψυχογονία. Goclenius may have picked up the word—at first or second hand—from Proclus ; for in fact he applies it to the discussions which he has brought together on the old question of ' The generation of the soul.' If this conjecture is right, it is very curious : the

Rational Psychology. Empirical Psychology professed to give a description of the inner or mental life, and in doing so it confined itself mostly to such methods and statements, and to the use of such terms as had already been laid down in Aristotle's celebrated treatise. This Empirical Psychology had been cultivated not so much in a methodical manner as by popular writings, among which the most brilliant were furnished by the French moralists from Montaigne and Pascal, through La Rochefoucauld and La Bruyère, down to Rousseau and Diderot. Lectures on this subject belonged to the recognised course of German University studies, and were as such delivered also by Kant, who—except for the distinction between thinking, feeling, and willing, to which he gave its subsequent importance by adopting it from Tetens — did not add anything very novel to the subject. Besides this Empirical Psychology, there was another definite philosophical science which was termed Rational Psychology; this treated of the highest questions, such as the nature of the soul, its fate, its destiny, its origin and future. It formed together with Cosmology and Rational Theology that large branch of philosophical inquiry which went under the name of Metaphysics. The relation of empirical and rational psychology may be compared with the relation which exists for instance between a treatise on the nature of things (such as the great poem of

names 'psychology' and 'metaphysics'—both so exactly adapted to the subjects—would have come in alike by a sort of historical accident." The word did not become current in French or English literature before the nineteenth century, and seems to have been introduced into the latter through Coleridge's connection with Germany, and into the former in the school of Victor Cousin.

Lucretius or the recent Philosophy of Nature of Schelling's
school) and the modern natural philosophy which has
grown up since the time of Galileo and Newton.   Empirical psychology dealt with detailed facts and phenomena in the life of the soul, rational psychology dealt
with questions of principle and with fundamentals.

9.
At the
beginning of
the century
rational
psychology
mainly
studied in
Germany.

Whilst in Germany, up to the beginning of the nineteenth century, little methodical work was done in
empirical psychology, English, and notably Scotch,
thinkers had devoted themselves almost exclusively to
the cultivation of this field; many works of lasting
merit having appeared, among which those of Thos. Reid

10.
Empirical
psychology
chiefly
British.

and Dugald Stewart as representative of Scottish, of
David Hartley and James Mill as representative of
English, philosophy are prominent.[1]   We may therefore
say that in the beginning of the nineteenth century

---

[1] One of the most popular representatives of Scottish philosophy
in the nineteenth century was
Thos. Brown, whose Lectures were
published in four volumes after his
death in 1832, and had a wide influence, running through nineteen
editions.   It seems, however, that
he was less original than his popular
reputation would suggest, having
borrowed much from contemporary
French writers, notably from Destutt de Tracy, as has been remarked by Sir Wm. Hamilton, and
more recently by M. Picavet ('Les
Idéologues,' 1891, p. 494; also article, "Thomas Brown," in the
'Grande Encyclopédie').   With him
occurs the term "physiology of
the human mind," as expressive of
what we now term Psychology,
which may have been suggested as
much through his acquaintance
with French thought—a work with
the title 'Physiologie de l'Esprit'

having been published by M.
Paulhan — as by his professional
medical studies.   He laid great
emphasis upon the muscular sense,
or sense of resistance, distinguishing
it from touch, as an additional or
sixth sense, and it is in connection
with this much controverted point
that his name still occurs in recent
psychological literature.   There is
a short but appreciative notice of
him by the late Prof. R. Adamson
in the ninth edition of the 'Ency.
Brit.'   It is interesting to see how
two very different thinkers (Brown
and Lotze), both starting from
medical studies, should have described their psychology as "Physiology of the human mind" or the
soul.   In more recent times the
importance of Brown's philosophy
has again been insisted on by Prof.
Stout who, in a valuable series of
articles ('Mind,' vols. 13 and 14)
on Herbart and the difference of

rational psychology had its home in Germany, empirical psychology in Great Britain. In addition to these two branches of research appertaining to the things of the inner world, to the life of the soul, a third and independent line of research had sprung up in France as the immediate outcome of the great development of the mathematical, natural, and medical sciences. The life of the soul was there studied in its outer manifestations, partly as a physiological and pathological[1] problem, partly also in those creations such as language, grammar, and logic, in which it has become, as it were, externalised. Cabanis and Broussais are representatives of the former, the Idéologues, notably Destutt de Tracy, of the latter way of thinking. The French school as represented by these thinkers preserved accordingly its independent position, whether compared with the purely introspective psychology in this country or with the metaphysical psychology of Germany. It took up such an extreme position, notably in the writings of Broussais, and was frequently supposed to be so much allied with materialism, that it provoked as much as it opposed the reaction which adopted the more moderate or common-sense attitude of the Scottish school; it was later also much influenced by some of the leading German meta-

11.
French
physio-
logical
psychology.

his psychology from that of the British or Associational school, has singled out Brown's exposition of the latter as deserving prominence, "because he expressly discusses and formulates many ultimate principles which in other writers are more or less blindly presupposed" (loc. cit., vol. xiv. p. 1).

[1] D. de Tracy in his 'Éloge de Cabanis,' whose place he took in the Academy (1808), ventured to say that Cabanis had performed the double task which he had set himself, of carrying philosophy into medicine and medicine into philosophy (see Picavet, loc. cit., p. 288).

physicians. It allied itself with the political tendencies of the Restoration.

These three distinct ways of approaching the pheno-mena of the inner world, *i.e.*, the life of the soul, came together in Germany and asserted themselves with equal strength about the fourth decade of the century, when after the death of Hegel the exclusive dominion of the metaphysical method began to be attacked. The most powerful and persistent opposition was carried on by Johann Friedrich Herbart (1776-1841). But, although Herbart through his psychological writings did probably more than any other German philosopher of that period to counteract the one-sided idealism which then ruled supreme, he did not break with the metaphysical method : he still put into the foreground of his psychology defini-tions regarding the nature and the location of the soul. Inasmuch, however, as his psychological interest was primarily educational, and as in his early practical experience he had come in contact with the realistic tendencies of that great school of educationalists which was headed by Pestalozzi, he imported into his meta-physics a much greater knowledge and appreciation of actual realities than was to be found among his opponents. Accordingly he calls his philosophy Realism, maintaining that the main task of philosophy consists in a process of elaborating consistent ideas out of the frequently in-consistent and contradictory conceptions which are furnished by experience and common-sense. Philosophy was, so to speak, a clarifying process, the endeavour to arrive at clear and consistent notions. In his text-book of Psychology which was published in 1816, and still

12.
Herbart.

more in his 'Scientific Psychology' (1824), he emphasised experience as the main foundation of the
doctrine of the soul, but he significantly added to this
principal foundation also metaphysics and mathematics.
The object of the metaphysical inquiry was to arrive at a
clear and consistent notion of the essence of the soul.
The mathematical treatment was introduced in analogy
with the then current mechanical foundations which had
been gained for the physical sciences. Impressed with
the fact that the inner life consisted in a continual movement of ideas (called in German *Vorstellungen* [1]), which

[1] It is probably through Herbart's influence that the recent school of introspective psychology in England, of which Prof. James Ward may be considered the leader and Prof. Stout the best known representative, has abandoned the older term Ideas—used since the time of Locke — for the more appropriate term Presentations. It is evidently a translation of the German "Vorstellungen," and permits of introducing the distinction between the mental fact or process of presenting and that which is presented; corresponding to the double meaning of the word "Vorstellung" as a psychical phenomenon on the one side and its definite content on the other. To a foreigner the use of the term "Vorstellungen" in Herbart's psychology with its two aspects occasions as much difficulty, whilst it affords at the same time as much helpful insight, as the term "Anschauung" in the philosophy of Kant and some of his successors. The rendering of the latter term by intuition was much less successful than the rendering of the former by presentation. Both terms have this in common, that they suggest a double aspect. "A presentation may be considered in two points of view, either as having intrinsically a certain qualitative content, or, mechanically, as a condition of change in the total mental system of which it forms a part. It is in the former way, not in the latter, that presentations are usually regarded by all who are not students of psychology. From this point of view, attention is fixed either on resemblance and difference and other relations constitutive of the presented content, or on its relation to objects which it is in some way supposed to represent. In either case there will appear to be an entire absence of anything that can be called agency in the presentations considered. Variations in our idea of a thing do not alter the thing itself, and resemblance and difference are not in any sense modes of interaction. Most persons find it difficult to grasp the conception of a psychological mechanism, because they habitually regard presentations purely as having a presented content. Nevertheless, the mechanical standpoint is a legitimate one, provided that its nature and limitations are duly recognised. Presentations act and react on each other in manifold ways. They exclude each other

rise, vanish, and chase each other, he conceived the plan of
a psychical mechanics, divided into statics and dynamics.
To these processes, *i.e.*, the conflict of ideas in the soul,
he attempted to apply mathematical calculation through
which the resultant intensities of the different ideas
could be ascertained.   Although the elaborate scheme of
Herbart has in the main been abandoned, there is no
doubt that he left upon German Psychology lasting marks
of his work in two distinct directions.   With an eye for
the continual change and movement of ideas within the
human soul, he attached much more importance to the
tracing of this dynamical process than to a rigorous
definition of the faculties of the soul, which was then
current and which had been adopted even by Kant.
Herbart probably did more than any other contemporaneous thinker to destroy the old faculty-psychology in
Germany.[1]   And secondly, in looking upon the conscious

from distinct consciousness, they
reproduce each other, they support each other, and so forth.
Now, the clear recognition of this
distinction between presented and
mechanical relation forms a leading
feature in Herbart's psychology.
He has embodied it in his use of the
terms Presentative Activity and
Presented Content, and he has
made it the basis of his general
method in dealing with psychological problems.   He is perpetually
inquiring what connection of presentative   activities   corresponds
either to a certain connection of
presented contents, or to feelings of
pleasure and pain, or to desire.
Now, if we turn to English writers,
we meet with traces, but traces
only, of this distinction.   Nowhere
do we find a thorough and consistent application of it, such as

characterises the Herbartian system"   (Stout in his article on
"Herbart compared with English
Psychologists,"   'Mind,'   vol. xiv.
p. 2).   It is interesting to see that
a similar position is taken up by
Renouvier in the 1st ed. of the
'Critique Générale' (part 1, sec. iii.):
"Ce qui frappe d'abord dans la
représentation, ce qui en est le caractère déterminatif, c'est qu'elle est
à double face et ne peut se repré-
senter à elle-même que bilatérale.
Ces deux éléments que toute représentation suppose, je les signale
et ne les définis pas en les nom-
mant l'un *représentatif* et l'autre
représenté.
    [1] Herbart seems to have been led
to his peculiar view through the
influence of Fichte, who conceived
of the mind as an original, assertive,
and creative agent.   Herbart, how-

inner life as the playground of rising and vanishing ideas, he introduced the conception of the limit or threshold of consciousness, suggesting through this, if not elaborating, an idea which has since been variously worked out: that of the unconscious, the subconscious, and the subliminal.

In addition to this, Herbart urged the necessity of conducting psychological inquiries by the exact method of observation, measurement, and calculation, and although he did not succeed in this endeavour he had a clear notion of what would be required in order to convert

ever, did not follow Fichte in his process of abstract thought through which the term Mind (Self or Ego) ceases to denote the individual and becomes a general or absolute mind, for Herbart was as much influenced by the individualism of Leibniz. He confines his ontology and psychology to that of individual beings, considering the conception of a general or absolute mind as an illegitimate abstraction. Accordingly he consistently opposes the higher Hegelian logic and psychology which, as it were, represents the life and thought of the Absolute, and he confines himself to the lower or formal logic, and to the psychology of individual human minds. The principal difference which existed between Herbart's psychological position and that of contemporary thinkers in this country was that Herbart, quite as much as the Idealists whom he opposed, came to psychology from the metaphysical point of view, i.e., from the discussion of the problem of reality. This problem hardly existed for English and Scotch thinkers at that time. The Idealists, however, did not apply their metaphysical solutions of the problem of reality to that special reality which we call the Soul or the inner personal life

of the individual, but dealt rather with cosmological and theological problems, as also with problems of human history and society. On the other side, the early educational interests of Herbart led him back to views current in the Leibniz-Wolffian school, which did not lose sight of the existence and independence of a plurality of individuals in the conception of an underlying unity or substance after the model of Spinoza. A new problem, however, existed for Herbart as it already existed for Leibniz — how is the plurality of existing beings (called by Herbart, "Reals") to be reconciled with the universal order? Leibniz had solved this problem in his "Monadology" by the conception of a central monad and the theory of a pre-established harmony. This solution Herbart does not adopt. For him the unity or order of the existing things and beings is that of a system, and as such he also conceives of the unity of mental life. This idea of a systematic unity, as differing from that of a substantial unity, has since the time of Herbart, and probably much through his influence, gained ground in modern psychology both in this country and abroad.

14.
Exact
method.

psychology into an exact science. His followers in consequence adopted this term as characteristic of Herbart's
school, and started in the year 1861 a periodical for
exact philosophy. Of other developments which had
their origin in Herbart's psychology I shall speak
further on.

15.
Beneke.

Almost simultaneously another German psychologist
started in direct opposition to the current idealistic
philosophy. This was Friedrich Eduard Beneke [1] (1798-
1854). He did not succeed in impressing the German
mind in the same way as Herbart had done, or in influ-
encing philosophical thought. Yet he deserves to be
specially mentioned in this connection as the only
genuine representative in Germany of that important
and original psychological school which had its origin in

[1] Beneke was influenced as much
as Herbart by an educational interest, but he differs from Herbart,
with whom he agrees in his opposition to idealism, by discarding all
preliminary metaphysical discussions. For him psychology is the
main part and foundation of all
philosophy—much in the same way
as philosophy of the human mind
was considered in this country.
The publication in 1822 of a work
on 'Physics (not metaphysics)
of Morality' ('Grundlegung zur
Physik der Sitten'), drew after it
the prohibition of his lecturing at
the Berlin University, where he had,
though unsupported by an official
position, gathered a considerable
audience. Beneke received verb-
ally from the Minister Altenstein
"an explanation that it was not
single passages which had given
offence, but the whole scheme, and
that a philosophy which did not deduce everything from the Absolute

could not be considered to be philosophy at all" (see Hertling in 'Allgemeine Deutsche Biographie,' article
"Beneke "). The supposition that
Hegel personally influenced this remarkable decision can, according to
Kuno Fischer ('Hegel's Leben,' &c.,
vol. i. p. 156), not be proved. It is
rather a testimony to the enormous
weight which Hegel's line of thought
possessed in the eyes of statesmen
like Altenstein, Johannes Schulze,
and others. Beneke's view can be
summed up in the statement that
"the soul is a system of forces or faculties, under which name we have not
to think of the faculties of the older
psychology but of a systematic and
completely unified complex " (ibid.,
vol. ii. p. 328). We are indebted
to Prof. Stout for the first comprehensive appreciation in this country
of Beneke's as well as of Herbart's
psychology in his articles in 'Mind'
referred to above.

this country,[1] where, up to the present day, it has preserved its fundamental characteristics, exhibiting an unbroken historical continuity. This is the genuinely introspective school of psychology. Its greatest representatives during the first two-thirds of the century are James Mill and Alexander Bain. Before entering on an

16.
British
intro-
spective
psychology.

[1] Beneke differed from Kant inasmuch as he did not admit that knowledge of mental phenomena or states revealed to us by the inner sense was merely phenomenal, as is the case with our knowledge of external things through the outer senses. On the contrary, he reduces all knowledge to that afforded by introspection and dealt with in empirical psychology. He therefore agrees to a large extent with English thinkers of the Associational school "on two fundamental points—(1) the dependence of all other branches of philosophy on psychology; (2) the dependence of psychology on introspection and, in the last resort, on introspection only. These capital points of agreement with English thinkers are at the same time capital points of disagreement between him and Herbart. Further traces of English influence in Beneke are perhaps to be found in his assiduous study of all facts likely to throw light on psychological problems, and at times also in his treatment of special questions. It must, however, be confessed that there was one lesson which he failed to learn from his favourite English writers. He did not learn from them to be cautious. . . . He claimed with reason the right of framing hypotheses to explain observed facts. But he pushed his hypotheses far beyond what the exigencies of psychological explanation required. . . . Nevertheless, it is right to treat him as a kind of link between English associational psychology on the one hand, and the psychology of Herbart on the other" (Stout, 'Mind,' vol. xiv. p. 25, &c.) The fact that Beneke did not accept the older view which considered the soul or mind as possessed of different faculties, but reduced the latter to mere dispositions which had to be developed by external stimuli, made his teaching even more acceptable than that of Herbart to educationalists; for the task of education as well as its value was clearly defined and emphasised. He had, accordingly, a considerable following among educationalists in Germany. On the other hand, von Hartmann emphasises the fact that "Beneke did not content himself with pointing to introspective phenomena as affording a secure and certain starting-point for psychology and philosophy, but that he went behind the phenomenal in search of unconscious origins and dispositions for the existence of which he could offer no empirical or metaphysical proof" ('Die Moderne Psychologie,' 1901, p. 11). There is, however, no doubt that Beneke's acceptance of psychical experience as ultimate and self-evident—giving the only knowledge of reality accessible to the human mind—is akin to a view which has found expression in quite recent times, though it can only be upheld by an altered conception of reality. Fr. Ueberweg (1826-71), the well-known historian of philosophy, was much influenced by Beneke, as notably in his 'System of Logic' (English translation by J. M. Lindsay, 1871).

account of this school, to which we probably owe the greater part of the important psychological work of the century, it may be interesting to refer briefly to the causes which prevented the purely introspective methods of psychology from ever receiving due recognition in Germany. The reason will probably be found in what may be called the essentially metaphysical turn of the German mind. The principal aim of all prominent thinkers in Germany down to the present day is to arrive at first principles, to lay firm foundations of knowledge and practice. This has seemed a necessary requisite because, ever since, through the political and ecclesiastical wars and controversies which followed the Reformation and accompanied the Revolution in Germany, not only the material progress of the nation had been arrested, the historical traditions and foundations of society destroyed, but also the fundamental beliefs criticised and variously attacked. This general unsettlement in the political, economical, social, and religious world urged upon thinkers as their first and paramount duty the laying and perfecting of solid foundations and principles. This was the task which Descartes had set himself in France, and which Leibniz, though in a less systematic manner, took up for the first time in Germany at the end of the seventeenth century. It has been considered as such by all prominent German thinkers down to the present day. It was most distinctly put forward by Kant and his immediate followers, and not less by those who stood in opposition than by those who professed to follow the lines which he had indicated.

So far as the special branch of philosophy with which

I am now concerned is affected, it might have appeared
natural if the desire to make psychology, or the doctrine
of the soul, a definite science, should have led out of
metaphysics through observation of facts to that exact
treatment which Herbart foreshadowed and which has
to some extent—though on other lines—been realised
in our days. Instead of that, the intermediate phase
between the metaphysical and the exact treatment was,
with the exception of Beneke, left out at the time.
With the intention of arriving at the foundation of a
reasoned or rational creed, and with the distinct assertion
that the idealistic systems had failed to do so, it seemed
natural to the German mind to take up those principles
which had proved to be of such value in the exact and
natural sciences. These had at the time of the collapse
of the ruling idealistic philosophy attained to great
prominence at some of the German universities; a new
science, that of Physiology, had been founded by German
thinkers, and great practical results in medical and
industrial practice had already resulted mainly through
the efforts of Johannes Müller and Liebig. To many
enthusiastic inquirers and forceful minds nothing seemed
simpler than to elevate the supposed elementary notions
with which the natural sciences operated and which
were in current use, such as matter and force, to the
rank of fundamental principles for the mental sciences
or even to that of articles of a new creed.[1] The errors

17.
Attempt
to base
psychology
on ele-
mentary
scientific
principles.

[1] It may be well to remark here
that to follow the example of the
natural sciences had been likewise
the aim of the representatives of
mental philosophy in this country
at a much earlier date; the difference being mainly this, that it was
the method and practice rather
than the principles of the natural
sciences which recommended themselves to British thinkers. This
opened out the large field of ex-

which were committed by the logic of these thinkers were manifold, but two of them may be singled out not only as fatal to ultimate success but also as highly dangerous, inasmuch as their seductive nature prevented them from being readily detected, and because they were extremely difficult to destroy when once the popular understanding had given them an entry.

18.
Errors of
this pro-
cedure.

To begin with, the terms matter and force referred to notions which might appear clear to the popular mind, inasmuch as they were in daily use in common language, and as such seemed to convey a definite meaning. It was therefore an irony of fate that just about the time when these terms were placed at the head of a new philosophy and made the foundations, as it were, of a new creed, these same terms were being discarded from strict scientific treatises, and others being introduced which were capable of rigorous definition. The term matter was to be replaced in dynamical treatises by the word mass or inertia, and the word force had to give way to the less equivocal term, energy. Both mass and energy could be mathematically defined in terms of the

perience and observation, whereas the introduction of the so-called principles or fundamental notions of physics and chemistry led rather to an abstract and contracted view of mental phenomena, to hasty generalisations, and, in the end, to purely verbal distinctions. In this country, in spite of the fact that the principles of exact science, the laws of motion, were first laid down and clearly defined in the 'Principia' of Newton, little was done to examine clearly and to define the range of applicability of these principles. Natural science was limited almost exclusively to observation and ex-periment. It was only through the French mathematicians, in the course of the eighteenth century, that the Newtonian principles were more clearly brought out, and only through Lavoisier that the con-servation of mass, or rather the constancy of the weight of bodies, was made the foundation of modern chemistry. In Germany, on the other hand, the principles of dy-namical and physical research were discussed in a philosophical spirit by Leibniz, in whom the tendency of the German mind to deal with fundamental questions was for the first time clearly exhibited.

measurable quantities, time, space, and velocity. It became quite clear in the course of the controversies carried on between the years 1840 and 1870, that the familiar term matter was not clearly definable, and that the word force was used to denote two entirely different conceptions. It was therefore unfortunate that in dealing with psychological questions, with things pertaining to the soul, two conceptions were placed at the head of the new doctrine which could not stand the test of rigorous definition.[1] The second error committed by the new school of thought was this, that in spite of all criticism which they rightly levelled against the vagueness of the older philosophy, they did not really break with the metaphysical method and resort to that method suggested by Beneke and to some extent by Herbart, the empirical method of introspection, but simply continued, on a lower plane, the same sort of abstract and *a priori* reasoning which they condemned in their opponents. By the time that this inherent defect of both idealism and materialism was recognised, another way had been opened by which access could be gained to the phenomena of the inner world: this was the method that studied them in their concomitant, physical and physiological manifestations. As I showed in former chapters,[2] the phenomena of consciousness began to be studied from the physiological side.

In the meantime, and only slightly influenced by German metaphysics, the introspective mode of dealing

[1] For a further discussion of the value of the fundamental notions of physical science for philosophical purposes, see chapter vi., *infra*, which deals with the philosophical problem of nature.

[2] See chapter xi., vol. ii. of this History.

with mental phenomena had been largely developed in
this country, the results of this inquiry having found
expression in the great psychological treatises of Alexander
Bain (1818-1903),[1] which appeared shortly before the

[1] Of all philosophers during the
nineteenth century Alexander
Bain deserves pre-eminently to be
called a psychologist. Others
equally great in psychological
analysis have nearly always been
tempted to enter the arena of
general philosophy, making psychology the fundamental doctrine
from and through which metaphysical problems might be approached,
or they have found psychology insufficient for this purpose. Bain
moreover furnishes the best example
of that tendency mentioned above
(note 1, p. 23), of following in psychology the lead of the natural
sciences. "Be it noted that Prof.
Bain was, as most British philosophers have been, under the influence of the leading scientific conceptions of the moment. It may be
affirmed generally that the advance
in psychology in our land has very
much followed the advance in
physical research. The theory of
sound, for instance, was the outstanding physical theory in the
time of Hartley. Consequently he
proceeded to interpret mind according to the analogy, and to represent
the nervous process as simply
propagations of vibrations as in
sound. Chemistry, in like manner,
came to the front in the days of
Mill. Consequently the process of
Association was interpreted in terms
thereof—it was set forth as a kind
of mental chemistry. So, in Dr
Bain's time, physiology was attracting much attention, and the work
of Johannes Müller, in particular,
was greatly in evidence, and there
was also an awakened interest in
biology. Hence the physiological
reference became prominent, and

the method of natural history
pointed the way to Dr Bain's mode
of procedure" (Prof. W. L.
Davidson in 'Mind,' 1904, p. 162).
Prof. Sorley has, however, pointed
out that the influence of physiology
in Bain's writings is of a different
kind from that in which chemistry
influenced Mill : the latter being
of the nature of analogy, whereas,
in Bain, we find the tendency to
explain mental facts and processes
by physiological facts and processes.
Bain's principal works ('The Senses
and the Intellect,' 1855, 'The Emotions and the Will,' 1859) were written before the evolutionary theories
of the influence of heredity and
environment had been generally
recognised. This further stage in
natural science, fully established in
this country only later by Darwin,
led accordingly to a new scientific
formulation in the region of psychology which is represented mainly
by Herbert Spencer ('Principles of
Psychology,' 1st ed. 1855, 2nd
ed. 1870, 1872). It has been
frequently remarked of Bain's
writings, as likewise of those of
Lotze in Germany, that they belong
essentially to the pre-evolutionary
period of thought. M. Ribot finds
Bain deficient likewise in morbid
psychology : " Je regrette, pour ma
part, que M. Bain ait été si som-
maire sur les phénomènes qui font
la transition de la psychologie normale à la psychologie morbide
(rêves, sommeil magnétique, &c.),
et qu'il semblait si bien en état
d'étudier. Mais le manque de
méthode comparative est une des
lacunes de l'ouvrage. Ajoutons-y
l'absence trop fréquente de l'idée
de progrès, d'où par suite l'étude

new school of psycho-physical research made its début in Germany. The British school had latterly benefited greatly by taking notice of the critical works of Kant and the physiological labours of Johannes Müller. It was mainly owing to Sir William Hamilton of Edinburgh, that the analysis of the intellectual constitution of the human mind, instituted by Kant in reply to the scepticism of Hume, received due recognition by one of the foremost representatives of the empirical school—John Stuart Mill.

The introspective school was not content to confine itself to purely descriptive work. It had elaborated a psychological theory of its own, which held a place in the labours of English writers similar to that occupied for a time in Germany by the theory of Herbart: this was the theory of Association.

19.
Association-
psychology.

The psychology of this school, usually termed association psychology, differed as much from the older faculty psychology as did the psychology of Herbart. It dates from the writings of Hume, perhaps even from those of Hobbes, as well as from those of David Hartley (1705-57). With the latter it starts from the idea already expressed by Locke, that the phenomena of the inner life can be traced back to sensations. But the way in which this idea was expressed suggested from the beginning a twofold development. It

dynamique des phénomènes a été quelquefois négligée" ('La Psychologie Anglaise Contemporaine,' 1870, p. 294). On the other side, it must be remarked that the mathematical treatment of psychical phenomena as it originated in

Germany first through Herbart and more successfully through Prof. Wundt has never found much favour in this country. It is mainly through American writers that English psychological literature has been represented in this branch.

did not only imply that the world of our senses supplies all the material for reflection and thought and the great development of abstract ideas, but also secondly, that this totality of sensations consists of separate elements into which it can be broken up, and out of which it can be put together again in the same way as we put together in chemistry physical bodies out of their elements. The first of these two aspects has been adopted by all the representatives of the empirical school, and also by those philosophers who make a definite distinction between the matter and the form of thought. But the second way of putting the truth which was implied in the sensational theory of knowledge led to a kind of atomism of thought, to what John Stuart Mill called a mental chemistry. We may say that the rigid views of the older faculty psy-chology were opposed in the German school of Herbart by emphasising the conflict and movement of ideas, these being conceived in analogy with mechanical forces, and that it was on the other side opposed in the English school of Hartley and James Mill by the attempt to show how the higher and more complex ideas were compounded out of simpler elements by the various processes of associa-tion.[1]   The agency, however, which brought about this

[1] Prof. Stout in his analysis of Herbart's psychology has some valuable remarks as to the differ-ence between the German and the British ways of approaching the subject. One of the principal dif-ferences lies in the much greater importance and prominence which both Herbart and Beneke, especially the former, attached to the unity of consciousness or of the soul. This characteristic of the inner life stands with Herbart in the foreground of psychological investigation ; with contemporaneous British thinkers it is kept in the background, or rather implied. For Brown, "the unity of the mind is rather an abstract unity excluding difference, than a concrete unity including and connecting differences. Herbart also regarded the soul as a unity excluding difference. He even held this doctrine in a more rigid and uncompromising form than any other philosopher" ('Mind,' 1889,

union of simple into complex ideas was left very much in the dark; as in chemistry, for a long time, chemical affinity remained unexplained and obscure. Hume, in trying to account for the conception of cause and effect, for the inevitable connection which we recognise in the succession of phenomena, reduced this fundamental fact of all experience to the custom or habit which the repetition of the same sequence inevitably produces. Hartley, adopting a similar explanation, confirmed and strengthened it by supposing that this habit was acquired through the physical constitution of the nervous system. He held

p. 18). "For Herbart, as well as for Locke and his successors, the unity of the mind was primarily an hypostasised abstraction of unity. But the German thinker differs from the English both in the manner in which he arrived at this conception and in the psychological consequences which he deduced from it. It was through exclusive reliance on the immediate evidence of internal perception that the countrymen of Bacon fell into this error. With Herbart, on the contrary, it was an integral part of an elaborate and highly speculative system of metaphysics. He was led by a process of abstract reasoning to maintain the simplicity of the soul in so absolute a sense that he was compelled to exclude from its intrinsic nature all variety and difference whatever, including even successive modification in time. Thus he cannot, like Locke, treat the mind as essentially a combining agency, or, like Brown, as a substance passing through a series of states. He is therefore unable to introduce into his psychology the metaphysical conception of the unity of the soul, except by transforming it, however inconsistently, into a conception of synthetic unity, which takes a twofold form in its application to presented content and to mechanical interaction respectively" (ibid., p. 19, et seq.) Herbart, as we know, was influenced by Leibniz. Now Leibniz in his well-known criticism of Locke laid stress on the fact that in mental science we have not only to do with what is in the intellect but also with the intellect itself. This puts the question of the combining agency or unity of the soul into the foreground. Herbart was further influenced by the mechanical sciences of his age. But in dynamical reasoning we deal with the composition of forces acting on a point and merging into a resultant. And it seems likely that putting these two aspects together Herbart found his way from the unity of the soul to the multiplicity of psychical phenomena under the conception of the play of different forces, whereas English psychologists, such as Mill, fastened rather upon the analogy of chemically different substances combining in the unity of a compound with different properties. In fact, Herbart thought mechanically, the Associationists, chemically.

in fact that sensation is the result of physical vibrations in the nerves, which leave behind them the tendency or habit of vibrating, this being the physical explanation of memory. Hartley took note of only one kind of association, viz., association by contiguity, sensations being together, either in space (synchronous) or in time (successive). James Mill took up the theory of Hartley, but he, like Hartley, confined himself to association in space (synchronism) and association in time (succession), whereas Hume had recognised three forms of association, viz., contiguity in time or space, resemblance, and causality.

20.
James Mill's
mental
chemistry.

James Mill also laid stress upon the fact that, in the same way as in chemical compounds, the result or product may appear to be simple, and that the elements out of which it is compounded may from various causes become imperceptible. And he as well as Hartley attempted to show how simple mental states may, through the union with others, lead to apparently quite different states. For instance, disinterested love might have been developed out of originally selfish emotion. The principle of association was thus employed to bring unity and simplicity into the chaotic mass of the phenomena of the inner world, and it cannot be denied that the simplicity with which this complicated subject was thus represented did much to recommend the whole scheme. It was further elaborated with a very large amount of evidence drawn from original observation, as well as from physiological research,

21.
Alex. Bain.

by Alexander Bain in his two well-known treatises mentioned above.[1] Bain, however, remedied in addition one

[1] See p. 27, note 1.

of the principal defects in the psychology of the empirical school, a defect which had been noticed not only in this country but also in France. Of this I shall speak later on.

In the meantime it will be of interest to draw attention to some of the general characteristics of the British schools of philosophy. There never has existed in this country, up to quite recent times, a ruling system of philosophy in the sense in which we may speak of the ruling systems of Descartes, of Leibniz, Kant, and Hegel abroad. It is quite true that Hobbes elaborated a system of philosophy and Berkeley suggested one, but neither had acquired any widespread following or currency. More than by systems of philosophy the British mind has been led by methods of thought. Such methods are, for instance, the inductive methods usually connected with the name of Bacon, the common-sense and the introspective methods usually connected with the name of Thomas Reid and the Scottish school. One of the results of this attitude of the British mind has been the absence of completeness and finality in many of the arguments of English and Scotch thinkers. In spite of great acuteness and originality, they have rarely pursued their leading ideas to their ultimate conclusions. Instinctively they have mostly been satisfied with the attitude peculiar to the natural sciences, where definite methods are employed and principles applied so long as they prove to be useful; being frequently abandoned when it becomes evident that their usefulness has come to an end. Thus, for instance, the division which in the Baconian

22.
Want of system in British philosophy.

philosophy was set up between the knowledge of natural and spiritual things, amounted to a merely temporary division of mental labour, signifying a truce rather than a final reconciliation.   This truce lasted for more than two centuries, when, in the end, it became evident that the growth of natural knowledge gained by the appli-cation of the inductive methods would entrench upon those regions which had been reserved to theology and to the formation and development of a practical creed. What the Germans call " zu Ende denken," the thinking out or pursuing of a course of thought into its remote conclusions, is a thing rarely practised in this country as it is abroad.   As soon as any argument, however logical it may appear, comes into conflict with common-sense, or with strongly held beliefs, it loses its hold of the British mind in the same way as any theory in science would do as soon as it came into conflict with facts.   The consequence is that many original lines of thought which were started in this country have, when adopted abroad, acquired quite a different complexion from what they presented in their native country.   Examples of this are the appearance of Newtonianism in France and Darwinism in Germany.   In philosophy the teachings of Locke led to sensationalism and materialism under the hands of French thinkers, such as Helvetius and Con-dillac.   In the controversy between Leibniz and Locke's younger contemporary, Clarke, it was quite evident that the former realised more clearly the ultimate outcome of Locke's reasoning and the necessity of dealing with it. In this country these ultimate conclusions were probably first realised by Berkeley and Hume.   The former replied by a system of philosophy which remained unnoticed at the time, receiving merited attention only quite recently. Hume was content to leave matters in the state of special problems which he defined but did not attempt ultimately to solve. It must also not be forgotten that none of the great thinkers, from Bacon to Hume, were charged with teaching, *i.e.*, with imparting their ideas to younger minds. They held no official positions which necessitated them seriously to consider the educational side of their doctrines.

The educational demand arose in this country prominently through the teaching at the Scotch Universities. These were, as I mentioned on a former occasion, modelled upon the continental system ; on that system which obtained in France and the Netherlands. They were Universities in the true sense of the word. Their task was to cultivate the complete circle of knowledge. In this they differed, up to quite recent times, from the two great English universities, which excelled rather in a few special branches of knowledge, and which approached the ideal of a university, compassing the whole circle of learning and thought, only within the second half of the nineteenth century. The same peculiarity which has characterised the teaching at the older English universities, that it nursed excellence in single and unconnected branches of learning, is characteristic of all English thought as opposed to that of the Continent : it utters itself freely in works of individual excellence and originality, with little regard for systematic completeness. But wherever the latter, as expressed in the term " universitas," is attempted,

23.
University
teaching in
Scotland.

it becomes inevitable that subjects have to be treated and matters discussed, for which an assembly of even the greatest scholars cannot guarantee adequate and equal treatment. Du Bois-Reymond, the great physiologist of Berlin, has truly and honestly admitted this fact in saying that the teacher of physiology has indeed to teach a great many things which he does not know. We may express this fact, which has exerted an enormous influence upon the development of philosophic systems, and, indeed, on all comprehensive doctrines, by saying that the position of an official teacher imposes upon him obligations which the unofficial and extramural scholar has never to face. These demands, which the position of a university professor officially imposes, made themselves felt when the Scotch universities took up the teaching of moral and mental philosophy in the eighteenth century;[1] they were accentuated when that

[1] "The Parliamentary Commission for visiting the Universities, appointed in 1690 and following years, directed in 1695 the Professors of Philosophy in St Andrews to prepare the heads of a system of Logic, and the corresponding Professors in Edinburgh to prepare a course of Metaphysics. The compends drawn up in consequence were passed from one college to another for revision ; there is no evidence that they were finally sanctioned, but they may be accepted as giving a fair idea of the instructions in philosophy conveyed in the universities of Scotland at the close of the seventeenth century — at the very time when Locke's Essay was finding its way so rapidly over the three kingdoms. Logic is called the instrument to acquire other sciences, inasmuch as it prescribes rules for rightly apprehending, judging, and arguing. . . . Metaphysics are said to be defined by some as a science of being as being; by others as a speculative science, which considers being in general and its properties and kinds as abstracted from matter. The benefits arising from the study of metaphysics are said to be, that treating of undoubted truths and axioms we are enabled by their assistance the better to discover truths generally and avoid errors. . . . That . . . it aids the understanding in every kind of learning, and specially in theology, in which use is made of metaphysical terms. . . . Such was the pabulum on which college youths fed during the century" (M'Cosh, 'The Scottish Philosophy,' 1875, pp. 22, et seq.)

crisis of thought had to be faced, which was marked by the writings of David Hume.[1] Similar demands presented themselves when in Germany the original but fragmentary ideas of Leibniz had to be worked into a system which should form the basis of university teaching. Again, the same practical problem had to be solved when during the Restoration in France the great teachers of philosophy had to meet the demands made upon them by the official system of higher instruction. The way in which this practical problem was solved differed in all the three cases according to the genius of the nation, the prejudices, the exigencies, and the surroundings of the age. There are two distinct ways in which the teacher of any large subject can make up for the deficiencies which his personal knowledge or that of his age must necessarily contain. No doubt both ways are generally resorted to. He can either appeal to custom and tradition, or he can extend the principles and ideas which have proved fruitful in the treatment of restricted fields to the whole of the region which he desires to cultivate. In the degree in which he gives more weight to the one or to the other of these methods, his teaching will become practical or abstract, conventional or revolutionary, satisfying on the one side

---

[1] We know that in 1744 David Hume was anxious "to be appointed Professor of Moral Philosophy in the University of Edinburgh, but public sentiment could not bear the idea of one so sceptical being appointed a teacher of youth" (M'Cosh, p. 124).

"People have often speculated as to what Hume would have taught had he been elected Professor of Moral Philosophy in Edinburgh. I believe he would have expounded a utilitarian theory, ending in the recommendation of the pleasant social virtues; speaking always respectfully of the Divine Being, but leaving His existence an unsettled question" (ibid., p. 153).

the inherent common - sense, on the other the ideal demands of our nature.

There can be no doubt which of the two courses was mainly favoured by those teachers of philosophy beginning with Francis Hutcheson (1694-1746) and ending with Sir William Hamilton (1788-1856), who together form the Scottish school of philosophy.[1] They all appealed to what was early called by them common-sense, a term which the historian of Scottish philosophy, James M'Cosh, has traced to the writings of Shaftesbury. With some correctness it may be said that the opposition to the theoretical movement in English philosophy which began with Locke and was continued by Berkeley and

24.
Philosophy of common-sense.

[1] The history of this school has been written by James M'Cosh, who gives a very complete account of the different members and their teaching. He traces the beginnings of this school back to Bacon, Locke, and Shaftesbury in England, and includes a great number of names of local importance, but little known outside of their own country. The Scottish school, though it educated James Mill, led to an independent development when the latter left Scotland for London, where he came under the influence of Hartley's philosophy and Bentham's political theories. Besides, "it is not uncommon for Scotchmen, when they bury themselves in London, to lose their religious faith, which is so sustained by public opinion—as Mill would have said, by association of ideas—in their native land" (M'Cosh, *loc. cit.*, p. 372). He also abandoned Scottish metaphysics for the more fruitful and practical problems of economics and political philosophy. The other development which led Scottish thought out of the precincts of the native school came through Sir Wm. Hamilton who adopted some of Kant's doctrines and prepared the way for that more recent school of thought which centres in the names of T. H. Green and Edward Caird. In Germany the Scottish school is known only through the scanty information which Kant possessed of some —and these not the most important —of Hume's and Reid's writings. This was, however, enough to start in him an independent line of reasoning, so different from that of the Scottish thinkers that for German thinkers, with the exception of Beneke, Scottish philosophy lost all interest and attractiveness. As to the relation at the Scottish universities between theological and philosophical teaching, M'Cosh singles out Thos. Chalmers (1780-1847) as the principal thinker in whom the reconciliation between Scottish philosophy and Scottish theology was effected. Before his time there existed "a severance, at times an opposition, if not avowed yet felt, between the Scottish philosophy and the Scottish theology" (*loc. cit.*, p. 393).

Hume, started in the popular and elegant writings of Shaftesbury, but received a more professional expression in the writings of the Scottish university teachers.[1] The great problem with which they were concerned was to define what is meant by common-sense, and to what extent the appeal to common-sense is legitimate and ultimate. So far as the subject is concerned with which I am dealing at present, Thomas Reid, who occupies the central position in this Scottish school, appeals to common-sense against the scepticism of Hume, as immediately revealing to us two facts: the existence of an external world, and that of the soul. These two principles are elements of our original nature as it came from the hands of the Creator. Every sensation which I receive brings with it the belief in an external object and of myself, the experiencing subject. Reid, in fact, appealed to what in more recent philosophical phraseology are called the data of consciousness, and, in doing so, he opened out and cultivated the great field of observation of the phenomena of the inner world. He has been blamed for multiplying too much the number of these immediate data, but he and his followers have the merit of taking due note of the breadth and fulness of the human mind, of its active as well as its intellectual powers, and of counteracting the one-sided intellectualism and the exclusiveness of those who would find the solu-

---

[1] None of the principal representatives of the English, as distinguished from the Scottish school of philosophy, beginning with Bacon and ending with John Stuart Mill and Herbert Spencer, were university teachers. Like so many of the great naturalists and natural philosophers in England, they developed their ideas in treatises dealing usually with one or a few special problems without any attempt towards completeness or systematic unity. The latter appears for the first time, as has already been said, in Herbert Spencer.

tion of the philosophical or psychological problem in a single principle. It is true that they frequently seemed content with a description where others would seek for explanations, and that, as for instance in the lectures of Thomas Brown,—who, however, approximated, on many points, to the English school,—rhetoric frequently takes the place of argument.

In this country the labours of the Scottish school of psychology were to a great extent cast into the shade by the more critical and penetrating writings of James and John Stuart Mill, and by the new phase of thought which has its beginning in the last representative of the Scottish school. In the writings of Hamilton, and those of his disciple Mansel, the slowly elaborated arguments of the English and Scottish schools came into contact with the foundations of religious belief. The Bampton Lectures on the "Limits of Religious Thought" put an end, once for all, to that truce which Bacon had established between philosophical or scientific and spiritual knowledge.[1] But outside of

[1] The history of the earlier school of Scottish philosophy down to its latest representative, Sir Wm. Hamilton, has been written by Prof. Pringle-Pattison (Andrew Seth) in the first part of his Balfour Lectures. He there very lucidly deals with that special problem through which Scottish philosophy came into contact with German thought: the problem of knowledge. It is, therefore, not so much the psychology of the school, in which we are for the moment mostly interested, that he discusses. It is rather the problem of knowledge, which will occupy us in one of the following chapters. He shows that the influence of Kant upon Hamilton signifies a departure from the genuine spirit which pervades the earlier representatives of the Scottish school—notably the writings of Thos. Reid,—and he maintains that the agnostic conclusions of Hamilton and Mansel led "Scottish philosophers (to) set about a more careful revision of their premises" (A. Seth, 'Scottish Philosophy,' 1885; 3rd ed. 1899, p. 186). How this led, through a study of Hegel, to a philosophical position not unlike that occupied by Lotze in Germany, I shall have opportunities of showing in the sequel of this History.

this country the philosophy, and especially the psychology, of the Scottish school met with due recognition by the French philosophers of the time of the Restoration.

As is well known, and has been mentioned in the course of this History, the philosophy of Locke was introduced into France mainly through the influence of Voltaire, who made it, as well as the natural philosophy of Newton, a prominent subject in his 'Lettres sur les Anglais,' published in 1731.

The new ideas which were contained in this philosophy fell upon a more genial soil in France, where everything was prepared to receive the seed of the mental revolution which they contained. M. Taine has eloquently set forth the reasons why the philosophy of the eighteenth century, which was born in England, met with its full development in France. "The new seed fell upon a suitable soil in the country of the classical spirit. In this country of logical reasoning it did not meet any of those rivals which choked it on the other side of the Channel, and it not only acquires immediately the force of the rising sap, but also the organ of propagation which was wanting. This organ is the art of language : eloquence applied to the most serious subjects, the talent of illuminating everything. The good writers of this nation express things better than those of any other nation. Their books teach little to genuine scholars, but it is by the art of language that men are ruled, and the mass of them, continually driven away from the sanctuary of the sciences by the severe style and the execrable taste of other learned works, cannot

25.
British ideas
carried over
to France.

resist the seductiveness of the French style and method." [1]   Accordingly M. Taine maintains that "the fever of demolition and reconstruction remained superficial and momentary in England. Deism, atheism, materialism, scepticism, ideology, theories of the return to nature, proclamation of the rights of men, all the audacities of Bolingbroke, Collins, Toland, Tindal, and Mandeville, all the darings of Hume, Hartley, James Mill, and Bentham, all the revolutionary doctrines remained there, greenhouse plants confined here and there in the isolated cabinets of a few thinkers : in the open air they quickly degenerated after a short blossoming, through the heavy competition of the older vegetation which still occupied the land." [2]

This older vegetation was the inductive spirit, the healthy common-sense and the constitutional life of the nation which then already " slowly broadened down from precedent to precedent." Locke had something else to do than to work out a system of philosophy by drawing out with slender logic the extreme conclusions of a theory which worked with the two conceptions of sensation and reflection and started with the human soul as a *tabula rasa*. His writings on questions of government, on toleration, and education, had the object not of upsetting but of reforming the existing political and social conditions. The extreme consequences of his line of reasoning, drawn by Hume, were — when the appeal to common-sense was allowed—easily refuted by Thomas

---

[1] See H. Taine, ' Les Origines de la France Contemporaine' (L'Ancien Régime), 15th ed. 1887, p. 331, &c. The above quotation includes a passage from Joseph de Maistre referring to French style.
[2] Taine, *loc. cit.*, p. 330.

Reid and others by appealing to common-sense. To this school, which had to teach the youth of Scotland, common-sense included the universally admitted conceptions of an enlightened form of Christian doctrine. This had, in their country, received a very strong popular confirmation by the evangelical movement which opposed free thought as much as extreme clericalism, and which trusted to immediate evidences and inner light. This immediate evidence or common-sense told man that the world had a Creator, that he himself had a soul and a spiritual destiny. Such a broad basis of common-sense, such a fruitful field for social reform and popular instruction, did not exist in France. Writers of the most opposite schools have eloquently described the condition of things there. Not only M. Taine but Victor Cousin has described the reception which Locke's ideas met with in France, where the logical and systematic mind of Condillac reduced them to an extreme sensationalism which took no notice of all the surrounding conditions and the background of Locke's philosophy.

If we leave out this background and the evidence of common-sense, if we abandon, as Hume did, the doctrine of the substantial nature of the soul, the psychology which remains reduces the inner life to a passive receptivity, the mind to a *tabula rasa*, to a blank page which receives passively the impressions of the senses; and even the word reflection, which denotes the process by which general ideas and knowledge are formed, does not help us to understand the two great facts of the inner world : its unity and its activity. Hume recognised the difficulty, but he contented himself with leaving it standing as an insoluble dilemma. In France the successors of Condillac early recognised that the theory which reduced all inner life to an automatic occurrence with the semblance only of a spiritual reality was neither theoretically nor practically satisfactory. Practically the opponents of the Revolution saw in the anarchy of the latter the proof that something was wanting which should govern and direct the aimlessness of human actions when abandoned to complete freedom. This something they found in the return to that authority which in church and society had been destroyed by the Revolution. It was the philosophy of pure reaction, it found its classical expression in the writings of Joseph de Maistre (1754-1821). This position led to no further philosophical development, but only to an attempted rehabilitation of the spiritual despotism of the Roman Catholic church with its dogma of infallibility. But the followers of Condillac, notably Cabanis (1757-1808) and De Tracy, actuated by a truly scientific spirit, pointed out what was wanting in Condillac's system, which emphasised unduly the passive and receptive side of the inner world, being mainly interested in an analysis of the processes of understanding and reasoning. These had, through the enormous development of the mathematical and abstract sciences during that period, absorbed by far the greater and the most original part of the intellect of the age. Condillac had in the second edition of his 'Treatise on Sensations'[1] already pointed out one of the defects in his earlier edition; he incidentally makes the remark that our knowledge of external things as outside

26.
Reaction and development.

[1] Ravaisson, pp. 13, 14.

of our sensations has its origin in the reaction from outside against our own activity, and De Tracy had significantly added that the principle of our action is the will and that the latter is our personality. "Within the torrent of our sensations there is nothing but appearance, there is neither a self nor a not-self; surfaces as it were without an inside or an outside; through the consciousness of our own willing we learn at once ourselves and something other than ourselves: that there are on this side and on that side of sensations an inner world and an outer world: two realities opposed to each other and which, in the act of concurrence, touch and penetrate each other." [1] As M. Ravaisson says, it was tantamount to finding again the soul itself below the passivity of sensations, which since Hume seemed to explain everything.

By referring to this principle of activity, the point was defined at which psychology would separate itself as a mental science from the physical sciences that threatened to absorb it.[2]   Both positions, that of re-

[1] Quoted by Ravaisson, ' La Philosophie en France au XIXᵉ Siècle,' 1868, p. 13, &c.
"Sous la passivité des sensations, qui, depuis Hume, semblait tout expliquer, retrouver l'activité, c'était, sous le matériel, retrouver l'esprit même.   Forte de cette découverte, la philosophie devait bientôt se dégager de la physique, sous laquelle Locke, et Hume, et Condillac lui-même l'avaient comme accablée. Deux hommes surtout y aidèrent : Maine de Biran et Ampère."

[2] This point is well brought out by M. Ferraz in his ' History of French Philosophy in the Nineteenth Century' (vol. iii., ' Spiritual-

isme et Libéralisme,' p. 55 and following).   "Les philosophes écossais croient que, si les sciences morales sont moins avancées que les sciences physiques, cela tient à ce qu'elles ne suivent pas la méthode de ces dernières ; qu'elles la suivent donc et elles ne tarderont pas à les atteindre. Or, la méthode des sciences physiques consiste à observer les phénomènes matériels et à déterminer par induction les lois qui les régissent, sans se préoccuper ni de leurs causes ni de l'essence de la matière.   Les sciences morales devront donc, de leur côté, se borner à observer les faits psychologiques et à en induire les lois, sans s'inquiéter ni de leurs

ducing the study of the phenomena of the inner world to a study of natural phenomena, and that of looking upon them as constituting a reality within themselves, were represented in France during the first half of the nineteenth century by prominent and original thinkers. The first thesis aimed at including psychology within the new science of biology which had been founded in the beginning of the century by Bichat. For its adherents the word soul had no meaning. The second strove to establish psychology and all the mental sciences upon an independent principle, maintaining the reality and substantiality of this principle. This would amount in the end to a definition of what is signified by the term soul and its synonyms such as mind, spirit, the inner and the higher life.

28.
Maine de
Biran.

The man who probably conceived the psychological problem most deeply was Maine de Biran (1766-1824). He was a disciple of Condillac, but in insisting untiringly upon the process of introspection as the only way

causes ni de la nature de l'âme elle-même. Cette conséquence, nous ne l'imposons pas aux Écossais et à Jouffroy ; ils la tirent eux-mêmes. Reid et Stewart, si prodigues de détails, quand il s'agit de décrire l'imagination ou l'association des idées, ne parlent guère que pour mémoire de la spiritualité de l'âme. Ils l'admettent plutôt comme hommes et comme chrétiens que comme philosophes et semblent y voir un mystère inaccessible à la raison humaine. Jouffroy bien que plus hardi que ses maîtres de l'Écosse, recule devant la question de l'immortalité du principe pensant et déclare qu'il faut la laisser mûrir quelque temps encore, la science n'étant point pour le moment en mesure de l'aborder. Ce philosophe ne s'aperçoit pas qu'en s'en tenant à la méthode inductive, c'est-à-dire à la méthode des sciences physiques, la science ne sera pas plus en mesure d'aborder cette question dans mille ans qu'aujourd'hui. L'immortalité de l'âme, en effet, repose sur sa causalité, son unité, son identité ; or, ce sont là des attributs qui se constatent ; ils ne s'induisent pas. Pour résoudre de telles questions, il ne faut pas recourir à la méthode des Écossais, qui n'est que la méthode de Bacon généralisée, mais à la méthode de Biran qui est celle de Descartes perfectionnée."

to find the essence of the inner life, by searching for it deeper and deeper, he separated himself more and more from the system of his master. In many ways his position and his career differed from that of other prominent thinkers of his age; for he was neither a politician nor a teacher of philosophy. His practical occupation consisted in administrative work, holding official positions during the Revolution, the Empire, and the Restoration. In passing, we may note that he thus belonged to that organisation which preserved all through the rapidly succeeding catastrophes and changes of the age that continuity and stability which did so much for the French nation: I refer to the organisation of administrative and legislative work. He has been called the greatest French psychologist of the nineteenth century. His influence was to a great extent personal, his works are fragmentary, and the most important and interesting among them were not published till long after his death; nevertheless he may be considered as a centre of philosophical thought, and as such he has recently received increased appreciation.[1] He marks the trans-

[1] French psychology during the first half of the nineteenth century had at the time little direct influence on European thought as a whole. Accordingly we do not read much about it either in English or in German contemporary philosophical literature, and it is only since the more recent development of French philosophy has attracted attention and appreciation outside of France that the larger histories of philosophy have begun to assign to it an important place in the History of European Thought. Among these Prof. Höffding's History, written from an international point of view, gives the fullest and most satisfactory account, though he himself, in a later work ('Moderne Philosophen,' 1905, p. 67), declares that he has not been able to give it that exhaustive study which it deserves. M. Ferraz has written its history in three volumes, dealing separately with three currents of thought, called respectively Socialism, Traditionalism, and Spiritualism. The first includes Naturalism and Positivism; the second, Ultramontanism; and the third, Liberalism (1877,

ition from the professedly naturalistic to the professedly
psychological treatment of mental phenomena.   The
former was represented within the teaching profession
by the medicals and by the lecturers at the École
Polytechnique, the latter by the lecturers at the École
Normale.   Auguste Comte, himself a student and
lecturer at the former institution, refers in a letter
to the impending " struggle between the *Normaliens*
and the *Polytechniciens*, which he regarded as a special
form of the struggle between the metaphysical and
positivist schools." [1]

&c.)   By far the most interesting
account is the brilliant " Rapport "
on French philosophy during the
first two-thirds of the century which
M. Ravaisson wrote at the instiga-
tion of the Ministry of Public Instruction under the Second Empire ('La Philosophie en France au
XIXᵉ Siecle,' 1868).   It forms one
of a series of reports on the progress of Letters and Science in
France, suggested no doubt by, and
as a sequel to, the Reports which
the first Napoleon ordered the
Academy to prepare in the beginning of the century.   Modern
French philosophy first attained to
a prominent position in European
thought through Auguste Comte,
who, as we shall see later on,
opposed not only metaphysics but
also the psychological or introspective method emphasised in the
school of Victor Cousin in opposition to the scientific method of the
naturalistic school.   Nevertheless,
it must be admitted that through
taking note of the different schools
of thought prevalent in neighbouring countries, such as the common-
sense philosophy of the Scottish
school—mainly through Royer Collard, and the idealistic philosophy
of Germany—mainly through Ma-
dame de Staël (1766-1817, in her
'Sur l'Allemagne,' 1813), and by
Degerando, as also by reviving the
study of Descartes and of the
Ancients, the spiritualistic school,
through its very eclecticism, brought
together a very large body of
thought and much material.   More
recent thinkers, with whom we
shall become acquainted in the
sequel, have criticised and developed
this in an original manner.   In
itself the psychology of the earlier
part of the century in France appears uncertain and inconclusive,
being in search rather than in possession of a new principle wherewith
to oppose the purely intellectual conception of the school of Condillac
with its materialistic tendencies.
Most of the prominent members of
this school, such as Maine de Biran,
Jouffroy, and Victor Cousin, are
continually changing their attitudes, and must have been to the
young and ardent spirits of that
age suggestive and stimulating on
the one side, unsettling and un-
satisfying on the other.

[1] H.   Höffding, 'History of
Modern Philosophy,' English trans.,
vol. ii. p. 319.

Maine de Biran influenced mathematicians like Ampère and Sophie Germain, as well as leaders of the higher instruction such as Royer Collard and Victor Cousin.

With the intention of escaping from the materialism of the opposite school, and with a desire of impressing younger minds with the realities of the inner world, Royer Collard, who like so many others had gone through the disillusionment of the Revolution, adopted the method of introspection, which in the course of his studies he found to be most genuinely represented by Thomas Reid. He was animated by the "idea of transferring into the domain of philosophy the method of observation to which we owe the discovery of so many truths in the natural sciences, and of abandoning the tendency to systematise, that inexhaustible source of error."

Royer Collard was appointed to the chair of History of Philosophy at the University by the Emperor Napoleon in 1811. This new departure in philosophical teaching, which Royer Collard continued for only four years, was taken up and brilliantly carried on for a long period by Victor Cousin (1792-1867). The centre of gravity of his teaching lay in the history of philosophy, the exhaustive exposition of which by means of a fascinating but frequently fanciful rhetoric had the result of interesting a large number of younger talents in the study of the various philosophies of the ancient and modern world from an ideal point of view. Biran recognised that this teaching led away from the true psychology which he had in view, but he himself did not escape the

29.
Royer Collard and Cousin.

influence which more than any other, and largely through Cousin himself, made itself felt in the development of philosophical thought in France. I refer to the influence of Kant and of German idealism.

Before considering this new influence which spread, in the course of the century, over the whole of European thought, it is well to remark that the French psychology of the earlier part of the century, though much influenced by the purely psychological interest of the Scottish school, nevertheless assumed quite a different character. Whereas at the Scottish universities empirical psychology was for the first time cultivated in a broad spirit and by introspective methods, psychology in France showed a tendency to become metaphysical, aiming at the solution of problems which in the terminology of Wolff's school belonged to rational, not to empirical psychology. This was no doubt one of the reasons which made Comte doubt its value and discard it as useless. We have seen how French thinkers criticised the psychologists of the Scottish school as dealing merely with the phenomena of mental life and not with the main problems, such as the nature of the soul and its destiny. That Scottish psychology was in much of its teaching and original research able to move in narrower and defined limits has been to its advantage. It was enabled to do so through its more or less intimate alliance with Scottish theology as taught at the same universities. This has been pointed out by M'Cosh, the historian of Scottish philosophy. The fundamental questions of the nature, the origin, and the future of the human soul were dealt with in the theological, not in the philosophical lecture-room.

They formed the recognised groundwork, and were accepted by the philosophical teachers in the form of truths—be it of natural or of revealed religion—and as little analysed as the axioms of geometry or natural philosophy were analysed in their respective lecture rooms. This exclusion of what, on the Continent, was considered to be included in the task of the mental philosopher, really formed the strength of the Scottish school, through which it has become the founder of British psychology, *i.e.*, of psychology proper, excluding—though not uninfluenced by—metaphysics on the one side and natural science on the other. French as well as German thinkers having, unlike their Scottish contemporaries, assumed an independent attitude with regard to traditional beliefs as taught in the ruling churches of their countries, had to seek and establish that metaphysical or rational groundwork which contemporary thinkers in Scotland found ready made, and which they, on their part, had little inducement either to challenge or to prove. The consequence was that in Germany, in certain schools, for a considerable time, psychology was entirely neglected in favour of metaphysics, and that in France the spiritualistic school conducted a continued search for metaphysical principles.

II.

The far-reaching influence which the idealistic philosophy of Germany had on the conception of all philosophical problems has shown itself prominently also with

31.
Kant and
psychology.

regard to all those questions which refer to the inner life, to the soul. To the historian of philosophy, and still more to the historian of thought, this influence announces itself not only by the appearance of quite a new vocabulary, but also by the altered meaning of older and well - known terms. Nothing is more perplexing, more difficult to understand, for the student who approaches for the first time the works of the German philosophers, from Kant to Schopenhauer, than the words and phrases which they employ and which lend themselves only awkwardly to a rendering in other modern languages. This new terminology is in itself an indication that we have to do with quite a new body of ideas, that the discussion of all philosophical problems has been moved on to an entirely different plane.[1] We shall meet this change of level in the dis-

[1] This point is well brought out by Prof. R. Eucken in his ' Geschichte der Philosophischen Terminologie,' Leipzig, 1879 : "Especially in the theory of knowledge, that high-water mark of Kantian thought, we find much that is independent. The traditional also is here moved into a new aspect, in particular we may remark, e.g., the following distinctions and oppositions : theoretical and practical knowledge, sense and understanding, understanding and reason, empirical and pure intuition, concepts of the understanding and of the reason, analytical and synthetical judgments, constitutive and regulative principles, immanent and transcendent principles, ' thing in itself ' and appearance, semblance and appearance, phenomena and noumena, intellectual and intelligible. In these and in other distinctions we recognise throughout the specific diversities of knowledge as a whole ; so far as the substance is concerned we recognise the endeavour to keep the subjective and the objective apart. In physics we find the opposition of mechanical and dynamical philosophy, of the inorganic and organic, of mechanism and teleology, of internal and external purpose, &c.; in psychology, the separation of the mechanical and the chemical senses, of effort and passion, &c." (p. 146).

"Kant sometimes adopts notions as he received them by tradition, brings them into the crucible of his own thought and elaborates them. We have then something that is novel, but a residue remains and a certain discordance is unmistakable. That Kant, in psychology, starts with much that is taken from Wolff and Tetens, has been frequently remarked, but not less is this the case in logic, metaphysic,

cussion of philosophical questions in every instance where, in the course of this History, we deal with other matters than those pertaining to psychology or to the soul. It will therefore be useful to state in as few and simple words as possible wherein this radical change of aspect consists. Perhaps it can be more readily understood in contrasting the treatment which psychological phenomena received in the idealistic schools with that which obtained in the English and French schools during the eighteenth and the early part of the nineteenth century. The latter had collected a large amount of detailed knowledge of the various sides which the inner life presented, but the problem of the unity and essence of the soul had been either neglected or kept in the background as belonging to a different province, or it had been pronounced to be insoluble. The first of these three positions was that of Locke, the second that of the Scottish school, the third that of Hume. Kant was induced to take up the question in the course of the study of some of Hume's later writings, and the problem which he fixed on was the problem of the unity of thought.[1] He did not start

and the philosophy of religion ; this awkward circumstance throws its shadow on his terminology. The same word may in the beginning and the end of a discussion mean something very different, though a clear explanation is wanting " (p. 149). The change in the philosophical language of Germany, which Prof. Eucken brings out in this passage, and in his further references to post - Kantian terminology, becomes still more evident and is liable to create still greater confusion for those who approach the study of this philosophy from outside.

[1] Looked at from the position at which psychology has arrived in the course of the nineteenth century, we now see that the difficulties which presented themselves to Locke and his followers may, to a large extent, be traced to the atomising habit of their mental analysis, and that this is very likely owing to the fact that they desired to imitate the processes of observation and reasoning which had been adopted in the natural sciences. This atomising tendency of thought, so successful, and yet, as we now know, so one-sided in its application to external nature, which readily submits to a disintegration into sep-

with the second and equally important question as to the essence or nature of the soul. He confined his investigations in the beginning to the question how unity of thought and knowledge was attained. In the sequel of his researches which, for reasons which we need not dwell on at present, he termed critical, he was inevitably led to deal with such questions as the essence of the soul, but the fact that he, to begin with, limited his investigations to the question how unity and order came to be introduced into the casual and fleeting mass of single sensations of which experience consists, gave to his whole philosophy the appearance as if it dealt in a one-sided manner with the intellectual life of the mind. In fact, the connection of his practical with his theoretical philosophy remained always a difficult point, although the

arate and definite things and processes, was still further aggravated by the fact that psychical phenomena do not become subjects of discussion before they have been externalised, so that they, to some extent, become observable objects for many minds; whereas they originally are the possession and property only of individual minds. This process of externalisation is carried out by us unconsciously in the acquisition of language, which consists of many words put together in many ways, and very frequently with very different meanings attached to them. In this way the natural "together," in time and space, of mental states is broken up into a multitude of different parts, in the same way as the sciences of dynamics, physics, and chemistry start by showing how the complex things, facts, and phenomena of nature can be divided up into separate more or less similar parts, and to some extent put together

again out of them. But this reverse process of synthesis, by which we again arrive at natural objects, meets with very great difficulty if we deal with things of the mind, and this for obvious reasons on which I need not dwell at present. For the moment and in the present connection it is only useful to remark how, after taking for granted that our conscious inner experience is made up of a succession or assemblage of definite elements called ideas, sensations, perceptions, or by other terms, the difficulty has arisen how to account for the unity or synthesis which seems to us so characteristic of the inner life. Anticipating, we may say that this difficulty which distinguishes internal from external experience is fully recognised only in recent psychological literature, since Prof. James Ward put the conception of a presentation-continuum prominently at the entrance of psychological discussions.

practical or ethical problem was in his later writings put into the foreground. For our present purpose it is sufficient to note that by far the most important psychological question with which Kant dealt was the problem of the unity of thought as it appears in the exact knowledge which we possess in the sciences. There being on one side the casual mass of unordered sensations, on the other an orderly arrangement of scientific knowledge, the question arose, How must the human mind be equipped so as to be able to make order out of disorder, to import unity into the multiplicity and variety of the material given by our senses ?[1] We may note that pure

[1] In defining the problem in this way, we see at once that Kant adhered to the thesis developed in the writings of Locke, Berkeley, and Hume : that knowledge and science is an attempt to bring unity and order into the contingent and chaotic material supplied by our sense-impressions, termed by them ideas. In opposition to this view, which he termed the ideal system, Reid showed a deeper psychological insight when he searched for the unity and order in what was *given* to the observing and thinking mind, when he distinguished between sensation and perception. According to his view, single sensations or ideas were not the original given components, but these consisted of perceptions, *i.e.*, of single elements already joined together. He thus may be considered as the first psychologist who maintained that the thinking process in the adult intelligent person is not the putting together of loose material, but that the beginning of this synthesis is afforded already in our perceptions. The single sensation is itself a mental abstraction, and as such never given in experience alone. Reid in this way goes behind the words and terms of language. To him, relations or judgments are the material with which we work, not the separate and single sensations into which we, by a process of abstraction, may scientifically and artificially divide them. Whereas for Kant, the synthesis of the given loose material seemed to be the main function of the thinking mind, this synthesis existed already for Reid in the simplest original data of perception or experience. In this respect Reid stood nearer to modern views and theories in psychology than did Kant. But wherein he failed was in his enumeration of the original complex data of consciousness and in the precise definition of the subsequent processes of thought which are partly analytical, *i.e.*, dissecting, partly synthetical, *i.e.*, leading on to higher or more comprehensive unities of thought. For an English reader, the best exposition of the permanently valuable contributions of the Scottish school to the psychology of the intellectual process is to be found in Prof. A. Seth's 'Balfour Lectures on Scottish Philosophy,' notably Lectures

Q

psychology, of which, *e.g.*, at a later period, Maine de Biran is a true representative, looks deeper and deeper into the conscious self in order to find the essence of the inner world.   To Kant, on the other side, the latter became as it were a mathematical or formal problem, and this was so much more the case as Kant, in his analysis of knowledge, directed his main attention to such knowledge as was laid down and crystallised in definite judgments, *i.e.*, in the sentences and words of language, and in the theories of mathematics and natural philosophy.[1]

III. and IV. : " The essence of Scottish philosophy, as it appears in Reid, may . . . be described as a vindication of *perception*, as perception, in contradistinction to the vague sensational idealism which had ended in the disintegration of knowledge. Sensation is the condition of perception ; but so far from the two terms being interchangeable, sensation, as a purely subjective state, has no place in the objective knowledge founded upon it ; that is to say, the philosophical analysis of knowledge cannot pass beyond the circle of percepts. It is significant that the two points on which Reid takes his stand should be (1) the proclamation of a general distinction between extension, as a percept, and any feeling or series of feelings as such ; and (2) the assertion that the unit of knowledge is an act of judgment. These are the hinges, it is hardly necessary to add, upon which Kant's philosophy also turns—in the Æsthetic and the Analytic " (3rd ed., p. 96).

[1] One of the principal subjects of psychological as well as of logical interest with which Kant was concerned was the problem of the certainty of knowledge, of the necessary, not merely contingent,

connection of ideas. Locke had reduced all certainty in the natural sciences to more or less of probability, and Hume, to custom or habit of thought.   This did not satisfy Kant, who, following in this Descartes' line of reasoning, sought for certainty in the constitution or nature of the human mind.   This seemed to explain satisfactorily mathematical certainty, but not the certainty of knowledge referring to external phenomena.   To explain this, the phenomena of the outer world must, as it seemed, have something in common with the processes of pure or logical thought.   This common feature was explained by Kant in his special theory of the ideality of time and space.   With his followers it took more and more the form of the ultimate identity of the subject (the thinking mind) and the object, and led, through various phases, ultimately to Hegel's conception of thought as the nature and life of the absolute mind, as being the essence both of the external world of nature and history and the internal world of the human mind.   It then became a task of philosophy to develop a logic as well as a psychology of the abstract mind, or of thought in its most ab-

In adopting this course the beginning was made of a development that later on became characteristic of the whole school which historically started from Kant's position and ended in Hegel and Schopenhauer. Philosophy in England and France had become purely psychological, or, if it did not confine itself to the inner world which lies open to everyone in his own consciousness, it extended its field in the direction of taking in bodily phenomena, *i.e.*, the physical outside of the inner world, or of dealing with the collective existence of man in the life of mankind and society. The natural development of English, Scottish, and French philosophy lay therefore in the direction of biology, anthropology, and sociology. The development on the other side, which was initiated by Kant, was not psychological, but on the contrary logical, or, to use a more modern phrase, epistemological. If it was not professedly so in Kant's own deliverances, it tended to become so in the systems of his followers. There is no doubt also that a tendency in this direction lay already in the enterprise of Locke, who in his celebrated Essay dealt mainly with the human understanding, *i.e.*, with the intellectual side : the problem of thought and knowledge. In this respect he followed, probably unconsciously, in the line of Descartes, who placed the thinking process in the beginning of his philosophy as the main characteristic of human person-

32.
Epistemological development in Germany.

stract sense. This higher psychology was contained in Hegel's first and most original work, the 'Phenomenology of Mind.' This coincided neither with the empirical nor with the rational psychology of the Wolffian school, and left far behind and below it the painstaking mental analysis of the human mind, as it was developed in this country, and later on by Herbart and others in Germany. In this psychology of the Hegelian school the conception and term of the Soul or individual Mind was gradually displaced in favour of the term Mind or Spirit.

ality. This pure intellectualism, which in the British
schools of philosophy was overcome by studying from
various points of view, not so much the human intellect
as the human mind, human nature, man and mankind,
became a pronounced feature in the German idealistic
systems, and ended in what has been termed the Panlogism
of Hegel. This tendency of the idealistic schools was
to a great extent inherited from ancient philosophy,
notably from Plato and the Neoplatonists. Plato had
already looked upon concepts as independent realities,
not merely as phenomena of the human mind; and in
the neoplatonic system the sum of concepts was in a
manner personalised as the universal "Nous" or Mind
that comprehends in itself the intellectual essence of
all things.

This tendency to personify what to the ordinary
observer were only processes, phenomena, or manifestations
in the human mind—*i.e.*, of the inner life of the human
being—runs through the whole school of thought I am
now referring to. It was there taken in real earnest,
whereas in general literature similar expressions were
used only in a figurative sense. If we add to this inherited tendency, which on the Continent was vigorously
opposed only in the monadology of Leibniz and by
thinkers influenced by him, the other vicious tendency
common to all the earlier psychological schools of looking
upon the human mind or the soul as compounded of
distinct faculties or powers, we understand at once the
origin of that extraordinary phraseology with which Kant
heralded his critical investigations; how it came that
instead of speaking of the human mind or the soul he

speaks of intuition (Anschauung), understanding, and reason, and of reason again as theoretical and practical, and of judgment, as if they were independent agencies, working together on separate lines and by definite laws in the production of all mental life and work. To these two tendencies, the tendency to divide rigidly mental phenomena and to personify independently mental processes or powers, we must add, as a third important factor, an extreme reliance upon the power of the human intellect to decide as to its own capabilities, and this not, as with Locke, by a psychological or historical investigation of the genesis of the thinking process, but by an analysis of general statements made in the form of language.

The very title of Kant's first and most important great work, ' The Critique of Pure Reason,' suggests the idea that it was possible to abstract from the actual and concrete existing examples of reasoning a definite pure form or scheme which existed as it were somewhere in the human mind anterior to the practical use of the reasoning faculties; that one could by analysis of what is given in the crystallised knowledge of experience and of the sciences find out that something, that *quid proprium*, of which the thinking mind must be possessed before it made any practical use of its faculties. It was an attempt to step beyond the purely descriptive or psychological position. This attempt to overstep the limits of a purely descriptive process Kant termed characteristically the transcendental method. This term has been variously criticised, and had no doubt a deterrent effect upon those students of his philosophy who approached it from a common-sense point of view and with realistic habits of thought. The term, however, was coined with the definite object of distinguishing the whole investigation, on the one side, from the purely empirical and psychological, and, on the other, from the older metaphysical or purely rational treatment which started, as in the philosophies of Descartes, Spinoza, and Leibniz, with certain abstract definitions of the nature or essence of the human mind or soul, trying to deduce from these definitions its properties, its behaviour, and its destinies. Kant never adopted the conception of Locke that the human mind was a *tabula rasa* or an unwritten sheet of paper; he believed in the significance of Leibniz' criticism that the human intellect was a something with a specific endowment, and he proposed to find out what this endowment was by analysing the product of human intelligence, viz., experience, knowledge, scientific thought, and further on its activity as shown in the precepts of morality and the judgments regarding the beautiful, the good, and the purpose of things. This way of putting the problem was perfectly legitimate. Given on the one side the perceptions of our senses, our impressions and feelings, and on the other side unified knowledge, definite precepts of morality and judgments of taste as they are elaborated through the activity of the human mind, it was a legitimate question to ask how the former are converted into the latter. But to many students of Kant's works it must at the time have appeared a mistake to think that this problem could once for all be solved by a critical analysis of the very meagre descriptions which the processes of knowledge, thought, or the precepts of morality and the canons of taste had received at that time in the literature of the schools. Nor did the pedantic formalism in which Kant's solution of the problems was clothed, and the great array of new terms which was employed, help to destroy the first strange impression which many even of Kant's followers, friends, and pupils received on the appearance of Kant's first great work. Nevertheless in this forbidding formalism, in this abstruse terminology, the great task of nineteenth century thought was for the first time fully grasped and announced. For its solution there was wanted a deeper and fuller psychological knowledge of that so - called material supplied by the senses, and on the other side a much clearer and fuller exposition of the methods of science, of the data of ethics, and of the precepts of taste and rules of artistic creation. To supply these preliminary and indispensable requisites, philosophical thought in this country had in Kant's time already made the beginning. The introspective school, assisted later on by physiological research, had, as we have seen, accumulated—from Hartley to Bain—a large amount of descriptive matter. Simultaneously and independently the science of morality or ethics was likewise developed in this country. A minute analysis of scientific reasoning was first given by John Stuart Mill in his Logic ; the principles of criticism and of literary and artistic taste were studied, as we shall see later on, on independent lines in all the three countries.

Thus about eighty years after the appearance of Kant's first Critique, and mostly if not always without any special reference to Kant's work, the preliminary steps had been taken for a renewed attempt to solve, in a less formal manner, the problem which Kant had defined for all time, namely this : How is the human soul passively and actively engaged in rearing the great edifice of knowledge, in instituting moral life and culture, and in producing and appreciating the creations of art and poetry ? Looked at in this way, we may say that Kant has formulated the psychological programme down to the present day, although it may be urged with some propriety that he himself was not pre-eminently a psychologist, and that his philosophy discarded the genuine psychological method.

33.
Kant's
psycho-
logical
programme.

But for those who do not look for the working of the human mind and the life of the soul only within the narrow limits of individual experience, but who use the terms mind, soul, and spirit in the larger sense, as denoting that unseen agency which underlies the history of mankind, the manner in which mental phenomena were studied in the philosophy of Kant, and still more in that of his immediate successors, constitutes an era in philosophical thought.   As I remarked above, the discussion of things referring to the soul was lifted on to an entirely different and higher plane.   We may call this transcendental if we choose to do so, but this term should not suggest the idea that we have not to do with actual realities.   Although it may be difficult or impossible to define these realities in such a manner that a minute analysis becomes possible, few persons will deny that such expressions as the spirit of the age, the essence of culture, the soul in nature and history, and thought—as used in the English language and by the writer of this History,—that all these terms have a

34.
The way out
of individu-
alism.

very real meaning, and that they refer to a definite though logically undefinable something which underlies all external events, alone making them subjects of general and lasting interest. It is true that in the writings of Kant, and still more so in those of Fichte, Schelling, and Hegel, we do not meet with any sustained effort towards that painstaking psychological analysis which we find in the writings of the English and French introspective schools: they were, as stated above, introduced in Germany by the opposition thinkers like Herbart and Beneke; but in the whole of the literature which followed the appearance of Kant's works, or which accompanied it, we meet with one of the most remarkable psychological phenomena in the history of human thought. The fact that speculations of such an abstract nature, frequently expressed in uncouth and forbidding terms, should have attained a firm and lasting hold on the great intellects of a great people for a long period, is a psychological phenomenon well worthy to be pondered. Nor is it likely that this phenomenon would ever have actually occurred had the movement been a purely individual [1] and academic one. The causes which brought it about are to be found as much in the

---

[1] " At a time when the universal nature of spiritual life has become so very much emphasised and strengthened, and the mere individual aspect has become, as it should be, correspondingly a matter of indifference, when, too, that universal aspect holds, by the entire range of its substance, the full measure of the wealth it has built up, and lays claim to it all, the share in the total work of mind that falls to the activity of any particular individual can only be very small. Because this is so, the individual must all the more forget himself, as in fact the very nature of science implies, and requires that he should ; and he must, moreover, become and do what he can " (Hegel, ' Phenomenology,' end of the Preface, J. B. Baillie's translation, 1910, vol. i. p. 72).

varying political temperament of the German people in
the earlier part of the nineteenth century as in the
independent rise and development of the creative powers
in literature, in poetry, in the fine arts, and in musical
composition.[1] We may indeed go a step further, and
say that those powers of the human mind which, in
Kant's philosophy, were perhaps unduly separated or
personified, became actually living forces in the great
individuals who form, as it were, the *dramatis personœ*
or characters in that great intellectual drama—never to
be forgotten and never to be acted again—which the

35.
General
causes of
this move-
ment.

[1] The connection of philosophy,
even of so abstract a nature as
that of Fichte, Schelling, and above
all of Hegel, with the literary and
poetical atmosphere which prevailed
in Germany at the end of the
eighteenth and the beginning of
the nineteenth century, has been
more and more appreciated in recent
histories of German philosophy and
German literature. The following
quotation from a recent thinker,
who has done more than any other
to make intelligible to the present
generation the elevated intellectual
character of that bygone age, may
serve in lieu of many others : "The
generation to which Hegel belonged
stood as much under the influence
of the idealism of Kant and Fichte
as of that of the French Revolution.
It was full of the idea of an elevation
of humanity and an approaching
higher order of society. Fichte
was the hero who proclaimed this
new era, and his philosophy was
devoted to bringing it about. The
disciples of Fichte in Jena, in Berlin, and in Tübingen were bound
together through these ideas. Hegel,
Schelling, Hölderlin retained the
ideals of their Tübingen years and
strengthened each other in them.
And as the movement which the
French Revolution had produced
bore a European character, as the
writers of the ideological school in
France, the defenders of the Revolution in England and in Germany co-operated in this movement,
the new ideals maintained themselves through their energy and
their extent, even in opposition to
the reaction which spread after the
execution of the King and the wars
of the Revolution. Hegel, among
others, remained steadfast and full
of courage. If one examines his
[early] theological fragments, one
sees them borne up by the spirit of
this movement. His deep historical
studies do not stand in contradiction to his endeavours after a
more perfect religious spirit and a
renovation of society, but rather he
brought, much more radically than
the average German 'Aufklärung,'
Christianity into the flow of historical development, in which also
this form of the religious spirit
must lead to something higher.
Taking this development in full
earnest, his labour for and his
belief in the future received added
energy and a more definite aim "
(Wilhelm Dilthey, ' Die Jugendgeschichte Hegels ').

history of German culture unrolls before our view.
Thus the powers of the human mind, which in the
various writings of Kant seem to co-operate in producing the intellectual, moral, and spiritual life of the
human soul, are characteristically represented in the
systems of his followers, not only by being emphasised
as leading principles; they are supported also in many
instances by the personal character of the authors of
those systems. For instance, if we read in Kant of the
primacy of the will over the intellect, no more practical
instance could be found wherewith to demonstrate
this power of the human will than the life and the
personality of Fichte. But it is not my intention to
enlarge further on this point or to indulge in fanciful
analogies. I desire only to arouse in my readers some
sense of the wider psychological problem which the
history of German idealism presents in its various
aspects as philosophical, classical, or romantic, and in its
appearance in science, poetry, and art.[1]

[1] Referring again to what was said in the note to page 65, we may look upon Hegel's first great work as the psychology of the universal or absolute mind, and upon his later logic as the stages and method of its development. Earlier writings of Hegel were preparatory to his final exposition, and had the object of defining the difference of his speculation from earlier attempts. This has been well brought out by Kuno Fischer in his brilliant analysis of Hegel's earlier tracts, in the last section of his 'History of Modern Philosophy' (vol. viii. p. 245 sqq.) Still earlier preparative studies are dealt with by Dilthey in the dissertation quoted in the last note. Hegel defends the new philosophy, which was to "lay aside the name of love of knowledge and be actual knowledge." As against the fragmentary philosophy of the "Aufklärung" the new philosophy was to be systematic; as against the philosophy of common-sense, represented in Germany by Krug, the new philosophy was not to be content with enumerating empirically the data of consciousness,— it had, following Kant, to deduce them from a higher principle; as against modern sceptics, represented in Germany by G. E. Schulze, it had to overcome the agnosticism suggested in Kant's mistaken doctrine of "the Thing in itself" as opposed to its appearance; as against the distinction of know-

The process of generalisation, of the sublimation of thought out of the concrete into the abstract regions, had, however, a very detrimental effect upon the study of all those questions which deal with the life and nature of the individual mind or soul. Psychology, in the older sense of the term, as an analysis of the human mind, *i.e.*, of the individual mind, had really disappeared. The data of consciousness were only discussed in a critical spirit and with the object of leading beyond an individualistic conception, of overstepping or transcending the limits of the self (or ego), and of conceiving such words as consciousness, mind, self, and idea in a more general and impersonal sense as denoting at once the unity and community of many minds, many selves, and many ideas. It was only by elevating the philosophical point of view above the consideration of the empirical world of many things, many minds, and many ideas into the sphere of the systematic unity of all and into a higher hierarchy of ideas that Fichte[1] found it possible

36.
Disappear-
ance of
psychology
in the older
sense.

ledge and faith, variously represented in the philosophies of Kant, Jacobi, and Fichte, it had to overcome this disturbing dualism, the mere subjectivity of religion; finally, as against Spinozism, renovated in German philosophy by Schelling, the absolute or universal substance was not to be dogmatically placed at the entrance of the system as an empty conception, but it was to be understood in its development in nature, the individual mind, and the mind of mankind. It was to be a subject, *i.e.*, a spirit. "The mind which knows itself in its development as such is science. There is its reality and the realm which it creates out of its own elements" (Hegel's 'Werke,' vol.

ii. p. 15). In this and similar passages contained in the preface to the 'Phenomenology' lies, as Kuno Fischer (*loc. cit.*, p. 293) says, "the whole of Hegel's philosophy."

[1] That Fichte's philosophy, for which he invented the new term "Wissenschaftslehre," was something very different from the ordinary psychological treatment of mental phenomena, was emphatically stated by Fichte in the earlier expositions of his doctrine. Yet if we advance to the study of his later writings, through which he gained a popular as well as an academic reputation, we find that Fichte himself recognised more and more the necessity of leading up from the position of introspective psychology

to escape from that purely subjective point of view, enclosed in purely introspective limits, which a logical development of Locke's and Kant's ideas seemed to necessitate. This consequence of Locke's sensationalism had been clearly pointed out by Hume, whereas the object of Berkeley's [1] philosophy was to overcome it.

to the higher level on which the whole of his speculation moved from the very beginning. "Philosophy starts from an observation of knowledge through introspection, and advances to its [supersensual] foundation" ('Werke,' vol. ii. p. 541). In consequence of this some of these later writings have distinct psychological value in the narrower sense of the word. Notably is this the case with one of his later courses of lectures dealing with the "Data of Consciousness" (delivered 1810-11, published posthumously, 1817). The lucid analysis with which this treatise begins drew, even from such a realistic thinker as Helmholtz (whose father was an enthusiastic follower and admirer of Fichte), favourable comment. And quite independently of his metaphysics Fichte had a powerful indirect influence upon thought in general, and more recent psychology in particular, through the fact that the fundamental doctrine in his speculation was the thesis that mind is primarily and essentially an active principle, and that he considered this to be a truth founded on immediate evidence and not deducible from any still higher principle. Through this statement, to which Fichte always adhered and which he expounded and illustrated from many sides, his influence is still felt at the present day. More definitely can this be traced through the writings of the Jena professor, C. Fortlage ('System der Psychologie,' 1885), to

Prof. Wilhelm Wundt in Leipzig. A purely metaphysical interpretation and development by no means identical with the one just named may be traced through Schelling to Schopenhauer.

[1] No philosopher of the first order seems to have been so much misinterpreted or misunderstood as Berkeley. He is classed by Reid among the "ideal" philosophers, beginning with Descartes and ending in Hume, and among German historians of philosophy he is very generally represented as a solipsist. This is to a large extent owing to the fact that only his earlier writings seem to have been taken into consideration by his critics, and that his later constructive philosophy remained for a long time unknown. It is only since Prof. Campbell Fraser devoted himself to an independent study and to the editing of Berkeley's Works that a correcter view has gradually gained acceptance, although we still find Ueberweg in Germany and Huxley in England maintaining the more traditional view. From Fraser's painstaking examination it is clear that Berkeley was as little a solipsist, starting from the purely subjective experience of the individual mind, as was Fichte. Berkeley, in speaking of the mind, seems always to take for granted the existence of many individual minds, though he never faced the criticism — most clearly put by Hume — that his arguments against the reality of external matter outside of the

It may be true and undeniable that everything to every
individual soul comes back to its own sensations and
subjective experience, but the fact that there are many
other individual souls claiming similar, though not
identical, experiences, raises the problem : How do we
in practice get out of the narrow limits of our own self
and, as it were, regard ourselves from outside as one
among many equals ?   Fichte did not linger to discover
or even to suggest how this transition from a purely
subjective to an objective point of view was actually
attained in the history of the individual soul, still less
did he form any theory how, alongside of the common
stock of ideas, individual life and individual conceptions

thinking individual mind would
apply with equal force to the existence of other individual minds
external to an individual mind.
Fichte, on the other side, overcame
the difficulty by taking the term
mind as meaning the universal or
general mind, of which individual
minds were only examples.   But
Berkeley seems to be nearer to the
more recent psychological view, inasmuch as he admits that we know
as little of the essence of the individual mind as we know of external
matter.   It is to him merely a
point of reference, a unifying principle manifesting its existence in the
use of the word "I," and as he finds
this unity in subjective experience
so he is likewise in search and convinced of the existence of such a
spiritual unity in the external or
general order of things which without it is inconceivable.   Nor does it
seem to him that a knowledge of
the Supreme Unity or the Deity is
less possible than our knowledge of
other men, or of our own self, as in
all the three cases what we do know
is merely phenomenal.   " Nor,

Berkeley might say, is this sight of
God which we have daily, a sight of
an unknowable Something.   We
find through inner experience what
conscious life is, though we have
no sense of phenomenal knowledge
of the 'I' or the 'You.'   We can
attribute this, can we not, to God
as well as to our fellow-men ? . . .
So 'God' is more than a meaning-
less name—more than the unknowable behind the sense-symbolism of
nature.   God means the eternally
sustaining spirit—the active conscious reason of the universe.   Of
God's existence we have the same
sort of proof as we have of the
existence of other conscious agents
like ourselves when we say we 'see'
them.   Of course we never see and
never can see another human spirit
even when his body, as a phenomenal
thing, is present to our senses ; we
can only perceive the visible and
tangible appearances behind which
reason obliges us to recognise an
invisible, individual spirit, &c."
('Berkeley,' by A. Campbell Fraser,
"Blackwood's Philosophical Classics," 1881, p. 165).

are maintained. In fact the phenomenon of individuality or personality of the human soul was lost sight of. The individual self was conceived as being merged into a general self, the individual mind in the general mind, and for a long time the interest of philosophical thought lay in showing how the general mind, which gradually drifted into the position of the Absolute, the spiritual One, developed and manifested itself in the many things and processes of nature and the community of individual minds which we call society or mankind. In the process of elevating the philosophical view above the individual, the casual, and the subjective, the greatest problem of psychology, the phenomenon of individuation, of Personality, was either forgotten or its existence was actually denied.

37.
Individual self merged into general self.

As I stated above, this process of raising the discussion from the empirical, subjective, and individual level on to a higher abstract, objective, and ideal level was only the philosophical reflex of that ideal movement [1] which char-

---

[1] That this movement was very general *before* the appearance of the critical philosophy may be proved in many instances to which I shall have occasion to refer in the sequel. That Kant himself was an independent representative of this movement before he became generally known may nowhere be seen better than if we study the personal life and development of Herder. This subject has been so fully and so ably treated by R. Haym in 'Herder nach seinem Leben und seinen Werken' (2 vols., 1880-85), that a perusal of this work will go a long way to introduce the reader to the connection in which the spirit of Kant's philosophy stands with the general thought of the age, as also to the very important contrasts which exist between them. Herder was an enthusiastic pupil of Kant, as he himself fully testified in many of his writings, even when he later on declined to adopt and entirely failed to grasp what was most original, stimulating, and fruit-bearing in Kant's systematic works. He has proclaimed, in terms which remind us of passages in the Prelude of Wordsworth, how he, a youth of eighteen years (1762), felt himself elevated and borne aloft by Kant's teaching which formed an epoch in his life. " I have had the good fortune," he says, " to know a philosopher who was my master. He, in the years of his prime, had the cheerfulness of a

acterised German thought, literature, and culture during the last quarter of the eighteenth and the first third of the nineteenth century, covering a period of about sixty years : I there defined this movement as being led by the ideal of humanity. We may now define it as an endeavour to elevate the minds of men, to introduce a higher conception of the object of life and of the dignity of the human mind. This endeavour to elevate by the creation of ideals was in one form or other common to all the great leaders in thought and life during that period. This process of elevation or of idealisation assumed a tangible form and became a historical force in two definite directions. The first of these was the educational movement, which itself has again two distinct issues. The earlier one was the widespread interest in popular education, the later one was that referring to the higher or learned educa-

38.
Creation of
ideals.

39.
The
educational
movement.

youth ; his open forehead, made for thought, was the abode of undisturbed cheerfulness and joy ; thoughtful speech flowed from his lips ; wit and humour were at his command, and his instructive utterance formed the most entertaining intercourse. With the same spirit in which he probed Leibniz, Wolff, Baumgarten, Hume, and unfolded the laws of Kepler, Newton, and the physicists, he also received the then appearing writings of Rousseau, his ' Émile ' and ' Héloïse,' as also the most recent discovery in nature, appreciated them and always came back again to plain natural knowledge and to the moral worth of man. . . . He encouraged and forced you, in an agreeable way, to independent thought ; despotism was quite foreign to his mind. This man, whom I name with the greatest thankfulness and esteem, is

Immanuel Kant ; his figure stands agreeably before me" (Haym, vol. i. p. 31).

Herder also followed Kant in his criticism of the prevailing philosophy of the Aufklärung, in his dislike of traditional metaphysics of the school which he characteristically terms Averroism, and in his proposal to define the powers and the limits of human reason. But when Kant stepped forward with his own transcendental philosophy Herder seemed incapable of following him. Kant, on his part, hardly did justice to the far-reaching and suggestive writings of Herder, which in a poetical, attractive, but desultory manner led the way into newly discovered regions of anthropology and the philosophy of history. All this will be found elaborately treated in Haym's volumes.

tion. The former aimed at an education and elevation of the masses; it centred in Pestalozzi, who was influenced by Rousseau. It had a distinctly religious side, based upon an enlightened interpretation of Christian doctrine. The later educational movement aimed at an elevation of the middle and higher classes through a reformation of the teaching at the high schools and universities. It had a distinctly classical, in some instances even a romantic bias, but in some of the greatest leaders of thought, such as Lessing, Kant, Herder, Schiller, and Goethe, the process of education and elevation took a still higher flight, being conceived as the process of the education of mankind under Divine guidance. This fruitful but somewhat vague conception assumed a more realistic aspect when the general tendency of the age towards elevation and liberation was led into the channels of political life during the Anti-Napoleonic Revolution, which crystallised into definite shapes in the administrative reforms led by Stein in Prussia, and culminated in the war of Liberation and the overthrow of foreign despotism. The general tendency towards liberation and elevation became a definite and real national movement, and, in this its realism, it was not infrequently opposed to the vagueness of those who would not descend from the ideal heights of Classicism and Romanticism. Something of this realism attached also to the endeavours of popular educationalists who experienced the necessity of descending from the transcendental heights occupied by Kant and Fichte on to the level of practical psychology and pedagogics. It is known that Kant's academic teaching was in a different

40.
The political movement.

R

style from that of his published works; Fichte, in the
course of his academic and political activity, modified
very considerably the manner in which he approached
what always remained his characteristic point of view;
but the actual return from a purely rational to an

**41.
Return to
empirical
psychology.**

empirical psychology was led by two educationalists—
Herbart and Beneke.   As stated in the beginning of
this chapter, it was through them that psychology proper
became a recognised branch of philosophical teaching.

**42.
J. F. Fries.**

To these two names we may add that of J. F. Fries
(1773-1843), who brought philosophy, as it were, back
again from the transcendental to the empirical level.[1]

In addition to this there were two distinct influences
at work which co - operated with the movement just
referred to in concentrating the attention of many thinking minds upon definite psychological questions, such as
the nature and destiny of the human soul.   The first
of these influences came from the side of the natural
sciences, which, mainly under the leadership of Johannes

[1] The importance of Fries' philosophy lay mainly in two very
different directions.   First, in his
philosophy of religion, in which he
assimilates ideas independently expressed by Jacobi and deals — as
Schleiermacher did more fundamentally—with religion as a psychological phenomenon.   Secondly,
in his philosophy of nature, which,
in opposition to that of Schelling,
approached more to the position
occupied in this country by natural
philosophy.   In this respect he was
probably the only contemporary
German philosopher who was
noticed and appreciated by Gauss.
The celebrated naturalist, Schlei-
den, tells us how Gauss referred to
Fries' 'Mathematische Naturphil-

osophie' (1822), in the following
words addressed to a student:
" Young man, if you manage after
three years of arduous study to
understand and appreciate this
book, you may leave the university
with a conviction that you have
employed your time better than
most of your fellow-students" (see
Henke, ' Jacob Friedrich Fries,'
1867, p. 226).   To both of these
directions of Fries' speculation I
shall refer in later chapters.   Fries
was also one of the first who led
psychological research in the direction of anthropology.   His ' Handbuch der psychischen Anthropologie' appeared in two volumes
in 1820.

Müller and E. H. Weber, had through physiological inquiries approached the phenomenon of consciousness in the highest forms of organic life. Single phenomena of conscious life, notably those referring to the organs or processes of sensation, had been subjected to minute observation, measurement, and experimentation; the question presented itself, What position has the physiologist to take up to the problems of the inner life? As already stated in the earlier part of this chapter, this serious and fundamental question was taken up by the editor and the writers of that important dictionary of physiology which began to be published in 1842. The editor was a celebrated professor of physiology at Göttingen, Rudolf Wagner. Among the contributors was his colleague, the successor to Herbart in the chair of philosophy, Hermann Lotze. The position which the former took up was essentially dualistic : soul and body were two substantial principles, the relation of which was not clearly defined or definable ; both principles, however, worked together in producing the higher life of organised beings. To a dualism in this form Lotze objected, inasmuch as he maintained that for the student of nature all observable processes within the organism came under the rule of a definite and all-pervading mechanism. Vital forces were not to be introduced into the study of nature, and, if they existed, they would be of no use to the physiologist, who has to look merely for such mechanical, physical, and chemical processes as can be explained by resorting to such laws and agencies as are laid down in the sciences of mechanics, physics, and chemistry. Nevertheless Lotze

43.
Influence of physiology.

in his ʻPhysiology of the Soul' not only retained this latter term as denoting a definite substantial existence, but he thought it necessary to introduce the study of " medical psychology " by a lengthy discussion on the essence, and even the location, of the soul in the body. Through these writings the problem was brought under the immediate attention of naturalists.

The second influence which forced the central psychological problem into the foreground was the searching analysis to which the arguments and conceptions of the Hegelian philosophy—that final consummation of the idealistic course of thought—were subjected by Ludwig Feuerbach. This analysis was very much provoked by the attempts of the disciples of Hegel to show that Hegel's philosophy of religion supported the orthodox conceptions regarding the soul, immortality, and the Deity, and still more when the whole doctrine became, as it were, an instrument of a reactionary and illiberal movement in Prussian ecclesiastical and political circles. The champions of freedom of thought, with which the systems of the ideal philosophy from Kant onward had hitherto allied themselves, were not slow or unsuccessful in showing that the philosophy of Hegel lent itself to an entirely different interpretation; that, in fact, the conceptions of individuality, personality, and immortality, harmonised very awkwardly with that general process of absorbing all individual life and thought in a general panpsychism, panlogism, and pantheism, which left no room for separate existences. Feuerbach, in drawing the ultimate consequences of the idealistic speculation, worked into the hands of many

44.
Feuerbach
on Hegel.

thinkers who had approached the subject from a purely naturalistic point of view. Thus we see that the age was ripe for a discussion of the soul problem, *die Seelenfrage.* Scientific, educational, psychological, philosophical, and religious interests combined to place it in the foreground. It was taken up, as I stated above, in a conservative spirit, as a question of the day, by Rudolf Wagner himself, in an address which he delivered at the meeting of the German Association of Sciences, which took place at Göttingen in the year 1854. The challenge which was thus thrown out was taken up by Karl Vogt,[1] who, in various pamphlets and by characteristic phrases, stigmatised the position as dualistic and untenable, spoke of the genuine Göttingen *Seelensubstanz*, and opened the long campaign which goes under the name of the materialistic controversy. In it thinkers of all shades and opinions took part. It resulted in an enormous popular literature, in which the extreme watchwords of the naturalistic school played a great part, being, if not really more intelligible, still seemingly more easily assimilated by the popular mind. In many instances they allied themselves with political and social radicalism, and, later on, with the growing industrialism and the newly-born material prosperity of the German nation, which they supplied with a shallow but convenient creed.

I have in the foregoing attempted to show how the great psychological problems were approached in the three different countries during the course of the first

45.
Die Seelen-
frage.

---

[1] See for details of the various authors and their publications the note to page 197 in the early part of this chapter.

half of the nineteenth century. In this country and in Germany we witness independent movements which, however, about the middle of the century, had in their natural development approached each other. The mutual influence of the philosophies of the two countries was not important up to the time when Sir William Hamilton introduced the study of Kant in this country, and when Beneke and others in Germany drew attention to some of the writings of Bentham, Mill, and others. In France, as we have seen, there existed a lively interest in psychological questions; the influence of Maine de Biran, however, the most original of French psychologists, remained somewhat in the background, whilst the great development of the natural and medical sciences favoured those researches which approached mental phenomena from their physical aspects, and among these prominently also from the pathological side. The greatest thinker of the scientific school, whose importance became gradually recognised since English philosophers had drawn attention to his writings, Auguste Comte, reduced, in his earlier writings, all psychology to biology. Psychology proper lived on under the influence of the Scottish school in the writings of the eclectic school, many members of which drew attention to the new origins which they announced as being contained in the writings of Maine de Biran. Psychological research in all the three countries, though mostly preserving its genuine character in this country, was nevertheless largely affected by the transcendental movement which, in Germany, for a long time kept psychology proper in check, which in France diverted it into the channels of eclecticism, but which in England attained to a marked influence only after the middle of the century. This influence of the transcendental movement may be defined by saying that it pushed into the foreground those problems which in the older philosophy had been dealt with under the title of rational psychology or pneumatology. In contradistinction to empirical psychology, which aims at a simple description of the phenomena of the inner life, rational psychology aimed at answering those questions which form the ground-work of a reasoned creed (*Weltanschauung*). Speaking in a general way, it may be said that in Germany the formation of a philosophical creed was the all-absorbing interest up till the middle of the century, after the failure of which the more empirical treatment received long - delayed attention ; that in England empirical studies which had been roaming about at large and without any definite systematic organisation, accumu-lating a large amount of valuable material, awakened, greatly under the influence of the transcendental move-ment, to the necessity of attacking the great questions of the soul, its nature, its destiny, and its place in the Divine Order,—in fact, to the necessity of forming a rational or reasoned creed. Among those who recog-nised that this task could no longer be postponed, stand out prominently Herbert Spencer, John Stuart Mill in his later writings, and George Henry Lewes.[1] The eclectic school in France, with Victor Cousin at

[1] G. H. Lewes' (1817-78) prin-cipal works referring to this matter are 'Problems of Life and Mind' (1st series), 'The Foundations of a Creed' (2 vols., 1874 and 1875) and 'The Study of Psychology ; its Object, Scope, and Method' (1879).

its head, oscillated between the empirical and transcendental, an idealistic and a traditional, point of
view, without consistently maintaining either.

III.

In consequence of the different points of view from
which the psychological problem had been approached,
and which began to influence each other shortly after
the middle of the century, a varied and widespread
interest was created in this, the oldest of philosophical
problems.   To grasp and do justice to the many-sided
aspects which it now presented there was required
an intellect of the high order represented in modern
European philosophy pre-eminently by Leibniz.   It had
to combine the common-sense aspect of Britain with the
metaphysical of Germany ; the physiological and pathological of the Continental naturalists with the spiritualistic of the religious thinker ; and lastly, the mathematical
with the poetical spirit.   At the same time, it had to
rise to a higher form of eclecticism than that which was
characteristic of the French school which bore the name.
There lived at that time only one thinker of the first
order who, through education and individual taste and
sympathy, possessed both the universal knowledge and the
high mental qualifications necessary for this task.   This
was Hermann Lotze (1817 - 81), who for this reason
stands, as it were, in the centre of the philosophical,
and especially the psychological, thought of the century.
His points of contact with all the then existing move-

47.
Lotze.

ments of thought are very marked. It is true that he was not a great student of modern French or English thought. We have seen, however, that the position taken up by the English school had already, in Lotze's time, been reached in the writings of Herbart and Beneke; and so far as the researches of French physiologists and medicals are concerned, they were at that time followed with the greatest interest in Germany, in the schools of Berlin, Leipzig, and Vienna, between which and the medical schools of Paris there existed a lively intercourse of students and studies.

In fact, Lotze himself came to philosophy from the side of the study of medicine; some of his earlier writings having the object of counteracting the vagueness of medical philosophy in Germany by introducing the clearer definitions of mechanical science. But Lotze was quite as much interested in the transcendental movement, and from the beginning of his literary career urged the necessity of approaching all philosophical problems from the point of view of a definite creed, a central conception. His training was also equally balanced by realistic and classical studies, and his spiritual home was in the classical ideals of the great period of German literature headed by Goethe and Herder. Next to Herbart, from whom he acknowledges having received much stimulation, he was the first systematic philosopher of Germany who gave psychology a prominent and foremost place in his speculations, and who made important contributions to empirical psychology.[1] Psy-

48.
Approaches philosophy from the side of medicine.

49.
Connection with the classical period.

[1] The broad view which Lotze took of psychological problems has hardly been sufficiently recognised by historians of philosophy, and this for several reasons. His first elaborate tract (' Seele und Seelen-

chology was to him not a purely empirical science, as
it was to the English school; it had to solve the great
problems referring to the soul, and was thus related
to metaphysics.[1] It is therefore not to be wondered at

leben') on the subject was published in the third volume of Rudolf Wagner's Dictionary in the year 1846. His latest contribution is the third section of his 'Metaphysics,' published in 1879 as the second volume of his (uncompleted) 'System of Philosophy.' Between these two publications, embracing a period of thirty-three years, there lie the Works, through which he became better known in wider circles, notably his 'Medical Psychology,' his 'Microcosmos,' and his courses of lectures, regularly delivered annually on the subject. Of these, in their final and most matured form, a syllabus was published after Lotze's death by Prof. Rehnisch of Göttingen. The inspection, however, of different copies of the lecture notes taken down by hearers shows that he approached and introduced the subject variously from different sides. Also the publication of the 'Kleine Schriften' in four volumes by D. Peipers proves sufficiently that all through his literary career Lotze recurred again and again to psychology as one of the principal subjects of his philosophical interest. It was a disadvantage that his first tract, which mapped out as it were the field of psychological research, was buried in the volumes of a special psychological encyclopædia, whereas it really was addressed as much to philosophers as to naturalists. In this respect it had a similar fate to that which has befallen in this country Prof. James Ward's psychological treatises—buried in the volumes of the 'Britannica' or of 'Mind.' In both cases original psychological aspects and a definite programme

of research became better known only through those who came primarily under the influence of these suggestive treatises and elaborated some of their ideas in independent works. Another reason why Lotze's deeper psychological speculations were for a long time little known and frequently misunderstood is to be found in the fact that his name was mainly connected with his theory of "Local Signs," a hypothesis which led to much controversy and various emendations, and to which I drew attention in the chapter on the " Psycho-Physical view of Nature," in the second volume of this History, p. 507 et seq. That Lotze adhered, all through his many deliverances, to a metaphysical as a necessary counterpart of the purely empirical treatment of psychology, and that he gave expression to this in the latest of his Works, was also a reason for passing them by during a period which prided itself on having found its way out of metaphysics. That nevertheless such discussions are inevitable and recurrent has of late become evident in the most recent psychological literature in Germany as in other countries.

[1] The peculiarity of Lotze's psychological as also of his other writings and of his lectures consists to a large extent in this, that he seeks, first of all, clearly to define the subject of which he treats, and notably the main problems of which it forms the centre. Thus, in his earliest tract, he starts with the question, What is it that induces us to speak of the soul as a special entity ? This question he

that he should have been the first among the then living thinkers to take up the soul problem when it reached its acute form in the beginning of the second half of the century, and that a large portion of his writings should be devoted to effecting a clearance in the materialistic controversy.

The circumspection which is characteristic of his dealing with this as with many other polemical questions explains how he was frequently misunderstood, classed now with the materialists, now with the obdurate metaphysicians, and again called a disciple of Herbart or of Leibniz, or of other earlier or latter-day thinkers. Again, he has, though uninfluenced by them, some points in common with the French eclecticists ; adopting, as he

51.
His circum-
spection.

answers by insisting on three points. First, the existence of phenomena of consciousness which are utterly incomparable with those of the outer world ; secondly, the existence of a unity through which they are connected ; and thirdly, the active principle for which we claim a certain amount of freedom. He admits that the last is not a proven fact, as the two former ones are, but that it acquires its importance through the overwhelming ethical interests which attach to it. The problem of the soul is thus for him not a purely scientific one, as is the case with other subjects of research —it is one in which we have a special interest for reasons which lie beyond both the empirical and the metaphysical, the descriptive and the explanatory, treatment of the subject. At the end of his earliest tract he sums up the object of psychology in words something like these : a complete psychology would have to put and solve the following problems, (1) a dialectic deduction of the phenomena of

psychical life, and an interpretation of their ideal importance in the significant totality of things ; (2) a consideration of the phases of development of psychical life. This would include an investigation whether a reality is conceivable, the inner nature of which is not essentially psychical ; (3) a description of the physical and mechanical conditions with which in our observation the life of the soul is connected, a physiology of the soul ; (4) a mechanism of psychical life, leaving it doubtful whether this applies in all individual cases and is not dependent on subjective coefficients ; (5) a psychology of individualities such as has been hitherto left to works of fiction ; (6) a confirmation of our ideas referring to the fate of souls in the totality of things (see ' Kleine Schriften,' vol. ii. p. 203). These problems remained before the mind of Lotze through all his writings, but he is fully aware of the limits placed in the way of the solution of some of them.

does, valuable ideas from many and apparently antagonistic sources.   But he is distinguished from them by his
frequently successful endeavours to harmonise apparent
contrasts in a higher unity.   Thus we find that he was
early regarded as a protagonist for a mechanical view of
all phenomena, and that much later his metaphysical
position has been adopted by theologians of the positive
school.   Accordingly, his philosophical writings occupy,
not only in time but also in importance, a central
position in the philosophical thought of the nineteenth
century, and we shall in the sequel have again and
again to revert to them.[1]

As I said above, modern psychology may be dated
from the appearance of Lotze's writings.   But if we
wish to find out what is meant by modern psychology,
it is of interest to note the very different conceptions we meet with on this point.   I single out
three prominent writers who have delivered themselves
on the subject, and who may be considered as represent-

52.
Various lines
in recent
psychology.

[1] Outside of Germany the writings of Lotze have received most
attention in this country and in the
United States of America, least
in France.   Most of his important
works have been translated into
English, and have run through
several editions.   I am not aware
that of any of his larger works a
complete translation has been published in France, though prominent
thinkers, such as Renouvier, Fouillée,
and Boutroux, take note of his
teachings.   I regret that the latest
edition of the 'Encyclopædia
Britannica' contains only a mutilated reprint of an article I supplied in the year 1882.   It was
written shortly after the death of
Lotze, when the Syllabus of his
Lectures was not yet completely
published, and when little had been
written in the way of criticism even
in Germany.   Since that time a very
large literature has sprung up both
in German and in English, and a
great deal has been done to explain,
to criticise, and to make his teachings better known.   To some of
these important contributions I
shall have occasion to refer in the
sequel.   There seems to me no
doubt that the spirit and manner
of his speculation is more and more
entering into philosophical literature, and that a study even of his
less known writings would be
peculiarly appropriate in the present
state of thought in all the three
countries I am dealing with.

ing the three principal lines on which psychology has developed in the course of the last forty years. The first writer is M. Ribot in France, the second Professor James Ward in England, the third Eduard von Hartmann in Germany.

In dealing with them as representatives of three distinct lines of research, I shall have occasion to mention many other names, some of which are of equal importance. But it is impossible, in a field so largely cultivated as has been that of psychology within the last forty years, to do more than sample the fruits which it has produced. The choice also of special authors and writings is a matter of individual taste, and cannot avoid being to some extent casual.

It has been claimed for psychology that it has grown into an independent science, that it has become detached from the parent stock. If this is so, it consists like other sciences to a large extent of knowledge brought together from many sides and by many workers, but only partially systematised and unified. As it is the youngest of the sciences, its fragmentary nature will be more pronounced. It will stand, as it were, at the furthest end in that hierarchy of the sciences, specified by Comte, which begins with the most perfect of all natural sciences, viz., physical astronomy. M. Ribot, who has himself contributed largely to modern psychological literature, both from the physiological and introspective points of view, is well aware of this. Probably no two works have done more to diffuse clear ideas as to the different lines of psychological research than his treatise on ' Contemporary English Psychology,' which appeared in 1870, and that

53.
Ribot.

on 'Contemporary German Psychology,' which appeared in 1879. M. Taine had already vigorously opposed the French psychology of the eclectic school,[1] and he published in the same year with Ribot's first-named

[1] Hippolyte Adolphe Taine (1828-93) may perhaps be considered as the first among French thinkers of the second half of the nineteenth century who aroused renewed interest in the science of psychology. He did so by a series of articles which he published in the 'Revue de l'Instruction Publique' in the years 1855 and 1856, and which appeared as a separate volume in the beginning of the year 1857. It was a virulent attack on the official school of philosophy headed by Victor Cousin, dealing with Laromiguière, Royer Collard (un dictateur), Maine de Biran (un abstracteur de quintessence), Cousin (un orateur), and Jouffroy (un homme intérieur). The title of the first edition, 'Les Philosophes Français du XIXᵉ Siècle,' was changed in later editions to 'Les Philosophes Classiques au XIXᵉ Siècle en France.' He there shows how the valuable ideas of the eclectic school can be traced back to the writings of Condillac, and that what was added under the influence of Scottish and German thought by means of a brilliant rhetoric and great personal influence does not mark a substantial progress,—such must be attained by the methods successfully introduced in the natural sciences; but he does not adopt the Positivism of Comte, which at that time condemned all psychology, reducing it to a branch of physiology. It is interesting to note that he approves of the general scheme of Hegel, though condemning its metaphysical elaboration. The preface to a later edition he concludes by say-

ing : "Such is the idea of nature expounded by Hegel through myriads of hypotheses, accompanied by the impenetrable darkness of the most barbarous style, with a complete reversal of the natural movement of the mind. One comes to see that this philosophy has for its origin a certain notion of causality. I have tried here to justify and to apply this notion. I have neither here nor elsewhere tried to do anything more." In his later work, quoted in the text, he gave a specimen of this new psychology, being largely guided by the writings of John Stuart Mill and of Bain, whom he may be said to have introduced into France; but he goes beyond them by bringing in, at the end, a kind of metaphysic. Of this, Mill in his review of Taine's book ('Fortnightly Review,' July 1870, reprinted in 'Dissertations and Discussions,' vol. iv. p. 111) says : "When M. Taine goes on to claim for the first principles of other sciences — e.g., of mechanics — a similar origin and evidence to what he claims for those of geometry, and on the strength of that evidence attributes to them an absolute truth valid for the entire universe, and independent of the limits of experience, he falls into what seemed to us still greater fallacies." Through establishing psychology on an independent basis, and notably through his doctrine of the milieu, Taine stands out as one of the principal founders of that modified Positivism which, as we shall see in the sequel, plays such an important part in recent French thought.

treatise his celebrated work 'De l'Intelligence,' in which, in addition to the influence of Condillac, he had drawn attention to the writings of John Stuart Mill and Bain, to that branch of English thought which had developed independently, and which stood latterly as it were in opposition to the Scottish school favoured in France by the eclectics. M. Ribot, in introducing contemporary English psychology to French readers, does not refer to the Scottish school at all, and only just mentions by name Hamilton, Whewell, Mansel, and Ferrier. His main object is to deal with Mill, Spencer, Bain, and Lewes. As M. Taine introduced the philosophy of John Stuart Mill, so M. Ribot introduced that of Herbert Spencer into France; moreover, the two introductions which he prefixed to his two treatises constituted a kind of manifesto : the earlier one in favour of the inductive as against the older metaphysical method, the later one recommending the experimental methods which had been developed in Germany, notably by Fechner and Wundt. Accordingly he not only places both the English and the German development in opposition to what he calls the older or metaphysical psychology, but he also draws a sharp distinction between the purely introspective or analytical methods of the English school and the novel experimental and exact methods of the German school. Both, he maintains, make large use of physiological discoveries ; but he significantly remarks, that on the one side the English psychologists enlarge and interpret their introspective data by borrowing from the labours of physiologists, whereas the later leaders and representatives of the German school are physiologists who have advanced from the study of physiology to that of the phenomena of conscious life. Thus his German treatise deals almost entirely with physiological and experimental psychology, the development of the Herbartian school in the direction of the psychology of the objective mind receiving only short notice, and no mention being made of important psychological analyses of fundamental psychical forces such as are, *e.g.*, contained in the works of Schleiermacher, Feuerbach, Schopenhauer, and Von Hartmann. Nevertheless it may be noted here that the very different psychological analysis of the phenomena of religious life by the two first-named thinkers, and the emphasis laid by Schopenhauer on the will and by Von Hartmann on the unconscious, have probably done more to change and deepen our ideas on the life of the human soul than all the purely psychological analysis and researches of the introspective and experimental schools put together. So far as the experimental or exact methods are concerned, I have reported so fully upon them in the chapter on Psycho-Physics in the second volume of this History that I need not in this connection say anything more about them.

But M. Ribot and the school which he represents in France have enlarged the field of psychological research in a special direction, of which already the older French psychologists, who are classed among the "Idéologues," had a very distinct notion. In their writings we read of a definite branch of science called "Nosologie," a theory of disease, and of the importance of this science both for psychology and medicine. In fact, the tendency to treat of the abnormal states, both of the body and the

54.
Morbid
psychology.

mind, in the interest of psychological research, goes back to the age of the Encyclopædists, Diderot having written a treatise on the deaf and dumb. Nothing of importance, however, was done till, within recent times, and greatly under the influence of M. Ribot,[1] experi-

[1] Théodule-Armand Ribot (born 1839) had already in his earliest work, mentioned in the text, on 'Contemporary Psychology in England,' marked out on a large scale the field of psychological research in the following words (1st ed., p. 36) : "We may comprise first of all under the name of *general psychology* the study of the phenomena of consciousness ; sensations, thought, emotions, volitions, &c., considered under their most general aspects. This study, which must be the point of departure and the basis of all others, is the only one which so far has been cultivated by psychologists. It is, however, clear that general psychology must profit by all the discoveries in its subordinated branches. It will be completed, first of all, by a *comparative psychology*, of which we have tried to show the object and the importance ; further, by a study of anomalies or monstrosities, which we may term *psychological teratology*. It is needless to demonstrate how useful the study of deviations is for the complete understanding of phenomena ; but what is remarkable is the neglect of psychology on this point. Outside of the 'Letter on the Blind,' by Diderot, which does not give what it promises, the pages of Dugald Stewart on James Mitchell, and some scattered observations, psychology has completely closed its eyes to anomalies and exceptions. It is the physiologists who have drawn from the curious 'History of Laura Bridgman' the conclusions which it suggests ; conclusions quite contrary to the doctrine of transformed sensation, and which, founded on facts, are by no means in the vague style of ordinary arguments. A deaf or a blind man, one originally deprived of some sense, is he not a subject specially fit to be observed, and to which we can apply one of the most rigorous processes : the method of differences ? Have the study of cases of folly, though quite incomplete as yet, been so far fruitless ?"

In his later work on 'Contemporary German Psychology,' the term "experimental," which in the earlier treatise meant rather "empirical," the psychology of observation, than the psychology of experiment, is extended to embrace the new psychology of Germany, which has recourse in a measure to experiment. It is there argued that the older method "is powerless to pass much beyond the level of common-sense." As its main representative the works of Bain are specially commended. "It is in the largest and best sense a descriptive study. In Germany, on the contrary, those who are working to construct an empirical psychology accord little place to description. To characterise their work we must employ a term which has been much abused in our day, but which is proper here, *i.e.*, *physiological psychology*. Almost all of them are physiologists, who, with their habits of mind and the methods peculiar to their science, have touched upon *some points* of psychology" ('German Psy-

mental research in psychology was pushed into the region of pathology. In France, within the last thirty years, a whole literature has sprung up, cultivating the large region of nervous affections and mental maladies, constituting what may be called abnormal psychology, to which would also belong the psychology of criminality, of degeneration, and of such exceptional conditions as the hypnotic state, &c. M. Ribot himself has published valuable and original treatises on 'The Diseases of Memory' (1881), 'The Diseases of the Will' (1883), and 'The Diseases of Personality' (1885). As is well known, these writings have opened out quite a new field of research on the Continent, and have influenced many neighbouring provinces which belong to the borderland of psychology, law, and economics.[1]

chology,' &c., Eng. trans., by Baldwin, 1899, p. 12). But M. Ribot does not omit to mention that the German method of experiment touches only a certain limited region of facts, and does not touch the central group of psychical states. This has become more evident since that time. (See above, vol. ii. p. 523.)

[1] It must not, however, be inferred that M. Ribot takes a narrow view of the problems of philosophy, or that he, so far as we know, belongs to the school represented in Germany by Fries, Beneke, and, in more recent times, by Prof. Theodor Lipps, who desire to found all philosophy upon psychology. The large and comprehensive view which he takes of philosophy in general is shown by the fact that he started in 1876 the monthly 'Revue Philosophique de la France et de l'Etranger,' which although, especially in the beginning, favouring the new psychology, opens its pages to every philosophical opinion, and contains very important contributions by writers of very different schools ; also by the article he contributed to 'Mind' in the year 1877 on "Philosophy in France," in which he gives a most lucid analysis of the then existing schools of philosophical thought and their leaders. He there also refers to a thinker who since that time has gained increasing influence and, in a different way from M. Ribot himself, has brought some lines of French thought into closer contact with that of other European countries, notably with the movement which centres in Kant's 'Criticism.' This thinker is Charles Renouvier, who may be said to occupy in French thought a position similar to that of Lotze in Germany. In his 'Essais de Critique Générale' (1st ed. 1854-64), notably in the 2nd edition (1875-96, 8 vols.), he, by a careful and circumspect criticism of the different ways in which

Although in England this last-named branch of psychology has not remained unrepresented—as evidenced by the works of Henry Maudsley—the great bulk of psychological work has remained faithful to the traditions handed down since the time of Locke. It has remained essentially introspective, being an analysis of the normal individual mind. In the year 1876 a quarterly review was started under the title 'Mind,' and whilst this was intended to deal generally with philosophical subjects, it is significant that psychology is put into the foreground, for reasons clearly set out by the editor, Croom Robertson, in his introductory discourse. In fact, in England philosophy has—till quite recently—hardly professed to be anything else than philosophy of the human mind; but it has been found necessary to define, within this large domain, the narrower provinces which have shown themselves capable of special cultivation. Thus the older and common title of philosophy of the human mind has been imperceptibly supplanted by other titles describing treatises which deal with special well-marked phenomena. Among these psychology and ethics are the most important. A separate analysis of the processes of scientific reasoning had been given by J. S. Mill, and A. Bain had in his

55.
'Mind' and Croom Robertson.

the great philosophical problems have been approached, tries to clear the ground for the new philosophy, of which his ethical treatise, 'La Science de la Morale' (2 vols., 1869), is the most important outcome. We shall see in the sequel how it has gained considerable influence, especially in the teaching of morals in the modern French schools. So far as psychology is concerned, the second portion of the 'Critique Générale' deals with this subject, but, as is the case in Lotze's metaphysics, rather from a rational than a purely empirical point of view, dealing with such questions as the Essence and Nature of the Soul, Certitude and Free Will—subjects not infrequently excluded altogether from modern works on psychology.

two monumental works dealt with psychological phenomena in a purely descriptive and analytical fashion,
working much with the principle of Association. General
questions as to the Soul, its nature and destiny, are
not discussed, being considered as metaphysical. But
about the same time the necessity was felt of dealing
with the general and fundamental problems of knowing
and being in an independent way. In the same degree
as psychology has been made a special science, general
philosophy and epistemology have received due attention
from a different point of view and not infrequently by
the same thinkers.

The History of Philosophical Thought takes interest
in Psychology from two distinct points of view, which
are the same as it occupies with regard to all natural
science. This twofold aspect has become more clearly
defined, in the same degree as psychology has become a
distinct science. So far as the researches of this special
science are concerned, these lie outside and are independent of philosophical reasoning, and will, like the
researches in other natural sciences, change with the
progress of empirical knowledge and the facts disclosed
by observation, experiment, and analysis. But, like all
other sciences, psychology must start with certain fundamental conceptions, in the light of which the growing
mass of detail accumulated by external and internal
observation, or by historical records, is arranged, classified,
and made accessible for the purpose of deductive reasoning. Philosophy interests itself, firstly, in clearly setting
out those fundamental notions, criticising them, and
defining their scope and value, just in the same way as

it recognises, criticises, and appreciates the fundamental notions forming the starting ground in the
sciences of dynamics, physics, chemistry, biology, &c.
The second interest which philosophy takes in the
researches of psychology, as they are now very generally
carried on, is to answer the questions which, in this
chapter, we have specifically defined as the Psychological
Problem, the nature and essence of that special something which we term the Mind or Soul. In one of the
following chapters we shall, in a similar way, deal with
the Problem of Nature, *i.e.*, with attempts which have
been put forward all through the century to answer
questions as to Nature as a whole, its relation to Mind,
which it, from one point of view, includes as much as
from another point of view it is differentiated from it.

Now, so far as the first philosophical interest is concerned, no one has done more to pass in review and
criticise existing fundamental notions in psychology, and
to prepare the ground for more adequate scientific treatment, than Prof. James Ward of Cambridge. In several
articles which he published in 'Mind'[1] on "Psychological
Principles," he prepared his readers for an original and
comprehensive sketch of modern psychology, which he
gave in his article on "Psychology" in the 'Encyclopædia Britannica' (1886).[2] This article may be looked
upon as a kind of manifesto, as a programme for

56.
James Ward.

[1] "Psychological Principles"
('Mind,' vol. viii., 1883, and vol. xiii.,
1888); "Modern Psychology, a Reflection" (vol. ii., N.S.); "Assimilation and Association" (ibid., and
vol. iii.)

[2] The article was followed in the
10th ed. of the 'Britannica' by an
account of the general progress made
in psychology during the last fifteen
years of the century. The latest
edition of the 'Britannica' contains
(vol. xxii. pp. 547-604) a very condensed but comprehensive sketch
of psychological theory at the
present moment.

modern psychological work. In the carrying out of some parts of this programme no one has been more successful than Prof. Stout.[1] The new programme breaks with all the older psychologies, which it nevertheless estimates at their full value as preparatory phases in the development of the independent science of psychology. It will be useful to state shortly the main characteristics as they have been most clearly explained by Prof. Ward on repeated occasions. To begin with, the new psychology should discard all metaphysical questions as to the soul, its substance, essence, or destiny. At the same time it has regard to, and implies, a subjective reference.[2] It

[1] Notably in his 'Analytic Psychology' (2 vols., 1896). It is surprising to see how little the original contributions of Prof. Ward, in laying new foundations for psychological research, have so far been noticed in German and French literature. Prof. Stout himself admits Ward's great influence on his own work, and Prof. Wm. James in his 'Principles of Psychology' (vol. ii. p. 282, 1891) refers to Ward's article in the 'Britannica' as one to which he would have owed much had it appeared before his own thoughts were written down. Through his psychological treatises, as well as through his epistemological work ('Naturalism and Agnosticism,' being the Gifford Lectures for 1896-1898 at Aberdeen), we may consider Ward as occupying a position similar to that of Lotze in German and of Renouvier in French philosophical literature, representing on a comprehensive scale the inevitable criticism called forth by the uncritical use, as fundamental notions, of a great variety of conceptions in psychological, logical, and epistemological discussions in the existing schools of philosophical thought. This work had already been begun by John Stuart Mill, and to some extent by Sir Wm. Hamilton in Scottish philosophy. The fact, however, that Mill had somewhat prematurely adopted his father's Associationism in psychology, and Hamilton similarly a somewhat confused version of Kantism, had prevented both these thinkers from impartially and exhaustively reviewing the situation before they ventured on their own constructive speculations. In both cases, however, very striking dilemmas or paradoxes were the result of premature generalisations, and these as well as those handed down in the writings of Hume have furnished valuable material to Prof. Ward for his timely criticism.

[2] Prof. Sorley informs me that in one of his earliest writings ('A General Analysis of Mind,' privately printed in 1880, published in the 'Journal of Speculative Philosophy,' 1882) Ward remarks that, in previous works on psychology, "though the special analyses and descriptions are excellent, the *tout ensemble* of mind is never exhibited at all;

deals with the facts of consciousness, meaning by consciousness the individual self. To avoid falling back
into a discussion of abstract consciousness, the object of consciousness is defined as that continuum of
(sensory and motor) presentations which to every person
constitutes his actual self, as known by him. By introducing this term in the place of the more familiar expressions such as soul, mind, consciousness, ideas,
&c., the various tendencies of older psychologies to
become metaphysical, abstract, or intellectualistic, are
guarded against. Further, by speaking of feeling, knowing, and doing, instead of the intellect and the will, the
older faculty-psychology is avoided; the conception of a
continuum, instead of that of separate sensations and ideas,
guards the psychologist against that atomistic conception
of the mental life which was common to the association-
psychology in England, and to the psychology of the
school of Herbart abroad.[1] It is characteristic of Ward

we lose sight of the wood among
the trees" (p. 366); and he there
puts forward the view, afterwards
elaborated by him, that in every
concrete "state of mind" there is
presentation of an object or complex of objects to a subject; this
presentation entailing, on the part
of the subject, both attention and
change of feeling (i.e., pleasure or
pain). By "subject" in this connection, he proposes to "denote the
simple fact that everything mental
is referred to a self" (p. 368); but
adds that "it must be allowed that
the attempt to legitimate this conception as a constituent element
of experience is as much beyond
the range of psychology as the
attempt to invalidate it even as
a formal or regulative conception.
If Hume is wrong on the one side,

Reid is equally at fault on the
other" (p. 369).

[1] Although the metaphysical conception of the soul is discarded,
there remains in Ward's fundamental psychological position the
primary dualism of subject and
object; the former as a central and
uniting point of reference, the "I"
of our language as the knowing,
feeling, and willing subject which
in and through this knowing, feeling, and willing is connected with
and stands over against its sensory
or motor-presentations or objects.
Through this scheme the atomising
tendency of the older faculty-psychology, which analysed the one
subject into a variety of distinct
powers or forces, is quite as much
avoided as, on the other side,
through the idea of the continuum

to make a systematic attempt to elaborate psychology as
an independent science ; in this he contrasts with some
of his predecessors (*e.g.*, Bain), who endeavoured equally
to give scientific character to psychology, but helped
themselves out by reference to physiological facts.
Great care is also taken to get behind the words and
terms of language which are habitually used in describing mental states, and which have the tendency to put in
the place of the inner world an artificial and conventional picture or image of it.[1]

In his more recent deliverances on the subject Prof.
Ward gives further precision to the definition of
psychology as an analysis of individual experience. In
emphasising individual experience as not consisting of
definite and separated sensations or ideas, but as a
continuum or a plenum, a new problem arises for the
psychologist which did not exist for earlier schools, which,
starting from verbal expressions, dealt with what might

(or actual together) of presentations, the disintegration of the
association-psychology is got over.

[1] One of the most important
deliverances of Ward, especially for
an historian of thought, is his
article in 'Mind' (1893, p. 54),
entitled "Modern Psychology: a
Reflection." It was occasioned by
a controversy started in Germany
among the followers of Prof. Wundt
over the theory of the latter regarding apperception and his search for
a centre or organ of apperception.
Some of his disciples have not been
able to follow him into this speculation, which indicates the difficulty
of all purely psycho-physical or
physiological psychology in finding
an expression for, and dealing with,
the unity of mental life. In fact,
they cannot find an entry into that
central region which has always
been held sacred by the introspective school. "Spite of all," Ward
says, "there are, I believe, good
grounds for the view that the difference as regards the immediacy
between feeling and presentation
is a difference of kind ; that feeling
is not obscure cognition nor sensation objectified feeling ; that feeling, in a word, is always subjective
and sensations always objective,
objective of course I mean in a
psychological sense. According to
this view, the duality of consciousness or the antithesis of subject
and object is fundamental ; according to the opposite view, the difference of subject and object gradually
'emerges' as the result of development or 'differentiation'" ('Mind,'
1893, p. 62).

appear to them to be individual things or elements [1] in the human mind. The problem which arises is to explain how in this continual flow of the inner states, in this continuum of presentations, it comes that we single out and fix upon definite portions which, with the help of words, signs, and symbols, we are able to isolate and to describe. This is effected by the process of attention, of interest, or of conation. This brings at once the active factor into play. What in the older schools of psychology was looked upon as the passive and purely receptive side of mental life has disappeared. Not only do we hereby abandon Locke's *tabula rasa*, the unwritten sheet, but we do not separate and treat separately the intellect and the will in the way that even writers like Bain have still done.

And lastly, the new psychology has come under the influence of the genetic view of nature, not only inasmuch as it studies the genesis of individual experience through infancy and childhood, but also by recognising the existence of other and lower experiences than our own. These lead us to believe that, just like the external forms of organic life, the phenomena of consciousness or of individual experience are subject to the general law of development.[2]

---

[1] Faculties or powers on the subjective side ; separate sensations or ideas with their combinations or associations on the objective side. The whole of Ward's psychology may be considered as one of the most brilliant examples of the modern tendency of thought mentioned above (p. 104), to look at things in their "together" instead of in their isolation ; of the synoptical as against the analytical and synthetical view.

[2] The fact that psychology has come under the influence of the genetic view of phenomena not only enlarges very much the region of psychological research ; it also separates it once for all from any theory of knowledge. "Comparing psychology and epistemology, we may say that the former

57.
Avenarius.

In dealing with modern empirical psychology, I have confined myself mainly to the work of English thinkers, and notably to the expositions of James Ward. A movement in many ways similar has taken place among German psychologists; though perhaps nowhere in their voluminous writings has the matter been so simply and lucidly dealt with as in the expositions given in English philosophical literature. In Germany the philosophy of Richard Avenarius [1] aims apparently at a similar reduction

is essentially genetic in its method, and might, if we had the power to revise our existing terminology, be called biology; the latter, on the other hand, is essentially devoid of everything historical, and treats *sub specie æternitatis*, as Spinoza might have said, of human knowledge, conceived as the possession of 'mind' in general. The principles of psychology are part of the material, the logical worth and position of which a theory of knowledge has to assign; but they are not, neither do they furnish, the critical canons by which knowledge is to be tested. Yet, in three several ways, epistemology has been supposed to depend upon psychology, in so far, viz., as psychology might explain the origin of knowledge, the process of knowing, or the limits of the knowable. But it can answer none of these questions in the way required. To ask them at all betrays serious misconception as to the nature of psychology. . . . So far, knowledge has contained the means of its own advance, and mere psychology cannot tell us whether this is to hold always or must cease at some point, while there remain possibilities of knowledge still beyond. Psychology seems, in fact, far more intimately related to metaphysics, that is to say, to theories about being and

becoming, than to theories of knowledge" (J. Ward, "Psychological Principles,"—'Mind,' 1883, p. 167).

[1] Born 1843, Avenarius died 1896, as Professor of Philosophy, at Zürich. His philosophy, which certainly possesses the merit of originality both in form and substance, was elaborated under the influence of the different lines of thought which prevail in modern scientific and philosophical literature. Thus we find such heterogeneous aspects as the physiological (through Ludwig), the purely physical and descriptive (through Kirchhoff and Mach), the Herbartian (through Drobisch), and, above all, the pantheistic or parallelistic of Spinoza, brought together. The modern conception of science and philosophy as a unification of knowledge or thought takes with him the form of "economy of thought," as, in consequence of the limited nature of the human intellect, a condensation and simplification of ideas is inevitably called for. It seems, therefore, as if his object was to reduce the complex mass of our intellectual conceptions to a minimum of what he terms "pure" experience; the latter is, therefore, not, as in Kant's conception of pure reason, the fundamental endowment of the human mind; it is rather the ultimate outcome of a purifying process of

of psychology and philosophy to an analysis of experience, but with the fundamental difference that what is aimed at is not an analysis of individual experience, as with Ward, but an analysis of pure experience. The title of his great work as a ' Critique of Pure Experience ' reminds one of Kant's ' Critique of Pure Reason.' As Kant set himself the task of finding out the innate forms of the reasoning intellect, so Avenarius tries to arrive at a description of pure experience, *i.e.*, of such experience as is not contaminated and mixed up with a whole host of conceptions, images, and ideas, which are imported through tradition and habit and elaborated by fanciful analogies. Unfortunately the style of Avenarius' writings is no less peculiar than that of Kant's Critique, and it remains to be seen whether his disciples will succeed in extricating an intelligible and useful set of important and

analysis towards which we approach, but which is, after all, only a distant ideal. There seems no doubt that Avenarius was much influenced by the success attained in the abstract sciences of nature through reduction of qualitative to quantitative differences. Prof. Höffding in his independent statement of Avenarius' speculation (' Moderne Philosophen,' pp. 117-27) characterises it as the natural history of problems ; the attempt to show how, through the want of equilibrium between the external (physical) and the internal (psychical) series of events or processes, the desire and need for equalisation is produced. Through a repeated study of Avenarius' works, as also through personal intercourse with him, Höffding has come to the conclusion (against Wundt) that Avenarius cannot be stigmatised as a materialist, inasmuch as he himself declared that he knew neither the "physical" nor the "psychical," but only a third something. Nevertheless it has to be admitted that the attempt to penetrate from outside, from the brain processes to the mind processes, gives the whole the appearance of a purely physiological treatment. " This relation between psychology and physiology is characteristic, and contains a significant warning against the view that it would be more scientific in questions of this kind to proclaim the ' biological' as the only correct method " (Höffding, *loc. cit.*, p. 122). A very interesting though somewhat acrid criticism of modern psychology in Germany, from the position indicated by Avenarius, will be found in Rudolf Willy, ' Die Krisis in der Psychologie ' (1899). Hardly any notice is taken of modern English or French psychological work.

novel ideas. So far, their activity has consisted mostly in criticising the positions taken up by other leading psychologists, most of whom, they maintain, have not sufficiently liberated themselves from the metaphysical bias, and are continually falling back into fanciful speculations. The philosopher who has done most to give the general reader some conception of the deeper meaning which lies hidden behind the forbidding terminology of Avenarius is the Danish professor, Harold Höffding, who, in two recent works on 'Modern Philosophers' and 'Philosophical Problems,' refers at some length to the 'Critique of Pure Experience.' From these expositions we gather that the way adopted by Avenarius lies in the direction of a minute analysis of the physiological basis of the psychical processes. As such, it would hardly be acceptable to psychologists in this country, who have persistently upheld the introspective method, aided indeed by indications and suggestions furnished by physiology.

But the persistent polemics which are carried on abroad, as to the intrusion of metaphysics into psychological research, are indicative of a tendency of thought which, though continually criticised, will nevertheless continually recur. The question as to the essence, the *quid proprium*, of the inner life, will always be asked, and if psychology, as the analysis of " individual " or of " pure " experience, cannot give it, it will have to be sought elsewhere. Further, the position of the individual mind, or rather of individual minds in their collective existence as human society, in the whole economy of nature, and the developments of history, is also a question of such abiding interest that it will become inevitable to try to gain a higher point of view from which to judge the totality of mental life in its individual and collective appearance. These two problems, the essence of the inner life, of the soul, and its significance in the economy and connection of things, may be termed transcendental so far as the limits are concerned within which individual experience is confined. They characterise two independent lines of thought and constitute two independent fields of research by which psychological studies must be supplemented. Both were represented in the philosophy of Lotze. We may call the first, rational psychology, the second, anthropology.

In all the three countries we have, at the end of the century, to deal with prominent speculations as to the essence and main characteristic of mental life. We have in Germany, von Hartmann's 'Psychology of the Unconscious'; in England, Herbert Spencer's 'Psychology of Evolution'; and in France, M. Fouillée's 'Psychologie des Idées Forces.' None of the governing ideas contained in these speculations have been elaborated by purely introspective analysis. They are based upon generalisations arrived at from various sources, and afterwards supported by a more or less exhaustive survey of facts brought together from many sides; the natural sciences with their large accumulation of novel facts arrayed under the recent theories of energy and descent having been made to furnish valuable contributions. The 'Philosophy of Evolution' of Herbert Spencer originated in the genetic or genealogical view of nature, which was put forward in the beginning of the second half of the century from many sides, and which Spencer

58.
Hartmann,
Spencer, and
Fouillée.

himself embraced in a definite form before the idea had received general currency through the writings of Darwin and the watchwords of the Darwinian school. Herbert Spencer's psychology consists in an application of the metaphysical canons of the theory of evolution to the phenomena of mental life, which he maintains cannot be understood if we confine ourselves to a study of the individual mind. He had come to this study from that of human society, its history and progress. The latter he had attempted to analyse and comprehend by resorting to biological analogies. He thus illustrates the two points just referred to, viz.: that the study of the individual mental life must be enlivened by gaining from elsewhere the clue to its nature and significance, as also by looking at its collective existence in human society. The psychology of Herbert Spencer is an instructive example how, alongside—if not in the midst—of inductive and introspective schools of thought, a metaphysical construction could grow and flourish with much greater practical results and popular influence than the more cautious and sober teachings of those schools could ever boast of.

The historical antecedents of the two other philosophies, of those of von Hartmann in Germany and M. Fouillée in France, are to be found in the idealistic philosophy. In the case of M. Fouillée we have to go back to the source of all idealism, the ideology of Plato. His object is " to bring Plato's ideas from heaven on to the earth and to reconcile idealism and materialism." His psychology has been regarded as the best exposition of the psychology of voluntarism, *i.e.*, of that tendency in modern

marginalia:
59. Spencer's evolutional psychology.

60. Idealistic antecedents of Hartmann and Fouillée.

thought to look upon the will, the active principle, as the determining factor of all mental life which—as I stated above—plays an important part in what was once erroneously considered its purely receptive side. Still less purely psychological or realistic is the philosophy of Eduard von Hartmann. He considers the purely scientific mode of proceeding to be insufficient, and resorts to the assumption of an unconscious power which makes itself felt throughout the whole physical and mental world, and by which all the chasms left in our empirical knowledge of nature and mind are filled up. The terms and conceptions by which we in ordinary language describe the more mysterious sides of physical and mental life, such as instinct, natural selection, association of ideas, voluntary impulse, individual genius, and creative power, are all traced back to the working of the Unconscious.

The principles of von Hartmann's philosophy, which has had great influence abroad, especially in extra-academic circles, will occupy us in some of the following chapters. In the meantime it is interesting to note how von Hartmann himself has given an exhaustive review of modern German psychology. In this review he tries to show how modern German psychology, which he dates from Fechner and Lotze, is slowly but inevitably approaching recognition of the unconscious element. The main points of interest in modern psychology he considers to be the importance and scope of the doctrine of the unconscious, its relation to conscious mental processes, and the part it plays in all the principal psychological problems, such as, *e.g.*, the relation of willing to other mental processes, the problem of the

61.
The Unconscious in psychology.

unity of mental life, of psycho-physical parallelism, &c. He considers that in the second half of the nineteenth century philosophical thought has progressed from the conception of a metaphysical unconscious to that of a psychological unconscious existence. The difference between the treatment of the history of modern psychology in the accounts of such writers as M. Ribot in France, Professor Baldwin in America, Rudolf Willy and von Hartmann in Germany, and James Ward in England, is truly significant and instructive.[1] In spite of violent opposition and the persistent determination on the part of professional psychologists to ignore von Hartmann's ideas, some of the leading thinkers of the day have introduced the conception of the unconscious into their psychological discussions. It is already apparent that, under different names, the conception of the unconscious is gradually becoming domiciled in psychological treatises,[2] even if it should be no more

[1] Perhaps the most instructive piece of writing on the problems of modern psychology is to be found in Jas. Ward's address before the section of General Psychology of the Congress of Arts and Sciences, held at St Louis, September 1904, reprinted in the 'Philosophical Review' (vol. xiii. pp. 603-621). Referring to the "actuality" theory of Wundt, "already more or less foreshadowed by Lotze," Ward takes up the fundamental dualism of subject and object, and refers to "three recent writers of mark," representing "three conflicting positions : (1) subject activity is a fact of experience, but psychology cannot deal with it because it is neither describable nor explicable ; (2) subject activity is not a fact of experience, but it is a transcendent reality without which psychology would be impossible ; (3) subject activity is neither phenomenal nor real ; the apparent 'originality' and 'spontaneity' of the individual mind is for psychology at any rate but the 'biologist's' 'tropisms.' " Ward concludes his article by saying that "the definition of psychology, the nature of subject activity, and the criticism of the atomistic theory, seem now fundamentally the most important" psychological problems.

[2] In English psychology the Herbartian term of the "threshold" or limit of consciousness, implied already in Leibniz' conception of the *petites perceptions*, or, as it were, the twilight of consciousness, has been domiciled in such expressions as the "subconscious" or "subliminal." In Germany, the majority

than a name for the intrinsic mystery which is also the most characteristic feature of the inner life. The most important psychical phenomenon which forces us to lay our account with the unconscious is the phenomenon of memory. In a study of this phenomenon, unique in the large circumference of the inner life, we may hope to gain clearer notions of that central and paradoxical fact that the main characteristic of consciousness is to include the unconscious.

Having now arrived at the latest positions taken up with regard to the inner life of the human mind, it may be of value to my readers if I briefly state in what the great changes consist which, during the nineteenth century, have come over our conceptions of the inner world or of the soul.

First, then, the discussion of the soul-problem as it was carried on in the middle of the century, notably in Germany, has resulted in a distinct change in the vocabulary which we make use of in psychology. The word soul has almost disappeared out of psychological treatises, and, if the soul-theory is still occasionally

62.
Change in vocabulary.

of psychologists are still opposed to the introduction of anything suggesting the unconscious element into psychological discussion. A notable instance is the endeavour to identify the soul with consciousness, as is very ably done (otherwise not without some similarity to James Ward's position) by J. Rehmke, who, in his very interesting tract, "Die Seele des Menschen" (3rd ed., 1909), takes the term soul *au sérieux*, but subsequently identifies it with consciousness. Helmholtz, fifty years ago, adopted the notion of unconscious logical processes in the mind to explain certain phenomena of sensation and perception, and Wundt followed him, but subsequently dropped this conception. Prof. Stout, on his part, has introduced the term "anoetic" (see his ' Analytic Psychology,' vol. i. p. 171). A very interesting examination of the whole question will be found in Prof. Theodor Lipps' address to the Third International Congress for Psychology, held at Munich, 1896 : ' Der Begriff des Unbewussten in der Psychologie ' (Report, p. 146).

referred to, it is admitted that in modern psychology, *i.e.*, in the methodical study of the phenomena of the inner life, we can dispense with that time-honoured word. Psychology, instead of being the doctrine of the soul or of the mind, is now variously described as a treatment of the individual human self, as a study of the things of the inner world, as that of the normal flow of consciousness, of the unity of thinking, feeling, and willing, or, lastly, as the science of individual experience. All these definitions, if we contrast them with those that were in use in the older treatises of the soul, agree in this, that the object of psychology is not a definite thing, but a series of occurrences or happenings which make up the continuous stream of our conscious life; more or less importance being at the same time attached to the intervals or the background of unconsciousness, and the breaks in the continuity by which the conscious and continuous flow is accompanied or interrupted.

Secondly, the older conceptions, which divided the subjective unity of mind into different faculties or the objective field into separate sensations or ideas, have been abandoned; it being more and more recognised that thinking, feeling, and willing are not in reality distinctly marked off, but that they proceed through continual interchange, alternation, and blending. In two distinct directions modern psychological treatises stand in a marked contrast to the earlier ones. The intellectual process is now generally conceived as being dependent quite as much on the active as on the receptive functions of the human mind. And, so far as feeling is concerned, it now receives much more attention from psychologists

63.
Stress laid
on activity
and feeling.

than it used to do. I shall have occasion to refer to this latter class of psychological writings when treating of the psychology of religious experience.

Thirdly, as the treatment of separate faculties and separate sensations has been replaced by the study of the presentation-continuum of experience and the stream of thought, so the study of the single human individual has expanded to a study of the collective life in human society. Psychology is more and more extending in the direction of anthropology.

64.
Presenta-
tion-con-
tinuum.

65.
Anthrop-
ology.

Whilst all these characteristic features of modern psychology emphasise the continuity of mental life, the great fact of individuality, personality, of the unity of self, stands out as the highest unexplained phenomenon. No scientific theory can explain away the discontinuity of separate individual existences. This seems to consti- tute the very characteristic, the *quid proprium*, of the individual soul or mind, and not only are we apt to lose sight of this discontinuity through the modern scientific methods of studying the inner life; we have also to face the fact that the whole interest of mental existence lies in qualitative differences, and in sudden and unexpected occurrences, the products of individual energy and the creations of imagination, *i.e.*, in phenomena of discon- tinuity. No one has given clearer expression to this characteristic of mental life than Charles Renouvier, and Professor Höffding has drawn special attention to the psychological aspect of the problem of discontinuity. In respect of this he says, " The relation of continuity and discontinuity touches the highest interest of personality as well as of science. In both directions we aim at

66.
Discon-
tinuity—
Renouvier.

unity and connectedness; and in this regard the discontinuous appears as an obstacle which has to be overcome.   On the other side it is just this discontinuity (difference of time, of degree, of place, of quality, of individuality) which everywhere, in the realms of science as well as of life, brings something new, releases the bound-up forces, and places before us the great tasks. Neither of the two elements appears *prima facie* to be the only legitimate one, and it is of undoubted interest to follow up their mutual relations from different points of view.   In the philosophy of the nineteenth century the importance of the continuity problem stands out characteristically.   In the first half of the century philosophical Idealism insisted in its own way on the continuity of existence, and looked down upon empirical science on account of its fragmentary character, whilst positivism (as upheld by Comte and Stuart Mill) emphasised the discontinuity of the different groups of phenomena.   Towards the end of the century it is Realism which, with the help of the evolution hypothesis, urges continuity, whereas the idealistic school is inclined to lay stress upon the inevitable discontinuity of our knowledge.   In this way the different directions of thought change their position in the great contest through which truth is to be won." [1]

It is evident from this that the highest psychological problems lead us out of psychology into other and more general regions of thought.   Not only are we told that psychology proper has nothing to do with the soul, *i.e.*, with the essence of the inner life, but wherever this

[1] Höffding, ' Philosophische Probleme,' p. 5.

problem is touched upon by recent thinkers we see how they find it necessary to approach the subject from an outside, not purely psychological, point of view. In fact we are referred to a discussion of what constitutes Reality. This is the main problem of metaphysics. On the other side such terms as unity and continuity point to distinctions which the thinking mind imports into its consideration of every matter with which it deals. Accordingly we find that psychological analysis leads on the one side to metaphysical discussions and on the other to a more minute examination of the methods of thought and the processes of acquiring knowledge. In some cases these two interests have entirely cast into the shade the purely psychological aims. It will now be necessary for us to take up separately these two problems : the problem of Knowledge and the problem of Reality, into both of which the nineteenth century has introduced novel and interesting points of view.

CHAPTER IV.

OF KNOWLEDGE.

I.

OF all the processes in the inner life of the human mind, those referring to knowledge have always attracted the greatest attention of thinkers. At a very early age of philosophical thought, the problems of the nature and origin of knowledge, of the means of acquiring it, and of the difference between correct and incorrect, useful and useless knowledge, have presented themselves as amongst the most important questions in philosophy. Nor does it seem as if, in spite of the very advanced nature of the speculations referring to this subject in ancient philosophy, the problem of knowledge, of its nature, its origin, and its usefulness, has at all lost its freshness, its interest, or its difficulties. Thus we find that also during the nineteenth century the problem of knowledge has again been attacked by foremost thinkers with much eagerness, and that various solutions have been attempted. It has even been maintained that theory of knowledge formed the characteristic occupation and the most important outcome of philosophical thought during the nineteenth

1.
Early appearance of the problem of knowledge.

2.
Re-emergence characteristic of nineteenth century.

century. This assertion might justify itself by pointing to a number of new terms introduced into philosophical language referring to the subject in question. From this point of view Kant's critical labours have been appraised and represented as the starting-point for the later contributions of Continental thinkers; whereas in this country the earlier studies dealing with this subject are more directly connected with the writings of Bacon, Locke, and Hume, to which Kant himself was likewise largely indebted.

During the last years of the eighteenth century Fichte had introduced the problem of knowledge under the new term and conception of *Wissenschaftslehre*,[1] professing that such was no more than a general theory of methodical knowledge (termed in German *Wissen-*

3.
Fichte's
Wissen-
schaftslehre.

[1] The term *Wissenschaftslehre* appears for the first time in 1794, in Fichte's correspondence with Reinhold, and had probably been fixed upon during a course of Lectures which he delivered at Zürich before a small circle of friends interested in his philosophy. These included Lavater, the physiognomist. Shortly after that time Fichte was installed at Weimar in the chair vacated by Reinhold, and there he published his first tract "On the Conception of *Wissenschaftslehre* or the so-called Philosophy" as a syllabus for the attenders of his Lectures. It was republished four years later with a new explanatory preface. In this tract he defines his aim as being to give to philosophy, as a science, unity and certainty, or necessary connection. This undertaking, the success of which he hypothetically supposes, and which he intends to establish, should warrant a new name in order to distinguish it from existing sciences and from existing philosophy as a preliminary investigation. Should such a fundamental science be possible, it would deserve, he says, to "drop the name which it hitherto bore in consequence of a by no means exaggerated modesty. . . . The nation which should invent such a science would indeed deserve to give it a name in its own tongue, and it might well be called *die Wissenschaft* (*i.e.*, science *par excellence*) or *Wissenschaftslehre*" (Fichte, 'Werke,' vol. i. p. 44). In a note he also indicates that through such an achievement the nation and its language would attain to a distinct preponderance over other languages. In passing it may be noticed that not the term chosen by Fichte but the later one of *Erkenntnisstheorie* has in a manner attained to the leading position he indicates, though both terms share the disadvantage of not being easily and intelligibly translatable into other languages.

4.
Erkennt-
nisstheorie.

schaft or Science) in the spirit of Kant's own speculations. Sixty years later the term *Erkenntnisstheorie*
(in English Epistemology) marks the beginning of a new
series of attempts to deal with the problem of knowledge, with the distinct aim of going back to Kant, of
reverting to the problem of the critical philosophy.
This direction of philosophical thought manifests itself
independently in all the three countries with which we
are mainly occupied. It was most loudly proclaimed
in Germany by F. A. Lange and supported by Eduard
Zeller, both having turned away from the metaphysical
systems of Kant's immediate successors. In this country
somewhat later the study of those very systems, which
Germany rejected, led the opponents of Mill, Comte,
and Spencer to go back to Kant as a necessary
preparation for carrying out more satisfactorily and
consistently the great scheme propounded by Hegel.

5.
Renouvier's
Neo-
criticism.

In France Charles Renouvier took up quite an original
and unique position in opposition to the prevailing
official philosophy of his country,[1] and in distinct recog-

---

[1] The foremost works referring
to this movement which have
appeared in Germany and in this
country are in general well known,
and have had a widespread influence.
But the equally important and
equally original labours of Renouvier
remained for a long time unknown
and unrecognised beyond a narrow
circle of followers in his own
country. And even there his influence as one of the leading thinkers
of recent times has only gradually
made its way. The reason, *inter
alia*, given for this, is that the
works of Renouvier are deficient in
style and elegance of expression,
defects which French literary taste

cannot forgive. See, *e.g.*, what M.
Ribot says in his otherwise appreciative mention of Renouvier in
'Mind,' 1877, vol. ii. p. 379 : "I
regret to have to state that in
France Renouvier's works have not
been sufficiently read, and that
they are far from obtaining the
success they deserve. The fault
lies in the author's style, and still
more in a want of art and composition, not easily forgiven by
French readers. It should be remarked, however, that of late years
the diffusion of his doctrines has
begun to make way ; not so much
perhaps on their own account, as
because they are related to the

nition of the beginning made by Kant. In this sense he termed his philosophy Neocriticism. We have thus Neo-Kantianism in Germany, Neo-Hegelianism in England, Neocriticism in France; all three starting with and putting into the foreground the theory of knowledge. It is interesting to note that neither of the two above-mentioned terms, neither *Wissenschaftslehre* nor *Erkenntnisstheorie*, has a current synonym in the French language, but, on the other side, that language has contributed largely to the fixing of modern views on the subject by the introduction of the term " Positivism," which denotes and characterises a special conception of the nature of knowledge, of which I shall have to say more in the sequel.

The contributions of this country to the terminology of the subject came later, but are probably more incisive and, for the general intelligence, more significant. Following upon Herbert Spencer's doctrine of the Unknowable, Huxley coined the term " Agnosticism," and towards the end of the century a very different turn was given to popular philosophical discussions by the introduction in this country of the American term

6.
Agnosticism and Pragmatism.

movement which is known by the name of Neo-Kantism in Germany, and of which the influence is now being felt in France." See also important articles " On Renouvier and French Criticism," by M. Beurier, in the 'Revue Philosophique,' vol. iii., 1877. In order to show the chronological sequence of works referring to the return to Kant in the three countries I give the following dates :—

1847. Ch. H. Weisse. 'In welchem Sinne die deutsche Philosophie jetzt wieder an

Kant sich zu orientieren hat.'
1854. Ch. Renouvier. 'Essais de Critique Générale.'
1862. Ed. Zeller. 'Ueber Bedeutung und Aufgabe der Erkenntnisstheorie.'
1866. F. A. Lange. 'Geschichte des Materialismus.'
1874. T. H. Green. 'Introduction to Hume's Treatise on Human Nature.'
1877. Ed. Caird. 'A Critical Account of the Philosophy of Kant.'

"Pragmatism." Whereas all the theories of knowledge emanating from Locke and Kant, both in England and abroad, treated the problem of knowledge by correlating Knowing and Being, or by contrasting Truth and Error, the new turn given to the treatment of the subject by the introduction of the term "Pragmatism" fastens upon the correlation of Knowing and Doing; leading us back to an early period of Greek philosophy.

7.
Preparation
in logic and
psychology.

Both in Germany and England, where the problems of knowledge have been, in recent times, independently attacked, leading to original theories, these discussions were preceded by minute and extensive logical and psychological studies; as witness the very large number of treatises pertaining to Logic and Psychology which had been published in both countries before the middle of the century. French philosophical literature, on the other hand, had during the period which preceded what we may call the "return to Kant," contributed no important works upon either Logic or Psychology.

It is indeed a remarkable literary phenomenon, well worthy of examination, that the nation whose language and literature excel all others in logical clearness, simplicity, and elegance, and which has exhibited in the domains of fiction and popular philosophy a large amount of psychological insight and refined analysis, should have, for a long period, produced hardly any exclusively psychological or logical treatises.

Although it is conceivable and has been the ambition of some thinkers that the process of knowledge should be approached in an unbiassed spirit, and studied in an unprejudiced manner as a definite object belonging to the natural history of the human mind, we can never-theless easily recognise how, in modern philosophy, the different theories of knowledge have sprung up under the distinct though frequently unconscious influence of those habits and tendencies of thought which, in general and scientific literature, were at the time most acceptable and dominating. And in this we may possibly find an explanation of the different ways on which leading thinkers have in different periods and countries approached the same problem. The *Wissenschaftslehre* of Fichte sprang up under the dominant impression of a great change which had recently taken place in men's minds, and which had found a partial expression in Kant's philosophy. But it was not an exclusively academic interest which directed Fichte's earliest speculations. Before he became, as he tells us, accidentally acquainted with Kant's philosophy, he had come under the influence of Lessing's theological polemics in Germany and of the educational interests which emanated from Rousseau in Switzerland. Both produced in him that mental unrest, that "storm and stress" which was common to many other prominent writers and thinkers of the day. He partook, in his way, of that yearning for liberty in religious belief and social life which was as widespread as it was indefinite. It was the problem of liberty which he tried to solve for himself. Inclined for a moment, under the influence of Spinoza, to adopt the determinist solution, he first found relief and satisfaction in Kant's doctrine of the higher life of the human mind in which it is able to assert its autonomy, or self-imposed law of duty and conduct. At that moment the storm of the Revolution

8.
Influence of
current
literature
and science.

9.
Effect of the
French
Revolution.

broke out in France, and brought with it more definite social and political problems. Fichte's first writings of importance referred to the religious problem and to the social problem. It was only after he had gained a considerable reputation through these writings that he found it necessary to lay a deeper foundation for his speculations by dealing with the fundamental problems approached by Kant. This was the origin of the *Wissenschaftslehre*. But what Fichte would have called the purely scientific and logical treatment of the fundamental question of knowledge was very soon interrupted by the influence of the creative, in opposition to the critical, spirit which sprang up in German literature, poetry, and art, and attained its greatest sway during his Jena period.

When, half a century later, the general interests of literature and science had undergone a great change in the direction of Realism, when the creative spirit had exhausted itself, we find philosophical thinkers approaching once more the problem of knowledge. But this time it is not the belief in an ideal world which strives for philosophical grasp and expression, but rather the new and rapidly growing region of knowledge opened out by the natural sciences and their exact mathematical treatment. It is no more the logic of the autonomous, nor that of the creative human mind, but the logic of patient observation and mathematical reasoning that is required; in fact, the ideas of knowledge have undergone a great change. The exact sciences begin to assume the position of types and models of the most perfect human knowledge, which the philosophical theory tries to understand,

10.
Later
dominance
of exact
science.

to formulate, and to explain. With the transition from the Idealism of the classical to the Realism of the exact period of thought, knowledge has, even in the eyes of the professedly unprejudiced thinker, acquired a different aspect, demanding a new Logic and a new Psychology.

If we now turn from German to British philosophy of the last hundred years, we find that a distinctly new effort to solve the problems of knowledge was put forward by John Stuart Mill, the first of a long line of psychologists and logicians, whose labours have largely influenced philosophical thought not only in this country but also abroad. But here again the tendencies of thought as exhibited in general literature exert a very distinct influence, not to say pressure, on the minds of even the most secluded thinkers. Two characteristics have here to be noted. The rapid growth of natural knowledge, based almost exclusively on observation and experiment, had already, in the eighteenth century, created a desire for an analogous study of the human mind and human nature, placing as it were the natural history of the human soul in a position parallel to that of the knowledge of external nature. Rightly or wrongly, it was generally thought that the Inductive methods of research, practised by the great naturalists and appraised by Bacon, furnished the principal instruments by which to attain correct and useful knowledge, and these inductive methods formed therefore a prominent aspect in the study of the problems of knowledge. But even more determining for these philosophical speculations was a second influence. This was the widespread atten-

11.
J. S. Mill.

tion which economic and social questions had attracted through the growing wealth, industry, and population of the country. It was with the distinct intention of contributing something towards the development of a political science that John Stuart Mill and many of his contemporaries and followers attacked the problem of human knowledge.

**12.
Influence
of social
questions.**

The influences which general literature and scientific thought exerted upon philosophy in France were quite different from those which existed in Germany or in England. Indeed, the most prominent characteristic which existed in the scientific thought of that country was almost entirely wanting both in Germany and England in the beginning of the century; although these countries had furnished in former centuries two brilliant examples in Newton and Leibniz. I refer to the mathematical spirit, the analytical as distinguished from the experimental method, which pervades the speculations of the greatest French philosophers such as Descartes, Pascal, and Malebranche, nay, even of Buffon and Voltaire. The analytical method had at the beginning of the century risen supreme, revealing its great power in the highly abstract, but also in the more popular works of Laplace and some of his contemporaries. Against this we find it, after the age of Newton and Leibniz, almost absent both in English and German philosophical thought.[1] In Germany the great genius who probably

**13.
Influence of
mathe-
matics in
France.**

[1] This generalisation might be objected to, considering that Germany had Euler and Gauss. But, to disregard the fact that Euler was not a German but a Swiss, it must be noted that he only indirectly influenced German thought as represented by the High Schools

represents nineteenth century thought more fully than
any other, who influenced men's minds more lastingly,
and gave them certainly a higher flight, that of Goethe,
sympathised with almost every fruitful line of thought
and aspiration except the mathematical. And in England also the wisdom of Bacon was blind to the power
of the mathematical methods. Thus it comes that what
was wanting in the theories of knowledge in the school
of Mill and had to be supplemented by his later followers was an appreciation of just that factor which
dominated French thought, being reflected in the best
style of some of the classical French writers. But the
clearness, simplicity, and elegance which this dominant
trait imparted to French thought misled it also into
the belief that psychological theories, in which English
and German philosophy abounded, were superfluous for
the attainment of exact knowledge, even in the region of
morals, economics, and politics. It led to that neglect
or contempt of logic and psychology which is characteristic of the positivism of Auguste Comte, whose ideal

and Universities ; he was an acade-
mician, not a professor, and passed
a great part of his life outside of
Germany. And as concerns Gauss,
he stood outside and above the
general current of German thought.
His earliest and most original mathematical work was written in Latin,
and was practically unknown in
Germany. He was a younger contemporary of Goethe, and, alongside of him, probably the greatest
German intellect of the age. Personally they seem to have been
unknown to each other, nor is there
any reference, so far as I know, in
the writings of either of them to
the other. The mathematical precision which Wolff gave to his
philosophical writings was purely
formal, as was also that of Spinoza,
after the manner of Euclid. The
modern analytical methods of
Leibniz, developed and perfected
by mathematicians such as the
Bernoullis and Euler, and most
successfully applied by French
physicists, remained, as it seems,
unknown to the majority of German mathematicians, and possibly
also to Kant. Even the study of
the ' Principia ' would hardly reveal
to him the power of the analytical
method.

of knowledge, like that of Laplace, was to be found in mathematical astronomy.[1]

14.
Reaction in
British
thought.

As a great change came over the ideals of human knowledge about the middle of the nineteenth century in Germany, so likewise a reaction set in in this country though somewhat later. It is frequently suggested that this was brought about largely through the tardy influence of German literature and philosophy.[2] But though this has no doubt been considerable, especially since

[1] I have in the first volume of this history (p. 237) given extracts from a pamphlet entitled ' On the Alleged Decline of Science in England' (1831) which bear upon this subject. It was published anonymously, but is known to have been written by Dr Moll of Utrecht. *Inter alia* he refers to the exclusive culture of the higher analysis promoted by the great teachers at the École Normale and to the discouragement of classical studies. See also page 149 as to the fate and the temporary suspension of the ' Académie des Sciences morales et politiques.' The idea that the philosophical sciences should be entirely founded upon the physical and natural sciences was not original, though it was fundamental in Comte's early positivism. " We find it everywhere at that time, with Vicq-d'Azyr, who treats psychology as a branch of physiology ; with Destutt de Tracy, who considers Ideology as a simple chapter of Zoology ; with Volney, who gives to his ' Catechism of Natural Law ' the sub-title ' Principles of Morals ' ; it is the last word of the sensationalism of the age, as it is of that of to-day. To these contested views Saint-Simon joins others which are extremely paradoxical and which border on the ridiculous. . . . God appears to him (he does not say whether in a dream or otherwise) in order to declare to him that Rome, the Pope, and the Cardinals have ceased to receive His inspirations, and that He will in future communicate them to a sacred college composed of twenty-one sages elected by entire humanity, and presided over by a mathematician. . . . The great Council will have, above all, the mission to study gravitation, the only law — if we may believe our author, who in this agrees with Charles Fourier — to which the universe is subjected, &c., &c." (Ferraz, ' Histoire de la Philosophie en France.' — ' Socialisme, &c.,' 3rd ed., 1882, p. 8 *sqq.*)

[2] " The German mind, awakened into *a priori* speculation by Leibniz, continued in it on the new lines of Kant, and from Kant to Hegel tended steadily towards the speculative construction and systematic unity of absolute all-explaining Idealism. This philosophy, introduced into Britain at first by Coleridge and by the criticisms of Hamilton, has . . . gradually transformed our insular manner of thinking, and inverted, for the time, Locke's ' plain, historical ' matter-of-fact procedure " (Fraser in ' Locke,' " Blackwood's Philosophical Classics," p. 286).

several of the outstanding works of that philosophy have been brought out in English translations, this alone would not account for the entirely altered attitude now taken up by prominent thinkers, in general philosophy as well as to the special problem of knowledge. The deeper cause of this change must indeed be sought in a different direction, and again in that pressure which the diffused thought of general literature, the clearer principles of science and the demands of practical life, exerted upon the most secluded and abstract philosophical speculation. In this instance what influenced philosophy was a circumstance to which I have had occasion to advert already in the foregoing chapters, namely, the growing necessity that was felt for the formation of a philosophical or reasoned creed.

Up to the middle of the nineteenth century free inquiry into the nature and essence of fundamental beliefs had not been a desideratum with the large number of educated and thinking persons in this country. The Reformation [1] was not accompanied in England or in

---

[1] The Reformation in this country is in fact not one startling event such as was connected with Luther's appearance in Germany. It was a process which had several stages, occupying, in all, three centuries before it manifested, and then only partially and imperfectly, its inherent tendencies. As I am not writing for British readers only, who may, or may not, be well acquainted with the historical development of religious thought in their own country, I refer to two works in which that History is very lucidly explained. The first is written by one inside what is termed 'The Church,' i.e., from the Anglican point of view, which looks upon movements outside as representing Dissent, be they in the direction of the older Romanism or in that of independence in religious organisation or doctrine. It is the 'Bampton Lectures,' by G. H. Curtis, entitled, 'Dissent in its Relation to the Church of England' (1872). On p. 287 he says : "The controversies which mainly characterised the sixteenth and seventeenth centuries were of a dissimilar type, the cause of divergence in the sixteenth century being the merely exterior question of Church-polity —on which the Independents se-

U

Scotland by a desire for an independent justification of
personal beliefs and for a philosophical interpretation of
religious doctrines such as existed, from the very beginning, in German Protestantism.   The highest problems

ceded, and drifted away in the
direction of excessive liberty and
of ultimate anarchy. . . . In the
seventeenth century . . . the matters
in dispute were of a more interior
nature. The use or disuse of the
Church's *Sacramenta* or external
means of grace was the question
mainly at issue. And here the
Baptists represented one tendency
of thought and the Quakers the
diametrically opposite one. . . .
The controversies of the eighteenth
century, and the two principal
secessions in which those controversies terminated, [are] Unitarianism on the one hand and
Wesleyanism on the other. The
questions on which those two controversies hinged are of extreme
interest and of paramount importance. . . . They belong to a still
more interior department of the
Church's life ; . . . they are, in a
word, questions relating to the
Church's *system of doctrine*, to her
educational method of procedure.
. . . And here Unitarianism . . .
went off in the pursuit of an unlimited intellectual freedom ; while
Wesleyanism . . . handled, with
an almost sublime self-confidence,
the tremendous spell of an appeal
to the mere *feelings* of half taught
and half civilised men." The other
work I wish to recommend is by
John James Taylor, a Unitarian
minister, with the title 'Retrospect
of the Religious Life of England'
(1845). As the title indicates, the
subject is here treated under the
three headings of The Church,
Puritanism, and Free Enquiry. In
Chapter III. (p. 131 *sqq.*), the
author proceeds "to contrast with
[the Anglican hierarchy] the nature

and operation of the antagonist
principle of Puritanism. It is
from the conflict of these opposing
tendencies that the peculiar character of our religious life results.
The spirit of Puritanism must not,
however, be confounded with the
principle of Free Enquiry and
mental independence, which ultimately grew out of it, and by
those who were capable of reasoning to consequences, might have
been seen to be implied in it. The
fundamental idea of Puritanism, in
all its forms and ramifications, is
the supreme authority of Scripture,
acting directly on the individual
conscience—as opposed to a reliance on the priesthood and the
outward ordinances of the Church.
. . . With Puritanism, the range
of enquiry is shut up within the
limits of the written Word ; it does
not venture to sally forth beyond
them, and survey the Scripture
under a broader aspect from some
point of view external to it."
"The strict letter of Scripture was
received by [the Puritans] as a
final absolute rule, ever present,
ever applicable, standing in close
immediate contact with the exi-
gences of man's outward life
through the revolutions of centuries. On the other hand, the
Anglicans regarded Scripture as
indeed the original depository of
Christian truth, in which its germs,
as it were, and first principles were
shut up, but acknowledged ecclesiastical tradition as its legitimate
exposition ; Scripture and Tradition being viewed by them as
equally under the superintending
direction of Providence. . . ." (p.
286).

of life, death, and immortality, of evil, sin, and redemption, which are now freely and largely discussed
by philosophical writers in all the three countries, did
not in English and Scottish philosophical literature find
any exhaustive treatment. They were relegated, after
the example of Bacon, to the separate domain of Theology
or Divinity,[1] where they received adequate treatment on
the basis of historical tradition. This was either confined—as with the Nonconformists and Presbyterians—
to the Scriptures, which were interpreted, but not criticised, in the light of Reason, or it was the combined
authority of tradition and the Church which prescribed
the correct canons for explanation and interpretation of
the Scriptures. To the English mind the doctrines of the
Christian religion, taught in a more or less orthodox
spirit, and the unique historical records connected with
its mysterious origin, presented themselves quite as much

[1] See a remarkable passage by
George Ripley in his Introductory
Notice to Jouffroy's Philosophical
Essays, pp. 23, 24, quoted by
Robert Flint in his 'Philosophy of
History in France and Germany'
(1874, p. 4): "There is a little
book," says George Ripley, "which
is taught to children, and on which
they are examined in the Church.
If we read this book, which is the
Catechism, we shall find a solution
of all the problems which have been
proposed; all of them without exception. If we ask the Christian
whence comes the human race, he
knows; or whither it goes, he
knows; or how it goes, he knows.
If we ask that poor child, who has
never reflected on the subject in
his life, why he is here below and
what will become of him after
death, he will give you a sublime
answer, which he will not thoroughly
comprehend, but which is none the
less admirable for that. If we ask
him how the world was created,
and for what end; why God has
placed in it plants and animals;
how the earth was peopled; whether
by a single family or by many;
why men speak different languages;
why they suffer, why they struggle,
and how all this will end,—he
knows it all. Origin of the world,
origin of the species, question of
races, destiny of man in this life
and in the other, relations of man
to God, duties of man to his fellow-
men, rights of man over the creation,—he is ignorant of none of
these points; and when he shall
have grown up, he will as little
hesitate with regard to natural
right, political right, or the right
of nations: all this proceeds with
clearness, and as it were of itself,
from Christianity."

in the character of reality as the data of experience and observation in the outer world. Both these realities were considered by common-sense philosophy to furnish material for reflection and interpretation. In the opinion of most thinkers from the time of Bacon down to the beginning of the nineteenth century, these two separate sources of knowledge and reflection stood sufficiently apart to admit of being independently recognised and studied. This view was probably most clearly represented in the writings of Locke, who, more than any other among those thinkers who acquired a widespread reputation and influence, may be looked upon as typical of the ruling philosophical thought in this country from the time of Bacon till well on into the nineteenth century. His attitude to knowledge gained by observation through the senses as well as to that based upon religious beliefs has been characterised as a kind of *via media*. But it did not emanate from the desire, and still less from an attempt, to reconcile the two realms of thought, as was the case with his famous contemporary on the Continent, Leibniz; it rather sprang from a dislike of dogmatism, be that dogmatism theological or scientific: for, according to Locke, neither the theologian nor the naturalist could attain to such certainty as would allow either side to disregard the evidence furnished by the other. "Thus for 130 years after its publication the ' Essay ' of Locke gave to philosophy in this country its groundwork and its method. The Anglo-Saxon mind cautiously leans to that side of human life which is instinctive and determined by its custom, overlooked, as outside philosophy, altogether by those who would confine its speculations to the ultimate presuppositions and who despise *axiomata media* as external to the sphere in which it moves."[1] It is quite true that there were exceptions, and that attempts had been made to build up coherent or monistic systems similar to those which abound in the nineteenth century; and this both with a materialistic tendency—as by Hobbes—and with that towards spiritualism—as by Berkeley. But these systematic attempts were disregarded and stood outside of the prevailing currents of philosophical thought. This was, in general, occupied with a discussion of special problems, and did probably more than either French or German philosophy to lead up to special philosophical sciences, such as Psychology, Logic, Theory of Method, Ethics, Economics, &c. Even the most influential and far-reaching discussions which mark an era in philosophical thought, those of David Hume, appeared in the form of essays which stimulated thought without exhausting their subject, and aimed as little at building up a systematic whole as they emanated from a *universitas scientiarum et literarum*. The opinion sometimes expressed by foreign historians of philosophy, that thinkers like Bacon, Locke, Newton, Mill, and others shrank, through timidity, from expressing their convictions regarding matters of faith or subjecting them to the same penetrating analysis which they practised with regard to science and natural knowledge, can hardly be upheld.[2] It was rather a correct and

15.
Dispersive character of earlier British thought

[1] Fraser, 'Locke,' p. 286.
[2] This opinion is, however, to some extent borne out by what John Stuart Mill tells us about his father, James Mill, in a well-known passage of the 'Autobiography,' p. 43. "I am one of the very few examples, in this country, of one

deep-seated, though frequently an unconscious, conviction that the foundations of natural knowledge were not sufficiently firm, nor its principles sufficiently clear to permit of indiscriminate application beyond a limited region. We are acquainted with Newton's final verdict regarding the Law of Gravitation, or of action at a distance, unduly extolled later on in the school of Laplace,[1]

who has not thrown off religious belief, but never had it : I grew up in a negative state with regard to it. I looked upon the modern exactly as I did upon the ancient religion, as something which in no way concerned me. It did not seem to me more strange that English people should believe what I did not, than that the men I read of in Herodotus should have done so. History had made the variety of opinions among mankind a fact familiar to me, and this was but a prolongation of that fact. This point in my early education had, however, incidentally one bad consequence deserving notice. In giving me an opinion contrary to that of the world, my father thought it necessary to give it as one which could not prudently be avowed to the world. This lesson of keeping my thoughts to myself, at that early age, was attended with some moral disadvantages, though my limited intercourse with strangers, especially such as were likely to speak to me on religion, prevented me from being placed in the alternative of avowal or hypocrisy. I remember two occasions in my boyhood on which I felt myself in this alternative, and in both cases I avowed my disbelief and defended it." At a much later period he wrote ('Autobiography,' p. 189), "With those who, like all the best and wisest of mankind, are dissatisfied with human life as

it is, and whose feelings are wholly identified with its radical amendment, there are two main regions of thought. One is the region of ultimate aims, the constituent elements of the highest realisable ideal of human life. The other is that of the immediately useful and practically attainable, . . . and, to say truth, it is in these two extremes principally that the real certainty lies. My own strength lay wholly in the uncertain and slippery intermediate region, that of theory of moral and political science ; respecting the conclusions of which in any of the forms in which I have received or originated them, whether as political economy, analytic psychology, logic, philosophy of history, or anything else, . . . I have derived a wise scepticism, which, while it has not hindered me from following out the honest exercise of my thinking faculties to whatever conclusions might result from it, has put me upon my guard against holding or announcing these conclusions with a degree of confidence which the nature of such speculations does not warrant, and has kept my mind not only open to admit, but prompt to welcome and eager to seek, even on the questions on which I have most meditated, any prospect of clearer perceptions and better evidence."

[1] See vol. ii. of this History, p. 29.

and we have in Locke's Essay the repeated assertion that natural knowledge gives only probability and not certainty.

We are thus indebted to Locke and his successors not for any attempt towards a complete and systematic theory of knowledge, but rather for leading philosophical thought into separate and definite channels of research; dealing as it were with the different regions of knowledge which were being cultivated or opened out in modern times, thus laying the foundation for separate philosophical inquiries. In each of these separate regions of knowledge, such as Psychology, which deals with the phenomena of the inner life; Logic, which deals with the principles of scientific knowledge; Ethics, which deals with the principles of action; Economics, which deals with the principles of industry and commerce; Æsthetics, which deals with the principles of taste,— English Philosophy can boast of having produced treatises of standard merit, distinguished by careful and penetrating analysis. But what was wanting from the point of view occupied by Continental thinkers from Descartes to Hegel was systematic unity based upon completeness and intrepid trust in the conclusiveness of purely logical argument. If we except Bishop Berkeley's Idealism, no attempt had been made in this country before the middle of the nineteenth century to construct a comprehensive and consistent philosophical creed, which should afford definite answers to all the more important problems of theory and practice. It can be easily shown that the prominent feature of British philosophical thought up to quite recent times

16.
Its want of systematic unity.

was a kind of dualism. No principle or position, however clearly enunciated in the beginning, was ever by
its first propounder carried to finality : there seems
always to have been a reluctance to attach much
credence to extreme consequences drawn out by slender
logic. Thus we have in Locke's Philosophy the two
principles of Sensation and Reflection, and further on
the two forms of natural and revealed knowledge. The
latter dualism is characteristic of all the philosophy of
the Scottish school, and it was revived in a different
form by Dean Mansel as an outcome of the latest
phase of Scottish philosophy, that represented by Sir
William Hamilton. But the extreme conclusions of
every logical argument will in the end be drawn, if not
by those who propounded it still without fail by some
of their followers, and thus we find that, in spite of the
realism of the English mind which clings to facts and
practical requirements, the time did arrive when attempts
had to be made to overcome the dualisms and latent
contradictions contained in the writings of philosophers,
from Bacon and Locke down to Hamilton and Mansel,
and to lay the foundations of a reasoned and consistent
philosophical creed. In the present connection it is
well to note that endeavours in this line of thought
existed long before and outside of the influence which
the study and criticism of German Idealism exerted, in
the same direction, in more recent times. The history

17.
Beginning
of search for
a creed.

of British philosophical thought can point to a distinct
and tolerably coherent search in quest of a philosophical
creed, beginning with James Mill and ending with
Herbert Spencer. It forms only an episode, though an

important episode, in nineteenth century thought. It began and ended with Agnosticism, though this term, with the special meaning attached to it, was only adopted at the end. James Mill [1] was, according to the testimony of his son, neither a believer nor an unbeliever in any ultimate theory of the origin and destiny of the world. In spite of his acquaintance with the pronounced opposition to religious beliefs contained in the writings of some of the French encyclopædists he was never an avowed atheist. The writings of his son, John Stuart Mill,[2] notably his 'Autobiography,' and the post-

[1] "My father, educated in the creed of Scotch presbyterianism, had by his own studies and reflections been early led to reject not only the belief in Revelation, but the foundations of what is commonly called Natural Religion. . . . Finding no halting-place in Deism, he remained in a state of perplexity until, doubtless after many struggles, he yielded to the conviction that, concerning the origin of things, nothing whatever can be known. This is the only correct statement of his opinion ; for dogmatic atheism he looked upon as absurd ; as most of those, whom the world has considered atheists, have always done" ('Autobiography,' p. 38). James Mill's Agnosticism was, however, as we are told further on, founded, not upon intellectual difficulties, nor upon a mechanical or naturalistic direction of thought, but upon the difficulties which surround the problem of physical and moral evil in the world. It is, at the same time, remarkable that, living so near the age during which the philosophy of Kant had made a lasting impression upon Continental thought, his philosophical interests should not have led

him to take some notice of the critical and idealistic philosophy of Germany. In his 'Life of James Mill,' A. Bain has published a reference to Mill's 'Commonplace Book' "as a clue to his studies." From this it is interesting to see that among the many authors, ancient and modern, English and foreign, there is not one representative of German philosophy, nor even of the great and broad current of speculation which began with Descartes and was continued by Spinoza and Leibniz, leading on to contemporary German transcendentalism.

[2] Although earlier and contemporary French thought played a considerable part in the development of J. S. Mill's convictions, we find no reference to the 'Discourse on Method' of Descartes, nor did the shallow philosophy of Condillac satisfy him. Starting, as he said, without any creed, he felt the necessity of finding and possessing one. Satisfied at an early age with the "principle of utility " as understood by Bentham, he found in it " the keystone which held together the detached and fragmentary component parts of [his] knowledge and beliefs. . . . It gave him a

humously published 'Essays on Religion,' revealed a
continued search after a reasoned creed which, however,
led to nothing really convincing. Much more decided
was the position taken up by George Henry Lewes,[1]
through whom, as also through Hamilton, Herbert

creed, a philosophy, a religion"
('Autobiography,' p. 67). At the
age of twenty he came to the
conclusion that the direction of
his thought had become too analytical; he had lost, as it were, the
substance of things over an attempt
to dissect them; though he never
"ceased to consider the power and
practice of analysis as an essential
condition of improvement," he
"thought that it had consequences
which required to be corrected"
(p. 143). Under this "sense of
want" the cultivation of the feelings became . . . "a cardinal point
in his ethical and philosophical
creed" (ibid.). This led him
to an appreciation of poetry and
art, and through the love of music,
such as that of Weber and Mozart,
and a disappointment with Byron's
pessimism, he accidentally came
upon the 'Miscellaneous Poems'
of Wordsworth, which "proved to
be the precise thing for [his]
mental wants at that particular
juncture" (p. 147). From Wordsworth he "seemed to learn what
would be the perennial sources of
happiness, when all the greater
evils of life shall have been removed" (as the utilitarian philosophy was hopeful of removing them)
". . . and the delight which
these poems gave [him] proved
that with culture of this sort,
there was nothing to dread from
the most confirmed habit of analysis" (p. 148).

[1] In 1874 and 1875 G. H. Lewes
(1817 - 1878) published the first
series of his 'Problems of Life and
Mind,' with the sub-title, 'The

Foundations of a Creed.' With
much less caution but with a
vastly superior knowledge of the
natural, especially the biological
sciences, than Mill possessed, Lewes
came to the conclusion that a reconciliation of knowledge and belief
in a "creed" founded upon scientific methods of thought could be
elaborated. He, as well as Spencer,
and probably largely through the
influence of the latter, entertained
an exaggerated belief in the power
of the genetic view to solve the
fundamental problems of life and
mind. This view had been established in Spencer's mind before
Darwin gave to it convincing
strength through his 'Principle of
Natural Selection.' But beyond
collecting much material, interesting especially to the psychologist,
Lewes did not advance far in his
original design, nor did he really
tackle the main difficulty as Renouvier had done before him in
France. He did indeed realise
the necessity of dealing with the
problem of certitude, but did not
advance to a "science of morality" like that which Renouvier
had put forth already in 1869. It
is interesting to note that one of
the weakest points of Spencer's
system lies likewise in his Ethics,
as fully explained by Henry Sidgwick, but that Spencer, unlike
Lewes, propounded the doctrine
of the Unknowable, thus closing
this search for a reasoned creed by
that Agnosticism with which, two
generations earlier, James Mill
had, according to the testimony of
his son, already started.

Spencer must have acquired at least a superficial knowledge of some of the ideas current in Kantian and post-Kantian speculation. But the search for a creed ended with the latter in exactly that doctrine of the unknowableness of the origin of things at which James Mill had arrived sixty years earlier, and which received popular expression when Huxley coined the term Agnosticism. The circuit of thought which thus began and ended in an agnostic attitude preceded historically the deeper and more scholarly study of Continental Idealism, and has, through it, been pushed somewhat into the background.

18.
The first
episode
ends in
Agnos-
ticism.

Besides this very prominent episode we have, in this country, the original studies and speculations of James Martineau, an independent thinker, of whom we shall have to take notice in some of the subsequent chapters of this History.

The introduction of the term Monism [1] into recent

---

[1] The term Monism has cropped up in recent philosophic literature from different sides and with somewhat different significance. It is opposed by some writers to the various forms of dualism existent in contemporary thought and, more recently by others, to pluralism, which they consider to be the necessary presupposition for a consistent application of the principle of Evolution. In Germany the term has been usurped by Ernst Haeckel for the materialistic creed which is developed in his popular writings. Some of his followers have joined hands with an earlier tendency of thought, represented by the Society for Ethical Culture, which aims at giving to morality a foundation independent of any religious creed. This direction of thought is represented by a special periodical founded in America, with the title, ' The Monist.' It aims at representing a unitary philosophical creed by no means identical with the Positivism of Comte or the Materialism of Haeckel, but nevertheless influenced by both. Quite recently there has been held at Hamburg the " First International Monist Congress," of which Ernst Haeckel, the great naturalist, Wilhelm Ostwald, the celebrated chemist, Friedrich Jodl, author of an important ' History of Ethics,' and others, mostly naturalists, seem to have been the leading spirits. The term Monism has thus become, as it were, the Shibboleth of a sort of religion of Free Thought, and cannot now, any more than the term Positivism, be used in the wider sense which its etymology suggests.

philosophical literature indicates a widespread tendency to overcome the latent dualism characteristic of the earlier philosophies in this country.

This dualism in human knowledge is, however, not a special characteristic of modern thought, but can be traced in the earliest systems of ancient philosophy, and was nowhere more apparent than in the middle ages with their avowed antithesis of Divine—or Revealed—and of Human Knowledge.

19.
Continental
efforts to
transcend
dualism.

Unlike English philosophical thought, thought on the Continent set out in modern times with the bold attempt to overcome the existing dualism in know-ledge by starting from some supreme principle or idea in the light of which the whole of human science—be it spiritual or natural—could be organised, being systematically co-ordinated or subordinated. The two great systems in which this was carried out, and which have had lasting influence on Continental thought up to the present day, are those of Descartes and Spinoza.

Up to quite recent times, when the independence of the development of philosophical thought in this country has been clearly recognised by Continental writers, the leading historians of philosophy, who belong nearly exclusively to Germany, were in the habit of represent-ing the history of modern philosophy as an unbroken chain from Descartes to Hegel and Schopenhauer; [1]

[1] This view is mainly represented by Kuno Fischer in his monu-mental work on the 'History of Modern Philosophy.' He does not include in it the History of the realistic movement in philosophy, to which he, however, devoted a smaller work with the title, 'Franz Bacon von Verulam, Das Zeitalter der Realphilosophie' (1856, 2nd ed., 1875). The continuity of the Idealistic movement is also sketched by Schopenhauer in the first Essay contained in his 'Parerga and Paralipomena,' and by Schwegler in his well-known 'Short History

Locke and Hume being the only British thinkers to whom was accorded an influence, the main importance of which lay in the fact that Locke provoked the elaborate refutation of Leibniz in the 'Nouveaux Essais,' and that Hume "roused Kant out of his dogmatic slumbers." Against this view it must be recognised that the philosophical thought of this country presents from Bacon to Spencer an independent line of development which was no doubt influenced by Descartes and Kant very much as the unbroken tradition of Continental thought was influenced by Locke and Hume. Towards the end of the nineteenth century it seems as if these two independent lines of philosophical tradition have crossed each other in a characteristic manner. When the need of a philosophic creed made itself felt in this country, several thinkers of the first order recognised that this problem was exactly that which had occupied Continental thought from the time of Descartes. Accordingly the philosophical writings not only of Kant but of Hegel, of Spinoza, of Lotze, and latterly of Leibniz, have been studied in this country with growing interest, and a school of thinkers has arisen which tries to assimilate, to co-ordinate, and to systematise the ideas contained in those formerly neglected or forgotten writings. On the other side, when, after the

20.
Two lines of development.

21.
Union of these.

of Philosophy.' The important works on 'History of Philosophy' by Erdmann (see *supra*, p. 37 note 1) have, in later editions, taken more and more notice of other collateral schools of thought previously ignored. But the one-sidedness of giving undue and exaggerated prominence to Idealistic, or even only to German, philosophical thought (as, *e.g.*, is the case with v. Hartmann) has now been finally overcome and a new spirit infused into the treatment of the subject by Windelband and by Höffding. A still more one-sided but opposite view of the History of philosophy is represented by G. H. Lewes's later work on the 'History of Philosophy.'

traditional Continental philosophy had led to scepticism and pessimism, and was generally—though erroneously —believed to be fruitless, the critical spirit attacked the principles of exact science and of moral conduct, it must have been with some surprise that it was found that this critical analysis had been begun and successfully practised long ago by prominent thinkers in this country. A growing appreciation in Germany of the writings of Mill and Spencer and other English thinkers has been the consequence.

Looking at philosophical thought in the nineteenth century as a whole, we may thus say that it is based upon two independent traditions: that which prevailed in this country and that which prevailed on the Continent. They were to some extent complementary, and may, besides, in other ways, be characterised by the different position which they took up to the problem of knowledge.

The problem of knowledge presents among others two principal sides to the philosophic thinker. He may inquire as to the means and methods of extending knowledge, or he may inquire into the difference of correct and incorrect, of true and false, of certain and doubtful knowledge. Each of these inquiries will lead in due course to the other. We cannot discuss the means of increasing knowledge without some kind of definition of what knowledge is. And on the other hand, we cannot discuss the question of certainty and validity of knowledge without casting a glance at the large body of actually existing and increasing knowledge. For, in actual practice, the pursuit and extension of knowledge does not wait till the philosopher has settled the criteria of certainty, nor, on the other hand, is the problem of certainty settled, in the eyes of the logician, by simply pointing to a body of existing and generally accepted knowledge, however extensive this may be. Still, the extension and growth of knowledge, especially of useful knowledge, may be the more attractive side of the problem to certain thinkers in certain times and surroundings, whilst to other thinkers, in other times and placed in a different environment, it may appear more important to arrive at some ultimate ground of certainty than to examine into the methods by which existing knowledge is extended. There is further no doubt that, whether we start with the first or the second of the two questions involved in the problem of knowledge, we shall in the end have to deal with both.

From what we have learnt of English philosophy in this chapter, as also on former occasions, it will appear natural that in the beginning of the modern era of thought, the problem of the extension of knowledge should, in this country, have presented itself first, that the question of the nature of knowledge and the grounds of certainty should have come later, that it should have gradually been narrowed down to the search for an ulti- mate foundation of all knowledge quite independent of the particular regions of knowledge which surround us, and that the attempt to establish unity and harmony should have come last.

But about the time when this characteristic and perfectly logical succession in the different phases of the theory of knowledge was started in this country by

22.
Continental
thought
began with
scepticism.

Francis Bacon, quite different conditions prevailed on the Continent. There a pronounced scepticism as to the capacity of the human intellect to reach certainty in matters of fundamental importance had got hold of men's minds. It found expression mainly in French learned and polite literature: in the writings of a man of the world like Michel de Montaigne [1] (1533-1592); of Pierre Charron [2] (1541-1603), a lawyer and preacher; and of François Sanchez [3] (died 1632), a professor of medicine and philosophy at Montpellier. Out of this general scepticism, which rested more on the uncertainty that pervaded the thought of the age than on the fruitlessness of the philosophy of the schoolmen or on the want of advance in useful knowledge in the dark ages, it is the great merit of Descartes to have sought a way to

[1] Montaigne's 'Essais' appeared in 1580, an augmented edition in 1588. "As the most important among them may be considered the 'Apologie de Raymond Sebond' (ii. 12), which contains important discussions on Faith and Knowledge. Montaigne founds his doubt upon the diversity of individual views: every one has a different opinion, whereas truth can only be one; there is no certain, no generally admitted knowledge. Human reason is weak and blind in all things, knowledge is deceptive (especially contemporary philosophy, which explains explanations and not things); and the laws of the country, which reason advises us to follow, are a seething ocean of opinions of a people or a Sovereign" (Falckenberg, 'Geschichte der Neueren Philosophie,' 1886, p. 34). If theoretical certainty is impossible, practical conduct must rely on nature and revelation.

[2] Charron develops Montaigne's

sceptical and practical position into a system. In his work 'De la Sagesse' (1601), "doubt has the double purpose to keep alive the spirit of research and to lead us to Faith. As reason disposes of no means by which to distinguish truth from falsehood, it follows that we are born to search for truth but not to possess it. Truth abides only in the bosom of the Deity, &c., &c." (Falckenberg, ibid.)

[3] The principal work of Sanchez is entitled 'Tractatus de multum nobili et prima universali scientia quod Nihil Scitur,' and appeared one year after the first edition of Montaigne. It is directed against Aristotle and scholastic philosophy. Another work, intended to give the true philosophy, never appeared. It is interesting to see how views independently expressed by more recent thinkers can already be found in these the earliest representatives of the modern critical spirit.

certainty and light. He recognised that certainty in the highest sense of the word implies trust and confidence. In the then prevailing insecurity of external conditions and the strife of political and religious parties, such certainty could according to him be found by the individual thinker only through retiring into the depths of his own mind and seeking there for a central fact or self-evident principle from which to start. This he found in the process of thought itself. But Thought implies a thinking Subject; it gave him besides an indication how to proceed further in the search for truth and certainty by suggesting an inquiry into the method of thought and into its content. As to the former he was led to fix upon the mathematical methods, inasmuch as they lead to clearly defined conceptions which bear intuitive or immediate evidence of their truth. But human thought is also characterised by the fact that it leads beyond itself, *i.e.*, beyond the limit of the finite thinking subject. Applying the idea of causality, Descartes comes to the conclusion that what we now term the transcendency of thought cannot have its foundation in the thinking subject alone, but implies the existence of a higher intellect which he identifies with the Divine Mind. In this manner he finds the way out of the limits of subjective thought to a belief in another reality and into that of external things. In contradistinction to the immediate evidence of the subjective mind, the nature of which is thought, the nature of the objective world consists in extension, *i.e.*, in the mathematical properties of number and measure. Descartes thus establishes the contrast or dualism of a thinking

23.
Descartes'
constructive
effort.

and an extended reality, and he thereby fixed the immediate problem for the speculations of his followers.

For our present purpose it is unnecessary to dwell upon the questionable logic in Descartes' reasoning; it is sufficient to point out that nearly all the different aspects which the problem of knowledge presents, and which have occupied thinkers up to the present day, are either implied or distinctly brought out in Descartes' speculation. Such are, *e.g.*, the question of innate ideas, of the deductive as compared with the inductive processes of thought, the identification of certainty with mathematical precision or clearness, and many others. The way out of the uncertainty of knowledge, which for Continental thinkers was at that time by far the most important problem, seemed indeed to be solved in a promising manner by the appeal to the mathematical method. This was exactly that aspect of thought for which the philosophy of Bacon had no appreciation. The latter seemed to be unaware of the important part which the application of mathematics was to play in the extension of natural knowledge as well as in giving it precision and value.[1] The exact methods practised by Galileo were extended and

24.
Mathematical methods.

[1] It is, however, well to remember that Bacon (1561-1626) preceded Descartes (1596 - 1650) in time; that his most important works dealing with the "advancement of learning" were written in the first years of the seventeenth century; that at that time neither ' Kepler's Laws' (1609-1618) nor Galileo's 'Laws of Falling Bodies' (1612) were yet known or published; that the principal discoveries which were accessible to Bacon, such as those of Gilbert ('de Magnete,' 1600) and Harvey (' Circulation of the Blood,' 1619), had nothing to do with mathematics. The Works of Hariot and the 'Logarithmic Tables' (1594-1614) of Napier, on the other side, were probably too exclusively mathematical to come within the sphere of Bacon's interest in the extension of natural knowledge. Descartes' 'Discourse on Method' appeared in 1637. He had thus before him much of the best that, during that age, had been achieved in astronomy and physics through the application of measurement and calculation.

perfected by Descartes himself in the application of Algebra—the general arithmetic of the Arabians—to Geometry; it changed the latter from a science which, though rigorous, was somewhat casual, to a methodical doctrine by which configurations in space could be generally and exhaustively treated. It must indeed have been a seductive prospect for those acquainted with the great development of mathematical science which followed the invention of the analytical and infinitesimal methods to acquire in the uncertain regions of philosophic thought the grasp and mastery exhibited by the mathematical sciences. Nearly all the great Continental, notably the French, thinkers of the seventeenth and eighteenth centuries came more or less under the spell of this idea. That it did not exert a similar spell in this country was largely owing to the fact that here the foremost mathematical genius, Newton, retained in his immortal works the synthetic methods of the ancients, which in the hands of all but the very greatest mathematicians remained specific and did not rise to abstract generality.[1]

The detailed arguments by which Descartes elaborated the two main principles of his philosophy, viz., that certainty can be found only in and by thinking, and

---

[1] The synthetic methods of the ancients which were, following the example of Newton, retained for a long time in the teaching of higher mathematics in this country, attained nevertheless, under the hands of French geometricians (notably of Monge and Poncelet in the beginning of the nineteenth century) a systematisation equal in importance to the analytical principle of Descartes. This was by means of the 'Principle of Projection.' An analytical interpretation of this principle led in the course of the nineteenth century to an approximation of the two methods and in the sequel to an extraordinary development of mathematical thought and knowledge (see vol. ii. of this History, p. 658 *sqq.*)

that knowledge depends on the conviction that unity
and order pervades everything, need not occupy us at
present. The fact that he identified this principle of
unity and order with the personal Deity of religion
permitted him to bring spiritual and natural knowledge
into connection and gave to his philosophy a twofold
interest. For it was capable of being on the one side
mystically interpreted by spiritual thinkers, whilst on
the other side the emphasis laid upon mathematical
reasoning attracted those who had successfully begun to
explain mechanically many phenomena in nature.
Whilst the former line of thought led to the religious
conception that we know and "see all things in God"
(Malebranche), the mechanical philosophers on the other
side recognised that for their purposes the supposition of
a definite (mechanical) order in the universe was all that
was wanted, and that the task of the natural philosopher
consisted in tracing in detail some lines of this inwoven
cypher of all Reality. Towards this Descartes had already
made a beginning in his celebrated theory of Vortices.
But the thinker who most consistently devoted himself
to carrying forward the line of thought suggested by
Descartes, viz., the ascent through abstract thought to a
conception of the true order and unity of the world, and
the working of this by a mathematical method, was

25.
Spinoza and
Leibniz.

Spinoza, whose writings, however, acquired their importance in modern philosophy much later, and need not
occupy us at present. A more striking immediate
reaction upon the course of thought on the Continent
than was exercised by the philosophy of Spinoza, who
nevertheless influenced contemporary thinkers more than

has been generally admitted, emanated from Leibniz, and this influence has, with important fluctuations, continued up to the present day. One of the reasons why this influence has again and again made itself felt is because none of the great thinkers of modern times has studied with such equal interest and sympathy the most opposite lines of thought, and because hardly any one has been qualified in the same degree by genius and education to appreciate seemingly contradictory tendencies. Ancient and modern, English, French, and Italian philosophies were alike known to him; he was a mathematician and abstract thinker as well as a naturalist and historian, a practical man of the world as well as a theorist. The two great objects which he seems to have had in view all through his life were, first, to reconcile apparently opposed views, to harmonise existing differences in philosophy, politics, and religion; and secondly, to lead his theoretical and abstract meditations into practical channels.

Turning now to the special problem with which I am dealing in this chapter, the problem of knowledge, we find in the philosophy of Leibniz a great advance in his conception of the nature of Knowledge and the means possessed by the human mind of acquiring it. With Descartes the criterion of truth consisted in clearness of thinking and immediate evidence, two qualities which were nowhere more conspicuous than in the reasoning of the mathematical sciences.[1] A similar predilection for

[1] This conception of Descartes was more fully elaborated by Leibniz. What with Descartes was not sufficiently distinguished received in Leibniz's treatment a somewhat more definite expression. He dis-tinguishes between what is clear from what is also distinct. "Clear" is opposed to "obscure," "dis-tinct" to "confused." A notion is clear if readily recognised; it is distinct if analysable into its parts

the mathematical form of knowledge is to be found in Spinoza, though the latter in the course of his metaphysical expositions arrives at the conception that discursive knowledge must, in its highest form, become intuition,—mediated or rational knowledge having finally to pass into intuitive or immediate knowledge.[1] This idea was revived or independently enunciated by many

and their connections. ('Meditations on Cognition, Truth, and Ideas,' 1684). "Accordingly the *a priori* or eternal geometrical or metaphysical truths are both clear and distinct. On the other side the *a posteriori* or actual truths are clear but not distinct. The former are therefore fully transparent, accompanied by the conviction of the impossibility of their opposite ; with the latter the opposite is conceivable. With the former, intuitive certainty rests on the principle of contradiction ; with the latter, their possibility, which is proved by their actual reality, requires further explication through the principle of sufficient reason. . . . In course of its further development this distinction acquired, for Leibniz, metaphysical importance. He distinguished between absolute necessity, which implies the logical impossibility of the opposite, and a conditioned necessity which is merely factual. He divides the principles of things into those the opposite of which is inconceivable, and those of which it is conceivable " (Windelband, 'Geschichte der Philosophie,' 4th ed., p. 334). Prof. Windelband also shows that Leibniz originally considered that the difference between conceptions which are clear and those which are in addition fully defined or transparent applied only to the human or finite intellect, whereas in the Divine Intellect this difference did not exist ; but that in the

sequel, in order not to fall into the absolute necessitarianism of Spinoza, he emphasised the difference of necessary and contingent truths. Leaving out of consideration, as alien to the subject of this chapter, the metaphysical aspect, we may say that Leibniz approached the problem of the difference of certitude and precision of knowledge, *i.e.*, the difference between knowledge which we acquire (by observation and reflection) and ultimate convictions which we must possess.

[1] With Spinoza "the cognition of all finite things and states leads to two highest conceptions—extension and consciousness ; they both acquire a higher metaphysical importance than finite things possess, they are the attributes [of the absolute substance], the finite things are only their modes. But as abstract thought rises from these ultimate distinctions to the most general, the *ens generalissimum*, the conception of the latter loses all definite content and there remains only the empty form of substance. And for Spinoza the Deity is All—and as such—Nothing. His theology follows entirely the lines of mysticism. . . . To this corresponds also his threefold theory of knowledge, which places, beyond perception and reflection, intuition as the immediate apprehension of the eternal emanence of all things out of God, cognition *sub specie æterni* " (Windelband, *loc. cit.*, p. 342).

thinkers during the nineteenth century. But the fact
which must have troubled all those thinkers who
worked at the unification of thought and the criteria of
certainty—viz., the existence of the actual knowledge of
science on the one side and the spiritual knowledge of
faith on the other—was not sufficiently explained or
traced to its psychological sources either by Descartes
or by Spinoza. Leibniz works out the theory of knowledge in opposition to the Cartesian view as well as to
that of Locke. It is not correct, according to his view,
that all true knowledge is limited to that which can be
clearly defined, as the Cartesians maintained, nor is the
soul originally a *tabula rasa* as Locke and the empiricists
maintained. Only a portion of our soul is at any time
fully illuminated, only a portion of our thoughts arrive
at the clarity of discursive knowledge.[1] Behind and

[1] The two most important ideas
which Leibniz has the merit of
introducing into the theory of
knowledge, and for which he coined
two distinct terms, are the doctrine
of the "petites perceptions" and
that of "apperception," as distinguished from "perception." Both
these ideas, which have become so
fruitful in recent philosophy, are
contained in Leibniz's later, mostly
posthumously published, works and
correspondence. Originally mainly
interested in a development or
correction of the Cartesian system
as a comprehensive reasoned creed,
he had devoted himself to the
study of the two most prominent
problems that Descartes had bequeathed to his successors. Those
were; first, the problem of method;
secondly, the central metaphysical
conception of the ultimate reality
—the notion of substance. His
important psychological, and his

still more important epistemological, discussions seem to have
come to the fore much later,
notably through his acquaintance
with the writings of Locke and
Newton; the former suggested the
'Nouveaux Essais,' the latter led
to the correspondence with Clarke.
Leibniz's earlier labours were in
the direction of the development
of the mathematical methods, and
resulted *inter alia* in his invention
of the calculus, but also in his
fruitless attempts to import greater
precision into philosophical reasoning by the invention of a general
combinatorial method or logical
calculus which should not only
prove, but also lead to the discovery of new truths. "From
early youth he had the hope to
find such an art, and it is remarkable that a man of his mental cast,
and with his appreciation of the
meaning of individuality, should

around this illuminated portion there lies the region of the "petites perceptions," the half illuminated storehouse of thought. These "petites perceptions" accompany as a background all our thinking, as they also form the source and guarantee the continuity of all our thoughts. This suggestive view put forward by Leibniz has also been taken up in various forms by thinkers during the nineteenth century. But Leibniz's immediate successors took more interest in the process by which what was unclear and mystical might be drawn into clear daylight than in emphasising those internal possessions of the human mind which can never be completely rationalised.[1]

believe in the possibility that the highest faculties of the mind could some day be reduced to a mechanism; in fact, he did not shrink even from the consequence that if once such a method were found it would require only experience and ingenuity to find new truths: a genius himself, he strove to make genius superfluous" (Windelband, 'Geschichte der Neueren Philosophie,' vol. i., 4th ed., 1907, p. 468). The term "petites perceptions" was characteristic of Leibniz's manner of looking at things, and had no doubt its origin in the infinitesimal method which he perfected and applied in the calculus: it combined the spirit of analysis with the principle of Continuity which forms another fundamental notion in Leibniz's speculation. What in recent psychology is termed the "presentation-continuum" or the "plenum of consciousness" was mathematically represented in Leibniz's mind by the totality or continuous background of the "petites perceptions," in the same way as geometrical structures may be treated as the

integrals of their infinitesimal elements or differentials. The question then arose, how, on this continuous background or out of this half illuminated store of perceptions, certain among them rose into distinct vision. This led to the doctrine of apperception, which involved at the same time an activity of the human intellect; likewise an idea which we meet with again more fully developed in recent psychology. (See *supra*, p. 290.)

[1] The study of Leibniz's philosophy and its continued influence on philosophical thought ever since affords a good example of the difference between a history of philosophy or of philosophical systems and a history of philosophical thought. Leibniz, more like Descartes, and in contrast to Spinoza, published no concise and connected statement of his reasoned creed. Nearly all his writings seem to have been suggested by those of other thinkers, or for special persons, and on special occasions. Thus the 'Monadology' was written in 1714, for Prince Eugene of Savoy, in order to promote a better

Just as the position taken up by Descartes lent itself to a twofold development, the one leading into

understanding of what he had expounded in his 'Théodicée' and in his various contributions to contemporary learned periodicals in which, as he says, he "accommodated himself to the language of the schools or to the style of the Cartesians," it being first written in the German language. The 'Théodicée' had been written some years earlier at the request of the Queen of Prussia, in order to counteract the sceptical spirit which was spread through the writings of Hobbes, Bayle, Gassendi, the Socinians and Arminians, &c. His most important work, the 'Nouveaux Essais,' was similarly composed after the appearance of Locke's famous 'Essay,' and forms a kind of running commentary to Locke's doctrines. Whilst the two former works were published during Leibniz's lifetime, the latter, which is by far the most instructive and permanently important, was not published by Leibniz himself— because Locke had died in the meantime—but very much later, in the year 1765, nearly fifty years after Leibniz's death. In consequence of this disjointed form of composition, and still more, of publication of Leibniz's Works, it has been impossible to settle with even approximate certainty many important features of his system, the latter still remaining a problem to historians of philosophy. The same circumstance further had the effect of allowing a very one-sided and insufficient version of Leibniz's ideas to get hold of the philosophical mind in Germany during the first two-thirds of the eighteenth century. Leibnizianism was no more identical with Leibniz's real teaching than Newtonianism in France, or Darwinism in Germany, have

been identical with the doctrines of their respective authors. "When the 'Nouveaux Essais' were printed in 1765 they excited great attention. Lessing was going to translate them. That the life of the soul transcends all that is clear and distinctly conscious, and is rooted in dimly traceable depths, meant insight of the highest value for literature ; this was just struggling out of the intellectual dryness of the Enlightenment, and out of insipid correctness to an unfolding full of genius ; it opened a view all the more valuable, as coming from the same thinker whom Germany honoured as the father and hero of its Enlightenment. In this direction Leibniz worked especially upon Herder; we see it not only in his æsthetic views, but still more in his prize essay 'On Knowing and Feeling of the Human Soul.' Under the preponderance of the methodological point of view, the Leibnizo-Wolffian school had strained the opposition between rational and empirical knowledge as far as possible, and had treated understanding and sensibility as two separate 'faculties.' The Berlin Academy desired an examination of the mutual relation of these two separated powers, and of the share which each has in human knowledge. Herder represented the true Leibniz — as he appeared in the 'Nouveaux Essais' — against the prevailing system of the schools : he emphasised in his treatise the living unity of man's psychical life, and showed that sensibility and understanding are not two different sources of knowledge, but only the different stages of one and the same living activity with which the 'monad' comprehends the universe within itself" (Windelband loc. cit., p. 388).

the mathematical sciences and the mechanical explanation of things, the other to a mystical and spiritual
view, so also the philosophy of Leibniz pointed in
two directions. It suggested the attempt to rationalise
the whole of our knowledge, be it natural or spiritual;
but it also pointed to the unexhausted wealth of
inner life out of which a new world of ideas might
spring up at the right moment. Thus Leibniz unconsciously heralded, as it were, the two great developments
which took place in German thought after the middle of
the eighteenth century; the earlier rationalising movement during the age of the " Aufklärung " and the later
spiritual deepening and consequent ideal elevation during
the age of classical literature and art. We have seen in
an earlier chapter how the former movement of thought
led to more and more methodical treatment in all the
different regions of knowledge; how criticism, in the
larger sense of the word, developed out of it and became the great instrument of academic education in all
the branches of learning which were not covered by
the mathematical and physical sciences. But we saw
at the same time how this critical movement derived
its higher meaning and importance from the existence, in
the minds of its foremost representatives, of an ideal
background, which the critical processes hoped, in the
end, to reach and bring into daylight. This ideal
background had become a reality through the creative
genius during the classical and romantic periods of
German literature and art.

26.
Diverging
directions
after
Leibniz.

II.

If we, for a moment, adopt an expression which has been coined and become current in modern philosophical literature, and according to which philosophy consists in unified knowledge, its highest aim being the unification of thought, we may say that modern philosophy on the Continent consciously worked from its very beginning in Descartes towards the attainment of this end, whereas, in this country, it only arrived at a recognition of this, its highest task, during the latter part of the nineteenth century. I have expressed the same idea in other words by saying that modern philosophy on the Continent aimed at the establishment of a consistent and comprehensive philosophical creed. The boldest attempt to solve this problem is no doubt the system of Spinoza, whereas Descartes had contented himself with enunciating certain leading principles. In Spinoza philosophy attained to an elevation of spirit and diction which has only been reached in rare instances. It became to its author an expression, as it were, of his deepest religious convictions; it rose to inspiration. Such had been the philosophy of Plato in antiquity, such was the philosophy of Spinoza in modern times. Both are conspicuous by their grandeur and sublimity. But in the same way as Plato's philosophy in ancient times was followed, and to a large extent superseded, by the sober and judicious treatment of Aristotle, so the creative effort of Spinoza was superseded, for the time being, by the harmonising endeavours contained in Leibniz's

27.
Aim at unity in Continental thought.

28.
Spinoza and Leibniz contrasted.

philosophy. In another point also Leibniz can be
compared with Aristotle, inasmuch as he was equally
acquainted with the teaching of other earlier or contemporary thinkers, and built upon their foundations.

There are other causes why with Leibniz philosophical
thought had entered on a new phase, and, instead of
venturing on a bold attempt of creation and systematic
construction, was largely occupied with reconciling existing doctrines and apparently contradictory aspects
of thought. This task of reconciliation and of arriving
at unification, not so much by constructive effort as
by a process of harmonising, was pushed into the foreground and became a desideratum to many thinking
minds through the writings of a contemporary of
Leibniz. It was Pierre Bayle who in several of his
writings had asserted the conflict between religion and
reason, between the tenets of faith and the doctrines
of philosophy ; and had exemplified this by pointing to
the difficulties involved in the problem of evil and
sin.[1] Bayle's criticisms gave the occasion to Leibniz

29.
Leibniz
and Bayle.

[1] Pierre Bayle (1647-1706) was
one of the most influential writers
of the seventeenth century, as
much through the sceptical tenor of
his works as through the enormous
erudition displayed in his 'Dic-
tionnaire Historique et Critique'
(1695-1697, 2nd augmented ed.,
1702). It formed a principal channel of historical knowledge for several generations, continued the scepticism of earlier French writers like
Montaigne, and led on to the still
more celebrated and influential writings of Voltaire. It preached tolerance in all matters of doctrine, especially of religious beliefs. It was
the forerunner of the great Encyclopædia of d'Alembert, who, nevertheless, as Voltaire indignantly remarks, did not sufficiently acknowledge his real predecessor. It
is supposed that Locke, who met
Bayle in Holland, received his
ideas on toleration in great part
from Bayle. Bayle was the great
exponent of the absolute separation
of matters of knowledge and matters of faith, but not in the sense
expressed by Bacon and Locke,
which led to the natural religion
of the Deists in England, but in
the older sense, according to which
religious beliefs would have no
meaning if they could be logically
demonstrated. It was this dualism

for publishing, in 1710, his most popular work, the 'Théodicée.' In doing so he gave further expression to an idea which had been familiar to him for some time. He had early recognised that knowledge presents two forms—the knowledge of efficient causes and the knowledge of final causes, the mechanical and the teleological view of things, that it is a desire of the human

which Leibniz desired to counteract, for wherever it is admitted, it leads, in most minds, to a strong assertion of scepticism and a corresponding indifference, if not antagonism, towards religion. It must be added that Bayle anticipated likewise the modern school of thought, which relies upon the possibility of establishing morals and a system of ethics without the assistance of any religious or philosophical creed. This side is fully expounded, *e.g.*, in Prof. Jodl's 'Geschichte der Ethik' (vol. i., 2nd ed., p. 418 *sqq.*). As Bayle was quite unsystematic in his writings and expounded his fundamental convictions as occasion presented itself, suggesting, and frequently only insinuating, his real meaning, his influence may be considered from very different points of view. The fact that, for him, religious truths were not rational but superrational, and that morality did not depend upon them but had its foundation in human nature itself, put such truths out of contact both with reason and moral conduct, removing them—without a distinct avowal of unbelief—into a region which presented little interest. They were not an essential factor for either the intellectual or the moral life of humanity. In spite of many passages which may be construed as revealing personal belief in Bayle's own mind, this seems nowhere to be a clear and

necessary conviction. Thus different writers have put various sides of Bayle's reasoning into the foreground. M. Picavet (in the 'Grande Encyclopédie,' art. "Bayle") emphasises his doctrine of tolerance; Prof. Jodl hails with approval his doctrine of the independence of ethics from religion and metaphysics; and Prof. Windelband represents him as a pronounced exponent of the doctrine of the twofold truth. "Religion is for him possible only as an actual revelation; in contradiction to philosophical knowledge, he represents quite rigidly the twofold truth; and, whilst he might, therefore, personally claim credit for a faith contrary"—or superior—"to reason, his writings, and especially the articles in his Dictionary, were not less dangerous to the doctrines of positive religion than to those of the Deists" (Windelband, *loc. cit.*, p. 413). Voltaire, who quotes Bayle frequently, does not accept his dictum that a society of atheists would be quite possible. With Voltaire some religious beliefs are required to regulate and restrain the conduct of men at large. Bayle had admitted that true religion, which he identifies with the love of God, would indeed do so; but this, he thought, was too rare an occurrence, and the conventional religion of the Churches did morally more harm than good.

mind to trace phenomena back to their antecedent causes, but not less so to understand their purpose and meaning.[1] He appreciated the philosophies of Descartes and Spinoza inasmuch as they laid stress upon the deductive mathematical treatment, but he could not agree with Spinoza, who discarded altogether and treated with scorn all teleological explanations. In Leibniz philosophical thought arrived at the position which, with certain interruptions, it still occupies at the present day; its task being, not to afford new knowledge, but to mediate between the claims of two kinds of knowledge: that which deals with things

[1] From the point of view of the problem of knowledge we may thus say that Leibniz distinctly announced three kinds of knowledge, founded upon the law of contradiction (mathematical or metaphysical truths), the law of sufficient reason (all contingent truths found by observation and experience, tracing the causal connection of things), and the law of final causes through which the apparent contingency in nature is raised to the position of necessity, inasmuch as in and through the contingent facts and events in the world a definite plan, the design of the Divine Creator, is realised. Lotze remarks that this reduces the whole scheme of Leibniz to a mathematical conception. "The whole world has its reality from God, and indeed in this way that in the mind of God there existed many consistent schemes, among which He admitted that which contained the smallest amount of evil and the greatest perfection. Such a scheme he could not alter or improve, but only admit or reject, as a whole. We see from this that also with Leibniz the whole content of reality resembles a mathematical formula in which each part is rigidly determined by others and itself determines them, so that not only does the past include the future, but also the latter the past" (Lotze, Syllabus of Lectures on 'German Philosophy since Kant,' 1882, p. 7). We shall see further on how Lotze himself attempted to modify this scheme of Leibniz, giving it a freer, not purely logical, consistency. Whether we admit this rigidity in Leibniz's conception or not, it is quite clear that, so far as the problem of knowledge is concerned, Leibniz admitted the necessity of considering the purpose or meaning of things as a clue for finding the mechanical causes through which it was attained: a rule which was applied in the shallow and popular philosophy of the *Aufklärung* to put forward trivial explanations which made the whole ridiculous. This was quite contrary to the spirit of Leibniz; for we may say that if Spinoza taught us to contemplate things "sub specie æterni," Leibniz taught us to contemplate them "sub specie universi."

surrounding us in time and space, and that which deals with the highest questions of our life, our destiny, and our duties.[1] Occupying this position, the object of the philosopher is not to increase our knowledge of things natural or spiritual, but to appreciate the difference and importance of these two regions of knowledge, to show how we acquire each, what kind of certainty is attainable in either, and, if possible, to make sure that neither of the two should overstep its true limits and interfere with the other. But the immediate followers of Leibniz on the Continent did not maintain this judicial attitude, but, as I stated above, devoted themselves more exclusively to a rationalising of all knowledge. This attempt was somewhat justified by the necessity of teaching philosophy in the High Schools and Universities. It entailed a systematisation of the Leibnizian ideas, which by their author himself had never been developed in a final, systematic, and complete form. In this attempt many of the best suggestions of Leibniz were lost—to be taken up again at a much later period, as I shall have ample opportunity to show in the sequel.

30. Systematisation of Leibniz's ideas.

All the foremost thinkers in the seventeenth and eighteenth centuries on the Continent were guided by the desire to arrive at a unity of philosophic thought and to establish a consistent philosophic creed, which should do justice to the claims of science as much as to those of religion, affording equally the means of increasing knowledge and of arriving at the ultimate grounds of

[1] Lotze has given a clearer definition to this twofold aspect by distinguishing between the world of things with their connections and the world of values or worths.

certainty and truth. The outcome of their labours, however, was not very encouraging. It seemed rather as if the attempt to unify and harmonise had succeeded only in showing up more clearly the existing differences. At the same time, the growing volume of actual knowledge attained in the different empirical sciences, and especially the increasing precision which the introduction of the mathematical methods afforded, made these sciences more self-reliant and dogmatic. On the other side, the vagueness and seeming uncertainty of all philosophical speculations referring to the general order of the world and the destiny of human life produced in many thinking minds doubt and indifference, and among believers the conviction that salvation could only be found by a strong dogmatic assertion of the truths of traditional faith, which were guaranteed by their historical origin and confirmed to the believer by an inner light which was not assisted by philosophical reasoning.

31.
New way
opened by
Kant.

The existence of this dogmatism on both sides, as well as the growing doubt and indifference with regard to the most important questions which confront the serious thinker, led, in the mind of Kant, to what seemed to him to be a new way out of the existing dilemma and perplexities. It seemed to Kant that, before entering on a discussion of the higher problems of philosophy— problems which he termed transcendent—it would be necessary, systematically and methodically, to examine into the processes of observation, experience, and reasoning. Although this had already been, to some extent, undertaken by Locke, and before him by Descartes, it had not been undertaken for the definite purpose of answering the question, how is knowledge possible which refers to those things that transcend our senses? This kind of knowledge Kant termed metaphysical. It was not the "plain historical method" which Locke had adopted that seemed to Kant to lead to a useful solution of the problem. The investigations of Locke, pushed to their seemingly inevitable consequences, had led to the scepticism of Hume, which was followed either by abandonment of the whole problem or by, what seemed to Kant, an uncritical appeal to common-sense. A better way for dealing with the questions started by Locke seemed to be indicated by the position taken up by Leibniz in his 'Nouveaux Essais.' These had been posthumously published just about the time (1765) when Kant had been strongly influenced by Locke's and Hume's writings. This suggestion was contained in the formula which Leibniz succinctly opposed to Locke's formula. The latter maintained that our intellect contains nothing which was not given by our senses. To this Leibniz agreed, with the addition, "except the intellect itself." This formula suggested an examination of the intellect as such, or, as Kant termed it, the criticism of pure reason. In deliberately placing this problem before philosophers as an introduction or preliminary investigation which should precede any attempt to decide whether the human mind was capable of arriving at knowledge or certainty regarding things spiritual and transcendent, Kant founded that philosophical discipline termed later on *Erkenntnisstheorie*, Epistemology, or Theory of Knowledge. The result which Kant arrived at, and which appeared to him to contain a reply to all

the vexed questions which then exercised the minds
of thinkers, was not reached by a detailed psychological investigation such as has since been carried
out through the labours of independent thinkers in
all the three countries, *e.g.*, Mill, Renouvier, Wundt,
and their successors; it was gained by a much
shorter and much more abstract process. Kant relied
on two points which he considered were well established. The first and most important of these was
the existence of a definite amount of perfectly certain
and assured knowledge contained in the sciences of
mathematics and mathematical physics; the second was
a definite body of doctrine contained in the formal logic
and the empirical psychology of the schools, both of
which Kant himself taught in his academic courses.
So far as the first point is concerned, Kant had a
broader foundation to build on than Descartes before
him, inasmuch as he could not only point to pure
mathematics, but had in addition also, what he considered the ideal of scientific achievement—the natural
philosophy of Newton.[1] So far as the second point is

---

[1] It has, however, been shown (*e.g.*,
by E. Dühring in his 'Kritische
Geschichte der Allgemeinen Principien der Mechanik,' 3rd ed., 1887)
that Kant's notions as to the principles of dynamics and physics were
still extremely inaccurate and confused. Although in the minds of
some of the great mathematicians,
such as Newton in England and
d'Alembert in France, very precise
views existed, these have only very
slowly become the property of
philosophical thinkers. Nor does
it appear as if Kant himself contributed much to this important
clearance of ideas. Neither his

early tract, which deals with the
measure of *vis viva* (1753), nor
his treatment of dynamical and
physical conceptions in the celebrated 'Natural History of the
Heavens' (1755), shows any strict
definition or consistent use of
dynamical principles. And it is
significant that Ernst Mach in
his historical Treatise on these
subjects ('Mechanik in ihrer Entwickelung,' 1883, Eng. trans. by
M'Cormick) has no occasion to
refer to Kant. With Kant the
fundamental notions of arithmetic
(numerical and general), of geometry (synthetic and analytic), of

concerned, he was hampered by the formalism in the logic as well as in the psychology of his day, both of which he gratefully accepted.

In spite of the strong recommendation of the inductive methods by Bacon, the science of logic dealt, at that time, mostly only with deductive and syllogistic reasoning, without attempting to analyse the processes by which knowledge was extended in the natural sciences, such as the methods of inference and of proof. And Kant's psychology was the empirical faculty-psychology of the school of Wolff, improved by some of his followers, such as Tetens and Baumgarten.

The theory of Knowledge had been independently attacked by Locke and Hume; but Kant was able to go beyond the position they had reached, for he had before him the significant and suggestive answer which

**32.
Relation to
Locke,
Hume, and
Leibniz.**

phoronomy (kinematics), of dynamics (kinetics), and of physics (gravitational and other) were none of them clearly distinguished. That in each of these sciences an additional notion, principle, or axiom is involved was not clear to thinkers—certainly not to philosophers—of that age, nor for a long time after. Kant identified numbering with the temporal series in analogy with geometry, which deals with spatial series or dimensions. The purely phoronomical science of "kinematics," of which Kepler's Laws were the most brilliant example, was not separated from "kinetics," which is based on Galileo's experiments and Newton's laws of motion, implying the conceptions of force and inertia (mass). Again, Newton's natural philosophy, which to Kant was the ideal of a science, brought in the notion of attraction (action at a distance), a purely empirical fact, based upon a synthesis of Kepler's and Galileo's discoveries. To these notions Kant added in his cosmological theories the correlated notion of repulsion, following the vaguer theories of the ancients, and suggested also by elementary electric and magnetic phenomena. The modern conception of energy was, so far as mechanical phenomena are concerned, anticipated by Leibniz, who suggested a measure for mechanical action. That the celebrated controversy which raged over this matter between the Leibnizians and the Cartesians had been finally settled by d'Alembert in his 'Traité de Dynamique' (1743) seems to have been unknown to Kant ten years later. In the last chapter we have seen how Kant was also influenced by the traditional psychology of his day.

Leibniz had given to Locke's sensationalism in the 'Nouveaux Essais' published in 1765.[1] It is probable that the study of the latter helped to give to Kant's speculation its peculiar and characteristic form.

33.
Locke and
Kant.

From the Introductions to their respective works which treat of the theory of Knowledge, the 'Essay' of Locke and the first 'Critique' of Kant, we learn that both thinkers were led to their investigations by the desire to explain and possibly to aid in settling differences of opinion which they met with among thinking persons and in the teaching of the schools. But these differences were, with Locke, enclosed in a narrower circle—we may say they were Confessional differences. During the period of more than two generations which

[1] This opens out an interesting historical question, which may be somewhat differently answered according as our interest lies in the development of thought or in that of Kant's own ideas. Kant was wont to compare the revolution in Thought, which he suggested, to that worked by Copernicus in physical astronomy. As the latter had changed the centre of the universe from the earth to the sun, so Kant proposed to change the centre of Ideology from the external world of experience and science to the internal active principle of the human intellect. But this was indicated already in Leibniz's formula. Historians of the Kantian philosophy tell us, as Kant did himself, of a turning-point in his speculations, and assign this to a period somewhere about 1769 or 1770. This is represented sometimes as a kind of awakening out of his dogmatic slumbers, and is then connected with the influence of Hume (e.g., by Paulsen), some-times as a continuous development under various influences, that of Rousseau being also specially mentioned. This view of the continuity in Kant's development is mainly represented by Prof. Höffding in his interesting articles in the seventh volume of the 'Archiv für Geschichte der Philosophie' (1894). Neither he nor F. Paulsen ('Immanuel Kant') refers to the fact that the 'Nouveaux Essais' of Leibniz were made known to the world in 1765, just before the time when the Copernican change in Kant's views was being established. This is brought out by Prof. Windelband in an article in the 'Vierteljahrsschrift für wissenschaftliche Philosophie' (1876), and referred to in his works on history of Philosophy, quoted above. It is somewhat remarkable that Höffding in his important Discussion does not refer to Windelband's article; Paulsen mentions it only incidentally, and attaches little importance to it.

lie between Locke's and Kant's Treatises, the circle of interests had widened as much through the influence of Locke's speculations themselves in this country, and still more in France, as through that religious and political unrest which, in the sequel, led to the French Revolution. The difference between political, social, and religious creeds had become more and more accentuated till it became a question, not of different shades of belief but of belief and unbelief, not of different orders of society but of the maintenance or dissolution of any order, of scepticism, of indifferentism, and subsequently, of anarchy. The problems which presented themselves to Locke in a limited sphere had gradually assumed the largest dimensions, and required much deeper research and more drastic methods for their solution.[1] As an example, we need only point to the

[1] That Kant's main object in publishing his 'Critical Philosophy' was to settle the conflict between Knowledge and Faith is clearly brought out by Paulsen in the Introduction to his Work. It is mentioned by Kant himself in the preface to the first edition (1781), but still more emphatically in that to the second edition (1787). Whereas in the earlier preface he treats the subject more from a purely scientific point of view, attacking mainly the dogmatism and indifferentism of the age, and mentioning only incidentally in the Introduction the higher problems, he very emphatically urges the practical consequences of his doctrine in the later preface. This was no doubt done in order to explain more clearly what he had secretly at heart: to establish beyond doubt and cavil the sacredness of the moral law and the religious beliefs which it entails. "A cursory view," he says, "of this Work may suggest that the value of it is purely negative, to induce us in speculation never to venture beyond the limits of experience ; and this is indeed its first merit. . . . But such a criticism . . . is indeed of very great and positive value if we consider that there exists a necessary, practical, the moral, use of pure reason, in which it inevitably extends itself beyond the limits of our sensuous experience " (Pref. to 2nd. ed., Rosenkranz' ed. of 'Kant's Works,' vol. ii. p. 675). "In this way the teaching of morality maintains its position, as does likewise natural science its own. . . . And just this Discussion shows the positive gain of the critical principles of pure reason with regard to the conception of God and of the simple nature of our Soul (p. 678). I had accord-

wider view on religious toleration of Bayle in France
and later of Lessing in Germany compared with that
of Locke in England. How much more important a
correct theory of knowledge and the problem of ultimate
certitude had become in the interval and to foremost
thinkers on the Continent is shown by the tone of the
two Introductions referred to above. The plain historical method of the friend of Bayle and Sydenham and
the tutor of Shaftesbury in England, contrasts significantly with the boldness of the solitary thinker of
Königsberg (the "All-Destructive"), who sweeps away
all the existing philosophy of the schools, proclaims
a new era of thought, and anticipates that within twenty
years the new doctrine, with all its important and reassuring consequences, might be generally accepted.[1]

Kant, indeed, had at heart a vindication of the fundamental verities of religion: of the belief in the existence
of God, the Immortality of the soul, and the Freedom of
the Will. Was the human intellect able to reach in
these matters of belief something like that certainty
which belonged, according to his view, to the sciences of

ingly to remove knowledge in order
to gain room for faith. The dogmatism of metaphysics . . . is
the real source of all unbelief
which contradicts morality (p. 679).
This is not a performance which
should be undervalued: once for
all by a Socratic method, *i.e.*,
through a clear proof of the ignorance of their opponents to put an
end to all attacks on morality and
religion " (p. 679).

[1] At the end of his first 'Critique'
Kant gives what he terms the
'History of Pure Reason,' and
closes this short chapter by con-

trasting his method with that of
Wolff on the one side and of Hume
on the other. "The critical way
is the only one open. If my
reader has been obliging and
patient enough to follow this in
my company he may then judge
whether . . . what many centuries
have not been able to attain might
not be achieved before the end of
the present one, namely, to give
to human reason complete satisfaction regarding that which has
always, but hitherto unsuccessfully,
engaged her curiosity."

applied mathematics; and, if not, on what foundation had this belief to rest? Mere experience could not give to knowledge the characteristics of universality and necessity—it could not make it generally valid or convincing. The question then presented itself, how does some of the knowledge we possess, viz., mathematical knowledge, arrive at this generality and convincing evidence? Leibniz had suggested that empirical knowledge did not consist merely of a collection of sensations, but that there was the intellect itself which collected them. And with Kant the problem of knowledge took the form of asking: What does the intellect supply so as to bring into the casual material gained by experience, the logical qualities of universality and certainty? And this question was asked with an eye to the higher interests of the human mind, the truths of morality and religion.

By formulating the problem in this way, Kant issued, as it were, the programme of philosophical thought not only for his age but down to the present day. It is, however, well to recognise that, so far as the theory of knowledge is concerned, he was not in a position, nor in possession of the necessary preliminaries, to carry out his programme successfully. This has been done, to some extent, by thinkers in all the three countries since his time. In Germany, and largely also in France, it has been done mainly under the influence of Kant's own doctrine; in this country—as we have seen above— an independent beginning was made by John Stuart Mill, who, probably only through the study of Hamilton's philosophy, was induced to lay his account with Kantian ideas.

34.
Kant's
philosophy
a central
point.

Be this as it may, the philosophy of Kant has, as the nineteenth century advanced, been more and more considered as a central point in the development of modern thought. Especially so far as the problem of knowledge is concerned, we find that the different sides which this problem presented to different thinkers in different countries were already explicitly given or implicitly contained in the writings of Kant. Here his lasting influence may be shown in the great number of preliminary and subsidiary problems which he formulated, and into which he divided the main problem itself; not least also in the large array of new terms which he introduced for the definition of these problems. Through them he succeeded in fixing the attention of his own and subsequent ages. For our present purpose it may be convenient to gather this formidable body of thought under three headings.

35.
Relativity
of Know-
ledge.

First, Kant gave to the ancient theory of the Relativity of Knowledge a new form and expression. He did away with the primary (mathematical) properties of external things, which even Locke considered to afford a real, not merely a phenomenal, knowledge of things. He showed that these properties, which refer to the existence of things in time and space, are not less dependent on the nature of the human mind than the so-called secondary properties which depend on the nature and operation of our several sense-organs. Also he showed that to the forms of time and space belonged a special definiteness, that the conceptions of extension and duration, and the properties of things connected therewith, possess a greater convincing evidence, more generality and stability than attaches to the casual and fleeting impressions of our senses. This view crystallised in the doctrine of the Ideality of time and space.

Secondly, having deprived external reality of all the attributes with which the human mind describes it, maintaining that these refer only to its appearance in time and space, not to its intrinsic essence, he nevertheless did not destroy what remained in the human mind as a definite, though empty, idea of a thing. This essence of reality, the truly real, as opposed to the merely phenomenally real, Kant described as the Noumenon, that which we are obliged to think though we cannot see or describe it. For this he coined the characteristic term, the "Thing in itself"; the unknowable substance and cause which lie behind the phenomenal world. He identified it with the Intelligible as opposed to the merely Sensible. This remaining phantom, a relic of earlier metaphysics, which Kant did more to perpetuate than to explain and correct, has done incalculable mischief in subsequent systems of philosophy.[1]

36.
The sensible and the intelligible.

[1] It was especially unfortunate that this doctrine of the "Thing in itself" became, for a considerable time, the central point of interest in the literature which sprang up abundantly around the Kantian philosophy with the object of confirming or refuting it. The novelty of the term gave it exaggerated importance, as did likewise a mistaken explanation given of it by Reinhold, who otherwise, as we shall see presently, was one of the most successful expounders of Kantian ideas. "In all these discussions it is important to note that they referred only to the 'Critique of Pure Reason,' and that none of those who led them understood at all the ultimate connection of the Kantian 'Critiques.' Just for this reason the notion of the 'Thing in itself' which, with Kant, was the connecting link between theoretical and practical philosophy, was here considered only in its theoretical meaning, and as such, it was rightly found to be untenable. Thus it has come about that this conception, which

Thirdly, having distinguished the two worlds, the intelligible and the sensible, the world of things in themselves and the world of mere appearance, he applied this distinction to the human mind itself, and maintained that so far as our own self and nature are concerned, we possess an entrance into the world of the truly real. Following on the lines indicated already in antiquity in the Ideology of Plato, he distinguished the world of ideas from that of phenomena: for Kant, however, ideas did not add anything to, they served only to regulate, experience. Foremost among these regulative ideas stands out the self-regulating freedom of the human Will. Indeed to safeguard this and the moral law was a prompting idea in Kant's whole speculation. Here we meet with our real nature, we gain a glimpse of the existence of a universal mind. This view has become a leading idea in many of the foremost ethical systems since the time of Kant : we shall have specially to consider it in a later chapter. So far as the theory of knowledge is concerned, it had the important influence of representing the human mind, not as merely receptive or reflective, as was the case in the philo-

37.
The regulative ideas.

for Kant's theory of Knowledge recedes into the background compared with that of *a priori* knowledge, was in the sequel pushed into the foreground, and that the main object of the 'Critique' was sought . . . in this doctrine of the 'Thing in itself.' And this tendency was nursed by the fact that the majority of the opponents was composed of popular philosophers and teachers whose interest consisted primarily in disproving Kant's refutation of a reasoned knowledge of 'Things in themselves.' As these objections reacted upon the followers of Kant, these strove to clear the notion of the 'Thing in itself' . . . of its inherent contradictions. . . . Accordingly the further development of the critical philosophy was mainly occupied with the disintegration of the notion of the 'Thing in itself'" (Windelband, 'Geschichte der Neueren Philosophie,' vol. ii. p. 201).

sophies of Locke and even of Leibniz, but as an active principle. Knowledge is not merely collected, arranged, and abstracted, it is essentially also created by the human mind, or, as Kant said, by human Reason.

It is not only in the Kantian theory of knowledge that we find a novel treatment of these three main points —the nature of time and space, the difference of appearance and reality, and the formative or active principle of the human intellect; even thinkers who, like Comte, Mill, and Herbert Spencer, elaborated their theories independently, have eventually arrived at conclusions which were more or less in harmony with views explained or indicated by Kant himself.[1] His philosophy, and as

[1] Among the contemporaries and early critics of Kant three deserve notice as dealing specially with the theory of Knowledge and connecting or contrasting Kant's doctrine with earlier speculation. Gottlob Ernst Schulze (1761-1823) wrote under the name (with its sceptical suggestion) of Aenesidemus (1792). He shows that the critical philosophy does not solve the problem left over by Hume ; for, according to Kant, causality, being a necessary form of thought and applicable only to things of experience, is not applicable to the "Thing in itself," to that which transcends experience. The new philosophy thus contains an inherent contradiction, and the great problem of knowledge remains where Hume left it. Salomon Maimon (1754-1800) came from the Jewish religion through great vicissitudes of life and thought to study Kant's philosophy, after having become acquainted with the works of Spinoza, Leibniz, Locke, and Hume. He attempted to remodel the Kantian theory of knowledge by doing away with the unknowable "Thing in itself," and reducing the evident difference as to clearness and certainty of knowledge to that indicated already by Leibniz in his doctrine of the *petites perceptions*. Kant had a high opinion of Maimon's ability, and went even the length of saying that he was the one of his followers who had understood him best. The best and most concise of his writings is considered to be that on the 'Categories of Aristotle' (1794). It is interesting to note that he undertook to write a philosophical dictionary, evidently recognising the important part which verbal terms play in philosophy. The third and most constructive among the earlier critics is Jacob Sigismund Beck (1761-1842), who led on to three important developments of philosophic thought, to Fichte, Herbart, and Schopenhauer. He likewise rejected the Kantian solution as contained in the doctrine of the "Thing in itself." "He found the only possible position from which the critical philosophy could be judged in this, that what

part of it also his theory of knowledge, may thus be regarded as a focus in which the different lines of earlier thought, both ancient and modern, were collected and brought into mutual contact, and from which they emanated with altered shades and colours. And still more has the general tenor of his thought, his critical attitude, as shown in an earlier chapter, been almost universally adopted in the course of the nineteenth century, and more so towards the end than in the beginning of the period. Kant is, therefore, a representative thinker. His philosophy looks backward and forward and all around, and consciously or unconsciously mirrors the thought of his own and the subsequent age: that of his own country as well as that of the neighbouring nations. To show this, we need only take up the two aspects which I mentioned above. Consider, first, the emphasis which Kant laid upon the existence of a body of certain and assured knowledge contained in the mathematical and mechanical sciences. Here he not only inherited the predilection for mathematical treatment characteristic of French philosophers as well as of Spinoza and Leibniz, but he also assimilated the spirit

38.
Acceptance
of extant
body of
scientific
knowledge.

to an individual consciousness is given as an 'object' must be contained in an original hyper-individual consciousness which is accordingly authoritative, so far as empirical knowledge is concerned. In the place of 'things in themselves' he put Kant's 'consciousness in general.' In this way he explained the *apriority* of mental forms and categories, so that what is given in the manifold of sensation remained also for him the unsolved residue of the Kantian problem" (Windelband, 'Geschichte der Philosophie,' p. 485). Prof. Windelband shows also how near he comes in some respects to Berkeley's Idealism. "It cannot be denied that between the standpoint of Beck and that of Berkeley the dividing lines are difficult to draw. But neither Kant nor Fichte occupied Berkeley's position. Kant did not, inasmuch as he stuck to the reality of things in themselves; neither did Fichte, inasmuch as he was far removed from the spiritualistic ground of the English thinker."

of the Newtonian philosophy in the exaggerated form in which it was later proclaimed by the school of Laplace in France.

And so far as the second point mentioned above is concerned, Kant's acceptance of traditional psychology and his reliance upon definite categories or forms of judgment suggested by the Aristotelian logic, supplied a fruitful subject for discussions among followers and opponents. These showed the necessity for that deeper psychological and anthropological treatment which logical doctrine subsequently received at the hands of English, German, and French thinkers.

39.
And of traditional psychology.

In the following chapters we shall have abundant occasion to realise the central position which Kant occupies in philosophical thought. At present we are specially concerned with the new lights which, as we have seen, he was able to throw upon the problem of knowledge. And here one of the great defects of Kant's method has revealed itself as much through the labours of his followers as through the criticism of his opponents. This defect consisted in the apparent want of unity in his doctrine. That this was to a large extent only apparent has been shown by recent historians of philosophy, and more fully in the researches of a whole series of writers who have made the study of Kant's works their principal task.[1] That it struck his contemporaries

40.
Apparent want of unity.

---

[1] Among these may be mentioned a series of publications which was started in 1896 by Prof. Hans Vaihinger under the title 'Kant-studien,' and which has been continued up to the present day ; further, a number of independent works by thinkers all over Germany and latterly also in other countries, the titles of which may be found in the tenth edition of the 4th part of Ueberweg-Heinze's 'History of Philosophy,' p. 225. This extensive literature has been fully consulted in their respective 'Histories of Philosophy' by Höffding

so forcibly is owing to various circumstances, among
which the two following are of special interest in a
History of Thought. The first refers to the internal
character, the second to the external fate, of the new
doctrine.

41.
Criticism
pre-
dominant.

In Kant, the critical and analytical, the dividing and
dissecting spirit, cast into the background the synthetic
and constructive process of thought, and still more the
synoptic and comprehensive view.[1] Although Kant had,
as stated above, a central conviction which was in the
end to be the crowning idea of his system,——the supreme
reality, importance, and dignity of the moral principle,——
this was not put forward with sufficient clearness and
emphasis as a constructive principle in the first of his

and Windelband, who themselves
have made important contributions.
Prof. Vaihinger was also active,
on the occasion of the Kant
Centenary, 1904, in creating a
"Kant-foundation" and a "Kant-
Society." The Berlin Academy has
been publishing since then a complete
edition of Kant's Works and Correspondence. As Professor Heinze
says, "a real comprehensive digest
of the results of recent Kant researches has not yet appeared."

[1] Anticipating what I shall endeavour to bring out more clearly
in this and following chapters, I
may say that the synthetic and
constructive spirit gained the upper
hand in the most prominent of
Kant's immediate followers, in
Fichte. Subsequently, the synoptic
view was that peculiar to Schelling,
in whose writings the power of
synthesis and of construction, and
still more that of criticism and
patient analysis, was much less
conspicuous. The synthetical process, although opposed by Kant
himself to the analytical in his

celebrated distinction between synthetic and analytic judgments,
leads always only to an artificial
product in which the constituent
elements are still discernible, as
the stones are in a building, the
particles in a mosaic, or the parts
in a machine. In order to come
nearer to the true nature of real,
physical or mental, things, we must
start with their Together as it presents itself in the expanded world
of time and space, or as it is concentrated in the totality of human
intellect and character. This was
the starting-point of Schelling's
original speculations, reached, to a
great extent, under the influence
of Goethe's poetical insight into
the world of nature and of mind.
Hegel, in his conception of the
absolute mind, tried to combine
the synoptical view of Schelling
with the constructive spirit of
Fichte, and in doing so has, in a
different way from Kant, issued
what has become the programme
of philosophical thought ever since.

great works, nor did Kant ever carry out his intention
of giving the new metaphysic or reasoned philosophical
creed which he had in his mind, and which was implicitly contained in what he modestly represented as
merely preparatory works. The result was that he was
often misunderstood and misrepresented. Some mis-
interpretations, even of his followers and admirers, he
tried to correct in his later writings, but it was left to
others to import unity into the seemingly disconnected
parts of his doctrine. As this unity was not that which
Kant himself had in view, it led away from the main
line of thought which he had marked out.

So far as the second point is concerned, it is important
to note that the first successful attempt to introduce
the Kantian philosophy to the general intelligence of the
nation, and subsequently to the students of the German
universities, happened to issue from that centre which
had already become the home of the creative genius in
German poetry, literature, and art. It was there, in the
innermost circle of German culture, at Weimar and
Jena, that the earlier Kantian school of philosophy was
founded by a man who had started from entirely different
beginnings, but who was troubled by the same religious
and doctrinal perplexities as Kant himself had in view,
and who had personally experienced, in the depths of
his own soul, the reassuring and strengthening influence of the Kantian doctrine. This was Reinhold[1]

42.
Reinhold.

[1] Karl Leonhard Reinhold was born in Vienna and received his education in a Jesuit College, which he had to leave when the Order was suspended by Pope Clement XIV. in 1773. Thence he entered a freer atmosphere in another Roman Catholic College, in which he subsequently became a teacher of philosophy. Carefully watched by the Order to which he still belonged, he escaped to Leipzig,

(1758-1823), who, as Kuno Fischer says, is "in a certain
sense a compendious expression of the development of
[German] philosophy during the last decade of the
eighteenth century." An ardent admirer of Kant's first
'Critique,' which he had read five times, he set before
himself two distinct tasks.

The first of these was to make Kant's doctrine more
easily and more generally understood, to mitigate the uncouth terminology in which it had been propounded, bringing the leading ideas of his teaching into contact with
the general thought of the age and making it a fit subject for academic instruction. The second was to import
a greater unity and harmony into the Kantian doctrine, to
fill up the gaps which had apparently been left between
the different parts of the system, and to arrange the
whole according to one all-embracing principle. The first
task he brilliantly accomplished in his 'Letters on the
Kantian Philosophy,' which were published in Wieland's
literary journal five years after the appearance of Kant's
first 'Critique,' and which may be said to have trans-
planted Kantian philosophy from its eccentric position

and from there, through an introduction of the Austrian poet Blu-
mauer to Wieland, he came to Weimar and became an inmate of the
family of Wieland, whose daughter
he subsequently married. A contributor, and later on the editor of
Wieland's literary periodical, 'Der
Deutsche Merkur,' he first came
across Kant's writings in a review
of Herder's 'Ideen' which Kant
had published in the first volume
of the recently founded 'Jenaer
Litteraturzeitung.' To this he replied, but was led to a profound study of Kant's first

'Critique.' Captivated especially by the practical and religious
ideas contained therein, "he finds
here the foundations of faith independent of all metaphysical knowledge, and, in consequence, the
doubts solved which free thought
creates. He is convinced that
the Kantian philosophy, correctly
understood, must produce a bene-
ficial and radical change of human
thought, and he determines to do
his part to let this light be kindled
in men's minds" (Kuno Fischer,
'Geschichte,' &c., vol. v. p. 43).

in the extreme north-east into the centre of Germany. From there it spread to Göttingen, Leipsic, and subsequently to all the Protestant and to some of the Roman Catholic teaching centres of Germany. At Weimar it came into contact with, and was eventually greatly influenced by, the new literary—at once poetical and religious—movement. The importance and promise of this new movement[1] had been early recognised by the spirited Duchess, Anna Amalia of Weimar, a Brunswick princess and niece of Frederick the Great, who, after the early death of her husband, ruled the small State with remarkable intelligence, and with an equal regard for the welfare of the people and the culture of art, science, literature, and learning. For the education of her two sons she had engaged the celebrated author, Wieland; his recommendation being that in one of his writings he had discoursed with much freedom and liberality on the education of princes and the administration of the State. By this step she laid in 1772 the foundation of the leading position which Weimar occupied for a long time during the golden age of modern German literature and art.[2]

[1] Many recent historians of literature and philosophy have tried to convey to the present more prosaic and realistic generation an idea of the great change which took place in German culture at that period. I quote only one passage among many. "The whole culture of the age had arrived at a great turning-point. It began to descend into more profound depths of thought and sentiment. Feeling and passion began to waken from slumber, imagination stirred gently and ventured, here and there, to penetrate through the surface dried up by rationalism. To act, to suffer, and to enjoy with one's whole being—this striving had awakened in deeper minds such as that of Hamann. In the poetry of the youthful Goethe it found vent in stirring revelations. It worked in no one so actively and in so many-sided a manner as in the soul of Herder," &c. (Haym: 'Herder, nach seinem Leben und seinen Werken,' vol. i., 1880, p. 577).

[2] During the fourteen years previous to the importation of Kantian philosophy into the literary circle, enormous changes had

Through the transportation of Kantian ideas into this centre the fate of the new doctrine was for long decided in advance. The exclusively critical character which the titles of Kant's larger works perhaps unduly emphasised, had, under the influence of a great national, educational, and literary movement, soon to be abandoned or left to secluded thinkers. The doctrine had on the other side to contribute what it could to that movement itself, which, as I have had frequent opportunity to remark, was destined to bring about nothing less than the poetical, literary, artistic, and, in the sequel, the political elevation and regeneration of the German nation. That in the midst of such interests the problem of knowledge would occupy an important position was just as clear as it was certain that this problem would not be conceived in a

taken place in the small Duchy, which comprised only 750 square miles. Three years after the arrival of Wieland the regency had been terminated by the accession of the young Duke, Karl August, who having, in the company of his military tutor, Knebel, a man with many literary and intellectual interests, become acquainted with Goethe at Frankfort, invited the latter to Weimar offering him a high position in his Administrative Council. Not long after this he had, at Goethe's suggestion, appointed Herder to fill the highest clerical position in the country, admiring in him a liberal and spiritual theologian, qualified to oppose the prevailing narrow orthodoxy. The University of Jena flourished likewise under this enlightened government, and counted among its professors many eminent scholars and naturalists. Among these were Schütz and Hufeland, who, as editors of a renowned literary paper, represented, as did Wieland in a different way, the new literary spirit in opposition to the prosaic 'Aufklärung' which had its centre in Berlin. As Goethe wrote to Eckermann, the Duke "possessed the talent to take the measure of different minds and characters, and to assign to each its place." And as the latest biographer of Goethe, A. Bielschowsky, says, "By means of this great gift, and with his generous temperament and his rich talents, he not only succeeded in gathering around him the first minds of the nation, but, what was much more, he retained them" (vol. i., 7th ed., 1905, p. 276). For the third time, as Julian Schmidt says, "after 1517 (Luther) and 1675 (Leibniz), one of the small States monopolised the intellectual movement in Germany and gave to it a special character" ('Geschichte der Deutschen Litteratur,' vol. ii., 1886, p. 240).

narrow and purely logical spirit. The consequence was that the critical movement which in philosophy was initiated by Kant's writings was for a long time cast into the background, being superseded by the more enticing and, as it seemed, more promising constructive movement of thought. The purely scientific position which starts from a definition and seeks for a criterion of knowledge was abandoned in the attempt to give expression to an actually existing higher kind of knowledge, an ideal content, which was labouring into birth in the writings of the great representatives of German literature, notably in the works of Herder and Goethe.[1] Those

43.
Criticism superseded by construction.

[1] In order to realise the new influence which was to make itself felt in the development of Kantian ideas, it is well to recall some facts and dates showing the great activity in the literary world during the decade which preceded the arrival of Reinhold at Weimar. Herder had published the most important and stirring of his theological writings, having progressed from his early critical, through a poetical, to a deeper philosophical treatment of the religious problem. During the decade from 1774 to 1784 he published, *inter alia*, the following Works :—

'Vom Erkennen und Empfinden der Menschlichen Seele.'
'Auch eine Philosophie der Geschichte.'
'Aelteste Urkunde des Menschengeschlechts.'
'Provinzialblätter an Prediger.'
'Erläuterungen zum Neuen Testament.'
'Volkslieder.'
'Theologische Briefe.'
'Vom Geist der Ebräischen Poesie.'
'Ideen zur Philosophie der Geschichte.'
Lessing's 'Nathan der Weise' appeared in 1779; Wieland's 'Oberon,' 1780; Bürger's 'Lyrics,' 1781 to 1785. Above all there towered the enormous productivity of Goethe, who had given to the world 'Götz von Berlichingen,' 'Prometheus,' 'Werther's Leiden,' 'Klavigo,' 'Faust' (first form privately circulated), 'Wilhelm Meister,' 'Iphigenie.' Turning away from his earlier critical and lyrical writings, and liberating himself from the influence of the "storm and stress" literature, Goethe had assimilated the spirit of the Antique : through it and through a simultaneous study of nature and art during his journeys to the Harz, the Alps, and Italy, he rose to that unique conception of the world and life, and that philosophical calm which separated him for some time from Schiller, whose early stirring dramatic works began to appear in the year that saw the publication of Kant's 'Critique.' To this we must add the renewed influence of Rousseau, whose 'Confessions' appeared after his death in 1778, and the still greater influence which the study of Spinoza exerted on all these thinkers.

who were inspired by this new world of ideas saw in it a definite something which strove for realisation, and which only awaited a suitable form, the right word, the adequate expression by which it should be rendered intelligible to the expectant and receptive minds of the younger generation; a possession not limited to a few creative intellects, but the common property of the many that came under the influence of the great educational movement which was spreading over most of the countries and nations of Europe. In fact, the problem of knowledge was for them not contained in the questions, What is knowledge, and where and how is it to be found? They rather saw with their mind's eye the existence of a higher kind of knowledge in the shape of definite ideals, and the problem of knowledge consisted in realising these ideals and finding a suitable expression for them. No one had uttered himself more clearly in these matters than Goethe himself, who at that time had already in many ways declared that the Highest reveals itself to the human mind only through intuition,—that it is not elaborated by thought but felt and seen : he had in his own creations made it actually visible to the increasing number of his admirers. If some of the contemporaries of Kant, notably Hamann, Jacobi, and Herder, had contented themselves with emphasising the independence of feeling, belief, and faith, as the ultimate original sources of knowledge, Goethe succeeded through the wonderful intuitive powers of his mind in embodying in the poetical creations of his artistic genius what others only believed and felt, thus strengthening enormously the constructive and creative movement of thought.

These influences did not make themselves fully felt in the region of philosophical thought till ten years later. In the meantime a new element was imported into the philosophical and literary circles of Jena through the arrival of Reinhold's successor, Fichte. He took up and proposed to fulfil the second task which, as I stated above, Reinhold had set himself but had not successfully carried out—the unification of the Kantian doctrine. A great personality, a strong and unbending character, self-reliant in abstract thought as well as in action, he was the very man to bring out the moral power, as well as the ideal sides, of the Kantian system.

He professed to understand Kant better than did his immediate followers, including Reinhold.[1] Nor was it difficult for him to find in the writings of Kant, especially in the two later Critiques,[2] many valuable suggestions which would aid him in the accomplishment

---

[1] After having lectured for three years Fichte found it advisable to publish an authentic Introduction to his philosophy (1797); partly in order to correct certain misunderstandings, partly also to emphasise that his intention always had been to expound the true Kantian system. He remarks that Kant's intention to give to the philosophical thought of the age an entirely new direction had completely failed. "Kant is up to now, with the exception of one recently published suggestion, . . . a sealed book, and what has been read into it is just what is not adequate and what he desired to contradict. . . . I have not to do with the correction and extension of current philosophical views, but with the complete routing of them and an entire reversion of thought"

(Fichte, 'Werke,' vol. i. p. 420). The one exception which Fichte refers to is the philosophy of Beck.

[2] After the publication of the first 'Critique' in 1781 Kant published in 1785 'Principles of the Metaphysics of Ethics'; in 1788 his 'Critique of Practical Reason'; and in 1790 his third 'Critique,' which was to give unity to the whole of his system, the 'Critique of Judgment.' Fichte published in the true Kantian spirit in 1791 his Essay on 'Criticism of Revelation,' in which he applied Kant's principles to the religious problem. This was followed by the last of Kant's important works, 'Religion within the limits of Pure Reason' (1793). It was in the year 1794 that Fichte came to the University of Jena.

of his task. But he also very soon became convinced
that the Kantian scheme would require considerable
modification in order to meet what he considered to be
the demands of the age. What attracted Fichte most
in Kant's philosophy was that Kant assigned to the
practical reason or the moral principle in human nature
the supremacy over the purely intellectual side.   In
this moral region were not only to be found the answers
to the great fundamental questions, which the purely
logical analysis was unable to give, but it also appeared
that the "categorical imperative" or moral law was the
greater, the only, reality with which man was able to
confront the otherwise overwhelming and crushing
reality of the external world. What in Kant's philosophy came at the end of a long and wearisome logical
and dialectical process seemed to Fichte to be worthy
of being elevated to the position of the initial and
dominating principle of all speculation. This was the
fact that the human mind was primarily not reflective
and passive, but active and assertive.   Action, self-
assertion, comes before reflection ; a primary synthesis
precedes the subsequent reflective analysis. The many
opposites and dualities which played such an important
part in the 'Critique of Pure Reason,' such as sense and
intellect, understanding and reason, form and content,
cause and effect, appearance and reality, the phenomenon
and the noumenon (or the thing in itself), freedom and
necessity,—all these appeared to Fichte to be mere
abstractions which were made out of the original unity
by the activity of the intellect or pure reason, apart from
which they could not be understood.   This unity itself

indeed did not exist in the form of individual minds, but in that of the all-embracing mind or consciousness which formed the background of everything. To get hold of this the philosophical thinker had to retire into the recesses of his own mind and rise through a process of intellectual intuition. And that such was possible, and not only an interesting and poetical fiction, was made evident by the existence in every one of the prompting Will or active principle. This conception of an intellectual intuition,[1] of an intuitive understanding, had already been suggested by Kant in the first, and more fully developed in the last, of his three Critiques, in which he had thrown out the idea of an intellect which was not merely discursive and analytical, but which was synthetic and intuitive. The existence of organised beings in nature, and of the creations of the poetic and artistic genius, proved, according to Kant, that sense and intellect, the world of external appearance and the world of reason (freedom), are not absolutely separate, but are rooted in an original synthesis or common ground.

[1] Fichte has given several explanations of what he means by intellectual intuition. "This contemplation of his own self which we expect from the thinker, and through which he becomes aware of himself, I call intellectual intuition. It is the immediate consciousness that I act and what I am performing : it is that through which I know something, because I do it. That there exists such a faculty of intellectual intuition cannot be demonstrated nor developed through reasoning. Every one must find it immediately in himself. . . . The demand that one should prove it through reasoning is much stranger than the desire of one born blind that one should explain to him what colour is without his being able to see it. . . . Every one who claims to be active appeals to this intuition. In it lies the source of life, and without it there is death. . . . It is a remarkable thing in modern philosophy that it has not been perceived that what can be said against the existence of an intellectual intuition may also be said against sensuous intuition [perception]" (vol. i. p. 463).

Having once arrived at this conviction of an underlying spiritual unity, the difficulty for Fichte was how
to descend from it into the diversities and contradictions
of the actual world which surrounds us, or philosophically
to explain how it comes that that which is essentially
and originally united should have unfolded itself in the
world of many things, many persons, and many contradictions. This difficulty Fichte does not profess to solve :
he merely interprets it. The existence of materiality, of
the mechanical, of all that destroys the original unity
and harmony, is for him just as much an immediate and
inexplicable fact as is the conception of the spiritual
and deeper unity. But of the two facts the latter is
for us human beings the greater and more important,
brought home to us continually by the necessity to act,
to do something, and by the possibility of self-determination according to some ethical principle or moral law.

The attempts of Fichte to elaborate the logical and
psychological details of his great conception must now
be regarded as unfortunate, and indeed at the time
they tended to bring discredit upon the whole of his
philosophy, exposing it to much criticism, and even to
ridicule.[1] His greatness lay, not in the direction of
logical analysis, but rather in the personal fervour with
which he emphasised the principle of freedom and self-
determination according to high moral standards. He
did this in an age when the sense of liberty was making
itself felt everywhere among the rising generation.
With them it was frequently apt to run riot, and

---

[1] Fichte himself complains of this in the above quoted Introduction of
the year 1797.

nothing was more wanted than the gospel of duty, of self - restraint, and the strong belief in the existence of high and realisable ideals.

Although Fichte called his philosophy " *Wissen-schaftslehre*," a kind of theory of knowledge which was to precede the different doctrines in which special knowledge was communicated, we find little in his writings of those kinds of investigation which nowadays go under the name of Epistemology. Fichte's contributions to the problem of knowledge lay in a different direction; [1] and though he found it necessary

---

[1] Though Fichte's writings are now little read, it is well to note that we find in them many tendencies indicated which have been further developed in subsequent philosophical thought. Thus he suggested that only two systems of philosophy are conceivable, the materialistic and fatalistic on the one side, the idealistic on the other. This has been borne out in the history of subsequent thought. He terms the former dogmatic, whereas the latter is, following Kant, supposed to be critical. Not to decide which of the two to accept is the attitude of scepticism. The decision or choice itself depends on the resolution of the character. We shall see in the sequel how this view is also that of Lotze. What is peculiar to Fichte is that he sees more clearly the logical difficulties which stand in the way of the materialistic hypothesis than those which stand in the way of the idealistic. This is largely owing to the fact that he stands quite outside of the exact and natural sciences which were making such great progress during his age. A further important idea which has become fruitful in recent philosophy takes with Fichte the form of denying the existence of the "Thing in itself" which remained in Kant's philosophy as a limiting conception, a tribute to the common-sense way of looking at things. In modern philosophy this argument has taken the form of a denial of the conception of substance as a fundamental principle, and of replacing it by that of process. With Fichte the idea of substance, matter, or "Thing in itself" was in the course of the activity of the universal (hyper-individual) intellect or self produced as a necessary conception. The intellect, or pure reason, was not merely the form, as with Kant, with which to comprehend the material content given by our senses; it was not only the form but also the matter or content of knowledge. Thus Kant's idea of what he termed the transcendental unity of apperception became with Fichte identical with Kant's fictitious intuitive understanding. The unity of apperception became identical with intellectual intuition. Further, with Fichte the problem of knowledge received an extension in a direction indicated already by Leibniz, and brought out in the clear-

in his later years to enter into more detailed logical
and psychological discussions, the principal interest he
took in it was to enforce by argument, as well as by
the influence of his powerful personality, a conviction
of the existence, for the human mind, of a definite
and immediate source of certainty regarding the highest
problems of conduct, action, and duty.   In fact, he
laboured perhaps more than any other thinker at the
establishment of a philosophical creed that should
be of practical value in the solution of the great
problems which were then being ventilated on the

est terms subsequently by Lotze.
Knowledge does not deal only with
an increasing number of purely
empirical data, the things and
events which surround us ; it does
not, secondly, consist in addition
only in certainty—that is, in the
necessary connection or relation of
things (laws physical and mental) ;
but it consists, thirdly, also in a
comprehension of the meaning of
things, of their purpose, of the
all-embracing system or order of
the whole.   Thus Knowledge is,
first, descriptive, and as such continually accumulating and extending itself ; secondly, constructive
and synthetical, joining together to
a necessary system ; and, thirdly,
synoptic, viewing and interpreting
the whole in a general scheme, revealing the meaning and purpose of
things.   And, lastly, we find two
modern ideas foreshadowed already
in Fichte's doctrine.   The beginning of philosophy is not a logical
principle which would require proof,
and thus lead to an endless regres-
sion of thought.   The beginning of
philosophy is a postulate : you must
do something, you must act.   The
idea of action nvolves that of overcoming a resistance.   In following

out this train of thought, a meaning
is assigned to the objects or tasks
which present themselves to be
solved ; ever reappearing in new
forms, they constitute the activity
of the intellect.   Difference and
opposition is always required to
maintain action.   The overcoming
or solution of existing differences
and difficulties produces ever new
and higher tasks.   Logically this
scheme is indicated by the formula
of thesis, antithesis, and synthesis ;
in Fichte's system we find the
birth of the dialectical method
practised and extolled later on by
Hegel.   Inasmuch, however, as
Fichte is forced to throw back the
whole of the active process of the
intellect into a hyper-individual
region, he leads the way to the
world of the unconscious, out of
which the difference of subject and
object, of self and other selves,
emerges in the minds of finite
persons.   The conscious activity of
the conscious and moral self leads
us back to the conception of an
unconscious striving or instinct as
the source and essence of all reality.   This idea we also meet with
under various forms in recent
philosophy.

Continent: the problems of education raised in France by Rousseau, and practically worked out by Pestalozzi; the problem of reason and faith raised by Kant and Jacobi; the problem of liberty raised by the French Revolution; the problems of the reconstruction of the State and society which followed in the sequel of that great movement,[1] and of the breaking down of all the old landmarks during the Napoleonic wars. He found a foundation whereon to build in Kant's doctrine of the primacy of practical over theoretical reason, and he filled in the seemingly empty forms or categories of Kantian morals by emphasising a higher spiritual reality. The existence of such a higher reality was not merely a personal conviction of Fichte's; he only saw, felt, and expressed more clearly and tried to define what an ardent younger generation were striving for, and what had found expression and become an active power in a new literature and a new poetry.[2] In urging the necessity that all thought and

45.
Fichte representative of a new generation.

---

[1] The earliest of these problems was that raised simultaneously by Kant in his first 'Critique,' and by Jacobi in his publication, after Lessing's death, of his conversation with the latter on the philosophy of Spinoza. Jacobi himself treated of it in his subsequent writings, in which he took up an independent position to Spinoza, Kant, Hume, and, later on, to Fichte. The problem of education assumed a definite form and received a practical and realistic treatment through Pestalozzi, who published the first of his popular Works in 1780, with a significant appeal to Goethe to identify himself with the new movement, just at the time when the latter was already, as is shown in 'Wilhelm Meister,' moving away from the purely classical to a more practical ideal of life. Fichte himself, before approaching theoretically the problem of knowledge in his 'Wissenschaftslehre,' had contributed to the solution of these various practical problems in his earlier writings on 'Revelation' (1792), on 'Freedom of Thought' (1793), on the 'French Revolution' (1793), and on the 'Vocation of the Scholar' (1794).

[2] Schiller had stirred the minds of the younger generation by a brilliant succession of poetical and dramatic productions; had been appointed to fill the Chair of History in the University of Jena (1787); had, under the influence

knowledge must be ultimately based upon the immediate evidence afforded by the senses, he did not limit the word sense to mean only the external or bodily senses, upon the evidence of which ordinary knowledge is based ; he extended its meaning to denote the existence of a higher sense which, though latent in every human mind, requires, nevertheless, to be nursed and educated so as to furnish the entrance into the region of spirituality and form the beginning of the higher life.[1] And he

of Herder and others, developed independent theories on historical, æsthetical, and educational subjects ; and had latterly, in prose and poetry, given a new turn to Kantian ideas on ethics and the vocation of art in the development of culture and society. Above all, there had appeared in the year 1790 the first rendering of Goethe's greatest and immortal work ' Faust,' in which there occur the memorable words : "*Im Anfang war die That.*" Kuno Fischer, with an equal knowledge of modern poetry and modern philosophy, was the first, in his ' History of Modern Philosophy' and in his smaller writings, to show the intimate connection which existed between the literary and the philosophical movement at Jena and Weimar at the end of the eighteenth and at the beginning of the nineteenth century. This interconnection, which nevertheless did not deprive either of the two movements of their independent and original character, has been more fully traced by Prof. Windelband and also by recent biographers of Goethe, Herder, and others. Using a modern phrase, we may say that Fichte preached Pragmatism—but on a higher level than

is done in America and England at this moment.

[1] More recent expositions of Fichte's philosophy and the development of his ideas have brought out clearly that he laboured up to the end of his comparatively short career (he died in 1814 from hospital fever which he, as well as his wife, caught whilst devoting themselves, during the War of Liberation, to the nursing of the sick and wounded) to give more precision to the fundamental conception from which he had started twenty years before. This view, established notably by Kuno Fischer and Windelband, contradicts to some extent an earlier conception which had its origin mainly in the polemic of Schelling, who tried to show that Fichte, under his influence, had modified the character of his speculation. There seems no doubt that Fichte himself was aware that his fundamental idea required clearer exposition, a more thorough logical and psychological grounding ; but he refused to see that what was lacking in his own treatment had been at all supplied either by Schelling or by Hegel. His independent attitude of thought is

maintained that the certainties which this higher sense reveals to those who cultivate it depend just as much upon immediate evidence, upon intuition and insight, as all the truth of external reality depends ultimately upon the evidence of our external senses. By this doctrine of the immediate certainty afforded by the perceptions of our lower and higher senses, he repeated the truth which has been many times urged by the greatest thinkers, and many times forgotten by those

brought out with much power in the last rendering of his ' Wissenschaftslehre,' which is contained in the last course of lectures which he delivered at the University of Berlin in the year 1813, published posthumously by his son, J. H. Fichte, in the year 1834. The immediate source of all higher speculation is asserted there very distinctly : the fact that all knowledge is based upon immediate conviction afforded by some lower or higher (physical or spiritual) sense. Starting with the declaration that neither Kant nor he himself had been correctly understood, he proceeds to state what he, in the beginning of his career, had represented as the cardinal point of his doctrine; what had not been quite clear to Kant ; and what, after a lengthy acquaintance with this attitude of thought, had become clear to himself, viz., that " this doctrine presupposes an entirely new inner sense-organ through which a new world is opened out which does not exist for the ordinary human mind. This is not to be understood as an exaggeration or a rhetorical phrase thrown out only to claim so much more—with the secret reserve that so much less would be given,—but it is to be

understood literally as follows : for human beings as they are through birth and ordinary education this doctrine is distinctly unintelligible ; the things of which it treats don't exist for them, because they have not got the sense through and for which these things exist. . . . They cannot understand it, they must misunderstand it. The first condition, therefore, is that the sense be created in them for which these things exist" (Fichte's 'Nachgelassene Werke,' vol. i. p. 4). He then goes on to explain by analogy with the physical senses the nature of this higher sense. It aims at a reformation of the whole man, a renewing and expansion of his whole existence out of a contracted into a wider circumference. He further explains that this sense exists potentially, but must be drawn out or developed. That such a sense exists is not a new doctrine : it has been used ever " since human beings existed, and what is great and excellent in the world and through which alone humanity is preserved comes from the visions of that sense. That such a sense exists is not new, but it has only been clearly seen in recent times," &c., &c. (ibid., p. 7).

who do not penetrate to the fundamental questions. It is
the doctrine with which Descartes started and with which
Spinoza ended,—the reliance on the certainty afforded by
intuition or vision, be this physical or intellectual.

46.
Schelling.

Still less did Schelling, Fichte's immediate successor
and disciple, make any important contribution to what
we nowadays call the theory of knowledge; but he
laboured, as did Fichte, at imparting a definite kind of
higher knowledge which he believed he possessed, without being able in the course of the many phases which
his philosophy traversed to satisfy himself that he had
found the right and adequate expression. There is no
doubt that he saw the task of the philosopher in his
age to consist in the formation of a philosophical creed;
but whereas Fichte was essentially a strong character
and a man of action who taught and inspired the youth
of the nation, Schelling was more of an artist and a poet.
Addicted to symbolical expressions and to reasoning by
analogies, he possessed a finer insight into the workings
of the poetical genius and the mind of the artist. This
led to, and was sustained by, his intimacy with Goethe;
in fact, he seems to have been the only one among the
great philosophers of the idealistic school for whom
Goethe preserved a lasting interest and appreciation.
Some of his deliverances embody, as it were, a few of
Goethe's favourite ideas.[1]   Thus he occupied a position

[1] One example instead of many
may suffice. It shows the abstract form which Schelling gave
to such ideas, and his assimilation
and appreciation of the latest
philosophy in Goethe's poetical
creations. It refers, as Kuno
Fischer has pointed out, to Goethe's
'Faust' in its earliest rendering.
"As in consequence of their
common origin, the inner nature
of all things must be one, and as
this may be seen to be necessary, so
likewise this necessity lives in any
construction which is founded
thereon. Such, therefore, does not

to the philosophical problem of the age entirely unlike that of his master, from whom he separated when it became evident that the philosophy of the latter had but little love of nature.

One of the reasons which prevented the great thinkers with whom I am now dealing from contributing anything appreciable, beyond occasional brilliant suggestions, to a truly scientific theory of knowledge, was that they possessed neither the critical spirit of Kant nor the sceptical spirit of Hume, and that they had not, what Kant possessed, a personal acquaintance with what we now call exact or mathematical knowledge. One of the prevalent notes of their teaching was indeed the endeavour to counteract the scepticism of Hume and Voltaire, and the sceptical consequences of Kant's criticism; and further,

47.
Want of criticism and exactness.

require to be confirmed by experience, but is sufficient of itself, and can be continued beyond the limits which experience cannot transcend, as, for instance, into the innermost mechanism of organic life and of universal motion. Fate does not exist only for action ; Knowledge also is confronted by the essence of the totality of nature as an unconditional necessity ; and if, according to the dictum of an ancient thinker, the strong man in conflict with circumstances is a drama on which even the gods look with pleasure, so likewise the struggle of the mind for a sight of the real nature and the eternal essence of the phenomenal is a not less inspiring spectacle. As in the tragedy, the conflict is not solved by the downfall of either necessity or freedom, but only through elevating each to a complete equality with the other ; so also the mind can only step victoriously out of its conflict with nature in so far as nature becomes identical with mind and transfigured in the ideal. To this conflict, which arises through an unsatisfied longing for a knowledge of things, the poet has attached his creations in the most characteristic poem of Germany, and opened an ever fresh source of enthusiasm which alone was sufficient to rejuvenate science in this age, and to throw over it the breath of a new life. Whoever desires to penetrate into the sacred interior of nature may nourish himself with these tunes out of a higher world, and imbibe in early youth the power which emanates, as it were, in solid rays of light from this poem and moves the innermost centre of the world " (Schelling, 'Werke,' sec. i., vol. v. p. 325, &c. ; Kuno Fischer, 'Geschichte der Neueren Philosophie,' vol. vi. (1872) p. 836).

to impress upon the minds of their hearers and readers the existence of a higher, more unified, and more spiritual knowledge than that which the separate sciences afforded. With the conviction that such a higher field of mental activity really exists, and is within the reach of the human intellect, they started on their way. We must remember that they were neither surrounded by growing material prosperity and industrial enterprise, to which contemporary thinkers in this country might direct their attention, nor had they grown up in the midst of the great achievements which the exact scientific spirit could boast of in France at the end of the eighteenth century. Industrial progress and economic wealth were just as much wanting in Germany at that time as was the correct appreciation of the exact methods of research, notably of applied mathematics. The only thinkers of importance who were acquainted with what we nowadays look upon as exact knowledge were Fries and, somewhat later, Herbart. Both these thinkers stood, however, too much outside of the interests and aspirations which then guided German literature and German thought to earn speedily from their contemporaries the recognition which they deserved. No better example exists of the defects as well as the peculiar kind of inspiration which characterises the more impressive deliverances of the idealistic school, than the introduction to the series of lectures which Schelling delivered at Jena in 1802 "On the method of academic study." Without leading up to the elevated position which he desires to occupy, he at once propounds the idea of an unconditional and unified knowledge, and he bases this on the conviction that the truly ideal is alone the truly real. He admits that even in philosophy this essential unity cannot be strictly proved, as it rather furnishes the entrance to all that can be called science,[1]—the only possible proof consisting in this, that what claims to be science aims just at realising this identity, at merging the real in the ideal, and *vice versâ* at converting the ideal into reality. Such announcements, which to us nowadays sound oracular and rhetorical, would no doubt have had only a passing and deterrent effect had the majority of German students been aiming (as they do nowadays) at becoming scientific, professional, or industrial experts. To such, in however noble a light their vocation might present itself, it would soon have become evident that this doctrine of the Immediate and of the Identity of the ideal and the real did not condescend to indicate the practical ways and means of research. They would have sooner or later turned away

---

[1] "The appropriate training for a special profession must be preceded by a knowledge of the organic whole of science. He who wishes to devote himself to a special pursuit must know the place which it occupies in the whole and the special spirit which enlivens it, as also the kind of culture through which it fits into the harmonious structure of the whole; the way also by which he has to approach his science, that he may not be a slave but free to move in the spirit of the whole. It will therefore be seen that an academic study can only proceed out of a genuine insight into the living connection of all sciences, that without it every precept would be dead, soulless, and narrow. But perhaps this demand has never been more pressing than in the present age when everything in science and art seems more strongly to aim at unity, when even things most distant come into contact, when every movement which takes place in the centre spreads more immediately into the different parts, and when a new organ of intuition is everywhere being created. Such an age cannot pass without the birth of a new world which leaves those who have no part in it buried in nothingness. It must be left mainly to the fresh and unspoiled powers of a youthful generation to preserve and develop this noble endeavour, &c., &c. . . . No one is excluded from co-operating. . . . He must contemplate his science as an organic member and recognise in advance its task in this new-born world."

from it. Illustrious examples of this kind are to be found, *e.g.*, in J. von Liebig, Johannes Müller, E. von Baer,[1] G. T. Fechner,[2] who nevertheless in their further development retained a large share of the idealistic spirit. Fortunately, however, for the idealistic school, it could count on the support of two movements which were then much more prominent in Germany than the culture of the exact sciences, whose only great popular exponent and later patron, A. von Humboldt, was then travelling in the tropical regions of the New World.[3]   These two

[1] See vol. i. of this History *passim*, especially pp. 207, 208.

[2] The influence of Schelling upon Fechner is important and probably typical. It is described by Fechner himself in a characteristic passage quoted by J. E. Kuntze ('G. T. Fechner,' 1892). "Through my medical studies I had become a complete atheist, alienated from religious ideas ; I saw in the world only a mechanical scheme.   At that time I came across Oken's 'Naturphilosophie,' which I began to read with a friend.   A new light seemed to me all at once to illuminate the whole world and the science of the world.   I was as if dazzled by it.   In truth I did not really understand anything properly—how could that have been possible ?—and I did not advance beyond the first chapters ; but, in effect, I had at once gained the position for a grand united view of the world, began to study Schelling, Steffens, and other philosophers of nature, failed indeed to find in any of them clearness, but thought I could myself do something in that direction, of which some Essays in 'Stapelia Mixta' (1824) bear testimony.   But even now I remember that I once put to myself the question : Could anything, by the ways of Oken-

Schelling, have been found of the beautiful and orderly connection of optical phenomena which Biot lays before us with such clearness ? Certainly natural science does not lie in these ways. . . . The influence of that period in the direction of a uniting activity and a spiritual penetration of nature has remained for me and has found expression in later writings, although I could then no longer consider the view of Schelling - Oken to be adequate" (pp. 39, 40).

[3] There lived in Germany at that time, at the University of Göttingen, another prominent representative of the genuine scientific spirit, the great mathematician, C. F. Gauss. Although, however, he had already published in 1801 his most original work, 'Disquisitiones Arithmeticæ' (see vol. i. of this History, p. 120), he was practically unknown to German scholars and thinkers.   Not a great teacher, he belonged to the small international society of foremost mathematicians and astronomers of the age, for many of whom his labours furnished the starting-point of entirely new developments. His 'Theoria motus corporum cœlestium' was published in 1809 (see ibid., p. 324).

movements were, as I have had occasion to point out before, the higher educational movement and the growth of the critical spirit in literature, art, history, and theology. For both of these movements the ideal aims, though vague, were nevertheless of inestimable value : indeed history has shown that both these movements have fallen to a lower level in proportion as these ideal aims have lost their meaning and their hold upon them.

But also within the idealistic school itself the want was felt of a distinct method by which the beginner could be gradually introduced into the region of philosophical thought. There must be some way of leading up from the position of common-sense and ordinary reasoning to the heights of speculation. There was wanted what the ancients called a special dialectic which should traverse the different stages of the intellectual process, leading the mind on from lower to higher, from familiar and concrete to larger and more abstract conceptions. The great work which was dictated by a feeling that this was the desideratum of the age, and which had for its aim to exhibit this gradual rise of the philosophic mind to the heights of speculation and the establishment of a comprehensive philosophic creed, was Hegel's 'Phenomenology of Mind.'[1] This work appeared in 1807.

48. Hegel aims at supplying the want.

[1] The 'Phenomenology of Mind' may be studied from various points of view, and the important position which the work occupies in the history of Thought becomes evident as we realise how many different sides and interests it represents. It may be considered as a logical development of the main idea which governed the philosophical and poetical thought of the age, and which was most clearly expressed in advance by Spinoza when he identified the order which prevails in things with the order which prevails in our thoughts about things. The philosophy of Spinoza introduced to the age by Lessing, Jacobi, and Herder came as a welcome and inspiring solution of the

In the preface Hegel breaks with what he calls the philosophy of reflection, and proposes to bring into connection the different elements of thought and the different philosophic positions which, in the critical philosophy and in the systems of Fichte and Schelling, had remained disconnected, as it were improvised at random, forming postulates in the former, and, in the latter, solutions

dualism which had been created as the result of the Kantian doctrine that no proof existed that the human intellect (the order of thought) was identical with, or an expression of reality (the order of things). To realise this solution Fichte had clothed the Spinozistic conception in that of a moral order or fundamental activity of mind. Schelling, inspired by Goethe, had proclaimed that the union of the ideal and real lies beyond nature and mind, and is exemplified to us in artistic creation; whereas Schleiermacher, about the same time, maintained that this union existed only in religious feeling. These three thinkers drew their philosophical inspiration equally from Spinoza and Kant, for the latter had exalted the moral law as the supreme reality, had suggested the unifying power of intuition, and had cleared the way for religious faith. One step more was required, and this was to give a scientific or logical expression, not only to the reasoning of the human mind, but also to the fundamental unity proclaimed in these various forms under the name of the Absolute. The method was to be a scientific process, and the Absolute was to be conceived as a subject or a spirit. This task was what the 'Phenomenology' professed to perform. Hegel had pre-

pared the way in his earlier writings contained in the philosophical journal which he edited together with Schelling. Another point of view from which this work may be considered is that it is an attempt to show how, in the historical development of thought from the dawn of philosophy in the ancient world, that comprehension or definition of the Absolute was gradually matured which constituted the central conviction in the philosophical creed of the age; the timeless substance of Spinoza was to become a living process, the moving spirit in science and art as much as in religion and life. Again, we may see in the 'Phenomenology,' to a large extent, a personal history of Hegel's own mental development as it has become better known through the labours of Dilthey and others (see *supra*, p. 250, note). And lastly, we may regard the 'Phenomenology' as a programme, defining the highest intellectual task of subsequent thought, and giving the first sketch of a triumphant solution, to be followed by more detailed exposition. As such a programme, it has lived—perhaps unconsciously — in many historical and many critical labours since Hegel in Germany. It has been explicitly adopted by a modern school of thinkers in this country.

gained by intellectual intuition, *i.e.*, by a kind of in-spiration which not infrequently degenerated into guess-work.[1]

In the conventional histories of philosophy, the ex-position of Hegel's method and doctrine follows immedi-ately and naturally after the exposition of the systems of Fichte and Schelling; but for our purposes, since we are at present interested in the problem of knowledge, we must desist for the moment from entering into an exposition of Hegel's ideas, and this for the following reason. It is quite true that Hegel's philosophy is much occupied with the question of knowledge, but it does not contain what we nowadays call a theory of knowledge. If it solves the problem of knowledge at all, it solves it not by an analysis of existing knowledge, but by unfolding the new and higher kind of knowledge compared with which the actually existing knowledge was not considered to be real knowledge at all, but only a lower stage of merely apparent or preliminary knowledge. Desiring to estab-lish a philosophical creed, a reasoned and consistent view of life and its great questions, Hegel, as little as his predecessors Fichte and Schelling, considered it worth while to spend much time and labour in analys-ing such forms of existing knowledge as had proved themselves incapable of meeting the wants of the age, *i.e.*, of solving the great practical questions. In fact, the

---

[1] The most lucid exposition of Hegel's relation to the philosophy of his predecessors, and of their merits and defects, is to be found in the latter part of his posthumous-ly published lectures on 'History of Philosophy' (see 'Werke,' vol. xv. p. 534 to end). This course he delivered—as the editor, K. L. Michelet, tells us in the Preface—ten times during the last twenty-five years of his life.

interest of these thinkers lay more in replying to the question, What is the truly real?[1] than in solving the critical problems which Kant had put forward in his writings: they desired to solve the problem of reality rather than the problem of knowledge. Accordingly I propose to relegate the exposition of the more systematic views of these thinkers to other chapters, where we shall deal with the problem of reality and other related problems which again and again present themselves to the philosophical mind. At present we must look for the beginnings of the modern theory of knowledge in a different direction.

III.

49.
J. S. Mill's
logic.

In spite of the small interest that J. S. Mill's 'System of Logic' aroused in philosophical circles in Germany,[2] it is nevertheless true that what is now

---

[1] "With Schelling the speculative form has been re-established, and philosophy has become again something specific; the principle of philosophy, thought in itself, reasoned thought, has again received the true form of thought. Thus in Schelling's philosophy the content, truth, has again become the principal object, whereas in the Kantian philosophy interest attached mainly to this, that knowledge, understanding, subjective reasoning, were to be examined: it appeared plausible, first, to investigate the instrument, the process of reasoning. It is the story of the σχολαστικός who would not go into the water before he could swim. To examine the reasoning process means, to

reason about reasoning, but how we can reason without reasoning cannot be stated" (Hegel, 'Werke,' vol. xv. p. 657).

[2] It was owing to the influence of Liebig, who probably came across Mill's writings during his repeated visits to England in the 'Forties, that the 'System of Logic,' which appeared in 1843, was translated into German by J. Schiel (1849), and published by the firm of Vieweg in Brunswick, who for a considerable period brought out the principal scientific works in physics, chemistry, and the natural sciences. It does not appear to have had any influence on philosophical thought till much later, when the same subject—viz., the foundations and

termed *Erkenntnisstheorie* in Germany, and Epistemology in this country, is for the first time distinctly put forth in that work. It was prepared by the Baconian philosophy, the traditions of which, through Locke, Berkeley, and Hume, were inherited by the Scottish school, whose principal exponent in the first quarter of the century was Dugald Stewart. All these thinkers were impressed by the existence and growing volume of a definite kind of knowledge termed natural knowledge. This knowledge existed before an attempt was made to analyse it logically and understand it philosophically as a mental phenomenon. A serious attempt to do so was made by a group of thinkers who about the year 1830 marked the new era of mathematical science in England. Most of

method of scientific reasoning and research — had been taken up independently by German naturalists, among whom Prof. Wundt of Leipzig stands foremost. Wundt approached the problem of knowledge primarily from the side of the physiology of sense-perception, to which he added an original examination of the "axioms of the physical sciences and their relation to the principle of causality" (1866). Coming twenty-five years after Mill, when the exact and mathematical methods of research had, by him and others, been introduced and successfully applied in many fresh fields of natural science, he was able to approach the theory of knowledge with a much greater command of existing material and a better personal acquaintance than Mill possessed. It is interesting to note what Prof. Wundt himself says regarding Mill. "If the historian of science in the nineteenth century should wish to name the philosophical works which during and shortly after the middle of the century had the greatest influence, he will certainly have to place Mill's 'Logic' in the first rank. This only slightly original work has hardly had any important influence on the development of philosophy. It was first recommended by Liebig to the German scientific world, which at that time possessed few philosophical interests, and was frequently consulted when philosophical questions had perforce to be considered. Thus also the labours in the 'physiology of the senses' of Helmholtz . . . moved decidedly under the sign of Mill's 'Logic.'" Wundt then goes on to explain that it was not the association-psychology of Mill, but the Logic proper and the theory of the syllogism and of induction, that attracted Helmholtz, independently of their psychological truth or importance. (See W. Wundt in Windelband, 'Die Philosophie im Beginn des zwanzigsten Jahrhunderts,' vol. i. p. 28, &c.)

these, such as Sir John Herschel, William Whewell, George Peacock, A. de Morgan, belonged to the Cambridge school: they not only aimed at enlarging and deepening the mathematical sciences by introducing the French methods, but they also strove to understand more clearly the logical foundations of the mathematical or exact sciences. They felt the necessity of rewriting the *Novum Organum* of Bacon. Each of them worked in an independent way at the same task. Herschel published in 1831 his "Preliminary Discourse on the Study of Natural Philosophy," where in a number of examples he showed how the generalisations and discoveries of science were actually arrived at. William Whewell published in 1837 his "History of the Inductive Sciences" as Prolegomena to a "Philosophy of the Inductive Sciences founded upon their History" (1840). Peacock was one of the first who expounded the logical premises of general arithmetic. De Morgan's publications begin in the year 1831 with an essay "On the Study and Difficulties of Mathematics," which was followed by a series of writings dealing with the borderland of Logic and Mathematics, such as his essay "On Probabilities" (1838) and his "Logic" (1839). Some of these writings helped to stimulate Mill to the composition of his Logic, the first edition of which appeared in 1843. But there were two other influences which combined to give to Mill's work its representative character, both of which came from his father, James Mill. The first was the Association-psychology to which I referred in the last chapter; the other was the strong political bias which Mill inherited from his father, as well as from his father's friend,

Jeremy Bentham. This was strengthened by his early acquaintance with the political philosophers of France, notably those of the school of St Simon. Mill's acquaintance with Comte began before the publication of the Logic, but belongs mainly to a later date. Mill's Logic was the first systematic attempt in the direction of a theory of knowledge, and it starts by referring to " the modes of investigating truth and estimating evidence, by which so many important and recondite laws of nature have in the various sciences been aggregated to the stock of human knowledge." It is not likely that Mill had at that time any knowledge at first hand of Kant's ' Critique of Pure Reason.' Nevertheless it is significant to note how both he and Kant take for granted the existence of a body of correct knowledge as it is contained in the mathematical and natural sciences. But he at once separates himself by indicating as the final aim of his book " to contribute towards the solution of a question which the decay of old opinions and the agitation that disturbs European society . . . renders as important . . . to the practical interest of human life as it must be to the completeness of our speculative knowledge—viz., . . . how far the methods by which so many of the laws of the physical world have been numbered among truths irrevocably acquired and universally assented to can be made instrumental to the formation of a similar body of received doctrine in moral and political science." It is evident from this that Mill did not take, with regard to the problems of practical life, the same view as Kant and his successors, notably Fichte—viz., that the certainty in such matters starts

50. Ground common to Mill and Kant.

from a different and opposite pole to that from which natural knowledge takes its beginning.

It must, however, be admitted that in the course of his philosophical writings Mill came more or less explicitly to admit the existence of a something, of a mental factor, which could not be found and definitely traced by the process of analysis which he practised. And this admission dates from an early period in his life when he already, in opposition to his father, recognised the importance of Coleridge's influence, when he felt the power of Carlyle's oracular sayings, and when he was himself coming under the spell of Wordsworth's poetry. Regarding this hidden factor in mental life he nowhere expressed himself with sufficient clearness, though he rejected all the various attempts by contemporary English or foreign thinkers to define or locate it in a comprehensive philosophical creed. But there is no doubt that we find foreshadowed in Mill's writings the conception of the Unknowable which plays such an important part in later English philosophy. At present it is important for us to remark that we find in Mill something analogous to that position which, on a much larger scale, existed a generation earlier in German philosophy. As I have mentioned before, the constructive efforts of German speculation after Kant, the dogmatic assertion of a higher insight, which in single instances rose to a kind of inspiration, was derived from the regions of poetical, or creative, thought as it manifested itself in the great classical literature of the age. Similarly the poetical creations of the new school of poetry in England, notably of Wordsworth and Coleridge, the revelations of which were brought together by Carlyle, with cognate elements which Coleridge and he discovered in German literature, produced in the mind of Mill the impression of an actual reality, and elicited from him, in spite of his cautious and un-impassioned habit of mind, some very remarkable admissions.

Next to Mill and to those writers named above, all of whom continued the tradition of the Baconian philo-sophy, the thinker in this country who at that time laboured most effectually at the problem of knowledge was Sir William Hamilton [1] of Edinburgh. His writ-

51.
Sir W.
Hamilton.

[1] In point of time it would perhaps be more correct to say that the theory of knowledge in this country was first distinctly put forward as a special investigation and the problem of knowledge solved in a definite form by Sir Wm. Hamilton in a series of brilliant articles communicated to the 'Edinburgh Review' from 1829 to 1839. But the fact that they appeared anonymously and were more critical than systematic, also that they created what may be called a new style in the philosophical literature of this country, prevented their due appreciation till much later, when Hamilton exerted a great personal influence on Scottish and English thought through his (posthumously published) Lectures on 'Logic' and 'Metaphysics' at the University of Edinburgh from 1836 to 1856. The late Prof. Veitch of Glasgow defines Hamilton's conception of the philosophical problem as follows : "Science is knowledge—a form of knowledge. Whence knowledge in this form ? If we seek a cause of the fact of experience, we may, nay must, equally ask for a cause of our know-

ing the fact. Knowledge has its cause or source in what we call mind, and it is possible only under certain conditions. The primary problem of philosophy is thus to investigate the nature and necessary conditions of knowledge,—the conditions of its own possibility. What is knowledge ? and what are the laws of knowledge ? Such is Hamilton's conception of the problem of philosophy proper. Keeping this in view, we can see how the philosophy of Hamilton rises to its highest question — that of the nature of our knowledge of the absolutely first or of the uncondi-tioned. The line of causality in finite things leads backwards and upwards to the problem of an ultimate or primary cause, and we have the points—is this a necessity of inference ? is it an object of knowledge ? in what sense is it an object of faith ?" (Veitch, 'Hamil-ton' in "Blackwood's Philosophical Classics," 1882, p. 36, &c.)

As to Hamilton's philosophical antecedents Veitch says : "Even in his youth he had gone far beyond the range of reading in philosophy then usual in Scotland. He had

ings, most of which appeared anonymously in the 'Edinburgh Review,' date somewhat further back than those of the Cambridge mathematicians, and formed in a certain sense an opposition to the arguments employed by what we may call the empirical school. At the same time Hamilton's philosophy worked quite as effectively in the direction of generating the agnostic attitude of the succeeding period. Hamilton was as much influenced by Reid's original refutation of Hume as he was by Kant's 'Critique.' He believed quite as strongly in the truthfulness of our sensuous experience as he did in the relativity of all that we may call knowledge. To this latter doctrine he gave the name of the Doctrine of the Conditioned, maintaining that all that deserves the name of knowledge cannot rid itself of its inherent conditional character. To possess knowledge meant, for him, to move in the region of the

studied the 'Organon' of Aristotle, and had acquired a mastery of it at an early age, rarely paralleled at the close of the long and laborious efforts of a lifetime. Even at Oxford he knew it better than all the tutors. He was familiar with the principal schoolmen. . . . Descartes and the Cartesian school had been matter of minute investigation ; and from Descartes he gathered the ultimate principle in his theory of knowledge, viz., the subversion of doubt in the fact of consciousness. He had mastered German at a time when few people in the country knew anything about its literature or philosophy. He had given a quite competent attention to the 'Critique' and to the logical writings of Kant. He had traced the course of subsequent German speculation through Fichte, Schelling, and Hegel, as his unpublished notanda especially show. The influence of Kant both upon the cast of his thought and his philosophical phraseology is marked enough. In point of positive doctrine, however, the two men in Germany he most nearly approached were Jacobi and G. E. Schultze. . . . When he made his first published contribution to philosophy, in the Essay on 'Cousin' in the 'Edinburgh Review' of October 1829, the first impression, even among people who professed some philosophical knowledge, was that of astonished bewilderment rather than admiration or even appreciation. The Essay on 'Cousin' dealt with a question regarding the reach and limits of human knowledge which was wholly new, in form at least, to British speculation" (ibid., p. 26).

Conditioned. The Unconditioned, though it exists, is not an object of knowledge, not even to the extent that Kant conceived it to be—viz., as a limiting idea and regulative principle. To accept it as such is, in Hamilton's opinion, the great error of the Kantian philosophy, which opened the door to the vagaries of Kant's successors, who attempted to superimpose upon the existing knowledge of the Conditioned—*i.e.*, upon the only knowledge that is possible — a higher kind of knowledge, the knowledge of the Unconditioned or Absolute. Hamilton's criticisms are directed as much against Schelling and Hegel and their pupil Victor Cousin in France, as against that philosophy in England which starts from the knowledge we possess in the mathematical and physical sciences, and aims at penetrating by their methods into the region of mental and moral phenomena, as Mill hoped to do. For, according to Hamilton, our moral ideas are based upon the Unconditioned, which we approach only by faith, and upon the idea of freedom, through which the human being is elevated beyond the laws of a purely natural order.

On a larger scale than Sir John Herschel had attempted in England, an exposition of the leading ideas and methods of the exact and natural sciences was attempted about the same time by Auguste Comte in France. In many respects the influences which governed the early development of Comte's mind were similar to those which made themselves felt in the case of John Stuart Mill. Both had a precocious development; the ideas attained in childhood, which in the case of most, even of the great, thinkers are characterised

52.
A. Comte.

by vagueness, seemed to have acquired, both with Mill and Comte, definite forms at an unusually early age. Both also took at this early age a lively interest in social questions. But whereas for Mill the private and personal influence of his father ruled supreme and fixed permanently some of his mental characteristics, the great school for Comte was the *École Polytechnique* in Paris. According to his own statement,[1] in a letter to

[1] The letter to Mill is dated 22nd July 1842 ; to the same year belongs also the publication of the sixth and last volume of the 'Cours de Philosophie Positive.' This contains an elaborate preface occupied mostly with personal explanations. Comte there complains of the want of support and appreciation of his philosophical labours on the part of the members of the governing body of the École Polytechnique. To this he attributes his failure to gain a professorship, his connection having been limited to that of an entrance examiner. A reactionary spirit very different from that which governed the earlier period, when in 1814 Comte had entered the school, had, after a crisis in 1816, gradually supervened in the direction of the establishment. This change corresponds in time with the change which took place in Comte's own ideas, when, in the course of the composition of his great work, he came to deal with the biological and political sciences. He recognised more and more, what he had already indicated in an earlier tract (see above, p. 193, note), that the purely mathematical spirit, the analytical method, or, as he called it, the *esprit de détail*, must as we ascend in the sciences be supplanted or compensated by the *esprit d'en-semble*. This development of his own opinions, to which he gave

full expression in the 57th chapter of the 'Cours,' is significant, and was accompanied by his personal experience of the disproportionate encouragement which the mathematical or analytic spirit enjoyed at the expense of what we may now term the synoptic spirit. He had at one time hoped to introduce what he termed *la vraie spiritualité moderne*, through Guizot, whom he reluctantly approached with a proposal of founding, at the Collége de France, a Chair devoted directly to the general history of the positive sciences. But the want of sympathy which Guizot himself exhibited towards the purely mathematical tendencies resulted finally not in a support of the *philosophie positive*, but in the "dangerous restoration of an academy happily suppressed by Bonaparte." This was the restoration of the "Académie de Science Morale" referred to in vol. i. p. 145 of this History. "It is necessary," Comte says, "carefully to distinguish the two schools which, spontaneously antagonistic, divide between themselves, though so far very unequally, the general rule of rational positivism : the mathematical school, properly so called, still dominating without serious contention the whole of the inorganic studies, and the biological school, striving feebly at present to maintain, against the irrational ascendancy of the former,

Mill, he found in the studies and the methods which were pursued in that great educational establishment the first beginning of a true scientific corporation. There he also met with the republican spirit among the pupils, and an enthusiasm for the practical value of the studies which united them. These studies embraced mainly what we now call the exact sciences. The foremost representatives of this large and novel region of knowledge, the founders of new sciences, were the teachers of that institution. It is no wonder that this great body of knowledge came to Comte as a kind of revelation, and that the methods which it employed fastened themselves on his mind as models of the highest form of thought. In opposition to the vagueness of the popular philosophy outside this circle of interests, and the scepticism promoted by the critical school of thought, there must have been something as restful and invigorating in the serene calmness and assurance which is characteristic of the mathematical methods. Comte early fixed this character in his mind by the term positive, and the aim of his life became to expound and extol the canons of the positive sciences and to apply them to the solution of social and political problems. His great treatise, the 'Cours de Philosophie Positive,' was published between the years 1830 and 1842 in six volumes. In it he leads up, from the mathematical and exact sciences,

the independence and dignity of the organic studies. In so far as the latter understands me, it is at heart more favourable than hostile, because it feels in a confused way that my philosophical endeavour is directed towards liberating it from the oppression of the mathema-ticians. I have found there not only complete scientific appreciation in the person of my eminent friend M. de Blainville, but also numerous and respected adherents, &c., &c." ('Cours,' vol. vi. p. 22, &c.)

beginning with astronomy, through the biological to the
sociological sciences. Significantly he leaves out psychology and metaphysics. Through omitting the former
he stands in opposition to the then ruling school of
philosophy in France, headed by Royer Collard and
Victor Cousin; through omitting the latter he stands
in opposition to the ruling philosophical systems in
Germany. Though we read a great deal in Comte's
philosophy of the three stages of knowledge, the theological, the metaphysical, and the positive, and though
he emphasises the fact that positive knowledge is not
limited to that of facts, but looks for the connection
of things or the laws of nature, Comte does not contribute anything material to the theory of knowledge.
The exposition of the methods of exact research was
not followed as it was in England by a psychological
analysis of these methods. This was effected later [1] by

[1] Though English and, later on,
German thinkers have gained a
general reputation as having mainly
dealt with the logic and methods of
scientific thought, it is well to note
that France all through the nineteenth century possessed an extensive literature on the subject
which, on the whole, has attracted
little attention in other countries,
and has, even in France itself, been
very insufficiently appreciated.
There are notably four representatives of the mathematical, physical,
and natural sciences who occupied
themselves with the principles and
the philosophy of the sciences in
which they themselves had, through
their original researches, gained
great distinction. Foremost among
these stands André-Marie Ampère
(1775-1826). He was professor at
the École Polytechnique as well as
at the Collége de France, and one
of the greatest physicists of the
century, having earned through his
memoirs on electro-dynamics the
title of the "Father" of that
science. Of his philosophical writings his classification of the sciences,
differing from that of Bacon, became
known in England through Whewell
in his 'Philosophy of the Inductive
Sciences.' Somewhat later another
teacher at the École Polytechnique,
J. Duhamel (1797-1872), a contemporary of Comte, through his text-
books on the Calculus and on
'Analytical Dynamics,' exercised
for some time an important influence upon the teaching of higher
mathematics in France and Germany. He published in 1866-
1872 a large work in five volumes, 'Des Méthodes dans les
Sciences de Raisonnement,' in

other writers, such as Duhamel and Cournot. These latter writings, however, appeared at a time when other interests had already attracted European thought in all the three countries into other channels.

The conception which we form as to the nature of thought and its possible achievements, the attitude which an age takes up to the problem of knowledge, the natural history of the Logos which it believes in, does not depend so much upon theoretical investigations as upon those kinds of knowledge which are at the time prevalent and active, which are fruitful in new discoveries and suggestions, and increase the resources of the human intellect. A new region of knowledge opening out new fields of research is more interesting and

which he insists upon analysis as the true method not only in mathematics but also in other sciences. Contemporary with Comte and Duhamel was A. A. Cournot (1801-1877), a pupil of the Ecole Normale, who, beginning with a mathematical treatise on the 'Theory of Probabilities,' published a series of writings all dealing more or less with the methods and fundamental ideas of the various mathematical, historical, and economic sciences. Though original, his works had little influence at the time, but his memory has been quite recently revived since a new interest in the various subjects of his researches has sprung up (see 'Revue de Métaphysique et de Morale,' 1905, pp. 291-543). As eminent and original in physiology as Ampère in physics, Claude Bernard (1813-1878) produced a great impression through his 'Introduction à la Médicine expérimentale,' 1865, and 'La Science expérimentale,' 1878, in which he successfully combated the older vitalism still

prevalent in the medical schools of France without going to the opposite extreme represented by contemporary thinkers in Germany and some later biologists in France (see vol. ii. p. 409 of this History, where he is compared with Lotze in Germany). The traditional interest which some of the most eminent of scientific thinkers in France have, especially in later life, taken in the fundamental principles, the philosophy, and the history of their science has been maintained in quite recent times by such foremost thinkers as MM. Henri Poincaré, Jules Tannery, Duhem, and others, to some of whose writings I may have occasion to refer in the sequel. It is interesting also to inquire into the causes which gave notoriety to some of these writings, whereas others equally important and original were treated with comparative neglect. (See Lévy-Brühl in 'Revue de Mét. et de Mor.,' 1911, p. 292.)

eloquent than an abstract treatise on logic. The latter solves the problem of knowledge theoretically, the former does so practically. The second quarter of the nineteenth century witnessed the growth and recognised towards its close the existence of new fields of knowledge in various directions.

53.
Revival and deepening of the historical sciences.

The first great movement of this kind consisted in the revival and deepening of the historical sciences, under the influence of the critical spirit on the one side and the great ideals of classical literature on the other. On this I have discoursed in an earlier chapter. But this movement was very much strengthened by the peculiar development of the abstract philosophical systems themselves. In Hegel's system emphasis was laid on the genesis of ideas, on the gradual development of these ideas in the course of the history of the human mind. The consummation of the system itself was to be found in the History of Philosophy, which Hegel was the first to include as an integral and culminating portion of the whole edifice of philosophical thought. In the history of the different philosophical systems Hegel recognised the appearance in time of those categories or leading principles of thought which the 'Phenomenology' had traced in the individual mind, which the 'Logic' had brought into abstract expression, and which, with more or less success, had served as the leading canons through which to understand the development in nature, in art, in society, and in religion. This idea of mental development, of the movement and working of ideas in history, was put forward by Hegel with such force and supported by so many happy illustrations that it made a great impression upon the younger generation. What was merely suggested by Leibniz, Lessing, and Kant, what remained vague and elemental in Herder and found poetical expression in Goethe, seemed to be raised to the position of a definite science by Hegel. What was the subject of a kind of inspiration with earlier and less methodical thinkers became now, as it seemed, a teachable method. The great idea of development became suggestive of researches on a larger or smaller scale in many regions of historical, literary, æsthetic, and theological criticism. Other thinkers who did not follow Hegel into the same daring abstractions, and who could not find in the rhythms of the dialectical process the key for the understanding of the phenomena of mental life or their historical development, supported nevertheless through their historical studies the same movement. If they did not possess, they at least sought for, the right points of view, the leading ideas, from which to comprehend the mental life of earlier ages. Foremost among these stood Schelling and Schleiermacher. Notably, so far as philosophical thought is concerned, a great gain must be recorded when the study of the leading systems of ancient philosophy, pre-eminently of Plato and Aristotle, was revived, the first by Schleiermacher, the latter by Trendelenburg. In the year 1862 Trendelenburg could write: "Had such a powerful mind as Schelling begun his philosophical studies with Plato and Aristotle instead of going in the reverse order, backward from Fichte and Kant to the analogies of Herder, then to Spinoza, then to Plato and Giordano Bruno, then on to Jacob Böhm, and only finally to Aristotle,

. . . a chapter of German philosophy would have come out differently, larger, more lasting, and more fruitful. So important is it to march with history and to follow the historic development of the great ideas in mankind." [1] Gradually almost the whole philosophical interest in Germany—with two or three brilliant exceptions— threw itself into historical studies, bent upon tracing everywhere the movement of ideas, and thus elaborating on a larger and more accurate scale the programme of Hegel's philosophy. But as the lofty ideas of the classical period of German literature, where philosophy itself had found its inspiration, receded into the past, and what Hegel had done and Schelling attempted appeared to the critical eye to be untenable or shadowy, the flood of historical literature descended more and more to lower levels, spreading out in the study of mere detail. A loss of grasp, a disintegration of philosophical thought as a whole, was the inevitable consequence. Not unnaturally, therefore, a generation succeeded for whom the earlier leading ideals had lost their meaning, and who would accordingly seize with eagerness any new suggestion which afforded the prospect of arriving at that unification of thought which had been temporarily lost, but without which no fruitful progress could be made in any large department of knowledge.

Through the working of the scientific spirit as well as through that of the critical spirit, with both of which my readers have become acquainted in earlier chapters of

[1] See the preface to the second edition of 'Logische Untersuchungen.'

this history, a great body of new knowledge had been launched into existence during the first half of the century. To this all the three countries contributed, though, as has been shown before, science was most systematically cultivated in France and the higher criticism in Germany, whilst English learning preserved its traditional character by adhering to the experimental, historical, and inductive methods of investigation and exploration, without attempting that unification of thought which was such a prominent characteristic of Continental learning. This country has, however, the merit of having, under the influence of Mill and Hamilton, laid the beginnings in the theory of those modern processes of thought and methods of research which were practised with so much success in the exact and historical sciences abroad. The problem of know-ledge became accordingly a definite subject of a new science about the middle of the century: in England through Mill and Hamilton, abroad as a reaction against the perplexities which the criticism of the abstract, not-ably the dialectic methods had revealed. In Germany and France [1] the problem of knowledge became identified

---

[1] I must here draw attention, as I did on a former occasion (*supra*, chap. iii., p. 274, note 1), to the work of Charles Renouvier, who attempted from the year 1854 onward a reconstruction of the fundamental doctrines of logic and psychology on the lines of Kantian criticism. He proposed—as did, twenty years later, a school of thinkers in this country with reference to Hegel — to do the work of Kant over again, adhering more strictly than Kant himself to the lines of criticism and discarding the dualism which Kant had introduced into his system by adopting, in a special form, the old Platonic conception of the difference of appearance and reality. By doing this Renouvier deserves not only to be termed the first in time of the Neo-Kantians, but also the first of modern thinkers who aimed at a consistent system of pure phenomenism. This has been well brought out by Mr Shadworth H. Hodgson, who in two articles in

with a solution of those questions which Kant had
placed at the entrance of his celebrated Critiques. It
may, however, be doubted whether these purely theoretical, logical, and psychological investigations would have
brought about, by themselves, that great change which
has come over our ideas on the nature and value of
knowledge during the last forty years, had it not been
that the exact sciences themselves, about the middle
of the century, outgrew the boundaries which the older

'Mind' (vol. vi., 1881) has given,
as it seems to me, what is still the
best exposition of Renouvier's
fundamental conceptions, which he
classes with his own as "Phenomenism." "Had I," he says (loc.
cit., p. 32), "been acquainted with
M. Renouvier's Works when I
published the 'Philosophy of
Reflection' [2 vols., 1878] (as I must
now confess with shame I was not),
I should not have laid claim, in the
unqualified way I did, to have been
the first to dispense in a system of
philosophy with the notion of
substance" (vol. ii. p. 189), "though
basing that claim on my views
with regard to time and space.
It is equally dispensed with in M.
Renouvier's system, though its
place is not supplied in the same
way ; and this retractation, unimportant as it may be, is therefore
his due." Mr Hodgson states,
however, that "a prior name ought
not to be omitted when we speak
of a critical philosophy, the name
of a younger contemporary of Kant
himself, that of Salomon Maimon.
He too was phenomenist and criti-
cist, but he did not live to bring
his philosophical system to completion. M. Renouvier's originality,
too, is in every way beyond question. He can in no sense be called
the successor of Maimon. Their
ways diverge widely, though it is

from a point within phenomenism.
Both go together up to the point of
complete correlation between consciousness and its objects, which is
the note of phenomenism ; but
when they come to the analysis
of phenomena within consciousness,
then immediately their differences
begin, differences which are of a
fundamental kind."
If the painstaking investigation of the psychological and
logical foundations of philosophical
thought may be considered as one
of the most appropriate subjects
for philosophical teaching, then it
seems to me that a careful study of
M. Renouvier's earlier works would
serve as an Introduction quite as
valuable as that of Lotze's Logic
and Metaphysic in German or Mr
Bradley's Logic (assisted by Prof.
Bosanquet's 'Treatise on Logic,'
2 vols., 1888) in English literature.
Renouvier has the further advantage of being equally acquainted
with the two independent movements bearing upon the problem of
knowledge, that originating with
Kant in Germany and that beginning with Mill in England, also
with the one-sided development of
the former in the direction of
Idealism and Absolutism in Hegel,
and of that of the latter in the
direction of empiricism and naturalism under Spencer in England.

principles had fixed, and were thus forced to introduce new conceptions. These new conceptions have not only opened out in their application vast regions of natural and historical knowledge, but have also tended to change our ideas regarding its nature, leading up to a new theory of knowledge and novel solutions of the everlasting problem. It may be useful to consider somewhat more in detail some of the more important steps by which this change has been brought about.

Foremost in this respect stand the modern definitions of two terms with which older science operated, frequently unconscious of the ambiguity inherent in them. These two terms are, matter and force. They have been supplanted in the exact or mathematical sciences by two other terms, viz., mass and energy,[1] which are capable of strict definition as measurable quantities in time and space. Upon them is built up the purely mechanical explanation of things and phenomena. It is true that in those natural sciences which deal with the individual things of nature we cannot yet discard the older terms, matter and force. But this—according to an opinion which can neither be proved nor disproved—only shows that where they have to be employed, as when we, for instance, deal with chemical

55.
Greater precision.

[1] Some thinkers would prefer to say Mass and Motion, and to define energy in terms of Mass (or Inertia) and Velocity (or rate of motion). If this is done, it is evident that phenomena in which mechanical motion does not primarily present itself must be translated into these mechanical terms before they can be treated with exactitude. On the other side, the leaders of the energetic philosophy abroad, with Prof. Ostwald at their head, conceive of energy as a fundamental quantity possessing two distinct factors, that of quantity (capacity) and that of intensity. With them mechanical energy is only one form of energy, and the term is conceived also to embrace non-mechanical (psychical) forms of energy.

substances and affinities or with the instincts and impulses visible in organic nature, there remain dark
points into which the daylight of exact science has not
yet penetrated,—relations which are not yet accessible to
strict definition in terms of measurable quantities.

In the seventh chapter of the first portion of this
History I have shown how the conception of energy has
been gradually evolved out of vaguer conceptions, and
how the two principles of the conservation and the
dissipation (degradation or disgregation) of energy have
been established which respectively maintain that the
amount of energy in the physical world remains constant, and that this amount tends to change from a
more to a less available or useful condition. It was
shown how the experimental proofs of the conservation
of energy were furnished mainly in England, the
theoretical in Germany; how the idea of dissipation
originated in France; and how the whole doctrine of
energy, so far as mechanical processes are concerned,
was brought into clear relief and mathematically
formulated mainly by the experimental and theoretical
labours of Lord Kelvin. At the same time I showed
how a school of natural philosophers has arisen in
Germany who see in the theory of energy, or energetics,
the fundamental doctrine which is to explain all physical
phenomena. Unfortunately, so far as philosophical
writers are concerned, almost the whole literature down
to quite recent times is permeated and vitiated by a
want of clear distinction between the mechanical definition of the older term force, which is now superseded by
the less ambiguous term energy, and the still prevailing

meaning according to which force is the hidden cause or spring of motion. For, in the same degree as the modern definition of energy has brought clearness into physical science, where the tendency is to look upon all natural processes as transformations of energy or of various modes of motion, it has been found more and more impracticable to comprise in this attempt, in the same way, a definition of life and an explanation, or even an adequate description, of vital phenomena.

Accordingly, this first great step [1] by which the physical sciences have been more completely elevated into the region of exact research would have left the biological and psychological phenomena at a comparative disadvantage, inasmuch as, the older sense (the duplex meaning) of the word force being destroyed, the connec-

---

[1] The dualism which, according to the modern conception, attaches to the term knowledge, and which differs from that which was characteristic of the middle ages, which distinguished divine and human knowledge, may—in one aspect—be defined by looking at the meaning of the term force. In the older and popular use of the term there lurks a reference to the subjective element, that connected with volition and conscious exertion, what we may term the active principle as known to us through personal experience or introspection. If on the one side the clarifying and simplifying process in scientific thought consists in removing this subjective element, then, on the other side, we may say that a parallel movement in philosophical thought consists in the increasingly distinct recognition how this subjective factor of volition enters into all mental phenomena. A one-sided and extreme expression of this fact is to be found in the philosophy of Schopenhauer, who, in his first great work (1819), influenced, no doubt, not only by Kant but also by Fichte and Schelling, identified the unknown "Thing in itself" of Kant with the Will. It is interesting to note that, when materialistic philosophy in the middle of the century had emphasised the purely mechanical aspect of the forces of nature, at a time when the conception of vital forces was banished from German physiology, many of those who still longed for the spiritual view of things were powerfully attracted by the philosophy of Schopenhauer, the fundamental idea of which in endless different forms permeates the whole of modern philosophy, as we shall have occasion to see in subsequent chapters.

tion between the exact and the biological (including the mental) sciences was removed. But, fortunately for the biological sciences, a second and equally important step was taken about the same time, by which one of the fundamental conceptions through which we fix our comprehension of the phenomena of living matter received likewise a clearer definition. The older terms of development and progress, denoting not merely change but change from the lower, simpler, and less interesting and valuable, to the higher, more complex, more interesting, and more valuable, received likewise a more definite expression by which the natural as well as the mental philosopher were enabled to connect facts which before seemed unconnected, and to give to their descriptions and classifications a deeper meaning; enabling them also to some extent to know beforehand in which direction to look for the discovery of new and significant facts and phenomena. This second step may be identified with Charles Darwin's work and the appearance in the year 1859 of the 'Origin of Species.'

57.
Darwin and
develop-
ment.

The title of this epoch-making book was not without ambiguity; for, in the course of the diffusion and criticism of the ideas contained in it, it has become more and more evident that the process of natural selection could not explain the origin of living matter, but only the origin of separate species, the greater differentiation which is continually going on in all natural and mental processes. The genetic view of natural phenomena has become limited to a genealogical record, without being able to deal with first beginnings.

The same position has arisen with regard to that great movement of thought which originated abroad in the second half of the eighteenth century, of which Leibniz and Herder were the first exponents, but which received greater distinctness in the philosophical systems of Schelling, Schleiermacher, and especially of Hegel. Both in the history of nature and in that of mankind what was originally aimed at—viz., an exposition of the origin or genesis of things—has more and more had to content itself with a record of genealogies, generations, and transformations, *i.e.*, with a theory of descent or ascent, without being able to penetrate to first beginnings or origins. In the theories of the inanimate world, notably in the celebrated attempt of Kant and Laplace to explain the development of the solar system, the whole scheme reduces itself to a rearrangement of the constant quantities of masses and energy in space. This seemed feasible by taking into consideration the simple laws of motion, the law of gravitation, and—in the sequel also—the exchangeability of heat and mechanical motion. The question as to the ground or sufficient reason for the whole of this process which goes on in space and time could be left out altogether as unnecessary for the mechanical explanation of things. In the development of organic life, however, and still more in that of the mental life of individuals and of mankind, a new principle appeared. This was the principle of growth, including order, progress, and, at a later stage, what have been appropriately termed spiritual values and their increase.[1]

[1] The principle of growth, *i.e.*, of an increase which cannot be defined by the categories of more or less alone, but implies a certain arrangement or order, a Together of things accessible only to the

Already before Darwin, Malthus had pointed out that the main characteristic of social development consists in the growth of population. This idea put Darwin on the track of his theory of natural selection,[1] which appeared

synoptic, not to the analytic, view, forms really the fundamental and characteristic principle of the whole of the living, as differentiated from the non-living, world. Though the idea of order and arrangement as distinguished from mere quantity is a mathematical, or, if we like to call it so, a mechanical conception, this would not necessarily lead to the simpler or more complicated phenomena of living matter and of the animated world, were it not for the further characteristic that where certain forms of order and arrangement, of matter and motion exist, they have a tendency to spread in space like a vortex which draws surrounding things into its action. Through this property living things are not only, to a certain extent, self-centred and self-contained ; they are also mutually exclusive, as in a world in which the sum of matter and of motion are constant quantities, an increasing absorption of these constituents in certain places must mean a diminution in other places. This leads to the phenomenon of crowding out, to unconscious or conscious selection, and underlies all the phenomena of physical and mental life. In the whole of this process there are involved two principles which among recent thinkers, as it seems to me, Prof. Wundt has the merit of having most prominently put forward in his analysis of mental life, namely, the principle of creative synthesis and the principle of the growth of spiritual values. But what is created in the process of creative synthesis exists only for the synoptic intellect, and this had

been pointed out in various ways by other thinkers before Wundt. Allowing, however, that he has more clearly recognised the supreme importance and the connection of those two principles, it must be regretted that he has not devoted himself more exclusively to explaining and illustrating them. As it is, they are rather hidden away in the enormous bulk of his voluminous writings, and have hardly in recent histories of philosophical thought been duly appreciated.

[1] A remarkable passage is to be found in Lotze's early Tract entitled 'Leben Lebenskraft,' published in 1843 and reprinted in 'Kleine Schriften' (vol. i. p. 139 *sqq.*) Referring to the importance of Metabolism (*Stoffwechsel*) in plants, he says : " With reference to this point, we must admit that wherever a successive development of a form is to take place assimilation of matter is necessary ; but that likewise rejection of matter, *i.e.*, metabolism, should take place can only have its reason in this, that the elements which are necessary for growth are not supplied in the suitable form, but in a connection which has to be dissolved, and of which only one part is utilised, whereas the other is rejected as a bye-product. Metabolism would, in plants, appear almost inconceivable if it consisted in anything else than in a rejection of that which is unsuitable, so that in this case it is not something unused by the organism, but something unsuitable that is rejected " (p. 206). This recognition of the connection of growth and selection is significant. Prof.

to be the necessary consequence of overcrowding and the cause of the survival of the fittest. But this idea of the increase of population, which was applied by Darwin to the whole of the organic world on its physical side, can in the same way be applied to the growth of ideas and of ideal interests and values on the mental side of the organic world. In fact, in the whole extent of animated nature, we cannot leave out the question regarding the ultimate ground or sufficient reason as we do in the inanimate world, for the principles of the conservation of mass and energy do not suffice to explain the evident increase of that something which permeates all living things, from the lowest to the highest examples.

Now here we have to record another change in modern terminology and the striving after a clearer definition of ambiguous terms. As the word Force received, in the exact sciences, a purely mathematical definition, being supplanted by the word Energy, so likewise the terms Cause and Effect have undergone a

58.
Cause and effect defined.

Jas. Ward, in his "Gifford Lectures" on 'The Realm of Ends' (1911), referring to Wundt's conception of a creative synthesis, says: "The so-called conservation of mass and energy might be regarded as symbolising the initial state of the pluralistic world, and as symbolising too the mere permanence and abstract being of its many units. But it is notorious that these concepts are the result of ignoring those differences of quality which alone convert units into individuals. Without these we may have *Erhaltung* but not *Entfaltung*, as a German would say; we may have conservation and indefinite composition, but not development and definite organisation. In short,

the concrete integration of experience is the diametrical opposite to the mechanical resultant of a composition of abstract units: it is a *creative* resultant or synthesis, to use Wundt's happy and striking phrase." To this Ward adds the note that to Lotze belongs the credit of first signalising the fact to which Wundt has given the name; and Lotze even gets so far as to apply the term creation to this "relating activity," as he calls it (p. 103 *sqq.*) This "relating activity" spoken of by Lotze in his 'Metaphysik' (§§ 268 and 271) is really identical with the synoptic view, or the *esprit d'ensemble*, of Comte.

similar process of more precise definition. For the purposes of the mechanical sciences, cause and effect mean respectively merely the antecedent and the subsequent in time. But this definition, which is sufficient for the mechanical explanation of phenomena, and which can be mathematically expressed, does not embrace either the conception of the ultimate ground and sufficient reason of things, or of that power, of that principle of progress, of which we are conscious through our Will and our actions, and which we transfer by analogy to the explanation of the phenomena of growth in the region of organic and mental life.

This twofold development in quite recent times—the narrowing down of the meanings of the words force and cause to denote such relations as can be mathematically defined in terms of measurable quantities, excluding actual increase or decrease—has put an entirely different aspect on the problem of knowledge, and has, in its sequel, brought about the conception of two kinds of knowledge, corresponding to the two meanings of the word force and to the two meanings of the word cause. We have seen that Kant took up the problem of knowledge by asking the question, How is exact knowledge possible? He started from the admitted fact that such knowledge actually exists in the mathematical and mechanical sciences. We have also seen how, in the middle of the nineteenth century, the problem as it was defined by Kant was taken up again by Mill in England and by the Neo-Kantians in France and Germany. But, in the meantime, the nature of this exact knowledge which Kant took for granted has become more clearly understood, and it has also somewhat changed through the development of these sciences themselves.

A few examples of this change and of its causes will suffice to show how the problem of knowledge has assumed a different aspect. Kant's view of nature was to a large extent comprised in that circle of notions which I have in an earlier chapter termed the astronomical view of nature. He worked with the conceptions of attraction and repulsion, of action at a distance. These notions, which are as old as philosophy itself, had received an exact definition through Newton's principle of gravitation and through the measurement of electric actions, all of which came under the same numerical relation. Accordingly not only Kant, but still more specifically Laplace and his school, made this numerical relation which obtained in all actions at a distance the fundamental principle of their natural philosophy. The warning of Newton that the principle involved could not be considered as ultimate, but itself demanded a further explanation, was forgotten till well on into the nineteenth century. Even Helmholtz, who did so much in the middle of the century to bring about the great change I am speaking of, stated, in his celebrated tract " On the Conservation of Force," that natural phenomena might be supposed to be explained if they were reduced to a combination of central forces acting at a distance. Neither can it be denied that, to the popular mind, action at a distance, attraction and repulsion, are of such common occurrence, and are met with in so many different forms, that they have, through habit, become elevated to the position of ultimate, not further analysable processes, which afford to our understanding a convenient resting-place, a temporary and provisional foundation upon which to build. But this aspect upon which the astronomical view of nature is based, which governs almost half the exact science of the nineteenth century, and which still enjoys popular favour, was in the course of the century dispelled or superseded by the theory of action by contact. According to this view, empty space disappeared in the imagination of natural philosophers, a plenum being put in the place of the vacuum of intermediate space. This change of aspect, which was brought about mainly through the study of the phenomena of radiation, may be identified with the name of Faraday. To him and his school it seemed more natural to reduce mechanical action to processes in the immediate vicinity of the acting centres, and they accordingly filled empty space with an imaginary something called ether, and undertook the very fruitful task of defining in terms of measurable quantities the properties and the behaviour of this all-pervading substance or entity. What we may call the second school of French mathematicians after Laplace, those who were largely influenced by Fresnel's discoveries, adopted an intermediate position, looked upon the ether as an atomic structure, and attempted to explain the movements of this structure on the same lines as physical astronomy had followed in the calculation of cosmic phenomena. They employed attractive and repulsive forces acting at very small distances, as astronomers had used them at very large distances. This remnant of the astronomical view was finally destroyed in the school of

59.
Superses-
sion of as-
tronomical
view.

60.
Plenum
substituted.

Faraday by the British mathematicians of the Cambridge school, and by the introduction of the conception of energy and the theory of its distribution in the plenum of space. In passing, it may be remarked that an absolute plenum and perfect contact present as much difficulty to the thinking mind as action at a distance does, but this does not prevent these conceptions being of great use as soon as they can be mathematically defined.

But this change in the fundamental notions with which the new school of natural philosophers, headed by Faraday, worked, not only proved extremely fruitful by opening out new vistas of research and avenues of thought leading to the discovery of many quite unexpected facts ; it had also the philosophically far more important effect of shaking the confidence with which the popular mind regarded, not the results, but the processes and contrivances, of mathematical and mechanical reasoning. This was still more the case when it became increasingly difficult to construct mechanical models of those elementary motions and mechanisms through which the mathematician pictured to himself the fundamental processes of nature. The construction of such models, though only mentally, seems to the present day to be a desideratum for some of the greatest minds as often as they attempt to give mechanical explanations. But as these models grew more and more complicated, the conviction gradually dawned upon philosophical thinkers that such devices could no longer be considered as describing the real processes of nature, but that they were merely convenient and helpful means by which to start a train of reasoning, the results of which might or might not be true, according to the verification—or otherwise—afforded by experience and observation.

Thus it has come about that what Kant, and before him Hume, looked upon as exact knowledge, has in the eyes of more recent thinkers acquired quite a different aspect from that which it presented to them. Mathematical and mechanical calculations are only a convenient method of joining together various facts and phenomena which surround us in time and space, a means by which we can fix, define, and describe them, and arrive at a knowledge of other facts and phenomena which, but for these methods, would remain hidden and unknown to us. The present aim of scientific knowledge is, to describe the occurrences round about us in the simplest form and as completely as possible. The object is on the one side to attain to a greater simplicity and accordingly to a more complete unification of knowledge, and on the other side to make this more and more complete. In order to do this, it has been found necessary to supplement what we can see and observe by imaginary pictures of that which we cannot see, either because it is too remote, too far away in space and time, to come within our horizon, or because it is too minute, and accordingly escapes our notice. But unless we return on these circuitous paths—which lead us beyond our horizon or underneath that which lies on the surface— into the limits of what we can see and observe, ending up with the visible, the tangible, and the finite, all those complicated theories, built up with so much ingenuity and elaborated with so much care, are of no use whatever, and have no right to be called knowledge, however exact they may be. A recognition of these fundamental truths, and of the real nature of scientific knowledge, is gradually making its way into philosophical literature. It is also more and more being allowed by the leaders of scientific thought themselves, some of whom have probably done more than philosophers by profession to lay bare the roots and foundations of scientific reasoning. At best it has been, and is still, a slow process by which these plain truths are being elaborated and promulgated, nor is it possible to give any single names with which we could identify in anything like completeness the modern theory of knowledge. In a note [1] I have tried to collect references to the more

61.
Limitation
of scientific
knowledge.

[1] The most important enunciation of the nature of exact science, viz., that it aims at describing and not at explaining natural phenomena, is probably to be found in the introductory sentence of G. Kirchhoff's Lectures 'On Dynamics.' On the idea expressed in this simple sentence the whole of the purely scientific discussion of the principles of natural philosophy hangs, together with the more recent interest taken by philosophical writers in this subject. The sentence has been quoted over and over again, not only in text-books of natural philosophy but also in philosophical treatises. It is, on the one side, the result of the labours of mathematicians and experimentalists, on the other side the starting - point for a clearer separation and recognition of the different aims of scientific and philosophical thought. Among German thinkers it is especially E. du Bois Reymond who, in many passages of his various Addresses, has referred to this subject. Shortly before Kirchhoff's Lectures there appeared E. Dühring's 'Critical History of the general Principles of Mechanics' (1873), a book which would have exercised a greater influence had it not been for the polemical invectives introduced into the later editions. Kirchhoff's definition should be contrasted with the closing sentence of Lotze's 'Logic' (1874), in which he expresses the hope that "German philosophy will always rise again to the attempt to comprehend and not only to calculate the order of things." The next important and epoch - making discussion of this subject is the 'Critical Exposition of the Development of Dynamics,' by E. Mach ('Die Mechanik in ihrer Entwicklung,' 1st ed., 1883), a book which has now acquired a world-wide reputation, and should be studied by every teacher of natural as well as of mental philosophy. Somewhat later, Karl Pearson published his 'Grammar

important works which deal with this subject since the age of Mill in England and the return to Kant in Germany. But it is hardly from a philosophical point of view—*i.e.*, from the point of view of the theory of knowledge as such—that the more important investigations have been undertaken, or that the great revolution regarding the aspect of the problem of knowledge is being prepared. This has been done in the interests of science itself, which everywhere has been brought face to face with fundamental problems, having outgrown the language and terms in which it was clothed a hundred years ago. With the intention of providing more suitable expressions, more elastic notions, and wider principles, some of the foremost scientific thinkers have, within the last fifty years, attacked the fundamental conceptions with which science operated in their time. This I showed, at sufficient length, in the first part of this History,[1] where the leading principles of modern science were discussed, and the different stages

of Science' (1892), in which he refers to Kirchhoff and Mach, and develops independently correcter notions of the principles of science; following on the lines indicated in this country by Mill and Stanley Jevons on the one side, by Clerk Maxwell and Clifford on the other. French literature, after having in the early years of the century, notably under the influence of Lagrange and later on through Poncelet and Carnot, contributed so largely to the clearing up of the principles of pure science, has quite recently produced two original works on the subject by M. Henri Poincaré, entitled 'La Science et l'Hypothèse' (1903 and 1905). But it should also be noted that already in his 'Essais de Critique Générale' Renouvier gave some very clear and correct definitions of fundamental mechanical principles, at a time when both in Germany and in this country the notions on this subject were still generally in a state of great confusion.

[1] I shall return to this subject in a later chapter, which will deal not so much with the leading principles of scientific research as with the philosophical problem of nature, *i.e.*, with the various attempts to comprehend the totality of things as revealed to us by our outer senses,—what we may term the cosmological problem.

of their gradual development identified with the leading representatives of the various mathematical, physical, and natural sciences.

If we now look at the whole of this change, in the midst of which we are living, from a different point of view, we are led back to the observation with which I opened the Introduction to this, the second, part of our historical survey. We may say that this change consists in finding and fixing new meanings to the existing words of our current language; occasionally also in coining new terms wherewith to fix certain ideas and meanings which are unconsciously striving after clearness and adequate expression. Prominent examples of this kind are afforded by the words force, cause, and development. It is a clarifying process. But every definition has not only the advantage of producing clearness and exactitude; it has also the disadvantage of narrowing the field of vision, of limiting the view, leaving out much that lies outside, but which, though less defined, is not necessarily less real and important. If the scientific definition of the word force tends in the direction of making the word superfluous in mechanical science, it does not therefore destroy the deeper meaning of force as the cause or origin of motion which we continually experience individually in our voluntary efforts. If the terms cause and effect are discarded for the more easily defined terms antecedent and subsequent in time, we do not hereby get rid of looking for the sufficient reason and ultimate ground of this sequence and for the final end and purpose. If we are told that the object of science is to describe phenomena as simply and as com-

pletely as possible, we do not thereby satisfy the desire
of having things explained—*i.e.*, of seeing their hidden
sense and deeper meaning.   And lastly, if we reduce
the meaning of the word development, or evolution, to
mechanical processes of differentiation and integration,
we do not thereby satisfy the abiding conviction that
through these mechanical processes and their ever-recur-
ring repetition something is developed or evolved, that
the more advanced stage is richer in this something,
containing more of that which is of value and interest to
us human beings.

We may further describe the most recent phase into
which the problem of knowledge has entered by saying
that we are confronted by a twofold meaning of the
word.   Everywhere we meet with a twofold aspect, a
dualism in the nature and aims of knowledge.   This
dualism has been impressed upon the modern philosophical mind in many ways, and has found expression
in various systems of philosophy and through many
thinkers.   I will at present refer only to four distinct
lines of thought which are conspicuous amongst others.

62.
Dualism in
the problem
of know-
ledge.

The first distinct recognition of the twofold aspect of
the philosophical problem, and also of the problem of
knowledge, will be found in the writings of Hermann
Lotze.   He continued in Germany about the middle of
the century the traditions of the idealistic systems as
well as those of the Leibnizian philosophy.   Although
he did not elaborate a special theory of knowledge and
stood somewhat isolated, belonging neither to the school
of Herbart nor to that of the Neo-Kantians nor to the
historical school, he revived a conception of knowledge

63.
Recognised
by Lotze.

suggested already in the writings of Leibniz. He recognised that a description of the phenomena of nature and
mind would not permanently satisfy our thirst for knowledge or our search after truth, but that the human
mind would look for an explanation in addition to a
description of things, and that the highest task of science
in the larger sense of the word—that is, of *Wissenschaft*
—would always consist in an attempt to interpret or find
out the hidden meaning of the phenomena which lay in
and around us. He distinctly formulated this idea by
emphasising the all-pervading, but also the subordinate,
rôle of mechanism, and the necessity of penetrating to
the deeper sense or meaning of this all-pervading
structure. In his largest and most popular work, the
' Microcosmus,' he endeavoured to reconcile the view of
things which was being elaborated in the natural
sciences with the demands of the moral and emotional
side of our nature, by trying to fix the meaning and
significance which belongs to man and mankind within
the larger universe, the position of the microcosm in the
macrocosm.

As in many other instances the progress of thought
has been dependent on, and assisted by, the introduction
of a new vocabulary, so again it is the merit of Lotze
that he has raised to the rank of leading conceptions
familiar terms which before him had only restricted
meanings. Appreciating as he did the growing importance of the exact or mechanical treatment of all natural
phenomena, of the world of things and events which
surround us, he recognised, earlier probably than any
other thinker, how the growth and diffusion of

mechanical ideas would more and more leave out of consideration the existence of a different world which the idealistic systems had conceived as the world of ideas uniting and culminating in the idea of the Absolute. The importance of this other world which contains all that is of supreme interest to the human soul, the ideals of Truth, Goodness, and Beauty, requires to be placed on an independent foundation as the realm of human interests appealing to the emotional and moral side of our nature. To this he gave the designation of the world of Values or Worths,[1] and he conceived it to

64.
His doctrine
of Values.

[1] German philosophical literature, after having for a considerable time done but scant justice to the originality and independence of Lotze's position, has latterly made partial amends for this neglect by very generally absorbing at least the terminology introduced by him into current philosophical language. In addition to the appreciative references to his philosophy, as the last important philosophical system, which are to be met with in the closing chapters both of Erdmann's 'History of Philosophy' and of Kuno Fischer's 'Exposition of Hegel's System,' we are mainly indebted to Falckenberg and Windelband for creating a renewed and deeper interest in Lotze's writings. Shortly after the writer of this History had, in the year 1882, been obliged to state (in an article contributed to the 'Encyclopædia Britannica' which has unfortunately been reprinted without the necessary enlargement and revision in the latest, the 11th, edition, 1911) that Lotze's system had met with little criticism, a large literature on the subject sprang up in Germany, and R. Falckenberg wrote in 1886 : "The most important among the post-Hegelian systems, that of Lotze, proves that the scientific spirit does not refuse conciliation with idealistic convictions on the highest problems, and the esteem in which it is everywhere held proves that a strong desire exists in that direction" ('Geschichte der Neueren Philosophie,' 1st ed., p. 471). More specifically Windelband has drawn attention to that side of Lotze's teaching referred to in the text. "Since Lotze emphasised forcibly the conception of value, and placed it at the head also of Logic and Metaphysic, we meet with manifold attempts in the direction of a theory of values as a new and fundamental philosophical doctrine" ('Geschichte der Neueren Philosophie,' closing section). And in a recent work ('Grosse Denker,' ed. E. von Aster, vol. ii. p. 376) Windelband still more emphatically says : "Historical philosophy has its most promising support in the greatest thinker whom German latter day nineteenth century thought has produced, in Lotze. During the critical and empirical period he was wellnigh forgotten, as one among the remaining metaphysicians, and it is only recently that the fundamental ideas of his phil-

be the highest object of philosophy to show forth the realisation of these higher interests and values through human thought and action in the world of things. With this object before him, he conceived that the processes of thought which, working by the methods of scientific research, are more and more impressing on us the existence of an intellectual order, the so-called laws of nature, must be studied with a renewed interest. The philosophic mind is not contented to trace merely the formal connections of ideas, but desires to show also how, in ascending from the lower to the higher regions of thought, those supreme interests are consciously or unconsciously always at work. In this connection he introduces two other conceptions defined by the terms, the *validity* of our notions and the *meaning* or significance of thoughts and things. Around these three terms of validity, meaning, and value,[1] a new logic has sprung up which, suggested

osophy are coming again victoriously forward. This indeed shows itself in an assimilation of these ideas by the critical movement. . . . It is in the spirit of Lotze that the knowledge of the Actual is handed over to other sciences, while the recognition of values is claimed for philosophy. The elaboration of these principles, due to their origin in the critical movement, has shown itself mainly in the province of logic. Here it is that, through the researches of Rickert and Lask, the conception of validity, coined by Lotze, has in its relation to empirical and metaphysical reality been made the central philosophical problem."

[1] The philosopher who has most prominently put forward the problem of value is Prof. Höffding, who, I believe, has coined a new term: *Das] Wertungsproblem.* See his latest writings: 'Religions-Philosophie'(1901); 'Philosophische Probleme' (1903); and 'Moderne Philosophen' (1905). It is, however, remarkable that in this, his original development of a distinctly Lotzian idea, he expresses no allegiance to Lotze, and that the treatment of Lotze in Höffding's 'History of Modern Philosophy' does not emphasise what to us seems the most important conception of his system. When the writer of this History came to Göttingen in the year 1860, the principal writings through which Lotze's central philosophical views became known (the third vol. of the 'Microcosmus' and the two vols. of the 'System of Philosophy') had not appeared, and it was extremely difficult really to understand what

first by Lotze, has been independently treated by original thinkers in this country.[1]

Indeed, nowhere has the change which has come over philosophical thought in the course of the nineteenth century been more conspicuous than in the science of Logic. According to a well-known dictum of Kant, this had remained stationary for two thousand years. Shortly after this expression the very fact that Kant himself, in his first ' Critique,' introduced a section under the title of transcendental logic as an integral part of his theory of knowledge, gave rise to various attempts to remodel the traditional logic of the schools to which Kant had so contemptuously referred. A real advance was, however, not accomplished till Hegel boldly conceived of logical and metaphysical notions as forming the stages of the development of the Absolute—*i.e.*, of the Spirit or Thought which lives and moves in the progress of the individual human as well as in that of the universal mind in nature and history. This development gave a deeper sense or meaning to the otherwise lifeless forms of logic, connecting them in the dialectic process of thought which moved in the orderly rhythm of thesis, antithesis, and synthesis, as suggested already by Fichte.

65.
Hegel's new conception of Logic.

—to use a popular phrase—Lotze was driving at. The first light that came to the writer was an expression of Heinrich Ritter, Lotze's elder colleague, that the central idea of his system was the *Werthbegriff*, the conception of Value or Worth. Before Lotze, Herbart had already separated æsthetics and ethics from metaphysics by introducing the idea of valuation or judgments of value which are concerned, not with realities, but with the relation that exists between realities. From this view, the influence of which on Lotze deserves to be appreciated, Lotze's idea of a world of Values or Worths, as distinguished from a world of Things, differs in principle.

[1] Notably by Bradley and Bosanquet.

This new conception of logic, which holds its position as one of the ideals of recent philosophic thought, gave rise to an extensive critical literature. It provoked, on the one side, a reaction in favour of the older purely formal logic, bringing the same into connection with psychology; and, on the other side, various attempts to show that the genuine Aristotelian logic stood really much nearear to the demands and positions of modern thought than either the new dialectic or the traditional logic of the schools which professed to be that of Aristotle. The former movement was in Germany represented mainly by Beneke, the latter by Trendelenburg.[1]

Both in this country and in France independent attempts were, as we have seen, mainly in the direction of understanding the applied logic of the exact sciences, not infrequently with a tacit supposition that the historical, notably the social, sciences should, or could, be submitted to similar treatment. The splendid results, however, which had been achieved

66.
Reaction against this.

---

[1] Both these movements stood in opposition to the principal idea of Hegel's philosophy, and contributed to bring the latter into discredit. They came together in the logical writings of Ueberweg, who was also influenced by Schleiermacher. The latter had, like Hegel, revived the term dialectic, but his dialectic is something very different from that of Hegel. "Schleiermacher attacks the Hegelian position, that pure thought can have a peculiar beginning distinct from all other thinking, and arrives originally at something specially for itself. He teaches that in every kind of thinking the activity of the reason can be exercised only on the basis of outer and inner perception, or that there can be no act without the 'intellectual' and none without the 'organic' function, and that only a relative preponderance of the one or other function exists in the different ways of thinking. Agreement with existence is immediately given in inner perception, and is attainable immediately also on the basis of outer perception. The forms of Thought, notion and judgment, are made parallel by Schleiermacher to analogous forms of real existence—the notion to the substantial forms and the judgment to actions" (Ueberweg, 'System of Logic,' transl. by T. M. Lindsay, 1871, p. 70).

in Germany by the historical school, under the influence of the idealistic in combination with the critical spirit, attracted the attention of a few thinkers in this country who did not approve of the growing mechanical philosophy. They instituted a search[1] for the *rationale* of that line of thought which had produced abroad such an original and long-sustained intellectual effort. It was natural that the interest centred for a time in a study of Hegel, of that system which was supposed to contain the most mature expression of the logic of the mental and spiritual, as distinguished from the mechanical and naturalistic, movement of thought.

67.
Lotze and
English
Hegelian-
ism.

The philosophy of Lotze, which became known in England through the translations of the 'Microcosmus' (1885) and the 'System' (1884), came at an appropriate time to give to that current of thought which was moving away from the lines prescribed by the writings of Mill, a specific character somewhat different from the stricter Hegelianism which for a time was represented by Edward Caird and his school in Glasgow.[2] The Logic of Lotze began to be studied

---

[1] The merit of having started on this search belongs to J. Hutchison Stirling, who published the 'Secret of Hegel' in the same year (1865) in which Mill published his 'Examination of Hamilton's Philosophy.' This beginning of a European, as distinguished from the earlier exclusively German, interest in Hegel's philosophy was contemporaneous with that which started independently in Italy, mainly under the influence of Vera.

[2] The study of Hegel led to two distinct developments of thought in this country. We may distinguish them as the historical and the logical. Both were critical: the former studied the origin and genesis of Hegel's ideas, going back to Kant and to earlier thinkers—notably those of classical antiquity. The leading spirit in this movement was Edward Caird, whose Works on Kant mark an epoch in British thought, casting somewhat into the shade kindred labours such as those of Ferrier and Martineau, who likewise in-

in the University of Oxford in the place of Mill, and
—what is of prime importance—always in conjunction
with the Logic of Aristotle.[1] This fusion of two dis-

troduced aspects gained by a study
of Continental thought. The second
undertook to elaborate the Hegelian
programme on independent lines, a
task distinctly formulated already
by T. H. Green. For this purpose
its representatives studied not so
much the historical as the logical
foundations of Hegel's system,
closely scrutinising what Lotze had
already done in that direction, moving frequently in opposition to him,
but with him also away from
genuine Hegelianism. The former
school had taken no notice of Lotze's
writings, but subsequently formulated its opposition to the drift
of his ideas in the first critical
attempt which was made in this
country to estimate the value of
his system as a whole. This
was done by Henry Jones in his
' Critical Account of the Philosophy
of Lotze' (1895). After criticising
in the Preface what others have
termed the "theologising" tendency of Lotze's thought, he says :
"Lotze's investigation of thought
has had other and more valuable
consequences. It has led modern
writers to investigate the nature
of thought for themselves, with a
result that, particularly in this
country, there has been a remarkable development of logical theory
on Lotze's own lines. I refer more
especially to the logical works of
Mr Bradley and Mr Bosanquet.
. . . This development of Lotze's
position seems to me to issue in
its refutation ; and there are indications that the main contribution of Lotze to philosophic
thought, the only ultimate contribution, consists in deepening
that Idealism which he sought to
overthrow[1]" (p. xii). The quarrel,
then, of the genuine Hegelians

with Lotze is that "if his view of
thought be true, . . . the power
of that idealistic reconstruction of
belief, which has so strongly influenced the modern mind, is entirely
broken" (ibid., p. xi). We must
be thankful for this clear and
concise statement, as it is very
helpful in trying to understand
the aims of recent philosophical
thought as conceived by opposite
schools. It also leads us on
to the metaphysical problem, of
which I shall treat in the next
chapter.

[1] The philosophical studies in the
University of Oxford would merit a
special historical treatment. The
only approach to this, so far as I
know, is to be found in an article
by Prof. Mackenzie in the ' Revue
de Métaphysique et de Morale,'
which in the year 1908 published
a series of articles aiming to represent the state of philosophic
thought in different countries. The
articles are of value to such readers
as have already a fair knowledge of
the problems which now occupy
philosophic thought ; but they nearly all suffer through being over-
crowded with names, and exhibit
a prevalent tendency of such
writings in the present day — the
desire to do justice to everybody.
They bear testimony to the general
inconclusiveness of recent thought.
I would suggest to those of my
readers who, being outsiders like
myself, wish to gain some idea of
the position of one prominent side
of philosophical thought represented in this country by the University of Oxford, to read the three
articles on Logic contained in the
three last editions of the ' Encyclopædia Britannica ' : the first, by
the late Prof. R. Adamson, was

tinct currents of thought, which in Germany were represented by two different schools, has helped to give to recent works on Logic in this country—notably to those of F. H. Bradley and B. Bosanquet—a character of originality and comprehensiveness which places them in the forefront of modern treatises on Logic and the theory of Knowledge. As logic has, mainly through their labours, fully justified its traditional position as an independent science, the special doctrines elaborated therein hardly enter into a general history of thought. The latter, however, has to take note of the change which has come over the general points of view from which, and the interest in which, logical science has been reconstructed. In this respect there are two points which seem to me to have a general bearing on the development of modern philosophical thought.

The first refers to the breaking down of the older

68.
Bradley and
Bosanquet.

written in the year 1882, and in consequence does not embrace the more recent developments largely to be traced to the influence of Lotze. As being of permanent value up to this point, it is gratifying to know that it has been republished. The second is an article published in the "New Volumes" just twenty years later (1902). This article is written by Prof. Case, and contains a very trenchant criticism of recent logic, which in its distinctive and hopeful reforms is considered by the author to be approaching the position occupied by the genuine Aristotelian logic in antiquity — a view which was held similarly by Trendelenburg in Germany a generation earlier. In addition to the strong recommendation of the Aristotelian 'Organon,' it is

strange to see the 'Novum Organum' of Bacon recommended for the study of inductive logic. Prominent authorities on the Continent—such as Prof. Alois Riehl (see his article in 'Systematische Philosophie,' 1907, p. 84) — maintain that this distinction does not belong to Bacon, "a schemer and dilettante," but to Galileo—a view initiated on the Continent by a celebrated pamphlet of Justus Liebig (1862), and destructive of the *fable convenue* of the Baconian method so prevalent in this country. The third article, in the 11th edition (1911), is by Mr H. W. Blunt. It is thoroughly up to date, and does full justice to the influence of Lotze and the new era in the science represented mainly by Bradley and Bosanquet.

separation between the form and the content of thought. This tendency is one of the most valuable bequests of the Hegelian Logic, which in this respect may be looked upon as the first brilliant attempt to carry out an idea which in Germany was kept alive by Lotze, and which was independently taken up at first hand by students of Hegel in this country. In both we find the desire to get at the deeper sense or meaning of words, terms, and symbols, to which the purely formal logicians, misled, not infrequently, by the mathematical forms of reasoning, gave exclusive attention. This is intimately connected with a second important tendency according to which units of thought are not to be found in distinct ideas, notions, or concepts, but in judgments; so that the older analytical and atomising treatment, from which even Lotze did not fully emancipate himself, must be abandoned in favour of what I have termed the synoptic treatment; all thought as well as all experience starting from a " Together," which is, for practical and scientific purposes, subjected to the processes of artificial analysis and subsequent synthesis. In this respect more recent treatment of logical theory in this country, perhaps even more than abroad, falls in with that general tendency of thought to which I have already had occasion to refer in earlier chapters of this History.

Whilst Lotze was working at a new conception of philosophy which has since been adopted by many thinkers, Herbert Spencer in England, starting from very different beginnings, put forward a definition of philosophy which in some respects coincides with that

69.
Lotze and
Spencer.

of Lotze, and which has become similarly popular. He sees in philosophy the complete unification of Knowledge, as distinct from the different sciences which afford only a partial unification of Knowledge. But he has paid the inevitable tribute to the trend of modern thought by introducing into the foundation of his system that inherent dualism which, as I said before, seems everywhere to confront us. Continuing the traditions of earlier English philosophy, and influenced as much by Hamilton as by Mill, he draws a sharp distinction between the Knowable and the "Unknowable." The former is really only concerned with mechanical connections, although the language in which these connections are expressed by Spencer retains many of the older attributes by which a duplex meaning is conveyed. But the deeper desire of arriving at an explanation and not merely at a description of phenomena is recognised and satisfied in Spencer's philosophy by acknowledging the existence of an unknown power which is at once the origin and the sustaining ground of everything.

70.
The 'Un-
knowable.'
Through this doctrine of the Unknowable, Herbert Spencer has become the father of that School of Thought to which Huxley has given the pertinent name of "Agnosticism."

Somewhat later than Lotze in Germany and Spencer in England, philosophical thought in France came prominently forward with contributions to the solution of the problem of knowledge. The most important among these contributions are to be found in the writings of Charles Renouvier, a contemporary of Lotze, though his influence belongs to a much later date. In the present connection it is of interest for us to note that Renouvier, from an entirely different beginning, combats the attempt to lay down any one principle by which all our knowledge is governed. A complete unification of knowledge on the purely scientific basis is not possible.

71. Renouvier on Discontinuity.

This contention finds in Renouvier's System a characteristic expression. He attacks the law of Continuity which, since the time of Leibniz, has played such an important part in modern Thought. According to Renouvier, we are everywhere confronted with discontinuities, with new beginnings, with breaks in what we would fain consider the orderly development of things.

The period during which, under the sway of the ideas of uniformity and continuity, science has made its enormous strides, will be followed by a new era of philosophical thought, by a new conception in which the idea of personality will be utilised for the explanation and interpretation, as opposed to the description and construction, of the phenomenal world.

72. And Personality.

The essence of personality is to be found in our individual experience and in the process of willing. The Will affords by analogy the key to the deeper explanation of everything.

With this conception Renouvier touches another and prominent development of modern Thought, which, no less than the three developments already mentioned, emphasises the dualism which everywhere surrounds us. The movement I refer to centres on the Continent in the philosophy of Arthur Schopenhauer. It was prepared independently by the study of the ethical problem in the English school. Beginning with Hume, who significantly turned away from the fruitless attempt to solve the problem of Knowledge, and betook himself to the more fruitful study of moral, political, and historical questions, English thinkers have the merit of having established the study of morality or ethics as an independent philosophical discipline which has latterly been enlarged into the modern science of Sociology.

73.
Schopen-
hauer's
Voluntar-
ism.

The interest which led Schopenhauer to emphasise the problem of the Will was very different from that which had led or was to lead English or French thinkers. His aim was neither epistemological nor sociological, it was purely metaphysical. He desired to give what he considered the only possible answer to the problem left over by Kant, as it was understood by Kant's early disciples. What Kant called the "Noumenon" or the "Thing in itself" which underlies the phenomenal world, reveals itself, according to Schopenhauer, in its real nature in our will. What Spencer more recently termed the Unknowable is conceived by Schopenhauer in analogy with the human Will.

By emphasising the existence of the active factor, not only in the human mind but in the whole of nature, Schopenhauer perpetuated on the one side that dualism which exists already in Kant's philosophy between the theoretical and the practical reason, and on the other side drew attention to that region of psychology which had been unduly neglected by the contemporary systems of German philosophy, but which had been specially cultivated in this country—the region of the Emotions and the Will. Although it cannot be said that the ethical theories of Schopenhauer are satisfactory, or that they follow with necessity from the initial position which he takes up, there is no doubt that he has powerfully influenced philosophical thought on the Continent during the second half of the century, as I shall have frequent occasion to point out in the sequel. He thus belongs to those thinkers who have combined to overthrow that extreme intellectualism which was characteristic of some of the prominent philosophies during the earlier part of the nineteenth century. It is now generally recognised that alongside of the problem of knowledge and of the intellect, the problems of action and of the will, including feeling and emotion, demand an equally independent study. The problem of knowledge, in the modern phase which it is passing through, thus leads us on to other problems, such as the problem of reality or the metaphysical problem, the problem of action or the ethical problem, and many more. The history of these we shall study in separate chapters.

74.
Overthrow
of extreme
Intellectual-
ism.

In the meantime my readers may expect me to sum up in a few words the present position of the problem of knowledge. This cannot be done without some risk, as the discussions referring to this subject are very diverse, indicating the unsettled position of opinion in this matter.

Nevertheless it seems to me that the following may be said with some approach to accuracy, though I cannot point, in the very extensive literature, to any single and prominent writer who has given expression to the view we are historically led to. It seems to me that the problem of knowledge, at the end of the century, is narrowed down to the distinction between certainty and exactness.

Up to the middle of the century the conception of exact knowledge grew in importance with the growth and diffusion of the scientific spirit. To many thinkers it may have appeared as if the definiteness and exactitude which increasingly characterises natural knowledge carries with it the impress of certitude, and might, in due course, lead to that certainty of conviction which we are seeking to attain in questions of conduct, and as the foundation of a reasoned creed and a system of Morality.

The later developments of scientific or exact knowledge, the spread of the mathematical spirit, and the criticism of the foundations of the mathematical and mechanical sciences, have not realised this expectation.

More and more it has become evident not only that the mechanical view does not satisfy us as an explanation of things, but that its character of being exact, definite, and accurate does not include the feature of certainty. Lotze would call it *eine Gemüths-sache ;* Renouvier, *une affaire passionelle.*

If knowledge is limited to that which is defined with exactitude, it appears to be doomed to be hypothetical, provisional, and uncertain.

This forces upon us the conclusion that we must seek for certainty in a different direction, that the foundations of our convictions must lie elsewhere, or that we must extend the meaning of the word Knowledge beyond the narrow and shifting region of that which can be clearly defined.

CHAPTER V.

OF REALITY.

I.

HISTORY of philosophy shows us several instances when the philosophical mind started on new beginnings, initiating a new phase of thought, by attempting a fresh solution of the problem of knowledge. The statement that before taking up the important problems of philosophic thought it is necessary to settle the method and define the way by which we may hope to attain to their solution, has been repeatedly put forward both in ancient and modern times. Thus we find that in many instances philosophical systems have been introduced by preliminary discussions, of which the Organon of Aristotle, the Novum Organum of Bacon, the Discourse on method of Descartes, the Critique of Kant, and, to some extent, the First Principles of Herbert Spencer, furnish well-known examples.[1] Their object was to define the

1.
Epistemology and systems of philosophy.

[1] It must, however, be noted that the search after first principles of Thought has, in modern times, acquired a different aspect from that which it possessed in Antiquity or the Middle Ages; and this is owing to the fact that the pioneers in modern philosophy, both Bacon and Descartes, could refer to or build upon a certain amount of generally admitted and accepted knowledge, that of the mathematical and mechanical sciences which, as it were, did not require any preliminary discourse for their recommendation. The epistemological investigations of

starting-point and to justify the methods of advance which were to be adopted. At the end of the century which precedes the period we are dealing with this was done with much detail and patience and unexampled completeness by Immanuel Kant; his philosophy has accordingly been rightly and consistently termed Criticism, and the nineteenth century itself has marked its indebtedness to Kant, and to the thinkers who immediately preceded him, nowhere more than by continually and repeatedly urging the necessity of a theory of knowledge. And yet it can hardly be maintained that those systems which have had the deepest influence and have marked the great eras of philosophic thought are exclusively characterised by that cautious and critical spirit which would not venture on any bold generalisation without a previous patient examination. It is not always to the careful and accurate surveyor; often it is rather to the daring explorer of an unknown country that we owe the greatest discoveries, the enlargement of our knowledge and the revolution of our views. Though we must admit that the critical spirit, which during the last fifty years has acquired an almost undisputed sway over all but the purely exact and experimental sciences, favours the

Bacon, Descartes, Locke, and Kant, referred, therefore, not to knowledge in general but more exclusively to philosophical knowledge; scientific knowledge being considered as firmly established, in fact, frequently as a model of true knowledge. Investigations as to the hidden and unconscious principles which guided such exact knowledge have latterly been undertaken, not so much in the interests of science itself as rather with the intention of placing philosophical thought on a similarly secure foundation. Accordingly we find that scientific authorities themselves show, as a rule, little interest in the philosophy of their respective sciences. The widespread modern interest in scientific first principles is not purely scientific, it centres in the question: To what extent are they capable of supporting a moral and spiritual view of things?

cautious way of proceeding which I allude to, we are at the same time bound to acknowledge that this period is poor in creative efforts and new aspects of thought, and that to the small extent that such have made their appearance, they stand outside of, and sometimes in opposition to, the orderly movement of thought, being frequently stigmatised by representatives of the latter as unscientific and uncritical.[1]

2. Some systems start with theories of Reality.

In recent times this difference, which we may call the difference between the critical and the dogmatic attitude, has been much influenced by the requirements of academic instruction. This has variously laid the greater stress upon one of the two requisites of higher culture : the imparting, on the one side, of a strict mental dis-

[1] Examples of this are to be found in all the three countries, but most in Germany. During the last fifty years three names have risen to celebrity in philosophical literature, which, in the beginning, were either neglected or denounced and even violently denied a place by the ruling philosophy of the age. They are : Schopenhauer, von Hartmann, and Nietzsche. All three gained a considerable influence over the philosophic thought of their age and country before adequate notice was taken of their writings in academic circles or in some of the prominent works on History of Modern Philosophy. There is, however, no doubt that Schopenhauer contributed, probably more than any other individual thinker, to counteract a one-sided Intellectualism, to prepare the way for that Voluntarism which is a characteristic feature of recent thought. Von Hartmann's reputation has latterly rested more on his critical and historical writings, some of which are of the first order, than on the idea of the Unconscious which played such a prominent part in his earliest work. And, so far as Nietzsche is concerned, it is interesting to note that he has, after being violently proclaimed unphilosophic, gained at last a place among the 'Grosse Denker' (ed. E. von Aster, 2 vols. 1912), an honour not vouchsafed to thinkers like Comte, Lotze, or Spencer. In France, leaving out such eccentric thinkers as, e.g., Saint - Simon and Proudhon, we have, in recent times, the remarkable writings of Jean Marie Guyau ; and, in this country, a group of writers who have had a marked influence on philosophic thought, though the fundamental principles of their teaching are so little defined that it is difficult to do them justice in an account of the methodical philosophical thought of the century. They are : Coleridge, Carlyle, and Ruskin. A real appreciation of their views belongs to the section which should treat of poetical and religious thought.

cipline and, on the other side, the establishment of
leading aspects of thought, whereby firstly to gain knowledge, and secondly to grasp and organise it. During
the first half of the nineteenth century so many new
fields of research were opened out, especially on the
Continent, by the labours of the Academies and Universities, that the necessity was felt of gathering the newly
accumulated knowledge into systems and of organising
it under leading ideas. Accordingly it was the age of
the great scientific systems of the mathematicians and
naturalists in France, and of the equally celebrated
systems of philosophy in Germany. Academic teaching
then emphasied, perhaps unduly, the constructive ideas
which governed those systems. Gradually, however, the
critical spirit acquired a mastery over the dogmatic and
constructive spirit. The necessity was felt of sifting the
existing knowledge, much of which proved to be incorrect; also of examining the leading ideas and theoretical aspects under which it had been organised.
Many of the conclusions which had been drawn
appeared premature, and some of them dangerous.
Theoretical and systematic teaching acquired accordingly much more caution and circumspection, and this
tendency has been encouraged and strengthened by
another influence which has made itself increasingly
felt in quite recent times.

This is the practical influence : the demands of actual
life with its specific problems and difficulties. Everywhere these have made themselves felt, though in the
different countries in different ways. The German
Universities which, during the first half of the century,

3.
Interests of
academic
teaching

4.
and of prac-
tical life.

had elaborated the ideal of Wissenschaft, *i.e.*, of science and erudition combined,—the union of the exact and the historical spirit,—have more and more become obliged to train specialists in definite branches of knowledge; and these specialists, who in earlier times were mostly occupied with purely theoretical or learned work, have latterly become largely practical experts, for whom professional experts have had to make room. In France the two great schools, the École Polytechnique and the École Normale, assumed more and more the leadership in higher education, which was for a time exclusively identified with instruction.[1]

In England the two older Universities had, in modern times, never aimed at that universality and completeness of learning which is the ideal of the German University, having always put in the foreground the imparting of a liberal education,[2] which appeared indispensable to those who would occupy high positions in the Church, in the State, or in professional or social life. Accordingly we do not find that at the latter—*i.e.*, at the English Universities—any comprehensive teaching of philosophy existed at all. To the Scottish Universities belongs, almost alone in this country, the credit of having kept alive the philosophical tradition in academic teaching. This has had the result that, in England at least, the higher branches of philosophy were for a considerable time cultivated almost exclusively outside the schools and, in consequence, with only a subordinate regard for the requirements of teaching or

[1] See vol. i. of this History, p. 112.   [2] See ibid., pp. 255 and 262.

for systematic unity and completeness. On the other
side, whatever of theoretical and systematic philosophy
existed in this country, stood in close connection with
the practical interests and the social demands of the
age.

In France the teaching of philosophy had to accommodate itself to the demands of the higher schools,
which were, at that time, under the influence of the
clergy.[1]

[1] On this point see the account
given by M. Ribot in the year
1877 ('Mind,' vol. ii. p. 382 *sqq.*)
"The Courses at the *Lycées* and
Colleges (secondary instruction) are
much less free than those of the
Faculties (superior instruction),
since they are not addressed to
men but to youths preparing for
an examination, and must besides
keep within the one programme
drawn up for the whole country.
The professor is closely watched
by the Faculties, the State, the
bishops, and the families. Thus
an official philosophy is formed
which is rigorously orthodox. It
has unvarying solutions for all
problems, a fixed number of proofs
of the existence of God and of the
immortality of the Soul, &c., &c.;
a student who does not answer in
conformity with the programme is
rejected. The consequence is that
many think one thing and say another. I must add that the same
is often true of their masters,
though it is only fair to acknowledge that latterly many young professors have endeavoured to introduce the new doctrines under the
form of historical expositions and
discussions. Many of the students
in our *Lycées* know something of
the Logic of Stuart Mill and of the
Psychology of Bain and Spencer,
but the heads of Spiritualism are

little in favour of these innovations.
Spiritualism, such is, in fact, the
name of this official philosophy. It
would be useless to dwell at length
on this doctrine which has reigned
amongst us for fifty years, and
which consists in a collection of
opinions founded on common-sense,
and adapted to the religious beliefs
of the majority. If we extract
from the different religions subsist-
ing in Europe the common basis
that is called Deism or natural
religion, and deduce from this
Deism the theology, the morals, and
the psychology which it involves,
we shall have Spiritualism; the rest
is only matter of detail. It is a
timorous, a fearful doctrine, that
abhors all disturbance, and is very
compliant to the clergy; many of
its supporters are avowed Catholics"
(p. 384). Those who are interested
to see the difficulties of steering a
middle course between Roman
Catholicism on the one side and
German Idealism on the other, resulting in a species of Cartesianism,
should read the 'Life of Victor
Cousin,' by Barthélemy-Saint Hilaire (3 vols., 1895). In his interesting 'Rapport,' already referred to, M. Ravaisson said, in
the year 1868, somewhat prophetically: "A bien des signes, il est
permis de prévoir comme peu éloig-
née une époque philosophique donc

The teaching of philosophy in Germany has of late, through the growth of the scientific and industrial spirit, moved somewhat towards that position which has always existed in England. This we may define by saying that the solution of the highest philosophical problems must be found, not in and through the schools, but outside of them, under the practical influences of life. To this end the work of the schools can only be preparatory and introductory. But that such preparation must be complete, circumspect, and systematic, and not casual and fragmentary, this the English Universities have learned in modern times largely through acquaintance with and appreciation of the German systems and method.

In the course of the nineteenth century the position of philosophy, as an element of culture and a subject of higher teaching, has thus undergone two great changes. The failure of the constructive systems first of all impressed lastingly on the thinking mind the necessity of bringing philosophic discussions into immediate contact with the methods and the results of the special sciences. We now hear it proclaimed that no thinker is qualified to deal with the great problems of philosophy who has not been trained and disciplined through some special research where he has practised the true methods of inquiry, be they exact or critical; pref-

le caractère général serait la prédominance de ce qu'on pourrait appeler un réalisme ou positivisme spiritualiste, ayant pour principe générateur la conscience que l'esprit prend en lui-même d'une existence dont il reconnaît que toute autre existence dérive et dépend, et qui n'est autre que son action " (p. 258).

In the light of the development of philosophical thought during the last fifty years, especially in France, the last pages are well worth reading.

erence being usually given to the exact methods. This is equivalent to saying that the best preparation for the philosopher is to be found in the training of the scientific expert or learned specialist. And in quite recent times a further step has been taken, inasmuch as it is being more and more recognised that an acquaintance with the practical objects of life, a familiarity—in some form or other—with the actual work that goes on around us, is indispensable as a preparation for higher speculation : assuming that this is to be of real use to humanity and to the furtherance of culture. The one - sided influence which the much vaunted training of the scientific specialist exerts has to be balanced by the very different interests and methods which govern practical work and application. In passing I may remark that here again we are only reviving views which are as old as philosophy itself; that Plato had already proclaimed geometry as the best training for the philosopher, and that philosophy with him was not a purely theoretical occupation.

5.
Discredit
of Meta-
physics.

All the different changes which I refer to, work in the direction of bringing discredit upon that central branch of philosophy which is usually termed Metaphysics ; so much so that we find it frequently stated that no definite branch of knowledge exists which deserves this name. Scientific, religious, and practical interests have combined in denouncing metaphysics as a useless occupation, as an undertaking which has no foundation and method, no beginning and no end. Some have tried to save the dignity of philosophy by giving to the word quite a different meaning from that which it originally

had, identifying it, for instance, with the theory of knowledge or with some branch of psychology. It is, of course,
needless to fight over words. Still the existence and
the continual reintroduction of a term which we thought
discarded shows that it covers some meaning and has
some significance. Many passages might be collected
from recent writers—Continental as well as British—
where the word metaphysic is used although the existence of such a thing is denied. It is more useful to
observe how in Germany lectures on Metaphysics have
become rare at the Universities; but that nevertheless
philosophical literature shows there, though perhaps to a
smaller extent than it has done during the last generation in this country and in France,[1] a tendency to

[1] In general it may be stated that
the revival of the interest in metaphysics commenced in France and
in this country just at the time
when in Germany it had almost
entirely disappeared. So far as
British philosophy is concerned, the
change which has come over philosophical thought is shown, for instance, in two treatises on Metaphysics which appeared respectively
in the 8th and the 9th editions of
the 'Encyclopædia Britannica,' both
by thinkers of the first order, representing definite schools of thought.
The earlier one was written in the
year 1857 by H. L. Mansel (1820-
1871), a pupil of Sir Wm. Hamilton;
the latter by Edward Caird (1835-
1908), the centre of the independent
Hegelian movement of thought, in
1883. Both articles are important
treatises, from very different points
of view. In the earlier article Metaphysics is mainly concerned with
psychology; the ontological problem,
or the problem of reality, receives
only subordinate treatment—in fact,
the principal metaphysical problem
as treated in the present chapter
is, by Mansel, thrust beyond the
limits of philosophical speculation,
and philosophy is reduced to pure
phenomenalism which, according to
this view, has to be supplemented
in the acceptance by faith of revealed truth; a position from
which it required only one step
to the philosophy of the Unknowable of Herbert Spencer.
This extreme development of a
view which originated in the school
of Hamilton, and which was more
popularly explained in Mansel's
'Bampton Lectures,' reacted as
much in the direction of phenomenalism and naturalism as it did on
the other side in the direction of a
transcendentalism modelled very
much on the Hegelian type. The
latter is, together with the History
of Metaphysics, expounded in a
concise and masterly manner 'in
Caird's article, reprinted in the
second volume of his 'Essays on
Literature and Philosophy' (1892).

6.
Revival of
Meta-
physics.

revive those inquiries which were once termed metaphysical, and which for some time had been neglected
and wellnigh forgotten.[1]

It is significant to see how in the
later editions of the ' Encyclopædia
Britannica,' as was the case with
Logic so also in Metaphysics, the
Aristotelian predilections of the
Oxford school have again asserted
themselves. The article on the
subject by Prof. T. Case opens
with the following significant sentence : "Side by side with psychology, the science of mind, and
with logic, the science of reasoning,
metaphysics is tending gradually to
assert its ancient Aristotelian position as the science of being in
general. Not long ago, in England at all events, metaphysics was
merged in psychology. But with
the decline of dogmatic belief and
the spread of religious doubt about
the creation and government of the
world ; as the special sciences also
grow more general and the natural
sciences become more speculative
about matter and force, evolution
and teleology ; men begin to wonder
again, like the Greeks, about the
nature and origin of things, and
half unconsciously discover that
they are metaphysicians. Nor
must we expect any great difference between the old and the new
methods of dealing with these problems when the causes have been
similar."

In France the revival of metaphysics may be traced to the influence of Renouvier and Jules
Lachelier (1832-1875). Like Hamilton and Caird in this country,
Renouvier and Lachelier were
influenced by the Criticism of
Kant. It is interesting to note
also that France alone possesses
since 1893 a periodical which
prominently puts forward the metaphysical interest : the 'Revue de
Métaphysique et de Morale.'

[1] So far as Germany is concerned,
the metaphysical interest in the
sense of ontology was kept alive
for a considerable period almost
exclusively by the philosophy of
Lotze, and the revival of this interest attaches itself significantly
to a renewed study and appreciation of Lotze's position,
especially of his doctrine of validity and value. To understand
the most recent movements of
thought in this direction we may
consult two publications to which
I have referred on former occasions. The first is the Kuno
Fischer 'Festschrift' (1904), the
second the 'Systematische Philosophie' (1907). The former contains no chapter on Metaphysics,
the latter contains a chapter on
Metaphysics by W. Wundt : against
this the former contains a chapter
on 'Philosophy of Religion' by
Tröltsch ; in the other this subject is wanting. But the article
by Windelband on Logic in the
earlier work is important as showing how the treatment of the
problem of knowledge is gradually
leading over to the metaphysical
problem of reality ('Festschrift,'
vol. i. p. 183 sqq.). In the latter
work we find in the chapter on
Metaphysic no reference to the
problem of reality and the truly
Real. Metaphysics is there treated
as poetical, dialectical, or critical,
and, as examples of these three
aspects which run through ancient
and modern philosophy, we are surprised to find Haeckel as representing poetical and Ostwald dialectical metaphysics, whereas Mach
is selected as representing the
critical position. In reference to
the recent history of Metaphysics,
the name of Lotze does not occur,

In the present instance I propose to use the word Metaphysics to denote all those investigations and discussions which refer to the problem of Reality. It is the central problem of philosophy, a problem not treated specially and prominently by any other branch of philosophic thought nor in any one of the different sciences. It is true that the metaphysic of the schools used to be divided into three distinct parts: of these the first, termed Ontology, dealt with Being or Reality in general; whilst the second, termed Cosmology, dealt with the Universe or the outer world; and the third, termed Psychology, dealt with the Soul or the inner world. As it is now generally admitted that questions referring to the outer world, to nature and to the Universe, cannot be answered except on the foundation of natural knowledge, nor those referring to the inner world or the Soul otherwise than on the basis of Empirical Psychology, there remains as the specific problem of Metaphysics and the central problem of Philosophy, the question concerning Reality, or, what we may call real.[1]

though the formal task of philosophy is defined by Wundt (p. 133), as likewise by Paulsen (see his 'Einleitung in die Philosophie,' p. 2), very much in the words used by Lotze fifty years ago (see Lotze, 'Diktate, &c.,' 'Logik,' p. 85). The view that Metaphysics and Philosophy have not only the formal problem of the unification of knowledge to solve, but that they have to interpret reality, to show the meaning of things, and that they, therefore, find their ultimate ground in Ethics—an idea contained already in Lotze's 'Metaphysik' of the year 1841 (p. 329)—is not referred to in this most recent deliverance of a leading representative of German philosophical thought.

[1] The earlier work of Lotze on 'Metaphysik' published in the year 1841 is purely ontological, and deals, in three sections, with Reality, with Appearance, and with the Validity of Knowledge. This work was followed by a Treatise on Logic (1843). The substance of both these earlier Treatises, which preceded the physiological, psychological, and anthropological writings of Lotze, through which he became known in wider circles, was incorporated after an interval of thirty years in his 'System of Philosophy' published

8.
The problem
of Reality.

And here it is well to note that the word real was already in ancient philosophy, notably in that of Plato, used to denote that which is opposed to the merely apparent, and that it received an even greater accentuation by the introduction of the term, the truly real. In the first instance, then, if we speak of Reality, we do not merely place it in opposition to that which is non-extant, the nothing which is the negation of existence, but we place it in opposition to that which *seems* to exist, but

during the 'Seventies. In the 'System,' Logic precedes Metaphysic, but the treatment of both subjects is much enlarged, the Logic by the treatment of applied Logic, the Metaphysic by an application of ontological principles to cosmological and psychological problems. This elaboration of the original programme, from which Lotze did not materially deviate, is contemporaneous with the clearer definition of the principles and methods of the exact and natural sciences to which the philosophical literature in all the three countries contributed during the fifth, sixth, and seventh decades of the century. The change also in the position of Logic and Metaphysics in the arrangement of Lotze's 'System' indicates the decline of the influence of Hegel, which was more prominent in Lotze's earlier writings. It is to be regretted that Lotze never gave an adequate treatment of the ethical problem to which he points back in his earlier Metaphysics, and forward as intended to form a portion of the third and concluding part of the 'System.' In many earlier works on Metaphysics we meet with a section entitled Rational Theology. This has dropped out of Lotze's 'Metaphysik.' His attitude to such ques-

tions may be gathered from the introduction to his 'Diktate; Religionsphilosophie' (1882): "Could religious truth be found entirely through human reasoning, philosophy would be the organ for its definition and exposition. Could it, on the contrary, not be found through reasoning, but required an outer or inner revelation, philosophy would still have a task to perform: it would have to show in what connection the revealed content stood with other of our opinions, demands, and duties. Lastly the hopeless view, that religion is only a psychologically explainable error, could only then be held if philosophy could first give us the truth about the supersensuous world; for then only could it be shown why psychological processes, in consequence of the course they take, must necessarily miss such truth. For itself alone, however, the historical origin of any conception can never decide as to its correctness. The object of our investigations will thus be: first to find out how much reason by itself can tell us regarding the supersensuous world; further, to what extent a revealed religious content can be brought into connection with these fundamental positions."

which, on closer examination, reveals itself as merely apparent. In the second instance we make a distinction between that which, though possessed of reality, does not seem to us to have the true or full reality. We thus introduce the conception of a higher and a lower reality or of degrees of reality. These distinctions are not merely logical or metaphysical quibbles, but carry with them a deep meaning which pervades all the higher forms of thought and which finds expression in the language and literature of all civilised nations. In poetry as well as in prose, in science as well as in popular literature, we are continually brought face to face with two problems: we are asked to distinguish appearance from reality, that which merely seems to be from that which is; and among those things which are real and actually exist we are asked to distinguish those which have a higher and fuller reality from those which are poorer in reality. Thus, to give examples, we distinguish the real movement of the sun or planets from their apparent movement; the real events and facts of life from the merely apparent ones presented in a dream or in fiction, the true colours and dimensions of an object from those which, owing to the imperfections or distance of view, are merely apparent. And on the other side, some things have for us more reality than others; thus wealth and possessions may be more or less real than fame and honours, mind may be more or less real than matter, and there are probably few persons who would not admit that goodness or "the Good" is the highest reality of all; though they may differ in their conceptions of the nature of goodness and as to where its supreme existence is to be found.

That these aspects of Reality, these different meanings of the word " real," constitute the central and everlasting problem of philosophic thought, can be gathered, *inter alia*, from the fact that the oldest among the great systems of philosophy that have influenced speculation ever since, that of Plato, had already coined simple terms wherewith to express these meanings, and that they form the subject of elaborate discussion in the latest prominent metaphysical treatise published in this country—Mr Bradley's 'Appearance and Reality.' Thus, however often metaphysical discussions have been denounced as aimless and futile, the problem of reality has survived all vicissitudes of opinion ; and its questions : What is Reality ? What is the truly Real ? will occupy the human mind, again and again, as long as it is capable of elevated thought.[1]

[1] The earliest discussion of the problem of reality in its threefold meaning expressed by the terms, the Real ($\tau\grave{o}$ ὄν), the Unreal ($\tau\grave{o}$ μὴ ὄν), and the truly Real ($\tau\grave{o}$ ὄντως ὄν), is to be found in the Platonic Dialogue, 'The Sophist,' and Benj. Jowett, in his Introduction to the translation of this Dialogue, has brought the treatment of the problem into juxtaposition with that of Hegel. Through the latter, indeed, the problem passed into its more recent forms, one of which, that adopted by Lotze, identifies the truly Real with that which has value or worth ; whereas another, that of Mr Bradley, deals with the problem in the doctrine of ' Degrees of Reality ' (see his ' Appearance and Reality,' chap. xxiv.) It is interesting to read in the Introduction to this work the following statement, very much in the tone of the passage quoted from Lotze in the last note : " The man who is ready to prove that metaphysical knowledge is wholly impossible has no right . . . to any answer. . . . He is a brother metaphysician, with a rival theory of first principles. And this is so plain that I must excuse myself from dwelling on the point. To say the reality is such that our knowledge cannot reach it, is a claim to know reality ; to urge that our knowledge is of a kind which must fail to transcend appearance itself implies that transcendence. For if we had no idea of a Beyond, we should assuredly not know how to talk about failure or success. And the test, by which we distinguish them, must obvi-

In the last chapter I have shown how the philosophy of Kant has influenced all discussions bearing upon the problem of knowledge which have appeared during the nineteenth century. The modern theory of knowledge seems to centre in Kant. I have now to report that Kant occupies a similarly central position with regard to the problem of reality. In fact, Kant's immediate followers, and among them certainly those who exercised, at the time, the greatest influence on philosophic and general thought abroad, made the problem of reality the most prominent theme of their speculations. With them philosophy became again dogmatic and assertive, instead of remaining critical as Kant had desired it to be. The critical side of the new doctrine was cultivated by some of the less known disciples of Kant, and was raised to the prominence which it deserves only after the constructive effort had seemingly exhausted itself—*i.e.*, since the middle of the century. With this change of interests which, as I have shown before, had a deeper historical meaning beyond the region of philosophical speculation, the

9. Modern problem of Reality centres in Kant.

ously be some acquaintance with the nature of the goal. Nay, the would-be sceptic, who presses on us the contradictions of our thoughts, himself asserts dogmatically. For these contradictions might be ultimate and absolute truth, if the nature of the reality were not known to be otherwise." No better proof could be given of the renewed interest which the problem of reality commands than the remarkable appreciation of Mr Bradley's own work, as shown by the appearance in less than ten years of four editions and the important literature which deals with it (see the 10th ed. of Ueberweg's 'Grundriss,'

part iv., p. 524). It is significant that this literature is almost entirely English and American. The student of Lotze cannot help being reminded, almost at every turn of Mr Bradley's many-sided argument, of sundry passages as well as of the general tone of Lotze's writings. If, and as, the study of Lotze is resumed in his own country, there is no doubt that the important philosophical writings of the Oxford school will have to be appreciated in their orginality : a beginning of this is to be found in the closing chapter by Windelband in 'Grosse Denker' (vol. ii.)

critical spirit revived, metaphysics being thrust into the background. Theories of knowing became more attractive than theories of being, Epistemology usurped the place of Ontology. In spite of this reaction the first half of the nineteenth century, and the systems which succeeded Kant's doctrine, deserve the credit of having elaborated certain views as to the problem of reality which are of lasting value, having left their mark on philosophic thought in the literature of all the three countries.

One of the reasons why Kant, whether he intended it or not, became the leader in metaphysics as well as in the theory of knowledge, may be found in a circumstance on which I have had frequent occasion to lay stress. Kant enriched our metaphysical vocabulary,[1] he coined certain words to denote deeper-lying conceptions, he defined what had been vague, and he brought into currency terms which for a long time exerted an influence, not to say a spell, over philosophical reason-

---

[1] The Kantian vocabulary has not only enriched philosophical thought ever since, but it has also created new difficulties and perplexities and increased those that existed before. Accordingly it has been the subject of much writing and many expositions. English readers will find the best introduction to the subject — as least, so far as the theoretical philosophy is concerned —in an excellent article on "Kant's Terminology" in Baldwin's 'Dictionary of Philosophy and Psychology' (3 vols., 1901, &c.) It is written by Josiah Royce, who contributes a similar article on Hegel's Terminology. In that article will be found references to all the important German writers on the subject, including Eucken's little tract on 'History of Philosophical Terminology,' referred to above (see *supra*, p. 238 note; also vol. i. p. 21). The analysis of Kant's vocabulary began almost immediately after the appearance of his writings, the earliest work to take up the task being Mellin's 'Dictionary' (6 vols., 1797). All important later works on Kant— notably those of the Neo-Kantians in Germany and of Edward Caird in this country—contain elaborate explanations; and yet Royce can say that "a thorough history of Kant's terminology is still to be written."

ing. One of these terms was "the Thing in itself," another was "the Categorical Imperative." These two terms fix, as it were, Kant's position with regard to the two main problems of reality, his answers to the two questions, What is Real? and What is the truly Real?

To begin with the first, with "the Thing in itself." When Kant analysed our knowledge of things which we call real, he not only, with Locke, discarded as apparent and purely subjective the secondary qualities, dependent upon the nature of our senses, but he also discarded the primary qualities, the space which things occupy and the time during which events happen, as arising out of the form of our perceiving intellect. Depriving thus what seemed to be external realities, the phenomena of nature, both of their secondary and their primary qualities, treated as mere appearance, there remained over only an indefinable something by which real things were distinguished from purely subjective images. This something we can, according to Kant, only *conc*eive by thought, we cannot *perc*eive it. It was a Noumenon in distinction from the Phenomenon; the former he termed "the Thing in itself," or "Things in themselves," in opposition to the Thing or Things as they appear.[1] This is equivalent to saying that ex-

10.
The "Thing in itself."

---

[1] A concise and lucid history of the influence of the conception of the 'Thing in itself' and its cognate but not synonymous designations as the Noumenon, the transcendental object or the *x* of the Kantian philosophy, is to be found in Windelband's 'History of Philosophy' (§ 41) frequently referred to already. Jacobi's pertinent remarks, made so early as 1787 ('Werke,' vol. ii. p. 304), "that *without* this assumption he was unable to enter the system, and *with* it unable to remain inside of it," indicates the difficulty of thinking of something of which we know nothing. Accordingly the Kantian

istence is the only thing we know about the reality of things, and that all detailed information which we possess about them is mere appearance, originating in the nature of our senses and the forms of our intellect. It has frequently been observed that this way of stating the problem of reality involves a latent contradiction, inasmuch as of a thing regarding which we know absolutely nothing, we cannot even maintain its existence. The same objection has been raised in more recent times against the statement of Herbert Spencer, who, in a more direct way than Kant before him, asserts the existence of the Unknowable, and places this at the entrance of his philosophy.[1]

position was unstable and, as Windelband has shown, led to two separate developments: the first, that indicated by Jacobi as unavoidable and necessary, was to throw this conception of an unknowable Thing in itself overboard and resort to pure Idealism, as was done in various ways by Fichte and his successors, who all took great pains to show how Kant's position was untenable. The second was to endow the empty idea of a Thing in itself, the x of the Kantian philosophy, with a definite meaning, whilst maintaining in substance the Kantian argument. The way to accomplish this had been indicated already by Fichte as well as by another philosopher of the Kantian school, Fr. Bouterwek (1766 - 1828), and was, without appreciation of either, consistently followed up by Schopenhauer. Thus the pure idea of reality either lapses into nothingness, the Unreal, or it acquires a higher meaning as the truly Real. It either degenerates, as Windelband says, "into a quasi-rudimentary organ without any function in the body of thought," or it rises to that highest object of contemplation on which the closing pages of Schopenhauer's first great work contain an eloquent rhapsody. A third investigation belongs to more recent times, and is not yet concluded. It would have to show how, psychologically, the perplexity has arisen out of the three notions of Self, which we involuntarily form in early life and which are continually intermingled and superposed in all our reflective and practical mental operations: the Self as one among many other Selves, its equals; the Self as pictured to us through the memory of past experience; and the Self as the sensations and feelings of the present moment. Beginnings of this psychological analysis are to be found in Renouvier's 'Essais de Critique Générale.' See also papers by Josiah Royce in 'Philosophical Review' (Sept. 1894, Sept. and Nov. 1895).

[1] We may get out of this difficulty, which applies as much to Kant's as to Spencer's Unknowable, by looking upon it as a limiting

There were several reasons which prevented Kant from destroying the remnant of reality which he assigned to external things. When it was pointed out to him by some of his critics that the logical consequence of his doctrine would be to negative altogether the conception of Things in themselves, and that this would lead inevitably to the position taken up by Berkeley, he strongly objected to the statement, maintaining that this would be leading back to the position of idealism, the refutation of which was one of the main objects of his critical philosophy. Whilst he insisted that all we know about things was what followed from our own sensuous and

11.
His objection to Idealism.

conception. An analysis of external phenomena (Kant) or of experience in general (Spencer) seems to leave an unexhausted Something without which neither the Unity, nor the "Together," nor the immediate evidence of phenomena, can be explained. We seem to have lost the kernel of reality and to grasp only the shell. Examples of a similarly unsatisfactory state of knowledge are, however, so to speak, of daily occurrence. A prominent example is the impossibility of defining life, that Something which distinguishes a dead from a living organism. We seem to grasp this only by the synoptical function of some sense, be this lower or higher, physical or spiritual. It can, so to speak, only be seen and experienced but not reproduced by any synthetic action of the intellect. A more serious objection attaches to Kant's Unknowable which does not in the same degree apply to that of Spencer. It recurs again in dealing with Schopenhauer's doctrine. Both Kant and Schopenhauer, following Hume, consider Causation as a subjective form or habit of

thought, but they nevertheless —as Jacobi had pointed out in dealing with Kant's view—apply this category to the "Unknowable Thing in Itself" which lies, as it were, beyond or beneath the region of experience, whereas causation refers only—it is maintained—to things as they appear. A third objection which has been urged against Kant's Unknowable, and which does not apply to that of Spencer, is this: that Kant does not only speak of the Thing in itself, but goes even the length of speaking of Things in themselves. This plural is, as Lotze amongst others has remarked, quite unjustifiable, as no reason exists to conceive of the Unknown as a plurality and not as a unity. In fact, as the former error consisted in transferring and applying the phenomenal category of causation to that which is supposed not to enter into the phenomenal world at all, so, in the other instance, the error arises through tacitly applying distinction which depend on time and space to a content which is supposed to be outside of time and space.

intellectual nature, he as strongly insisted upon the
reality of at least a portion of our perceptions—viz.,
those which were not merely subjective creations or
illusions, but which were supported by some underlying
ground or substance. This was evident through the fact
that, not only our own subject or person, but likewise
other persons around us, participated in the same experience. An agreement with other observing and thinking
beings would not be possible without some common point
of reference. Kant also employed the intellectual categories of substance and cause—unjustifiably as his critics
maintained—to define more clearly the relation of the
Noumenon or Thing in itself to the phenomenal world.
But probably the greatest interest which, in his mind,
attached to this purely noumenal and intelligible,[1] but
not perceptible, entity was the importance that this
distinction acquired when applied to our own personal
self. Here, in the region of our inner experience, he
found a similar dualism, a similar contrast, between
what he called the phenomenal and the real self. In
opposition to the phenomena which constitute our changing experience, the fleeting moments of our inner life, he
detected a unifying principle, a regulative agency. This
was Reason itself, which was intellectually a regulative,
practically an active principle, and the very essence of this

[1] In the Kantian vocabulary, following earlier usage, the word
" Intelligible" had a different
meaning from that which it has
acquired in the English language.
Intelligible means with Kant that
which we can think about but not
see or perceive by our senses. It
is the noumenon as distinguished
from the phenomenon ; it has

therefore quite a different meaning, in fact an opposite meaning,
to the word as used in current
English, where it signifies that
which we can understand. The
difference is clearly marked in
the title of one of Kant's earlier
Treatises : ' De mundi sensibilis et
intelligibilis forma ac principiis '
(1770).

unifying and active principle—our Will—he conceived to stand in a relation to the changing events of our inner life like that of the Thing in itself to the changing phenomena of that outer experience which we call the external world, and which we have in common with other intelligent beings, our fellow-men. In fact the Will, in its self-restrained freedom, was as much the noumenal ground of our own self, its intelligible character, as the Thing in itself was the noumenal ground of external things with their merely apparent reality. From this point onward the real importance of Kant's philosophy is to be found in the stress which he laid upon the self-restraining freedom of the Will that brought with it its own law, the " Categorical Imperative," the " Ought " of our moral nature, the second and higher Reality which he regarded with wonder and veneration.[1]

12. His " Categorical Imperative."

Before we proceed to see how the various suggestions contained in Kant's doctrine were taken up by his successors, it is important to point out again how much of the novelty of Kant's teaching lay in that strange, yet telling and impressive, terminology which he invented, and through which he laid stress upon the different aspects in which the Real makes itself apparent to us. It is possible and has since been variously attempted to put Kant's ideas into the language of earlier philosophers, employing the terms used by Aristotle in older, or by Spinoza in more recent times, also to show how almost every one of his single statements was anticipated by one or the other of his predecessors. But this would not efface the historical fact that Kant, through his original way of

13. Importance of his terminology.

[1] See the celebrated passage quoted *supra*, p. 29.

stating the eternal truths and formulating the everlasting problems of knowing and being, succeeded in imparting to these subjects a fresh interest, inspiring his age with the courage to attack them once more and with the belief in their ultimate solubility.

In the last chapter, when dealing with the problem of Knowledge and Kant's epoch-making contributions to its solution, I pointed out how in his various suggestions may be found indications of the several further developments which the problem underwent in the course of the nineteenth century. Dealing now with Reality, we can similarly point to Kant's writings as containing or suggesting the different aspects which the problem assumed with his successors, and we can accordingly classify their contributions according to these different aspects contained implicitly in Kant's teaching. Fichte,

14.
Fichte on
Kant's terms
for Reality.

the greatest among Kant's immediate followers, has pointed to the threefold meaning which the word reality had for Kant: see a remarkable passage [1] in his lectures on "Wissenschaftslehre" from the year 1804. In this passage he uses the expression, the Absolute,—a term frequently employed in earlier philosophies, and which in the present connection may be considered synonymous with what I have termed the central Reality or the truly Real. Fichte finds that Kant made three important attempts to determine the Absolute, corresponding to the three critiques. "In the Critique of Pure Reason sensuous experience was for him the absolute, . . . in a consistent exposition of the principles which he there adopted the supersensuous world would have to disappear altogether,

[1] Nachlass II., p. 103.

and, as the only Noumenon, would remain, that which
' is ' since it can be realised in experience. . . . The high
moral nature of the man, however, corrected the philosopher, and so there appeared the Critique of Practical
Reason. In it appeared the ' self ' " (or subject) " through
the inherent categorical notion " (*i.e.*, through its self-
assertion) " as something by itself; and thus we get the
second absolute " (or reality), " the moral world. Yet all
the phenomena of human nature were not thereby explained. . . . Moreover, what is still more important,
the empirical world was now lost in the moral world as
the one world in itself " (*i.e.*, as the truly Real), "—a just
retribution for its former victory over the moral world :
and now there appeared the Critique of Judgment, and in it
. . . the confession that the supersensuous and sensuous
worlds must have some common though quite unknowable root, which root was the third absolute." From this
passage we can see how three distinct ways were opened
out to Kant's successors. Which of the three ways was
adopted would depend upon the mental bias of the individual thinker, but also upon the practical interest by
which his speculations were prompted. To those who
move in the world of external realities, of the actual
observable things and phenomena which surround us,
i.e., to the natural philosophers, the problem of reality
would primarily consist in seeking an answer to the
questions—What is the criterion of reality in external
things ? What is their essence ? How is the real and
actual to be distinguished from the imaginary or illusory ?
For a second class of thinkers whose interest lies in the
mental and moral, as opposed to the physical, life of

mankind, those who are termed philosophers *par excel-lence*, the paramount question would be: What is the essential reality of the moral life of man and mankind? and what is its relation to the physical world? No doubt either of the two types of thinkers would in due course be led to the consideration of the other or opposite reality; the natural philosopher would have to ascend from matter to mind or to penetrate from the outer to the inner phenomena; the moral philosopher would try to gain an understanding of the outer world, of the environment upon which the development of mind and character depends. But there is a third position possible, a point of view suggests itself which, if attainable, would transcend or supersede equally the two aspects just mentioned. It is a view which has naturally suggested itself at all times to youthful and ardent minds when first confronted with the problem of reality. It is the attempt to assume at once that the two realities are essentially one, that they have, as Fichte says, a common root. This finds confirmation in the fact that, in the higher spheres of mental activity, notably in poetry, art, and religion, this higher unity is presupposed, and that the greatest work in these regions emanates from a belief in it.

To those of my readers who have realised the importance which the Ideal of Humanity, in an elevated sense of the word, had acquired in German culture at the end of the eighteenth century, how it was upheld and represented at Weimar and Jena by leaders of thought such as Herder, Goethe, and Schiller, and how from there, as a centre, a new spirit and a new life spread all over Germany, it will not be surprising that, of the three aspects of reality just mentioned, the last should be held up and proclaimed by Fichte and Schelling, and that their predecessor in the philosophical chair, Reinhold, should find in Fichte's version of the Kantian doctrine the realisation of what he and other followers of Kant were striving after. In the passage quoted above from his lectures, Fichte goes on to say that his independent speculation was historically connected with Kant in this, its essence: "that it explores the root which to Kant seemed undiscoverable, but in which the sensuous and supersensuous worlds are united, and that its task consists in the actual and intelligible deduction of these two worlds from one principle." Once proclaimed by Fichte, this task became and remained the grand problem of philosophy for a whole generation of thinkers. At the same time Fichte admitted that this higher unity could not be reached by a psychological or logical train of reasoning, by an analysis such as Kant had employed, but that it must be reached by a process of intellectual intuition,[1]—i.e., it must, as Lotze says, be guessed or

15.
Fichte and Schelling.

16.
"Intellectual Intuition."

[1] It is unfortunate that the English language possesses no term equivalent to the German *Anschauung*. The word intuition seems to imply something akin, though perhaps inferior, to inspiration, whereas the German word *Anschauung* implies something akin, though perhaps superior, to seeing or perceiving by means of the senses. *Anschauung* is thus more nearly equivalent to sight; *Intellectuelle Anschauung* might be rendered by "intellectual sight." The German term plays an important part in the philosophies of Fichte and Schelling, but was discarded by Hegel as too vague. The use which the two former thinkers made of the term connects them with Kant as well as with Spinoza. Kant did not use the term in his 'First Critique,' but, as Kuno Fischer has pointed out, employs instead "pure apperception" and "transcendental apperception," the unity of the perceiving and thinking subject or, as Fichte termed it, the *Ego*. But through the influence of Spinoza's writings, with which, as already stated, German thinkers after Kant became acquainted through Lessing and Jacobi, the term acquired a meaning somewhat akin to the *amor intellectualis Dei* of Spinoza.

divined, for it presents itself to the human mind in the immediacy of feeling and not by discursive thought.

Fichte emphasises in this way an important truth which, again and again, rises up in the history of thought, be this philosophical, poetical, or religious : If the human mind is at all capable of understanding, interpreting, or ideally reconstructing the world which surrounds it and of which it forms a part—*i.e.*, if it is at all capable of approaching the essence of reality—some point must exist where it is at one with the Absolute, the truly Real ; and only when this point is reached—*i.e.*, *sub specie unitatis et æternitatis*—will it arrive at, and support, the conviction of the universal Order and meaning of things. From this point of view, so difficult to reach and so easily lost again, we should then be able to grasp

---

Therefore, as Kuno Fischer has remarked : " In the first use of the term Fichte agreed with Kant in maintaining an intellectual intuition as equivalent to the immediate self-consciousness of the subject. The principle of *Wissenschaftslehre* is the intellect in its self - observation. This self-observation of the intellect or the original act through which consciousness becomes its own object is called by Fichte *Intellectuelle Anschauung ;* it is the original act of self-consciousness or of the *Ego.* Whoever ascribes to himself an activity appeals to this *Anschauung ;* in it is the source of life, and without it there is death" (Kuno Fischer, ' Geschichte der neueren Philosophie,' " Fichte," 1st ed., p. 476, with quotations from Fichte's 'Second Introduction,' Works, vol. i. pp. 451 *sqq.*) Subsequently, through a remark which Kant made in his ' Third Critique,'

the term acquired a more pregnant meaning. " Kant demonstrates from the conditions of human reasoning the impossibility of an intellectual sight, or of an intuitive intellect ; the impossibility of a faculty for which the Thing in itself would be an object ; the incognoscibility of Things in themselves and the impossibility of an intellectual sight are for Kant one and the same thing. In this sense Kant denies intellectual sight ; in this sense Fichte denies it likewise " (Kuno Fischer, *loc. cit.*, p. 478). But it is just this suggestion made but not accepted by Kant in his ' Third Critique ' which had a special attraction for Schelling, to whom it seems as if Lotze's remark applies more immediately than to Fichte, though the latter subsequently, not unlike Jacobi, seems to admit a similar conception under the designation of religious faith.

the meaning of those dualities and contrasts which we find around and in us, the difference of self and not self, of mind and matter, of subject and object, of appearance and reality, of truth and semblance. Fichte's endeavour is to bring, in many ways, this truth home to his hearers and readers: nor is there any doubt that he found as much in them an expectant and appreciative audience as they, on the other side, found in him an expositor of these sublime reflections; for he had understood the signs of the times, the want of the age, and also the way to satisfy it. The very fact that he appeared to his listeners as continually seeking, and never quite finding, the right expression for his central idea, kept them alive and intent upon following and assisting him in this arduous enterprise; for he only gave expression to conceptions which others around him had likewise, though vaguely, formed for themselves, and to express which was the untiring endeavour of that age.

But it was not in the spirit of Fichte's philosophy to remain content with an intuitive knowledge of the existence of this underlying unity of the Absolute. His was not a contemplative nature like that of Spinoza, who, before him, had given expression to the same idea, whose writings were at that time much studied in the circle to which Fichte belonged, and who had a growing influence upon the successors of Kant. Fichte's was an eminently active and practical nature, not practical indeed in the lower and everyday meaning of the word, but practical in that elevated region in which the great minds which surrounded him were living and into which

17.
Fichte's practical aims.

it was their and his object to raise the interests and thoughts of the academic youth of Germany. That this was not only an aim which he had constantly in view, but that he also, to a large extent, realised it, is known by the reform which he worked among the students of the University of Jena. From this reform emanated, to a large extent, a wave of elevated feeling and aspiration; it stirred up the life which had for a long time been stagnant in the German high schools and universities. From that age onward they entered into a new phase and put on an entirely changed character. In this respect Fichte joined hands, from the highest regions of philosophic thought, with Pestalozzi who worked upwards from the innermost recesses of the hearts of the people. Fichte did for the select few what Pestalozzi did for the many. This practical tendency in Fichte's nature allowed him to realise, better than any other disciple of Kant's, the great moral influence of Kant's practical philosophy. He felt distinctly what Kant meant by the Categorical Imperative, by the self-restraining power of the human Will. In his search for an expression wherewith to describe the essence of the truly Real or the Absolute, he fixed upon this idea contained in Kant's philosophy; the truly Real was to him—Action or Self-realisation.

18.
"Self-real-
isation."

Now, if we try to analyse this idea of Self-realisation which seems to me to be the most suitable rendering of the somewhat abstruse sentences and oracular sayings in which Fichte's discourses abound, we shall at once see how this conception led Fichte away from the position occupied by Kant into entirely different lines of reasoning, which for a long time became characteristic of German philosophy.

Kant's analysis, though it called itself transcendental, moved nevertheless almost entirely within the region of Psychology and Logic, that is to say, within the enclosure of an individually thinking, feeling, and willing personality. It is true that what he related or described in his several Critiques professed to refer to what all thinking, feeling, and willing minds have in common. His psychology and theory of knowledge moved, as little as did that of Locke and his school, within the region of the purely subjective; nevertheless all his statements refer to what any individual mind could—or must—personally observe and realise within itself. There is no doubt that, in various passages of his two later Critiques, Kant hinted at the conception of a position which was elevated above and beyond the casualties of ordinary experience or of merely subjective impulses. The Categorical Imperative, the "Ought" of our moral nature, the highest moral law as well as the possibility of an intuitive intellect, all these conceptions refer to something which antecedes or supersedes casual, subjective, and temporary facts and events. | This suggestion Fichte took in real earnest. He postulated, at the entrance of his philosophy, an elevation of the thinking mind into that region where the everyday distinctions of subject and object and of many persons or selves would disappear. He here met with the same difficulty of "solipsism" which confronted Berkeley when he started from his own idealistic point of view. The existence of many minds or selves with a common world of objects obliged Berkeley to fall back on the theological conception of a transcendent mind, and Fichte to take the word mind or self to mean a kind of universal mind, in which all single minds are merged or united. With this step his speculation, and German speculation in general, left the region of actual psychological analysis. It became not only transcendental but transcendent.

19.
Fichte's
Absolute is
a process.

The second important step which Fichte took was involved in his attempt to conceive the nature of the truly Real or the Absolute as activity, or, as he also calls it, as a sequence of impulses towards action. In this conception is involved the admission that the truly Real is a process, not a substance in the sense of Spinoza. And Fichte is at considerable pains to differentiate his system from that of Spinoza, inasmuch as it takes a genetic, in opposition to a statical, view of the ultimate Reality. Further on his important philosophical writings deal mainly with the practical questions involved in the state and society, in history and the life of mankind. Here he deals with the realisation of the Absolute, with the unfolding of the truly Real in a world of many individuals. Beyond the very early introduction into his reasoning of a something which he calls the Not-self, and which others would call the external world or nature, he does not approach the outstanding problem of Kant's philosophy—the essence of things in themselves. In fact these have, for him, no essential or true reality.[1]

[1] Fichte, as well as Schelling, in his published Works exhibits the strivings of the thinking mind to arrive at a reasoned creed. The consummation, however, of this searching process of thought is not to be found with either but only in their successor Hegel. Whilst Hegel kept the gradual development of his final conception from the world, Fichte's writings and lectures laid open his repeated

It was natural that the position taken up by Fichte should provoke much criticism and opposition, that his one-sided accentuation of the subjective side of reality should appear unsatisfactory.   At that time a twofold interest was spreading in the study of natural phenomena, especially of the phenomena and forms of living or animated nature; it was also the age that witnessed the discovery of galvanic phenomena, which for a time seemed

more or less successful attempts to arrive at, and give expression to, a reasoned body of thought or a creed.   With Schelling the process becomes still more tentative and changing, and this was the more the case as he lived long enough to realise the insufficiency of the whole idealistic movement of thought.   From the beginning to the end of his career Fichte had a definite purpose before him.   He was, more than any of the other leading thinkers of the century, a man who had a conscious message to deliver to his age and nation. He was influenced by other thinkers, but they did not divert his thinking and teaching into new courses ; they furnished only new aspects and new ways, with the help of which he could find a more and more adequate expression of his guiding idea and fulfil his mission. This view of Fichte's speculative labours is now, thanks to the pains-taking researches and the lucid expositions of historians like Kuno Fischer, Falckenberg, and Windel-band, generally established.   Earlier writers of the history of modern philosophy, following misrepresent-ations and misunderstandings of Fichte's main object, which can be largely traced to the influence of Schelling, were wont to speak of an earlier and a later system of Fichte's philosophy.   This view is now replaced by the conviction of

the consistency of Fichte's main argument.   For our purposes it is of special interest to note how, with Fichte, the interest in one and the same fundamental idea—the supre-macy of moral law and order—moved away from the significance which this idea had for the prob-lem of knowledge to that which it had for the problem of reality. The initial theory of knowledge (Wissenschaftslehre) in the light of the same central conception gradually developed into a theory of being (Ontology), an answer to the question ; What is the truly Real ?   Of all the earlier philo-sophies the only one, in modern times, which has answered this question definitely was that of Spinoza ; all other thinkers, such as Descartes, Leibniz, and even Kant, not to speak of the realistic school in this country, found the Real in something which was given or known already in some other way.   This is owing to the essenti-ally receptive attitude which all these thinkers took up to the exist-ing regions of knowledge occupied by common-sense, science, or reli-gious doctrine.   The question : What is the truly Real ? in perfect simplicity, directness, and independ-ence presented itself in modern times first in Spinoza, and after he had been neglected and almost for-gotten, in Fichte.

to bridge over the two regions of the inanimate and the animated creation. We know how in the beginning of the century these phenomena attracted great attention, and how, especially in the medical sciences, great importance was attached to electrical, magnetic, and galvanic forces. But, outside of this scientific interest in natural phenomena, nature itself as a whole had become an object of a new interest, not to say veneration, in all the three countries I am dealing with, from an artistic, literary, and poetical point of view. A return to nature was proclaimed and practised in many ways and took many forms: Rousseau in France was the exponent of one very prominent form of this modern naturalism. He opposed the artificiality of society and the logical aridity of eighteenth century life and thought. He became the founder and the greatest master in a peculiar form of poetical prose, which had an enormous influence on Continental literature. In this country Goldsmith, Gray, Cowper, and Burns represented a quite independent and less pretentious school of naturalism, which opened out an entirely new vein of poetical feeling and created new forms of poetical diction. Both these products of poetical and creative thought had a great influence on German literature. There, an independent contribution to this line of thought was given by Herder, who, in his studies on the problems of humanity, the origins of language and history, had recourse to the elemental forces of nature as conditioning and producing historical developments. He created an interest in primitive cultures and in the popular poetry and songs of nations all over the world. All these influences, that of

Rousseau, that of the earlier poetry of the English naturalistic school and that of Herder, combined, as it were, to form the mental environment in which Goethe's original genius grew up; they found expression in his intuitive comprehension of nature, which forms such a prominent characteristic of his poetical genius. The speculative philosopher who came most under the influence of this twofold interest in nature and natural things, the scientific and the poetical, was Schelling. He was, after Wieland and Schiller, the third great personality in whom the South of Germany made its contribution to the assembly of representative minds which formed the circle at Weimar and Jena. Herder and Fichte came from the North and East of Germany, whence also had come the influence of Lessing and Kant.

It appears that, in the case of Schelling, the scientific interest in nature succeeded the artistic or poetical interest, and that the latter remained always the dominant one.

20.
Schelling.

In spite of the more matured labours of Kant and the more comprehensive and systematic speculations of Hegel, Schelling deserves to be looked upon as the central figure during the idealistic period of German philosophy,[1] and this for several reasons. In the long

21.
His central
position in
German
Idealism.

[1] This is being more and more recognised and brought out by the latest historians of philosophy in Germany. The standard work on Schelling is still that of Kuno Fischer, forming the 6th vol. of his History (1st ed. 1872). And yet, even this monumental work stops short of an adequate and complete comprehension of Schelling's philosophic development : the last phase of his philosophy is not treated. The reason of this is that forty years ago, when Kuno Fischer completed this section of his History, that phase of Schelling's thought appeared to stand outside of the historical progress of German philo-

course of his philosophical career he came under the influence of almost all the prominent systems and doctrines of ancient and modern times. He assimilated successively many of the suggestions and leading ideas thrown out by his predecessors and contemporaries. He was thus an eclectic in the best sense of the word, in the sense in which Aristotle in ancient times, Leibniz in more recent, Schleiermacher and Lotze in quite recent times, may be called eclectics. Though very different from Aristotle and Leibniz, who aimed at putting their ideas into exact scientific language, and more akin to Plato in his love of the poetical form of diction, he nevertheless resembled Leibniz in his endeavour to reconcile existing differences and contrasts, to mediate between seemingly opposite points of view. His was an exceedingly receptive mind, whose originality consisted in finding unity among diversities and establishing suggestive analogies. To him were attached also prominent workers in very different regions of thought and learning : from the naturalistic pantheist Oken to the mystical theosophist Baader, from the pathologist Kieser to

sophy. For Kuno Fischer saw the consummation of this philosophy and the programme for its future in a form of spiritual rationalism towards which Hegel had given, as it were, a first approximation and a comprehensive programme. He did not recognise, as his disciple Prof. Windelband has done, that before this programme could or would be more adequately carried out a great reaction against the whole of rationalistic thought would set in and have to be dealt with. Accordingly Windelband's profound and advanced insight into the courses of quite recent thought has led him to add a new chapter to the history of German—as indeed also to that of European—speculation. This chapter bears the title of 'Irrationalism,' and comprises such names as Schelling in his latest phase, Feuerbach, Hartmann, and others, ending for the moment with Nietzsche. Out of the hopelessness of this final ending of the philosophy of Reason in Unreason the way to new vigour of speculative thought is, as is indicated in the closing page of Windelband's 'History of Philosophy,' to be found in the conception of value.

the æsthetical philosopher Solger, from all - embracing founders of systems like Hegel to specialists like Ast in history, Nees von Esenbeck in botany, G. F. Puchta and Fr. J. Stahl in law.[1] Schelling also occupies a central international position in the history of modern thought.[2]

[1] Many more names might be mentioned : intimate admirers such as, foremost of all, the poet Platen, who has given in his ' Diary ' a graphic account of the thrill which Schelling's Lectures in Erlangen (1819) sent through his large audiences, confessing that during the whole Exposition the " to be or not to be fell on his heart with its whole weight, and that he felt as if for the first time a real comprehension of it had entered his soul." And on the other side cases of great disappointment and aversion, such as Justus v. Liebig, who in his autobiographical Memoir refers to the baneful influence of Schelling's teaching. Between enthusiastic admirers and angry opponents there stand the more temperate appreciation and criticism of such leaders of thought as K. E. v. Baer (vol. i. of this History, p. 207, note), and Fechner (vol. iii. p. 370).

[2] Schelling himself was well aware that he had led philosophy into wider fields and opened to it extensive realms of thought. In the remarkable Introductory Lecture which he delivered in the year 1827 on his appointment to the Chair of Philosophy in Munich, he said : " When, nearly thirty years ago, I was first called upon to take an active part in the development of philosophy, the different schools were dominated by a philosophy full of life and vigour but estranged from actual realities. Who would have then thought it possible that a teacher with no name, in years still a youth, should become the master of a philosophy so powerful and, in spite of its empty abstruseness, yet in intimate contact with some of the favourite tendencies of the age ? And yet this has happened —indeed not through his merit and special worth, but in consequence of the nature of the Cause itself, through the might of an invincible reality which pervades all things ; nor can he ever forget the grateful and joyful appreciation which then came to him from the first minds of the nation. Though nowadays only few know from what fetters and limits philosophy had then to be liberated in order to force an entry into the free and open field of objective science—a freedom and vigour of thought which they themselves now enjoy and the effects of which they experience. Now again philosophy seems to have arrived at a point beyond which she cannot progress, whilst what is offered as the last and best meets, in the opinion of the foremost, with a general opposition difficult to move. The invisible Spirit which rules over all calls forth at the right time and moment, in every case of arrest, such mental conditions as increase the power of conquest and make minds receptive of help when it arrives. Under such circumstances, in our land, our age, and our science, I come to you and appear in your midst. I greet you with love, receive me also with love. I shall live, work, and strive for you as long as it pleases God " ('Sämmtliche Werke,' vol. ix. p. 366).

It was in the form which he gave to some of the leading ideas in modern German philosophy that these became known in this country through Samuel Taylor Coleridge, and it was he also who among German thinkers made the deepest impression upon Victor Cousin and, through him, upon French thought.[1] And though so much has been said against the " philosophy of nature," some of the leading ideas of its way of looking at natural phenomena found their response partly independently and partly through Schelling's indirect influence in France as well as in this country.

We have already seen that in Fichte the philosophical interest had moved away from the critical position to the dogmatic and constructive, that the problem of knowledge had to give way to the problem of Reality. In Schelling we find little interest in the critical problem of Knowledge and no contributions to its solution. But this interest was not overcome, as it was in Fichte, by the ethical or practical interest; both of these were thrust aside by the artistic or poetical interest. The first Kantian school studied mainly the first Critique and its doctrines. Fichte threw the whole weight of his personality on to the moral and practical teaching as initiated in Kant's second Critique. Schelling's starting-point is that of the third Critique, which deals with final causes in nature and the conception of art, with the meaning and beauty of things.

But nowhere is the central position which Schelling takes up more marked than in this, that he made the

22.
Practical
and poetical
interests.

[1] And even further afield the influence of Schelling is to be found in the writings of Emerson, as is hardly generally known and appreciated.

central problem of philosophy, the problem of Reality, the continued object of his speculation. His philosophy is, more than any other, an attempt to fix the truly Real, to find an expression for the highest form of Reality, for the ultimate ground and essence of things. It is pre-eminently a philosophy of the Absolute. This term he again introduced and made familiar in German philosophical literature. By this more than by any other term—*i.e.*, as a theory of the Absolute—has this philosophy been praised and extolled on the one side, vilified and ridiculed on the other. And Schelling's philosophy is, more than any other, the living proof for the correctness of the view which has been held in various forms and will again and again recur, that the Absolute or the truly Real is the highest object of our search, yet, at the same time, that for which we shall never find a lastingly satisfactory philosophical expression. But Schelling has enriched philosophical language and literature with many valuable suggestions which give us, if not a full view, at least glimpses of the truly Real.

In the first period of his philosophical career, when he saw in Fichte the greatest philosopher of modern times, Schelling conceived the idea of supplementing the one-sided emphasis which Fichte laid upon the subjective side of the truly Real or the Absolute, by a more appreciative treatment of the objective side—*i.e.*, of the phenomena of nature, of the external world which surrounds us. Fichte had seemingly reduced this to a secondary position, looking upon nature, which he defined by a pure negation as the Not-self, merely as the means in and through which the Self or the Absolute arrived at a knowledge of itself and wherein it found a field to display its own activity. In this way of fixing the relation of mind and matter, all reality seemed to be contained in the former; the latter was degraded to a something which did not possess full reality, having its end and meaning, not in itself, but in something else; this being the universal consciousness which it, as it were, helped to arrive at self-consciousness. This existed in the form of many individuals and their reunion in human society. Schelling's love of nature and his admiration of the philosophy of Spinoza, which centred in the idea of an underlying ground or Substance with its two attributes of extension and thought (*i.e.*, of nature and mind), led him to consider that Fichte's view of the external world as a Not-self was a degradation of nature which did not do justice to its manifold purposes and beauties, nor to the fact that consciousness itself made its appearance at the highest point of the natural order of beings. The first

23. Rehabilitation of Nature.

step which he accordingly took, was an attempt to show how the forms and things of nature exhibit in their way a realisation of the Absolute, analogous to, though essentially different from, the realisation which Fichte's philosophy had tried to demonstrate in the region of mind. In this endeavour of Schelling's we find a resuscitation of that parallelism between the external and internal worlds and their phenomena, which played such a great part in Spinoza's philosophy and which, in more recent times, underlies the doctrine of psycho-physical parallelism. But, whereas Spinoza's system centres in the idea of the eternal substance, Schelling conceived the Absolute after the fashion of Fichte, not as a substance but as a process, as activity; an idea which has also been revived in many shades in quite recent speculation. Schelling's idea of the process of the Self-realisation of the Absolute is, however, more akin to that of Leibniz, who introduced into philosophy the ideas of development and continuity. We may therefore say that Schelling's philosophy was much more a reconciliation of Spinoza's and Leibniz's views than a development of the critical philosophy of Kant, or the ethical of Fichte. From Leibniz, Schelling also inherited the tendency which is inevitably connected with the idea of continuity, that of reducing qualitative differences to those of quantity; the latter having the property of a continuous flow, a gradual and imperceptible transition from one to another.

The correct and valuable ideas which underlie Schelling's earliest philosophy are twofold. They have asserted themselves in recent times in a more definite form, having become divested of that admixture of the fanciful element by which they attracted, and also misled, many of Schelling's contemporaries. And I may here remark that it is hardly correct to speak of disciples of Schelling, inasmuch as he began to publish his ideas when quite young and only put into language conceptions which were at the time common to many, though in a much less developed form.[1] Of the two

[1] In many passages of his History Kuno Fischer has pointed to the fundamental difference which separates the philosophical attitude both of Fichte and Schelling from that of Kant before, and of Hegel after. The two former philosophies represent a continual unsatisfied

ideas I refer to, through which Schelling connects earlier systems with more recent thought, the first is the idea of the successive development of natural

striving, such as is peculiar to youthful minds. "In very remarkable contrast to Kant, who proceeds thoughtfully and in measured step from problem to problem, all of which he equally masters, an impatient and impetuous striving now takes hold of philosophical thought. In the life also of ideas there are turning-points and crises which require for their decision the freshness of youthful vigour. It appears as if philosophy in its progress from Kant to Fichte and Schelling tries with each step to rejuvenate itself. Kant was fifty-seven when he brought out his fundamental work, Fichte was thirty-two when he introduced his *Wissenschaftslehre* (1794), Schelling stands at twenty on the height of Kant-Fichtian philosophy (1795) and entered two years later (1797) on the course which is peculiarly his own. Hardly had Fichte spoken the first word of his new doctrine when he was understood by no one better than by the twenty-year-old Schelling, who now, together with the master, developes the doctrine, and plans already the transition to the philosophy of nature whilst Fichte is still occupied with his system of Ethics." This absence of finality in the writings of Fichte and Schelling — of whom Fichte was the greater and more impressive personality, Schelling the more suggestive and inspiring thinker — is probably the reason why the philosophy of neither has met with due appreciation outside of Germany. But this want of finality appears in very different forms in the two philosophies. Fichte's *Wissenschaftslehre*, of which his Works

contain several apparently different renderings, is based upon a fundamental and unvarying conviction, not only of the supremacy of the moral principle in man and mankind and, in consequence, of moral obligation and of the necessity of the development of character, but also of the immediate requirements of his age and country. On the other side Schelling is continually progressing. Beginning with the knowledge of Self, he advances to that of the World, and from thence to that of the Divine Principle ; *Wissenschaftslehre*, philosophy of Nature, Cosmology, Theosophy. "This necessary succession of problems marks the stages of Schelling's philosophical development. The first years are dominated by *Wissenschaftslehre*, the second period comprises Philosophy of Nature and the doctrine of Identity, the third and longest, Theosophy. The philosophical development which Schelling presents to the eyes of his contemporaries covers hardly more than fifteen years ; they are the most brilliant and active period of his life. He was nineteen when he entered on this important period, thirty-four when he ceased to let the world witness his mental labours" (Kuno Fischer, 'History,' vol. vi. pp. 6 and 7). The ethical problem which was, as it were, solved in Fichte's great personality but not in his philosophical rendering, became in Schelling's mind more and more the great enigma at the solution of which he laboured during the last forty years of his life. It was the problem of Evil and Redemption.

forms. This has become extremely valuable to naturalists through the greater precision given to it by French
transformism (Lamarck), von Baer's Embryology, Darwin's Theory of Descent, and Spencer's Evolutionism,
though it has probably also misled many through one-
sidedness and exaggeration. The second valuable idea
leads us away from the position taken up by the pure
naturalist. It has been most clearly defined by Lotze,
who was the first to see in Schelling's philosophy of
nature the attempt, not only to describe natural
phenomena and to calculate them — this being the
specific task of science—but to interpret them, *i.e.*, to
show their deeper sense and meaning.

In carrying out this scheme Schelling made use of all
the new ideas and discoveries which were then revolu-
tionising the natural sciences. Among others the polar
forces, as exhibited in electric and magnetic phenomena,
are considered to be symbolic of the two sides of reality
which confront us everywhere; also the phenomena of
light, and generally the properties of what was then
termed imponderable matter, were opposed to its ponder-
able properties and looked upon as symbolical of many
contrasts which nature exhibits, such as, *inter alia*, the
maternal and paternal principles. Everywhere also the
formula appears of positive and negative factors or
elements which neutralise each other, leading up to and
producing a new reality. Great stress is also laid upon
organisation. In fact, in the phenomena of organised
nature the different activities of the Absolute are seen
as it were on a smaller and more easily observable scale.

24.
Formulæ of
"polarity."

By means of repeated steps from lower to higher poten-
cies or powers (to set forth which algebraical symbols are
employed) the soul of nature as it were unfolds itself,
rising to higher and higher developments, culminating
in the phenomena of sensibility, with which the natural
or external order of things comes to an end, to be
again absorbed and carried into a different region
in the philosophy of mind with its three regions of
intellect, activity, and the union of both in poetry
and art.

This latter region acquires in Schelling's ever-progres-
sive mind more and more reality. This was due to the
influence of the artistic life, interests, and creations which
surrounded him, to Schiller's inspiring doctrines, and
above all to the intuitive and poetical comprehension
of nature peculiar to Goethe, under whose personal influence Schelling came during those years. For a time
at least he conceived Art to be not only the highest
identity of the Real and Ideal which is accessible to the
human mind, but also the union of the latter with the
Absolute, the actual manifestation of the truly Real:
the intellectual intuition of Fichte has become with
Schelling an artistic or poetical intuition. In and
through it the truly Real becomes an immediate, not
merely a mediated reality. This extremely fruitful and
inspiring idea was taken up in many versions by
Schelling's contemporaries, notably by the representatives of the romantic school. It was the melody which
lent itself to endless variations, being enriched by all
the harmonies and resolved discords of which the creative mind is capable; the whole musical orchestra becom-

ing emblematic of the world-process in its symphonal presentation and development.[1]

A further stage in Schelling's successive attempts to fix the essence of the Absolute or the truly Real was

[1] For the understanding of the development of philosophic thought in Germany at the turn of the centuries it is essential to realise the shortness of the period during which it took place, the unusual congregation of minds of the very first but very different order at the same place, the limited duration of concord, the causes of arising differences and discord, and, lastly, the breaking up of this concourse followed by the dispersion of the new wealth of ideas into the different centres of life and learning in Germany. Schelling himself, whose sensitive nature was quick to detect nascent developments, speaks of the disruption of what had hitherto been the point of indifference of North and South in Jena, whence one part is thrown to the south, another to the north. (See 'Aus Schelling's Leben,' vol. i. p. 482.) We read also in the 'Life of Schiller' that in the last years of his life, in the beginning of the nineteenth century, he had to deplore the loss of many of the first intellects which surrounded him at Jena. The principal centre of attraction seems to have been Berlin, where, with the reign of Frederick William III. and his highly gifted Queen, a new era in literature and art had arisen, to be followed, later on, by political regeneration and social reform. The extravagant expectations with which the beginning of the new reign had been heralded had indeed not all been realised, but a hopeful view existed. Many who had migrated to Berlin, as, e.g., Fichte, felt themselves stimulated in the great moving life of the capital, where the indications of increasing political weakness were known to few, and where most felt as if they were surrounded by new and aspiring life. (See Karl Berger, 'Schiller, Sein Leben und Seine Werke,' 1911, vol. ii., 5th ed., p. 702.) On the other side, the poetical element which came from the South of Germany felt itself repelled by the rationalising tone which ruled in the Prussian capital. This antagonism is represented in philosophic thought by the rupture of Fichte and Schelling. It showed itself publicly when Fichte, after leaving Jena, allied himself with the larger political, social, and educational interests centred in Berlin, and gave a turn in this direction to his unfettered academic influence at the Prussian University of Erlangen and in several popular courses in Berlin. This turn was entirely opposed to Schelling's own conception of what was needed to further and deepen the philosophical movement of thought. And this antagonism, this parting of the ways, is very clearly indicated by the polemics and criticisms which Schelling published about the year 1806, on a Course of Lectures ('Über das Wesen des Gelehrten') delivered by Fichte in the year 1805 at Erlangen. Fichte must indeed have felt the great want in the exposition of his System. Through Schelling the apparent depreciation of nature and of the sensuous and intuitively receptive sides of mental life which characterised his doctrine must have become evident to him. He had also, as he says himself, made a profounder study of the religious problem with

reached under influences which made themselves felt when he left the Weimar circle, migrating to Munich and later to Berlin. But before referring more explicitly to this further advance of his speculation, it will be necessary for us to understand and appreciate the last great step which the idealistic philosophy took, and by which it for a time riveted the attention of all thinking minds in Germany, and later on also in other countries of Europe.

25.
Hegel.

This last step was taken by Hegel, who had for some time (1800 to 1806) worked together with Schelling, who was a younger countryman and friend of his, in editing a critical journal of philosophy. The object they had in view was to bring out more clearly the characteristics of the latest form of the idealistic philosophy, the Philosophy of the Absolute, as opposed to the earlier teachings of Reinhold and Fichte. It has, however, been correctly remarked that the orbit in which Hegel's ideas moved and developed was different from that of Schelling; that their courses met only for a short time in order to separate again and to diverge more and more. This divergence was clearly manifested when Hegel published, in 1807, his first great work, the 'Phenomenology of Mind.'[1] Perhaps it would be more correct to

its ethical and educational importance. The endeavour to give expression to these two new lines of thought, but in the original spirit of the *Wissenschaftslehre*, is manifest in those lectures. Schelling, rightly or wrongly, in his Tract of the year 1806, regarded this as an indication of a change of front, brought about through his own "philosophy of nature," and henceforth lost all sympathy with what he termed Fichte's "improved" doctrine.

[1] The estrangement between Schelling and Hegel was of quite a different kind from that between Fichte and Schelling, and not accompanied by violent mutual recriminations before the eyes of the world. It seems as if Schelling had been taken by surprise when he read the

translate the title of this book as the Phenomenology of
Spirit, for by this word (in German *Geist*) the philosophy
of Hegel is most clearly distinguished from that of
Schelling. Both philosophies profess to be, as was that
of Spinoza, philosophies of the Absolute. With Spinoza
the Absolute was conceived as substance, with Schelling
it meant at that time the identity or indifference of
matter and mind, of the inner world and the outer, the
hidden ground, source, or unity of both. From that
point where he conceived the Absolute as the deeper
lying unity or identity, Schelling went on in search
of other fuller and more adequate expressions, at the
moment when Hegel, after many years of preparatory
work, conceived the essence of the Absolute to be Spirit.

Preface to Hegel's ' Phenomenology ' in the year 1807. The last
letter which he addressed to Hegel,
six months after receiving the great
work of the latter, is accompanied
by a copy of his own celebrated
Address before the Munich Academy
which created such a sensation.
The contrast between Schelling's
and Hegel's minds, as well as that
between their work, is indeed
significantly expressed by these
two characteristic products of the
genius of each. On the one
side, a ponderous volume, full
of enigmas, which has ever since
its appearance furnished material
for philosophical thought and on
which the last word has not yet
been spoken. On the other side,
a finished oration, one of Schelling's
best productions, admired by many,
full of artistic and poetical life and
suggestion, comparable to some of
Goethe's best writings in German
or Ruskin's in English. And at the
same time we have Schelling's own
expression of the deep-lying difference which separated him after-

wards and increasingly from Hegel.
"Our real difference of conviction
or opinion—an irreconcilable difference — can be shortly and
clearly found and decided : for
indeed everything might be reconciled, one thing excepted. Thus,
I must confess, that I can so
far not understand your meaning
when you oppose the notion [Be-
griff] to the intuition [Anschauung,
i.e., 'seeing']. You cannot possibly
under the former term mean anything else but what you and I have
called the Idea, the nature of which
is to have one side from which it is
' notion ' and one from which it is
'intuition'" (Ibid., vol. ii. p.
124). Expressed in terms which
I have used several times already,
we may say that Hegel represents
the analytical method to be completed by a subsequent synthesis ;
Schelling on his part started from,
and remained permanently in, the
region of synopsis, of seeing things
in their Together. (See *supra*, p.
192 note.)

26.
Philosophy
of the Ab-
solute
Spirit.

We may therefore say that Hegel's philosophy is the philosophy of the Absolute Spirit. The word Spirit combines many meanings, in the same way as the German equivalent *Geist* does. We express by it the essence of the highest, of the Divine mind as well as of the human mind, and we also speak of the Spirit of nature, and the Spirit of the age. It further includes the idea of life and development, as opposed to that of rest and stability which is implied in the word substance. The very title, therefore, of Hegel's work was happily chosen.[1] It gave some definiteness to what had been left quite vague in contemporary philosophy, and it also gave expression to an idea which underlay the best of German thought since the time of Leibniz, the idea of development, the history of the various phenomena [2] in which Reality, the

---

[1] The German term *Geist* is even more comprehensive than the English term Spirit, for it includes what we mean by Mind as well as by Spirit. This work of Hegel has quite recently been admirably translated into English by Prof. J. B. Baillie in the 'Library of Philosophy,' edited by J. H. Muirhead (2 vols. 1910). He has chosen the term " Mind " to represent *Geist*, whereas I note that Ed. Caird (see ' Hegel' in Blackwood's Philosophical Classics) speaks of the " Phenomenology of Spirit " (p. 62). The translator of Höffding's 'History of Philosophy' uses the term " Mind " (vol. ii. p. 177). This twofold rendering exhibits the ambiguity of the German word *Geist*, which in its derived adjectives *Geistig* and *Geistlich* shows more clearly that it comprises the two meanings of Mental and Spiritual.

[2] The ' Phenomenology' is not more intelligible to the student of to-day than it appears to have

been to Hegel's contemporaries. Fortunately, however, in our days, over a century after the appearance of the book, two important works have been published which have done much to promote a better knowledge and appreciation of Hegel's great design—which, in a certain sense, may be considered to furnish the programme of thought for a certain class of intellects that will never die out. The first of the two works I refer to is Kuno Fischer's 'Paraphrase of Hegel's Teaching' in the last part of his monumental History. As Prof. Windelband says, the present generation will resort to this as the best guide to a just appreciation of Hegel's doctrine. The other work is Lord Haldane's 'Gifford Lectures' (2 vols., 1903-4), the very title of which most happily represents what Hegel was striving for, The Pathway to Reality. That the independent position taken up by the English school of Hegel's interpreters

essence of the truly Real, manifests itself in the actual world of facts and events. In the preface to this work Hegel clearly puts his finger upon the weak points of the philosophy of Schelling or—as Schelling himself tried to understand it—of the philosophy of many of Schelling's followers and admirers: the want of method, the licence with which vague analogies, poetical images, and fanciful *aperçus* had been put in the place of strict definitions and logical analysis. In this he only gave expression to a conviction which must have been that of many leaders of thought at that time, who felt that the wholesome discipline exerted by the writings of Kant

is perhaps not yet sufficiently recognised abroad may be gathered from the following passage in Windelband's 'Geschichte der Neueren Philosophie' (vol. ii., 4th ed., p. 331). Speaking of the obscurity of Hegel's 'Logic' he says : "We can only recommend the German reader of to-day to acquire through Kuno Fischer's 'Exposition' a detailed and clear insight into the wealth which Hegel's mind has woven into the System of the Categories: we possess in it a translation, intelligible to the present age, of Hegel's work that greatly excels the manifold attempts which before this have already appeared in foreign, especially English literature. It is to be hoped that through it the prejudices under which Hegel's memory has long suffered will be increasingly dissipated." In order not to leave my readers quite in the dark, I may here state that the great difference which separates Neo-Hegelianism in England from genuine Hegelianism is, in my opinion, to be traced largely to the influence of Lotze, who was the first to attempt in a truly Hegelian

spirit an exposition of the logical forms of thought or of the categories in connection with the content of such thought and with the object with which it is carried on. And this seems also to agree with Windelband's own words (*loc. cit.*) : "Only by adhering to the principle [of an epistemological logic] that all forms of thought have meaning only with reference to their object-matter is it possible for Logic to preserve contact with the actual reality of human thinking. Hegel is, next to Aristotle and Kant,—in spite of all the arbitrariness of his constructions,—the greatest logician whom History has known, and he is, together with them, the proof that a truly original and creative treatment of Logic is possible only to such as have gained, through a rich and scientific experience, a comprehensive view of the intellectual work of man." As might have been expected, the Oxford School has also brought Hegel into closer connection with the philosophy of Aristotle. This is eminently characteristic also of Lord Haldane's Lectures.

and by the earlier lectures of Fichte was gradually being relaxed, thus rendering philosophy unfit to be a training school for the youthful minds of the nation. This suspicion that the philosophy of romanticism contained dangerous elements which would unfit it to be a definite subject of University teaching, was significantly confirmed by Schelling's subsequent career when, for various reasons, he ceased to give regular courses of lectures, confining his utterances to casual discourses and dissertations; which, however, rose to great distinction and had a deserved influence on thought in very wide circles. *Inter alia*, it may be noted that in the year in which Hegel's ' Phenomenology ' appeared, Schelling delivered his celebrated address at Munich " On the relation of the fine arts to nature." [1]

---

[1] See *supra*, p. 42, note 2. Through the labours of Kuno Fischer and Windelband as contained in the Works frequently referred to, and to a large extent also through the appearance in 1905 of W. Dilthey's 'Jugendgeschichte Hegels,' a new and altered view has been gained of the historical succession of the idealistic systems of German philosophy. Earlier historians, both those who looked upon Hegel's System as the last word of Idealism and those others who, like Zeller and Ueberweg, had thrown off the traditions of Idealism and given entry to the spirit of exact research, were in the habit of representing Hegel as a follower of Schelling and his philosophy as the last act in the speculative drama in which Kant represented the first act. This view was also introduced and accepted in this country through the earlier writers, beginning with J. H. Stirling, who introduced Hegel to English students. The result has been that the philosophies of Fichte and Schelling have never received adequate attention in this country. It is now quite evident that Hegel's philosophy stands in as immediate a connection with Fichte, and through him with Kant, as that of Schelling. A close friendship existed between Schelling and Hegel, both having received at Tübingen the same training within the same intellectual surroundings; both studied Fichte's philosophy and were, for a time, fascinated by it; both experienced the necessity of transcending the subjectivism of Fichte's earlier speculation—as indeed Fichte did himself. But the courses they took were very different, and of the three courses that of Hegel was the most independent, the most thorough, hence also the latest to reveal itself. Schelling's was the earliest, his mind was the most receptive and, though not the least original,

According to Hegel, the essence of the Absolute as Spirit was not revealed only by intellectual or artistic intuition; it was to be reached by a process of severe thought. And this process was at the same time conceived not to be merely a logical scaffolding by which the human mind rises to an eminence from which it comprehends the truly Real, the Spirit of things; the process was considered at the same time to exhibit the different stages in and through which the Spirit itself unfolds its reality in the regions of nature and mind, of history, art, and religion. It was accordingly not only a process of thought; it was also a process of actual development. In this way, what were in earlier systems considered to be merely logical forms and categories were elevated in Hegel's doctrine to be the successive stages of the development or evolution of the ultimate Reality or Spiritual ground of things. Logic, with Hegel, meant not merely the laws and forms of thought; it meant the development of the Logos, the living and moving

27.
Logical process identified with world-process.

certainly the least independent of external influences. Fichte came under the influence of Jacobi and Schleiermacher and, though not avowedly so, under that of Schelling. With all three he had, for a time, intimate personal intercourse, living and moving in the same circle. Hegel did not move in this circle, — his contact with it was maintained mainly through his correspondence with Schelling. He had carried on deep studies mainly in the history of ancient classical and Christian thought and religion ; had written elaborate dissertations upon historical and theological subjects, — among these a 'Life of Jesus.' An analysis of these unpublished remains which were to some extent accessible already to Rosenkranz and Haym, is given fully in Dilthey's work. After reading this we are driven to the conclusion that from Kant and Fichte there emanated four tolerably distinct developments of idealistic thought in Germany, viz.: Schelling's later philosophy, that of Hegel, that of Schleiermacher, and that of Schopenhauer. They are historically co-ordinated and cotemporaneous. The old formula of Kant, Fichte, Schelling, Hegel, which even by Kuno Fischer was only awkwardly broken up by a somewhat incongruous Introduction of Schopenhauer, must, so far as the deeper History of Thought is concerned, be abandoned.

principle of the world. In describing the categories of
thought, Hegel thus meant to describe also the forms
and stages of the world-process. The detailed account
of this, which was significantly called the dialectical process, must necessarily follow the order of the abstract
notions with which the human mind operates and in
which it is, as it were, forced to move onward from one
idea to another. The Logic or the evolution of the
Logos exhibits therefore at the same time the deeper
meaning of the formal categories of the ordinary logic,
and brings into a scheme, intelligible to the human
mind, the life and movement of the underlying spirit
and essence of things. The different philosophies which
preceded Hegel had already suggested the formula or
rhythm which seems to govern the various stages of
human thought. Thus Kant had already pointed out
how affirmation and negation become united in limitation; how the notion of unity and its opposite, the
notion of plurality, are united in the notion of the all.
Fichte had employed the rhythm of thesis, antithesis,
and synthesis; Schelling had conceived the idea of an
identity which splits up into opposites and comes
together again in the position of indifference. Following these suggestions and partial applications of what
he considered the general process of thinking and being,
Hegel conceived that every content, be it the highest idea or only a lower stage of its manifestation,
finds its first definition by its contrary or opposite,
by something which it is not, and from which it is
differentiated; that a second and fuller definition consists in finding what is common to the two opposites,

and that in the discovery of this common ground consists the progress to a higher conception, which again
requires to be subjected to the same process of contrasting and harmonising, of going out of and resuming itself
in a higher unity. The peculiarity with Hegel is that
this process is not only a process of human thought, but
is emblematical, a conceivable image, of the development
of the highest content itself. This, at the time, novel and
fascinating general conception was applied in many particular instances; the general process being illustrated by
an extraordinary wealth of examples drawn from all the
existing regions of knowledge. Foremost stood history
and, in the large region of history, principally that of
society, art, religion, and philosophy. In fact, it may be
said that many of the modern branches of the history of
culture, civilisation, and the higher manifestations of the
human mind were for the first time systematically treated
and co-ordinated to a living whole in the writings and
lectures of Hegel.

The extraordinary impression which Hegel's philosophy
made in an age when the mind of the nation was in a
state of ferment, but when it also put forward its greatest
creative efforts, is not difficult to understand. For this
philosophy came forward in many ways as a realisation
of the ideals of that period. It understood the greatness
of Goethe and Schiller and the aims of the Romantic
movement, without following the latter into the dreams
and vagaries of the purely imaginary. It had at the
same time a full appreciation of the strictness of
scientific method and of the critical spirit which was
then slowly but surely making itself felt in many de-

28.
Reason of
Hegel's
success.

partments of knowledge. It further participated in, and to a large extent directed, the historical interest, being nursed and brought up in the same school, that of classical literature and learning, in which so many of the leading minds of the nation have been trained. And lastly, it took as the highest subject of philosophic thought the religious problem, the attempt to put something better in the place of the narrow orthodoxy or the prosaic rationalism of the eighteenth century. All this was to be done by ascending to, and getting hold of, the living spirit that pervaded everything; by rising beyond mere forms and categories, but through them, to the truly Real which manifests itself in all actual facts and processes in nature, mind, and history, giving to them their deeper meaning and value. This philosophy must have appeared to its disciples to be the very Rationale, the abstract exposition, of the various aims and endeavours which then formed the programme of many an eminent academic teacher. Notably in two directions and on two independent fields of research, the thought of the age had at that time put forward definite problems. Foremost stood the task which F. A. Wolf had defined as that of the new science of Philology : the reconstruction of classical antiquity, the task of finding again, through patient study of the remains of Greek art and literature, the spirit that lived in that greatest era of bygone human culture. The other and independent movement I refer to was the birth of modern German theology,[1]

---

[1] It is well to remember that nearly all the leading thinkers of that age in Germany, beginning with Lessing, onward through Kant, Herder, Fichte, Schleiermacher to Schelling and Hegel, came originally through theology to philosophy, and that they all preserved a genuine

or rather the regeneration of the conventional theological and religious teaching through a critical study of the Scriptures on the one side, and a philosophical fathoming of the deeper meaning—*i.e.*, of the spirit of the sacred

theological interest. Others of equal or, in one instance, of even greater eminence, such as Goethe, Schiller, Fr. Schlegel, though without theological bias, had a genuinely religious interest. And this formed one of the important connecting links between what we may term the spiritual and the profane or secular literature of the whole classical period. The entire circle of their interests, the whole body of thought which they put forward, was antagonistic only to two extremes: narrow clericalism on the one side and soulless materialism on the other. An idea or an ideal common to them all was the unity of the Divine and the human. And to this Goethe added and Schelling adapted the idea of the immanence of the Divine in nature. It was only for a moment that Fichte, under the influence of Spinoza, seemed to be contented with representing the Divine as the moral order of the Universe; he soon adopted again a more spiritual view. And at a very early stage both Schelling and Hegel identified the Absolute with the Divine principle, using interchangeably the terms Mind, Absolute, and God. This reintroduction of the words and terms used in specifically religious writings into philosophical and scientific discussions—a habit, if we may say so, not indulged in by Kant—gave again to the philosophies of Schelling and Hegel from the beginning and likewise to the later philosophy of Fichte, not only a poetical but distinctly also a spiritual character, and this in addition to the intellectual and ethical tone peculiar to Kant. But

it was in reality more than a mere habit of thought—it was the central conviction that the truly Real, the ultimate Reality, is what religion terms God, a living and active Spirit and, as such, a Personality. Whether the latter conviction can be logically defended (if not also demonstrated) is a problem which occupied a later and more critical generation and has produced an enormous literature. The perusal, however, of the philosophical literature of that age does not, as it seems to me, permit any doubt that a conviction that the truly Real is a Spirit essentially identical with the God of religion underlies the thought and the writings of the foremost thinkers of that age, and that thinking readers and listeners expected from its great leaders in thought a demonstration of this truth; that this formed one of the main attractions which their speculations possessed and that, at a later period, the interest in them declined in the same degree as a general impression gained ground that this expectation was not—or could not be—fulfilled. And when, in the year 1865, J. H. Stirling initiated that serious study of Hegel's Philosophy before which Ferrier recoiled, but which has been continued in this country ever since, it was one of the main points which he urged that this philosophy was destined to stem the tide of materialism and scepticism and strengthen the spiritual or religious view of things which was threatened in this country. A similar interest seems also to have drawn T. H. Green to a study of Hegel, though his foundations lay

records and of the Revelation which they contained—on the other.

What was demanded in these two great scientific tasks and stood out in tolerable clearness and definiteness, thus becoming a fit subject for academic teaching and study, existed, though less clearly and definitely, in many other branches of literature and learning. What was common to all these movements and endeavours and enlivened the lectures of many prominent academic teachers from that time onward, was the attempt to penetrate beneath forms and facts which had become dead through age, routine, and convention, to the moving spirit which had once vivified them. This was to be done by hard work and severe method, not only in the form of a poetical fancy. That this could be done was the common faith of all the great founders and leaders of German *Wissenschaft*, notably in the historical and philosophical sciences. Of this common faith the philosophy of Hegel appeared as the methodical and abstract enunciation : a statement which would serve as introduction to all critical, historical, and philosophical studies, but also as their consummation. As such it was announced by Hegel himself and accepted by a whole generation of eager and thoughtful listeners.

The further elaboration of the scheme put forward by

in a different quarter. Nor is there wanting in this age and in this country a parallel to the disillusionment which was widespread in Germany two generations ago. This is, *e.g.*, expressed in the 19th chapter of Mr A. W. Benn's ' History of English Rationalism in the Nineteenth Century ' (2 vols., 1906); in reference to which it may be remarked that this author takes no note of Lotze and of his influence on English thought, nor of the altered position which he occupies with regard to the relation of science and religion.

Hegel in his first great work occupied him up to the end of his life. During his enforced retirement from the academic career (1806 to 1816), he wrote and published 'The Science of Logic.' In 1816 he again took up this career at Heidelberg, and published there in 1817 his 'Encyclopædia of the Philosophical Sciences.' In 1818 he migrated to Berlin, where, for thirteen years, he expounded his system in various courses of lectures which treated not only of the abstract principles of his philosophy but also of their application to legal and social problems and to those of æsthetics, history, and religion. One of the most inspiring of these courses of lectures was that on 'The History of Philosophy,' which he was the first to treat as the manifestation of the hidden but inevitable movement of human thought, the condensed epitome of the growth and development of human ideas, philosophy being throughout conceived as the highest form of intellectual life, destined to embrace and exhibit the essence and latent truth contained in all the other higher regions of culture. What he there attempted to do with a few bold strokes has ever since his time been the theme taken up with more or less success by historians of Thought. Knowingly or unknowingly, they have been influenced by his ideas, even though the principle of progress has been variously sought in other than the purely intellectual forces which Hegel saw at work in the advancement of the human mind.

It was, however, inevitable that the problem which Hegel had set before himself, and which he had the ability, energy, and courage to attack, transcended even his powers and his erudition; that the whole scheme was much more in the nature of a postulate, of a great task which he set before the age and the nation,—a programme which had to be worked out by many labourers, by the co-operation of many minds, and after generations of research. It is, however, quite as certain that this programme, which covers really, up to quite recent times, the best work of many minds,— not only in Germany, but also in other countries,— would not have become intelligible if Hegel himself had not made an attempt to carry it out; the philosophical spirit, which culminated in him, would— without his efforts, his successes and his failures—not have got such a firm hold of the thought of the nineteenth century, that all attempts to supersede it—as, for instance, by the exact or the critical spirit—have proved vain. Hegel did not create this philosophical spirit, he only represented it in its most abstract form; but he proclaimed, formulated, and introduced it into many regions which it has since enlivened. Nor can he justly be blamed for having clothed it in terms which were too abstract, or encased it in formulæ which were too rigid. As Francis Bacon was held up in the seventeenth century as the herald of a new movement of thought in spite of the errors which abound in his enunciation of its methods, so Hegel deserves to be looked upon as the greatest representative of philosophical thought in the nineteenth century; who has done more — and this more effectually — for modern philosophical thought than the great Chancellor did for scientific thought. Those who first see the general importance and far-reaching power of a new movement

29.
Compared
with Bacon.

in thought or life, are rarely those who carry it on in the most judicious manner or give the best examples and proofs of its application. Their boldness and enthusiasm leads them into error, but they nevertheless conquer in the end. We have in another sphere and more recent times a telling example in Ernest Haeckel's labours in the theory of descent. Who could deny that his "Generelle Morphologie" gave currency to Darwinian ideas and created Darwinism on the Continent, if not also in this country? but who would look upon this work as anything but a suggestive, yet premature, *mise en scène* of those ideas?

II.

When trying to define the position which Schelling occupies in the idealistic movement of thought, I observed that this is, *inter alia*, characterised by the fact that he put the problem of reality at the centre of his speculation. The same may be said of Hegel. With him this problem gained even greater importance than it had with his predecessors, through the fact that he gave a distinct, and, to his age, intelligible answer to the question, What is the truly Real? and that he combined with the solution of the problem of Reality that of the problem of Knowledge, which was the central problem in the Kantian philosophy. The answer to the first question was, the Real is Spirit; the answer to the second question is, Knowledge, in the highest sense, is the self-realisation of the Real or the Spirit. I must repeat again that these answers, which may nowadays appear to us vague and unscientific, were not so for an age which thought itself in possession of a new inspiration, which had brought forth great creations in many regions of thought, art, and life, which was in fact conscious of having got hold of the underlying ground and essence of the truly Real in a fresh and original manner. In countries and times where this inspiration has disappeared, the understanding of Hegel's answers has disappeared likewise. That the problem of Reality acquired this foremost position in Hegel's speculation, may be seen in innumerable utterances of his—in none more emphatically than in his well-known saying : "What is rational is real," and "What is real is rational." This statement has been variously interpreted. It has been explained to mean that in all reality we must look for a deeper sense and meaning, and that this meaning is intelligible. It has been criticised as implying that everything that exists is justifiable, and as denying the existence of things or relations which are to us not only unintelligible but also irrational — such as evil and sin. It is not necessary at the moment to discuss what position the Hegelian philosophy took up to these gravest problems of human life; it is sufficient to indicate that this, like many other of Hegel's oracular sayings through which his philosophy has become popular and proverbial, can only be understood if we give to the word Reality a double meaning—the twofold meaning, in fact, which I have all through this chapter tried to impress upon the minds of my readers, and

30.
Meaning of
the identifi-
cation of the
Rational and
the Real.

which has come down to modern thought from the
great thinkers of antiquity, notably from Plato. We
must distinguish between the truly Real and that which
is only apparently so, between that which possesses and
deserves to possess full reality and that which has
only a semblance of reality or exists only by and for
something else, which shines only with a reflected light.
Further, we may note that Hegel, in a similar manner,
in speaking of that which is rational and intelligible,
distinguished, as Kant did before him, between a higher
and a lower stage of intelligence. He distinguished
between understanding and reason. And one of the
great points which he continually urges is this—that
it is the object of the highest science, *i.e.*, of philosophy,
to rise from a mere understanding to a conception of the
reason of things. This is identical with saying that we
must rise from a merely apparent and mechanical knowledge to an insight into the meaning and value of reality.

Before we proceed to see how in recent philosophical
thought this idea of the twofold or manifold meaning
of the word Real has more and more asserted itself, it
is of importance to note how other contemporary speculations co-operated—though sometimes quite independently—in creating an opposition to what we may call
the monistic tendency of the idealistic school of thought.
The latter tendency began with Reinhold and Fichte,
with whom the aim prevailed to find in consciousness
the point of unity, to overcome the dualism of the
theoretical and practical reason which had been established by Kant; it went on to Schelling, who took a
greater interest in the problem of Reality than in the

31.
Opposition
to the
monistic
tendency.

problem of Knowledge, trying to establish the underlying identity of mind and nature; and it finally culminated in Hegel, whose speculation is not only based
on the conception of the uniting principle in all
knowledge and the unity in all that is real, but who
also reverted to the antique conception of the unity
of knowing and being. This dogmatic assertion of the
monistic view was opposed by two quite independent
thinkers — by Herbart[1] on the one side, and by

[1] Herbart (1776-1841) is a unique
and isolated figure in modern philosophy. But though he had a considerable influence in various, only
slightly connected, directions of
thought, it cannot be said that
he has left a permanent mark on
philosophical thought as a whole
or outside of his own country.
The great revolution which has
come over philosophical thought
through Kant is only partially represented in Herbart's writings ; and
though he called himself a Kantian,
it has been correctly pointed out
that he really stands nearer to the
philosophy of Wolff, to some of
Leibniz's ideas, and to others peculiar to ancient Greek philosophy.
Nothing strikes one more in Herbart's writings than the want of
reconciliation of different lines of
thought which he takes up and
follows out independently; and this
is so much the more remarkable, as
his fundamental methodical precept
was that philosophy consists in
removing contradictions met with
in the philosophy of common-sense
and in the sciences. Not only is
his conception of reality pluralistic,
but his manner of thought is unsystematic. In religious matters
he was conservative, not to say
orthodox ; but there is no attempt
to give a philosophical interpretation to religious doctrines, as was
the aim of the idealistic systems,
or to deal with religious belief as
a psychological phenomenon, as
was done in an original manner
by Schleiermacher ; nor does he,
lastly, deal with the great problem
of Evil, Sin, and Redemption, as
was done by Schopenhauer. The
truly Real and the doctrine of degrees of Reality are not to be met
with, and his metaphysics present,
in consequence, no religious or ethical interest. Although one heard
at one time a good deal about the
Herbartian school, this seems to
have died out after having, through
some of its representatives, produced important works in special
limited regions of research ; in one
direction, that of anthropology, even
pioneer work. Some of his disciples have cultivated such branches
of philosophy as were only sketched
by Herbart himself—such as Æsthetics, Ethics, and Philosophy of
Religion. In those chapters of this
History in which I shall deal with
special philosophical problems, we
shall meet with Herbartian ideas,
as we have already done in the
chapter on the "Psychological
Problem" ; and notably we shall
find in Lotze's philosophy marks
of Herbartian influence which led
some early critics of Lotze to place
him erroneously in the Herbartian
school.

Schopenhauer on the other. These thinkers both start from that outstanding problem of Kant's philosophy— the conception of the "Thing in itself" or "Things in themselves." Herbart agrees with Kant that no direct answer can be given to the question, What is the Thing in itself? Though he thus introduces or retains what we nowadays should call the agnostic position regarding the ultimate nature of Reality, and agrees with Kant that we only know appearance, he at once adds the significant remark, characteristic of his whole philosophy, that appearances, though not Reality, are indications of Reality. He maintains that we can make use of these indications to arrive at a consistent conception of the Real — the object of philosophy being, through a re-modelling of our empirical notions, to introduce into them agreement in the place of seeming contradictions. The first result of this process of remodelling is the necessity of acknowledging the existence of many things in the place of only one substance; whereupon we may remark that Kant himself never thoroughly explained the relation of the "Thing in itself" to "Things in them-selves," and the precise usage of the two terms. Thus Herbart opposes to the monistic view which the ideal-istic systems had inherited from Spinoza's Substance the pluralistic view inherited from Leibniz's Monads. In doing this he approaches, as Leibniz did before him, the atomistic view. At that time this view prevailed and was being greatly developed in the natural sciences. By adopting it Herbart prepared the way for a mechan-ical construction of phenomena which he, as already stated, subsequently introduced also into psychology. In

32.
Herbart.

addition to this pluralism in his solution of the problem of Reality,[1] Herbart draws a sharp distinction between theoretical and practical philosophy. Our ideas regarding the ultimate nature of Reality have nothing whatever to do with the principles of our conduct. The latter must be sought quite independently in ultimate judgments of Æsthetical and Ethical approval and disapproval, and of the corresponding value or worth which we attach to things or actions.

33.
Schopen-
hauer.

With Herbart, Schopenhauer is in agreement on one point.[2] He looks the question of the ultimate nature

[1] We may say that the solution of the problem of Reality remains with Herbart on a lower level. The common-sense view of Reality and the notions developed by science lead him to conceive of the phenomenal world as consisting of a finite multitude of independent entities which he terms "Reals," of which we know nothing but their existence or that they are "posited." The manner in which, out of this plurality of independent Reals, an orderly scheme or system results, is nowhere clearly explained by Herbart. He indeed maintains that relations exist between this multitude of Reals, but "it is really very difficult to say what we are to understand by the hazy conception of a relation which is quite indifferent to its related entities. And it is equally difficult to combine with this the other conception that there exists a certain kind of relation in which two entities are no longer quite indifferent to each other, but where the difference of their qualities acquires such an importance that what we usually term interaction takes place. This relation, which is the condition of a causal connection between the Reals, Herbart terms 'their

Together': to begin with only in an abstract sense; further on, however, without any clear reason, as a 'Together' in Space" (Lotze, in 'Geschichte der Neueren Philosophie,' Lecture Syllabus, 1882, p. 91). Further on we learn "that what happens consists in a change of relations between the Reals, and what is really new takes place only in the consciousness of an observer to whom those Reals present different phenomena accordingly as they are variously connected, like the trees in a wood which to the approaching eye separate but at a distance merge into one mass, whereas they themselves experience no change whatever" (Ibid., p. 92; also Herbart's 'Works').

[2] There was another and a personal trait common to Herbart and Schopenhauer, though they in other respects represent a peculiar contrast in thought and personality. Neither of them had any theological interest. They are the first two eminent thinkers of modern times who did not come to philosophy from the side of theology. But whereas Schopenhauer had a deep sympathy with the mystical side of religion, this was quite foreign to

of Reality full in the face. He does not shirk the
task of finding an answer to the outstanding problem of
Kant's philosophy : What is the " Thing in itself "? [1]

Ignoring the complicated nature of the problem—
which results from the fact that in discussing the
question of the difference of the subjective and the
objective side of reality, each individual mind mixes up
what is its own inner experience with what it knows by
considering itself, as it were, as one of the many persons
which exist around it—Schopenhauer treats the problem
of the Thing in itself in its most abstract form.
Starting from the statement that our own self is
certainly a reality, he maintains that we must be able
to find within ourselves the essence of reality, the nature

Herbart. With the latter the central interest was the ethical, and
through this he had a genuine
understanding for Kant and Fichte,
especially for Fichte's personality,
though he soon developed a marked
aversion to the constructive attempts of the earlier, and the
mysticism of the later, form of
Fichte's speculation.

[1] Schopenhauer in philosophy, like
Goethe in literature and life, seems
through external circumstances to
have been at liberty to choose his
career without what are usually
termed pressing worldly considerations. He was thus, of all the
thinkers of that period, the only
one who came to philosophy with
no other interest. This is shown
in an interesting anecdote of an
interview which took place, about
the year 1811, between him and
the aged poet Wieland. When
Wieland tried to dissuade Schopenhauer from following the philosophical career, the student of
twenty-three replied to him : " Life

is an awkward affair : I have resolved to pass my life in thinking
about it." This answer impressed
the aged poet so much that he
recognised in him the born philosopher. When, shortly after, he
met Schopenhauer's mother at
Court, he addressed her as follows :
" I have lately made a highly interesting acquaintance ! Do you
know with whom ? with your son.
I was delighted to see this young
man ; something great will some
day become of him " (see Kuno
Fischer, 'Arthur Schopenhauer,'
1893, p. 29). Schopenhauer was in
other respects the very opposite of
Herbart, who was driven to philosophy through an early interest in
education and the desire to be a
teacher, a vocation which Schopenhauer only tried for a short time
when his pecuniary independence
seemed threatened, and which he
very soon abandoned in order to
devote himself exclusively to the
working out of his System.

of the Real, the core and kernel of existence. He there finds in addition to our external sensations, perceptions and impressions, the fact of the Will: this manifests itself in striving and feeling, in pleasure, pain, and desire. The whole of these manifestations of the Will he opposes to the region of the intellect and, by analogy, explains the reality of the not-self, *i.e.*, of things around us, as consisting in a similar activity, which, in the form of resistance, they oppose to our own reality, *i.e.*, to our Will. Schopenhauer maintains that this is the last and only step which can be taken beyond Kant's agnostic position. In the place of the unknown and unknowable *x* of Kant's philosophy, he boldly places the Will, which we know by inner or immediate experience, *i.e.*, intuitively, and a large part of his writings is occupied with showing how something analogous to the Will, *i.e.*, to the active principle within us, is to be found everywhere, and how the whole world consists of the two principles of the Will and the Intellect, the active and the receptive sides of Reality. To this purely metaphysical conception he gives further significance and interest by attaching to it an ethical interpretation. This will occupy us in a subsequent chapter. It does not form a necessary conclusion from the metaphysical position, but it differentiates Schopenhauer's philosophy from the main idealistic movement; to the optimism of which it opposes an equally decided pessimism. Through this it became, after having been ignored for more than a generation, the favourite philosophy of all those who turned away in disappointment when they found that Hegelianism did not fulfil the hopes it had created, and who had lost or never taken part in the inspiration which characterised the age that gave birth and substance to the whole idealistic movement. Outside of this ethical interpretation, which forms by far the most popular — though not the most important — side of Schopenhauer's teaching, the points of contact which unite his treatment of the problem of reality with that contained in the writings of Fichte are numerous and striking.[1] For Fichte had already emphasised the active

[1] These relations are well brought out by Herbart himself in the only really important Review, so far as I know, of Schopenhauer's great work which appeared at the time of its publication, 1819. In quite recent times, notably through the influence of Windelband, the philosophies of Herbart and Schopenhauer have been placed in contrast and appreciated in this position. This is very suggestively done in the two brilliant chapters written on these philosophers in the 2nd vol. of 'Grosse Denker' (ed. E. von Aster, p. 269, &c.), by Prof. Rud. Lehmann. Herbart's 'Review,' however, is so exhaustive, and brings out so clearly the fundamental difference of his and Schopenhauer's points of view, that it should be read by every student interested in the subject. The Reviewer recommends Schopenhauer's work as a fine literary production, well worth reading, and as a stimulating reflection and criticism, though he fundamentally disagrees with the principles as well as the result of his doctrine. With great knowledge he shows how nearly Schopenhauer agrees with some of Fichte's earliest enunciations. He remarks that Fichte's doctrine might quite as suitably be entitled : 'Die Welt als Vorstellung und Wille,' so much so that "the Reviewer believed, at first, that he had to do with a Fichtian, and was much surprised when, in reading further, he came upon the hardest judgment of Fichte which has probably ever been put in writing." He blames the author further for apparently not having read Fichte's 'Sittenlehre,' and goes on to say : "In truth the *Wissenschaftslehre* is no more than an ingenious exercise which should have remained unprinted because it frightens away the reader from the more mature works of Fichte. Nevertheless Fichte may be illustrated through Schopenhauer. The same metamorphosis of Kantian doctrine which occurred twenty years earlier in Fichte's mind has . . . repeated itself in Schopenhauer ; and may, after another twenty years, occur for a third time ; but a better result will never proceed from it than hitherto. Invariably the theoretical side of Kantian doctrine will develop itself more completely into idealism ; ever also the last foundation of a true realism will be wanting,—and then the gap will be filled by the Will which the 'Critique of Practical Reason,' if not in so many words, had already stamped as the 'Thing in itself' : ever also a mystical yearning for the One which is considered to be the Real will be the last sentiment

principle as the kernel and source of reality ; and the further attempt of Schopenhauer to show how this principle manifests itself in nature, rising from blind impulses and instincts through many stages to the height of conscious life, reminds us in altered terms of Schelling's expositions in his ' Philosophy of Nature ' ; also the ideas of the two thinkers on the function of art have much in common.

Schopenhauer's writings remained without influence on the main currents of thought till after the middle of the century.   In the meantime a great change was taking place in philosophical thought in Germany, a change which brought it nearer to the currents in which philosophical thought was moving in the neighbouring countries, notably in England and France.   We may define the purport of this movement by saying that the tendency of thought was in the direction of positivism.

whereinto such a philosophy will resolve itself. But whether Plato, or Spinoza, or the Indians should be admitted ? As good friends we shall always have them near us ; whether they gain influence over the system depends upon in-dividuality. A thinker so accu-rate, so valiant and independent as Fichte was, at least in his earlier years, does not permit them to come along. They have too many foreign features ; they do not agree amongst each other. But the majority does not take matters so minutely ; every plausible testimony is welcome ; the oldest and the remotest witnesses count as the most valid ; how could one despise Plato and the Indians ? " (See Herbart's ' Sämmtliche Werke,' ed. Hartenstein, vol. xii. p. 369 *sqq.*) Further on Herbart objects to what Schopenhauer has in com-mon with Kant—viz., " the secret effect of practical needs which show themselves in every system in which the practical and the theoretical are not most carefully and distinctly separated as completely indepen-dent, and to be kept from mutual influence" (p. 378), and he repeats (p. 379) " what no doubt will appear very strange to Schopenhauer, that to the Reviewer he seems only to repeat Fichte, though in a new and formally improved edition." The analogies with Fichte are followed up with considerable detail in the sequel (p. 382) of this interesting document, in which many diffi-culties are referred to which later historians of philosophy have dis-covered and criticised in the writ-ings of Schopenhauer as well as in those of Herbart.

It is interesting to note that, in the beginning of the second third of the century, the word positive was used by two of the leading thinkers in Europe, probably without knowing of each other's designs and not quite with the same meaning. Schelling in Germany used the word positive as indicating the opposite of negative, by which latter term he characterised that development of idealism which had culminated in Hegel's logical system. Comte in France about the same time introduced the word positive to denote a philosophy which stood in opposition to the whole tendency of idealism.[1] With him positivism meant more nearly what we should call realism. From this point of view he opposes his philosophy to the older metaphysics which he desires to see banished and altogether overcome. For him reality is not a problem but simply a fact, or rather a body of many facts which are connected by certain regularities or laws. All the favourite problems of philosophy of

34.
The term
"positive."

[1] We owe to Kuno Fischer the bringing together of these two names in the closing paragraph of his great work on Schelling which forms the 7th vol. of his 'History of Modern Philosophy.' But he does not proceed to give us a detailed analysis of the latest phase of Schelling's speculation. This has been done in quite recent times. The expectancy with which Schelling was received, ten years after Hegel's death, in Berlin, and which led to the dramatic incident of his opening address (15th Nov. 1841) — impressive as much through its intense seriousness as through its dignified self-assurance — was soon to be disappointed. This disappointment led to a complete neglect of philosophy under which no great thinker suffered more than Schelling himself. It is again to Prof. Windelband that we are indebted for a renewed interest; and quite recently there has appeared in the 2nd vol. of 'Grosse Denker' mentioned above, a highly original chapter on Schelling by Dr O. Braun, including a personal characterisation of him, which I recommend to my readers, especially to those among them who may have been influenced by the summary way in which Mr A. W. Benn disposes of this great figure in modern philosophy in the closing lines of his Review ('Mind,' N.S., vol. xvii. p. 281) of the new edition of 'Schelling's Selected Works,' published by A. Drews (4 vols., 1907).

which I have been treating so far, the problem of the Soul, the problem of Knowledge, the problem of Reality, do not exist for Comte. He starts with a belief in the certainty and finality of exact or scientific knowledge, and finds the problem of philosophy merely in understanding and accepting the existing methods of this knowledge and in extending the use of them into those regions where they have not been successfully introduced, notably into the historical and social sciences. Thus we shall not expect to find in Comte's writings any valuable contributions to the solution of the central problem of philosophy, though we may find many useful beginnings and suggestions in the direction of the methodical or exact treatment of social or practical questions. When we come to deal with these we shall meet with many of Comte's suggestions and shall have to recognise the importance of his influence.

35.
Schelling's
positive
philosophy.

For the moment it is more interesting to understand what Schelling really meant by his continually repeated demand of a positive philosophy to supplement and complete the then current negative philosophy of the Hegelian school. Schelling had recognised that the purely logical development of thought, even if it were capable of reaching up to the highest reality or descending to the ultimate source and root of all existence, would end in a mere formalism, being at best able only to unfold the necessary stages in which any or every reality must be conceived by us to move and develop, without further affording an insight into the varied nature of all the real things which surround us in space and time, and which exhibit individual life and freedom. In opposition therefore to Hegel, who regarded the necessary forms of thought and the stages of the logical process as representing also the phases of existence, the life of the Logos, Schelling thought it incumbent upon philosophy to recognise in the existing world an element of freedom or, as it has since been frequently termed, the contingent in contradistinction to the necessary. His later philosophy, which existed however only as a postulate or an unfilled programme, was therefore significantly characterised by him as the philosophy of Freedom. In the actual existing world of things and phenomena he recognised something that might also, so far as we could understand, have been otherwise, and which, though following the necessary and eternal laws of all reality, was only one of the many ways in which the Absolute or ultimate ground of everything realised itself. To this idea Schelling in his later philosophy gave a distinctly religious colouring by conceiving the actual or contingent world as having come into existence by a falling away from the original identity in which it lived in the bosom of the Absolute or Divine Being. This religious turn in his speculation will occupy us on a subsequent occasion. Here it is only necessary to point out how Schelling, though unable to give a satisfactory solution, put his finger upon the difficulty which was inherent in Hegel's scheme, and which became more and more apparent as the manifold examples and applications of this scheme had to submit to rigorous tests and to meet the attacks of criticism.[1]

36.
His religious turn.

[1] We may thus say that Schelling's mind, during the last forty years of his life, wrestled with the two great problems which have since been brought out more clearly and on which philosophical thought

The middle of the century thus found the problem of Reality pushed into the foreground from many sides. A multitude of ideas was floating about in the philosophical atmosphere. They were largely remnants of the idealism which pervaded the earlier systems as well as the classical and romantic literature of the first third of the century; they were partly also new suggestions coming from the recently cultivated and prolific fields of the natural and the historical sciences, and they were lastly in no small degree revivals or reminiscences of the

has more and more become concentrated. These two problems are not kept sufficiently separate in Schelling's writings. To have separated them is, *inter alia*, one of the merits of Lotze's philosophy; to have attempted the solution one of the claims of two systems, both of which have had an important influence upon Continental thought. I refer to the philosophy of the Unconscious (v. Hartmann in Germany) and the system termed "Personnalisme" (Renouvier in France). Of both these we shall have to take cognisance in the sequel. For the moment the simple statement of the two problems may suffice. The first problem has not necessarily an ethical or religious meaning. It is most clearly defined by Schelling in the well-known Preface which he wrote in the year 1834 to a translation of the lengthy explanation which Victor Cousin prefixed to the 2nd edition of his 'Fragments Philosophiques' (1833). It contains also the distinct enunciation of Schelling's objection to the development which his and Hegel's common position had found in Hegel's own doctrine. He there explains that if the purely Rational, that which we cannot help thinking, is pure subject, then that other

subject which rises through becoming objective to higher subjectivity is no longer the purely rational, but is endowed with an empirical specification. "One who has come later and whom Nature seems to have predestined to give to our age a new Wolffianism, has removed that empirical element, putting in its place the logical notion to which he attributes by a remarkable feat of hypostasis a similarly necessary movement. . . . The logical movement of thought sufficed so long as the system moved within the purely logical; as soon as it has to take the weighty step into reality the thread of dialectical movement breaks; a new hypothesis is necessary so that the idea—we do not know why—may happen to fall asunder into its different moments, so that nature might originate" (Schelling's 'Werke,' vol. x. p. 212). This means, expressed in modern language, that to the necessary must be added the contingent. But, of all that is merely contingent, a matter of accident or of free choice, the most mysterious and inexplicable is the problem of Evil; upon this problem Schelling concentrated his thoughts during the latter half of his lifetime.

philosophies of bygone ages, notably of Plato, Spinoza, and Leibniz. The systematic unity, however, of these ideas had been broken up, they existed as scattered fragments of an edifice which had fallen, but which it was the duty of the philosophical mind to reconstruct on broader and safer foundations and with more careful workmanship. On this task the philosophical mind has spent its labours ever since, not only in Germany but also in the neighbouring countries. In consequence of this the character of modern philosophy has become to a large extent critical and eclectic. In many instances it has not gone beyond the limits of a critical and historical survey of the valuable materials handed down by former ages and prepared by the original efforts of ancient and modern thinkers. But we must not forget that criticism can lead to no valuable and positive result unless the point from which it is undertaken is clearly defined, and that history cannot be written except in the light of definite ideas and convictions which are implied if not expressly stated.

37.
New eclectic spirit.

The philosopher who during the third quarter of the nineteenth century approached the philosophical problem in the critical and eclectic spirit just indicated, but who, at the same time, possessed more than any other the firm individual position and the central conviction which was to irradiate all his writings, was Hermann Lotze. In him we find united almost all the best characteristics of recent thought, with perhaps one exception, and it is probably just this one defect in his philosophical attitude which has been the cause that his works did not, for a long time, receive that attention which they deserve and

38.
Lotze.

which is only now beginning to be bestowed upon them. We find in Lotze a full appreciation of the critical and the scientific movements of thought, of the great aims, if not also of the specific formulæ, of the idealistic systems, and we find an equally genuine understanding of the methods of exact research, which he in fact handled himself with conspicuous success. In addition to all this his mind had a distinctly poetical and artistic side, which shows itself nowhere more than in the elegance and refinement of his style.

Through Kant and Hegel, as also through some of the purely systematic writings of Fichte, philosophical style in Germany has, not undeservedly, acquired the reputation of obscurity. Some of Schelling's writings, as well as those of Jacobi, are characterised on the other side by much simplicity and literary grace, and those of Herbart by directness and clarity. But Schopenhauer was the first great thinker of modern Germany who raised philosophical style to the level of excellence which literary style had attained through Lessing and Goethe. Lotze's style is not marked by the same directness and lucidity. Though his sentences are not as heavy as those of Kant nor as enigmatical as many of Hegel's, there is in them a certain round-aboutness and laboured structure which makes the prolonged study of his works exacting and sometimes fatiguing. In his reviews, criticisms, and polemical writings[1] he is as dignified as Kant and Herbart

[1] Unfortunately one of the most instructive writings of Lotze, the 'Streitschriften' (1857), has not been reprinted in the collection of his smaller works. It is directed against Fichte the younger, and is a model of decorous and dignified polemic, containing, moreover, Lotze's first attempt to fix his own philosophical position with reference to the idealism of Schelling and Hegel on the one side and to Herbart on the other, notifying especially his indebtedness and allegiance to Weisse.

had been; he is never impolite as Fichte and Schelling frequently were; nor does he fasten upon his opponents any stigma as Hegel frequently succeeded in doing;[1] he is quite above that virulent and unmannerly invective by which Schopenhauer tries to crush, but actually never damages, the arguments of thinkers whom he chooses to regard as enemies. But the style of Lotze reflects one characteristic trait of modern thought. The confidence and self-assurance of Kant, Fichte, Hegel, Schopenhauer, and of the earlier Schelling have disappeared. It is the style of a period of transition and uncertainty; much of the light which the preceding age thought it possessed has vanished and the new light has not yet dawned.[2]

[1] The ill-disguised contempt with which Hegel treats contemporary thinkers of eminence, such as Jacobi, Fichte, and Schleiermacher, in his contributions to the 'Critical Journal,' is less objectionable, though probably more effective, than the unpardonable rudeness with which Schelling treated some of his opponents and even friends, such as Jacobi, Eschenmayer, and Windischmann (see 'Aus Schelling's Leben').

But lasting harm was done to the cause of philosophy by the antagonism which existed between Schleiermacher and Hegel. The frequently quoted criticism in which Hegel, in mature years (1822), attacked Schleiermacher's conception of religion, as arising out of a feeling of absolute dependence which would put it on the level of "the feelings of a dog," was never forgiven by Schleiermacher. It appears that he prevented Hegel's election as a member of the Berlin Academy, and, on the other side, Hegel threatened to leave Berlin if the proposition to secure Schleiermacher's co-operation in an intended philosophical Review was persisted in : the result being that this Review ('Jahrbücher für Wissenschaftliche Kritik,' 1827) did not include, in the list of its celebrated patrons, the important name of Schleiermacher, and was subsequently regarded as an exclusive organ of the Hegelian party (see Kuno Fischer, 'Hegel, &c.,' vol. i. p. 180).

[2] With Lotze as with all of the best of recent thought the labour and search seem to be much greater than the achievement; the criticism quite out of proportion to the result. The latter consists frequently merely in indications, in suggestions, or in conclusions which are intentionally termed subjective ; in fact, Lotze seems to draw a sharp line between knowledge and conviction, and we are reminded of a dictum of David Hume that arguments may be logically unanswerable and yet carry no conviction. In this there is involved a psychological problem which no line of thought has done more to force upon the present age than that initiated by Lotze.

39.
Defect in
historical
sense.

But to characterise Lotze fully, we must take into consideration the above-mentioned defect in his philosophical attitude, through which he, to a large extent, placed himself out of the current of philosophical thought as it existed during the last third of the century. The latter was dominated by the idea of Evolution, which in many instances was narrowed down by the watchwords of Darwinism and the categories of the theory of Descent. For this narrowing down of the larger idea of development as it had enlivened the writings of Leibniz, Herder, and Schelling, within the limits of a purely mechanical and automatic succession, which is termed evolution, Lotze had no more appreciation than he had for the logical triads of the Hegelian philosophy. This in itself is not a defect of his philosophical temperament; it becomes such only to the extent that it implies an absence of the genuine historical sense. The latter, as I have had repeated occasion to remark, has grown enormously during the nineteenth century, with the result that the in itself meritorious exposition of the successive phases and stages of thought and art, of religion and life, has largely taken the place of a genuine interest in these things themselves, culminating in the marked tendency of many modern philosophical writers to see in a continual unfolding process the essence of existence, the definition of all ultimate Reality. Those who are satisfied with this revival of an idea represented in antiquity by Heraclitus and the Sophists, will have little understanding for the ever-repeated assurance with which Lotze urges that the truly Real is a definite something, a substance, not merely a shifting unreality, an existence which carries in itself the ground of its being, and is worthy to exist for its own sake, being not a mere relation but a value in itself.

This conception leads us at once into the centre of Lotze's philosophy. In his earliest philosophical publication, the 'Metaphysik' of the year 1841, he introduces us at once to the great theme of which his later writings treat in endless variations and illustrations: the idea that the truly Real is that which has supreme worth, and that the whole scheme of existence possesses reality only to the extent and in the degree that it is a realisation of this supremely valuable content. From the following passage of this early work the reader will at once get a large glimpse of the region of ideas in which Lotze's philosophy is moving. "This valuable and only truly Real cannot be grasped through any finite form of thought; only the terms: the Eternal, the One, the Infinite are suggestive and fluctuating enough to give it for a moment definiteness and objectivity. Out of this it always again retires, through the loss of a definite meaning, into the Void, the Immeasurable and Ineffable. That supremely rich content is therefore only what the mind *means* by it; it possesses no fixity of thought by which it exists outside of this meaning and by which it could be severed from the silent consciousness of an individual soul or by which it could be imparted to others. Wherever this is to take place, appeal must be made to the feelings, that they may create by a similar mood a similar content. As therefore meaning and opinion change, so also the essence of that inner world will seem to change, which is nevertheless supposed to

40.
Doctrine of Values.

be the imperishable and unchangeable substance of all
that appears. Wanting in every special determination
which could protect it from the many-coloured interpretations of the changing moods of the human mind,
what we mean by the real world is a product of these
variable moods, just as variable quantities determine
each other in nature : whilst in sublime and beautiful
moments it appears surrounded by all the splendour of
the most actual reality, it vanishes in moments of satiety
and reaction into absolute void and nothingness.   It is
the fate of all such inspired vision to possess that which
seems to be an immensely rich and glorious content ever
only in fleeting transition to nothingness ; the beautiful
world of the one moment does not continue into the
next ; it is given only to a few beautiful souls to retain,
through the troubles of life, the old possession as a
reflection, it may be, but nevertheless as an enduring
mental undertone." [1]

According to Lotze the truly Real is thus, as it were,
a silent possession of the human mind, which reveals
itself only in favoured moments and favoured individuals.

[1] Lotze, 'Metaphysik' (1841),
p. 6 *sqq.* Lotze then goes on to
state that although we have
primarily to do with what is given
to us, as it were, only in reflected light, this reflection is not
meant to be merely that of a casual
and evanescent mood but *should be*
the reflection of the truly Real, and
that to prove it such forms the
inducement to speculate, the impulse which produces philosophical
thought. "That infinite content
must, if it is to be valid, present
itself to the thinking mind in single
definite thoughts ; only by gaining
such objective presentation can it
be secured and elevated beyond the
uncertainty of sentiment. We cannot abandon the content of that
inspiration ; . . . and thus it is a
duty to protect what we consider
to be the Highest from the fluctuations of our own feelings, and to
advance from a purely subjective
aspect to the serious work of logical reasoning which is the region
common to all thinking minds"
(p. 8). And thus philosophy is at
one with other endeavours which
all have the aim to secure the real
content of our mental life from
being destroyed through the casual
nature of individual conditions.

Nevertheless what is seen by them in such moments is deposited in the various products of art and life and in external creations such as the laws of the State, the rules of society, the doctrines of religion, and the rituals of the Church. All these put together form what we call culture: the objective manifestations of the truly Real, in which it finds a changing and fluctuating embodiment. But inasmuch as this great body of thought, art, and life is created by an automatic fusion of an infinite number of casual, momentary, and fragmentary individual experiences, it is not an harmonious whole, but merely an aggregate wanting everywhere in consistency, completeness, and unity. Now it is, according to Lotze, the object of philosophy or of philosophical thought to impart unity and completeness to this existing aggregate of ideas, which are supplied by general culture, by the special sciences, by poetry, art, and the interests of life. But he is careful to add a further caution. Philosophy is a science in the wider sense of the word, but only a science; it appeals only to the intellect, not to the whole soul; it has indeed the task to exhibit to the thinking mind as a definite possession the truth which is contained in existing meanings, opinions, and aspirations, to present to the soul the content of its own self, to interpret the dream by which it is haunted;[1] it is, as it

[1] "The object of philosophy is not to start from an unmediated position, but to convert into a general possession that truth which, in an elemental form as opinion and intuition, is common to all; to show to the soul what is the content of its own self and to enlighten it regarding the dream by which it is haunted. Whilst philosophy, therefore, appeals to the free movement of the thinking mind without forcing upon it a ready-made doctrine, on the other side it appeals *only* to the thinking, not to the whole mind; the result is that possession of the general mind in the fixing of which

were, the knowledge which the objective mind possesses
of the essence of things; and yet this knowledge and
truth only becomes a reality for the whole soul through
the higher activity of faith and practice, through submission to law and order.

From this we see that Lotze recedes from the purely
intellectual attitude of the Hegelian school. The realisation of the Absolute is not to be found in the intellectual
process but in practice. Accordingly the root of Metaphysics lies in Ethics. The essence of Reality, the truly
Real, is an ethical ideal, a moral conception. It is the
conception of the highest moral worth. All the forms
of existence have true reality only to the extent that
they contribute to the realisation of this highest
moral ideal. Their reality consists in their value for the
attainment of this end—*i.e.*, in their intrinsic worth.

41.
Ethics the
root of
Meta-
physics.

Before giving somewhat more explicitly the final expression in which Lotze summarises his answer to the
problem of Reality, it is interesting to note how he
assimilates the leading ideas contained in the earlier
philosophies with which we have become acquainted.
With him the problem of Reality, of the truly Real, and
of degrees of Reality, becomes again the central problem
in philosophy: as such it is introduced on the first
pages of his earliest work.[1] From the speculations of

the individual mind has no merit;
it is only through the higher
activity of faith and conduct, in
the submission to custom and right
[law], that what has been accepted
as truth is confirmed as a reality
for the individual mind itself "
(p. 10).

[1] It is to be regretted, as has

already been pointed out by Erdmann in a well-considered digest
of Lotze's doctrine ('Geschichte
der Philosophie,' 3rd ed. vol. ii. p.
841 *sqq.*), that Lotze's earliest work,
the 'Metaphysik,' has been unduly
neglected in favour of his later
scientific, popular, and systematic
writings. For the history of

Schelling and Hegel, Lotze adopts the conception of the Absolute—*i.e.*, of something expressive of supreme reality, and he conceives with them the existing world of things and processes which surround us to be a realisation of this truly Real. In the emphasis which he lays upon the practical side of life and upon the ethical value of this supreme Reality as the beginning and end of the world-process, he reminds one of the energy with which Fichte developed, in his philosophy, the active principle, the self-restrained freedom of the human Will. But Lotze does not follow Fichte in attempting to deduce

Thought, it is, together with the above-mentioned 'Streitschriften,' by far the most important of Lotze's writings, and this for two reasons. It shows that in addition to the special interests which led to the publication of his biological and medical treatises, his whole thought stood on the firm ground of an original conviction which, as he himself says, he found in later life no reason to change materially. And further, it shows the distinct transition from the position occupied by Hegel and, especially, the influence of the 'Phenomenology.' Students of Hegel in the present day may rightly see in Lotze's 'Metaphysik' a paraphrase of the Introduction and the earlier sections of Hegel's first great work, as indeed Lotze's later 'Microcosmus' repeats likewise, on a larger scale and with more abundant material, Hegel's attempt to trace the life and workings of the mind in all the labyrinthine and devious paths of its growth and development in the history of the human individual and the human race. What T. H. Green conceived to be the task of philosophy a generation later, that the work of Kant and Hegel had

all to be done over again, was exactly what Lotze attempted in a concise manner in his earliest 'Metaphysik' (1841), and 'Logik' (1843), and, more fully, in his 'Microcosmus.' In the interval of more than thirty years which elapsed between his earliest works and his later "system," the interest in Hegel had almost entirely disappeared in Germany, and the references to Hegel's logical and metaphysical deductions, so frequent in the earlier work, have gradually disappeared, as indeed they were then no longer likely to facilitate an understanding of the main objects of speculation or the task of philosophy which Lotze had in view. A recognition, however, of these historical connections seems at the present moment to be particularly opportune, and is certainly of prime importance in a history of Thought. It can only be hinted at in this connection. A republication of Lotze's early 'Metaphysik,' with full references to passages from Hegel's and Herbart's writings, supplemented also by relevant extracts from the 'Streitschriften,' would indeed be a useful performance in the present state of philosophical thought.

from this active principle the forms of actual existence in the world, but maintains with Herbart that for us there remains an inherent dualism between the forms and things which exist or appear to exist and the rules and precepts of that which ought to exist. He bridges over this dualism by the initial thesis of all his teaching: that we have to comprehend though not to construct the phenomenal world in the light of the idea of that which ought to be: the world of things and forms which are, finds its interpretation in the world of worths or values which *ought* to be, and, *vice versa*, the latter are realised for us only in the former.

We thus see how Lotze continues and brings together lines of thought which found independent and frequently one-sided development in the systems of his predecessors. Though he believes with the idealists in the existence of an Absolute or highest reality, of which the real world is merely a reflection or appearance, he replaces their attempts to construct the phenomenal by the more modest task of merely interpreting it; yet he does not believe, with Herbart, that we can by a mere process of remoulding empirical notions arrive at an adequate conception of the underlying reality. Of the latter we not only require to have, but actually possess, an intuitive, though fleeting and fluctuating, knowledge. It is the object of philosophy to insist on this primary insight or possession, to try to fix it more precisely and, in the light of it, to effect that reconstruction, rearrangement, and completion of our empirical knowledge which Herbart proposed to carry out by a purely logical analysis. And lastly, we may remark that Lotze's philosophy, like all other important systematic attempts, owes its influence to certain characteristic terms in which it has crystallised its central ideas. By untiringly putting forward the notions of Value and Worth, by opposing to the world of Things the world of Values, he has introduced into recent philosophy a leading thought which has become more and more the central theme of speculation.

But Lotze is not content merely to give an answer to the question, What is the truly Real? This, the metaphysical problem, is indeed to him the central problem of philosophy, the point from which his speculation starts and to which it returns again in the end. The earliest and the latest of his works dealt with Metaphysics—*i.e.*, with the problem of Reality. But having quite early in life risen to a conception of what the truly Real in the world is—to a conception indeed which he saw no reason in after life to forsake—he for a time abandons the highest problem of philosophy in order to study and understand Reality in the world of phenomena which surrounds us. For he had fully imbibed the modern scientific or exact spirit which seeks for knowledge only in the world of many things which we can observe, measure, and calculate. In other words, after having settled in his own mind what the truly Real is— the core and essence of reality—he now descends into the actual manifestations of this highest reality in the world of many things, many forms, and many processes.

42. Detailed interest in phenomena.

To some of his contemporaries he then appeared, not as an idealist, as we know him to be, but as a realist, a

Herbartian, nay, even as a materialist.[1] After having answered the question, What is the nature of the *truly* Real or Absolute? he proceeds to answer the further question, What is the nature of the *apparently* Real? His answer to this question is not a monistic one. For Reals are things which exist, events which happen, relations which endure, conceptions and truths which are valid. But relations which endure and events that happen, imply things in and between which they subsist. And if we further try to understand what we mean by the essence of these things, we find that no answer is forthcoming, that the question concerning the Thing in itself has no meaning : the reality of things reduces itself in fact in our minds to a system of relations of things. That is Real which stands in relation to other things, to all things ; to exist means to stand in relations. Thus it is this network of relations in space and time—*i.e.*, their geometrical and causal connections, which constitutes the reality of the empirical world. If we further consider that these relations cannot exist as the invisible threads of a network of indefinable entities, we are driven to the conclusion that we must resort to the conception of a universal Order, of one underlying all-comprising Substance, of which the apparently separate things are the states, parts, or modi ; and that the apparent action of one thing on another is really only what happens in the interior of this universal substance—*i.e.*, within the sphere of this universal order. Further than this conception of a universal substance, in which Lotze unites the Monadology of Leibniz with the Pantheism of

[1] See above, chap. iii. p. 264.

Spinoza, the purely logical and psychological analysis of what we mean by Reality cannot advance, were it not that we ourselves, in our own consciousness, possess an example how the many is combined into one. Accordingly this phenomenon of our conscious personality solves for us, by analogy, the problem of Reality, and the highest ideal which we can form of a conscious, mental, or personal existence must be, for us, the definition of the essence of the underlying ground of everything—*i.e.*, of the truly Real. Formally, the one supreme Reality appears to us in the form of a universal order or mechanism, the nature of which we have to learn by experience and observation ; actually, however, the sense or meaning of this universal order or mechanism is the highest Good or Worth, which we can conceive to exist only as a personality or living Spirit. Of this living spirit, human personalities, the human spirits which are in and around us, are merely a dim reflection ; they only partake of Reality, and are not real by and for themselves.

The speculations of Lotze thus rise to a conception which the higher religions have embraced through the belief in a personal Deity, and to which the Christian religion has given final expression and sanction. For the reality that philosophy tries to grasp through an analysis of our highest intuitions, by trying to understand their meaning as well as the deeper sense of the world which surrounds us (the Macrocosmus) and the world within us (the Microcosmus) ; for that highest and deepest reality, Religion, the " Metaphysic of the general or popular mind," has already found certain terms and expressions and embodied them in definite articles of faith. To

43.
At the summit a religious conception.

show that speculation arrives finally at conceptions which harmonise with the essence of these beliefs, although it could not have produced them, is the task of the philosophy of religion. Philosophy thus establishes an understanding between these two regions of mental activity, the region of the intellect on the one side and the region of the emotions and moral impulses on the other. Ever since the time of Leibniz this has been the aim of the idealistic philosophy abroad. Even Kant, in whose writings the critical spirit supervened, acknowledges this to be the aim of his criticism; in Fichte, Schelling, and Hegel the dogmatic spirit asserts itself again with a greater confidence in the constructive powers of the human intellect. In Lotze, as already to some extent in Herbart, philosophy returns again to the more modest task of understanding, interpreting, and harmonising the two large and independent regions of thought—the intellectual and emotional, the mechanical and spiritual view of things, both of which spring from independent but equally real sources in the human mind.

Having arrived at this position, philosophical thought encounters several new problems which had been temporarily overlooked or forgotten during the creative epoch. The differences which again and again manifest themselves in human thought, point to different sources from which human thought takes its beginnings. This is a psychological problem which demands a special investigation as to the grounds of certainty in matters of knowledge and in matters of belief—i.e., regarding things sensuous and intellectual on the one side, and things spiritual and emotional on the other. This investigation would accordingly divide itself into a theory of knowledge (*Erkenntnisstheorie*) and, as its complement, a theory of belief. Lotze prepared this psychological turn which speculative thought has taken since his time, but he did not follow it up. In distinguishing between the world of forms on the one side and the world of worths on the other, he, as it were, invited the manifold discussions and investigations which sprang up during the last quarter of the century in all the three countries alike. A beginning had been made in Germany long before that time, in both directions, by Kant and by Schleiermacher. To Schleiermacher the essence of religious thought and life was as much a fundamental problem as the essence of scientific thought in the widest sense of the word had been to Kant. For Kant the problem was: How is exact knowledge possible? For Schleiermacher there stood out the parallel problem: How is Religion possible? In the last chapter I dealt with the former problem; in one of the subsequent chapters I shall take up the latter problem, which is now engaging, in many ways and from many sides, the attention of philosophers.

Lotze is the latest thinker abroad who placed the problem of Reality in the centre of his speculations, who arrived for himself at a definite solution of this problem before he took up special philosophical problems. He is also characterised by developing the twofold conception of Reality—that of the truly Real and that of Reality as it appears in and around us. He answers the question: What is the highest Reality as such? and after having arrived at a satisfactory answer to this question, he puts the further question : How does Reality manifest itself or appear to us in the actual world ? By his answer to the first question, he becomes the true follower of Fichte, who developed in a pronounced manner the idea thrown out by Kant in his doctrine of the primacy of the moral Will or the practical Reason. In his answer to the second question, he is, among the metaphysicians of the nineteenth century, the first, and probably the greatest, representative of the scientific spirit, and in his method of solving this question he adopts the formula of Herbart, according to which philosophy consists in a re-moulding of our empirically gained conceptions of Reality so as to make them consistent. In addition to this Lotze exercises a growing influence upon recent philo-sophical thought through many suggestive single ideas which he has thrown out in almost every department of speculation, and not less through enriching philosophical language by many happily chosen terms and expressions. By the latter he has succeeded in fulfilling, to a large extent, that task which he announces in his earliest writings—viz., to give definite expression to ideas and conceptions which exist for us mostly only as fleeting opinions, or in the form of a hidden, but none the less real and important, meaning.

45.
The problem of Reality since Lotze.
The contributions to the solution of the problem of Reality which have appeared since the time of Lotze are neither many nor conspicuous for their originality. Their value is mostly to be found in an analysis of the different leading ideas which have, since the seventeenth century, appeared in the successive philosophical systems

on the Continent of Europe. The Universal substance of Spinoza, the Monads and pre-established Harmony of Leibniz, the Categorical Imperative of Kant, the Active Principle of Fichte, the Absolute of Schelling and Hegel, the Will of Schopenhauer, and the World of Worths as distinguished from the World of Forms of Lotze, all these terms have become the embodiment of conceptions towards which the thinkers of to-day have to take up definite individual positions. Alongside of this array of abstract terms, through which philosophical thought has striven to express its conception of the supreme and truly Real, there stands the notion of a personal Deity. Through the whole of the professedly religious speculation of the ages, it is preserved in unaltered words which have the sanction of antiquity and tradition. Much thought has been bestowed upon the relation which exists, or should exist, between the one unaltered religious and the many fluctuating philosophical conceptions. A school of thinkers has arisen, notably abroad, whose main object has been to vindicate the meaning and deeper sense contained in the belief in a personal Deity and a Divine World-order, in the face of the many difficulties which beset every attempt to make it the foundation of a consistent and reasoned philosophical creed.

Among these difficulties two are conspicuous, and have been the subject of much speculation. The first refers to the idea of Personality. It has been maintained that personality implies limitation, and the problem has been, how to reconcile the idea of an infinite and omnipotent Being with that limitation which seems to adhere to our notions of individuality and personality.

46.
The idea of Personality.

Lotze has fully dealt with this problem, which seemed to be pushed into the foreground by the Panlogism and seeming Pantheism of the Hegelian philosophy, a defect which was prominently before the mind of Schelling in the later phases of his speculation. A voluminous literature sprang up in Germany about the middle of the century, which was mainly occupied with an analysis of the idea of a Deity and the idea of Personality. The most prominent thinker of the school was Ch. H. Weisse, who exerted an important early influence upon Lotze's ideas. I intend, in a later chapter, to deal specially with this phase of thought, which starts from, and tries to substantiate, the conviction that the Christian version of the doctrine of the Deity and the Divine Order affords the highest solution of the problem of Reality so far as this is accessible to, and demanded by, human reason.

47.
The problem
of Evil.
The second great difficulty refers to the moral side of Reality. It has been maintained that the existence of Evil and Sin is irreconcilable with the conception of a Divine and moral World - Order. This problem also seemed to many to have been insufficiently treated in the Hegelian philosophy, and it was this which occupied Schelling throughout the last fifty years of his life. Also the systems which stand outside of that continuity which characterises the idealistic movement, notably those of Schleiermacher and Schopenhauer, as well as the whole class of thinkers who came under the influence of the latter, make the problem of Good and Evil the most important part of their speculations. Lotze has fully analysed the different trains of thought which are suggested by this problem. It is, if not the highest,

certainly the most important problem from the point of view of practical human interests. In pronouncing it to be logically and metaphysically insoluble, he has admitted the necessity of seeking for a solution in a different direction, and in doing so he has, more than is generally acknowledged, helped to support views which have sprung up independently from many sides and in many regions of modern thought. But these speculations will be more fittingly dealt with in separate chapters, which will treat of the important labours that have been bestowed during the nineteenth century on the ethical and religious problems.

It is significant that, in the same degree as the meta-physical problem—the problem of Reality—has been pushed into the background through many influences, ethical problems, which for a long time had been neglected, are increasingly attracting attention abroad. For it has been clearly recognised that if it is possible and expedient, for a time at least, to ignore the question, What is the truly Real ? and to content oneself with that Reality which is merely apparent but which lies around us, through space and time, in overwhelming fulness and complexity; it is on the other side not possible, nor expedient, to neglect the solution of the problem of Conduct. We may, and can, for a moment refuse to consider the question: What *is* ? but we cannot refuse to answer the question: What *ought* to be ? and not infrequently we find that resignation with regard to the first question is accompanied by the greater emphasis which urges the second. The more difficult it is to arrive at a definite religious or metaphysical

48.
Ethical
problems.

creed, the more necessary it seems to be to establish
firmly and definitely the principles and postulates of
morality—*i.e.*, a moral creed. A great part of modern
speculation abroad is, at the end of the century, occupied
with this latter, the practical, problem, and has thus
arrived at a better understanding of what philosophical
thought has been occupied with in this country during
the whole of the nineteenth century. For it has
always been characteristic of British philosophy that it
has given independent and special attention to the
ethical problem. This problem was of equal interest to
those who took the metaphysical problem, the problem of Reality, to be satisfactorily solved in the ruling
religious creed—as was the case throughout the Scottish
school of common-sense—and to those who, following
Hume, despaired of satisfactorily solving either the
problem of Knowledge or the problem of Reality.
Generally speaking German philosophy has arrived,
towards the end of the nineteenth century, at a doubt
regarding the capacity of the human intellect to solve
these problems, similar to that expressed, more than a
hundred years earlier, by David Hume.

49.
Ethical
spirit of
British
philosophy.

English philosophers, in approaching the ethical problems, have after all not been so very far away from the
metaphysical problem as is sometimes supposed and represented ; for in attempting to define the highest ends
and aims of human conduct, they have implicitly approached the question : What is or should be the highest
reality for us human beings ? In the end also, notably
in the later writings of J. S. Mill, when the metaphysical
support which current religious beliefs afforded was

50.
Return of
British
thinkers to
Meta-
physics.

withdrawn, the problem presented itself : what conception have we to form of the Universal World-order so that the moral ends and aims of human life may appear realisable ? Mill not only, as we saw in the last chapter, led the way to an entirely altered comprehension of the problem of knowledge, but also through this as well as through his moral and economic studies, he was forced to tackle the problem of Reality. After Bishop Berkeley, he and Herbert Spencer were the first British philosophers to take up this problem independently of the solutions contained in the doctrines of the Christian Church on the one side, and in the metaphysics of the Continent on the other. For the whole of the Scottish school of common-sense came under the influence of the first, whilst Hamilton and his followers came in addition also under the influence of the second body of doctrine.

But the most prominent and dominating contribution to a solution—if we may call it so—of the problem of Reality, which has emanated from British thought, is to be found in Herbert Spencer's doctrine of the " Unknowable." It was prepared through Mill's and notably through Hamilton's speculations, and has gained much acceptance through the support that was given to it in the lay writings of Huxley. In fact, through the watchwords of the " Unknowable " and " Agnosticism," this view of the problem of Reality has become fixed and crystallised into a definite popular creed. Herbert Spencer is, moreover, the only English philosopher in modern times who places an answer to the problem of Reality at the entrance of his philosophical system. He had the ability and the courage to elaborate a definite philosophical

51.
Spencer's
"Unknowable."

creed such as should satisfy those who had discarded the ruling religious creed as well as the idealism of Continental thinkers. The simple answer which Herbert Spencer gives to the problem : What is Reality ? is this, that what we have so far termed the truly Real or the ultimate Ground of everything, is unknowable to us, though it exists as an underlying Power ; and, secondly, that all we can know about Reality is confined to the phenomenal world or to appearance. Though not exactly in the same words, Herbert Spencer's philosophy thus admits that twofold meaning of the word Reality on which I have dwelt in this chapter, and which has come down to us from antiquity, notably through the writings of Plato.

Through this doctrine of the Unknowable, English philosophy has arrived at a similar position to that occupied by several thinkers abroad, for it takes as its fundamental principle that we do not know Reality, directly and immediately, by intuition or instinct, but that we know it only in its appearance through the many things and events which lie in and around us or are known to us historically. As these different regions which make up the phenomenal world offer plenty of occasions for observation and study ; as, moreover, this study has to be pursued on definite lines and by precise methods, there is room for a science of First Principles, in addition to the various sciences which carry out their investigations by adopting and using those principles without a previous critical examination of their scope, origin, and validity. Such an examination can be termed metaphysical, although it either disregards, or puts aside as unanswerable, the highest metaphysical question — viz., What is the truly Real ? The first is the position taken up by the foremost representative of phenomenalism abroad, Professor Wilhelm Wundt; the latter is the position taken up by the foremost representative of phenomenalism in this country, Herbert Spencer. This difference is fundamental. Herbert Spencer has defined the philosophical task to be the unification of knowledge. Science, according to him, is partially unified knowledge, philosophy is completely unified knowledge. Many thinkers abroad, beginning with Herbart and going on to Lotze, Fechner, Wundt, Paulsen, and others, would probably to a large extent agree with this view. But there is a marked difference in the exact position which different thinkers take up to this generally accepted definition of philosophy. Herbert Spencer thinks it necessary to explain, at the entrance of his system, that the unity which holds together everything is an actual something, though a knowledge of its essence is not possible for us ; Lotze maintains that we have an intuitive, immediate, but not a discursive knowledge of the truly Real. For him accordingly the unification of knowledge in the sense of Spencer is only a formal enterprise : through the examination of first principles we arrive at best only at a formal unity. This empty form is in Spencer's philosophy all that we can expect to attain to. His highest principles, such as the principle of the " Instability of the Homogeneous," the alternation of the processes of " differentiation " and " integration," &c., are merely the most abstract descriptions of the ever-repeating phases in which the World-Process is developed, the stages of the evolution of the Unknowable Absolute. Lotze, following the later Schelling, would no more see in this mechanically conceived movement of the Absolute a solution of the ultimate philosophical problem than he saw it in the logically conceived Triads of Hegel. He believes that the human mind possesses an immediate knowledge of the ultimate Reality which passes through these mechanical or logical forms of development.[1]

[1] The position which Spencer takes up is so well known and has become so popular that it is unnecessary to give here special references to passages in his writings in which the doctrine of the Unknowable is explained. Nevertheless I believe that an attentive perusal of the concluding pages of the first part of 'First Principles' forms one of the best introductions to the study of philosophy ; further, that a comparison of it with the first thirty-eight pages of Lotze's early 'Metaphysik' will be one of the best means of introducing the philosophical student to the fundamental difference which exists between the two leading tendencies of philosophical thought at the present day. Some of the important arguments for dealing with the metaphysical problem of the truly Real (Lotze) or the Absolute (Spencer) are common to both. But nevertheless the main drift of these arguments is entirely different. According to Lotze, and more or less according to all thinkers who represent the same tendency of thought, the idea of the truly Real is formed by a process of gradual adaptation of definite notions and terms of language for the purpose of expressing a deep-lying thought which the human mind desires to fix ; for this the soul is considered to possess an immediate sense, it has

a definite meaning and is the subject of supremest interest, being as such the pivot upon which all moral distinctions turn. "There must exist a principle of certitude according to which we are able to decide as to the correctness of any result of our reasoning. . . . We must assume that philosophy does not create the rules for this decision, but that the whole soul is present with a sense of that verity which it possesses and practises before it scientifically explains it. Wherever we wish to determine something unknown through definite terms, we make the tacit assumption that we must in some way be able to know what notions are expressive of it and what not ; in case this judgment were impossible, the possibility of an investigation would vanish. The internal nature of the content we are in search of, whilst yet unknown to us, is not present in separate definitions of thought, but existing, as it does, in the form of a meaning, it nevertheless possesses implicitly a defensive power to reject that which is not adequate to it. . . . By rejecting what is inadequate and negating false determinations it gains in content itself, . . . acquiring for our consciousness in this way a positive expression of its own essence. This is the simple nature of every process of thought which, through defining

The position which, on the other side, Wundt takes up is, it seems to me, again different both from that of Spencer and from that of Lotze. He did not start his

and improving the definition, produces a knowledge of what we mean " (Lotze, 'Metaphysik,' p. 33). The process, on the other side, which is employed by Spencer to reach his conception of the Absolute, is that of abstraction. By generalising and refining more and more the conceptions suggested by common-sense and scientific research we arrive at a highest principle of unity, but this is only definable by removing all definitions and distinctions with which common-sense and science operate. As being and remaining purely negative the Absolute is therefore for us unthinkable except as a limitation or as the opposite to every determination which we are accustomed or obliged to make. Although therefore Spencer speaks of this Absolute or ultimate ground as something eminently Real, even as "the background of our consciousness," it is a thought which, not only for scientific but also for philosophical purposes, we have entirely to put aside. That this is not actually carried out in his elaborate system of philosophy, which deals only with the Knowable, we shall have ample opportunity to show in subsequent chapters, notably when dealing with the conception of Nature as a whole (the cosmological problem) and with the foundation of Ethics. For the moment I desire only to point out how the two ways of dealing with the problem of the truly Real or the Absolute may be described as exemplifying the two opposite ways of contemplating things based respectively upon what Comte termed the *esprit d'ensemble* and the *esprit de détail*. The former I have repeatedly referred to as the synoptical view

which generates—but is essentially opposed to—the combined processes of analysis and subsequent synthesis. It is true that, all scientific and philosophical reasoning being carried out only by adult minds, and among these only by such as have attained to a high proficiency in defining, distinguishing, and neatly putting together again, the natural beginning or starting-point is always an enormous mass of separate observations, thoughts, or conceptions present, within larger or narrower regions, to the mind of the thinker. But that this mass of detail, cleanly separated and neatly to be put together again, is itself the result of a long process of mental development which must have started from a confused and bewildering, yet eminently vivid and real, presentation of the whole—what in recent psychology is termed the presentation - continuum or the stream of consciousness — is just as much a matter of fact as the opposite assertion that fruitful and useful thought only begins when this fundamental psychical reality has been consciously or unconsciously dissected and disintegrated. And thus the difference between the two ways of philosophising consists in this, that the philosophy of the Knowable considered it unnecessary to bring into its manifold investigations that supreme reality which it acknowledges but keeps out of sight ; whereas thinkers belonging to the other side maintain that this underlying reality must be continually before the mind of the thinker, as without it even a correct description, not to say an interpretation of the world which surrounds us and is within us, is impossible.

philosophical career by publishing at the age of twenty-three, as Lotze did, a treatise on Metaphysics; nor did he, with Herbert Spencer, introduce his completed synthetic system at a mature age by a treatise on First Principles. Having an essentially philosophical interest which would have led him from any field of restricted and special inquiry into that which lies beneath and beyond it, and having taken up the physiological problems which in the middle of the century drove many naturalists on to the border-land of psycho-physical phenomena, he was led to an inquiry into the first principles of his science, from this to the first principles of all exact science, and further of the mental, moral, and historical sciences.   Still later he saw the necessity of giving a satisfactory systematic co-ordination of all his researches and of arriving at a metaphysical result.   The answer to the problem of Reality stands thus at the end of his inquiry: it is a result, not a preliminary as with Spencer, nor an immediate intuitive conviction as with Lotze.   To many it would seem as if he arrived at a merely formal answer to this problem, and that the unification which his system affords does not—and can never—reply to the question: What is the truly Real?

53.
Lotze's,
Spencer's,
and Wundt's
pheno-
menalism
contrasted.

It thus appears that, alike through Lotze, Spencer, and Wundt, philosophy has been reduced to phenomenalism, with this difference; that phenomenalism with Lotze requires for its completion the assistance of some central idea in the light of which the phenomenal world can not only be described and analysed, but also interpreted and understood; that with Spencer this underlying conception is reduced to the empty form of a mere affirmation, and that it is of no use and contributes nothing towards a comprehension of the phenomenal world; and that with Wundt no outlying or underlying conception exists at all, but that any conception which we may form as to the essence of Reality is merely a highest abstraction resulting from the analysis of the phenomenal world. But both Spencer and Wundt mark in a certain way an advance upon Lotze, inasmuch as they have a greater appreciation for the processes of development, both having assimilated the leading ideas of Darwinism, towards which in fact Spencer himself furnished large and important contributions. With both these philosophers we are inclined to think that the historical process of development, an insight into the *becoming* of things, very largely takes the place of an insight into their *being*. With Wundt, indeed, the idea of an underlying substance is entirely discarded; the nature or essence of things is a process. The Absolute, which played such a great part in the systems of Schelling and Hegel, which, with Lotze, is conceived as something of intrinsic value or worth, and which, with Spencer, has retired into the background as an unknowable something, has entirely disappeared out of the sphere of ideas in which Wundt's speculation moves. There is also no doubt that for many thinking persons a historical account which connects existing phenomena with the past appears to be an explanation of the nature and essence of those phenomena and satisfies their spirit of curiosity and inquiry. Lotze always regarded this manner of looking at Reality as insufficient.

III.

In the foregoing account of the progress of Metaphysics—*i.e.*, of the various solutions of the problem of
Reality—I have not taken any notice of the writings of
Fechner nor of those of Eduard von Hartmann. The
former indeed is already well known to us, mainly from
the chapter which dealt with the psycho-physical view of
nature. Of this he was, if not the founder, yet perhaps
the most prominent representative during the nineteenth
century. Hartmann has had to be mentioned on several
occasions, notably in the chapter which dealt with
the problem of the Soul, where his doctrine of the
" Unconscious " was referred to.

So far as Fechner is concerned, he elaborated, under
the early influences of the philosophy of nature, a distinct metaphysical conception which centred in the idea
of a personal Deity. His earlier writings, in which he
expounded these speculations, made extensive use of
poetical, imaginary, and fanciful—*i.e.*, of purely subjective views. As such they were akin to some of
Schelling's best productions, and stood in opposition
to Hegel, who always dwelt upon the necessity of
logical analysis, though it is true that frequently this
only thinly covers a great depth and wealth of imagination. The age, however, in which Fechner's earlier
writings appeared, had adopted, from Hegel as well as
from the historical and exact studies, the critical
temper, and was more intent upon drawing logical
consequences and arriving at clear definitions than in-

clined to be satisfied with poetical constructions ; and
thus it came about that the really important and original
ideas of Fechner made little impression, that he did
not count as a systematic philosopher at all, and that
he was known outside of his purely scientific works
mainly as a humorous writer.[1] His name appeared in

[1] Before the year 1860, when the
'Elements of Psycho-Physics' were
published, Fechner was known
partly through purely scientific
works (notably his translations of
Biot's 'Physics' and Thénard's
'Chemistry'), partly through humorous writings (under the pseudonym of Dr Mises), and some semi-
religious Tracts ('Das Büchlein vom
Leben nach dem Tode,' 1836 ;
'Ueber das Höchste Gut,' 1846 ;
'Nanna oder über das Seelenleben der Pflanzen,' 1848) ; lastly
through his larger work ('Zendavesta oder über die Dinge des
Himmels und des Jenseits,' 3
parts, 1851). In the latter he
expounds in full earnest what
earlier writings had only hinted
at or fancifully put forward—
viz., that the earth, as a higher
spiritual Being, is the bearer of
human consciousness, the intermediate link between the human
and the Divine Being. The stars
also are conscious beings. This
appears absurd, but Fechner is
certain of it : "Either my thesis
or the prevailing ideas are incorrect, and must in consequence be
altered. I maintain and demand the
latter"('Zendavesta,'Introduction).
This doctrine is itself not new, only
forgotten ; the ancient religion of
nature in the 'Zendavesta' is to
be revived on the foundation of
modern natural knowledge. Zendavesta means the "living word."
The new Zendavesta is to be the
word which gives life to Nature.
See Kurd Lasswitz ('Gustav
Theodor Fechner,' 1896), who has
had the merit of giving, for the
first time, a coherent statement
of Fechner's doctrine, removing it
from the sphere of mere interesting, suggestive, and fanciful writing to the rank of a carefully
thought-out philosophical speculation well worthy of separate study
and replete with many valuable
suggestions.   Accordingly we find
that in quite recent philosophy
Fechner's ideas have become fruitful.   Thus Fr. Paulsen, in his
well-known 'Introduction to Philosophy,' acknowledges his indebtedness to Fechner ; ¦and Höffding,
in his 'History of Philosophy'
(Eng. transl., vol. ii. p. 524), treats
of him, together with Lotze, as
"The 'Dioscuri' of German philosophy in the latter half of our
century. They are alike in idealistic tendency, in wide scientific
knowledge, in poetic sense, and
in the desire for a unified conception of the world. They pursued kindred ends, although to a
certain extent along different paths.
. . . Fechner—like Kepler, whom
he strikingly resembles—is an interesting example of how bold and
imaginative speculations may lead
to positive and exact results, provided that the thinker never loses
sight of his fundamental thought,
and is able to divest it of its
mystical swaddling - bands. Just
as Kepler was gradually led from
mystical speculations to the discovery of the famous laws, which
satisfied his longing to find definite
mathematical relations obtaining in
the real world, so Fechner's bold

the history of philosophy for the first time when he published his 'Elements of Psycho-Physics.' Although therefore more modern philosophers — such as Wundt and Paulsen—have acknowledged their indebtedness to Fechner's metaphysical views, it can hardly be maintained that before the year 1860 he had any leading influence on the course of philosophical thought; and it is the history of the latter and not of philosophy as such that we are concerned with.

Eduard von Hartmann's position is quite different. He is frequently named together with Lotze and Fechner as being one of the three philosophers who, after Hegel and Schopenhauer, attempted to build philosophical systems on the broad basis of the inductive sciences. Again, we find him classed with Schopenhauer as a prominent representative of Pessimism. And lastly, his system may be characterised as an attempted reconciliation of the intellectualism of Hegel with the voluntarism of Schopenhauer, somewhat on the lines shadowed forth in the later speculations of Schelling. Personally his philosophical career differs from that of Schopenhauer, who remained neglected for a long time. The success of Hartmann's first and typical work [1] was quite phenomenal. It ran through many editions in a comparatively short

analogies led him to the conviction that there is a definite quantitative relation between the mental and the material. By working out this thought more exactly, he became the founder of psycho-physics or experimental psychology." One of the best characteristics of Fechner's personality and speculation will be found in Prof. Wundt's 'Centenary Address' (1901). It is published in separate form, and contains valuable additions and personal reminiscences.

[1] ' Die Philosophie des Unbewussten' (1st ed., 1869 ; 11th ed., in 3 vols., 1904).

period; it may be said that it attracted and satisfied for a time all the popular taste that existed for metaphysics in Germany; but it is only fair to add that it also kept this vanishing interest alive. Hartmann also belongs to that small number of independent and original thinkers who have devoted the whole of their life and strength to the elaboration and defence of their philosophic creed, who have led solitary lives and did not gain reputation either as academic teachers or through the application of their abstract ideas to practical questions.[1] In this respect he resembles Schopenhauer in Germany and Herbert Spencer in England, but differs from Comte in France and from Mill, who were prompted by a lively interest in social, economic, and political questions.

Nevertheless we cannot say that Hartmann made a

[1] The importance of Eduard von Hartmann (1842-1906) in the history of Thought is twofold. His early celebrity, referred to in the text, was based on the philosophy of the "Unconscious," as Spencer's is, to a large extent, based on the philosophy of the "Unknowable." But in Hartmann's case his earliest work has gradually receded into the background, and a more permanent place in the history of Thought is being gradually won for him through the influence of his later writings. Among these the 'Phänomenologie des sittlichen Bewusstseins' (1st ed., 1879) and his 'Kategorienlehre' (1896) are of special interest, inasmuch as they contribute, critically and constructively, much that is valuable for the discussion and solution of two problems which occupy a prominent place in philosophical speculation at the present moment. The first of these is the logical or epistemological problem referred to above (chap. i. p. 72), to arrange in scientific order the original forms of thought through which the human mind ascends from the position of common-sense to the higher regions of speculative thought and spiritual insight — a task begun by Aristotle, taken up again by Kant in modern times, triumphantly solved by Hegel, and since his time more carefully and circumspectly handled in Germany by Lotze, Trendelenburg, Hartmann, and others; in France by Renouvier; in this country by Bradley, Bosanquet, Haldane, and others. The second is the ethical problem, notably the question to what extent a system of morality and rules of conduct can be elaborated independently, or whether a religious or metaphysical foundation is required. In connection with this problem we shall have to deal with Hartmann's position in a later chapter.

novel contribution to the solution of the problem of
Reality.   He did indeed coin a new term in the
" Unconscious," which was to be a negative definition
of the Absolute ; but though it served to make his
philosophy popular and has become a watchword in
philosophical literature, it is little more than a name
for the " Unknowable," and is seductive largely through
the fact that it reminds us of the subconscious
region of mental life which has become a favourite
topic in recent Psychology.   The conception involved
differs, however, from the " Unknowable" of Spencer,
inasmuch as it does not remain in the background,
but is continually introduced in all of Hartmann's very
voluminous writings, where it is appealed to for the
solution of every formidable difficulty, and where it
is employed to fill up the gaps and chasms in our
knowledge of the phenomenal world.   And from the
subconscious it differs, at least professedly, inasmuch
as it distinctly refuses to be considered as a conception gained by analogy with our subjective and personal
human experience.   The historical and critical writings
of Hartmann contain many valuable contributions of
thought, but their usefulness is somewhat curtailed by
a monotonous and one-sided reference of everything to
the one central idea of the " Unconscious."

Were I to follow the lead of German historians
of philosophy, I should at this point close the history
of the problem of Reality in the nineteenth century.
With very few exceptions, comprehensive and general
histories of philosophy have appeared only in Germany.
English and French writers on modern philosophy have

rarely even professed to take any other than a national point of view. Moreover, this national point of view did not, as it usually has done in Germany, secure a complete or exhaustive survey even of its own restricted subject. The 'History of Modern Philosophy' of Professor Höffding is distinguished not least by the fact that it is, so far, the only work on the subject written from an international point of view; and the author has in subsequent writings[1] done still more to counteract the impression, not unusual in Germany, that higher speculation in modern times is an exclusively German occupation. That this has been the case until within the last generation is, however, quite as true as that it has now ceased to be so. And one of the indications that this change has taken place is to be found in the fact that the central problem of philosophy — the Ontological problem, or the problem of Reality—has in the same degree ceased to interest German thinkers as it has been taken up in this country and also in France.

55.
Return to Ontology in England and France.

The causes which have led to this change have to some extent been already pointed out in past chapters of this section of 'The History of Thought,' but it will be useful to dwell somewhat more fully upon them.

British thinkers have not, till quite recently, experienced the necessity of formulating a Philosophical Creed. I have stated before that this was, since the seventeenth century, the main task set before the mind of Continental philosophers — ever since

[1] See for these, *supra*, p. 57.

Protestantism heralded the era of independent thought
and free inquiry. And the task became still more
urgent when, in addition to the breaking down of
authorities in the region of Belief, the French Revolution
shook the very foundations of national, social, and
individual existence— *i.e.*, when not only the problem
of Knowledge but also the problem of Existence or
Reality was pushed into the foreground.

If this country for a long time partook of the
movement of the Reformation only so far as Church
government was concerned, the reforms of Ritual and
of Doctrine following deliberately and tardily,[1] still
less did it witness any subversion of the general
order of things equal to that which took place at
the end of the eighteenth century in France, and
which was felt all over the Western Continent of
Europe. The waves of this great storm did indeed
beat against the shores of this island, but they did
little more than create alarm and help to formulate
those problems which the industrial and commercial
progress of a country blessed with a settled government and a national representation brought necessarily
to the surface.

These problems were the problems of wealth in the
first instance, of political rights and social organisation
later on. The fundamental problem of existence, the
problem of Reality, had indeed been touched by David
Hume, but not with a full sense of its enormous and
ultimate practical importance; as he himself affects to
admit that a game of backgammon or a good dinner

[1] See above, p. 116.

was sufficient to dispel all his doubts. In fact, the general feeling of security and the belief in progress were not shaken. A spiritual solution in harmony with Christian beliefs had been offered by Bishop Berkeley; and Hume was refuted, through Reid and the Scottish school, by an appeal to common-sense—*i.e.*, by a return to the Order of the day and the Powers that be. Such an Order and such Powers existed in this country, but they did not exist abroad. Hence the problem of Existence, the question as to the Divine order of things, was emphasised by that section of thinkers on the Continent who regarded the Revolution as the beginning of a new era, who inherited its faith and hope in a better future and considered themselves the bearers of a new message and a new Revelation. Another section preached the doctrine of Reaction and heralded the era of the Restoration. The former section was mostly represented by the Idealistic and the earlier Romantic schools in Germany, the latter by the philosophy of the Restoration in France and by the later phases of Romanticism in Germany. We know how, with the representatives of both sections, the practical problems of social organisation, of law and morality, stood in the foreground; in Germany also the great problem of popular and higher Education. We also know how the critical spirit on the one side, and the scientific on the other, slowly but surely prepared the downfall of the Idealistic movement in Germany, and, with it, of the peculiar solution of the problem of Existence and Reality which it had attempted.

In fact, up to recent times, and with few exceptions,

which have not become generally known and appreciated, this country has not produced any foremost
thinkers who were burdened with the problem of
Existence and Reality as we find them burdened on
the Continent; the self - assurance of Fichte, the
triumphant confidence of Hegel, the mystical depth of
Schelling, Schleiermacher, and Novalis have no parallel
in this country.   But neither does it exhibit such
typical examples of spiritual unhappiness, doubt, and
despair, as we meet with abroad in Hölderlin, in de
Lamennais, in Mainländer, or of intellectual self-assertion
as in Nietzsche.   Nevertheless the influences which
worked abroad in a sudden and catastrophic manner,
amounting to a Revolution in thought as well as in
practical life, have made themselves slowly, and perhaps
more insidiously, felt also in this country.   The suddenness of the Revolution abroad, the extremes of its
doctrines and passions, had at least the advantage that
they produced an equally sudden and powerful reaction
in an age and in surroundings which had not yet been
saturated with criticism or corrupted through the
commercial and industrial spirit.   In this country all
these influences, which in Germany succeeded each
other, have towards the end of the nineteenth century
simultaneously combined to produce, slowly but surely,
in many thinking minds, the conviction that the solution
of the problem of Reality offered by the Beliefs of
former days requires to be either abandoned or brought
into some kind of harmony with the principles of science
and the results of criticism.   This has led to two distinct
and original attempts to face the great problem of

Existence fairly and impartially. And this means that the problem of Reality has risen from being of purely speculative interest to the position of a fundamental practical problem. The problem which Hume formulated and abandoned, and which Carlyle fantastically adumbrated in the "Everlasting No" and the "Everlasting Yea" of Sartor Resartus, has gradually dawned upon living thinkers as the great question on which all our culture, civilisation, and progress ultimately depend. Through 'Philosophic Doubt' we are seeking the 'Pathway to Reality.'[1]

The beginnings of these two independent movements reach indeed as far back as the middle of the century, and find, *inter alia*, an expression in John Stuart Mill's famous dictum, that every thinking Englishman was either a Coleridgian or a Benthamite. The two movements identified by Mill with these celebrated names grew in importance, definiteness, and volume through different alliances which each of them contracted. The movement which, in the opinion of Mill, centred in Bentham, but really quite as much in the teachings of his father, James Mill, sought a deeper foundation in the study of logic and psychology, and was, through these studies, brought into connection with the natural sciences, the methods of which it very largely took as its models. The other movement had already in the mind of Coleridge two distinct sides—the philosophical and romantic side, and the poetical and naturalistic side.

56.
The two movements of search in England: Realistic and Idealistic.

[1] This way of putting the matter was suggested to me by a passage —which I cannot trace — stating that students in some foreign English missionary college asked for such books as Balfour's 'Defence of Philosophic Doubt' and Haldane's 'Pathway to Reality.'

Both movements allied themselves accordingly with a fresh study of nature; the former by embracing the experimental, mathematical, and latterly also the statistical methods of the natural sciences; the latter by finding in nature a source of poetry and inspiration. In this direction the second movement acquired depth and substance through the poetical genius of Wordsworth, who, together with the great masters of landscape painting, inspired what is usually called the Victorian school of Poetry and Art. Both movements — the Realistic as well as the Idealistic—elaborated their own logic and metaphysic: the former stood in this respect on more independent ground, although it was, in the popular opinion, erroneously identified with the French positivism of Auguste Comte; the latter had already in Coleridge, and still more in Carlyle, pointed to German Idealism, and had, in Sir William Hamilton, assimilated a considerable portion of its doctrines. Mill, through his logical and political writings, exercised for a time a considerable influence on the studies of Oxford, where his clear and dispassionate analysis was hailed by many as a refreshing breeze after the perplexities into which Newman and the Tractarian movement had plunged many youthful and ardent souls. But the profounder working out of the philosophical problem, true to the traditions of Oxford learning, was found in an historical study of those speculations which stood in immediate connection with the classical systems of Plato and Aristotle. The influence of these systems was prominent in German Idealism, notably in Hegel. Mansel brought to Oxford the spirit of Hamilton's philosophy, conspicuous for its historical erudition. Jowett revived the study of Plato, and T. H. Green pointed to the great ideas contained in Hegel's philosophy, in which he rightly admired the underlying scheme more than its actual elaboration. About the same time a solitary thinker, Hutchison Stirling of Edinburgh, created a deep curiosity, as much through the title as through the oracular wording of his 'Secret of Hegel.' The immediate result upon English philosophy was a series of works which, in an independent spirit and with much originality, attempted to fathom and expound the deeper meaning and drift of the writings of Kant and Hegel. To these was added a renewed study of Spinoza, whose influence on German philosophy was so conspicuous, but whose works had almost fallen into oblivion in this country. The study of Hegel was followed in Oxford by that of Lotze. It must, however, here be remarked that the knowledge in this country of the constructive systems abroad has up to quite recent times remained incomplete; it did not, for instance, include any intimate acquaintance with the systems of Fichte, Schelling, and Schleier-macher, nor with those of Herbart and Leibniz, nor did it take any notice of the underlying influences of the Romantic movement.

Before what we may call the Oxford school arrived at an independent expression of its aspirations, the Realistic movement in Philosophy had already advanced to an original conception, not only of the problem of Knowledge, but also of that of Reality. That the abandonment of the conventional and common - sense solutions of these problems entailed upon philosophers the necessity of giving a correcter answer was felt already by Mill, and notably by Lewes; but a definite answer was not given before Herbert Spencer treated comprehensively the fundamental problems of philosophical Thought in his 'First Principles.' It is interesting to see how he made use of the argument of Sir William Hamilton, the same which had led Mansel to a re-assertion of that body of positive doctrine with which the school of Mill had broken long before. Huxley gave the popular name of Agnosticism to Spencer's philosophy of the Unknowable, though it is doubtful whether he himself remained satisfied with the position it assumed. Another great popular influence which did much to urge the necessity of a deeper study of the fundamental problems, showing at the same time the uncertainty which had taken hold of the foremost thinkers of the Age, was the appearance in 1875 of a new Periodical which professed to offer an arena for the discussion of important questions to writers of all shades of opinion.[1] The 'Fortnightly Review' had started ten years before as the organ of independent thought;[2] it

57.
Popular influences: the new monthly Reviews.

[1] This is finely expressed in Tennyson's Prefatory Poem ('Nineteenth Century,' No. I., March 1877):

"Those that of late had fleeted far and fast
To touch all shores, now leaving to the skill
Of others their old craft seaworthy still,
Have charter'd this; where, mindful of the past,
Our true co-mates regather round the mast;
Of diverse tongue, but with a common will
Here, in this roaring moon of daffodil
And crocus, to put forth and brave the blast;
For some, descending from the sacred peak

Of hoar high-templed Faith, have leagued again
Their lot with ours to rove the world about;
And some are wilder comrades, sworn to seek
If any golden harbour be for men
In seas of Death and sunless gulfs of Doubt."

[2] The 'Fortnightly' may be considered to have been the organ of what on the Continent is sometimes termed English Positivism. Since the time when Lord Morley, as second editor of the Review, repudiated the designation of it as "positivist," a term objectionable also to Huxley and Spencer, the

was opposed by the 'Contemporary,' which treated of fundamental questions of Knowledge and Belief in a conservative spirit; the 'Nineteenth Century,'[1] branching off from this, contained in its first volume, under the title of a "Symposium," a discussion by prominent thinkers of the great underlying questions of Knowledge and Belief, of Life and Existence. The very inconclusiveness of this remarkable discussion, and, later on, the appearance of Mr Mallock's articles entitled, "Is life worth living?" must have created in wider circles the conviction that it was the task of philosophers to approach afresh those great problems which had since the time of Descartes occupied thinkers on the Continent, but which had in this country only recently attracted the attention they deserve.

None of these various lines of thought, however, gave a sufficiently distinct formulation of the underlying problem; none of them said, in plain words, that our age had to a large extent lost what former ages possessed or thought they possessed, viz.: a definite conception of the truly Real—as distinguished from the many surrounding realities, which proved, on examination, to be merely apparent, devoid of intrinsic value, mere semblances

---

term has ceased to be identical with Comtism, not less in France itself than in other countries. When M. Brunetière said, France would not give up Positivism, he clearly did not mean Comtism.

[1] The 'Nineteenth Century's' appearance falls in time almost exactly between the appearance of two works which made a great impression. The first was John Henry (Cardinal) Newman's 'Grammar of Assent' (1870); the other, Mr A. J. Balfour's 'Defence of Philosophic Doubt' (1879). The latter was followed by a more comprehensive Treatise on 'The Foundations of Belief' (1895). These works form landmarks in the history of religious philosophy in England, and will be discussed in a later chapter, which, under the title "Of the Spirit," will deal with this subject.

of the Real.   What English thinkers had so far done in
the region of original philosophic Thought was limited
mainly to Psychology, Logic, and Ethics.   The latter
subject was treated mostly in its connection with social
and economic questions.   In the writings of T. H.
Green, however, ethical problems formed the entrance to
a more independent discussion of the problems of Knowing
and Being, and it was largely owing to his influence that
his pupils and followers were led to attack these latter
questions in a purely metaphysical as distinguished from
a practical interest.   In this interest Professor Caird
published his important works upon Kant, Wallace his
translations of, and commentaries on, Hegel; in this interest also the two volumes of Lotze's ' System of Philosophy' were translated at the suggestion of Green.   The
works of other thinkers of bygone times were commented
on and re-edited; among these, the editions of David
Hume's ' Treatise,' by Green and Grose, and Professor
Campbell Fraser's excellent edition of Bishop Berkeley's
works, were of great importance and assistance to
students.

58.
Caird,
Wallace,
and Green.

One is sometimes tempted to say in one's haste that
these thinkers who heralded a new spirit of thought spent
perhaps too much time and labour over purely historical,
critical, and expository work, and that the danger existed
that through the study of Kant, Hegel, and Lotze, English
speculation might follow the example of Germany, where
history and criticism had long usurped the position belonging to original thought, erudition having taken the
place of creation.   It was therefore of immense value
for the development of English thought that an inde-

pendent work should appear, in which the fundamental problems of Knowing and Being were systematically treated, without that learned ballast which so frequently obscures the way instead of marking it clearly. This explains the great impression which Mr F. H. Bradley's writings created, and among them notably his meta- physical treatise ' On Appearance and Reality.' It may be regarded as the centre of an independent movement of Philosophical Thought in this country. Nearly all that has since appeared in the English language in the realm of Logic and Metaphysics has started from, or been influenced by, Mr Bradley's analysis. It may be said that he has forced every thinker in this country to face the problem of Reality, or, as he calls it, of the " Absolute "—a term which Herbert Spencer and he have introduced into English philosophical literature. It is the problem of the truly Real, of the ὄντως ὄν as dis- tinguished from the ὄν and the μὴ ὄν of Plato. Mr Bradley's work has been very variously criticised ; a conclusive verdict has not yet been pronounced upon it. Nor is it in the spirit of this history to enter on a detailed exposition of its many-sided argument. It will be enough if we briefly note the special direction it has given to philosophical thought in this country, and the position it takes up with reference to the two great doctrines which dominated philosophical thought in the middle of the century—the psychological Atomism of the English school and the critical Transcendentalism im- ported from abroad, and which there emanated from Kant.

Students of philosophy who are intimately acquainted

59.
Bradley's
' Appear-
ance and
Reality.'

with the development of German thought, and with the latest phase which it reached in the critical eclecticism of Lotze, will not fail to compare Mr Bradley's enterprise with Lotze's 'Metaphysik,' which appeared in 1841. Both works may be looked upon as attempts to give a consistent meaning to the current philosophical terminology, most of which has come down to us from antiquity. Both works start, explicitly or implicitly, from the assumption that the several abstract terms employed in dealing with the problems of Knowledge, Truth, and Reality, are meant to convey a consistent and deeper sense which it is necessary to unfold and lay bare before we can start upon the discussion of any special problem. Formally, this undertaking amounts therefore merely to a distinct logical definition of the words employed in philosophical language; substantially, it means that we abstract out of the casual, fluctuating, and many-sided use of the standard philosophical terms a consistent system of ideas affording the nearest approach to an expression of Truth and Reality which the human mind is capable of.

But though the object pursued by Mr Bradley in his matured analysis presents much similarity with the youthful undertaking of Lotze, the central position which he arrives at differs markedly from that of Lotze. I have above given extracts from Lotze's work which indicate very clearly the character of his philosophy. I will now select a passage from Mr Bradley's work which similarly places us at the centre of his speculation. In the earlier part of his work he arrives at the result that the " Absolute " [1]—what I have throughout

_____
[1] See 'Appearance and Reality,' p. 144.

called " the truly Real "—" is not many ; there are no independent reals. The universe is one in this sense that its differences exist harmoniously within one whole, beyond which there is nothing, Hence the Absolute is, so far, an individual and a system, but, if we stop here, it remains but formal and abstract. Can we then, the question is, say anything about the concrete nature of the system ? Certainly, I think, this is possible. When we ask as to the matter which fills up the empty outline, we can reply in one word, that this matter is Experience. And experience means something much the same as given and present fact. We perceive, on reflection, that to be real, or even barely to exist, must be to fall within sentience. Sentient experience, in short, is reality, and what is not this is not real. We may say, in other words, that there is no being or fact outside of that which is commonly called psychical existence. . . . Find any piece of existence, take up anything that any one could possibly call a fact, or could in any sense assert to have been, and then judge if it does not consist in sentient experience. . . . I am driven to the conclusion that for me experience is the same as reality." [1] And further on he continues : " This is the point on which I insist, and it is the very ground on which I stand, when I urge that reality is sentient experience. I mean that to be real is to be indissolubly one thing with sentience. It is to be something which comes as a feature and aspect within one whole of feeling, something which, except as an integral element of such sentience, has no meaning at all. And what

[1] 'Appearance and Reality,' p. 146.

I repudiate is the separation of feeling from the felt, or of the desired from desire, or of what is thought from thinking, or the division—I might add—of anything from anything else."

In this characteristic passage from Mr Bradley my readers may possibly divine much of that which unites him with—or separates him from—Lotze. But this is hardly the object which I have in view in transcribing it. What I desire to convey is the impression how completely English philosophical thought has, in this thinker, overcome the atomistic view of reality on the one side and the transcendental on the other. For it is here clearly indicated that no analysis which starts, with Hume, from separate ideas or, with Herbart and natural philosophers, with independent Reals or separate atoms, can satisfy our conception of underlying reality. And, on the other side, no noumenal "Thing in itself"—still less, "Things in themselves" as opposed to their appearance or phenomenal existence—can be considered to be a fitting title for the Absolute. Mr Bradley objects to all separation into independent detail, to all division of the world into that which is Unreal and that which is truly Real. He always looks to the whole, which is harmonious, comprehensive, and individual, and which in this its nature absorbs also that which is merely apparent.

61.
Bradley's
opposition
to both
atomistic
and trans-
cendental
view of
Reality.

There is indeed one great truth regarding reality which Mr Bradley urges and defends in an original manner. It is a truth which took greater hold of thinkers as the century progressed. It indeed underlies or consciously governs nineteenth century thought in many directions; not only Metaphysics but also Psychology, Sociology, and—we may go further and say—not only all philosophical but also much of the best scientific thought. This truth can be broadly stated in these words : Nowhere in the world of facts and phenomena do we meet with things in their isolation; the phenomenal world is a connected whole, a continuum, in time and space, and to deal with single isolated or independent facts or phenomena leads away from an understanding of their true nature and a comprehension of their reality. It is indeed a remarkable fact that the very process which, in the regions of science, has produced so much knowledge, led to so many discoveries and predictions, and been followed by so many useful applications—the process of mathematical abstraction and definition—should, at the same time, have led us away from a real comprehension of the nature of things into an artificial world of our own creation. Thus it has come about that the greatest step taken in modern times within the natural sciences themselves has consisted in studying the objects of nature, not in isolation, but in their surroundings, and the processes of nature not independently but in their sequence in time. The whole vocabulary of modern natural science, such as "habitat," "environment," "evolution," and "solidarity," mark this change in thought; in fact, hand in hand with the increase of precision characteristic of the mathematical treatment, there has marched the opposite process of annulling conventional definitions and of breaking down traditional landmarks.

I have had occasion to point out how the science of

empirical psychology underwent a great change, notably
through the labours of James Ward and his followers.
They replaced the atomistic view imported from the
modern science of chemistry and represented, notably in
this country, through Mill and Bain, by the conception
of the inner life as a presentation-continuum, which is
divided up merely by the process of attention into supposed definite sensations and perceptions. This conviction that the nature or reality of things, facts, and
phenomena, reveals itself in their "Together" and not in
their artificial isolation, finds its abstract expression in
Mr Bradley's conception of the comprehensiveness and
individuality of one Absolute [1] which alone represents
all and everything that is truly Real. There is no
doubt that this bias of his mind led Mr Bradley to
appreciate much that was done and said by the idealistic
school of German thinkers, though it is hardly true that
what prompted them in their speculations was an equally
clear insight into the different processes by which the
human mind acquires knowledge. This insight has
really been gained only by the slow processes of minute
analysis such as Kant attempted, which the most celebrated of his followers did more to abandon than to
perfect, but which owe the cultivation and refinement
they have reached in modern times, first to the
English school and secondly to those followers of Kant
who were temporarily forgotten and cast into the shade
by the glare which for a time emanated from the bolder

---

[1] It is, in fact, one of the most
brilliant examples of the growing
emphasis whith is being laid upon
the *esprit d'ensemble*, the synoptic
view, as distinguished from the
esprit de détail, the analytic view,
as already frequently referred to;
see above, pp. 192, 193 *n*.

constructive thinkers. The belief which lived in the latter was that the human mind was somehow capable of an elevation into that higher region of thought where it would gain an immediate intuitive knowledge of the underlying ground and essence of things—*i.e.*, of the truly Real. The classical expression of this way of thinking is Hegel's 'Phenomenology of the Mind.' Philosophers in Germany have now mostly settled down to a conviction that this endeavour of the idealistic school was illusory. What remnant of truth it contains survives only in the deeper-lying premises of Lotze's philosophy such as I have indicated above, and the resemblance of which with some of Mr Bradley's teachings I shall have another opportunity of more fully pointing out.

But the more we leave the purely formal side of Mr Bradley's speculations, the less does it seem as if his conception stood in any agreement with the positive ideas of Lotze's philosophy. As stated before, one of Lotze's most characteristic conceptions is the distinction which he emphasises between the world of forms, the world of things, and the world of values. This distinction has frequently been understood as implying in Lotze's philosophy an intrinsic dualism or pluralism. However this may be, it is quite clear that Mr Bradley does not countenance any such distinction. " I do not," he says,[1] " mean that, beside our inadequate idea of truth, we should set up, also and alongside, an independent standard of worth. For . . . our two standards would tend everywhere to clash. They would collide

[1] 'Appearance and Reality,' p. 333.

hopelessly without appeal to any unity above them. . . .
Such a separation of worth from reality and truth would
mutilate our nature, and could end only in irrational
compromise or oscillation."

62.
His Monism
or Absolut-
ism.

It may here be remarked that Lotze has been reproved
by some critics for countenancing this indecision or oscillation. Mr Bradley, on the other side, is clearly a monist ;
he believes in one comprehensive Absolute, and he recon-
ciles the existence of this supreme unity with the apparent plurality and the many-sidedness of the phenomenal world by his doctrine of " Degrees of Reality."
This is indeed a most important idea, which Mr Bradley
has revived in an original manner, and, as it were, introduced into British philosophy. Though very sparing in
his quotations and references to earlier thinkers, he
distinctly acknowledges his indebtedness to Hegel when
he enters on an exposition of this his central conception.
Thus he emphasises quite as much that nothing phenomenal, neither external things nor the phenomena and
experiences in the regions of art, morals, and religion, are
true and comprehensive expressions of the Absolute, as,
on the other side, he maintains that they all partake of
the truly Real, in some degree ; that their reality is not
lost but preserved in the truly Real. " Throughout our
world, whatever is individual is more real and true, for
it contains within its own limits a wider region of the
Absolute, and it possesses more intensely the type of
self-sufficiency. Or, to put it otherwise, the interval
between such an element and the Absolute is smaller.
We should require less alteration, less destruction of its
own special nature, in order to make this higher element

completely real.[1] And again :[2] "The positive relation of every appearance as an adjective to Reality and the presence of Reality among its appearances in different degrees and with diverse values—this double truth we have found to be the centre of philosophy. . . . This conclusion—the necessity on one side for a standard, and the impossibility of reaching it without a positive knowledge of the Absolute,—I would venture to press upon any intelligent worshipper of the Unknown."

I have selected the last passage not only as containing a summary of Mr Bradley's teaching, but also as forming a fitting conclusion to this chapter which deals with the problem of Reality, and as an indication of the latest phase into which this problem has entered at the end of our period. We have certainly left far behind us any confidence in the capacities of the human mind permanently to solve this problem, a confidence which characterised the preface to Hegel's 'Phenomenology,' and we have lost quite as much the security which characterised the appeal to common-sense and traditional beliefs prevalent in the school of contemporary Scottish philosophy at the beginning of the century. In fact the problem of Reality is at the moment more of a problem than it ever has been : it has come to be a world-problem.

At the end of the century we can divide the foremost thinkers into two classes according to the position they take up to this problem. This position can be put quite clearly by asking: Does an answer to the question,

---

[1] 'Appearance and Reality,' p. 382. [2] Ibid., p. 551.

"What is the truly Real," form the beginning or the end of philosophical thought? Is it the requisite or the result of all philosophical reasoning? Those who affirm the latter, who start professedly without bias and prejudice, looking at the world around and within them in an impartial spirit, and hope to arrive, by patient analysis and by lengthened trains of reasoning, at a final result or highest abstraction, would fain offer the latter as their solution of the problem of Reality. These philosophers may be called Phenomenists. Opposed to them stands another class of thinkers who are convinced of the necessity of first attaining a definite standpoint, a fixed centre of reference, a fundamental conviction in the light of which to gain an understanding and an interpretation of the many-sided appearances in the worlds of nature and mind, of society and history. For them philosophy only begins when at least a preliminary answer is given to the question, What is the truly Real? This class of thinkers may be termed Ontologists. Both classes of thinkers are represented in this country and abroad. Professor Wundt of Leipzig is probably the foremost living representative of the former, Mr Bradley of the latter class of thinkers. The former class is, apparently, at the end of the century, in the ascendant in Germany, the latter in this country.[1]

63.
Phenomen-
ists and
Ontologists.

---

[1] The opinion expressed in the text, which was written six years ago, is, so far as British Thought is concerned, confirmed by the appearance, since the end of the century, of several important works dealing with the ontological problem, and notably by the publication in the current year (1912) of James Ward's Second Series of Gifford Lectures (1907-10): 'The Realm of Ends, or Pluralism and Theism,' and Mr Bernard Bosanquet's Gifford Lectures (1911-12): 'The Principle of Individuality and Value.' So far as German Thought is concerned, a revival of the metaphysical interest is unmistakable.

Between the two, Herbert Spencer interposes with the philosophy of the " Unknowable," which admits the Absolute as a necessary preliminary conception of all philosophical thought, but abandons it as an idea not fruitful in the course of further detailed philosophical speculation. The latter is, with Spencer, confined entirely to principles gained by induction and abstraction in the course of an analysis of the things, facts, and events of the phenomenal world.

CHAPTER VI.

OF NATURE.

I.

OLDER Metaphysics comprised four distinct branches. Of these the first dealt with the problem of Reality in the abstract, attempting, in the main, to answer such questions as "What is Real?" "What is the truly Real?" The conclusions arrived at were then applied to three separate special questions. First, there presented itself the question as to the reality of the external world : this was the problem of Nature; secondly, there was the question as to the reality of the internal world : this constituted the problem of the Soul ; and lastly, there was the question as to the reality which stood above and beyond the realities of the external and the internal worlds : this referred to the Divine Order of things, we may say that it constituted the problem of the Spirit. Thus Ontology was followed by Cosmology, rational Psychology, and rational Theology. Now, although most of these terms have become obsolete, the problems which they designated still remain. The principal reason why we do not generally adopt the older terminology is because it has been recognised that in all the three regions, in

1.
Nature : a
metaphysi-
cal problem.

the region of things natural, of things mental, and of things spiritual, a preliminary study of facts is required before the great problems themselves can be attacked. Thus Cosmology, or the Theory of Nature and the Universe as a whole, has been superseded by the study of nature in detail; Rational Psychology has been superseded by Empirical Psychology; and Rational Theology has either been altogether abandoned or it has been placed at the very end of a detailed study of spiritual phenomena in individual and social life.

There seems to be no doubt that the modern age has been more largely occupied with empirical studies in all the three departments, and that the discussion of the ultimate problems has been either postponed or pushed into the background. Nevertheless, at the end of the period with which I am dealing, the necessity of arriving at a philosophical or reasoned Creed has, as I have stated before, made itself more and more felt, and with it a renewed interest has arisen in the everlasting metaphysical [1] problems of Nature, Mind, and Spirit,

2.
Superseded
by empirical
studies.

---

[1] During the third quarter of the century lectures on Metaphysics had almost disappeared at the German universities, and, still more so, lectures on philosophy of Nature. This was owing to two distinct causes, both equally important. The first was purely negative: a widespread aversion to premature speculations, such as were contained in the systems of Schelling and Hegel, and which, notably in the regions of the empirical sciences and for the purpose of the acquisition of natural knowledge, were considered to have exerted a baneful influence. The second was a positive cause: the growth of the historical interest which idealistic and romantic philosophy had helped to stimulate quite as much as the diffusion of the critical spirit. During that period, however, philosophical thought cultivated other departments which had previously been somewhat neglected. These were notably psychology, logic (in a wider sense of the term), and philosophy of religion. In the period there was only one prominent teacher of philosophy who did as much to preserve the continuity of philosophical thought and the valuable traditions of the past as he did to infuse a new spirit into the treatment of the three

taken as a whole and not merely in their scattered
phenomenal existence. Of these three problems, that
concerning the reality and the phenomena of the inner
life has been dealt with in the third chapter of this
section : that concerning spiritual phenomena will form
the subject of a later chapter : the present chapter will
deal with the problem of Nature as a whole or with the
cosmological problem. It will attempt to pass in review
the different positions which nineteenth century thought
has taken up to this problem in the three countries,
and the several answers which have been suggested.

3.
Changes in
the thoughts
of the age.

Probably in no other department have the views put
forward been so numerous and varied, and the changes
which have come over the thought of the age so rapid
and fundamental. The century itself opens with three
distinct and original departures, marking three distinct
interests in nature and things natural. With one of

last - named subjects. This was
Lotze, whose Courses of Lectures
included, at regular intervals, and
with the aid of little encouragement,
Courses on Metaphysics and on
Philosophy of Nature. The latter
subject disappeared subsequently
altogether till it was revived, towards the end of the century, by
Prof. Ostwald, who published in
1901 his lectures on 'Naturphilosophie,' and commenced a periodical with the title, 'Annalen der
Naturphilosophie,' of which the
present year (1912) sees the publication of the XIth volume. Here,
however, more than in any other
direction, Lotze represents, consciously and almost alone, the
transition from the earlier to the
later philosophical thought of the
nineteenth century. As a sign of
the unsettlement of philosophical
thought in Germany at the end of
the century it is interesting to
refer to two works, already frequently mentioned, the 'Memorial
Volume' (1904), dedicated to Kuno
Fischer, purporting to give a review
of the state of philosophy at the
beginning of the present century,
and the volume entitled 'Systematische Philosophie' (1907). Whereas the latter deals in eight chapters
with the different philosophical
sciences, devoting separate treatment to Metaphysics (Wundt) and
Philosophy of Nature (Ostwald),
but contains no chapter on Philosophy of Religion, the former
work deals likewise in eight chapters with separate philosophical
sciences but omits Metaphysics and
Philosophy of Nature, whilst it
contains a most valuable chapter on
Philosophy of Religion by Tröltsch.

these departures we have already become intimately acquainted in the earlier part of this work. I have there called it the scientific or exact study of Nature. As a tolerably compact and consistent doctrine, it first presented itself to the French mind: in its extreme form to the mathematical genius of Laplace. The second original departure is to be found in the naturalistic school of English poetry and art. The love of nature and the return to it which arose in this country towards the end of the eighteenth century spread into Germany, and formed there one of the most important agencies in stimulating the national mind to individual and original productions in poetry and literature. It found there its greatest exponent in Goethe, whose personality and whose works have, to succeeding generations, become as great and as inexhaustible a subject of study and re-flection as nature itself had been to him throughout his long career. Somewhat influenced by the last-named movement, there sprang up as the third original contribu-tion to the solution of the problem of nature, that phil-osophy which called itself, *par excellence*, the philosophy of Nature. As I have already shown in the last chapter, this movement centred in Schelling, in whose mind it formed as much an opposition to the one-sided moralism and intellectualism of Kant and some of his followers as it also marked the desire to reconcile the mechanical with the ideal or artistic study of nature in the midst of which Schelling found himself placed. In this latter desire Schelling had indeed a forerunner to whom he frequently refers in the introduction to his 'Philosophy of Nature.' This was Leibniz, with whom, probably for

4.
The exact study of Nature.

5.
Naturalism of English poetry and art.

6.
Philosophy of Nature.

the first time, the modern way of putting the matter made its appearance—viz., that Nature demands from the human mind to be mechanically described on the one side, and on the other, to be ideally interpreted, or, in other words, that every fact and phenomenon is as much the consequence of a mechanical cause as it is the means towards an ideal end.

With the movement which originated in England and culminated in Goethe, we have not at present to deal. It was not a movement of philosophical thought, although it very largely influenced the latter. This I have had, and shall have in the sequel, abundant occasion to show. One of the principal aims of the present section of this history, indeed, will be to make evident to my readers how all philosophical thought leads us back, for its ultimate sources, to a deeper experience of the human mind which finds its immediate expression in the subjective regions of art, poetry, and religion.

For the moment we must confine ourselves to those contributions to a solution of the problem of nature which were either distinctly and directly put forward by Schelling and his followers or which, later on, indirectly resulted from the purely scientific or exact study of natural phenomena just referred to.

Now, although it has become the fashion violently to denounce the " Philosophy of Nature "[1] and to place it

---

[1] It is again Lotze who, first among more recent thinkers, put forward a just estimate of the aims of Schelling's 'Philosophy of Nature,' and whose own entire speculation turns upon the distinction between the mechanical and the teleological view, between the description and the interpretation of nature. This clear demarcation of two entirely different but complementary tasks, which will always occupy the thinking mind, is set forth in the earliest of Lotze's writings, and untiringly repeated on many occasions, most clearly

in opposition to the more fruitful "Natural Philosophy," which has its home in this country, it cannot be denied that it formed an important, though premature, step, and that many of the ideas put forward by its votaries have, in the latter half of the nineteenth century, been revived with little alteration, though with more precise

7.
Importance
of this last.

when he opposes or criticises the labours of others, such as Fechner's 'Atomenlehre' (1855; 'Kleine Schriften,' vol. iii. p. 215 *sqq.*), or the younger Fichte's 'Anthropology' ('Streitschriften,' 1857; 'Kleine Schriften,' vol. iii. p. 324 *sqq.*). The review of the former work contains the following passage, most clearly indicating what Schelling intended: "Criticism, which now so often does not go to the original sources but contents itself with a frequently blurred picture of a philosophical view as it has entered into popular consciousness, seems to me in combating Schelling's views only too customarily to overlook an important point. Schelling did not place before himself the tasks which physical science considers, and must consider, to be its own, and we are unavoidably unjust towards him if we accuse him of the failure of an attempt upon which he never ventured. What he in principle aimed at was to view things in the Absolute or *sub specie æternitatis*, a task which we may express in this way : that he tried to discover the ideal content which single phenomena, themselves parts of one incarnate idea, were destined to represent ; but he did not consider it to be the task of philosophy, but left this to physical science, to show through what means and through what mechanical connections and interaction they did succeed in fulfilling their vocation. All these means of realisation in the connection of a finite world seemed to him inferior objects of research, for they neither increase, nor are they the ground of, the ideal value of the result. As little as we deem that we understand better the æsthetic value of a play if we follow up the movements of the vocal muscles of the speaking performers, just as little did he think it possible to increase our insight into the spiritual connection of nature, which alone interested him, through an investigation of the genesis of single phenomena. I do not share this opinion, but I should like to point out that the supposition of any other intention imports faults and confusion into Schelling's views which at least in principle do not encumber him, though they may through inadvertence" ('Kleine Schriften,' vol. iii. p. 228). And he proceeds to give the following quotation from Schelling : "Generally speaking, if only that is truth which is cognised through the highest form of knowledge, then only those sciences can boast of truth in which this characteristic of absolute knowledge is to be found, and as the main criterion of this we have noted the absolute contrast to the law of causality and to the world in which this obtains." And Lotze concludes : "One cannot make such an astounding statement without meaning in earnest what is expressed in it : and this is nothing else but this, that the machinery which produces the image of a phenomenon is not identical with the meaning of this image" (p. 229).

definitions.[1]   And, on the other side, even those who
at the time most loudly declaimed against the doctrines
of Schelling were rarely free from philosophical generalisations or traditional prejudices which proved to be
equally misleading.

About the time when Schelling published his ' Philosophy of Nature,' which professed to be an ideal interpretation of nature, Laplace in France published
two works in which he made two important contributions to a mechanical philosophy of Nature.   At the
end of his ' Exposition du Système du Monde ' he propounded what is now termed the nebular hypothesis, and
in the introduction to his ' Essai Philosophique sur les
Probabilités ' he put forward in a similarly compre-

8.
Laplace.

---

[1] The most prominent thinker in
the middle of the nineteenth
century who adopted suggestions
contained in the writings of the
earlier school, and who forms,
as it were, a connecting link between the ideal and the mechanical view of nature, was Fechner.
Prof. Wundt, in an appendix to his
Centenary Address in memory of
Fechner (1901, p. 63), has collected
valuable references showing how
various suggestions, put forward by
writers belonging to the school of
Schelling, have survived and been
elaborated by Fechner.   Such anticipations of Fechner's views are
notably to be found in the ' Naturphilosophie' (1809-11) of Oken,
who, as Fechner himself says,
" Through his titanic audacity
raised me for the first time above
the ordinary view of nature and
forced me for some time into his
own channels of thought."   And
Prof. Wundt goes on to show how :
" In Oken a real familiarity with
the facts of the natural sciences
gave to his fanciful speculations a
direction through which he occasionally anticipates, though indeed
in a crude form, more recent conceptions.   This is notably the case
in his evolutionary digressions.
. . . If in recent times Schelling
has been occasionally extolled as
a forerunner of the theory of evolution, this is a complete mistake.
Schelling never understood the idea
of development otherwise than in
that ideal sense in which Goethe,
whose ' Metamorphose der Pflanzen '
mainly influenced Schelling, considered the flower to be a higher
stage of the leaf. . . . Oken is, so
far as I can find, the only one
among these philosophers who
clearly looked upon organic development as a real process and
applied this conception also to the
human race. He was, therefore,
in this sense a true forerunner of
the theory of descent, while his
' infusorial bubbles' and his ' prim-
eval ooze' anticipate certain conceptions of the cellular and proto-
plasmic theories " (p. 65).

hensive spirit the idea that the whole course of nature would appear to a mind vastly more knowing than the human mind, but not essentially different from it, in the form of an intricate mathematical formula, in which only the necessary values of the co-ordinates of time and space would have to be introduced in order to afford a positive knowledge of the largest as well as the minutest phenomena.

Neither the nebular hypothesis nor that which has subsequently been termed the Laplacian world-formula seem to have attracted much attention at the time. Both the astronomical theory of the Universe and the doctrine of Probabilities offered to students of science such an enormous number of definite mathematical problems leading to so many fruitful theories that the scientific mind hardly grasped the ultimate philosophical conclusions which were indicated rather than fully explained.

But in the further course of the century, when the desire arose to supplant in the popular mind the fanciful systems of the " Philosophy of Nature " by a sober and practical mechanical theory, the suggestions of Laplace were variously taken up, elaborated, and criticised.[1]

[1] The nebular hypothesis owes its introduction into philosophical literature in this country to Herbert Spencer, who, in one of his earliest Essays (' Westminster Review,' July 1858), made it do service in the interest of the development hypothesis, or what he had already, in the year 1852 ('Leader,' Jan. 1852 and May 1854), termed the "theory of Evolution." In Germany the larger cosmical view, which the nebular hypothesis afforded, received additional support when Helmholtz brought forward his theory of the generation and maintenance of the heat of the sun through the continued action of gravitational forces (see his Lecture, ' Ueber die Wechselwirkung der Naturkraefte,' 1854). Before that time it is remarkable how little attention it received on the part of scientific authorities of the first order. Thus neither Whewell in his ' History of the Inductive Sciences ' nor Humboldt

What prevented these suggestions receiving at the time that recognition which was later on given to them in a degree greatly exceeding the importance which Laplace himself presumably attached to them, was the circumstance that they contained no reference to the phenomena of organic or to those of conscious life. Laplace, like so many other philosophers, places himself, as it were, outside of the Universe which he wishes to explain; and like the spectator in a play, forgets himself entirely in the contemplation of the scenery before him.

9.
Absence of organic and subjective factors.

But what Laplace had thus forgotten, the subjective factor, the position, reflections, and emotions of the beholder, constituted exactly that problem which, since the time of Kant, was attracting thinkers of the opposite school, notably in Germany. Not a comprehensive exposition of the system of the Universe allured them, but the problem how the human mind came to contemplate and comprehend such a system and what part it played itself in this process of contemplation and comprehension. And so great became this subjective interest, notably in the philosophy of Fichte, that the details of the scenery were, so to speak, entirely forgotten in the interest of studying the attitude and the emotions of the beholder. Nature, or the external world, came to be regarded merely as an opportunity for developing and exercising the intellectual and active

in his 'Cosmos' does more than just mention it, attaching to it little scientific importance; and even at the present day it figures much more largely in popular than in scientific works on Astronomy. The so-called Laplacian world-formula gained popular reputation as an extreme expression, but also as indicating the limits of a purely mechanical view of nature, through an Address of Emil Du Bois Reymond, delivered in the year 1872 at the meeting of the German Association of Naturalists in Leipzig.

powers of the human mind, which was conceived as
itself producing, on the provocation of an unknown
external (Kant) or internal (Fichte) impulse, all the
manifold and interesting features of the scenery which
surrounded it.

Now it was the conviction that this view of nature
was slighting, unpoetical, and degrading, which prompted
Schelling to elaborate his "Philosophy of Nature." In
his mind the contrast which we are now accustomed to emphasise between "Philosophy of Nature"
and "Natural Philosophy" was not clearly marked.
Among the members of his school were many of the
foremost naturalists, and indeed some of his ideas
were adopted from an eminent biologist, K. F. Kielmeyer,[1] who published in 1793 his well-known address
on the 'Relation of Organic Forces.' He was an elder
contemporary and friend of the celebrated Cuvier, the
foremost naturalist of the age, who subsequently became
one of the most strenuous opponents of Schelling's
teachings. Nor can it be denied that Cuvier himself,
in spite of his virulent attacks on the "Philosophy of
Nature," inherited likewise many of the philosophical
prejudices of earlier times, and that he moreover failed
to recognise the great truth which that philosophy
contained, and which was to play such a great part in
the second half of the nineteenth century: the idea of

10.
Biological
appeal of
Schelling.

---

[1] Through his influence on Cuvier
(see preface to the 'Leçons d'An-
atomie comparée'), on Humboldt
(who dedicated to him a zoological
tract on 'Comparative Anatomy,'
1806), and on Schelling, we may
look upon Kielmeyer (1765-1844)
as a central figure in the early
history of a truly philosophical
conception of animated nature.
He published little, but his Lectures
as a Professor at Tübingen, which
were copied and circulated in manuscript, had an important and widespread influence.

Development.[1] And he was further probably quite as deficient as Schelling and his followers in recognising the *rôle* which the exact or mathematical methods were destined one day to play also in the historical sciences of nature.

If, in the light of our present knowledge, we read afresh the writings of such thinkers as Kielmeyer, Schelling, Steffens, Oken, and others, to which we may add the names of Lamarck and Geoffroy, of Treviranus and Von Baer, we meet with almost all the leading ideas which governed natural science at the end of the century except one, and that is, if I may say so, a mathematical

11.
An omitted idea: Malthus.

or arithmetical conception.[2] This idea, nevertheless, was put forward about the same time in this country by Malthus in his 'Essay on Population.' It refers to the disproportionate increase of all organisms if compared with their means of subsistence: it is the phenomenon of overcrowding which, combined with that of "variation," necessitates an automatic "selection" leading to the "struggle for existence" and the "survival of the fittest." But it was not till forty years after this period

12.
Afterwards taken up by Darwin.

that the reflections contained in Malthus's 'Essay' met in the mind of Darwin with the necessary conditions by

---

[1] This, however, with the qualifications contained in Lotze's and Wundt's criticisms of this school: see *supra*, pp. 549, 550.

[2] Since I wrote this passage, in the first years of the present century, a second important conception has been added, of which we find no trace among the naturalists and philosophers I am here dealing with, but which has likewise tended in the direction of introducing math-

ematical or arithmetical methods into the study of the living creation. This is the conception anticipated already by Francis Galton and rendered more precise by the acceptance of Mendel's theories, which had been neglected and forgotten. Though published far back in the nineteenth century (1865), they do not belong to the history of Thought during that period.

which they became fruitful in a direction not anticipated by their author himself.   Had Schelling and his
followers confined their view to the purely natural, as
distinguished from the abstract physical, sciences, their
writings would have done less harm and led to less
opposition.   Unfortunately, however, they applied it in
two directions where it proved to be either useless or
actually harmful.   The first of these was marked by the
attempt to find a formula which would not only explain
the organic living creation, but also, by analogy, the
phenomena of the inorganic world.   The second became
manifest in the sway which the ideas of Schelling
exercised over the medical sciences.

Now, the whole tendency of the new or French school
of natural, as distinguished from mental, science in that
age was in the direction not of a genetic or dynamic,
but of a statical or morphological conception of phenomena.   This showed itself in the confidence with which
certain arithmetical or geometrical relations—such as
the laws of attraction and of fixed proportions, the
types of crystalline and organic forms—were applied to
the mechanical explanation or classification of cosmic,
molar, and molecular phenomena, of lifeless and living
things.   And this view was confirmed by the many discoveries and explorations through which the aspect of
nature and of things natural became vastly widened and
deepened.

13.
Statical
view of
French
science.

This was the age which inspired one of the most prominent students of nature, A. von Humboldt, with the
idea of writing a physical description of the Cosmos, a
scheme which was not carried out till much later, when

14.
Insuffici-
ency of this.

the insufficiency of the statical view of nature as a great panorama was already beginning to make itself felt.[1] Schelling's view of Nature as a development of the counterpart of Mind, as a series of stepping-stones to Life and Consciousness, proved to be both premature and incomplete: it was a prospect rather than an achievement. The realisation of it demanded volumes

[1] This statical view of nature—a belief in the regular recurrence not only of the fundamental processes or laws of nature, but also of the types and forms of existing things—showed itself likewise in the birth and development of statistics, as I have shown in the twelfth chapter of the first section of this History. This one-sided faith in recurrent types and forms has been severely shaken during the second half of the century by a belief in continuous and slow variation, and threatens, at the end of the century, under the sway of pragmatism, to move into the opposite extreme, denying even the highest standards of truth and morality. As a matter of fact, the recognition of statical sameness and similarity in natural things and processes has always preceded and led to the search for similar underlying causes. Thus, before the nebular hypothesis was propounded, such regularities as the revolution of the planets in the same direction, the small eccentricity of their orbits and the small inclination of the latter to a common plane, the plane of the ecliptic, suggested to Herschel and others the existence of some common plan or scheme in the constitution, and consequently in the genesis of the planetary system. Again, the sameness in the types of organic beings, especially in their embryonic stage, suggested first the existence of a common plan or scheme, and later on, of a common cause in their origin and development. It was the peculiarity of the philosophy of nature to rely too much upon the ideal sameness and succession of the types of existence, and to put forward only tentatively and in a limited sense the genetic view which relies upon a continuously acting force, an immanent causality. It is interesting to see how Lotze, in 1855, before the modern theory of evolution, pointed out how the philosophy of Schelling and Hegel stopped half-way in its explanation of nature: "Only the One out of which the whole of nature arises has for these opinions a full and independent reality; all single and finite phenomena, standing in their importance beneath the Absolute, are apt to lose that solidity of genuine existence through which they themselves become again new and consistent, though secondary, starting-points of a living activity. Thus in their view of nature the wealth of phenomena which surrounds us is preferably traced immediately to the Highest and the Infinite as its only true source and support; disinclination to explain the finite through the finite leads to a neglect of the succession of mediating causes. This direction of investigation is doubtless not a necessary consequence to which the starting-point of these views was bound to lead; it is only an error to which the temptation lay on the

of research, in the course of which only gradually some definite features of the underlying scheme could reveal themselves,—some traces of the enwoven cipher could become visible. For development, in the sense of Schelling, implied two further conceptions, the conception of a process according to which the development takes place, and the conception of an end or purpose towards which it was directed. Neither the one nor the other of these two conceptions could at the time be clearly defined so far as things natural were concerned. But in the course of the century which followed, the first of these conceptions, that of an automatic and continuous process of evolution, was discovered; whereas the question as to the end or purpose still haunts the mind of the naturalist: perhaps with even less hope of receiving a definite answer than seemed to exist in the beginning of the century. For as I have had occasion to state before, the age and surroundings of Schelling were actuated by a definite idea: the modern form of the classical Ideal of Humanity. This humanistic ideal inspired, created, and governed all historical research: it did more, for, since the time of Herder, it led to various attempts to show how the beginnings of mental

---

way. Whatever we may consider to be the highest creative principle, it will always be, on the other side, a natural assumption that in its creative activity an actual connection exists ; not only that all its products, as co-ordinated examples, bear the same stamp in various forms, but also further that every single reality which emanated from it becomes the necessary condition of something that is to follow and is a partial result of something that came before. The dialectic development in which modern systems recognise how the creative principle manifests itself in an ascending and orderly succession of stages does not fully afford what we mean by this expected connection, for every single stage serves here only as a new and increased exertion of the creative virtuosity of the Absolute, &c., &c." ('Kleine Schriften,' vol. iii. p. 216).

life, the early stages of culture and society, of language and poetry, were connected with the elemental forces of nature. Nature was studied in a human interest as the *alma mater* of Mind.

15.
Vague ideas
of develop-
ment kept
back by
mathemati-
cal spirit.
These aims and tendencies of the Philosophy of Nature were entirely opposed to the tendencies of exact science. The tendency of the latter was, as I have shown in the first section of this work, to discover everywhere fixed mathematical relations, to reduce everything to definite quantities which could be measured and calculated. The ideal of this view was the mathematical formula, the geometrical figure, or the mechanical model. Wherever these could be found or invented, the scientific mind could apply the powerful engine constructed with so much skill from the time of Newton and Leibniz onward: the infinitesimal calculus. Through the workings of this, every fixed relation, form, or movement discovered in natural phenomena became the starting-point for the development of new ideas. A whole train of abstract reasoning was set in motion; this in its course led to new relations and forms requiring only to be reinterpreted in order to reveal phenomena and events which, except for it, would have remained hidden and unknown. Through this powerful engine of research, through this independent movement of thought, the mind acquired an undreamt of mastery over nature, and could for a moment imagine that it had arrived at some of the fundamental data of reality, that it had laid bare the very foundations of existence.

It is not difficult to realise how the many triumphs achieved within a very short period in the regions of mathematical physics and chemistry would create in the minds of those who wielded these powerful weapons of attack a feeling of triumph and exultation, and the consequent conviction that the means were at last discovered by which all the intricacies of natural phenomena would be ultimately unravelled. The human mind felt for a moment as if it had become or would eventually become the master of nature. This mastery was indeed something quite different from that understanding of nature's ways, from that fathoming of her secrets,[1] which Goethe in the very age and in the home of some of the greatest mathematical intellects prophetically declared to be unattainable by scientific methods. To his poetical soul the mathematical aspect was not only repugnant, but unintelligible : it remained one of the few human achievements which Goethe never appreciated.

A knowledge of higher mathematics and skill in its application will, however, always remain the property of a very limited number, even among the highest intellects ; nor is it likely that from this quarter a great revolution in popular thought would have emanated had it not been for the indirect influence which it exerted upon the problems of practical life. And it did this as much by enabling older and well-known modes of practice to be reformed and improved—such was, for instance, the case with the practice of medicine and agriculture,—as also by the creation of a large number

[1] " Geheimnissvoll am lichten Tag
Lässt sich Natur des Schleiers nicht berauben.
Und was sie deinem Geist nicht offenbaren mag
Das zwingst du ihr nicht ab mit Hebeln und mit Schrauben."
—' Faust,' First Part.

of novel occupations which followed in the wake of the inventions of steam, chemistry, and electricity.

The modern age has had to deal not only with the unsolved problems of former ages and of the old world —which it regards in a new light,—but also with new problems which have arisen in the new and artificial world of commerce, manufacture, and industry. This new and artificial world is the creation of science, mainly of mathematical or exact science, and through this its origin in the human mind itself it also contains and increasingly produces such problems as can be most easily and successfully handled by those very methods of exact research of which it is the out-come.

16.
A premature
rationale in
materialism.

Now it is to be regretted that the rationale of this revolution of ideas and pursuits was not given by those gifted minds with whom it originated, but that it was rather left to intellects of a lower order, who were not creators but onlookers merely, to frame a popular philosophy,—a reasoned creed which should stand in agreement with the new conceptions and be intelligible to thoughtful persons among the general public. With very few exceptions, creative intellects have not the leisure nor the taste to reflect upon the ulterior consequences of their theories. Bent upon creation, and frequently unable to control the stream of ideas which rush in upon them from some mysterious depth, they are as it were only instruments in the hands of some unknown power, intent upon incessantly moving forward and impatient of delay. Not infrequently, indeed, we find them in later years, when the rush of youthful ideas is past, pausing to take a speculative review of the general movement which they have let loose and not always been able to control. But such a review rarely does justice either to friends or opponents, as the philosophical and impartial temper must be nursed from youth upward if it is ever to be acquired at all.

All this explains how it came about that a new Philosophy of Nature sprang up in Germany, which in the middle of the century was, more than it is at present, a creative and receptive centre of all movements of thought. This new philosophy turned out to be a premature generalisation, prompted as much by admiration for the new science as by dismay at the apparent fruitlessness of the older philosophy of Nature. Having, besides, lost the understanding for poetical, artistic, and classical ideals which prompted such speculations as those of Schelling and Hegel, it appealed to the material interests which, in the middle of the century, were making rapid progress. This philosophy of nature is known under the name of Materialism.

Few philosophical sects can boast of having given to the world, in a short and lucid form, such a concise manual of its doctrine as the popular philosophy of Materialism has done. Ludwig Büchner's well-known book entitled 'Kraft und Stoff,' which appeared in 1855, may be looked upon as the gospel of Materialism.[1] It ran through many editions; it has been translated into many languages. The title was well chosen, not only,

17.
Büchner.

---

[1] As stated above (chap. iii. p. 197), the materialistic controversy arose in Germany over the psychological discussion as to the nature of the Soul. I have there also given the titles of the other principal writings of the materialistic school.

as was probably intended, because it appeals to familiar
ideas and employs current phrases ; but also, as it turned
out in the sequel, because it is easily translated into other
civilised tongues.   It was published at a time when the
materialistic controversy was at its height, with Carl
Vogt and Jacob Moleschott on the one side, and Rud.
Wagner and Liebig on the other.   It is important to
note that this controversy arose within the regions of
the newly developed science of physiology, which at that
time, through the labours of chemists and anatomists, was
just adopting the experimental methods and mechanical
conceptions which had been elaborated and firmly established in the sciences of dynamics and mathematical
physics.   It was especially the vague idea of a vital
force which had to be combated and expelled from
physiological inquiries.   This was done in a masterly
manner by Lotze [1] in his articles on "Vital Force"

[1] Although Lotze is by far the
most thorough critic of the principles which lie at the foundation
of the materialistic view, his writings (see a list of them *supra*,
p. 6, note) did not create at
the time the impression they deserved.   He was frequently misunderstood, and only that part of
his criticism was assimilated by
contemporary thought in which
he successfully combated the conception of a vital force.   Accordingly we find that in the 'History
of Materialism' of F. A. Lange
(first edition, 1866)—already frequently referred to—little notice
is taken of the important part
which Lotze's writings played in
that controversy.   "It is Lotze—
one of the acutest, and in scientific
criticism one of the surest, philosophers of our day—who did this
involuntary service to Materialism.
The article 'Vital Force' in Wagner's ' Handwörterbuch,' and his
' General Pathology and Thera-
peutic as Mechanical Sciences,'
annihilated the phantom of a vital
force, and introduced some degree
of order into the lumber - room
of superstition and confusion of
ideas that medical men called
Pathology.   Lotze had trodden
the right path ; for, in fact, it is
amongst the tasks of philosophy,
while making a critical use of the
facts supplied by the positive
sciences, to react upon them, and
to exchange for the gold of special
research the results of a wider
survey and a more rigid logic.
He would no doubt have met with
more recognition in this course if
Virchow had not simultaneously
appeared as practical reformer of

(1843) and "The Soul" (1846), as well as in his three works on Pathology and Physiology (1842, 1851, 1852). Ignorant or oblivious of the fact that these writings of Lotze contained only one side of his philosophical creed, Carl Vogt utilised some of the arguments contained therein to attack the somewhat dubious position which the celebrated physiologist Rudolph Wagner had taken up to the questions of the Soul, spiritual existence, and religious faith,—a view which Lotze himself did not share or support. It was easy to show how, by an application of the purely mechanical conceptions of Matter and Force, great progress had been made in the description and explanation of phenomena and processes within the living organism, and how the psychological or metaphysical conceptions of Mind, Soul, Life, and Consciousness contributed nothing towards an exact definition and understanding of these phenomena. It was not clearly recognised at the time, except

Pathology, and if Lotze himself had not adopted a peculiar metaphysic of his own, of which it is difficult to understand how it could maintain itself by the side of his own critical acumen " (English Translation by Thomas, 1880, vol. ii. p. 285). Lange then proceeds to show how Czolbe was stimulated through Lotze's critical destruction of the supersensible notion of vital force to make the destruction of the Supersensible as such the principle of a comprehensive philosophic creed. In this endeavour Lange shows, as had already been shown by Lotze himself in his review of Czolbe's principal work (1855, reprinted in 'Kleine Schriften,' vol. iii. p. 238), how materialism and sensationalism are apt to be insufficiently distinguished. "If

we wish to distinguish strictly between Sensationalism and Materialism, we must give the former name only to those systems which hold to the origin of our knowledge from the senses, and attach no importance to the power of constructing the universe from atoms, molecules, or other modifications of matter. The Sensationalist may assume that matter is mere representation, because what we have immediately in perception is only sensation and not 'matter.' But he may also, like Locke, be inclined to refer spirit to matter. So soon, however, as this becomes the essential basis of the whole system, we have before us genuine Materialism " (p. 286).

perhaps by mathematicians and mathematical physicists, that the manner in which they defined and used the terms matter and force was quite different from the conception of these things in common life and practice. In fact, it took a very long time before, even in the better text-books of physical science, not to speak of those of chemistry and biology, clear definitions were introduced.

In the many editions of Büchner's work which appeared during the second half of the nineteenth century, nothing is more evident than the change which has come over the meaning of such words as matter and force in the minds of naturalists themselves. The first edition appeared at a time when the conservation of energy was clearly understood only by very few of the foremost representatives of the physical sciences, and in later editions of the book, though the word energy is occasionally introduced, there is no explanation of the reasons which brought about the change of terminology. Also the book appeared at a time when the notion of action at a distance still appeared as an axiom in most of the scientific works published on the Continent. Helmholtz had, in the year 1847, published his celebrated tract on the 'Conservation of Force,' which, through its very title, perpetuated the vagueness which still adhered to the term. He also, characteristically of the school in which he was brought up, advanced the proposition that natural phenomena might be considered to be fully explained if they were reduced to attracting and repelling forces acting between particles at a distance. It was the age that was content with what I termed, in the first section of this history, the astronomical and the atomic views of nature. The kinetic view was still only very imperfectly developed. The conception and term energy did not exist. The peculiar properties which attach respectively to vibratory, rotational, and translatory motion, and the definite part which each played in the description of physical phenomena, were not clearly understood. Further, the second law of thermodynamics, the dissipation of energy, was unknown to all but a very small number of the foremost thinkers. And lastly, the theory of descent and of the transmutation of species had not yet been formulated in a manner which made it useful for an exact comprehension of biological phenomena. We can not therefore be surprised that Büchner's work was acceptable neither to the representatives of exact science nor to those of philosophy. It was the first bold attempt to develop a detailed creed by means of conceptions familiar to all naturalists as well as to commonsense, but clearly defined only in the minds of very few amongst the foremost thinkers. What characterised its attitude was a dogmatic assertion of theories which could never be proved, and the use of conceptions which were not clearly defined, and which were in fact assumed to be undefinable. Nevertheless, with terms such as matter and force, the popular mind is accustomed to connect a definite meaning which is founded upon special sensations such as extension, pressure, or weight. Now there is no doubt that the popular mind connects a definite meaning also with such terms as idea and spirit. This is evident from the fact that these

18.
Inadequacy, yet popularity, of "Matter" and "Force."

words can be as little dispensed with in language and literature as the terms matter and force. In using them we appeal in the one case as well as in the other to the meaning which every thinking person involuntarily connects with them, and which is based upon definite subjective experience. Now the two classes of experience, of which the terms matter and force on the one side, idea and spirit on the other, are typical, differ widely; they represent the inner and the outer worlds of experience. It is the desire of philosophy to bring them together in some conception, theory, or creed in which their mutual relation and respective importance are recognised. In this endeavour it is, *prima facie*, just as legitimate to start with the one class as with the other. It depends upon the reality and importance which the thinker attaches respectively to the two sides of experience which way he will choose. Practice, however, has shown that the terms referring to the outer world, such as matter and force, referring as they do to things located in space, are capable of a mathematical definition, and in consequence of a systematic elaboration, to which the other class of terms do not lend themselves. From this it of course does not follow that the latter do not refer quite as much as the former to real experiences, as we have slowly learned that ever so clear a definition is not identical with, and does not necessarily imply, certainty.

19.
Inexactness
of the popu-
lar term
Force.

One of the principal causes of the widespread misunderstanding which existed, and still exists, about the creed of materialism is to be found in the use of the word Force. Not till the term was mathematically defined through the labours of Galileo and Newton did the mechanical sciences start upon that assured way of progress which they are now following. The very fact that, in spite of much mathematical and mechanical knowledge in former ages, it took such a long time before the now current definitions were reached, is an indication how little the popular notions connected with the word force are immediately applicable and useful in scientific inquiry. The sensations which have led to the popular definition of the word force are connected with subjective experiences, such as effort, pressure, resistance, and many others which are not externally visible, which every person, in fact, only experiences for himself. This subjective origin and signification of the term force has led to two difficulties. First, in order to make the term useful for describing external phenomena, the conception must be cleared of those purely psychical or subjective attributes, and only such data must be retained as can be shown to exist for the external senses—that is to say, the conception must be defined by the measurable quantities of time, space, and mass. This was accomplished by measuring a force by the velocity which it imparts to a definite quantity of matter. In this way no knowledge of force as the cause of motion was required ; it was simply measured and defined by its effect; in mathematical language it was equated, or made proportional, to its effect. In the second place, however, the word force, in spite of the clearance through mathematical definition, retained in the popular understanding, as well as in the purely descriptive natural sciences, that subjective meaning

and colouring which is due to its origin in our sensations; and it was not clearly seen that the very same
attributes which made the word so expressive in common conversation and the descriptive sciences were just
those misleading features which had to be got rid of
or eliminated before the term could become useful in
the exact and logically progressive sciences. It was
not seen that the mathematical definition of force
makes the term inapplicable and useless except in cases
where visible and tangible matter and motion in space
are clearly distinguishable. In fact, the mathematically
calculable forces of nature meant nothing else than the
motions of something in space, and where neither
motion nor location in space exist at all, as in mental
phenomena, or where they are only incompletely defined,
as in many biological processes, the whole mathematical
theory of forces is inapplicable. In the early stages of
the materialistic controversy the word force governed
popular philosophy through a misunderstanding: it
appeared, as it were, under false colours.

This false position which the notion of force retained
in popular estimation was strengthened by a further
conception which had been introduced into the mechanical sciences about the time when Lagrange put the
Newtonian laws of motion into a final mathematical
expression: this was the atomic hypothesis upon which
modern chemistry was founded, and which was taken
for granted by the whole school of naturalists on the
Continent. This hypothesis permitted or even forced
the natural philosopher to look upon all those hidden
processes, which neither the naked nor the fortified

human eye could resolve into the movement of particles of matter, as nevertheless constituted in the same
fashion as its cosmic and molar arrangements : they
were conceived to be motions of particles in space.
As these all came under the mechanical theory of
forces, so also it seemed a matter of course that what
were called molecular phenomena must be regarded in
the same manner.

Had the new philosophy of nature contented itself
with clearing the way for a fruitful scientific study of
natural phenomena, and with combating the vague
notions which had been spread through the earlier
philosophy of nature, it would have performed a useful
task. Unfortunately, however, it did not content itself
with this important and well-defined task, but perpetuated the error committed by the earlier school : it
attempted to find a universal principle or principles
by which external and internal, physical and mental
phenomena could be treated alike. This error brought
it into discredit with those who were well aware how
universal, but at the same time how limited in their
application, were the principles of the mechanical
sciences, and equally with those who appreciated the
stimulating and fructifying influence of the idealistic
philosophy. In consequence of this, materialism was
early stigmatised as a dilettante thing, and this character
it has not been able to shake off up to the present day.
It neither understood correctly the nature and scope
of the mathematical principles of exact science, nor
appreciated the fundamentally different nature of all
mental life. In the attempt to bring about a com-

promise, to establish a monistic view, it sacrificed, as it seemed to the one side, mathematical rigor, and, as it seemed to the other, spiritual depth. In the middle of the century nobody saw this more clearly or expressed it more emphatically than Lotze; and the formula by which he explained the position has not lost its validity even at this day, though materialism has considerably modified its fundamental assumptions. What Lotze endeavoured to show was "how universal but, at the same time, how subordinate is the part which mechanism plays in nature."

20.
Lotze's
formula
regarding
mechanism.

But even with regard to the wider problems which legitimately belong to natural science and natural philosophy, materialism itself did not greatly assist in their solution; though, in the course of the controversy, a gradual but slow clearance of ideas took place. Among these problems two stood out as of paramount interest and importance. The first refers to nature as a whole: this we may term the cosmological problem. The second refers to the system of ideas by which we try to comprehend nature. So far as the first of these problems is concerned, there is no doubt that the writings of the materialistic school, and foremost those of Büchner, tended to spread among the reading public a large amount of useful knowledge referring to the discoveries which science had made in the course of the first half of the nineteenth century, by which great regions of knowledge had been opened out or remodelled, and which were especially interesting and useful in the departments of biology and medicine.

21.
Success and
failure of
Materialism.

This knowledge, however, though extensive, remained more or less fragmentary and purely illustrative. The unification which was attempted, but never carried out, consisted largely in a monotonous iteration of the terms Matter and Force which were never defined, and in an equally vague reference to Nature and the Laws of Nature, which the reader could hardly help regarding as active principles. The desire which is always felt in such discussions to collect the many statements, illustrations, and analogies into a comprehensive view, led involuntarily to the use of such words as Nature, Causality, Natural Laws, &c., in a way similar to that in which the older philosophy of Nature had used the terms Mind, the Absolute, &c., without clearly defining them.

In a former chapter which treated of the problem of the Inner World, I endeavoured to show how psychology, in its recent developments, has gradually eliminated the word Soul as a conception which was not useful in a methodical treatment of mental phenomena. Nevertheless the word Soul and its various synonyms have remained indispensable in general language and literature. In a similar manner natural philosophy continually uses such words as Nature, though, for scientific purposes, the idea of nature as a whole vanishes as a superfluous conception. The essence, reality, and unity of natural phenomena are as little explained or defined in natural science as the essence and reality of mental phenomena are discussed in many modern treatises on psychology. In both cases, conceptions such as Soul or Nature lurk in the background as personified agencies which comprehend and command the multiplicity of phenomena, recalling but not explaining to us their essential and underlying unity.

As is the case with the notion of force, so also the conception of "Laws of Nature" creates considerable difficulty, and this difficulty arises from similar causes. The word Law is taken from conditions of human society, and denotes written and acknowledged statutes by which the conduct of a number of human beings living together is regulated. In this instance the rule of conduct is superimposed upon the condition of things which would have existed if no definite order had been formed. Such laws are subject to change, can be enforced or disregarded; the law is, as it were, something outside of the society which is supposed to acknowledge and follow it. In a similar manner the popular mind is apt to look upon the laws of nature as something outside of natural things; the latter being considered to be in a state of chaos before the system of laws which constitute the order of nature is introduced. Just in the same way as the forces of nature figured in the popular understanding as something outside or behind the different motions which they bring about, so the laws or order of nature figure in the popular mind as a kind of formal arrangement to which the otherwise disorderly elements have to submit. Now, in the same way as the exact science of nature defines the forces merely by their physical effects in the motions of particles and masses of matter, so it sees and knows the laws of nature only through the actual behaviour of things external. This behaviour exhibits uniformity and regularity, and the law of nature is merely an abstract expression of this regularity of external occurrences. As forces can be seen and measured only in the motions they produce, so the laws of nature can be seen only in the multitude of examples or single instances and occurrences which exhibit sameness and regularity. In fact, laws do not govern the things of nature; they are simply the abstract expression of the properties of these things themselves. The attributes of the word law which recommend it to the popular understanding as a something which turns chaos into order and maintains it, are derived from the artificial statutes of a human society, and do not belong to the laws of nature.

It is easily seen that those views of nature which I termed above the astronomical and atomic views — through the conception of forces acting at a distance and of external things as consisting of larger or smaller but discrete particles of matter—lent themselves readily to those popular conceptions of natural forces and natural laws which it was the first duty of a true philosophy of nature to get rid of. And, indeed, these prejudices and hidden attributes which recommended the mechanical conception to the popular understanding were got rid of quite as much by a change in the scientific ideas themselves as through a critical analysis such as was contained in the polemical writings of Lotze and other prominent thinkers. The change I refer to has been fully described in former chapters, which dealt with the kinetic and physical views of nature. The former destroyed the idea of imponderable matter and of action

22.
Change in scientific conceptions.

at a distance, the latter put into the place of the forces
of nature the conception of Energy.   In the same
degree as these modern ideas have been introduced into
the scientific view of nature, the older astronomical and
atomic views have been somewhat discredited or thrust
into the background.[1]

It then dawned upon some of the leaders of scientific
thought that science when it deals with natural phenomena is not tied to one rigid system of conceptions, that
its aim is not to explain but simply to describe the
things and processes around us in the simplest and most
convenient manner ; that different methods exist by
which this can be done, but that none of these methods
or systems give an insight into the nature of things, but
only afford to the thinking mind the means of connecting the processes and phenomena of nature with
each other.   This logical connection leads from the

[1] As already shown in the first
section of this History, however
(chapter vii., p. 198), the atomic
or corpuscular view has latterly
been strengthened by recent research in electrical science, which
favours a corpuscular theory of
electricity, and to this we may add
the importance which Mendelian
theories attach to definite units
of character in living organisms :
these are assumed to persist and to
be transmitted through heredity,
frequently after having been apparently lost or become useless
"survivals." It seems, indeed, impossible for an ultimate explanation
to conceive of a plenum or continuum in space without assuming
at the same time that such a
plenum contains discontinuities
which admit of portions of this
plenum being defined, and preserving their identity : this introduces
again the atomic view, the conception of discrete particles.   The
vortex-atom theory of Lord Kelvin,
" the discovery of the types of
permanent motion, which could
combine and interact with each
other without losing their individuality," seems so far the only
image which we possess of discontinuities in a plenum depending
entirely on different modes of
motion of the same all-pervading
substance termed the universal
fluid or Ether.   It is, however,
also interesting to note how the
celebrated author of the vortex-
atom theory latterly abandoned his
own hypothesis — "the idea that
a mere configuration of motion
suffices " — as not likely to be
" helpful in respect to crystalline
configurations, or electrical, chemical, or gravitational forces." See
ante, vol. ii. p. 182, note 2.

known to the unknown, from that which is visible to that which is invisible, and constructs an artificial picture or model in and through which the external world can be mentally grasped and studied.

But it took a long time before this was clearly recognised by either naturalists or philosophers. The thinker who in the middle of the century probably represented the clearest views on the subject was, as I mentioned above, Lotze himself. His interest, however, did not lie in the direction of assisting the exact sciences,[1] but rather in defining the correct position of the biological sciences and in preparing the way for an idealistic conception of things by showing the insufficiency of all purely mechanical or materialistic reasoning. In the meantime a great variety of interests combined to effect that change in our fundamental notions which has taken place in the course of the latter half of the nineteenth century. Germany and England each made independent and original contributions; France, as we shall see, took up the subject much later, but then likewise in an original spirit.[2]

23. New criticism of fundamental notions.

To begin with this country: Mill had already in his ' Logic' analysed some of the fundamental notions em-

24. J. S. Mill.

[1] Lotze's earliest published tract, his "inaugural dissertation," had the title ' De futuræ Biologiæ principiis philosophicis.' 1838.

[2] It should, however, not be overlooked that Charles Renouvier already in the first edition of his ' Essais de critique générale' (1854-1864), and still more in the second edition (1875), gave a very clear analysis and criticism of the fundamental notions employed in the sciences of nature and mind, and it

is significant of the age when he wrote that his criticisms were as little estimated at their true value as were those of Lotze ten years earlier in Germany. Both Lotze and Renouvier seem to have been entirely unknown to Mill as well as to Spencer, whose writings, through their influence on followers as well as on opponents, effected a gradual clearance of first principles in this country. There is, however, no doubt that for a whole generation,

ployed in scientific inquiry. A great revolution in

scientific thought followed the publication of Thomson
and Tait's 'Natural Philosophy' and of Clerk Maxwell's
writings. We know that with these names is mainly
connected the introduction of the conception of energy
into all the better text-books of physical science. To
Thomson (Lord Kelvin) we owe two important steps in
the philosophy of nature as distinguished from natural
philosophy: first, the early recognition (1852) of that
universal property in natural phenomena in consequence of which they exhibit, not only the conservation,
but also the dissipation or degradation [1] of energy, a

which roughly covers the third
quarter of the century, Lotze was
the only thinker who in a consistent
and complete manner dealt with
the principles and conceptions
which underlie the natural sciences,
examining also critically to what
extent they could be utilised in
the formation of a comprehensive
creed. He did not, however, publish any concise exposition of his
views ; they are scattered about his
systematic as well as his polemical
and more popular writings. At
regular intervals he delivered
courses of lectures on the subject,
beginning with the year 1846,
and ending in the year 1877 ;
the dictated lecture syllabus of
the last course was published
in 1882. The following extract
shows how Lotze, long before this
view was generally entertained,
had a perfectly up-to-date conception of the task of natural science
and of the purposes for which
scientific principles are defined and
employed by scientific thinkers :
" The natural sciences are, indeed,
not exclusively led by the demands
of practical life : thus they do not
aim wholly at the practical com-

mand of the external world. They
are, indeed, contented with a certain theoretical command over the
same—i.e., they strive to determine from present facts their necessary antecedents and to foretell the
necessarily following ones, also to
determine those to us unobservable
circumstances which coexist with
these which are accessible to our
observation. They have gained this
object by analysing experience and
extracting general rules regarding
the connection of phenomena ;
further, by framing hypotheses
regarding the actual facts which
underlie the changing phenomena,
and which make it possible through
the application of those general
laws to calculate from the given
parts of the course of things the
continuation of the same in conformity with actual existence."
Introduction   to   Syllabus   on
'Naturphilosophie,' sect. 2.

[1] The term degradation imports
an attribute which is not purely
mechanical : it suggests that natural processes may belong to a
higher or lower grade. But for
the purely mechanical view the
difference is only that of more or

feature which distinguishes all physical (actual) processes from merely mechanical (artificial) contrivances;
secondly, in a very different direction he had already
(1845) taken a great step in advance by showing how
two seemingly quite different ways of approaching
electrical and magnetic phenomena—the "action-at-a-
distance theory" of Continental mathematicians, such
as Poisson, and Faraday's "Lines of force," filling space
continuously,—led, through mathematical language, to the
same results.[1] Tait carried on a lifelong battle with
the older conceptions of attractive and repulsive forces,
assisted in replacing in physics the conception of particles
moving about in empty space by the conception of a
plenum, and ended by suggesting that the word "force"
should be discarded as an unnecessary and misleading
term. Maxwell worked in the same direction, though
with more caution and impartiality, through his small
tract on 'Matter and Motion,' and still more by building
up a large portion of the sciences of electricity and mag-
netism on the basis of the conception of Energy and its
distribution in space, discarding latterly the mechanical
models which he had previously invented as illustrations of Faraday's "lines and tubes of force." Incidentally a controversy arose between Tait and Herbert
Spencer as to the illegitimate use which the latter

less, of larger or smaller; there is
no difference of degree in any other
sense. Another sense or meaning
is introduced only with reference
to the observing or thinking mind
which derives more pleasure, more
use, from some sensations than from
others, and accordingly puts a
greater value on the former than
on the latter. The well-known
"Demon" of Clerk Maxwell shows
by a fiction how, for beings otherwise constituted than we are, the
most degraded forms of energy or
motion might be of the same value
for practical purposes as molar
motions are for us.

[1] See *ante*, vol. ii. p. 72.

made of such vague conceptions as the "persistence of force."

In Germany the introductory lines of Kirchhoff's Lectures on "Mechanics" mark an era in scientific thought: "Mechanics is the science of motion: we define her task: to describe completely and in the simplest manner the motions which take place in nature." This definition implies a great deal more than it actually states. In confining itself to description it discards explanation — *i.e.*, the search after the causes, and, still more, after the ends of motion. And as to the simplest manner of the description Kirchhoff adds significantly: "It is quite imaginable that doubts can exist whether one or the other description of certain phenomena is the simpler; it is also thinkable that a description which to-day is the simplest that can be given may in the further development of science be replaced by one still more simple." Since Kirchhoff wrote these words, they have been endlessly repeated by men of science and philosophers alike, to all of whom they have given much occasion for reflection.

Kirchhoff's work appeared in 1876. Before that time two thinkers of eminence had been led, through purely scientific interests, to an analysis and discussion of the axioms of physics and dynamics. They were:

Wilhelm Wundt, who published in 1866 a tract "On the physical axioms and their relation to the principle of causality," and Ernst Mach, who published in 1872 a tract "On the history and origin of the principle of the conservation of energy." To these two writers we owe, in their further publications, the most successful attempts towards a systematic exposition of the fundamental conceptions on which the exact sciences are built up. Especially are we indebted to Prof. Mach for applying his epistemological principles in three important regions of scientific inquiry: in the science of dynamics, which he has to a large extent remodelled; in the analysis of sensations; and lastly, in the theory of heat. Views similar to his have been elaborated in this country, as it appears independently, and in an original manner, by W. K. Clifford, and, more systematically, by Prof. Karl Pearson in his 'Grammar of Science' (1st edition, 1892). In fact, they do not widely differ from opinions already expressed by Herbert Spencer in several of his earlier works, notably in his 'Principles of Psychology' (1st edition, 1855), and his 'First Principles' (1862); they had been popularly explained in his replies to criticisms that appeared in the 'Quarterly Review' (1874) and the 'British Quarterly Review' (1873). These replies are reprinted in the third volume of his 'Collected Essays.'

28.
Clifford and
K. Pearson.

The rationale and result of all these discussions can be summed up in the thesis: that the whole system of conceptions by which the exact sciences try to describe the observable and known phenomena of nature, and to predict those that are unknown and frequently escape observation, is symbolic, a kind of shorthand, unconsciously invented and perfected for the sake of convenience and for practical use; that the leading principle is that of Economy of Thought.

Through this latter conception Prof. Mach's opinions come into contact with those of Richard

29.
Economy of
Thought:
Mach and
Avenarius.

Avenarius, who published in 1876 a tract with the significant title " Philosophy as thinking of the world according to the principle of least action." On the other side Prof. Pearson comes in contact with Herbert Spencer in his attempt to conceive our fundamental notions as unconsciously elaborated and perfected through inheritance. This is supposed to work through adaptation; strengthening and firmly establishing in the human mind and in the course of many generations fundamental notions and axioms which are best fitted to symbolise and describe the experience gained through the senses. These are further elaborated by science into a convenient and practical system of abstract reasoning on things natural.

This idea of adaptation and inheritance explains how certain fundamental notions and axioms appear to be *a priori* (in the sense of Kant) for the individual human mind, although they are *a posteriori*—*i.e.*, empirically acquired, so far as the civilised human race is concerned; and it further explains how it comes about that the human mind is nowadays in possession of a framework of ideas with which it can construct a correct and useful, though merely symbolical, image or model of the facts and processes of nature. Another school, who do not necessarily accept the Spencerian or Darwinian theory of evolution and adaptation, are forced to consider this adaptation of human ideas to real phenomena as a matter of happy chance or good luck which might equally well not have existed at all.[1]

[1] Dr Kleinpeter has summarised the theories of Mach, Stallo, Clifford, Kirchhoff, Hertz, Pearson, and Ostwald in an interesting treatise, ' Die Erkenntnistheorie der Naturforschung der Gegen-

We thus see that in the second half of the nineteenth century great changes were effected, not only in the views which the scientific mind takes of nature, but still more regarding the importance and value which philosophers attach to any and every scientific view of nature and to the fundamental conceptions on which it is based.

In the first instance, we find that nearly all the leading ideas employed in scientific theory and explained in scientific text-books have been either replaced or remodelled. Thus the word force has been either more clearly defined and circumscribed in its meaning, all subjective attributes being stripped off which originally attached to it, or it has been discarded and replaced by the term energy. Something similar has happened with regard to the term matter, which has

wart' (1905). He closes his exposition with the following curious words : " A world could be conceived in which no science was possible. That it has come to be otherwise can only appear as an accident. Such an accident is, for us, the regularity of the course of nature in consequence of which our conclusions as to the succession of phenomena, which would have as such only provisional value, acquired practically unlimited value ; it does not occur to us so much as even to think of an alteration of the laws of nature, although we cannot say that such alteration were impossible. A second favourable circumstance which places our science practically much higher than it is theoretically, is the similarity of human beings with regard to the intellectual process : were this not so, then what one individual finds would have no meaning for another. Then not only the real, but also the formal sciences would be impossible. We see, therefore—what is frequently overlooked—that also their possibility depends on a supposition which, fortunately, is practically always fulfilled, although we have no right whatever to expect it. Thus we see that the actual existence of science in the ordinary sense of the word depends on the fortunate, but accidental, reality of two suppositions, to expect which we have no theoretical right whatever. In the foregoing, the ways have been described in which man has tried to gain knowledge : that he has succeeded in this is a mere accident ; from our point of view we cannot assert anything more " (p. 141).

been replaced by that of mass or inertia. And lastly, the term cause has not escaped a similar process of remodelling, both so far as efficient and final causes are concerned. The school represented by Prof. Mach inclines in the direction of abandoning, for scientific purposes, the special term cause, putting in its place merely antecedence and sequence in time; Prof. Wundt inclines in the direction of doing away with the conception of substance; and Prof. Ostwald opposes the conception of matter and substance in favour of the conception of energy, agreeing to some extent with—but further elaborating—the position already taken up by Tait in this country. Yet most of these thinkers have not refrained from constructing a philosophy of nature upon one or several of the older or more recent terms which are employed in purely scientific reasoning. Thus we have, *inter alia*, the modern cosmological theory of the gradual and ultimate equalisation of temperature in the universe, and the extinction of the phenomena of life;[1] a theory built up by Helmholtz, upon Lord Kelvin's conception of the degradation of energy and the irreversibility of all natural, as distinguished from purely mechanical, processes. We have Prof. Ostwald's recent "Philosophy of Nature," built up exclusively on the conception of energy, discarding the conception of matter and substance as leading to materialism, but introducing the conception of development in the form of the second law of thermo-

---

[1] It may be well to remark here that the discovery of radium by M. and Mme. Curie in 1898, and the remarkable phenomena of radio-activity, may very considerably change our ideas as to the sources of heat and the gradual cooling of the sun.

dynamics. And lastly, we have the theory of evolution *par excellence*, as set out in Herbert Spencer's synthetic philosophy, with its alternating processes of differentiation and integration, and its recurrent cycles similar to those elaborated by the Stoics in ancient times.

But whilst it is interesting to learn what are the ultimate consequences to which any special and useful line of exact reasoning leads, it cannot be denied that little philosophical interest attaches to most of these mechanical theories. In order to be scientifically consistent they have to strip the fundamental notions they employ of those psychological attributes, of that subjective colouring which attaches to them, and which alone makes them suitable for describing the phenomena of life and consciousness, so as to draw them into the circle of exact scientific discussion. They alone are of supreme interest to philosophical thought. So far as nature herself is concerned, these her most interesting traits seem to be preserved and revealed only in a synoptic (poetical and artistic) as opposed to a purely analytic and synthetic (scientific or exact) contemplation of her phenomena and events.

30. Want of philosophical interest attaching to mechanical theories.

In order to solve the problem of nature in the philosophical sense—*i.e.*, in the sense in which Schelling and the earlier philosophy of Nature understood it—it would be necessary to introduce into the system of purely mechanical ideas some term which specifically denotes, symbolises, or describes the essential character of the processes peculiar to the living and conscious world. And this term cannot itself again be reduced to purely mechanical conditions and attributes. Nor will it be

sufficient to leave this essential factor in a shadowy
background, as Schelling did with his " Absolute," Hartmann with his " Unconscious," and Herbert Spencer with
his " Unknowable." [1] The term must have a deeper
meaning, and this meaning must be founded on some
subjective or psychical experience accessible to every
thinking person, and possessing as much immediate
evidence and intuitive certainty as those fundamental
data—such as space, time, motion, and mass—upon
which exact science builds up her theories.

[1] To this we might add Haeckel's " Law of Substance "—which as a cosmological first principle includes the conservation of matter and energy—were it not for the fact that this contains really no new idea, but reminds us only of Spinoza and other precursors (such as Büchner) whose opinions Haeckel partially adopts. It may here be remarked that it is not pre-eminently among such natural philosophers as define and handle the fundamental principles of the mechanical view with the greatest accuracy and efficiency that we find the materialistic view of the world prominently put forward. It is rather by those thinkers—notably biologists—who are forced by training and habit to use such terms as mass, force, energy, cause, and purpose in a wider and more pregnant sense than a purely mechanical definition would permit, that we find these conceptions employed to explain both mechanical and mental phenomena and the claim put forward to establish a monistic creed. Mathematicians such as Gauss, Cauchy, Kelvin, Hertz, and others have always laid down their mechanical principles with the greatest caution, indicating or distinctly expressing the conviction that the phenomena of life and mind belong to an entirely different sphere of thought and research. A remarkable expression in this direction will be found in H. Hertz's posthumously published ‘Principles of Mechanics’ (1894): "It is certainly a justified caution with which we confine the realm of mechanics expressly to inanimate nature and leave the question open how far its laws can be extended beyond. In truth, the matter stands thus, that we can neither maintain that the internal phenomena of animated beings obey the same laws nor that they follow other laws. Appearance and common-sense favour a fundamental difference. And the same feeling which induces us to relegate as foreign to the mechanism of the lifeless world every purpose, every sensation of pleasure and pain, the same feeling makes us hesitate to deprive our view of the animated world of these richer and more varied attributes. Our principle, sufficient perhaps to describe the motion of lifeless matter, appears at least *prima facie* to be too simple and limited to describe the manifoldness of even the lowest phenomena of life " (p. 45).

The earlier philosophies of the century recognised this, and attempted in various ways to supply the want. Considering the prominent part which abstract theories had played at the time, both in the departments of the exact and the historical sciences, and the great change which had thus come over men's opinions, especially on the Continent, it was natural that thought itself, or as it was termed "the Idea," should be considered as a definite factor and propelling force in the world, and that the system in which this conception was carried out, the Hegelian system, should attract much attention and appreciation. It was owing to three distinct causes, to which I have already had occasion to refer, that this attempt was discredited, and that it lost favour in the eyes of thinkers of various degrees and opinions. The first of these causes was the difficulty of defining more clearly the different stages through and in which Thought or "the Idea" operated in nature and in history, and the arbitrariness which was thus introduced into philosophical reasoning. The second cause was the return to the purely critical position of Kant, according to which thought plays only a formal and regulative and not a creative part in mental progress. The third, and probably the most important, cause, however, was the fact that the ideals and aspirations which filled the minds of people during and after the epoch of the Revolution, and which were then living forces, faded gradually away before a great multitude of practical and detailed tasks which had to be performed and of obstacles which had to be overcome, and which brought in the wake of them much doubt and discouragement.

Thus the panlogism which found its extreme expression in the Hegelian philosophy lost its hold of the philosophical mind, or continued to live only in branches of inquiry which were either purely mechanical, like the exact sciences, or purely critical and expository, like the historical sciences.

II.

The possibility of approaching the philosophical problem of Nature from a different side had already been shown much earlier in the century. This was done in a short treatise which Schopenhauer published just at the time when the philosophy of nature as suggested by Schelling was losing its attractiveness, and when the new science of Biology was laying the foundations of its subsequent brilliant development.[1] It consisted in an application of the fundamental idea of Schopenhauer's system to a subject which had been only imperfectly handled in his first great work.[2] Although it is true

31.
Schopen-
hauer's phil-
osophical
view of
Nature.

[1] As to the chemical and physiological discoveries which produced the reform of Biology during the second quarter of the century, see the first section of this History (vol. i. p. 194 *sqq.*; vol. ii. p. 208 *sqq.*)

[2] The treatise appeared in the year 1835 with the title ' On the Will in Nature,' seventeen years after the completion of the principal work, and purported to be a " discussion of the verifications which the philosophy of the author since its appearance had received through the empirical sciences."

In the Introduction Schopenhauer lays great stress upon the fact that his metaphysic was the only one which harmonised with the physical sciences, inasmuch as both had independently arrived at the same point. In this way he considers that his metaphysic differs even from that of Kant, which " leaves a wide gap between its own results and experience, and still more from that of Schelling, which is secretly abstracted from the empirical sciences, and only discovers *a priori* what it had really learnt *a posteriori*."

that to the influence of Kant's practical philosophy, and of the extreme version which Fichte subsequently gave of it, the fundamental conception of Schopenhauer must be traced back, it is nevertheless his undoubted merit to have first attempted to elaborate a comprehensive philosophical creed in which the ultimate Reality, the foundation and root of all existence, is conceived to be that power which in human consciousness figures and operates as the Will or active principle.[1]

As the interest in the logical system of Hegel subsided, and the shallowness of the materialistic doctrines revealed itself, the position which Schopenhauer took up, and which he had defended with a great wealth of illustration and with much literary talent, attracted at last popular attention and exerted that influence upon scientific,[2] academic, and popular thought which it has

32.
Opposed to Paulogism and Mechanicism.

[1] Schopenhauer gives very lucidly the rationale of his whole conception in a passage which is worth transcribing. "The empirical confirmations which I am going to mention refer one and all to the kernel and main point of my doctrine, the real metaphysic of the same — i.e., to that paradoxical, fundamental truth that what Kant opposed as the 'Thing in itself' to its mere appearance (termed by me presentation) and what he considered to be absolutely unknowable, that, I say, this thing in itself, this substratum of all phenomena, and as such of the whole of nature, is nothing else than what is immediately known and familiar to us, what we find in our own inner self as the Will; that in consequence this Will, instead of being, as all philosophers have hitherto assumed, inseparable from the Intellect, or even a mere result of the same, is fundamentally different and quite independent of it, capable of existing and manifesting itself without it : such being the case in the whole of nature, from the animal creation downwards : further, that this Will, as the only Thing in itself, the only truly Real, the only original and metaphysical principle in a world in which everything else is mere appearance, gives to everything, whatever it may be, the power through which it can exist and act, &c." (Schopenhauer, Werke, ed. Griesebach, 2nd edit., vol. iii. p. 202.)

[2] In the second edition of his tract, which appeared in the year 1854, Schopenhauer shows that his fundamental principle as well as

not lost down to the present moment.   There is no
doubt that what has been termed the voluntaristic
tendency in recent philosophy is largely to be traced
back to the impression which Schopenhauer's writings
have made on many of the foremost representatives of
modern thought, although few of the latter now follow
the special lines into which he developed his central and
fundamental idea.

For we must not overlook the fact that Schopenhauer
was not primarily led to his speculations by a special
interest in nature and natural phenomena, such as
actuated Schelling.   He branched off from the main
trunk line of idealistic thought at a point anterior to
Schelling's philosophy of nature, which at the time does
not seem to have much impressed him.   His philosophical
tradition was Kantian, his inspiration came from Plato,
and, though he barely admitted it, he was influenced by
Fichte.[1]   And he remained completely entangled in the

other contributions of his had not
escaped the notice of eminent
scientists, notably medical authorities, such as the physician, J. D.
Brandis of Copenhagen, and the
ophthalmologist, Anton Rosas of
Vienna, but that they in an unpardonable manner did not acknowledge their indebtedness to him,
and this leads him into a lengthy
diatribe against the dishonesty of
German literary practice, taking the
opportunity to contrast with it the
gentlemanly tone of 'The Edinburgh
Review,'—an admission which he,
however, retracts in the third
edition.

[1] This apparent resemblance to
Fichte, from whose writings many
sentences may be collected which
are almost identical with some of
Schopenhauer's, is, however, accompanied by a fundamental difference
which separates him from Fichte
and Fichte's immediate followers,
and may probably be one of the
reasons why he never acknowledged his indebtedness to Fichte.
The difference is well brought
out in an excellent sketch of
Schopenhauer's doctrine by Dr
Lehmann in a recent publication
already referred to ('Grosse Denker,' vol. ii. pp. 269-297). "Schopenhauer's Will is a blind and aimless
impulse, and here lies the difference
which separates decisively his conception of Will from that of Kant
and Fichte.   Kant's Will is altogether a rational power opposed in
its nature to desire, not an impulse or something impulsive but
a power through motives of reason
to resist impulse : it has in reality

formula which contrasted the phenomenal and the noumenal worlds, the " Thing in itself " and its appearance. The main object and root of his philosophy was to define the " Thing in itself," and this he did by identifying it with the Will. And he still further emphasised and perpetuated this contrast by placing in opposition the Will and the Intellect, as the two fundamental principles or factors in all reality. In the sequel he certainly did utilise the discoveries and theories of the rapidly progressing natural sciences as illustrations of his main thesis, and in the tract referred to, " The Will in Nature," he arrived at a philosophy of nature and a conception of her innermost essence.

Still Schopenhauer belonged to the idealistic and romantic school of modern philosophy and retained many of the prejudices and preconceptions with which that school started, as also that supreme belief in the

33.
Schopenhauer an idealist and romantic.

nothing but the name in common with Schopenhauer's Will. Not less is Fichte in the fundamental traits of his philosophy rationalistically inclined, and in addition much more than Kant teleologically minded. Indeed, without exaggeration, we may say that his system is the most consistent attempt to explain without remainder what *is* by what *ought* to be. . . . The Self (or ego) is for Fichte essentially a rationally determined function, its real essence being rational and moral determination. . . . With Schopenhauer, on the other side, it seems at first problematical how moral categories can be applied at all to the blind and aimless Will which appears most directly in the forces of inorganic nature" (p. 285). Dr Lehmann then shows how, so far as the ethical problem is concerned,

the way was indicated to Schopenhauer by Schelling's tract (1809) on the " Essence of human freedom," which Schopenhauer praised as an excellent paraphrase of Kantian doctrine in which, however, Schelling did not give Kant his due. We shall revert to this when dealing in a subsequent chapter with the Ethical problem. It should be noted that Schopenhauer's introduction to the idealistic philosophy came through Schulze in Göttingen and Fichte in Berlin, at a time (1809-1813) long after Fichte's separation from Schelling, whose philosophy of nature lay outside Schopenhauer's course of studies. His interest in physical and physiological questions was probably awakened by Goethe, who, in 1814, secured Schopenhauer's interest in his own colour theory.

power of abstract human reasoning which characterised
it.   To the same school belonged likewise Eduard von
Hartmann, and, although it cannot be claimed for his
philosophy that it has had any direct influence on
European thought outside of Germany, it would be
unjust, in this connection, not to take note of this last
brilliant attempt to bring the fruitful and original ideas
which are contained in the idealistic systems of Schelling,
Hegel, and Schopenhauer into some connection and
harmony.   In the middle of the century there had
been created, and there continues to exist, among many
thinking persons outside of the schools, the desire for a
comprehensive and reasoned creed in which some fundamental principle is shown to pervade, and to afford an
interpretation of, all nature, mind, and history.   It
seems natural that the great world-problem which both
Hegel and Schopenhauer attempted to solve by speculation, and which Schelling never lost sight of, should not
have been entirely abandoned without a last and supreme
effort to solve it; and this with due recognition of the
enormous change which had come over modern thought
through the rapid development of the natural sciences.

At the time when Hartmann published his first great
work (1869), the leading ideas just referred to still
formed, if not active convictions yet certainly very living
reminiscences in the minds of many thinking persons in
Germany, nor was the expectation absent that some
new system would arise affording a rational and comprehensive answer to the foremost problems of life,
mind, and society, which had become more pressing

34.
As also Von
Hartmann.

35.
The philoso-
phy of the
"Uncon-
scious."

as time went on.[1] These circumstances explain, to a large extent, the quite unexpected welcome with which Hartmann's work was greeted. The name he gave his philosophy and the title of his book indicated that he combined the transcendental with the realistic movement of thought, and arrived at speculative results through inductive methods. Instead of opposing Will and Intellect, as Schopenhauer did, he co-ordinated them as equally real attributes of the Absolute, which he terms the Unconscious, and the existence of which, under different forms, he traces in nature, in mind, in art and language, as the deep-lying background or hidden agency. Whereas Hegel extols the Intellect and Schopenhauer depreciates it, Hartmann shows that

---

[1] A variety of more or less systematic attempts were made towards the middle of the century, some of which created, at the time, considerable interest, though most of them have not had any lasting influence on European thought as a whole. Leaving aside the writings of earlier philosophical naturalists, such as Oken ('Naturphilosophie,' 3rd ed., 1843), Steffens ('Anthropologie,' 1823), Schubert ('Geschichte der Seele,' 1830, and several subsequent editions), and Oerstedt ('Der Geist in der Natur,' 1850), these attempts dealt mostly with questions of mental and religious philosophy, less with the philosophy of nature. One of Schelling's contemporaries was the theosophist Franz von Baader (1765-1841), who in his 'Fermenta Cognitionis' (1822-1825) directed special attention to the writings of Jakob Böhme, after having already influenced Schelling in that direction. Chr. Fr. Krause (1781-1832), an original thinker, attempted to unite the "subjectivism" of Kant and Fichte with the "absolutism" of Schelling and Hegel in a system termed Panentheism. His originality, especially in ethics and philosophical jurisprudence, has been acknowledged by eminent writers on this subject. Anton Günther (1785-1863), a Roman Catholic priest, opposed the pantheism of Schelling and Hegel by a "dualism" and "theism" modelled upon Cartesian ideas. He had, in a certain circle, a considerable influence, and numerous followers and admirers, but his philosophy, like that of de Lammenais in France, was rejected at Rome (1857). The only thinker who, in addition to the leaders of thought mentioned in this chapter, has received increasing attention not only as a theologian but latterly also as an original philosopher, is Schleiermacher. I shall deal more fully with his speculations in later chapters of this section.

the Will and the Intellect are equally real attributes of the Absolute, similar to Extension and Thought in the systems of Descartes and Spinoza. And he arrived, more than any of his predecessors, at his result through inductive reasoning, based upon a wealth of material gathered from the most recent discoveries in natural science, psychology, and mental history.

For our present purpose it may be noted that Hartmann's principle of the Unconscious is the last suggestive conception utilised for the solution of the problem of nature in the sense in which this problem existed for the older philosophies, and that it has, in one form or another, found its way into the reasoning of many modern schools. Hartmann was not slow to detect this, and many of his subsequent writings had the object of showing how the leading idea of his system is more or less distinctly stated or implied in the writings of earlier and contemporary German thinkers.[1]

[1] But also of showing how they have failed in giving a definite expression to this principle. One of Hartmann's latest deliverances dates from the year 1900, when he published in the 'Archiv für Systematische Philosophie' (vol. vi. pp. 273-290) an instructive summary of the different ways in which the conception of the Unconscious has clearly or confusedly crept into modern philosophical literature; whereupon it may be remarked that, with the exception of Mill and Spencer, hardly any but German philosophers are referred to. He there finds no less than nineteen different uses of the term Unconscious, which he groups under four main headings :—

(a) The epistemological Unconscious ;

(b) The physical Unconscious ;

(c) The mental Unconscious ; and

(d) The metaphysical Unconscious ;

thus indicating how the conception makes its appearance in dealing respectively with the problem of Knowledge, the problem of Nature, the problem of the Soul, and the problem of Reality. In spite of the infinite pains that Hartmann has taken to drive home the fundamental idea of his philosophy, I doubt whether he has succeeded in making that idea generally intelligible and useful. Some of the fine distinctions which he makes, e.g., between the Unbewusste and the Bewusstlose are hardly translatable into other languages. His disciple Prof. A. Drews published, shortly after Hartmann's death in

But on the whole the ideal view of the problem of nature was gradually losing its hold of the thinking mind, and has had to give way to the purely naturalistic view, which limits itself to describing and calculating natural phenomena and to the elaboration of a system of conceptions by which this can be most conveniently and completely effected. The philosophical task is then reduced to a criticism of these conceptions, fixing their logical definitions and the range of their applicability and usefulness; and this with the further distinct object of showing whether the more complicated phenomena of life, mind, and society can be described and interpreted in terms of those fundamental conceptions which have done such eminent service in the exact sciences; or whether, on the other hand, a new principle will have to be introduced in order to make these phenomena intelligible. As stated above, this task had, in the middle of the century, been already approached more or less methodically and in a narrower or wider sense by such writers

36.
The ideal
view dis-
placed by
the natural-
istic.

1906, two articles which he has reprinted under the title ' Das Lebenswerk Eduard von Hartmann's,' and which together with Hartmann's own summary just mentioned may be recommended as an introduction to Hartmann's philosophy. Prof. Windelband in his ' History of Philosophy ' gives the following summary of Hartmann's view : "That higher consciousness which is termed the Unconscious, and which is supposed to form the common living background of all conscious individuals, Hartmann tries to trace as the active essence of all processes in physical and mental life : it takes the place alike of Schopenhauer's and Schelling's ' Will in nature,' of the vital force of earlier physiology, and of the entelechies of the system of evolution. It unfolds itself above all in the teleological connections of organic life. In this respect Hartmann has also very effectually combated materialism, inasmuch as his doctrine points everywhere to the uniting spiritual and living ground of things : he for this purpose employs in the happiest way a great wealth of natural knowledge, although he deceived himself when he thought that his speculative results were gained by inductive methods " (4th German ed., 1907, p. 542).

as the Mills in England, Comte in France, Lotze in
Germany, somewhat later by Du Bois Reymond, Charles
Renouvier, Claude Bernard, Stanley Jevons, and others.
But the merit of having devoted himself without prejudice and bias to the solution of this critical problem in
a comprehensive and exhaustive manner is undoubtedly
due to Prof. Wundt of Leipsic. It is interesting to
see how in the course of his researches he has been led
to adopt a position which, though arrived at on quite
different lines, has tended to confirm and strengthen
what we may term the voluntaristic movement of thought.
This emphasises the active principle of the will, and gives
clearer expression to a tendency of thought which we
find already in Maine de Biran in France, in Alexander
Bain in England, and, in an extreme form, in Schopenhauer and Hartmann in Germany : to it Prof. Wundt
has given an independent expression. How he gradually arrived at his position he has himself described
in an article entitled " On Psychical Causality and the
Principle of Psycho-physical Parallelism," published in
the year 1894.[1] " I learned first," he says, " in the

[1] The writings of Prof. Wundt
are extremely numerous and voluminous, covering an enormous
field of research unparalleled by
any contemporary thinker, with
the exception perhaps of Hartmann.
But whereas Hartmann put forward
the main idea of his philosophy in
one of his earliest works, giving
currency to certain watchwords
and a certain form of pessimism,
the one - sided accentuation of
which he has been at great pains
to mitigate in his later writings,
the really valuable and original
conceptions of Wundt's philosophy
— the notion of creative synthesis and that of the growth of
spiritual energy — lie buried in
such an enormous mass of detailed exposition, of criticism, and
of scattered articles, that it is only
with difficulty that the student arrives at any tolerably concise view of
Wundt's philosophical system. We
must therefore be especially grateful to Dr E. König for his excellent Monograph on Wundt (' From-
mann's Klassiker der Philosophie,'
xiii.), to which may be added
Prof. Höffding's account of Wundt's
philosophy in his ' Moderne Philosophen,' pp. 6-38.

processes of visual sensation, to appreciate that act of creative synthesis which became to me gradually a leader by whose hand to gain also a psychological insight into the development of the higher functions of the imagination and the intellect, towards which the older psychology had given me no assistance. As I then approached the temporal relations in the flow of our ideas, a new insight was given me into the development of the functions of the Will,—of the external out of the internal, of the complex out of the simple, an insight also into the intimate connection of all psychical functions, which we artificially separate by such abstract names as intelligence, feeling, and willing: in short, I recognised the indivisibility and homogeneity of mental life in all its phases." [1]

The idea mentioned in this passage has gradually gained the supremacy in Prof. Wundt's speculation. Actuality appears more and more as the central idea of his philosophical creed, and he traces this factor back not only into the elementary and primary functions of

37.
Wundt on
Actuality.

[1] This explanation was published in the year 1894 in the ' Philosophische Studien ' (vol. x.), and has since been reprinted in the 2nd volume of ' Kleine Schriften,' 1911, see p. 111. This collection of his scattered contributions in two volumes will much facilitate the study of Wundt's philosophy, though, in consequence of the alterations introduced in the reprint, a reference to the original articles would, in the interest of a history of the development of Wundt's ideas, be necessary. In a note on pp. 103 and 104 of the reprint, Wundt traces his valuable conception of creative synthesis far back into the period of his researches into the physiology of visual sensations. This happened in the year 1858 or 1859, when he combined the nativistic and empirical theories of visual perception in his theory of " complex local signs." He then recognised that he had " to do with a process which was fully intelligible through its elements, but which was nevertheless, compared with them, something new, — a creative synthesis of these elements. And so this simple process of perception seemed to me to throw a clear light on the essence of psychical processes in general, &c."

the conscious human mind, but also into nature, which appears to him as an earlier stage in the self-development of mind, not unlike that conception which inspired the earlier writings of Schelling. With Wundt, however, as with many modern philosophers, this idea of development of the conscious out of the unconscious, of the organic out of the inorganic, has gained greater definiteness through the assimilation of Darwinian ideas. As this conception gained the ascendancy in Wundt's speculations, he has devoted himself more and more to those regions of philosophical thought which, in this country, are comprised under the name of mental and moral, as opposed to natural, philosophy. He has therefore, less than Schopenhauer, Lotze, and Hartmann, developed a philosophy of nature. His thought is, moreover, governed by what may be termed a monistic tendency : it aims at finding a universal principle, which pervades and unites the different regions of existence.

This tendency he has in common with many other recent thinkers, some of whom occupy fundamentally different positions, according to the central principle or conception which they adopt. But however varying the latter may be in different systems, it leads essentially to one characteristic, viz., to the attempt to bridge over the great gulf which, to the common-sense view—a view termed appropriately by Wundt " Naïve Realism,"— exists between the outer and the inner world, between matter and mind. Alongside of those various attempts to arrive at a monistic conception of things there will always run another and equally powerful current of thought, which emphasises not only this fundamental dualism but also many more special discontinuities, which show themselves in all our varied experience, and which may possibly be reducible to that main difference or contrast ordinarily described by the terms nature and mind. This tendency has shown itself, in the second half of the nineteenth century, also in the philosophy of nature, and this quite as much with thinkers who have approached the problem of nature in the purely scientific interest as with those who have done so in a philosophical spirit. It is the phenomenon of Discontinuity which has, more and more, attracted the attention of a large section among recent philosophers.

38.
Rise of the problem of Discontinuity.

In fact, the most emphatic expression of this difficulty was given by a natural philosopher who marched in the van of those modern reformers of science who discarded not only as useless, but as harmful for scientific purposes, that entire complex of ideas which invaded German philosophy during the first third of the century : the idealistic and romantic movement. Emil du Bois Reymond had acquired considerable reputation among philosophers through his 'Researches in Animal Electricity' (1848), which contained in their preface a strong recommendation of the exact methods and an equally strong denunciation of the conception of vital forces.[1] He was accordingly classed for a long time among the

39.
Du Bois Reymond.

[1] This Preface, as also the Addresses hereafter referred to, are reprinted in the Leipsic edition of E. Du Bois Reymond's 'Collected Addresses' (2 vols., 1886-87). This collection, with its valuable literary notes and references replying to numerous criticisms, has now been republished with additional matter. The collection forms together an important record of the beginnings, the progress, and the gradual reform of philosophical thought on the subject of the study of nature, the principles of natural knowledge, and the comprehension of nature as a whole.

materialists, perhaps with more correctness than was the
case with Lotze and Virchow, the principal protagon-
ists in that celebrated battle with antiquated notions.
It was therefore with all the more authority that he
undertook, in the year 1872, to address the meeting of
German naturalists at Leipsic " On the Limits of Natural
Knowledge." The address created an enormous sensation, led to a great controversy and to many further
explanations by adherents as well as opponents, was
republished many times, and was latterly followed by
an equally celebrated oration before the Berlin Academy
(1880) entitled "The Seven World Riddles."[1] These
two deliverances contain a characteristic definition of
the ultimate bearing of recent scientific ideas upon the
great philosophical problems. And, inasmuch as they
emanated from a foremost representative of modern scientific reasoning, and out of the centre of that eminent
scientific circle which counted among its members Helmholtz, Kirchhoff, and Virchow, and perpetuated the traditions of Johannes Müller, it deservedly commands, up to

---

[1] This is the first and most concise specimen in modern literature
of those attempts to revive, solve,
or declare insoluble the ancient
riddle of the Sphinx. On this
Kuno Fischer has a fine ironical
remark in the concluding paragraph of his monumental 'History
of Modern Philosophy': "The
meaning of the world is not a
riddle as our modern *Welträthsler*
are fond of saying, in order either
to play or to vanquish the Sphinx,
but a problem which man puts to
himself, for he will and must know
the essence of his own being. The
progressive solution of this problem, which can only take place in
the course of the ages of the world,
is the history of philosophy, for
the ages of humanity belong to the
theme of the problem, as in olden
times the four-footed, two-footed,
and three-footed ages of man belonged to the theme of the Sphinx.
In this connection with the ages of
mankind, in this light of a progressive solution of the world-problem,
Hegel was the first to regard the
history of philosophy" (vol. viii.,
p. 1190).

the present day, the serious consideration of thinkers of all shades of opinion.

In the first of these addresses Du Bois Reymond adopts—probably without being aware of it—a view somewhat akin to that of Herbert Spencer, who had published, already in 1860, the first part of his System, in which he puts forward the conception of the Unknowable as the underlying ground or power in and of everything.[1]   Similarly Du Bois Reymond maintains that the natural philosopher must admit that the ultimate conceptions of all exact or mathematical science, the conceptions of matter and force, cannot be explained or further analysed,—that they constitute for him an insoluble enigma.   In addition to this he maintains that a further equally difficult problem arises when we attempt to explain how the underlying substance of which matter and force are the attributes can, under certain conditions, feel, desire, and think ; in fact, the psychical attributes of the underlying substance constitute a second enigma.   The second enigma has occasion-

---

[1] It is indeed remarkable that E. Du Bois Reymond's first address ends with the celebrated 'Ignorabimus' with which Herbert Spencer, more than ten years earlier, had started his systematic speculations, expressive of an idea which has received popular currency through Huxley's 'Agnosticism.' It is also significant that Du Bois Reymond rouses himself out of this humiliating and deadening conviction of our fundamental ignorance by the following reflection : The natural philosopher "now finds solace and elevation in work which augments the treasure of human knowledge, increases by wholesome exertion the powers and capabilities of our race, extends our dominion over nature, refines our existence through the enrichment of our mind and beautifies it through the multiplication of our enjoyments.   From that depressing 'Ignorabimus' the natural philosopher rouses himself again by the dying Septimius Severus's watchword to his legions : 'Laboremus'" (loc. cit., vol. i. p. 235).   Truly an anticipation of modern pragmatism !

ally been identified with the problem of the nature and origin of life or animation, and it is significant that Herbert Spencer himself, in one of his latest deliverances, admits the insolubility of this problem.[1]

In the second address mentioned above, Du Bois Reymond further analysed the two enigmas which respectively have to do with the most elementary, or molar, and the most complicated, or mental, phenomena into a larger number of definite problems. Of these he details seven. Four of them, the essence of matter and force, the origin of motion, the elementary sensations, the freedom of the Will, are declared to be insoluble. The further three problems : the origin of life, the apparent purpose in nature, and the origin of language, he does not hold to be eventually equally insoluble, though they are so at present. His view can be defined by saying that the mechanism which suffices to explain the processes in inorganic nature and plant-life does not suffice for the processes of sensation and consciousness : the latter bring into biological development something new, which, as an epiphenomenon, rises out of the inner essence or nature of matter. Du Bois Reymond, however, significantly allows the assumption that these different problems or enigmas may be essentially one, thus approaching still nearer to Herbert Spencer's view.

40.
Haeckel's
Monism.

A speculation somewhat on the same lines had already been started by Ernst Haeckel in his first and greatest work, the ' Generelle Morphologie.' As this work had only a moderate circulation, he further expounded and popularised his philosophical creed in a series of writings,

[1] See *supra*, vol. ii. p. 438.

of which 'The Riddle of the Universe' is one of the latest and best known. It cannot be said that philosophically anything essential has been added by him to the arguments advanced by Büchner on the one side and by Du Bois Reymond on the other.

It is true that Haeckel brings in a great wealth of illustrations largely derived from his own original work; also that he started with a full appreciation of the Darwinian ideas of development, whereas his forerunner, Büchner, introduced these ideas mostly only in the later editions of his work. Otherwise it makes little difference whether we call the underlying essence matter (with Büchner) or substance (with Haeckel); and, if we compare Haeckel's view with that of Du Bois Reymond, we find that both thinkers admit the necessity of introducing into their conception of the ground of everything a spiritual or psychical attribute without which they think it impossible to approach the World-problem. This is a distinct advance upon Büchner's apparently mechanical view,—an advance through which both thinkers rise, in a similar way to Herbert Spencer, above simple materialism. As stated above, neither Büchner's nor Haeckel's views have been taken seriously by philosophical thinkers, although both have had a marked influence on popular thought and literature, especially in Germany. The fact that their works are only incidentally mentioned by historians of philosophy abroad may be traced to the following causes.

It is not an unusual thing to find that scientific specialists who have attained to eminence through original discoveries in definite lines of research or through theoretical views which have opened out new vistas of scientific thought, are tempted to apply their principles and habits of reasoning to a larger region than that in which they were originally at home, and this without a previous critical examination as to the applicability or validity of the notions they have employed. The proof of the correctness of these notions lies for them in the practical success which they have achieved in a more or less restricted field. The temptation to extend the use of any serviceable tool or instrument applies as much to logical as to mechanical devices, and we find this to be the case as much in science and philosophy as in practical life, in the arts, industries, and business. And this temptation, so far as abstract thought is concerned, is greater where we employ ideas and terms which have a double meaning, pointing, as it were, in two directions. This is the case pre-eminently in the natural sciences as distinguished from the mathematical sciences on the one side and from the mental sciences on the other. All naturalists, including also eminent representatives of the medical profession, deal with fundamental notions which are applicable to phenomena lying on the border-land of the purely physical and the purely mental, of the outer and inner world, of inanimate and animated nature. The words or terms also by which these notions are expressed in language were originally derived from that border-land, and are, in their full and direct meaning, only applicable there. Those who successfully operate with these notions are frequently led to believe that they possess in them a master-key which unlocks both worlds, affording a view into the external and the internal alike.

Further, workers on this border-land can apply the rigid methods of the exact sciences only to a limited extent; they are everywhere led, by observation as well as reflection, into departments where rigid definition is impossible; especially the medical teacher is many times obliged—as Du Bois Reymond himself has honestly confessed—to teach things which he does not know. Like all practical professions, the medical profession embraces a totality of things, many of which are matters of conjecture rather than knowledge. Thus it comes about that philosophical speculations issuing from naturalists are in the same degree more intelligible to the popular mind as they are unsatisfactory to those who start with mechanical or mathematical notions and habits of thought on the one side, or with exclusively psychological and subjective notions on the other. For the former complain that the naturalist uses many words and terms not in a rigidly scientific sense, and the latter complain that he deals with purely psychical phenomena by analogy with external processes which are not really analogous, and give only a semblance of insight.

41. Loose use by naturalists of physical concepts.

As stated above, it has taken thousands of years before such terms as matter, force, energy, potential and actual, have been sufficiently cleared of their purely subjective attributes to enable them to be mathematically defined. In the literature of the naturalist, the physiologist, and psychologist, these terms, however, still occur in a wider sense and are indispensable, denoting something additional and different from the restricted sense in which they occur in the purely exact sciences. In addition to these terms we have others like substance, cause, life, &c., which lend themselves only with difficulty to any rigid definition at all.   The same is also the case with the terms of the more recent vocabulary introduced by the theory of descent, such as : selection, the survival of the fittest, the struggle for existence, and lastly, evolution.   No thinker has done more to show how all these notions, with their various expressions in scientific and popular language, are ultimately derived from subjective states, than Professor Ernst Mach of Vienna. His views are independently represented in this country by Prof. Karl Pearson.   The matter cannot be more clearly put than was done by the former thinker in the following passage taken from his 'Science of Mechanics.' [1] " The division of labour, the restriction of individual inquirers to limited provinces, the investigation of those provinces as a life-work, are the fundamental conditions of a fruitful development of science.   Only by such specialisation and restriction of work can the economical instruments of thought, requisite for the mastery of a special field, be perfected.   But just here lies a danger —the danger of our overestimating the instruments with which we are so constantly employed, or even of regarding them as the objective aim of science.   Now, such a state of affairs has, in our opinion, actually been produced by the disproportionate formal development of physics.   The majority of natural inquirers ascribe to the intellectual implements of physics, to the concepts, mass, force, atom, and so forth, whose sole office is to revive economically arranged experiences, a reality beyond and independent of thought.   Not only so, but it

42.
Mach on the
limitation
of mechani-
cal physics.

[1] 'Die Principien der Mechanik,' 1st. ed., 1883, p. 476 *sqq.*

has even been held that these forces and masses are the real objects of inquiry, and that, if once they were fully explored, all the rest would follow from the equilibrium and motion of these masses. A person who knew the world only through the theatre, if brought behind the scenes and permitted to view the mechanism of the stage's action, might possibly believe that the real world also necessarily had a machine-room, and that, if this were once thoroughly explored, we should know all. Similarly, we too should beware lest the *intellectual* machinery, employed in the representation of the world on *the stage of thought*, be regarded as the basis of the real world. . . . Such an overestimate of physics, in contrast to physiology, such a mistaken conception of the true relations of the two sciences, is displayed in the inquiry whether it is possible *to explain* feelings by the motions of atoms ? Let us seek the conditions that could have impelled the mind to formulate so curious a question. We find in the first place that greater *confidence* is placed in our experiences concerning relations of time and space; that we attribute to them a more objective, a more *real* character than to our experiences of colours, sounds, temperatures, and so forth. Yet, if we investigate the matter accurately, we must surely admit that our sensations of time and space are just as much *sensations* as are our sensations of colours, sounds, and odours, only that in our knowledge of the former we are surer and clearer than in that of the latter. Space and time are well ordered systems of sets of sensations."

Let us see what effect this modern analysis of the work of science and the processes of scientific reasoning

43.
Effects of
modern
analysis on
view of
nature as a
whole.

has had on our view of nature as a whole. For we must not forget that the problem of nature, taken philosophically, cannot be solved by detailed researches in restricted areas or by conceptions which refer merely to special phenomena; further, that even if we multiply these researches indefinitely, they will not lead to a comprehensive view of nature as a whole. Just as in psychology, the enormous growth of detailed knowledge in the domain of the sensations has not approached, but rather led away from, an answer to the problem of the Soul or the essence of the inner world, and has ended by throwing overboard the former term altogether; so likewise the enormous bulk of natural knowledge of the phenomena and relations in nature has led us away from a comprehension of nature as a whole, and this for two reasons :—

In the first place, the so-called unification of knowledge, of which we hear so much in recent times, and which has become a watchword among philosophical naturalists, such as Spencer, consists in reducing the great variety of forms and processes which we observe to a small number of general relations expressed in logical or mathematical formulæ. These tend to become more and more purely geometrical when we have to do with the study of natural forms (Morphology), and more and more genealogical when we have to do with living things (Biology). It is true—as I have had ample opportunity to show in earlier chapters—that one of the great influences of Darwinism upon natural science has been to lead the way out of the laboratory, the museum, and the dissecting-room, into the great world and expanse

of nature herself, to the study of the things and forms
of nature, not in their abstract and artificial positions,
but in the concrete and in their actual environment; also
to replace the statical by the dynamical view of things.
Nevertheless, the introduction of the general formulæ
of selection, adaptation, and evolution, especially when
generalised after the fashion of Spencer, is only another
instance of the tendency to bring the study of individual
things under general principles and rigid formulæ, to
look upon the actual things and phenomena of nature
merely as examples of general processes, in the same way
as earlier naturalists looked upon natural specimens as
modelled according to definite and rigid types.

Besides being the only way in which the human
mind seems to be able to grasp a great mass of detail
and make its knowledge applicable in individual cases
and for practical purposes, it seems to afford a special
delight to recognise in that which is novel and
unknown, traits of that which is familiar and known;
still more to find oneself in possession of a leading idea
and guiding principle, by the instrumentality of which
unknown regions can be explored and new phenomena
discovered which would otherwise have remained con-
cealed.   Such a fascination attaches, for instance, to
the "periods" of Mendeleef (in chemistry), and to the
search for the "missing link" of Haeckel (in biology).
Especially to those who are fortunate enough to find
out such a resemblance, their discovery acts with a
magical force, with a kind of spell, compelling them
and their disciples to regard the new formula or the
happy generalisation as a master-key which unlocks

everything.[1] From this spell of mechanical connections, geometrical configurations or genealogical trees,
to which we may add statistical regularities, it has
always been the object of a deeper philosophy of

[1] Three thinkers of the very first
order have given expression, quite
independently of each other, to
this reflection. The first is Goethe,
who frequently dwells on the subject, but most explicitly in a
conversation with Eckermann in
the year 1824 : " As soon as one
belongs in science to a narrow confession, the unbiassed truthful view
is at once gone. The decided
Vulcanist will always see things
through the eyeglass of the Vulcanist, in the same way as the
Neptunist and the adherent of the
recent ' elevation' theory will do
so only through his own. The
view of all such theorists, who
are obsessed by a special exclusive
aspect, has lost its innocence, and
objects no more appear in their
natural purity. Whenever such
students give an account of their
observations, we do not, in spite
of the greatest personal veracity,
receive in any way the truth of
the object ; we receive things ever
only with the taste of a strong
subjective flavouring. But I am
far from maintaining that an
unbiassed correct knowledge stands
in the way of observation ; rather
the old truth stands, that we really
have only eyes and ears for what
we know. The professional musi-
cian hears, in the concord of the
orchestra, every instrument and
every single note ; whereas an out-
sider remains embarrassed through
the massive action of the whole.
So also the man who merely enjoys
himself sees only the graceful surface of a green and flowery meadow,
whereas the eye of the observing
botanist is struck by the infinite
detail of the most various single

plants and grasses. . . . In science
we meet persons who, by dint of
too much erudition and hypothesis,
never get back to seeing and hearing. With them everything turns
rapidly inside ; they are so much
occupied with what they are pon-
dering, that it happens to them as
to a man in a passion who passes
his nearest friends on the road
without seeing them. Observation
of nature requires a certain quiet
purity of the inner self which is
disturbed by nothing, nor pre-
occupied. . . . Would to God that
we all were no more than good
labourers ! Just because we want
to be more, and carry about with
us a large apparatus of philosophy
and hypotheses, we spoil things."
The second is Ruskin, who, at
the end of the third volume of
' Modern Painters,' makes the same
reflection, though he applies it
somewhat differently : " This comparative dimness and untraceable-
ness of the thoughts which are
the source of our admiration is not
a fault in the thoughts at such
a time. It is, on the contrary, a
necessary condition of their sub-
ordination to the pleasure of Sight.
If the thoughts were more distinct
we should not *see* so well ; and
beginning definitely to think we
must comparatively cease to see.
. . . It is evident that a curiously
balanced condition of the powers
of mind is necessary to induce full
admiration of any natural scene.
Let those powers be themselves
inert, and the mind vacant of
knowledge and destitute of sensibility, and the external object
becomes little more to us than it
is to birds or insects ; we fall into

nature to liberate the human intellect; to point to the diversity and individuality of natural things rather than to their sameness and repetition, and to see in this divine confusion the very essence of nature and the source of all that makes her interesting and delightful to the human soul.

To this philosophical view, which touches the real problem of nature, all the labours of the purely scientific mind seem to unveil only the skeleton around which nature herself throws, in endless ways and varieties,

the temper of the clown. On the other hand, let the reasoning powers be shrewd in excess, the knowledge vast, or sensibility intense, and it will go hard but that the visible object will suggest so much that it shall be soon itself forgotten, or become at the utmost merely a kind of key-note to the course of purposeful thought." The third important contribution and confirmation of this reflection is to be found in Charles Darwin's own account of the development of his mind in the course of his life and through the influence of his studies: "In one respect my mind has changed during the last twenty or thirty years. Up to the age of thirty or beyond it, poetry of many kinds, such as the works of Milton, Gray, Byron, Wordsworth, Coleridge, and Shelley, gave me great pleasure. . . . Formerly pictures gave me considerable, and music very, great delight. But now for many years I cannot endure to read a line of poetry. . . . I have also almost lost my taste for pictures or music. . . . I retain some taste for fine scenery, but it does not cause me the exquisite delight which it formerly did. . . . This curious and lamentable loss of the higher æsthetic tastes is all the odder, as books on History, Biographies and Travels, and Essays on all sorts of subjects, interest me as much as ever they did. My mind seems to have become a kind of machine for grinding general laws out of large collections of facts, &c. " ('Life and Letters of Charles Darwin,' 1st ed., vol. i. p. 100). In the face of this self-depreciation, this honest and modest confession, we may safely maintain that only through the early delight in nature, the intimate communion with her and the breadth of observation, did Darwin's mind succeed in fastening upon some undiscovered features of her life as a whole: as he indeed has done more to cultivate and encourage the *vue d'ensemble*, the synoptic view of nature, and to counteract the purely analytic and synthetic methods of the earlier natural sciences, than any other naturalist in recent times. And having, from the deep source which the love of nature revealed to him, drawn such a full and overflowing measure, we may feel thankful that he spent his life in dispensing the same for the benefit of science and the delight of his many followers and admirers.

a clothing of flesh and blood which brings with it beauty, sublimity, and elegance, pointing to and revealing something deeper and higher: the individual and the spiritual, for which no mechanical formula can be found.

In the second place, the analysis of the methods of science, as it has been most exhaustively carried through by Prof. Mach, urges the reflection: that the conceptions of science, or what are usually termed the laws of nature, such as we know them, do not refer at all to nature as a whole, but that they are inevitably bound up with finite departments and occurrences. For, as they only refer to regularities—*i.e.*, to numerous repetitions in time and space, or to frequent examples,—they cannot, of course, be applied to the whole of nature, which is unique, and cannot be compared with limited portions of itself as they may exist in time and space. This argument alone suffices to prove how illegitimate it is to extend such considerations, for instance, as are afforded by the second law of thermo-dynamics (the dissipation of energy), to the world as a whole. Accordingly, here also we find a limit placed to our speculations as to Nature in her entirety, regarding which we cannot apply in any way the term finite or infinite; inasmuch as one thing is certain, that all our knowledge of things natural refers only to a portion, and that an extremely small portion, of the universe.

44.
Artistic
view of
nature.

Those thinkers who, in spite of these limits which encompass our scientific study of nature, nevertheless desire to gain a deeper insight into the very essence and meaning of the world which surrounds us, have attached themselves to the views that have found expression in the poetical and artistic representation of nature; nor is it merely accidental, it is, indeed, highly significant, that the nineteenth century, which has witnessed the ever louder proclamation of the mechanical conception, has, on the other side, witnessed the growth, in various forms, of naturalism in poetry and art: it has developed not only the mechanical, but also the poetical, interpretation of Nature.

This naturalistic tendency in poetry and fiction showed itself already in the latter half of the previous century, and this independently in the three countries which specially interest us. The greatest influence, however, which this movement has had upon philosophical thought emanated from the personality and works of Goethe, to whom we may trace back most of the attempts which have been made abroad to supplement the purely mechanical (abstract) by a spiritual philosophy of nature, which latter claims to approach nearer to her real essence than the former does. It is also notable in Goethe's conception of nature that, in spite of all the realism which is characteristic of it, the one aspect towards which it is absolutely blind is the mathematical aspect.

Following up a suggestion to which the history of philosophical thought has already led us on sundry occasions, we may say that the peculiar view of nature represented by Goethe, as well as by some of the fore-

45.
Goethe as representa-tive of the synoptic view.

most naturalists [1] of modern times, is the synoptic view. To this view every object of contemplation, be it large or small, physical or mental, is a whole, a totality, which, in the actual " Together " of its apparent parts, reveals to us something which is lost as soon as we start to dissect or analyse it. In the most emphatic way this view looks also at nature as a whole. Its rationale may

[1] It would be transgressing the limits of the present section of this History to do more than merely hint at this uniting link of the scientific and the poetical aspects of nature. The subject can only be adequately treated in the third section, which should deal with individual poetic and religious Thought, The instances of poetical or artistic minds of a high order being at the same time naturalists, in the stricter sense of the word, are not frequent, though they exist. Not to mention Lionardo da Vinci, who belongs to a much earlier age, we have, in the eighteenth century, Albrecht von Haller in Germany, Goethe in the beginning and Ruskin in the middle of the nineteenth century. On the other side many of the foremost naturalists of the earlier school, like Buffon in France and Humboldt in Germany, and an increasing number in more recent times, have displayed not only a scientific but a very keen artistic appreciation of natural objects and of nature as a whole. As quite recent instances I may mention Sir Archibald Geikie and Prof. John Arthur Thompson of Aberdeen. No doubt my readers will think of many other examples of the close alliance between the poetical and the scientific love of nature. But Goethe stands out as a unique instance of the immediate influence of poetry, both on science and on philosophy. He clearly pointed out that Sight, and not Thought, represents the beginning and first stage both for the poet and the naturalist. The German language has for this a distinctive term in the word *Anschauung*, which is not identical with Intuition, for it does not necessarily include the mystical element implied by the latter term. It is interesting to see how, probably without much knowledge of German or any acquaintance with Goethe's frequent discourses on this subject, Ruskin, in the 3rd vol. of ' Modern Painters ' (1st ed., p. 288), uses the word Sight in exactly the same meaning as belongs to the German word *Anschauung*. As in this sense it has not become current in psychological discussions, I have, as stated above (p. 193 n.), adopted the word "synopsis," denoting by this term " the power of fully perceiving any natural object." It "depends on our being able to group and fasten all our fancies about it as a centre, making a garland of thoughts for it in which each separate thought is subdued and shortened of its own strength in order to fit it for harmony with others,—the intensity of our enjoyment of the object depending first on its own beauty, and then on the richness of the garland. And men who have this habit of clustering and harmonising their thoughts are a little too apt to look scornfully upon the harder workers who tear the bouquet to pieces to examine the stems " (Ruskin, *loc. cit.*, p. 290).

be expressed in Goethe's words: "Nature is neither kernel nor shell; She is everything at once." To this view the distinctions of external and internal, and of the different parts of any natural object, or of nature as a whole, disappear. This view lies on the borderland of poetry and science; of the intuitive grasp of the artist on the one side and of the combined analytic and synthetic processes of the naturalist on the other. It produces, in some instances, the inspired creations of the poet and artist, and in others the ingenious contrivances of the artificer and mechanic.

But let it not be supposed that science, with all its analytical and synthetical devices, can, for any length of time, dispense with this synoptic view. New trains of reasoning, leading to new scientific theories, to fruitful generalisation and extensive applications, begin not with thought but with Sight. And if, by patient watching and observation, some small trace of the enwoven cipher is discovered and the scientific mind is tempted to follow this up by itself and to forget that it forms but an element of the whole, it nevertheless only as such enables us to take one new step in the comprehension of nature and the world in their actual reality.

46.
This view indispensable in science also.

It was under the immediate influence of Goethe's synoptic view of nature and its intimate connection with his poetical genius that Schelling strove to make it more immediately fruitful for that philosophical comprehension of nature which, during the most striking phase of his progressive speculations, saw also in art its final consummation. This attempt was doomed to failure;

the logical process is, by itself alone, incapable of grasping the whole, or can do so only to a moderate extent by that creative synthesis which has been remarked on by thinkers like Lotze and Wundt as a unique property of mental, as distinguished from mechanical, activity.

Though Schelling abandoned the task which he had set himself in his earlier philosophy of nature, led away by his growing interest in the ethical and religious problems, he, nevertheless, maintained to the end that the purely inductive processes of the natural, as well as the logical deductions of the philosophical, sciences formed only one way of approaching reality. He stigmatised it as " negative," and maintained emphatically that such must find its counterpart and consummation in what he termed a " positive" philosophy. To the end of his days he was in search of this without being able to find for it a satisfactory and adequate expression. Yet in the meantime, while he was labouring at this unfulfilled task, others, partly with and partly without the help which his earlier suggestive writings afforded, founded or developed that positivism which he was in search of.

47.
Double use
of the word
positive.

And it is significant to see how the very term Positive was used simultaneously by Comte in France and by religious thinkers in Germany to denote a return from metaphysical abstractions to experience and observation of things natural and human on the one side, to individual and historical religious experience on the other. And, besides this, we have the naturalistic tendency of poetry and art in this country represented by Wordsworth, Coleridge, and, later on, by Ruskin; whilst in

Germany the logical categories of Hegel's System guided, in many instances, historical research before the overwhelming volume and achievements of which they themselves gradually vanished into the background.

The two systems of philosophy, however, on which the twofold aspect of reality suggested by Goethe and Schelling had the greatest influence were those of Fechner and Lotze. The speculations of the former, as contained in his earlier writings, had, as already stated, little or no influence on contemporary philosophical thought, and have only recently received the attention they deserve. But in the writings of Lotze we find all through a distinct appreciation of Schelling's endeavour as well as a very definite and original expression of the truth which lay in Schelling's repeated cry for a positive, as opposed to a purely negative, philosophy.

48.
Fechner and Lotze.

In many passages of his earlier writings, most clearly, however, in the last book of his ' Microcosmus,' in which he gathers up the different threads of his many-sided reasoning, Lotze points out that, to the unbiassed human observer, the world presents itself in three distinct aspects. There is first of all the world of many individual things which are, to look at, bewilderingly intricate and overpowering. Into this apparent chaos and unceasing rush of phenomena the human intellect has, by degrees, imported a certain amount of order, by discovering fixed regularities termed " Laws of nature." The totality of these we can oppose as the world of forms, a definite and ever-growing complex, to that which we now term the world of things or realities.

49.
Lotze's distinction between things, and forms, and values.

These two worlds, of which the second is constructed
by the human intellect through the observation and study
of the first, become, as thought progresses, more and more
separate : the world of forms, the laws of nature, appear
as necessities, as a fixed and unalterable framework in
which individual things and occurrences are encased.
The other, the world of things, the endless examples in
which these forms and laws seem to be realised, appear
on the other side as if they might also have been quite
different.

It is conceivable to the human mind that the rigid
and eternal laws of nature might also be realised in
numberless other worlds than the world which surrounds us. The "this," the "here," and the "when"
present themselves accordingly as something fortuitous,
however much the many instances and examples may be
subject to the same fixed rule and order. To escape,
however, from this conception of a merely fortuitous
concourse of things, from this doctrine of chance, a
further system of realities offers itself to the unbiassed
human observer. These are not the things and processes
outside of us nor yet the phenomena of an inner life, but
the standards of value or worth which the human soul
involuntarily applies in its judgments, and in the culture
of which man finds the real task of civilisation. The
existence of this world of poetical and ethical values or
ideals furnishes, according to Lotze, the solution of the
world problem and also of the problem of nature in the
sense anticipated by Schelling, and the formula would
thus be : that the things which surround us are the
material *in* which, the laws of nature the forms *through*

which, the world of values, or the Ideals, are, or have to
be, realised.

This view of Lotze, which has been strengthened and
made more definite by subsequent analyses of the
scientific and exact methods employed in the physical
and natural sciences — among which those of Prof.
Mach have been by far the most thorough and exhaustive—involves two special problems for a philosophy
of nature. The first of these problems was also clearly
defined about the same time in the writings of British
psychologists. The most definite expression was given
to it by Dr Chalmers when he said that, in addition to
the rigid laws and forms or the mechanism of nature, we
must assume a definite "collocation" of the material,
the specific disposition of which at any moment constitutes the world picture or the empirical aspect of the
universe. This collocation might be considered by some
as a mere fortuitous concourse of elements, by others as
the work of design.

The attempt to get over the difficulty by moving
the initial collocation of things backward into a
shadowy past, and, in addition, by substituting a
simpler state of things than we now witness, does not
solve the problem, although much labour and ingenuity
have been spent over it. Also the assistance which was
derived from the mechanical theories of development or
evolution, firmly established through observation by
Darwin and philosophically' elaborated by Herbert
Spencer in England and later on by Haeckel in
Germany, though enthusiastically accepted in some
quarters, has nevertheless proved illusory. It has been

50.
New prob-
lems.

many times exposed as such,—nowhere more clearly than in Prof. James Ward's celebrated lectures.[1] Moreover, the pushing back of the definite collocation of things which is taken as the basis of mathematical or evolutional reasoning introduces further difficulties. As it was clearly recognised that, according to scientific discoveries, a period must have existed when our planetary system, at least, was without life, the problem arose to explain, on purely mechanical principles, how life, and later on conscious life, have been evolved out of dead matter. In fact, the manifest discontinuities which the history of creation presents had to be somehow explained away. This forms the second problem implicitly contained in Lotze's formula. To put it concisely: the problem of Nature involves, besides an explanation of the æsthetical or poetic value or meaning of her aspects, the two problems of the "Contingent" and the "Discontinuous." Lotze's own view as to these two cardinal questions may be shortly stated as follows.

The question of the Contingent—*i.e.*, of a certain collocation or arrangement of things in space, exhibiting, as Schelling had already stated, an element of freedom or choice, or, as others would state it, an element of chance —refers to the way in which, at any definite moment in time, things are spread out before us in space. And it may here be noted that it really does not matter very much what moment of time we choose as the basis of our

---

[1] 'Naturalism and Agnosticism' (2 vols., 1st ed., 1899). This important publication has been followed in 1911 by a further series entitled 'The Realm of Ends or Pluralism and Theism.' I shall have an opportunity of dealing with the systematic view developed in these writings in a future chapter of this section, which will be entitled "Of Systems of Philosophy."

speculations or as the beginning, not of things themselves, but of our logical and scientific reasoning about
them. The Discontinuous, on the other side, presents
itself when, adopting a certain definite collocation which,
it must not be forgotten, contains the feature of contingency, we attempt to explain how from this initial
state, which we have observed or assumed, the further
historical developments can be mechanically deduced.
And here it may again be noted that, if we include
already in our initial collocation the elements of life and
mind—as some so-called Monists, like Haeckel, do,—we
have nevertheless to explain the continual growth of
mental values, so clearly pointed out by Wundt, and the
unforeseen and erratic creations, inventions, and discoveries of genius.

These two problems of the Contingent and the Discontinuous remain, at the end of the nineteenth century,
the two principal outstanding problems in which the
great problem of nature specifies itself. The philosophy
of Lotze, in the æsthetical and ethical aspects which it
contains, points to a solution of these difficulties. As
this, however, leads us away from the present subject, I
shall take it up in later chapters.

51.
The prob-
lems of the
Contingent
and the
Discontinu-
ous ou-
standing.

The ideas of Lotze, which, as I have shown, reach
back to the speculations of Schelling, have not been
adequately appreciated and followed up in subsequent
German philosophy. This has moved mainly on other
lines. At the moment, however, it seems, as I have
already stated above, as if Lotze's views are creating a
renewed and deeper interest.

It is to French thought within the last thirty years

that we have to turn for a fuller appreciation and a clearer definition of the problems I refer to. In France the problems of the Contingent and the Discontinuous have found respectively independent and original treatment in the schools of which Jules Lachelier and Charles

Renouvier form the centres. The writings of the former are few—two or three essays,[1] showing great originality and depth of thought; but through his teaching at the École Normale, Lachelier has had a profound and far-reaching influence on recent French philosophy. On the other hand, Charles Renouvier has elaborated his views in many critical, historical, and constructive works.

From an historical point of view it is interesting to see how these two independent lines of speculation, as well as several others of a more exact nature, are leading the most recent current of French philosophical thought towards a renewed study and appreciation of Leibnizian ideas. Perhaps the most important and suggestive among these writings is the short tract by Lachelier entitled, 'Du Fondement de l'Induction.' It was published in 1871, and deserves to be regarded as a corner-stone in the edifice of modern thought. Readers of the earlier writings of Lotze will find in it a clear and elegant exposition of many ideas similar to his, though the subject is approached from a different side.

The main idea which runs through the whole of the discussion is that the inductive process of reasoning, as we actually employ it, depends not only upon the neces-

---

[1] The writings of Jules Lachelier (1832-1875) have been republished in a small volume (Félix Alcan, 4th ed., 1902).

sary connection of cause and effect—*i.e.*, of antecedent
and consequent, but quite as much upon the conception
of finality—*i.e.*, of a definite end or ends. For the employment of the category of causality alone reveals to us
in nature merely numberless series of connected phenomena; it does not deal with the interconnection of
these series themselves in a comprehensive scheme.[1]
We require indeed not only regularities but also a
harmony among these separate regularities. Now, harmony implies a reference to an *ensemble*, or together,
or a whole; in the end, to the totality of things.
It is therefore only through some conception referring to the whole or totality of things that we can
satisfy the inherent requisite of thought—viz., to bring
unity and order into our view of nature. It is quite
true that this reference to the whole of nature which is
identical with that of finality cannot be subjected to
the rigorous methods by which we establish the geometrical arrangements and changes in space and time;
it rests upon an anticipation with which we approach
the phenomena of nature. "Nature is," as Lachelier
says, "at once, a *science*, which never leaves off de-
ducing effects from causes, and an *art*, which without
end exercises itself in new inventions; and if it is given
to us, in some instances, to follow by calculation a uni-
form progress of that science which works at the
foundation of things, induction properly understood
consists rather in divining, by a kind of instinct,
the varying processes of the art which plays on the

[1] We may perhaps say that causality alone would reduce our image of nature to a bundle of threads, or at best a texture, which would give us no picture full of life and colour.

surface." [1] Moreover, Lachelier endeavours to show how
the mechanical connections are bound up with the
essence of human thinking and are as such purely
formal, whereas the actual content of this form is given
to us not through thought but through sensation or
sight. "Thought which would rest exclusively on the
mechanical unity in nature lies, as it were, on the surface of things without penetrating into the things
themselves: divorced from reality it would be itself
deficient in reality, and would be no more than the
empty form or abstract possibility of thought. We
must therefore find the means at once of making
thought real and reality intelligible; and this can only
be done through a second unity which stands in the
same relation to the matter of phenomena as the first
stands to their form." [2]

Whilst Lachelier thus dwells upon the contingent in
Nature, a subject which has received further treatment in
the writings of Émile Boutroux,[3] Charles Renouvier was
led away from the positivist creed which he originally
embraced by a different line of argument. He recognised the insufficiency of positivism by realising that
contradictions and discontinuities meet us everywhere
in our contemplation of the world of nature as well as
the facts of history. He thus abandoned his original
endeavour to bring unity and order into his philosophical views by reducing qualitative to quantitative
differences and by finding imperceptible transitions be-

[1] 'Du Fondement de l'Induction,' p. 73.
[2] Ibid., p. 77.

[3] 'De la Contingence des Lois de
la Nature' (3rd ed., 1898).

tween phenomena which stand ostensibly apart—*i.e.*, by
the study of the continuous. This attempt, he found,
could not be consistently and satisfactorily carried
through. It seems, as he himself tells us, that this
change in his opinions was brought about by a study
of the writings of Descartes and the Critiques of Kant.
In fact, he professes to continue and correct the work of
the latter which he considers to be fundamental. His
philosophy was therefore known, for a long time, as
Neocriticism, and retained this title till, in his more
recent constructive works, he dwelt on the positive idea
of personality as the ultimate conception we could
reach in philosophy.

Since that time his system is known under the name
of "Personnalisme." From this we see that his reasoning dwells more upon the ethical outcome of philosophy
than upon the æsthetical, which is characteristic of the
school of Lachelier. Renouvier was evidently much impressed by the ultimate contradictions or "Antinomies"
to which we are logically led by following out the lines
of thought suggested to us by experience and observation. He sees in this part of Kant's criticism the
most important contribution which he has made to
modern thought. But he does not agree with the
manner in which Kant tried to solve his antinomies.
He does not believe in the contrast of the phenomenal
and noumenal worlds, nor of the empirical and transcendental (intelligible). For Renouvier there is only
one world,—the world of phenomena; he is so far a pure
empiricist or phenomenist. But the contradictions in

the phenomenal world cannot be slurred over, nor the discontinuities got rid of,—in fact, they constitute the very essence, in opposition to the mere form, of reality. The way in which they are to be met is peculiar to Renouvier's philosophy. They are to be met by a free choice which every thinker has to make for himself. Thus we have, so far as nature is concerned, to choose between the infinite in time and space and the finite; in history, between continuity or necessity of events and their freedom (individuality); and, to sum up, we have to base our system of philosophy ultimately on free will or mechanism—that is to say, we have to choose between being Determinists or Indeterminists. The very fact that the Determinists themselves arrive only through a definite resolution at their final conviction is a proof that their conclusion is self-contradictory. This is an argument which Renouvier has adopted from his friend Jules Lequier. We are here reminded of the dictum of Lotze, that a final belief depends ultimately upon a resolution of the character; and of Fichte, who maintained that the philosophy a man chooses depends ultimately upon the kind of man he is. And further, Renouvier agrees—probably unconsciously—with Lotze in this, that a firm conviction gained by an act of free will—*i.e.*, of self-determination—is the beginning and not the end of every philosophical system.

The later writings of Renouvier do not interest us much in the present connection, though they contain a fanciful cosmology. The interest of his speculations lies in their critical and ethical portions, and in the strong emphasis which he lays everywhere upon freedom of development, — an idea which he identifies with discontinuity.[1]

53.
Transition
to æsthetic
and ethical
aspects.

We thus find that, at the end of the century, the problem of nature has become specified in a manner which points on the one side to the poetical and artistic, on the other side to the ethical and practical aspects as necessary complements to purely mechanical views such as have been elaborated and become fruitful in science. By a general consensus of opinion among the representatives of many schools of thought, the mechanical views of nature reveal to us only the necessary forms of thought by which we can acquire a mastery over natural things and processes ; they do not reveal to us either the essence or the meaning—*i.e.*, the soul—of nature. Nevertheless, this latter term has a definite sense, and can as little be got rid of in any true philosophy of nature as the term Soul or Spirit can be permanently eliminated from a study and comprehension of the inner life.

The problem of nature has, in the course of the nineteenth century, met with a fate similar to that which has befallen other philosophical problems. It has been taken over by the exact and the natural sciences ; and, so far as the deeper questions of the essence and meaning of things natural are concerned, the earlier philosophy

[1] The problem of the Contingent will occupy us again in later chapters. In the meantime I may mention that it forms the principal subject of discussion in Alfred Fouillée's critical account of the idealistic as opposed to the positivistic movement in modern French thought. He there ('Le Mouvement Idéaliste,' 2me ed., 1896, pp. 151-277) traces "la théorie de la contingence, telle que l'ont soutenue Lotze, M. Renouvier, M. Boutroux, M. Bergson," into what he considers its ethical consequences, according to which it should be judged. The best discussion of this side of the subject in English literature is to be found in the 4th of Prof. Ward's second series of 'Gifford Lectures,' 1911.

2 R

of nature has had likewise to give way to the poetical and artistic treatment, in which Goethe and Wordsworth on the one side, the great schools of modern landscape painting on the other, have shown us the way. We have thus two distinct and seemingly different aspects of nature. This has drawn forth the oft-repeated lament to which Schiller in his ' Götter Griechenlands ' has given classical expression. But Goethe and Ruskin have told us what they and other great masters on both sides have always felt, that the two ways of approaching and understanding nature are ultimately rooted in Sight, and not in Thought; to which source they must ever and again return for new guidance and inspiration.

As in other instances, when the old problem has been taken out of the hands of the philosopher, there still remains the philosophical task to examine the methods by which mental work is being carried on in these new fields, and the principles upon which it rests. We have seen how an analysis of the methods and principles of the scientific exploration of nature has, under the name of philosophy of nature, largely occupied philosophy in the latter part of the nineteenth century. It was to be expected that a similar interest would attach to the philosophical study of the principles of poetical and artistic creation. Accordingly, we find that this has, in the course of the century, more and more engaged the attention of thinkers, so that a new philosophical inquiry, under the name of Æsthetics, now forms a prominent subject of philosophical interest, centring in a definite problem,—the problem of the Beautiful.

This will be the subject of the next chapter.

PRINTED BY WILLIAM BLACKWOOD AND SONS.